Leadership and Supervision

This volume is dedicated to examining various points of view of what leadership is, and how the leader supervises those whom he trains.

It is divided into three conceptual sections: *The Leader,* which examines various dimensions of leadership and what it means to lead; *The Leader's Effect on Others*, which as the title indicates it looks at the effect and influence that a leader may have on others; and *Organizational Culture*, the effect of the leader on the culture of the organization or institution.

The chapters in this book were originally published in *The Journal of Psychology.*

Ami Rokach is a clinical psychologist who has been researching and teaching about loneliness, human sexuality, and psychotherapy for the past 40 years. Ami is Executive Editor of the *Journal of Psychology: Interdisciplinary and Applied*, and a clinical psychologist who combines offering individual, couple, and sex therapy with teaching and research. He is a member of the psychology departments at York University in Canada, and Walden University in USA.

Leadership and Supervision

Edited by
Ami Rokach

Routledge
Taylor & Francis Group
LONDON AND NEW YORK

First published 2022
by Routledge
2 Park Square, Milton Park, Abingdon, Oxon, OX14 4RN

and by Routledge
605 Third Avenue, New York, NY 10158

Routledge is an imprint of the Taylor & Francis Group, an informa business

British Library Cataloguing-in-Publication Data
A catalogue record for this book is available from the British Library

ISBN13: 978-1-032-15315-5 (hbk)
ISBN13: 978-1-032-15317-9 (pbk)
ISBN13: 978-1-003-24359-5 (ebk)

DOI: 10.4324/9781003243595

Typeset in Minion Pro
by codeMantra

Publisher's Note
The publisher accepts responsibility for any inconsistencies that may have arisen during the conversion of this book from journal articles to book chapters, namely the inclusion of journal terminology.

Disclaimer
Every effort has been made to contact copyright holders for their permission to reprint material in this book. The publishers would be grateful to hear from any copyright holder who is not here acknowledged and will undertake to rectify any errors or omissions in future editions of this book.

Contents

Citation Information

The following chapters were originally published in various issues of *The Journal of Psychology*. When citing this material, please use the original citations and page numbering for each article, as follows:

Chapter 1
Investigating Leader Role Congruity and Counterproductive Work Behavior
Benjamin Biermeier-Hanson and Patrick Coyle
The Journal of Psychology, volume 153, issue 8 (2019) pp. 820–842

Chapter 2
Predicting Leader Emergence with Bright and Dark Traits
Maureen A. Conard
The Journal of Psychology, volume 154, issue 1 (2020) pp. 1–14

Chapter 3
When Core Self-Evaluation Leads to Career Adaptability: Effects of Ethical Leadership and Implications for Citizenship Behavior
Xiao-min Xu and Kun Yu
The Journal of Psychology, volume 153, issue 5 (2019) pp. 463–477

Chapter 4
Leader–Follower Congruence in MD Propensity and UPB: A Polynomial Regression Analysis
Jun Song, Jin Yang and Changqing He
The Journal of Psychology, volume 155, issue 3 (2021) pp. 275–291

Chapter 5
Supervisor Incivility and Employee Job Performance: The Mediating Roles of Job Insecurity and Amotivation
Yuhyung Shin and Won-Moo Hur
The Journal of Psychology, volume 154, issue 1 (2020) pp. 38–59

Chapter 6
Inclusive Leadership and Innovative Work Behavior: Examination of LMX Perspective in Small Capitalized Textile Firms
Basharat Javed, Abdul Karim Khan and Samina Quratulain
The Journal of Psychology, volume 152, issue 7–8 (2019) pp. 594–612

Chapter 7
Trust in Supervisor and Job Engagement: Mediating Effects of Psychological Safety and Felt Obligation
Ameer A. Basit
The Journal of Psychology, volume 151, issue 8 (2017) pp. 701–721

Chapter 8
Work Engagement: Investigating the Role of Transformational Leadership, Job Resources, and Recovery
Amy J. Hawkes, Amanda Biggs and Erin Hegerty
The Journal of Psychology, volume 151, issue 6 (2017) pp. 509–531

Chapter 9
What Does Leaders' Character Add to Transformational Leadership?
Patrick Liborius
The Journal of Psychology, volume 151, issue 3 (2017) pp. 299–320

Chapter 10
Is Charismatic Leadership Effective When Workers Are Pressured To Be Good Citizens?
Dewaynna Horn, Christopher J. Mathis, Sammie L. Robinson and Natasha Randle
The Journal of Psychology, volume 149, issue 8 (2015) pp. 751–774

Chapter 11
Mitigating the Harmful Effect of Perceived Organizational Compliance on Trust in Top Management: Buffering Roles of Employees' Personal Resources
Dirk De Clercq and Dave Bouckenooghe
The Journal of Psychology, volume 153, issue 2 (2019) pp. 187–213

Chapter 12
Bouncing Back from Setbacks: On the Mediating Role of Team Resilience in the Relationship Between Transformational Leadership and Team Effectiveness
Isabel Dórdio Dimas, Teresa Rebelo, Paulo Renato Lourenço and Carina Isabel Pereira Pessoa
The Journal of Psychology, volume 152, issue 6 (2018) pp. 358–372

Chapter 13
Psychological Capital, Team Resources and Organizational Citizenship Behavior
Ronit Bogler and Anit Somech
The Journal of Psychology, volume 153, issue 8 (2019) pp. 784–802

Chapter 14
Servant Leadership and Follower Outcomes: Mediating Effects of Organizational Identification and Psychological Safety
Aamir Ali Chughtai
The Journal of Psychology, volume 150, issue 7 (2016) pp. 866–880

Chapter 15

When Supervisors Perceive Non-Work Support: Test of a Trickle-Down Model
Tsung-Yu Wu, Shao-Jen Lee, Changya Hu and Chun-Chi Yang
The Journal of Psychology, volume 148, issue 2 (2014) pp. 215–251

For any permission-related enquiries please visit:
http://www.tandfonline.com/page/help/permissions

Notes on Contributors

Ameer A. Basit is assistant professor of management at the Information Technology University, Lahore, Pakistan. His current research interests are employee engagement, leadership, performance, entrepreneurship, and technology-based firms.

Benjamin Biermeier-Hanson is assistant professor of psychology at Radford University, USA. His research interests focus on leadership and organizational culture.

Amanda Biggs is lecturer in the Griffith Business School at Griffith University, Australia. Her research investigates the management of psychological and physical health at work, including work engagement, stress, bullying, healthy behaviors, and positive organizational cultures.

Ronit Bogler is associate professor and Head of the Program in Educational Administration, Policy & Leadership at the Open University of Israel. Her research interests include educational leadership, organizational citizenship behavior, empowerment, organizational and professional commitment, and job satisfaction.

Dave Bouckenooghe is associate professor of organizational behavior in the Goodman School of Business at Brock University, St. Catharines, Canada. His research interests are organizational behavior, organizational theory, and human resource management.

Aamir Ali Chughtai is associate professor at the Forman Christian College, Lahore, Pakistan. His current research interests are employee engagement, trust, workplace commitment, and organizational leadership.

Maureen A. Conard is professor of psychology at Sacred Heart University, Fairfield, USA. Her research interests include personality, individual differences, and their effects on performance in various contexts.

Patrick Coyle is assistant professor of management at Lycoming College, Williamsport, USA. His interests focus on leadership and individual differences.

Dirk De Clercq is professor of management in the Goodman School of Business at Brock University, St. Catharines, Canada. His research interests are in entrepreneurship, organizational behavior, and cross-country studies.

Isabel Dórdio Dimas is assistant professor of organizational behavior and social sciences at the University of Aveiro, Portugal, and a researcher at GOVCOPP – Research Unit in Governance, Competitiveness and Public Policies. Her current research interests include team effectiveness, group dynamics, intragroup conflict, leadership, and emotions in the group.

Amy J. Hawkes is lecturer in the School of Applied Psychology at Griffith University, Australia. She teaches undergraduate and postgraduate organizational psychology. Her research interests include transformational leadership, leadership aspirations, recovery, well-being, and empowerment.

Changqing He is assistant professor at Nanjing University of Aeronautics and Astronautics, China. His areas of research include leadership, human resource management, and business decision-making.

Erin Hegerty completed a Bachelor of Psychology, with Honors, through Griffith University, Australia. Erin's particular interest areas are non-work recovery and applying recovery principles to maximize engagement and to effectively manage stress at work.

Dewaynna Horn is assistant professor of management at Texas Woman's University, Denton, USA. Her current research interests are organizational citizenship behavior and work–life interface.

Changya Hu is professor in the Department of Business Administration at National Chengchi University, Taipei, Taiwan. She received her doctoral degree in industrial and organizational psychology from the University of Georgia, USA. Her research areas include mentoring, abusive supervision, work stress, and measurement equivalence/invariance.

Basharat Javed is assistant professor at the Namal College Mianwali, Pakistan. His areas of research include religious work ethic, innovative work behavior, ethical leadership and inclusive leadership.

Abdul Karim Khan is assistant professor at the United Arab Emirates University, Al Ain, UAE. His areas of research include abusive supervision, religious work ethics, innovative work behavior, and organizational cronyism.

Shao-Jen Lee is doctoral student of the Department of Business Administration at the National Taiwan University of Science and Technology, Taipei, Taiwan. His research interests focus on work engagement.

Patrick Liborius is research assistant at the Technische Universit€at Darmstadt, Germany. His current research interests are the impact of leaders' character on their followers, and the impact of self-regulated learning among university students.

Paulo Renato Lourenço is assistant professor of Work, Organizational and Personnel Psychology (WOP-P) at the University of Coimbra, Portugal, and researcher at the Institute of Cognitive Psychology, Human and Social Development (IPCDHS). His research interests are in work teams functioning, including topics such as team trust, team cohesion, team effectiveness and leadership.

Christopher J. Mathis is associate professor at Morgan State University in the Earl G. Graves School of Business and Management, Baltimore, USA. His current research interests are work–family (life) interface, organizational citizenship behavior, and leadership/followership.

Won-Moo Hur is professor at College of Business Administration at Inha University, Incheon, South Korea. His research interests include emotional labor, workplace incivility, service employee–customer relationship, and micro-CSR.

Carina Pessoa is psychologist, specialized in the area of human resources and organizations, by the Faculty of Psychology and Educational Sciences of the University of Coimbra, Portugal. Her research interests are related to people management and attraction, leadership and its importance in the motivation, and performance of employees.

Samina Quratulain is assistant professor at the University of Sharjah, United Arab Emirates. Her areas of research include abusive supervision, envy, and psychological contract breach.

Natasha Randle is associate professor of management at Mississippi State University-Meridian, USA. Her current research interests are workplace weight discrimination, professional intimacy, work–life, and leadership.

Teresa Rebelo is assistant professor in the Faculty of Psychology and Education Sciences at the University of Coimbra, Portugal. Her current research interests are focused on organizational culture, organizational and team learning, nonlinear dynamical system theory, and team dynamics.

Sammie L. Robinson is assistant professor in the Jesse H. Jones School of Business at Texas Southern University, Houston, USA. Her current research interests are African American women entrepreneurs and leadership and ethical leader behavior.

Yuhyung Shin is professor at School of Business at Hanyang University, Seoul, South Korea. Her research interests include team processes and performance, person–organization fit, creativity, and extra-role behavior.

Anit Somech is organizational psychologist, and a full professor at the Department of Educational Leadership & Policy at the University of Haifa, Israel. Her research interests include organizational citizenship behavior, participative leadership, and teamwork from a multilevel and cross-culture perspective.

Jun Song is assistant professor at Nanjing University of Finance and Economics, China. Her areas of research include individual unethical behavior, abusive supervision, and employee voice.

Xiao-min Xu is Ph.D. student in the Business School at the University of Edinburgh, UK. Her research interests include justice, trust, and career development.

Chun-Chi Yang is associate professor of the Department of Business Administration at Fu Jen Catholic University, Taipei, Taiwan. Her research interests focus on organizational learning (innovation in particular), mentoring relationship, and human resource management practice issues.

Jin Yang is instructor at Southwest University of Science and Technology, Mianyang, China. Her areas of research include servant leadership and employee creativity.

Kun Yu is assistant professor in the School of Labor and Human Resources at the Renmin University of China, Beijing, China. His research interests include ethical/ unethical behavior, work–family interface, and career development.

Tsung-Yu Wu is professor of the Department of Business Administration at the National Taiwan University of Science and Technology, Taipei, Taiwan. His research interests focus on emotions in the workplace, abusive supervision, and supervisory support.

Introduction: The Many Shades of Leadership and Supervision

Ami Rokach

It appears that there is not one best leadership style, rather the leader considers different components of an individual situation to determine their choice of leadership style and techniques. Such an adaptive leadership style is well suited for organizational management, and particularly for the various layers of supervision within counselor training programs. Primary components of effective leadership leader's behaviors regarding the task to be completed, relationship behaviors and the readiness of the followers to follow (Kozachuk & Conley, 2020). Related to supervision, task behavior mirrors the supervisor's level of focus on skill building and decision regarding type of feedback to provide based on the supervisee's needs. Relationship behavior is that behavior which the leader displays in order to establish and enhance the personal relationship with their followers. Related to supervision, relationship behavior mirrors the dynamics of the supervisee/supervisor relationship and the supervisor's provision of high levels of support to help supervisees elicit their own answers and build self-confidence. Readiness relates to the ability and willingness of the followers in a specific situation depending on various variables, among them the leader's behavior and influence on his followers. A follower's willingness is the level of "confidence, commitment, and motivation to accomplish a specific task" (Hersey et al., 2001, p. 176). There are arguments to be made that in order to promote and sustain effective psychological service delivery, service managers need to have access to ongoing supervision, given that "Supervision is central to the delivery of high-quality psychological services" (Dunsmuir & Leadbetter, 2010, p. 2). This may be particularly important, given the complexity of the relationship between performance measures and management, efficient organizational working and outcomes for service users (Arnaboldi et al., 2015).

This volume is dedicated to examining various points of view of what leadership is, and how the leader supervises those whom he trains. It was divided to three conceptual sections: *The leader*, which examines various dimensions of leadership and what it means to lead; *The leader's effect on others*, which as the title indicates it looks at the effect and influence that a leader may have on others; and *Organizational culture*, the effect of the leader on the culture of the organization or institution.

The Leader

Biermeir-Hanson and Coyle (2019) sought to examine the role of fulfilled vs. unfulfilled expectations in work-related and non-work domains. Specifically, they examined how congruence and incongruence between implicit leadership theories (ILTs) of typical, ideal and effective leaders and characteristics recognized on one's supervisor affect leader-member exchange (LMX), work-family conflict (WFC) and subsequent counter-productive work behavior. This study's results showed that congruence between ILTs of typical, ideal and effective leaders and supervisor recognition, as well as incongruity between ILTs of ideal leaders and supervisor's characteristics, significantly impacts perceived LMX quality with supervisors. Additionally, it was found that incongruity between ILTs of typical and ideal leaders and supervisor recognition was also associated with higher ratings of WFC.

Conard (2020) focused on leader emergence as regressed on five-factor model (FFM) traits and four additional traits of achievement, dominance, aggression and Machiavellianism in a sample of 280 undergraduates. In an independent groups' analysis, significant differences were found in six of the nine traits, thus indicating that leaders are less neurotic and Machiavellian, and more extroverted, open, agreeable and dominant than we may think they are. However, in a logistic regression analysis which the authors performed, which controlled for shared variance among traits, only extraversion, openness and dominance predicted leader emergence.

The Leader's Effect on Others

Xu and Yu (2019) Drawing upon the career construction theory and the trait activation theory, the authors aimed to explore the interactive effect of core self-evaluation (CSE) and ethical leadership on career adaptability. In addition, they also investigated how career adaptability mediates the interaction effect of CSE and ethical leadership on organizational citizenship behavior (OCB). Their sample was comprised of 156 employees which were tested in two waves. Results showed that ethical leadership moderated the relationship between CSE and career adaptability. The authors noted that the positive relationship between CSE and career adaptability was stronger when ethical leadership was low. Career adaptability was found to mediate the relationship between CSE and OCB, and ethical leadership moderated this indirect relationship.

Song, Yang & He (2021) based their investigation on previous work on moral disengagement (MD) and balance theory, and the (in)congruence effect of leader and follower MD propensity on followers' unethical pro-organizational behavior (UPB). Their sample was recruited from 185 Chinese firms, and was composed of 185 CEOs and 555 followers. Results indicated that followers in the presence of leader-follower congruence in MD propensity conduct more UPB. They also found that followers conduct more UPBs with MD propensity in the presence of congruence. Asymmetrical incongruence effects were revealed. Followers engage more in UPBs when their MD propensity exceeds their leaders' MD propensity than when their leaders' MD propensity exceeds their own.

Shin & Hur (2020) focused their research on workplace incivility, the relationship between supervisor incivility and employee job performance, as well as its intermediary mechanisms. Drawing on the transactional model of stress and self-determination theory, they hypothesized that job insecurity and amotivation of employees as mediating mechanisms between supervisor incivility and employee job performance. They analyzed data collected in two-wave surveys from kindergarten teachers and their principals. Analysis showed, as is so intuitively apparent, that incivility perpetrated by kindergarten principals exerted a negative effect on teachers' job performance three months later by shaping job insecurity perceptions and amotivation.

Javed, Khan & Quratulain (2018), in contrast to Shin and Hur, examined the relationship between inclusive leadership, leader-member exchange (LMX) and innovative work behavior (IWB) in 150 supervisor-employee dyads, in textile firms in Pakistan. The researchers hypothesized that LMX mediates the relationship between inclusive leadership and IWB. Results suggested that inclusive leadership is positively related with IWB, and LMX partially mediates this relationship.

Basit (2017) explored the role of trust that employees have in their supervisor and the mechanisms mediating this dynamic relationship. They aimed to explore whether psychological safety and felt obligation may be the two psychological mechanisms mediating the effect of trust in supervisor on job engagement. Data were collected from 337 nurses employed in a public hospital located near Kuala Lumpur, Malaysia. Results fully supported the proposed serial multiple mediator model, and revealed that trusting the supervisor was indirectly related to job engagement via psychological safety followed by felt obligation. Based on their study, the authors opined that trust in supervisor makes employees feel psychologically safe to employ and express their selves in their job roles. This satisfaction of the psychological safety need is interpreted by employees as an important socioemotional benefit that, in turn, makes them feel obligated to pay back to their organization through their enhanced level of job engagement.

Hawkes, Biggs & Hegerty (2017) aimed to understand the upstream factors that shape job resources in order to enhance work engagement. The researchers investigated transformational leadership as an upstream job resource and the moderating role of recovery experiences. Their sample included 277 employees from a variety of organizations and industries. Results pointed to a direct relationship between transformational leadership and engagement, and transformational leadership and job resources. They also found a significant indirect path between transformational leadership and engagement via job resources. Recovery experiences did not significantly moderate the relationship between job resources and engagement.

Liborius (2017) was interested in the influence of leaders' characters, such as integrity and humility/forgiveness, on both followers' perceptions of leaders' worthiness of being followed (WBF) and stress. They studied a sample of 347 from a scenario experiment and 110 from a field study. Their data indicated that these aspects incrementally predict WBF above and beyond the impact of transformational leadership. Similar results were found concerning followers' stress with the exception of leader integrity in the field study. They observed that integrity and transformational leadership predict WBF equally well.

Horn, Mathis, Robinson & Randle (2015) commented that prior studies pointed out that charismatic leaders motivate individuals to be more engaged and to exhibit more organizational citizenship behaviors. In their study, the authors explored how citizenship pressure, affects how charismatic leaders might influence their followers to go above and beyond what's expected of them and become more productive. Using a sample of 243 workers, they found that charismatic leadership is negatively correlated to citizenship pressure as far as job engagement is concerned. Citizenship pressure did not moderate the relationship between charismatic leadership and organizational citizenship behavior. They suggested that based on their research we may increase our understanding of leadership factors that encourage increased effort from employees and greater employee engagement.

Organizational Culture

De Clerq & Bouckenooghe (2019) explored how employees' POC (Perceived Organizational Compliance), meaning their beliefs that the organizational climate stifles change and pressures for compliance with the status quo, reduce their trust in top management. It also explored how this negative relationship might be buffered by access to two personal resources that support organizational change: openness to experience and affective commitment to change. Their sample was composed of Pakistan-based organizations. They found that POC reduce trust in top management, though this effect is weakened at higher levels of openness to experience and affective commitment to change.

Dordio Dimas, Rebelo, Renato Lourenco & Pereira Pessoa (2018) wanted to clarify the role of team resilience on different facets of effectiveness. It is a given that team resilience is very important for the organizational context, and thus, they were interested in the conditions that promote team resilience, analyzing the role of transformational leadership. The authors also examined whether the relationship between transformational leadership and team resilience stimulates positive team outcomes. They studied 90 teams which were composed of 445 employees from 40 companies. The results showed a positive direct effect of team resilience on both team viability and the quality of the group experience. Moreover, transformational leadership and team resilience were positively correlated. They were able to support the observation regarding the mediated effect of team resilience on the relationship between transformational leadership and the dimensions of team effectiveness considered. The authors noted that their study highlight the role of team resilience as an intervening process between transformational leadership and team effectiveness.

Bogler & Somech (2019) aimed to explore the impact of team resources, such as team leader's optimism and learning values, as moderating variables affecting the relationship between team psychological capital (PsyCap) and organizational citizenship behavior (OCB), which can be assessed by team outcome. Eighty-two management teams involving 395 participants from educational organizations participated in this study. Analyses confirmed interactive effects of both moderating variables, which serve to enhance the impact of team PsyCap on the willingness of the team to engage in OCB. It was also found that team PsyCap served as a positive team resource that created an environment that induces exhibition of high levels of OCB. It was found that this relationship is strengthened when, both, team leader's optimism and team learning are high. These findings emphasize the necessity of certain situational features that need to exist in order to have an impact on organization outcomes.

Chughtai (2016) investigated the mediating role of psychological safety and organizational identification in the relationship between servant leadership and employee outcomes, specifically employee voice and negative feedback-seeking behavior. The author studied 174 full-time employees drawn from a large food company based in Pakistan. Results indicated that psychological safety and organizational identification partially mediated the effects of servant leadership on voice and negative feedback-seeking behavior.

Wu, Lee, Hu & Yang (2014) explored whether subordinates' perceived supervisory non-work support (subordinates' PSNS) mediates the relationship between subordinates' organizational citizenship behaviors and that of supervisors' perception of higher-level managers' non-work support (supervisors' PSNS). Data was collected from 132 employees and their immediate supervisors. Results supported the hypothesized mediation process. Furthermore, supervisors' perceived in-group/out-group membership of subordinates moderated the aforementioned supervisors' PSNS-subordinates' PSNS relationship, and consequently, this relationship is stronger for out-group subordinates.

To conclude, this volume may serve as an indication to researchers and clinicians regarding what and how leadership is expressed and how it affects employees; supervisors; and the organizational culture, atmosphere and morale. I hope that you will find the articles in this volume illuminating and enhancing your thinking regarding research and teaching aimed at improving the leadership quality in organizations and institutions.

References

Arnaboldi, M., Lapsley, I., & Steccolini, I. (2015). Performance management in the public sector: The ultimate challenge. *International Journal of Public Sector Management*, 31(1), 1–22.

Dunsmuir, S., & Leadbetter, J. (2010). *Professional supervision: Guidelines for practice for educational psychologists*. Leicester: DECP.

Hersey, P., Blanchard, K.H., & Johnson, D.E. (2001). *Management of organizational behavior: Leading human resources*. Upper Saddle River: Prentice Hall of India.

Kozachuk, L.A. & Conley, A.H. (2021). Development-oriented situational supervision: A leadership approach to supervision in counselor education. *Journal of Counselor Leadership and Advocacy*, 8(1), 44–55. Doi: 10.1080/2326716X.2020.1835586.

Part I

The Leader

Investigating Leader Role Congruity and Counterproductive Work Behavior

Benjamin Biermeier-Hanson and Patrick Coyle

ABSTRACT

The present study sought to examine the role of fulfilled vs. unfulfilled expectations in work-related and non-work domains. Specifically, we examined how congruence and incongruence between implicit leadership theories across multiple categories of leaders (typical, ideal, and effective leaders) and characteristics recognized on one's supervisor affect leader-member exchange (LMX), work-family conflict, and subsequent counter-productive work behavior. We tested our hypotheses using polynomial regression and response surface modeling. The results of this study showed that congruence between implicit leadership theories (ILT's) of typical, ideal, and effective leaders and supervisor recognition, as well as incongruity between ILT's of ideal leaders and characteristics recognized in one's supervisor, significantly impacts perceived LMX quality with supervisors. Incongruity between ILT's of typical and ideal leaders and supervisor recognition was also associated with higher ratings of work-family conflict (WFC). Finally, the results showed support for a significant indirect effect of congruence between ILTs of typical and ideal leaders and characteristics recognized in one's supervisor on CWB through WFC. These results add meaningful depth to literature on congruent implicit theories in two ways: (a) we add to existing knowledge of outcomes associated with congruence on ILT's, and, (b) we examine these associations using ILT's across multiple categories of leaders. Implications are also discussed.

Engagement in counter-productive work behavior (CWB) interferes with goal attainment by organizational leaders and costs organizations up to $200 billion per year (Bolino & Klotz, 2015; Dalal, 2005; Yam, Fehr, Keng-Highberger, Klotz, & Reynolds, 2016). Counter-productive work behaviors are volitional behaviors that harm the organization or its members and are typically motivated by environmental events that violate expectations (Bies & Tripp, 1996; Martinko, Gundlach, & Douglas, 2002; Spector, Fox, Penney, Bruursema, Goh, & Kessler, 2006). Absenteeism, theft, coworker or supervisor abuse are all examples of these behaviors. To understand how leaders can reduce counter-productive behaviors, we must expand our understanding of how employees make sense of their workplace to identify what may violate their expectations and lead to CWBs.

To this end, we use knowledge structures about individually held prototypes of leaders, or implicit leadership theories (ILTs), to specify expectations for organizational sense making. These prototypes, or ILTs, are schemas that individuals hold about leader attributes and have received considerable attention in their ability to shape organizational processes and outcomes (e.g. Epitropaki & Martin, 2005; Foti & Lord, 1987; Lord, Foti & De Vader, 1984). For example, ILTs have been used to predict employees' work attitudes and relations. However, very little research has examined the relationship between these prototypes and counterproductive behaviors (Rupprecht, Kueny, Shoss & Metzger, 2016). To more fully understand the role of fulfilled vs. unfulfilled expectations in volitionally harmful behavior, we must continue to examine the relationship between ILT's and CWB.

Expectations for leaders are fulfilled only when there is alignment between individuals' prototypes and his/her perceptions of the characteristics exhibited by their leader, or "supervisor recognition" (Epitropaki & Martin, 2005; Lord & Maher, 1991). There is evidence that congruence between ILT's and one's supervisor (supervisor recognition) positively influences perceptions of working relationships. Specifically, initial evidence suggests that an employee's quality of relationship with their leader, as characterized by leader-member exchange (LMX), is positively affected when there is congruence between one's ILTs and characteristics recognized in one's supervisor (Epitropaki & Martin, 2005; van Gils, van Quaquebeke & van Knippenberg, 2010). Despite these initial findings, research that examines the ways in which this congruence influences relationships outside of work (e.g. work-family conflict, or WFC) is necessary to more fully understand the impact of this congruence on the workplace. Indeed, perceptions of leader relational quality along with work-life issues have been found to impact work-related outcomes generally, and counter-productive behaviors specifically (Epitropaki & Martin, 2005; Michel, Kotrba, Mitchelson, Clark, & Baltes, 2011; Rupprecht et al., 2016). Yet, the ways in which congruence between ILT's and supervisor recognition influence both constructs and subsequent engagement in CWB are not fully known. As such, research that examines how congruence between ILT's and supervisor recognition impacts CWB via LMX and WFC may help us achieve a greater understanding of how fulfillment of expectations regarding leaders can impact engagement in harmful behavior.

The purpose of this study is to explore how the role of intra-personal congruence on ILT's (e.g. alignment between followers' ILT's and characteristics recognized in one's supervisor) affects LMX and WFC and subsequent engagement in CWB. Our study makes two primary contributions to existing literature. First, our study expands on existing knowledge of outcomes associated with intra-personal congruence on ILT's by examining the influence of ILT congruence on CWB via LMX and WFC, as called for by prior studies (Epitropaki, Sy, Martin, Tram-Quon, & Topakas, 2013; Rupprecht et al., 2016). Second, our study adds to literature comparing ILT's across multiple categories of leaders (typical leader, ideal leader, and effective leader) (Epitropaki et al., 2013; Epitropaki & Martin, 2005; van Gils et al., 2010). Specifically, congruence using ILT's of "typical" and "ideal" leaders have been studied (e.g. Epitropaki & Martin, 2005; Rupprecht et al., 2016; Topakas, 2011), yet have not been examined thoroughly in the context of the same study. As such, the benefits of studying the impact of the norm vs.

valence of leader prototypes remain unclear (Foti, Hansbrough, Epitropaki, & Coyle, 2017). Furthermore, the extent to which ILT's of ideal leaders vs. effective leaders are different has yet to be clarified. We examine ILT's of all three categories of leaders in comparison to characteristics recognized in one's supervisor in order to generate a deeper understanding of perspectives and outcomes of congruence using several basic-level ILT categories, as called for by prior researchers (Foti et al., 2017; Junker and van Dick, 2014).

Literature Review and Hypotheses

ILT's, or schemas specifying the characteristics and behaviors characterizing leaders, are used to guide and interpret an individual's behavior toward leaders (Lord, Foti, & De Vader, 1984; Epitropaki & Martin, 2005; Epitropaki et al., 2013; Lord & Maher, 1991). These ILT's are developed over time and experience with different types of leaders (Lord et al., 1984; Shondrick & Lord, 2010). If there is a match between characteristics exhibited by a leader and the ILT of a leader held by the perceiver, it is more likely that the perceiver will recognize that individual as a leader (Lord et al., 1984). Thus, the leader's identity is reinforced (DeRue & Ashford, 2010; Lord & Maher, 1991). ILT's, however, vary widely from individual to individual, and while one individual may see someone as a leader, a different individual may not (Foti, Bray, Thompson, & Allgood, 2012). In addition to individual variability, ILT's can also vary due to culture-level influences (Den Hartog et al., 1999). Thus, similarities and differences between one's ILT and one's actual supervisor play an important role in the leadership process and, consequently, affect related outcomes.

Given perceptions are shaped by individual experiences, ILT's of leaders across different basic-level categories (e.g. typical leader, ideal leader, effective leader) held by a perceiver differ (Lord et al., 1984; van Quaquebeke, Kerschreiter, Buxton, & van Dick, 2010; van Quaquebeke et al., 2011). In order to examine the effect of these differences on organizational outcomes, it is essential to evaluate the impact of intra-personal congruence on these different ILT's and characteristics recognized in one's supervisor (the match between an individual's ILT and the characteristics recognized in his/her manager; Epitropaki et al., 2013). Studies have shown that intra-personal congruence between characteristics recognized in an individual's current supervisor and (a) a *typical leader* as well as (b) an *ideal leader* improves outcomes such as performance, LMX, and organizational citizenship behavior (OCB) (Epitropaki & Martin, 2005; Rupprecht et al., 2016; Topakas, 2011; van Quaquebeke et al., 2010, 2011). ILT's of *effective leaders* are different from typical or ideal leaders, in that they specify characteristics of leaders who work well, but may not be preferred (Dinh & Lord, 2013; Offermann, Kennedy, & Wirtz, 1994). Because congruence between ILT's of effective leaders has not been empirically examined, however, the role of this ILT category is not fully understood. By examining congruence between ILT's of typical, ideal, and effective leaders and supervisor recognition, we can identify which ILT categories are most predictive of workplace relationships and outcomes.

Most research has examined the effect of ILT congruence using traditional regression (Epitropaki & Martin, 2005; van Quaquebeke & van Knippenberg, 2012). For example,

Epitropaki and Martin (2005) examined intra-personal congruence between ILT's and current managers by regressing LMX, job satisfaction, commitment, and well-being on ILT difference scores in a field study of 439 employees. Recent studies, however, have demonstrated the advantages of using polynomial regression (Edwards, 2002; Rupprecht et al., 2016; Shanock, Baran, Gentry, Pattison, & Heggestad, 2010) which allows for more nuanced hypothesis testing of both agreement and disagreement around an outcome. Rupprecht et al. (2016) used this methodology to examine the role of discrepancy and congruence between perceived and desired sensitivity and supported their hypothesis that congruence between ideal and actual sensitivity displayed by leaders predicts affect and, subsequently, CWB. The current study uses this approach to examine congruence between an individual's current leader and several basic level categories of prototypical leaders (typical, ideal, and effective leaders) and the effects of this congruence (or incongruence) on LMX, WFC, and subsequent CWB.

Prior studies suggest that discrepancy between characteristics recognized in one's supervisor and expectations specified in the form of ILT's negatively impacts LMX (Epitropaki & Martin, 2005; Rupprecht et al. 2016; Topakas, 2011). This negative impact is likely to occur regardless of whether the target leader displays more of an expected characteristic (e.g. leader displays more of a trait specified in an ILT) or less of an expected characteristic (leader displays less of a trait specified in an ILT) (Rupprecht et al., 2016). Specifically, an individual with an ILT specifying a certain level of a given characteristic (e.g. intelligence) is likely to expect a leader to embody this characteristic in the expected amount. Thus, a leader who displays less of this characteristic may not be identified as a leader and, therefore, relationship quality may suffer (Epitropaki & Martin, 2005; Lord & Maher, 1991). If a leader displays more of this characteristic, however, it is possible that this trait will overshadow other relevant characteristics. For example, a leader who displays more masculinity than expected may fail to be recognized as sensitive (Foti, Knee, & Backert, 2008). Consequently, the leader may be misidentified and incorrectly categorized. As such, the degree and direction of discrepancy between ILT's and supervisor recognition may impact perceptions of LMX.

While the degree and direction of discrepancy between ILT's and current supervisors are important predictors of LMX quality, congruence between ILT's and characteristics recognized in one's supervisor is associated with LMX as well (Epitropaki & Martin, 2005; Topakas, 2011). Research by Edwards (2002, 2007) suggests that congruence between ILT's and supervisor recognition may be as instrumental in predicting relationship quality as discrepancy. Research has shown that congruence between ILT's and characteristics recognized in one's supervisor positively impacts perceptions of relationship quality (Epitropaki & Martin, 2005; Topakas, 2011). Furthermore, research also suggests congruence between highly rated levels of prototypical leader characteristics and supervisor-recognized characteristics is more beneficial than congruence between lower rated levels of ILT's and supervisor recognition (Rupprecht et al., 2016). Consequently, we make the following prediction.

> Hypothesis 1: Greater discrepancy (i.e. incongruity) between ILT's of (a) typical, (b) ideal, and (c) effective leaders and characteristics recognized in one's current supervisor will be associated with lower ratings of LMX.

Hypothesis 2: Congruence between ILT's of: (a) typical, (b) ideal, and (c) effective leaders and characteristics recognized in one's current supervisor (i.e. greater similarity) at high levels will be associated with higher ratings of LMX.

WFC, a form of role conflict that is characterized by incompatible demands between one's work and family relationships, creates different forms of time-based and strain-based interference from work and interference from family (Carlson, Kacmar, & Williams, 2000; Greenhaus & Beutell, 1985; Netemeyer, Boles, & McMurrian, 1996). Because leaders are representative of the organization's values, the extent to which leaders are seen as prototypical may directly impact the extent to which followers experience work–family conflict (Major and Morganson, 2011). Furthermore, Lyu, Wang, Le, and Kwan (2019) found that perceptions of authentic leadership were linked to greater work-family balance via LMX and work-family enrichment, suggesting that perceptions of leaders are related to WFC through greater work-related resources. We argue that a leader must be recognized as prototypical by his/her followers in order to engage in practices that reduce WFC. As such, the degree of congruence or discrepancy between characteristics exhibited by a leader and those specified a follower's ILT is an important factor to consider. No study to date, however, has examined the impact of congruence between ILT's and supervisor recognition and WFC, thus, research is needed in order to generate a deeper understanding of this relationship (Foti et al., 2017).

When an individual perceives a match between characteristics exhibited by a leader and those specified in his/her ILT, the leader role is mutually understood (Lord & Maher, 1991). Therefore, this individual is more likely to perceive a high-quality interpersonal relationship with his/her leader (Epitropaki & Martin, 2005; Lord & Maher, 1991). In cases where there is a perceived mismatch, however, the leader role is not mutually understood and interpersonal relationships will be low. The effect of this match or mismatch on role conflict has been predominantly studied in the workplace (e.g. LMX), however, individuals experiencing trouble with interpersonal relationships with leaders at work are also likely to experience strain on interpersonal relationships outside of work due to exhaustion from stress experienced with trying to manage these key relationships (Brunetto, Farr-Wharton, Ramsay, & Shacklock, 2010; Golden, 2006). Thus, there is a spillover effect stemming from an ILT mismatch that would affect interpersonal relationships outside of the workplace as well.

Huang, Wright, Chiu, and Wang (2008) found evidence that while leaders develop schemas focused on work-related issues, employees with direct supervisory relationships are more likely to develop schemas focusing on interpersonal issues. Therefore, there are likely to be discrepancies between a leader's characteristics and those characteristics that his/her follower believes are representative of a leader (Lord et al., 1984; Lord & Maher, 1991; van Gils et al., 2010). Furthermore, followers may perceive a certain level of a characteristic (e.g. charisma) as optimal, despite a leader exhibiting more or less of this characteristic. We theorize that greater discrepancy in both directions (i.e. a leader who displays more of an expected characteristic *or* less of an expected characteristic) are both problematic and lead to high levels of WFC, while congruence between ILT's and one's current supervisor will be associated with low levels of WFC.

As previously mentioned, a supervisor who displays less of a characteristic than specified in one's ILT may not be identified as a leader, while a leader who displays more of that trait may be incorrectly categorized (Epitropaki & Martin, 2005; Foti et al., 2008; Lord & Maher, 1991). In both cases, this discrepancy is likely to lead to lower quality interpersonal relationships (Epitropaki & Martin, 2005; Litano, Major, Landers, Streets, & Bass, 2016; Major, Fletcher, Davis, & Germano, 2008; Michel et al., 2011). Given that lower quality interpersonal relationships are associated with higher levels of WFC (Major, Fletcher, Davis, & Germano, 2008), it is likely the aforementioned discrepancy would lead to higher levels of WFC. Intra-personal congruence between ILT's and supervisor recognition at high levels, by the same logic, would likely lead to lower levels of WFC due to the benefits of high-quality interpersonal relationships on WFC. We, therefore, make the following predictions.

> Hypothesis 3: Greater discrepancy (i.e. incongruity) between ILT's of (a) typical, (b) ideal, and (c) effective leaders) and characteristics recognized in one's current supervisor will be associated with higher reported WFC.

> Hypothesis 4: Congruence between ILT's of: (a) typical, (b) ideal, and (c) effective leaders and characteristics recognized in one's current supervisor (i.e. greater similarity) at high levels will be associated with lower reported WFC.

CWB is commonly motivated by environmental events and interaction with individuals that are unaligned with expectations (Bies & Tripp, 1996; Martinko et al., 2002). There is evidence that perceptions of misfit between an employee and his or her organization are associated with lower LMX quality and employee CWB (Liu, Luksyte, Zhou, Shi, & Wang, 2015; Rupprecht et al., 2016; Scott, Ingram, Zagenczyk, & Shoss, 2015). Specifically, Rupprecht et al. (2016) found evidence that congruence between ideal and actual leader sensitivity influences engagement in CWB, such that increased discrepancy between ideal and actual leader congruence was associated with higher levels of CWB, while greater congruence was negatively associated with engagement in CWB. Therefore, intra-personal congruence between characteristics exhibited by one's leader and other basic level categories (a typical leader and an effective leader) impact employee CWB as well.

There is also evidence that LMX and WFC impact the extent to which employees engage in CWB (Bergerson, 2007; Epitropaki & Martin, 2005). Epitropaki and Martin (2005) demonstrated that LMX mediated the relationship between ILT congruence and organizational outcomes (e.g. commitment, well-being, as well as job satisfaction). In contrast, numerous studies have linked LMX and CWB, showing that low relationship quality is associated with higher levels of CWB (Chernyak-Hai & Tziner, 2014; Sears & Humiston, 2015; Spector & Che, 2014). Additionally, individuals who have less flexibility with regard to their work and family are thought to spend less time engaging in OCB and more time engaging in CWB (Bergerson, 2007). Individuals with less time to dedicate towards work and family are thought to engage in CWB as well (Bergerson, 2007). We build on existing research (Bergerson, 2007; Chernyak-Hai & Tziner, 2014; Sears & Humiston, 2015; Spector & Che, 2014) to theorize that LMX and WFC could serve as a link between congruence between ILT's and supervisor recognition and engagement in CWB to make the following predictions.

> Hypothesis 5: Congruence between ILT's of: (a) typical, (b) ideal, and (c) effective leaders and characteristics recognized in one's current supervisor will impact CWB through LMX.

Hypothesis 6: Congruence between ILT's of: (a) typical, (b) ideal, and (c) effective leaders and characteristics recognized in one's current supervisor will impact CWB through WFC.

Method

Participants & Procedure

Participants were working adults (20+ hours per week) recruited for a two-wave data collection through Qualtrics Panels. Qualtrics Panels is a service aligned with the Qualtrics survey platform that recruits and matches participants based off the needs of the study and prescreen questions. Participants are compensated through Qualtrics Panels at the completion of each survey. In this case, separate prescreen questions were utilized by Qualtrics to ensure that participants were above the age of 18 and that they worked at least twenty hours per week. Survey measures were separated out into two waves to minimize common-method variance. Participants were first surveyed on their implicit theories, followed by relational (e.g. WFC) and outcome variables (e.g. CWB). 941 individuals responded to both data collections. Of these, 29.4% were male, 36.8% were female, and 33.8% did not respond or marked decline to respond.

The sample was 54.4% Caucasian, with 4.4% responding as Asian, 3.2% as African-American, 3% as Hispanic, and 34% declined to respond. 6.2% of the sample was aged 18-25, 16.5% was 26–35, 10.4% was 36–45, 14.3% was 46–55, 15.0% was 56–65, 3.9% was 65+, and 33.7% did not respond. 12.9% of the population worked 20–30 hours per week, 32.1% worked 30–40 hours per week, 20.5% worked more than 40 hours a week, and 34.5% did not respond.

Self-report data were used to test the indirect effect of intra-personal congruence between ILT's and supervisor recognition on CWB through LMX and WFC. The use of same source, self-report data is necessary given the purpose of this study is to examine subjective assessments (e.g. interpersonal relationships inside and outside of work) (Rupprecht et al., 2016). This approach has been used in prior studies determining the relationships of congruence between prototypical characteristics with LMX, CWB, and other relevant outcomes (Rupprecht et al., 2016; Zhang, Wang, & Shi, 2012).

Measures

Implicit Leadership Theories

ILT's of typical, ideal, and effective leaders were measured using Epitropaki and Martin's (2004) measure. This measure consists of 21 items across 6 dimensions of prototypical characteristics of leaders (sensitivity, intelligence, dedication, dynamism, tyranny, and masculinity). Participants were asked to think of their prototypical leader (typical, ideal, or effective) and to rate how characteristic these attributes are of that prototype. For example, the prompt for the "Typical leader" read: "Please take a moment to think about your image of a TYPICAL LEADER that you have had. Then rate how descriptive the characteristics presented are of your TYPICAL LEADER using the scale presented below, where 1 is "not at all characteristic" and 9 is "extremely characteristic."

The six dimensions were averaged to form a composite ILT score for typical, ideal, and effective leaders separately. Because 8 of these items represent negative prototypical characteristics of leaders (e.g. domineering, pushy, manipulative, conceited, selfish, and loud represent "tyranny") and are negatively valanced, these items were reverse coded when forming the composite scores (Scherbaum, Finlinson, Barden, & Tamanini, 2006). Thus, the overall composite average reflected the overall prototype of a typical/ideal/effective leader. All composite scores showed acceptable reliability (Typical α = .815, Ideal α = .805, Effective α = .832).

Supervisor Recognition

Supervisor recognition (e.g. characteristics identified and recognized in one's current supervisor) was measured using Epitropaki and Martin's (2004) measure of ILT's and executed as recommended by Epitropaki and Martin (2005). This measure prompts participants think about their current leader and to rate attributes using the same scale described for above. These attributes were averaged to form a composite score demonstrating adequate reliability (Supervisor Recognition α = .857). This composite average reflected the overall prototype of one's current leader for comparative purposes with the other prototypes.

LMX

LMX was assessed using the LMX-7 (Graen & Uhl-Bien, 1995), consisting of seven items measuring the participant's relationship with their supervisor (α = .922). Example items include "How would you characterize your working relationship with your leader?" (1 = Extremely ineffective, 5 = Extremely effective) and "How well does your leader understand your job problems and needs? (1 = Not a bit, 5 = A great deal).

Work-Family Conflict

Work-family conflict was assessed along four dimensions from Kelloway, Gottlieb, and Barham (1999): time-based work-interfering with family (WIF), Strain-based WIF, time-based family-interfering with work (FIW), and Strain-based FIW. There were 22 items across all four dimensions and each dimension demonstrated adequate reliability (WIF-Time α = .984, WIF-Strain α = .878, FIW-Time α = .933, FIW-Strain α = .943). Example items include "I have to change plans with family members because of demands of my job" and "My family life puts me in a bad mood at work" (1 = Strongly Disagree, 7 = Strongly Agree). An overall WFC scale score was also calculated (α = .964) by averaging the four subscales together.

CWB

Finally, Counterproductive Work Behaviors were assessed using a 20-item scale (Bennett & Robinson, 2000). Example items prompted participants to rate the extent to which they engaged in the following behaviors in the past and include items such as

"Cursed at someone at work" and "Put little effort into your work" (1 = Strongly Disagree, 7 = Strongly Agree). This measure demonstrated adequate reliability ($\alpha = .964$).

Results

Means, standard deviations, inter-correlations, and reliability statistics are reported in Table 1. ILT prototype scores were scale centered per the recommendations of Edwards (2002).

The factor structure of ILT's for all categories of leaders (e.g. typical leader, ideal leader, and effective leader) was assessed as individual 6-factor models, as proposed by Epitropaki and Martin (2005). Additionally, ILT's were assessed pair-wise as 6- and 12-factor models. In other words, characteristics recognized in one's current supervisor were examined along with ILT's for all leader categories (i.e. typical leader, ideal leader, and effective leader). The pair-wise 6-factor model combined each dimension of ILT's (e.g. items assessing sensitivity of a leader loaded onto the same factor as items assessing sensitivity in one's current supervisor) while the 12-factor approach modeled them separately (e.g. items assessing sensitivity of a leader loaded onto a different factor than items assessing sensitivity in one's current supervisor). This approach follows the practices laid out in Epitropaki and Martin (2005) to demonstrate the factor structure of ILT's and the differentiation between comparison ILT's. CFA analyses of ILT's using the structure proposed by Epitropaki and Martin (2005) demonstrated adequate fit for ILT's of all categories of leaders. Furthermore, the 12-factor models were found to fit better than the 6-factor models combining ILT's, thereby demonstrating differentiation between ILT's and evidence that ILT's were captured accurately for each category of leader (see Table 2). As such, we believe construct validity to be adequate.

Polynomial regression with response surface modeling was used to test the first four hypotheses regarding the effect of congruence between ILT's and supervisor recognition on relational and work-family outcomes (e.g. Edwards & Parry, 1993). Using congruence between ILT's of typical leaders and supervisor recognition as an example, the equation for this approach is listed as follows, where *b* is the regression coefficient for

Table 1. Descriptive Statistics, Correlations, and Reliability Estimates for all Variables.

Variable	M	SD	1	2	3	4	5	6	7	8	9	10	11
1. ILT of typical leader	.78	.73	(.815)	.719*	−.002	−.011	−.043	.179*	.194*	.277*	.226*	.276*	.248*
2. ILT of ideal leader	.77	.66		(.805)	.031	.003	−.040	.183*	.204*	.251*	.218*	.293*	.242*
3. ILT of effective leader	1.22	.97			(.832)	.652*	.271*	.033	.044	.041	.044	.084	.046
4. Supervisor recognition	.91	1.16				(.857)	.436*	.055	.049	.051	.055	.048	.060
5. LMX	3.74	.91					(.922)	−.059	−.030	.022	.034	.013	−.012
6. WIF-Time	3.35	1.82						(.984)	.762*	.651*	.603*	.400*	.871*
7. WIF-Strain	3.48	1.51							(.878)	.661*	.656*	.446*	.874*
8. FIW-Time	2.62	1.61								(.933)	.872*	.571*	.899*
9. FIW-Strain	2.45	1.41									(.943)	.587*	.877*
10. CWB	1.93	1.24										(.964)	.563*
11. WFC	2.98	1.40											(.964)

Note. ILT: implicit leadership theory; LMX: leader-member exchange; WIF: work interfering with family; FIW: family interfering with work; CWB: counter-productive work behavior; WFC: Composite measure of work-family conflict. Reliabilities are in parentheses along the diagonal. ILT scores were scale centered and range from −3 to 3. * $p < .05$.

Table 2. Confirmatory Factor Analysis Results & Model Comparisons.

Model	χ^2	df	$\Delta\chi^2$a	Δdf	CFI	TLI	RMSEA
ILT of typical LEADER	808.656	182			.949	.941	.072
ILT of ideal leader	799.046	182			.950	.942	.072
ILT of effective leader	2170.212	182			.940	.931	.079
Supervisor recognition	2436.761	182			.944	.936	.084
Congruence between ILT's of typical leaders & supervisor recognition							
6-factor	12395.481	813			.540	.513	.156
12-factor	1192.676	803	10101.805*	10	.941	.937	.056
Congruence between ILT's of ideal leaders & supervisor recognition							
6-factor	12286.135	813			.542	.515	.156
12-factor	2301.938	803	9984.197*	10	.940	.936	.057
Congruence between ILT's of effective leaders & supervisor recognition							
6-factor	30659.388	813			.615	.593	.145
12-factor	7946.646	803	22712.7342*	10	.944	.936	.084

Note: *$p < .05$.
[a]6-factor models were compared.

each variable. In this equation, "typical" represents ILT's of typical leaders and "recognition" represents supervisor recognition.

$$Z = b_0 + b_1\text{Typical} + b_2\text{Recognition} + b_3\text{Typical} * \text{Recognition} + b_4\text{Typical}^2 + b_4\text{Recognition}^2$$

Significant overall models were further tested by bootstrapping the resulting coefficients in 5,000 bootstrapped samples and testing coefficients along the response surface for significance using bias-corrected 95% confidence intervals. Specifically, we (a) modeled the polynomial regression results on a response surface and (b) calculated estimates of elements along this surface using bootstrapping procedures (see Edwards, 2007). We were primarily interested in the slope along the line of congruence (Typical = Recognition; slope $= b_1 + b_2$) and the curvature along the line of incongruence (curvature $= b_3 - b_4 + b_5$). The slope along the line of incongruence tests the effect of congruence between ILT's and supervisor recognition on an outcome variable, which relates to Hypotheses 2 and 4. The curvature along the line of incongruence tests the effect of incongruence between ILT's and supervisor recognition, or the degree of discrepancy on an outcome, which relates to Hypotheses 1 and 3. Additionally, it is possible to examine the slope along the line of disagreement (Typical $= -$ Recognition; slope $= b_3 - b_4 - b_5$), which does not relate to a specific hypothesis but does examine whether the direction of the discrepancy between ILT's and supervisor recognition (i.e. ILT > Supervisor Recognition) impacts the outcome. Given the nuance of the congruence tests, we opted to test each dimension of WFC separately even though they were not differentially hypothesized.

We followed the block variable approach suggested by Cable and Edwards (2004) to test the hypothesized indirect effects (Hypotheses 5 and 6). Unlike the more nuanced congruence tests, the block variable approach makes it possible to test indirect effects by having a single predictor. Specifically, the five polynomial terms were combined into a block variable, with each term weighted by their association with the indirect variable. This block variable was then used as a predictor in bootstrapped indirect effects tests, again using 5,000 bootstrapped samples. Given the high intercorrelations between dimensions and that we are testing more complex models for the indirect effects tests, we utilized an overall composite score of WFC for the sake of parsimony, as has been supported with similar constructs in the published literature (e.g., Hill, Matthews, & Walsh, 2016). A 2nd order factor structure using the four dimensions of WFC with a higher order latent variable demonstrated adequate fit to further support this approach ($\chi^2(205) = 1364.29$, RMSEA = .092, CFI = .92, TLI = .91). The block variable approach encapsulates both congruence and incongruence effects – thus any effects found using this approach are due to both congruence and incongruence and cannot be unpacked using response surface modeling. Instead, significant effects can be interpreted as being due to overall (in)congruence between ILTs and recognized supervisor characteristics.

Hypotheses 1a–6a tested congruence between ILT's of typical leaders and characteristics recognized in one's supervisor (e.g. supervisor recognition). The overall model for LMX was significant, $R^2 = .167$, $p < .001$. The a_4 coefficient, used to test Hypothesis 1a, was non-significant ($a_4 = -.042$), suggesting that the degree of discrepancy is not associated with ratings of LMX. The a_1 coefficient, used to test Hypothesis 2a, was significant ($a_1 = .322$), suggesting that congruence between ILT's of typical leaders and supervisor recognition at high rating levels of both is associated with higher levels of LMX, thereby supporting Hypothesis 2a (see Figure 1). Although not hypothesized, the significant and negative slope along the line of incongruence shows directional effects of incongruence, such that when there is incongruence LMX is highest when perceptions of the supervisor are higher than one's typical leader prototype ($a_3 = -.332$).

WFC was tested along each of its dimensions. The overall model for WIF-Time was significant, $R^2 = .044$, $p < .001$. The overall model for WIF-Strain was significant, $R^2 = .058$, $p < .001$. The overall model for FIW-Time was significant, $R^2 = .103$, $p < .001$. Finally, the overall model for FIW-Strain was significant, $R^2 = .077$, $p < .001$. Follow-up surface coefficients were calculated for each of these models. Significant effects along

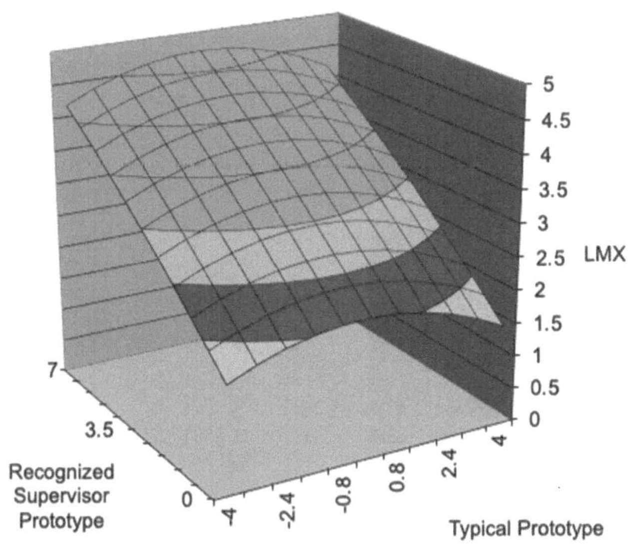

Figure 1. Typical-recognition congruence on LMX.

the curvature of incongruence were found for WIF-Strain and FIW-Strain (a_4 = .214, a_4 = .266, respectively), suggesting that greater discrepancy between ILT's of typical leaders and supervisor recognition is associated with greater strain-based conflict. No other significant coefficients were found. Thus, Hypothesis 3a was partially supported and Hypothesis 4a was not supported. See Table 3 for greater detail.

Figure 2 graphically represents these effects on FIW-Strain to provide a visual example.

Hypotheses 5a and 6a concerned the indirect effect of congruence between ILT's of typical leaders and supervisor recognition on CWB via LMX and WFC, respectively. There was not a significant indirect effect for LMX, $\beta = .01$ [−.03, .06). Congruence between the ILT's of typical leaders and supervisor recognition did not lead to CWB via LMX and thus hypothesis 5a was not supported. There was a significant indirect effect for WFC, $\beta = .16$ [.08, .24], providing evidence that congruence between ILT's of typical leaders and supervisor recognition leads to CWB via WFC, thereby supporting hypothesis 6a. These results suggest congruence between one's prototype of a typical leader and characteristics recognized in their current supervisor is associated with greater WFC, which, in turn, is associated with greater CWB. Given the block variable approach, described above, it is not necessarily greater congruence that is associated with WFC but instead the congruence and incongruence effects, combined, that were examined in 3a and 4a that are associated with WFC and CWB.

Hypotheses 1b–6b tested congruence between ILT's of ideal leaders and characteristics recognized in one's supervisor (e.g. supervisor recognition). The overall model for LMX was significant, $R^2 = .165$, $p < .001$. The a_4 coefficient, used to test Hypothesis 1b, was significant ($a_4 = -.053$), suggesting that greater discrepancy is associated with lower ratings of LMX, supporting hypothesis 1b. The a_1 coefficient, used to test Hypothesis 2b, was significant ($a_1 = .314$), suggesting that congruence between ILT's of ideal leaders and supervisor recognition at high rating levels of both is associated with higher levels of LMX, thereby supporting Hypothesis 2b. Similar to the typical prototype, the significant and negative slope along the line of incongruence shows directional

Table 3. Polynomial Regression Results for Intra-personal Congruence Between ILT of a "Typical" Leader and the Recognition Prototype of the Current Supervisor.

	LMX	CWB	WIF-Time	WIF-Strain	FIW-Time	FIW-Strain
Intercept	3.508	1.571	2.968	3.108	2.129	2.067
ILT of typical leader	−.005	−.003	.188	.130	.192	.064
Supervisor recognition	.327*	−.046	.065	.074	.104	.114
ILT of typical leader^2	−.033	.264*	.149*	.192*	.259*	.239*
ILT of typical leader × Supervisor recognition	.002	.074	.039	−.019	.000	.067
Supervisor Recognition^2	−.007	.024	−.006	.003	−.021	−.012
R^2	.167*	.126*	.044*	.058*	.103*	.077*
Congruence (ILT of typical leader = Supervisor recognition)						
Slope	.322*	−.049	.253	.204	.296	.178
Curvature	−.038*	.362*	.182	.176	.238	.188
Incongruence (ILT of typical leader = Supervisor recognition)						
Slope	−.332*	.043	.123	.056	.088	−.05
Curvature	−.042	.214	.104	.214*	.238	.266*

Note. * $p < .05$.

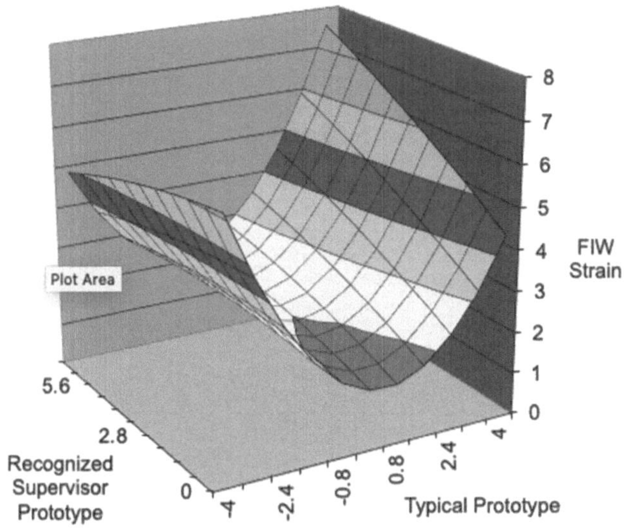

Figure 2. Typical-recognition congruence on FIW-Strain.

effects of incongruence. When there is incongruence LMX is highest when perceptions of the supervisor are higher than one's ideal leader prototype ($a_3 = -.316$).

Hypotheses 3b and 4b were tested along each dimension of WFC. The overall model for WIF-Time was significant, $R^2 = .057$, $p < .001$. The overall model for WIF-Strain was significant, $R^2 = .078$, $p < .001$. The overall model for FIW-Time was significant, $R^2 = .131$, $p < .001$. Finally, the overall model for FIW-Strain was significant, $R^2 = .123$, $p < .001$. Follow-up surface coefficients were calculated for each of these models. Significant effects along the curvature of incongruence were found for WIF-Time, WIF-Strain, FIW-Time, and FIW-Strain ($a_4 = .398$, $a_4 = .647$, $a_4 = .619$, and $a_4 = .619$, respectively), suggesting that greater discrepancy between ILT's of ideal leaders and supervisor recognition is associated with WFC. No other significant coefficients were found. Thus, Hypothesis 3b was fully supported and Hypothesis 4 b was not supported. See Table 4 for greater detail.[1]

Hypotheses 5b and 6b tested the indirect effects of the effect of congruence between ILT's of ideal leaders and supervisor recognition on CWB via LMX and WFC, respectively. There was not a significant indirect effect for LMX, $\beta = .01$ [−.03, .06). Congruence between the ILT's of ideal leaders and supervisor recognition did not lead to CWB via LMX. Therefore, hypothesis 5 b was not supported. There was a significant indirect effect for WFC, $\beta = .16$ [.08, .23), thereby supporting Hypothesis 6b. This effect suggests that the combined congruence and incongruence effects between ILTs of ideal leaders and characteristics recognized in their current supervisor are associated with WFC and, in turn, CWBs.

Hypotheses 1c–6c tested congruence between ILT's of effective leaders and characteristics recognized in one's supervisor (e.g. supervisor recognition). The overall model for LMX was significant, $R^2 = .203$, $p < .001$. The a_4 coefficient, used to test Hypothesis

[1]Note: Surface plots for the Ideal-Recognized comparison are similar, visually, to those presented for the Typical prototype comparison are available upon request.

Table 4. Polynomial Regression Results for Intra-personal Congruence Between ILT of an "Ideal" Leader and the Recognition Prototype of the Current Supervisor.

	LMX	CWB	WIF-Time	WIF-Strain	FIW-Time	FIW-Strain
Intercept	3.499	1.692	3.009	3.194	2.336	2.239
ILT of ideal leader	−.001*	−.36*	−.091	−.456	−.456*	−.504*
Supervisor recognition	.315	.006	.132	.169	.169*	.161*
ILT of ideal leader^2	−.031	.469*	.350*	.594*	.594*	.542*
ILT of ideal leader × Supervisor recognition	.016	.021	−.051	−.081	−.081	−.095
Supervisor Recognition^2	−.006	.017	−.009	−.028	−.028	−.018
R^2	.165*	.151*	.057*	.078*	.131*	.123*
Congruence (ILT of ideal leader = Supervisor recognition)						
Slope	.314*	−.354	.041	−.287	−.287	−.343
Curvature	−.021*	.507*	.290*	.485*	.485*	.429*
Incongruence (ILT of ideal leader = Supervisor recognition)						
Slope	−.316*	−.366	−.223	−.625	−.625*	−.665*
Curvature	−.053*	.465*	.398*	.647*	.619*	.619*

Note. * $p < .05$.

1c, was non-significant ($a_4 = -.138$), suggesting that the degree of discrepancy is not associated with ratings of LMX. As such, hypothesis 1c was not supported. The a_1 coefficient, used to test Hypothesis 2a, was significant ($a_1 = .437$), suggesting that congruence between ILT's of effective leaders and supervisor recognition at high rating levels of both is associated with higher levels of LMX, thereby supporting Hypothesis 2c. As with the other two prototype comparisons, the significant and negative slope along the line of incongruence shows directional effects of incongruence. When there is incongruence, LMX is highest when perceptions of the supervisor are higher than one's effective leader prototype ($a_3 = -.229$).

None of the models examining ILTs of effective leaders and supervisor recognition were significant for WFC. Follow-up surface tests were therefore not conducted, and Hypotheses 3c and 4c were not supported (see Table 5).

Hypotheses 5c and 6c were tested for indirect effects. There was not a significant indirect effect for congruence impact CWB via LMX, $\beta = .00$ [−.04, .05). Thus, hypothesis 5c was not supported. There was not a significant indirect effect for congruence impacting CWB via WFC, $\beta = .03$ [−.02, .08). Thus, hypothesis 6c was not supported. See Table 6 for a summary of the indirect effects tests.

Supplemental Analyses

In keeping with other congruence studies (e.g., Zhang et al., 2012), we tested for congruence effects between ILT's and supervisor recognition on CWB. While not hypothesized, we believed it useful to determine whether there were direct and nuanced congruence effects for CWB in addition to the effects hypothesized a priori.

The overall model for congruence between ILT's of typical leaders and supervisor recognition predicting CWB was significant, $R^2 = .126$, $p < .001$ though the surface coefficients relating to discrepancy or congruence were not significant. This suggests that while the congruence coefficients together predicted a significant amount of variance there were no specifically significant nuanced effects. The overall model for congruence between ILT's of ideal leaders and supervisor recognition predicting CWB was significant, $R^2 = .151$, $p < .001$. The a_4 coefficient was significant ($a_4 = .465$), suggesting that

Table 5. Polynomial Regression Results for Intra-personal Congruence Between ILT of an "Effective" Leader and the Recognition Prototype of the Current Supervisor.

	LMX	CWB	WIF-Time	WIF-Strain	FIW-Time	FIW-Strain
Intercept	3.424	1.771	3.279	3.408	2.522	2.363
ILT of effective leader	.104	.109	−.036	−.025	.063	.024
Supervisor recognition	.333*	−.020	.123	.073	.086	.059
ILT of effective leader^2	−.043	−.006	.015	.028	−.012	.002
ILT of effective leader × Supervisor recognition	.048*	−.019	−.018	−.010	−.012	.015
Supervisor Recognition^2	−.047	.034	−.005	−.011	−.011	−.026
R^2	.203*	.010				
Congruence (ILT of effective leader = Supervisor recognition)						
Slope	.437*					
Curvature	−.042*					
Incongruence (ILT of effective leader = Supervisor recognition)						
Slope	−.229*					
Curvature	−.138					

Note. * $p < .05$. Surface values were not calculated for models that were non-significant.

Table 6. Results for Tests of Indirect Effects of Congruence Between ILT's and Supervisor Recognition on CWB.

Model	LMX	CWB
Indirect effects of LMX		
Congruence between ILT of typical leader & supervisor recognition		
Coefficient of Block Variable (i.e. direct effect of congruence)	.43***	0.04
Coefficient of LMX		.03
Indirect Effect of Congruence via LMX		.01 [−.03, .06]
Congruence between ILT of ideal leader & supervisor recognition		
Coefficient of Block Variable (i.e. direct effect of congruence)	.43***	−.03
Coefficient of LMX		.03
Indirect Effect of Congruence via LMX		.01 [−.03, .06]
Congruence between ILT of effective leader & supervisor recognition		
Coefficient of Block Variable (i.e. direct effect of congruence)	.41***	.00 [−.11, .10]
Coefficient of LMX		.02
Indirect Effect of Congruence via LMX		.00 [−.04, .05]
Indirect effects of WFC		
Congruence between ILT of typical leader & supervisor recognition		
Coefficient of Block Variable (i.e. direct effect of congruence)	.29***	.13***
Coefficient of WFC		.54***
Indirect Effect of Congruence via WFC		.16 [.08, .24]***
Congruence between ILT of ideal leader & supervisor recognition		
Coefficient of Block Variable (i.e. direct effect of congruence)	.29***	.19***
Coefficient of WFC		.53***
Indirect Effect of Congruence via WFC		.16 [.08, .23]***
Congruence between ILT of effective leader & supervisor recognition		
Coefficient of Block Variable (i.e. direct effect of congruence)	.05	.00
Coefficient of WFC		.60***
Indirect Effect of Congruence via WFC		.03 [−.02, .08]

Note. Standardized coefficients are reported. LMX: Leader-member exchange; WFC: Work-family conflict. 95% Confidence Intervals for indirect effects are reported in brackets. * $p < .05$, ** $p < .01$, *** $p < .001$.

greater discrepancy is associated with higher levels of CWB. Finally, the overall model for congruence between ILT's of effective leaders and supervisor recognition predicting CWB was not significant. As a result, the surface coefficients for this comparison were not estimated.

In summary, the strongest pattern of results was found for the Ideal leader comparison. Incongruence and congruence effects were found for LMX, incongruence effects were found for work-family conflict, and mediation support was found for the work-family conflict mediator. A strong pattern of results was also found for the typical leader comparison. Congruence effects were found for LMX, incongruence effects were partially supported for work family conflict, and mediation support was found for the work-family conflict mediator. The effective comparison hypotheses found very little support. Only the congruence effects on LMX were supported for the effective comparison.

Discussion

The present study explored the effect of intra-personal congruence between ILT's (of typical, ideal, and effective leaders) and characteristics recognized in one's supervisor on relationship quality, work-family conflict, and subsequent counterproductive behavior. The results of this study showed that congruence between ILT's and supervisor recognition significantly impacts perceived LMX quality with supervisors. Specifically, greater discrepancy (i.e. incongruity) between ILT's of ideal leaders and supervisor recognition was associated with lower ratings of LMX. Congruence between ILT's of typical leaders and supervisor recognition, as well as ideal leaders and supervisor recognition, (i.e. greater similarity) at high levels were associated with higher ratings of LMX. Together, the results show that there are both positive effects of one's current supervisor being aligned with one's prototype and negative effects on LMX when there is deviation from one's prototype. Further investigation shows that, when there is deviation, LMX is highest when perceptions of one's current supervisor are high. While deviation alone is harmful to LMX, there is nuance as to when it is most harmful. When there is deviation, it is better for LMX to have higher perceptions of one's supervisor as compared to one's ILT, as opposed to having an ILT higher than perceptions of one's supervisor.

In addition, our results demonstrate that congruence between ILT's and supervisor recognition significantly impacts perceived work-family conflict. Greater discrepancy (i.e. incongruity) between ILT's of ideal leaders and supervisor recognition was associated with higher ratings of WFC. In the case of WFC, our results indicate that prototype match does not matter, as previous literature has suggested. Rather, match matters in the specific case of mismatch, or incongruence, when perceptions of one's current leader deviate from one's prototype. Our direct effects tests of congruence provide more nuanced findings around the differing effects of congruence and incongruence for both positive (LMX) and negative (WFC) outcomes. Taken together, they also suggest that the effects of congruence and incongruence are not, as we hypothesized, universally positive or negative across outcomes.

In addition, we tested whether congruence between ILT's and supervisor recognition impacts CWB via LMX and WFC. The results showed a significant indirect effect for WFC but not LMX. As such, we provide evidence congruence between ILTs of typical and ideal leaders and characteristics recognized in one's supervisor are related to WFC, which, in turn, is related to CWB. In sum, the results demonstrate that both congruence and incongruence between ILT's and supervisor recognition significantly impacts work-related outcomes (e.g. LMX) as well as non-work-related outcomes (e.g. WFC). Additionally, these results show evidence that the overall congruence effect is related to CWB and that this effect is, in part, due to WFC. This broader integrative model provides evidence for deviance-related outcomes, suggesting that the effect of negative congruence on felt strain can be one factor that leads to workplace deviance, while the positive effects of congruence on leader-follower relations do not protect against workplace deviance.

The present work adds to literature on ILT's and leader categorization in two important ways. First, we build on established research showing the impact of congruence between ILT's and supervisor recognition on LMX and CWB (Epitropaki & Martin, 2005; Rupprecht et al., 2016) by showing the nuanced effects of incongruence while exploring WFC as an additional outcome and process variable. Our results support assertions that congruence and discrepancy between ILT's and characteristics recognized in one's supervisor impacts LMX, and that discrepancy between ILT's and characteristics recognized in one's supervisor impacts WFC and CWB. We did not, however, find support for congruence impacting CWB through LMX. Although this does not align with expected results, based on prior studies (Chernyak-Hai & Tziner, 2014; Sears & Humiston, 2015; Spector & Che, 2014), it is possible that this relationship is moderated by immediate job and exchange characteristics and environmental factors not collected in this study. In contrast, we did find support for the assertion that congruence between ILT's of typical leaders and characteristics recognized in one's supervisor as well as congruence between ILT's of ideal leaders and characteristics recognized in one's supervisor impacts CWB through WFC. These results, combined with supplemental analyses showing incongruence effects on CWB, suggest unfulfilled expectations for the leader role lead to engagement in CWB.

Second, we tested ILT congruence in a broad sense by incorporating ILT's of multiple leader categories. As such, the present study also heeds calls from researchers to investigate how ILT's of different categories of leaders work within the framework of intra-personal congruence (Epitropaki et al., 2013; Foti et al., 2017). Table 7 presents a summary of the support for all hypotheses for each ILT category.

In addressing the differential effects of congruence between each individual category and supervisor recognition, we found the strongest support for our hypotheses when intra-personal congruence between ILT's and characteristics recognized in one's current supervisor when the ILT category was that of an "ideal leader." We found modest support for our hypotheses when the ILT category was that of "typical leader," and very little support for our hypotheses when the ILT category was that of an "effective leader." These results suggest that capturing the valence of leader prototypes in comparison with one's current leader is a more effective predictor of personal and organizational outcomes than capturing the norm of prototypes. There are several possible explanations for this. First, it is possible that ILT's of ideal leaders may be a clearer category to compare current supervisors to than ILT's of typical or effective leaders (van Gils et al., 2010; van Quaquebeke, van Knippenberg, & Eckloff, 2011; van Quaquebeke et al., 2010; van Quaquebeke et al., 2011). This supports prior research suggesting categorization plays a larger role with respect to "ideal" leaders than other categories of leaders (van Quaquebeke et al., 2011). Second, ILT's of effective leaders may be more reflective of the organization within which the leader and perceiver work (Dickson, Resick, & Hanges, 2006; Shondrick & Lord, 2010), thus not capturing the norm of leader prototypes accurately. Finally, it is possible that ILT's of ideal leaders are a more

Table 7. Support for Hypotheses for ILT's of Typical, Ideal, and Effective Leaders.

Hypothesis	ILT leader category		
	Typical leader	Ideal leader	Effective leader
Hypothesis 1 Greater discrepancy (i.e. incongruity) between ILT's and supervisor recognition will be associated with lower ratings of LMX	Not supported	Fully supported	Not Supported
Hypothesis 2 Congruence between ILT's and supervisor recognition (i.e. greater similarity) at high levels will be associated with higher ratings of LMX	Fully supported	Fully supported	Fully Supported
Hypothesis 3 Greater discrepancy (i.e. incongruity) between ILT's and supervisor recognition will be associated with higher ratings of WFC	Partially supported	Fully supported	Not Supported
Hypothesis 4 Congruence between ILT's and supervisor recognition (i.e. greater similarity) at high levels will be associated with lower ratings of WFC	Not supported	Not supported	Not Supported
Hypothesis 5 Congruence between ILT's and supervisor recognition will impact CWB through LMX.	Not supported	Not supported	Not Supported
Hypothesis 6 Congruence between ILT's and supervisor recognition will impact CWB through WFC.	Fully supported	Fully supported	Not Supported

comprehensive than ILT's of effective leaders (Lord et al., 1984). As such, ILT's of effective leaders may not capture the valence of prototypes as thoroughly as ILT's of ideal leaders.

There are several practical implications of our findings worth considering. First, our findings offer an additional explanation for counter-productive work behavior and work-family conflict. By identifying the extent to which leaders are seen as prototypical, it is possible employees could be more easily encouraged to engage in practices that positively impact work-family balance, thus reducing work family conflict and counter-productive behavior. Furthermore, organizations could, if necessary, match leaders and followers based on the extent to which perceptions of leaders match perceptions of supervisors of a workforce, as suggested by prior research (Engle & Lord, 1997). Second, training programs could be used to attempt to modify existing follower-held leadership schemas to better match or adapt to one's current supervisor. Such training programs would also benefit from processes proposed by DeRue and Ashford (2010), who noted that identification with a given role (e.g. follower) may coincide with granting an appropriate identity to one's dyadic partner (e.g. leader). Finally, managers should be cautioned about simply evaluating the extent to which leaders are seen as "effective," as this may not adequately address issues pertaining to relationships inside and outside of the workplace.

Limitations and Future Research

As with all studies, there are limitations that must be acknowledged. The primary limitation is the two-time point nature of our data collection, which precluded our ability to make causal inferences when testing hypotheses 5 and 6. The use of two time points does, however, minimize concerns over common method variance (Spector, 2006). Furthermore, the theoretical model was aligned with the causal precedent set by previous researchers for mediational research with implicit theories (Whiteley, Sy, & Johnson, 2012). A secondary limitation of the study is the use of single-source data. However, because this study focused on outcome assessments of associations of schema similarity, we believe that the central purpose of this study was still fully addressed. Thus, this limitation does not undermine the contribution of the study.

This study opens up exciting new avenues of future research. Primarily, the link between implicit theories and OCB with relational mediators should be investigated further. Examination of implicit followership theories (IFT's) as antecedents may be particularly fruitful (Whiteley et al., 2012). Future research should also use multi-level analyses to explore the extent to which ILT's of effective leaders are reflective of the organization within which the perceiver and target individual work (Shondrick & Lord, 2010). Finally, research should continue to examine specific incremental benefits of using implicit theories of specific basic level categories (e.g. ethical leaders) (Junker & van Dick, 2014).

Conclusion

In conclusion, the present study contributes to the literature in several ways. First, we expand on the existing knowledge of outcomes related to ILT congruence. We find that ILT congruence with characteristics recognized in one's supervisor relate to relational quality with one's leader and work-life outcomes. We also find that ILT congruence relates to counter-productive behaviors through WFC, providing initial evidence for an explanatory mechanism. Finally, we identify "ideal" and "typical" as the stronger comparisons to one's supervisor, suggesting that "effective" comparisons may not be useful in future research.

ORCID

Benjamin Biermeier-Hanson http://orcid.org/0000-0003-3839-1767

References

Bergerson, A. A. (2007). Exploring the impact of social class on adjustment to college: Anna's story. *International Journal of Qualitative Studies in Education*, *20*(1), 99–119. doi:10.1080/09518390600923610

Bies, R. J., & Tripp, T. M. (1996). Beyond distrust. "Getting even" and the need for revenge. In Kramer, R., & Tyler, T (Eds.), *Trust in organizations* (pp. 246–260). Thousand Oaks, CA: Sage.

Bennett, R. J., & Robinson, S. L. (2000). Development of a measure of workplace deviance. *Journal of Applied Psychology*, *85*(3), 349–360. doi:10.I037//0021-9010.85.3.349

Bolino, M. C., & Klotz, A. C. (2015). The paradox of the unethical organizational citizen: The link between organizational citizenship behavior and unethical behavior at work. *Current Opinion in Psychology*, *6*, 45–49. doi:10.1016/j.copsyc.2015.03.026

Brunetto, Y., Farr-Wharton, R., Ramsay, S., & Shacklock, K. (2010). Supervisor relationships and perceptions of work—family conflict. *Asia Pacific Journal of Human Resources*, *48*(2), 212–232. https://doi.org/10.1177/1038411110368467

Cable, D. M., & Edwards, J. R. (2004). Complementary and supplementary fit: A theoretical and empirical integration. *Journal of Applied Psychology*, *89*(5), 822–834. doi:10.1037/0021-9010.89.5.822

Carlson, D. S., Kacmar, K. M., & Williams, L. J. (2000). Construction and initial validation of a multidimensional measure of work–family conflict. *Journal of Vocational Behavior*, *56*(2), 249–276. doi:10.1006/jvbe.1999.1713

Chernyak-Hai, L., & Tziner, A. (2014). Relationships between counterproductive work behavior, perceived justice and climate, occupational status, and leader-member exchange. *Revista de Psicología Del Trabajo y de Las Organizaciones*, *30*(1), 1–12. doi:10.5093/tr2014a1

Dalal, R. S. (2005). A meta-analysis of the relationship between organizational citizenship behavior and counterproductive work behavior. *Journal of Applied Psychology*, *90*(6), 1241. doi: 10.1037/0021-9010.90.6.1241

Den Hartog, D. N., House, R. J., Hanges, P. J., Ruiz-Quintanilla, S. A., Dorfman, P. W., Abdalla, I. A., … Zhou, J. (1999). Culture specific and cross-culturally generalizable implicit leadership theories: Are attributes of charismatic/transformational leadership universally endorsed? *The Leadership Quarterly*, *10*(2), 219–256. https://doi.org/10.1016/S1048-9843(99)00018-1 doi:10.1016/S1048-9843(99)00018-1

DeRue, D. S., & Ashford, S. J. (2010). Who will lead and who will follow? A social process of leadership identity construction in organizations. *Academy of Management Review*, *35*, 627–647. https://doi.org/10.5465/amr.2010.53503267

Dickson, M. W., Resick, C., & Hanges, P. J. (2006). Systematic variation in organizationally-shared cognitive prototypes of effective leadership based on organizational form. *The Leadership Quarterly*, *17*(5), 487–505. https://doi.org/10.1016/j.leaqua.2006.07.005

Dinh, J. E., & Lord, R. G. (2013). Current trends in moral research what we know and where to go from here. *Current Directions in Psychological Science*, *22*(5), 380–385. doi:10.1177/0963721413486147

Edwards, J. R, (Eds.), (2007). Polynomial regression and response surface methodology. In C. Ostroff & T. A. Judge (Eds.), *Perspectives on organizational fit* (pp. 361–372). San Francisco: Jossey-Bass.

Edwards, J. R. (2002). Alternatives to difference scores: Polynomial regression analysis and response surface methodology. In F. Drasgow & N. W. Schmitt (Eds.), *Advances in measurement and data analysis* (pp. 350–400). San Francisco: Jossey-Bass

Edwards, J. R., & Parry, M. E., (1993). On the use of polynomial regression equations as an alternative to difference scores in organizational research. *Academy of Management Journal*, 3. 1577–1613. https://doi.org/10.2307/256822

Engle, E. M., & Lord, R. G. (1997). Implicit theories, self-schemas, and leader-member exchange. *Academy of Management Journal*, *40*, 988–1010. doi:10.2307/256956

Epitropaki, O., Sy, T., Martin, R., Tram-Quon, S., & Topakas, A. (2013). Implicit leadership and followership theories "in the wild": Taking stock of information-processing approaches to leadership and followership in organizational settings. *The Leadership Quarterly*, *24*(6), 858–881. https://doi.org/10.1016/j.leaqua.2013.10.005

Epitropaki, O., & Martin, R. (2004). Implicit leadership theories in applied settings: Factor structure, generalizability, and stability over time. *Journal of Applied Psychology, 89*, *89*(2), 293–310. doi:10.1037/0021-9010.89.2.293

Epitropaki, O., & Martin, R. (2005). From ideal to real: A longitudinal study of the role of implicit leadership theories on leader-member exchanges and employee outcomes. *Journal of Applied Psychology*, *90*(4), 659–676. doi:10.1037/0021-9010.90.4.659

Foti, R. J., Hansbrough, T. K., Epitropaki, O., & Coyle, P. T. (2017). Dynamic viewpoints on implicit leadership and followership theories: Approaches, findings, and future directions. *The Leadership Quarterly*, *28*(2), 261–267. http://dx.doi.org/10.1016/j.leaqua.2017.02.004

Foti, R. J., Knee, R. E., Jr,, & Backert, R. S. (2008). Multi-level implications of framing leadership perceptions as a dynamic process. *The Leadership Quarterly*, *19*(2), 178–194. https://doi.org/10.1016/j.leaqua.2008.01.007

Foti, R. J., Bray, B. C., Thompson, N. J., & Allgood, S. F. (2012). Know thy self, know thy leader: Contributions of a pattern-oriented approach to examining leader perceptions. *The Leadership Quarterly*, *23*(4), 702–717. https://doi.org/10.1016/j.leaqua.2012.03.007

Foti, R. J., & Lord, R. G. (1987). Prototypes and scripts: The effects of alternative methods of processing information on rating accuracy. *Organizational Behavior and Human Decision Processes*, *39*(3), 318–340. https://doi.org/10.1016/0749-5978(87)90027-6

Golden, T. D. (2006). The role of relationships in understanding telecommuter satisfaction. *Journal of Organizational Behavior*, *27*(3), 319–340. https://doi.org/10.1002/job.369

Graen, G. B., & Uhl-Bien, M. (1995). Relationship-based approach to leadership: Development of leader-member exchange (LMX) theory of leadership over 25 years: Applying a multi-level multi-domain perspective. *The Leadership Quarterly*, *6*(2), 219–247. https://doi.org/10.1016/1048-9843(95)90036-5

Greenhaus, J. H., & Beutell, N. J. (1985). Sources of conflict between work and family roles. *Academy of Management Review*, *10*(1), 76–88. doi:10.2307/258214

Hill, R. T., Matthews, R. A., & Walsh, B. M. (2016). The emergence of family-specific support constructs: Cross-level effects of family-supportive supervision and family-supportive organization perceptions on individual outcomes. *Stress and Health*, *32*(5), 472–484. doi:10.1002/smi.2643

Huang, X., Wright, R. P., Chiu, W. C., & Wang, C. (2008). Relational schemas as sources of evaluation and misevaluation of leader–member exchanges: Some initial evidence. *The Leadership Quarterly*, *19*(3), 266–282. doi:10.1016/j.leaqua.2008.03.003

Junker, N. M., & van Dick, R., (2014). Implicit theories in organizational settings: A systematic review and research agenda of implicit leadership and followership theories. *The Leadership Quarterly*, *25*(6)2. 1154–1173. https://doi.org/10.1016/j.leaqua.2014.09.002

Litano, M. L., Major, D. A., Landers, R. N., Streets, V. N., & Bass, B. I. (2016). A meta-analytic investigation of the relationship between leader-member exchange and work-family experiences. *The Leadership Quarterly*, *27*(5), 802–817. doi:10.1016/j.leaqua.2016.06.003

Liu, S., Luksyte, A., Zhou, L., Shi, J., & Wang, M. (2015). Overqualification and counterproductive work behaviors: Examining a moderated mediation model. *Journal of Organizational Behavior*, *36*(2), 250–271. https://doi.org/10.1002/job.1979

Lord, R. G., Foti, R. J., & De Vader, C. L. (1984). A test of leadership categorization theory: Internal structure, information processing, and leadership perceptions. *Organizational Behavior and Human Performance*, *34*(3), 343–378. https://doi.org/10.1016/0030-5073(84)90043-6

Lord, R. G., & Maher, K. J. (1991). Cognitive theory in industrial and organizational psychology. *Handbook of Industrial and Organizational Psychology*, *2*, 1–62.

Lyu, Y., Wang, M., Le, J., & Kwan, H. K. (2019). Effects of authentic leadership on work–family balance in China. *Journal of Managerial Psychology*, *34*(2), 110–123. doi:10.1108/JMP-08-2018-0340

Kelloway, E. K., Gottlieb, B. H., & Barham, L. (1999). The source, nature, and direction of work and family conflict: A longitudinal investigation. *Journal of Occupational Health Psychology*, *4*(4), 337. doi:10.1037//1076-8998.4.4.337

Martinko, M. J., Gundlach, M. J., & Douglas, S. C. (2002). Toward an integrative theory of counterproductive workplace behavior: A causal reasoning perspective. *International Journal of Selection and Assessment*, *10*(1&2), 36–50. doi:10.1111/1468-2389.00192

Major, D. A., Fletcher, T. D., Davis, D. D., & Germano, L. M. (2008). The influence of work-family culture and workplace relationships on work interference with family: A multilevel model. *Journal of Organizational Behavior*, *29*(7), 881–897. https://doi.org/10.1002/job.502

Major, D. A., & Morganson, V. J. (2011). Coping with work–family conflict: A leader–member exchange perspective. *Journal of Occupational Health Psychology*, *16*(1), 126–138. doi:10.1037/a0021727

Michel, J. S., Kotrba, L. M., Mitchelson, J. K., Clark, M. A., & Baltes, B. B. (2011). Antecedents of work–family conflict: A meta-analytic review. *Journal of Organizational Behavior*, *32*(5), 689–725. doi:10.1002/job.695

Netemeyer, R. G., Boles, J. S., & McMurrian, R. (1996). Development and validation of work–family conflict and family–work conflict scales. *Journal of Applied Psychology*, *81*(4), 400–410. https://doi.org/10.1037//0021-9010.81.4.400

Offermann, L. R., Kennedy, J. K., & Wirtz, P. W. (1994). Implicit leadership theories: Content, structure, and generalizability. *The Leadership Quarterly*, *5*(1), 43–58. https://doi.org/10.1016/1048-9843(94)90005-1

Rupprecht, E. A., Kueny, C. R., Shoss, M. K., & Metzger, A. J. (2016). Getting what you want: How fit between desired and received leader sensitivity influences emotion and counterproductive work behavior. *Journal of Occupational Health Psychology*, *21*(4), 443. doi:10.1037/a0040074

Scott, K. L., Ingram, A., Zagenczyk, T. J., & Shoss, M. K. (2015). Work–family conflict and social undermining behaviour: An examination of PO fit and gender differences. *Journal of Occupational and Organizational Psychology*, *88*(1), 203–218. doi:10.1111/joop.12091

Scherbaum, C. A., Finlinson, S., Barden, K., & Tamanini, K. (2006). Applications of item response theory to measurement issues in leadership research. *The Leadership Quarterly*, *17*, 366–386. https://doi.org/10.1016/j.leaqua.2006.04.005

Sears, K., & Humiston, G. S. (2015). The role of emotion in workplace incivility. *Journal of Managerial Psychology*, *30*(4), 390–405. doi:10.1108/JMP-11-2012-0373

Shanock, L. R., Baran, B. E., Gentry, W. A., Pattison, S. C., & Heggestad, E. D. (2010). Polynomial regression with response surface analysis: A powerful approach for examining moderation and overcoming limitations of difference scores. *Journal of Business and Psychology*, *25*, 543–554. doi:10.1007/s10869-010-9183-4

Shondrick, S. J., & Lord, R. G. (2010). Implicit leadership and followership theories: Dynamic structures for leadership perceptions, memory, and leader-follower processes. *International Review of Industrial and Organizational Psychology*, *25*, 1–33. https://doi.org/10.1002/9780470661628.ch1

Spector, P. E. (2006). Method variance in organizational research: Truth or urban legend? *Organizational Research Methods*, *9*(2), 221–232. doi:10.1177/1094428105284955

Spector, P. E., & Che, X. X. (2014). Re-examining citizenship: How the control of measurement artifacts affects observed relationships of organizational citizenship behavior and organizational variables. *Human Performance*, *27*(2), 165–182. doi:10.1080/08959285.2014.882928

Spector, P. E., Fox, S., Penney, L. M., Bruursema, K., Goh, A., & Kessler, S. (2006). The dimensionality of counterproductivity: Are all counterproductive behaviors created equal? *Journal of Vocational Behavior*, *68*(3), 446–460. doi:10.1016/j.jvb.2005.10.005

Topakas, A. (2011). *Measurement of implicit leadership theories and their effect on leadership processes and outcomes* (Doctoral Dissertation). UK: Aston University.

van Gils, S., van Quaquebeke, N., & van Knippenberg, D. (2010). The X-factor: On the relevance of implicit leadership and followership theories for leader–member exchange agreement.

European Journal of Work and Organizational Psychology, *19*, 333–363. doi:10.1080/13594320902978458

van Quaquebeke, N., Kerschreiter, R., Buxton, A. E., & van Dick, R. (2010). Two lighthouses to navigate: Effects of ideal and counter-ideal values on follower identification and satisfaction with their leaders. *Journal of Business Ethics*, *93*(2), 293–305. doi:10.1007/s10551-009-0222-x

van Quaquebeke, N., & van Knippenberg, D. (2012). Second-generation leader categorization research: How subordinates' self-and typical leader perceptions moderate leader categorization effects. *Journal of Applied Social Psychology*, *42*(6), 1293–1319. doi:10.1111/j.1559-1816.2012.00899.x

van Quaquebeke, N., van Knippenberg, D., & Brodbeck, F. C. (2011). More than meets the eye: The role of subordinates' self-perceptions in leader categorization processes. *The Leadership Quarterly*, *22*, 367–382. https://doi.org/10.1016/j.leaqua.2011.02.011

van Quaquebeke, N., van Knippenberg, D., & Eckloff, T. (2011). Individual differences in the leader categorization to openness to influence relationship: The role of followers' self-perception and social comparison orientation. *Group Processes & Intergroup Relations*, *14*, 605–622. https://doi.org/10.1177/1368430210391311

Whiteley, P., Sy, T., & Johnson, S. K. (2012). Leaders' conceptions of followers: Implications for naturally occurring Pygmalion effects. *The Leadership Quarterly*, *23*(5), 822–834. https://doi.org/10.1016/j.leaqua.2012.03.006

Yam, K. C., Fehr, R., Keng-Highberger, F. T., Klotz, A. C., & Reynolds, S. J. (2016). Out of control: A self-control perspective on the link between surface acting and abusive supervision. *Journal of Applied Psychology*, *101*(2), 292. doi:10.1037/apl0000043

Zhang, Z., Wang, M. O., & Shi, J. (2012). Leader-follower congruence in proactive personality and work outcomes: The mediating role of leader-member exchange. *Academy of Management Journal*, *55*(1), 111–113. https://doi.org/10.5465/amj.2009.086

Predicting Leader Emergence with Bright and Dark Traits

Maureen A. Conard

ABSTRACT

Leader emergence was regressed on five factor model (FFM; NEO Five-Factor Inventory) traits and four additional traits (achievement, dominance, aggression, and Machiavellianism) in a sample of 280 undergraduates (229 women (82%), 51 men; *M* age = 19.7 (*SD* = 1.4). The Jackson Personality Research Form (Jackson, *Personality research form manual* (3rd ed.). Port Huron, MI: Sigma Assessment Systems, Inc.) measured achievement, dominance, and aggression. Christie and Geis' (Studies in machiavellianism. San Diego: Academic Press) Mach IV scale measured Machiavellianism. In an independent groups analysis, six of the nine traits showed significant differences, indicating that leaders are less neurotic and Machiavellian, and more extroverted, open, agreeable, and dominant. However, in a logistic regression analysis, which controlled for shared variance among traits, only extraversion, openness, and dominance predicted leader emergence. Previous studies that did not use regression models showed significant differences for a large number of traits. Results from the present study indicate the importance of accounting for shared variance when analyzing personality traits in order to develop parsimonious models.

Personality trait theory asserts that a person's traits are stable over time, are important drivers of behavior, and therefore can be useful predictors of behavior. The trait theory of leadership predicts that personality traits of leaders and non-leaders will differ, can be useful in identifying future leaders and predicting their behaviors, which in turn correlate with the effectiveness of their performance (DeRue, Nahrgang, Wellman, & Humphrey, 2011). Most of the early evidence regarding leader traits predated the emergence of the five factor model (FFM) of personality, and focused on narrowly defined traits. For example, Bass (1990) review identified over 40 different narrow traits assessed in leadership studies. FFM traits, which are neuroticism, extraversion, openness to experience, agreeableness, and conscientiousness, evolved through a series of analyses of narrow traits with a goal of identifying a more parsimonious model, with fewer traits, that would still encompass the breadth of personality (Costa & McCrae, 1992). The resulting five traits, also called "global" or "super-traits" (Furnham & Crump, 2015) were factored from 30 more narrow traits, which are now facets of the super-traits (Costa & McCrae, 1992). Henceforth, super-traits will be referred to as FFM traits or traits. There has been a general level of agreement that the FFM of personality encompasses the necessary and sufficient number of traits to describe people (Digman, 1990) although such agreement is not universal (Block, 1995; Eysenck, 1992; Paunonen & Ashton, 2001). A corresponding interest in FFM traits as they relate to leadership has also emerged (e.g., Colbert, Judge, Choi, & Wang, 2012). However, relatively few leader emergence studies have measured all FFM traits within individuals. Studies that assessed additional traits together with FFM traits are not common.

Leader emergence and leader effectiveness are the most common criteria in trait research. Leader emergence is typically defined in one of two ways. Laboratory studies often define leader emergence by observers' ratings of a target person or persons engaging in leaderless group discussions (Judge, Bono, Ilies, & Gerhardt, 2002). Field studies usually define leader emergence in terms of whether or not the target person holds a leadership position (Aamodt, 2016; Arvey, Rotundo, Johnson, Zhang, & McGue, 2006). Albright and Forziati (1995) assessed leader emergence both ways, and showed that the two are correlated (ranging from .30 to .39).

FFM and Leader Emergence

The five traits of the FFM are neuroticism, extraversion, openness to experience, agreeableness, and conscientiousness. Neuroticism is characterized by negative emotions such as fear, sadness, embarrassment, and guilt. Individuals who are low on neuroticism tend to be emotionally stable, even-tempered, and able to cope calmly with stressful situations (Costa & McCrae, 1992). Individuals high on neuroticism were less likely to be perceived as leaders (Hogan, Curphy, & Hogan, 1994) in both laboratory and field studies (Colbert et al., 2012; Judge et al., 2002) and studies with students (Karnes, Chauvin, & Trant, 1984).

Extraversion is characterized by preferences for socializing, especially in large groups, being assertive and talkative and also optimistic and energetic. By contrast, introverts (low on extraversion) are reserved, independent, and even paced (Costa & McCrae, 1992). Previous studies found that extraversion and related narrow traits of sociability and dominance were strongly predictive of leadership across a wide range of studies, as well as leadership perceptions in group tasks (Colbert et al., 2012; Judge et al., 2002). Those perceived to be leaders talked more than non-leaders (Reynolds, 1984; Riggio, Riggio, Salinas, & Cole, 2003).

Openness to experience is characterized by intellectual curiosity, divergent thinking, and active imagination. Those who score highly on openness also desire a variety of experiences, independence of judgment, and eagerness to learn (Costa & McCrae, 1992; Hogan & Holland, 2003). Previous reviews found originality (divergent thinking) and openness were strongly associated with leadership and leader emergence (Bass, 1990; Judge et al., 2002).

Agreeableness is characterized by empathy, cooperation, altruism, and helpfulness (Costa & McCrae, 1992). Individuals who are low on agreeableness tend to be antagonistic, skeptical, self-centered, and competitive. The Judge et al. (2002) meta-analysis showed mixed results for agreeableness and leadership. *Rhos* were near zero for leader emergence studies. However, the *rho* was .18 when studies were limited to those with students as participants. Further, when leader emergence was regressed on all FFM traits, the coefficient for agreeableness became negative. Therefore, agreeableness may be predictive of leader emergence in studies involving students, or when other FFM traits are controlled.

Conscientiousness is related to self-control, academic achievement, planning, organizing, and accomplishing tasks (Costa & McCrae, 1992). Studies of conscientiousness and leadership have shown mixed results. Some previous studies showed that Conscientiousness was positively associated with leader emergence, whether in small task groups or across multiple studies (Judge et al., 2002; Lord, de Vader, & Allinger, 1986). Conversely, Colbert et al. (2012) found that conscientiousness was not predictive of a combined leader emergence/leader effectiveness criterion when all FFM traits were included, and their shared variance was partialed out.

Achievement, Dark Traits, and Leader Emergence

The FFM has proven to be a useful and parsimonious way to organize traits. However, there is disagreement on the comprehensiveness of the model (Block, 1995; Eysenck, 1992; Paunonen & Ashton, 2001). The FFM is also limited in that it tends toward positive or "bright" aspects of personality rather than "dark" aspects (Guenole, 2014; Jonason, Wee, & Li, 2014). Judge et al. (2002) meta-analytically regressed leader emergence on all FFM traits, and found an $R = .53$, which represents 28% of the variance in leader emergence. Clearly, there is variance that has not been captured. Further, Judge et al. presented evidence that additional, narrow traits (sociability, dominance, achievement, dependability) correlated positively with a combined criterion of leader emergence and leader effectiveness, however they did not provide separate analyses for leader emergence alone, and those studies generally did not include FFM traits. Therefore, common variance could not be partialed out. In order to confirm the meta-analytic findings, it is important to conduct studies that measure FFM traits as well as other traits together in the same individuals in order to develop a broad understanding of the domain of leader personality traits, and to develop a parsimonious model of traits and their relationship to leader emergence.

For the present study, four additional traits (achievement, dominance, aggression, and Machiavelliaism) were identified based on results of previous studies (Arvey et al., 2006; Judge et al., 2002). Pursuant to Hogan and Hogan's (2001) identification of leadership derailers, interest in what are called "dark side" traits has increased (Furnham, Hyde, & Trickey, 2014; Guenole, 2014). Judge, Piccolo, and Kosalka (2009) included both dark and "bright" traits in their heuristic model of leadership emergence and effectiveness, noting that dark traits have been largely ignored in leadership research and require more attention from researchers. Achievement is a "bright side" trait while dominance, aggression, and Machiavellianism are "dark side" traits.

Individuals high in achievement work toward distant goals and expend effort to accomplish difficult tasks (Jackson, 1999). In the FFM model, achievement is a narrow trait associated with conscientiousness and, as such, should be positively related to leader emergence. Previous studies showed that achievement was positively related to leader emergence (Arvey et al., 2006) and a combined criterion of leader emergence and effectiveness (Judge et al., 2002).

Individuals high in dominance attempt to control their environments, to influence others and they enjoy leadership roles. They also tend to be assertive and persuasive (Jackson, 1999). In the FFM model, dominance is a key aspect of extraversion. Although it is categorized as a "dark" trait, as Judge et al. (2009) noted, all traits can have bright and dark sides. Previous studies have found dominance to be positively related to leader emergence (Arvey et al., 2006; Gough, 1984) and combined leader emergence/leader effectiveness (Judge et al., 2002), although those studies did not measure extraversion and dominance separately.

People high in aggression are argumentative, combative, easily annoyed, hostile, and seek to get even or harm others. Conversely, those low on aggression are not easily provoked to anger, avoid confrontation and conflict, and are forgiving of others' mistakes (Jackson, 1999). In the FFM model, aggression would be inversely associated with agreeableness. Typically, studies of leader emergence focused on traits that were expected to be positively related. As such, aggression has not been widely studied in this context, although it is marked by tendencies similar to undesirable traits such as paranoid/passive-aggressiveness and narcissism that Hogan and Hogan (2001) identified as managerial (leader) career derailers. Therefore it would be expected to be negatively related to leader emergence.

Machiavellianism is another dark trait. The term derives from Niccolo Machiavelli's 1532 treatise *The Prince*, which gave advice about how to accumulate power, influence, and achieve conquests by any means (Christie & Geis, 1970; Crocker, 1963). Although Machiavellianism has not been widely studied in leader emergence, Judge et al. (2009) posited that Machiavellians aspire to managerial positions, are highly motivated to lead, and drawn to positions with extensive resources and power over others. As such one might expect leaders to be higher on Machiavellianism than non-leaders, at least when resources are available. However, Judge et al. noted that Machiavellians might be more likely to "get ahead" than to get along with others. Where leaders are expected to be team oriented and agreeable, leaders might be lower on Machiavellianism.

Few leader emergence studies have measured the complete set of FFM traits along with other traits intra-individually, rather than meta-analytically or by studying subsets of those traits (DeRue et al., 2011). Intra-individual measurement is advantageous because it controls for shared variance among traits. The Judge et al. (2002) meta-analysis established an important foundation for future inquiry. However, as Judge et al. noted, many of the studies available measured some subset of the traits of interest. Those that included narrow or facet traits typically did not include FFM traits. Therefore the meta-analytic findings represent pooled effect sizes rather than trait variance that occurred within individuals. They do not represent patterns of relationships that might emerge when FFM and lower order traits are measured in the same individuals. Because traits are integrated within people, rather than separate variables, researchers have stressed the importance of examining intra-individual patterns of traits (Foti & Hauenstein, 2007) as well as combinations of bright and dark traits (Paulhus, 2014).

The present study addressed several gaps in research. First, it included all FFM traits as well as four additional traits (achievement, dominance, aggression, and Machiavellianism) that may contribute to the prediction of leader emergence. Second, it included three "dark" traits, which have not been widely studied in this context. Third,

Table 1. Descriptive Statistics and Correlations.

	M (*SD*)	*E*	*O*	*A*	*C*	Ach	Dom	Agg	Mach
N	21.4 (8.0)	−36**	−04	−26**	−25*	−15*	−31**	19*	19**
E	33.3 (5.4)	–	06	35**	26**	18*	30**	15*	−36**
O	26.5 (6.0)		–	00	−11	10	07	−07	03
A	33.2 (5.4)			–	22*	07	−16**	−58**	−52**
C	33.7 (6.8)				–	55**	21**	−12*	−25**
Ach	9.9 (3.1)					–	26**	−10	−23**
Dom	8.9 (4.1)						–	23**	02
Agg	7.7 (3.4)							–	45**
Mach	52.5 (7.6)								–

*$p < .05$.
**$p < .01$.
Note. $N = 280$. N = neuroticism; E = extraversion; O = openness to experience; A = agreeableness; C = conscientiousness; Ach = achievement; Dom = dominance; Agg = aggression; Mach = Machiavellianism.

all traits were measured in each individual, which made it possible to identify a pattern of traits when their shared variance was controlled in logistic regression, and to compare the results to those of an independent groups analysis.

There are several overarching research questions to be addressed. First, are FFM traits are sufficient to account for leader emergence or do additional, narrow traits add to predictive efficacy? Second, what role do dark traits play when included with FFM traits? Third, will the pattern of results differ when shared variance among traits is controlled, compared to an independent groups model, and compared to previous studies which did not measure all traits at once. Based on previous single and meta-analytic studies, it was hypothesized that neuroticism, aggression and Machiavellianism would be negatively related to leader emergence. It was further hypothesized that extraversion, openness, agreeableness, conscientiousness, achievement, and dominance would be positively related to leader emergence.

Method

Participants and Procedure

A total of 280 full time undergraduates from a university in the northeast United States provided data for the study (229 women (82%), 51 men; *M* age = 19.7 ($SD = 1.4$); 96 freshmen, 64 sophomores, 65 juniors, and 55 seniors; 264 whites (94%), 3 African-Americans, 6 Hispanics, 3 Asian, 4 “other”). Data were collected over a period of several semesters in order to obtain an adequate sample size. Of the 280 respondents, 65 (23%) self-identified as leaders (51 women and 15 men) and 215 were non-leaders. Leaders and non-leaders had similar gender distributions (87% and 83% women, respectively). Of the 65 leaders, 39 were club officers, nine were team captains, five were resident assistants or head resident assistants, the remainder held various positions such as manager or coach. Several participants held more than one leadership position. Of the original sample of 289, nine participants were eliminated due to large amounts of missing data or because they were part-time, non-traditional or graduate students. Participants volunteered through the university subject pool, completed questionnaires in groups and received course credit for their participation. Non-participants could opt to do an alternate assignment.

Measures

The 60-item NEO Five-Factor Inventory, Form S (Costa & McCrae, 1992) measured FFM traits, using a 5-point scale (0 = *strongly disagree* to 4 = *strongly agree*) with 27 items reverse scored. Summed scale scores were entered in the present data set, rather than item level data. Therefore, Cronbach's alphas could not be computed for the present data. However, Costa and McCrae reported Cronbach's alphas of .86, .77, .73, .68, and .81 for neuroticism, extraversion, openness, agreeableness, and conscientiousness, respectively for their university student norm group used to develop and validate the measures. Further, Table 1 presents the *M*s and *SD*s for the scales of the present data, which are very similar to the *M*s and *SD*s reported for Costa and McCrae's university norm group data.

The Jackson Personality Research Form-E (Jackson, 1999) measured achievement, aggression, and dominance, with 16 items per trait, using a True-False format. Half of the items were reverse scored. For the present data, Cronbach's alphas were .57, .74 and .85, respectively. Jackson reported odd-even reliabilities for a university normative sample of .57, .63, and .67, respectively.

Christie and Geis (1970) 20 item Mach IV scale measured Machiavellianism with a 5-point scale (1 = *strong disagreement* to 5 = *strong agreement*). Items include "it is wise to flatter important people", and "the biggest difference between most criminals and other people is that criminals are stupid enough to get caught. Cronbach's alpha for the current data was .62. Christie and Geis reported a mean split-half reliability of .79 across nine samples.

Leader emergence was measured by respondents indicating if they held a leadership position (yes/no), and what the position was. A checklist prompted respondents with possible positions (officer of a club or organization, resident assistant, head resident assistant, team captain, or other). Checklists measuring leader emergence have been employed effectively in previous studies (e.g., Reichard et al., 2011). Respondents who indicated "other" were asked to specify what position they held. In previous studies, this elaboration beyond a simple yes/no reduced distortion in biographical self-reports (Schmitt & Kunce, 2002; Schmitt et al., 2003). Such self-reports are an established measurement method in leader emergence studies (see Arvey et al., 2006, for a review).

Results

Data were analyzed using the PASW 18 statistical program. First, means, standard deviations and correlations were computed. Then leaders and non-leaders were compared using *t*-tests. Then a two-step logistic regression was computed, and the results of the *t*-tests and regression were compared. Results are presented in the tables. Table 1 presents the means, standard deviations and intercorrelations among the variables. Patterns of correlations are similar to those found in other studies (Christie & Geis, 1970; Conard, 2006; Costa & McCrae, 1992; Farsides & Woodfield, 2003; Gray & Watson, 2002), and indicate acceptable levels of convergent and discriminant validity among the predictors. The correlations are also theoretically logical. For example, achievement, which is a facet of conscientiousness (Costa & McCrae, 1992) was strongly correlated with

Table 2. Mean Differences in Personality Between Leaders and Non-Leaders.

				95% CI		
	Mean leaders ($N = 65$)	Mean non-leaders ($N = 215$)	t	Lower	Upper	d
N	19.83	21.87	1.81	−0.18	4.25	.26
E	35.57	32.56	−4.00**	−4.48	−1.53	−.57
O	28.43	25.95	−2.99**	−4.11	−0.85	−.42
A	34.74	32.76	−2.61**	−3.47	−0.49	−.37
C	34.78	33.34	−1.48	−3.35	0.47	.21
Ach	10.55	9.65	−2.10*	−1.75	−0.06	.30
Dom	10.17	8.51	−2.91**	−2.79	−0.54	−.41
Agg	6.97	7.89	1.94	−0.01	1.85	.27
Mach	50.00	53.32	3.11**	1.22	5.42	.44

*$p < .05$.
**$p < .01$.
Note. N = neuroticism; E = extraversion; O = openness to experience; A = agreeableness; C = conscientiousness; Ach = achievement; Dom = dominance; Agg = aggression; Mach = Machiavellianism; 95% CI = 95% confidence interval. Negative *t* values indicate that means for non-leaders were lower than leaders.

conscientiousness. Agreeableness was strongly negatively correlated with aggression and Machiavellianism. Aggression was strongly correlated with Machiavellianism.

Table 2 presents the group means, test results, confidence intervals, and Cohen's *d* for leaders and non-leaders. Based on the independent groups model, six of the nine traits showed significant differences between leaders and non-leaders, and all six had confidence intervals that did not include zero. Leaders were significantly higher on extraversion, openness, agreeableness, achievement and dominance, and significantly lower Machiavellianism. There were no differences in neuroticism, conscientiousness, or aggression. Based on the sample size and Cohen's *d* values, power for the *t* tests ranged from .29 to .94. Five of the nine had power above .80. Unequal sample sizes result in lower power, however in a field study, one does not have control over how many participants are leaders or not leaders.

Because leader emergence was a dichotomous variable, the multivariate relationships of the predictors to leader emergence were assessed with a two-step logistic regression with FFM traits in the first step, and achievement, dominance, aggression, and Machiavellianism added in the second step. Table 3 shows the logit coefficients (*B*) and their standard errors, Wald statistics, and odds ratios (Exp (*B*)) as well as percent change in odds ratios for each predictor, and likelihood ratio tests. The Wald statistic is distributed as χ^2 and indicates the impact of individual predictors in the model (Cohen, Cohen, Aiken, & West, 2003). Although the Wald statistic is reported by the PASW 18 statistical program, according to Cohen et al. the likelihood ratio test, which also assesses impact of individual predictors and is also distributed as χ^2, is a more powerful test. The odds ratio indicates the extent to which the odds of being a leader are multiplied for each 1 unit increase in the predictor and is an indicator of effect size (Hernandez, Drasgow, & Gonzalez, 2004).The percent change in the odds ratio is the percentage of change in the odds of being a leader for each 1 unit increase in the predictor.

The Wald statistic and the more powerful likelihood ratio test both showed that three traits, extraversion, openness, and dominance significantly predicted leader emergence, in a positive direction, once other traits were held constant. Neuroticism, agreeableness, conscientiousness, achievement, aggression, and Machiavellianism were not significantly predictive when all traits were controlled for together. Those results differed from the

Table 3. Logistic Regression Predicting Emergent Leadership.

	Step 1					Step 2					
Var	*B*	*S.E.*	Wald χ^2	Exp (*B*)	%Δ	*B*	*S.E.*	Wald χ^2	Exp (*B*)	%Δ	Likelihood Ratio χ^2
N	00	02	0.01	0.99	−1	01	02	0.52	1.01	+1	0.45
E	09	03	8.08**	1.10	+10	07	04	4.15*	1.07	+7	4.32*
O	07	03	9.33**	1.08	+8	07	03	8.56**	1.07	+7	7.11*
A	05	03	1.75	1.05	+5	04	04	0.88	1.04	+4	0.89
C	01	02	0.53	1.01	+1	01	03	0.04	0.99	0	0.04
Ach						03	06	0.00	1.02	+3	0.26
Dom						11	05	6.46**	1.11	+11	5.39*
Agg						−04	06	0.47	0.96	−4	0.47
Mach						−04	03	2.10	0.97	-3	2.02

*$p < .05$.
**$p < .01$. $N = 280$.
Note. N = neuroticism; E = extraversion; O = openness to experience; A = agreeableness; C = conscientiousness; Ach = achievement; Dom = dominance; Agg = aggression; Mach = Machiavellianism; Exp(*B*) = odds ratio; %Δ = percentage change in odds ratio. Step 1 model χ^2 (5, $N = 280$) = 276.65, $p < .05$; Nagelkerke $R^2 = .14$. Step 2 model χ^2 (9, $N = 280$) = 267.48, $p < .05$; Nagelkerke $R^2 = .18$.

independent groups model, which showed significant differences for six of the nine traits. Based on Hsieh's (1989) tables, power for the logistic regression exceeded .80. Interestingly, dominance was the strongest predictor, followed by extraversion and openness. Based on the full model with nine predictors, the there is a 7% increase in the odds of being a leader with each 1 point increase in extraversion, a 7% increase in the odds with each one point increase in openness, and an 11% increase with each one point increase in dominance. Because dominance was measured on a different scale (range 0–16) than the FFM traits (range 0–48), the odds ratios are more comparable when the variables are standardized, and interpreted is in terms of one *SD* increases rather than one point increases. A second logistic regression equation with standardized variables was computed, resulting in odds ratios (Exp (B)) of 1.48 for extraversion, 1.53 for openness, and 1.56 for dominance. Therefore, controlling for all other traits, participants were 1.48 times more likely to be leaders with a one *SD* increase in extraversion, 1.53 times more likely with a one *SD* increase in openness, and 1.56 times more likely with a one *SD* increase in dominance.

Although the relationships did not reach conventional levels of significance in spite of adequate power, Machiavellianism and aggression were negatively related to leader emergence, meaning that the odds of being a leader were lower for those higher on those two traits.

Discussion

The present study adds to the rather limited domain of research that assessed all FFM traits with additional traits including dark traits. The results for the traits of extraversion, openness, and dominance were analogous to those found previously in studies that measured individuals or small groups of traits (Bass, 1990; Judge et al., 2002; Lord, de Vader, & Alliger, 1986). In terms of behaviors, leaders who are high on the three traits would likely be assertive and talkative, enjoy being in groups and teams, think divergently, exercise independent judgment, and be persuasive and exercise control over their environment (Costa & McCrae, 1992; Jackson, 1999). Considering the present results, dominance would appear to be a "bright" trait, particularly since aggression was not a significant predictor in the regression model. It is important to note that those scoring higher on the three traits have a tendency to become leaders more than those scoring lower. This is a tendency rather than a destiny. In a longitudinal study that included traits, Arvey et al. (2006) showed that both genetics and environmental factors accounted for a substantial proportion of variance in leader emergence, allowing for the possibility that people with different patterns of traits may emerge as leaders due to experiencing varying environmental circumstances over time, or finding themselves in various leadership situations that may involve different tasks or duties. It is possible for individuals who do not score highly on all three traits to, nevertheless, exhibit some of the characteristic behaviors associated with those traits. Leaders in the present study did hold a variety of leadership positions (i.e., club officers, team captains), so the results are not restricted to one narrow type of leader. Further, although the present study focused on leader emergence, one might expect that leaders possessing these traits and exhibiting the associated behaviors would also be more effective leaders than those who do not, as previous studies showed that extraversion and openness (dominance was not included) were positively related to leader performance (DeRue et al., 2011; Judge et al., 2002).

Interestingly, dominance added to the prediction of leader emergence, although in the FFM model it is considered to be a facet extraversion. That finding indicates that it is important to measure the narrow trait of dominance in addition to extraversion, and that narrow traits can add to the predictivity of leader emergence. These finding supports the calls for more attention to narrow traits, as well as dark traits (Guenole, 2014).

The present results differed from those obtained previously (e.g., Arvey et al., 2006; Judge et al., 2002) in that achievement, conscientiousness, neuroticism, and agreeableness were not predictive once their overlap with other traits was controlled. Further, neither aggression nor Machiavellianism were predictive, although they did show a significant difference in the independent groups model. The difference is likely attributable to the difference in analytic models used, because most previous studies did not measure all traits within individuals, and many found differences using an independent groups (t-test) analysis. Interestingly, one study that did analyze all FFM traits using a regression model, also found that extraversion and openness were the strongest predictors of leadership in a group discussion task, particularly when extraversion was measured by observers (Colbert et al., 2012).

Although dominance can be considered both a bright and dark trait, the clearly dark traits of aggression and Machiavellianism were not significantly predictive in the logistic model, although they were in a mathematically negative direction. The present results show the importance of the analytic model used to draw conclusions. The independent groups analysis misleads us to believe that six traits contribute to differentiating leaders and non-leaders, when the logistic regression model, which controls for shared variance among traits, showed that only the three traits of extraversion, openness to experience, and dominance were significantly predictive. Because traits occur together in individuals, the regression results highlight the importance of controlling for trait interrelationships in order to develop a parsimonious model of traits and leader emergence. The present results help to clarify which traits are most important, particularly in light of the mixed results found across previous studies, most of which either did not measure all FFM traits, did not measure FFM together with other traits, or were meta-analytic and drew from results across studies rather than integrated within individuals (DeRue et al., 2011). This study also addressed calls to study integrated traits with leadership (DeRue et al., 2011; Foti & Hauenstein, 2007).

Another strength of the study is that the large sample size gave adequate power to detect significant relationships. Therefore, non-significant relationships cannot be attributable to low power. Additionally, it was a field study in that participant leaders held real leadership positions, rather than being judged on their behavior in a laboratory based group discussion, which is the more common research design (e.g., Acton, Foti, Lord, & Gladfelter, 2019; Colbert et al., 2012; Emery, Calvard, & Pierce, 2013; Ensari, Riggio, Christian, & Carslaw, 2011; Morgeson, DeRue, & Karam, 2010).

Limitations

The study was limited in that it was based on undergraduate students and the results might not generalize to leader emergence in situations that relate to career advancement or economic outcomes. However, large scale research studies have demonstrated the stability of traits through the lifespan (Reichard et al., 2011; Roberts & DelVecchio, 2000), therefore the behaviors that correlate with those traits are likely to continue into adulthood. For example, Arvey et al. (2006) showed evidence for a genetic basis for leader emergence, which also points to the stability of traits. Further, a large portion of previous leadership studies have had undergraduates as participants (Judge et al., 2002).

The present sample had a high percentage of women. Results might not replicate in samples with high percentages of men. Normative samples of the NEO-FFI showed slightly different score distributions for men and women, such that there are separate T-score distributions (Costa & McCrae, 1992). Ensari et al. (2011) found that masculinity (not gender, per se) was associated with leader emergence in their meta-analysis that was limited to leaderless group discussions, although the separate measure of femininity did not differentiate. Notably, meta-analytic studies have shown that gender is not as important as other traits such as extraversion and conscientiousness in predicting leader effectiveness (DeRue et al., 2011; Indvik, 2004).

Leader emergence was self-reported and leadership positions were not independently verified. However, steps were taken to minimize the likelihood of response distortion, including maintaining anonymity of participants by using code numbers, and having participants elaborate as to what position they held, which has demonstrated effectiveness (Schmitt & Kunce, 2002; Schmitt et al., 2003).

The results of the present study are relevant to leader emergence, and not directly to leader performance or effectiveness. For example, neuroticism did not predict leader emergence when other traits were controlled. Studies have shown that neuroticism and aggression were negatively related to leader effectiveness (Hogan et al., 1994; Judge et al., 2002). Of course, a person must first emerge as a leader in order to perform as one. It may be that some of the bright and dark traits could be useful when leader performance is the criterion.

Implications and Future Directions

Conard (2006) showed that the trait conscientiousness predicted academic performance over and above Scholastic Aptitude Test scores. Given that universities are interested in having diverse groups of students who will participate in university life in various ways beyond academics, the current results provide a parsimonious group of traits that could be easily assessed and used in university admissions in order to promote admission of students who are likely to assume leadership positions. Since personality traits exhibit some changes up until around age 30 (Roberts & DelVecchio, 2000), it might also be possible to help students develop those traits, as well as the corresponding behaviors that are associated with effective leadership.

College students might be relieved to know that students who assume leadership roles tend to be extraverted and open to new experiences, and tend not to be aggressive or neurotic or Machiavellian. Many of the leadership positions held were club officers, team captains, and resident assistants who are elected or appointed after a screening process. It may be that those traits lead them to seek those positions. It is also possible that those electing or appointing are responding to those traits.

Future research can take a number of directions. First, the study could be replicated with samples of working adults in various organizational settings. Second, since leader emergence and leader effectiveness are two distinct criteria, new studies using the FFM and relevant traits are needed to establish the characteristics that predict leader effectiveness. If the present findings prove to be robust, they could have implications for systematic implementation in leadership selection and training. Third, some personality characteristics (such as aggression and dominance) show gender differences; therefore it is important to establish whether leader profiles differ by gender. Due to the relatively small number of men in the present study, there was insufficient power to do such analyses. Fourth, it is important to revisit the issue of situation specificity using a full range of personality traits. Studies are needed that will definitively establish whether different definitions of leader emergence (e.g., perceptions of leaders in laboratory-based group tasks vs. comparisons or actual leaders and non-leaders) and differences in research designs (e.g., group-based tasks with strangers vs. existing work groups) show different profiles of important traits. Lastly, the present study was conducted in the U.S. It would be interesting to compare traits and leaders in different cultures (for example, those in Southern Asia or Confucian Asia as identified by the GLOBE study), which show differences in the value of leadership styles such as team orientation, participativeness, or autonomous decision making (Den Hartog et al., 1999).

The study investigated both bright and dark traits, including the complete set of FFM traits as well as four additional traits intra-individually, when such studies are still uncommon. The present study showed that when a regression model was used to analyze traits and leader emergence, a more parsimonious pattern resulted which differed from studies that examined traits separately.

References

Aamodt, M. G. (2016). *Industrial/organizational psychology: An applied approach* (8th ed.). Boston, MA: Cengage Learning.

Acton, B. P., Foti, R. J., Lord, R. G., & Gladfelter, J. A. (2019). Putting emergence back in leadership emergence: A dynamic, multilevel, process-oriented framework. *The Leadership Quarterly, 30*(1), 145–164. doi:10.1016/j.leaqua.2018.07.002

Albright, L., & Forziati, C. (1995). Cross-situational consistency and perceptual accuracy in leadership. *Personality and Social Psychology Bulletin, 21*, 1269–1276. doi:10.1177/01461672952112003

Arvey, R. D., Rotundo, M., Johnson, W., Zhang, Z., & McGue, M. (2006). The determinants of leadership role occupancy: Genetic and personality factors. *The Leadership Quarterly, 17*(1), 1–20. doi:10.1016/j.leaqua.2005.10.009

Bass, B. M. (1990). *Bass and Stogdill's handbook of leadership*. New York, NY: Free Press.

Block, J. (1995). A contrarian view of the five-factor approach to personality description. *Psychological Bulletin, 117*, 187–215. doi:10.1037/0033-2909.117.2.187

Christie, R., & Geis, F. L. (1970). *Studies in machiavellianism*. San Diego, CA: Academic Press.

Cohen, J., Cohen, P., Aiken, S. G., & West, L. S. (2003). *Applied multiple regression/correlation analysis for the behavioral sciences* (3rd ed.). Mahwah, NJ: Lawrence Erlbaum.

Colbert, A. E., Judge, T. A., Choi, D., & Wang, G. (2012). Assessing the trait theory of leadership using self and observer ratings of personality: The mediating role of contributions to group success. *The Leadership Quarterly, 23*, 670–685.

Conard, M. A. (2006). Aptitude is not enough: How personality and behavior predict academic performance. *Journal of Research in Personality, 40*(3), 339–346. doi:10.1016/j.jrp.2004.10.003

Costa, P. T., Jr., & McCrae, R. R. (1992). *Professional manual for the NEO-PI-R and NEO FFI*. Odessa, FL: Psychological Assessment Resources.

Crocker, L. G. (1963). *Introduction to the prince by Niccolo Machiavelli*. New York: Simon and Schuster.

Den Hartog, D. N., House, R. J., Hanges, P. J., Ruiz-Quintanilla, S. A., Dorfman, P. W., Abdalla, I. A., … Zhou, J. (1999). Culturally specific and cross culturally generalizable implicit leadership theories: Are attributes of charismatic/transformational leadership universally endorsed? *Leadership Quarterly, 10*, 219–256.

DeRue, D. S., Nahrgang, J. D., Wellman, N., & Humphrey, S. E. (2011). Trait and behavioral theories of leadership: An integration and meta-analytic test of their relative validity. *Personnel Psychology, 64*(1), 7–52. doi:10.1111/j.1744-6570.2010.01201.x

Digman, J. M. (1990). Personality structure: Emergence of the five-factor model. *Annual Review of Psychology, 41*(1), 417–440. doi:10.1146/annurev.ps.41.020190.002221

Emery, C., Calvard, T. S., & Pierce, M. E. (2013). Leadership as an emergent group process: A social network study of personality and leadership. *Group Process and Intergroup Relations, 16*(1), 28–45. doi:10.1177/1368430212461835

Ensari, N., Riggio, R. E., Christian, J., & Carslaw, G. (2011). Who emerges as a leader? Meta-analyses of individual differences as predictors of leadership emergence. *Personality and Individual Differences, 51*, 532–536. doi:10.1016/j.paid.2011.05.017

Eysenck, H. J. (1992). Four ways five factors are *not* basic. *Personality and Individual Differences, 13*, 667–673. doi:10.1016/0191-8869(92)90237-J

Farsides, T., & Woodfield, R. (2003). Individual differences and undergraduate academic success: The roles of personality, intelligence, and application. *Personality and Individual Differences, 34*, 1225–1243. doi:10.1016/S0191-8869(02)00111-3

Foti, R. J., & Hauenstein, N. M. A. (2007). Pattern and variable approaches in leader emergence and effectiveness. *Journal of Applied Psychology, 92*, 347–355. doi:10.1037/0021-9010.92.2.347

Furnham, A., & Crump, J. (2015). Personality and management level: Traits that differentiate leadership levels. *Psychology, 6*, 549–559. doi:10.4236/psych.2015.65053 doi:10.4236/psych.2015.65053

Furnham, A., Hyde, G., & Trickey, G. (2014). Do your dark side traits fit? Dysfunctional personalities in different work sectors. *Applied Psychology, 63*, 589–603. doi:10.1111/apps.12002

Gough, H. G. (1984). A managerial potential scale for the California Psychological Inventory. *Journal of Applied Psychology, 69*, 233–240. doi:10.1037/0021-9010.69.2.233

Gray, E. K., & Watson, D. (2002). General and specific traits of personality and their relation to sleep and academic performance. *Journal of Personality, 70*, 177–206. doi:10.1111/1467-6494.05002

Guenole, N. (2014). Maladaptive personality at work: Exploring the darkness. *Industrial and Organizational Psychology, 7*(1), 85–97. doi:10.1111/iops.12114

Hernandez, A., Drasgow, F., & Gonzalez, R., V. (2004). Investigating the functioning of a middle category by means of a mixed-measurement model. *Journal of Applied Psychology, 89*, 687–699. doi:10.1037/0021-9010.89.4.687

Hogan, R., & Hogan, J. (2001). Assessing leadership: A view from the dark side. *International Journal of Selection and Assessment, 9*, 40–51.

Hogan, J., & Holland, B. (2003). Using theory to evaluate personality and job performance relations: A socioanalytic perspective. *Journal of Applied Psychology, 88*(1), 100–112.

Hogan, R., Curphy, G. J., & Hogan, J. (1994). What we know about leadership: Effectiveness and personality. *American Psychologist, 49*, 493–504. doi:10.1037//0003-066X.49.6.493

Hsieh, F. Y. (1989). Sample size tables for logistic regression. *Statistics in Medicine, 8*, 795–802.

Indvik, J. (2004). Women and leadership. In P. G. Northouse (Ed.), *Leadership Theory and Practice* (pp. 265–289). Thousand Oaks, CA: Sage.

Jackson, D. N. (1999). *Personality research form manual* (3rd ed.). Port Huron, MI: Sigma Assessment Systems.

Jonason, P. K., Wee, S., & Li, N. P. (2014). Thinking bigger and better about "bad apples": Evolutionary industrial-organizational psychology and the dark triad. *Industrial and Organizational Psychology, 7*(1), 117–121. doi:10.1111/iops.12118

Judge, T. A., Bono, J. E., Ilies, R., & Gerhardt, M. W. (2002). Personality and leadership: A qualitative and quantitative review. *Journal of Applied Psychology, 87*, 765–780.

Judge, T. A., Piccolo, R. F., & Kosalka, T. (2009). The bright and dark sides of leader traits: A review and theoretical extension of the leader trait paradigm. *The Leadership Quarterly, 20*, 855–875. doi:10.1016/j.leaqua.2009.09.004

Karnes, F. A., Chauvin, J. C., & Trant, T. J. (1984). Leadership profiles as determined by the 16PF scores of honors college students. *Psychological Reports, 55*, 615–616. doi:10.2466/pr0.1984.55.2.615

Lord, R. G., de Vader, C. L., & Alliger, G. M. (1986). A meta-analysis of the relationship between personality traits and leadership perceptions: An application of validity generalization procedures. *Journal of Applied Psychology, 71*, 402–410. doi:10.1037//0021-9010.71.3.402

Morgeson, F. P., DeRue, D. S., & Karam, E. P. (2010). Leadership in teams: A functional approach to understanding leadership structures and processes. *Journal of Management, 36*(1), 5–39. doi:10.1177/0149206309347376

Paulhus, D. L. (2014). Toward a taxonomy of dark personalities. *Current Directions in Psychological Science, 23*, 421–426. doi:10.1177/0963721414547737

Paunonen, S. V., & Ashton, M. C. (2001). Big five factors and facets and the prediction of behavior. *Journal of Personality and Social Psychology, 81*, 524–539.

Reichard, R. J., Riggio, R. E., Guerin, D. W., Oliver, P. H., Gottfried, A. W., & Gottfried, A. E. (2011). A longitudinal analysis of relationships between adolescent personality and intelligence with adult leader emergence and transformational leadership. *The Leadership Quarterly, 22*, 471–481. doi:10.1016/j.leaqua.2011.04.005

Reynolds, P. D. (1984). Leaders never quit: Talking, silence, and influence in interpersonal groups. *Small Group Behavior, 15*, 404–413. doi:10.1177/104649648401500309

Riggio, R. E., Riggio, H. R., Salinas, C., & Cole, E. J. (2003). The role of social and emotional communication skills in leader emergence and effectiveness. *Group Dynamics: Theory, Research, and Practice, 7*, 83–103. doi:10.1037/1089-2699.7.2.83

Roberts, B. W., & DelVecchio, W. F. (2000). The rank-order consistency of personality traits from childhood to old age: A quantitative review of longitudinal studies. *Psychological Bulletin, 126*(1), 3–25. doi:10.1037//0033-2909.126.1.3

Schmitt, N., & Kunce, C. (2002). The effects of required elaboration of answers to biodata questions. *Personnel Psychology, 55*, 569–587. doi:10.1111/j.1744-6570.2002.tb00121.x

Schmitt, N., Oswald, F. L., Kim, B. H., Gillespie, M. A., Ramsay, L. J., & Yoo, T. (2003). Impact of elaboration on socially desirable responding and the validity of biodata measures. *The Journal of Applied Psychology, 88*, 979–988.

Part II

The Leader's Effect on Others

When Core Self-Evaluation Leads to Career Adaptability: Effects of Ethical Leadership and Implications for Citizenship Behavior

Xiao-min Xu and Kun Yu

ABSTRACT

Drawing upon the career construction theory and the trait activation theory, the present study first aims to uncover the interactive effect of core self-evaluation (CSE) and ethical leadership on career adaptability. In addition, the authors examined how career adaptability mediates the interaction effect of CSE and ethical leadership on organizational citizenship behavior (OCB). Two-wave data from 156 employees were collected in a manufacturing company over a one-month interval. Results showed that ethical leadership moderated the relationship between CSE and career adaptability. Specifically, the positive relationship between CSE and career adaptability was stronger when ethical leadership was low. Moreover, career adaptability mediated the relationship between CSE and OCB, and ethical leadership moderated this indirect relationship. We discuss implications for career adaptation and organizational effectiveness.

The accelerated changes in employees' work duties and careers require them to adapt to different situations (Pulakos, Arad, Donovan, & Plamondon, 2000). To address this trend, Savickas (1997) proposed the concept of career adaptability, which refers to the psychosocial resources employees possess to improve their ability to cope with an uncertain environment. Career adaptability is beneficial in that it not only facilitates career performance (Zacher, 2014), career satisfaction and subjective well-being (Chan & Mai, 2016; Rudolph, Lavigne & Zacher, 2017), but also reduces work stress (Fiori, Bollmann, & Rossier, 2015), insecurity (Spurk, Kauffeld, Meinecke, & Ebner, 2016) and turnover intention (Merino-Tejedor, Hontangas, & Boada-Grau, 2016).

According to the career construction theory (Savickas, 1997, 2005, 2013), an individual's career adaptability continues to develop over the lifespan, "through interactions between the inner and outer worlds of the person" (Savickas & Porfeli, 2012, p. 663), which means that dispositional and contextual factors were not independently but interactively influence the development of career adaptability. Given that contextual factors acting as boundary conditions (Savickas & Porfeli, 2012) may not only enhance but also weaken or even eliminate the effect of dispositional factors on career adaptability, it is important to have contextual factors taken into account in examining the development of career adaptability. However, although dispositional factors such as proactive personality (Cai et al., 2015), emotional intelligence (Coetzee & Harry, 2014), and core self-evaluation (CSE; Hirschi, Herrmann, & Keller, 2015) were found associated with career adaptability (see Johnston, 2018 as a review), little research has addressed whether and how individual differences interact with contextual factors in the development of career adaptability (Autin, Douglass, Duffy, England, & Allan, 2017).

The first objective of this study was to address this void. Based on the trait activation theory that emphasizes the interplay between individual differences and contextual factors (Judge & Zapata, 2015; Tett & Burnett, 2003; Tett & Guterman, 2000), we attempt to explore the above issues by proposing a model focusing on the interaction between employees' CSE and their perceived ethical leadership on the development of career adaptability. Describing individuals' overall evaluations about their own worthiness, effectiveness, and capability (Bono & Judge, 2003; Judge, Locke, Durham, & Kluger, 1998), CSE is seen as a useful organizing framework to understand individual differences in the coping process (Kammeyer-Mueller, Judge, & Scott, 2009). According to the career construction theory (Savickas, 1997, 2013), CSE may serve as individuals' adaptive readiness and shape their career adaptability (Hirschi et al., 2015). Moreover, from the social learning perspective (Bandura, 1977), ethical leadership could be an especially salient contextual factor (Brown, Treviño, & Harrison, 2005) that shapes employees' attitudes, beliefs and behaviors through their adaption to the organization (Bauer, Bodner, Erdogan, Truxillo, & Tucker, 2007; Saks & Ashforth, 1997). Employees could learn from the ethical leader and build up positive psychological states and essential resources needed to increase followers' sense of control and autonomy over their job (Piccolo, Greenbaum, Den Hartog, & Folger, 2010). Based on the trait activation theory (Judge & Zapata, 2015; Tett & Burnett, 2003; Tett & Guterman, 2000), which argues that the relationship between personality traits and attitudes and behaviors should be stronger in weak situations, we propose that CSE will have a stronger effect on the development of career adaptability when ethical leadership is low.

Another objective of the present research was to test the mediation role of career adaptability in linking CSE-ethical leadership interaction and organizational citizenship behavior (OCB). Defined as a type of organizational behavior that goes beyond job duties and enhances the function of the organization (Borman & Motowidlo, 1997; Organ, 1988), OCB is an extra-role behavior that helps individuals to adapt to an uncertain working environment (Lam, Wan, & Roussin, 2015; Van Dyne, Cummings, & Parks, 1995). Given that OCB is one of the most critical outcomes in the workplace (Levy, 2003), it is essential to know whether, how, and when CSE, an essential predictor of employee and organizational outcomes (see Chang et al., 2012, as a review), associates with OCB. However, although there is a rich body of research regarding the antecedents of OCB (Babcock-Roberson & Strickland, 2010; Bolino & Turnley, 2003; Chiu & Tsai, 2006; Tang, 2009; Zhao, Peng, & Chen, 2014), surprisingly few studies have looked into the relationship between CSE and OCB. Drawing upon the career construction theory (Savickas, 2002, 2013), we conceptualize OCB as a management form of adapting behavior (Ployhart & Bliese, 2006) and propose that career adaptability mediates the relationship between CSE and OCB. Combined with the trait activation theory (Judge & Zapata, 2015; Tett & Burnett, 2003; Tett & Guterman, 2000), we argue that individuals'

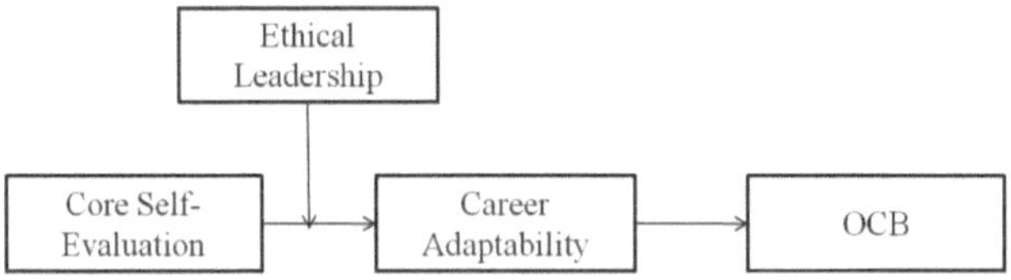

Figure 1. Theoretical model.

career adaptability gained from the interaction between CSE and ethical leadership will lead to more active adapting behaviors (e.g., OCB), testing a mediated moderation model (see Figure 1).

Theoretical Background

CSE and Career Adaptability

Career adaptability refers to the psychosocial resources to cope with the current or predictable tasks and unpredictable adjustments in their work (Savickas, 1997, 2012, 2013). In other words, career adaptability is a kind of self-regulation resource that helps employees cope with the change in the workplace (Savickas, 2005). Specifically, career adaptability consists of four sub-dimensions, namely concern (i.e., thinking and planning), control (i.e., making decisions and taking responsibilities), curiosity (i.e., exploring and investigating), and confidence (i.e., performing efficiently and solving problems; Savickas & Porfeli, 2012). Accumulated evidence showed its positive effects on organizational and individual outcomes. For example, career adaptability predicts work attitudes, such as career satisfaction (Fiori et al., 2015), work engagement (Rossier, Zecca, Stauffer, Maggiori, & Dauwalder, 2012) and career engagement (Nilforooshan & Salimi, 2016). In addition, career adaptability is important for individuals' career development, such as facilitating mobility (Ito & Brotheridge, 2005) and promotability (Chan, Mai, Kuok, & Kong, 2016).

According to career construction theory, four factors consist of a chain of putative effects: adaptivity → adaptability → adapting → adaptation (Savickas, 2002, 2013). Adaptivity refers to willingness or readiness to change; adaptability refers to the possession of psychosocial resources to change; adapting refers to the response to changing conditions; adaptation refers to the outcomes of the response (Savickas, 2002, 2013). As a typical indicator of adaptivity (Hirschi et al., 2015), CSE describes people's overall evaluations about their own worthiness, effectiveness, and capability (Bono & Judge, 2003; Judge et al., 1998), and is relatively stable over time (Chang et al., 2012; Ferris et al., 2011; Judge, Erez, Bono & Thoresen, 2002). Because individuals with a higher level of CSE have a higher overall evaluation of themselves (e.g., more confidence in their ability to succeed, more beliefs in their power to bring desired outcomes), they may deal with the change in the workplace better, and develop better adaptability (Chen, Gully & Eden, 2001). Indeed, some researchers have found a positive effect of CSE on career adaptability (e.g., Hirschi et al., 2015; Neureiter & Traut-Mattausch, 2017). Thus, we propose that employees' CSE will have a positive relationship with their career adaptability.

Hypothesis 1: Core self-evaluation is positively related to career adaptability.

The Moderating Role of Ethical Leadership

Ethical leadership describes the extent to which the leader's general behaviors (e.g., their actions and interpersonal relationships) are conducted based on ethical standards (Brown et al., 2005). From the social learning perspective (Bandura, 1977), an ethical leader serves as an explicit role model that employees could learn from, which helps the employees to build up positive psychological states and essential resources for coping with changes in the workplace (Gardner, Avolio, Luthans, May, & Walumbwa, 2005; Gooty, Gavin, Johnson, Frazier, & Snow, 2009). For instance, the leader's ethical values motivate the employees to adapt to changes in the workplace and become more innovative (Chen & Hou, 2016). Ethical leadership also affects the employee's psychological resources and improves follower–leader congruence, which can help employees perform more efficiently at work (Bouckenooghe, Zafar, & Raja, 2015). In addition, an ethical leader gives followers opportunities to express their opinions and participate in decision making, which increases followers' sense of control and autonomy over their jobs (Piccolo et al., 2010).

It is possible that employees' perceptions of ethical leadership may be affected by their CSE. It was found that CSE was correlated with employees' perceptions of their work environment, in which employees with higher CSE were likely to perceive higher satisfaction with their jobs (Judge & Bono, 2001). More importantly, CSE and perceived ethical leadership are likely to interact with each other and predict subsequent attitudes and behaviors. The trait activation theory (Judge & Zapata, 2015; Tett & Burnett, 2003; Tett & Guterman, 2000) suggests that the relationship between personality traits and attitudes and behaviors should be stronger in weak situations, and vice versa. For example, individuals' personality traits (e.g., pro-social values) were strongly related to their behaviors (e.g., helping behaviors) in a weak situation (e.g., low coworker support) than a strong situation (e.g., high coworker support; Kim, Van Dyne, Kamdar, & Johnson, 2013). In addition, for individuals with higher CSE, they tend to rely on their own judgment, whereas those with lower CSE are less confident with their own judgment and are more likely to rely on their perception of ethical leadership (Taylor & Pattie, 2014). Based on the trait activation theory (Judge & Zapata, 2015; Tett & Burnett, 2003; Tett & Guterman, 2000), we argue that ethical leadership, as a contextual factor, may play a buffering role in the relationship between CSE, a personal trait, and career adaptability.

When employees perceive low ethical leadership, they are less likely to build up positive psychological states and resources learned from the leader for coping with the environment, which creates a "weak situation." With a low level of ethical leadership, a leader's behavior is not consistent with appropriate norms. For instance, the leader is selfish and does not treat employees with consideration and respect (Brown et al., 2005). In this case, employees are less willing to report difficulties or ideas for improvement at work to the leader, because they don't trust that the leader will listen to their concerns and treat them fairly (Chen & Hou, 2016; Walumbwa, Morrison, & Christensen, 2012). In a low ethical leadership situation, it is necessary for employees to rely on their personality traits, such as CSE, to develop career adaptability. Indeed, research has found that personality traits are especially useful for building career adaptability when situational conditions are not helpful or supportive. Thus, we expect that CSE will have a stronger association with career adaptability for employees perceive a low level of ethical leadership.

In contrast, when employees perceive high ethical leadership, to learn from the leaders and build up positive psychological states and essential resources to develop their career adaptability (Gardner et al., 2005; Gooty et al., 2009), which creates a "strong situation." Under a high ethical leadership situation, it is less necessary for employees to depend on their CSE because they can obtain fairly sufficient resources from the leader. Thus, we expect that CSE will have a weaker association with career adaptability for employees who perceive a high level of ethical leadership. In summary, we propose that ethical leadership moderates the relationship between CSE and career adaptability, such that the relationship will be stronger when ethical leadership is low.

> Hypothesis 2: Ethical leadership moderates the relationship between core self-evaluation and career adaptability, such that the positive relationship is stronger when ethical leadership is low rather than high.

The Mediating Role of Career Adaptability

According to the career construction theory, adapting behavior refers to the behavioral response to changing conditions (Savickas, 2002, 2013). Adapting behavior is predicted by employees' adaptability, which is the possession of resources for coping with change (Savickas, 2002, 2013). Specifically, there are five types of adapting behavior, namely orientation, exploration, establishment, management, and disengagement, in which management means active role management at work (Savickas & Porfeli, 2012). OCB can be seen as an indicator of the management form of adapting behavior, which denotes employees' proactive actions regarding role management (Ployhart & Bliese, 2006).

Initial work has shown some evidence on how career adaptability is likely to influence people's adapting behaviors to the working environment, such as career engagement (Nilforooshan & Salimi, 2016) and job crafting (Wang, Demerouti, & Le Blanc, 2017). According to career construction theory (Savickas, 1997, 2013), employees who have a high level of career adaptability may be more likely to take actions that help them fit into the organization and facilitate career success. In the meantime, performing OCB could get more liking and higher performance evaluation from supervisors (Allen & Rush, 1998), which is critical for individuals to fit into the organization and obtain career success, respectively. Therefore, it is likely that employees with a high level of career adaptability will have more OCB in the organization. In other words, we proposed that career adaptability is positively related to OCB. Combined with the reasoning that CSE has a positive effect on career adaptability, we expect that career adaptability will play a mediating role in the relationship between CSE and OCB.

> Hypothesis 3: Career adaptability mediates the relationship between core self-evaluation and organizational citizenship behavior.

In sum, our hypotheses suggest a mediated moderation model, such that the interaction between employees' CSE and perceived ethical leadership affects their career adaptability that in turn affects their OCB. The effect of employees' CSE on OCB via career adaptability would be stronger when ethical leadership is low. In other words, the mediated effects are expected to be weaker when ethical leadership is higher. Thus, we predict:

> Hypothesis 4: Ethical leadership moderates the indirect relationship between core self-evaluation and organizational citizenship behavior via career adaptability. Specifically, the indirect relationship is stronger when ethical leadership is low rather than high.

Method

Participants and Procedures

We collected data at two points in time (separated by one month) from junior-level employees working in a foreign-invested manufacturing company located in Eastern China. Research assistants distributed questionnaires to the targeted respondents and sought their consent to complete the survey on a voluntary basis. At Time 1, we distributed surveys to a total of 200 employees and received 184 completed questionnaires (a response rate of 94.8%). At Time 2, we received 156 matched surveys from participants who took part in both Times 1 and Time 2 (a final response rate of 78%). Participants' average age was 33 years (SD = 6.0); average tenure with the current supervisor was 3.8 years (SD = 3.6). Of all 156 participants, 107 (68.6%) were male, and 49 were female (31.4%).

All measures were administered in Chinese. CSE, ethical leadership, and career adaptability were measured at Time 1; OCB was measured at Time 2.

Measures

We used Brislin's (1980) translation-back translation procedures to translate all survey items from English to Chinese.

CSE was accessed using a 12-item scale developed by Judge, Erez, Bono, and Thoresen (2003). Of the 12 items, six were positively worded, and six were negatively worded. Sample items were "I am confident I get the success I deserve in life," and "Sometimes, I do not feel in control of my work" (reverse scored). These items were rated from 1 (*very weak*) to 7 (*very strong*). Negatively worded items were reverse coded so that higher scores representing a higher level of CSE. The alpha coefficient of the scale in the current study was .84.

Ethical leadership was accessed using a 10-item scale developed by Brown et al. (2005). Specifically, we measured participants' perceptions of their leaders' ethical behaviors. Sample items were "She/he makes fair and balanced decisions," "She/he discusses business ethics or values with employees." These items were rated from 1 (*highly unlikely*) to 7 (*highly likely*), with higher scores representing higher ethical leadership. The alpha coefficient of the scale in the current study was .94.

Career adaptability was accessed using the Hou, Leung, Li, Li, and Xu, (2012) Chinese-version scale which translated from Savickas and Porfeli (2012). This scale has reasonably high reliability across different countries and different occupations (student, part-time, full-time). The 24-item scale is composed of four dimensions (concern, control, curiosity, and confidence). Participants were asked to evaluate the strength of their abilities. Sample items were "Preparing for the future," and "Overcoming obstacles." These items were rated from 1 (*very weak*) to 7 (*very strong*), with a higher score representing a higher level of career adaptability. The alpha coefficient of the current scale was .94.

OCB was accessed using a 16-item scale developed by Lee and Allen (2002). The scale is composed of two dimensions (OCB-interpersonal and OCB-organizational). Sample items were "Help others who have been absent" (OCBI), and "Attend functions that are not required but that help the organizational image" (OCBO). These items were rated from 1 (*highly unlikely*) to 7 (*highly likely*) with higher scores representing more OCB. The alpha coefficient of the OCB scale in the current study was .88.

Control variables—we also controlled for employees' gender (1 = male, 2 = female), age (in years) and tenure with the supervisor in the analysis because they often related with extra-role work behaviors (Berry, Ones, & Sackett, 2007).

Results

Preliminary Analyses

We first conducted the confirmatory factor analysis with Mplus 7.0 to test the discriminant validity of the current data, as some variables are measured in the same time (i.e., CSE, ethical leadership and career adaptability at Time 1 and OCB at Time 2.) Results showed that the hypothesized four-factor model (CSE, ethical leadership, career adaptability, OCB) provided a good fit to the data ($\chi^2(71) = 121.88$, $p < .01$, CFI = .94, TLI = .93, RMSEA = .068). Therefore, the results are favorable concerning the discriminate validity of the study variables in our model. The model fit of the four-factor model is significantly better than a single-factor model (i.e., all variables were combined), $\chi^2(77) = 603.52$, $p < .01$, CFI = .40, TLI = .29, RMSEA = .210, and the two-factor model, in which constructs were combined by the time measured (i.e., CSE, ethical leadership and career adaptability at Time 1 were combined; OCB at Time 2 was another factor), $\chi^2(77) = 547.30$, $p < .01$, CFI = .46, TLI = .39, RMSEA = .200. These results provide evidence for the discriminant validity of the current data.

Table 1 presents the means, standard deviations, correlations, and Cronbach's alphas for all the variables. All variables have acceptable internal consistency alphas of above .80. In line with expectations, CSE and ethical leadership were positively correlated with both career adaptability ($r = .43$, $p < .01$; $r = .31$, $p < .01$) and OCB ($r = .38$, $p < .01$; $r = .25$, $p < .01$), respectively. In addition, career adaptability was positively correlated with OCB ($r = .37$, $p < .01$). Age, gender, and tenure with the current supervisor in Time 1 remained as control variables for all analyses.

Table 1. Descriptive Statistics and Correlations for Independent, Dependent, and Control Variables.

	M	SD	1	2	3	4	5	6	7
1. Age	33	6.0	–						
2. Gender	1.31	.47	–.07	–					
3. Tenure with supervisor	3.82	3.64	.43**	–.05	–				
4. CSE (Time 1)	4.95	.86	–.01	–.14	.09	(*.84*)			
5. Ethical leadership (Time 1)	5.83	.95	–.09	.04	.07	.20*	(*.94*)		
6. Career adaptability (Time 1)	5.80	.57	–.04	–.08	–.05	.43**	.31**	(*.94*)	
7. OCB (Time 2)	5.19	.70	–.07	–.07	–.05	.38**	.25**	.37**	(*.88*)

Note. $N = 156$. OCB = Organizational Citizenship Behavior. Reliabilities (coefficient alpha) appear in parentheses on the diagonal.
*$p < .05$.
**$p < .01$.
***$p < .001$.

Table 2. Multiple Regressions of Hypothesized Relationships.

		Career Adaptability		
	Variables	Step 1	Step 2	Step 3
Step 1	Age	–.00	.00	.00
	Gender	–.10	–.03	–.03
	Tenure with Supervisor	–.00	–.00	–.00
Step 2	CSE		.29***	.27***
	Ethical leadership			.15**
Step 3	CSE × Ethical leadership			–.11*
	Adjust R^2	–.01	.17	.25
	ΔR^2	.01	.18***	.09***

Note. $N = 156$. Entries are unstandardized estimates.
*$p < .05$.
**$p < .01$.
***$p < .001$.

Testing the Hypotheses

A series of hierarchical regression analyses (Cohen, Cohen, West, & Aiken, 2003) was conducted to test the direct relationship between CSE and career adaptability, and the moderating effects of ethical leadership, while controlling for age, gender, and tenure with current supervisor. All independent variables were centered, and the interaction term was multiplied by the predictor variables (Cohen et al., 2003).

In the regression analyses, the control variables were entered in the first step; CSE was entered in the second step; ethical leadership and the interaction term (CSE × ethical leadership) were entered in the third step. As shown in Table 2, CSE was positively associated with career adaptability ($B = .29$, $p < .01$). Therefore, Hypothesis 1 was supported.

In addition, the results showed ethical leadership significantly moderated the positive relationship between CSE and career adaptability ($B = –.11$, $p < .05$). To further clarify the moderating effect of ethical leadership, separate plots were drawn for individuals whose scores on the moderator (ethical leadership) were one standard deviation below and above the mean (Aiken & West, 1991). As shown in Figure 2, the positive relationship between CSE and career adaptability was stronger when ethical leadership was low (–1 SD; $b = .32$, $p < .001$) than high (+1 SD; $b = .14$, $p < .01$). Therefore, Hypothesis 2 was supported.

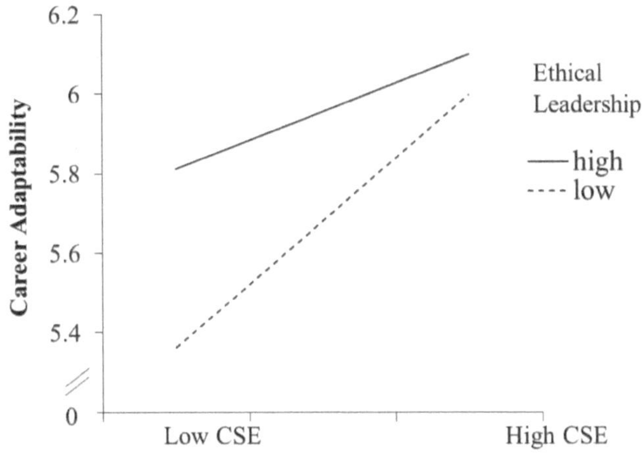

Figure 2. Interaction effect of CSE and Ethical Leadership on Career Adaptability.

Table 3. Bootstrapping Results for Test of Conditional Indirect Effects on OCB.

Moderator		Indirect effect	Boot SE	95% CI
Ethical leadership$_{Low}$	4.88	.114	.05	[.032, .234]
Ethical leadership$_{Mean}$	5.83	.083	.04	[.024, .178]
Ethical leadership$_{High}$	6.78	.052	.03	[.004, .145]

Note. $N = 156$. SE = standard error; 95% CI = 95% confidence interval.

Hypothesis 3 (i.e., the mediation hypothesis) was tested with Hayes' PROCESS macro based on a 1000 bootstrap sample (Hayes, 2013). In this mediation model, OCB was predicted by career adaptability and CSE, while career adaptability was predicted by CSE. Employees' gender, age, and tenure with the current supervisor were controlled. Results revealed that, the effect of CSE on OCB was .22, 95% CI = [.091, .353], while the effect of career adaptability on OCB was .31, 95% CI = [.113, .505]. These results suggested a partial mediation effect of career adaptability on the relationship between CSE and OCB (indirect effect = .10, 95% CI = [.031, .213]). Thus, Hypothesis 3 was supported.

Furthermore, a significant index of mediated moderation was generated through the PROCESS analysis (effect = –.03, 95% CI = [–.090, –.005]), which indicated that the indirect effect of CSE on OCB via career adaptability varied significantly with the moderator, ethical leadership. Specifically, according to Table 3, the indirect effect of CSE on OCB via career adaptability was stronger under the lower (effect = .114, 95% CI = [.032, .234]) rather than higher ethical leadership environment (effect = .052, 95% CI = [.004, .145]). Thus, the results fully supported Hypothesis 4.

Discussion

The present study tested the interaction effect of CSE and ethical leadership on career adaptability and the mediating role of career adaptability in the relationship between CSE and OCB. Results showed that CSE showed a stronger effect on career adaptability when ethical leadership was low. Moreover, we demonstrated that career adaptability mediated the relationship between CSE and OCB. Lastly, ethical leadership buffered the mediating effect of career adaptability in the relationship between CSE and OCB.

Theoretical Implications

The study contributes to the literature in the following ways. First, by exploring whether and how individual differences (e.g., CSE) interact with contextual factors (e.g., ethical leadership) in the development of career adaptability, we added novel knowledge to the career construction literature (Savickas, 2005). Although contextual influences are expected to be important for individuals to develop their career adaptability from a career construction perspective (Savickas, 1997), few studies have provided empirical evidence for this argument. Consistent with the trait activation theory (Judge & Zapata, 2015; Tett & Burnett, 2003; Tett & Guterman, 2000), this study proposed a moderation model in which the contextual factors and personality traits have an interaction effect on career outcomes. Our research demonstrated that the effect of individuals' CSE on individuals' adaptability would be more salient when contextual influence (i.e., ethical leadership) is low. The investigation of the interaction between personality traits and contextual factors on career adaptability would be helpful for a more comprehensive understanding of the development of employees' career adaptability.

Second, our research also adds to the literature on citizenship behavior. As one of the most densely examined topics in the field of organizational behavior (Levy, 2003), OCB has gained enormous attention from researchers in past decades (LePine, Erez, & Johnson, 2002; Podsakoff, MacKenzie, Paine, & Bachrach, 2000). However, whether and how OCB is affected by individuals' adaptability is largely unknown. The current study framed OCB as an adapting behavior reflecting active role management and uncovered the adaptability path between personality traits and OCB while ethical leadership acts as a buffer of the path. These findings shed some new light on the current understanding of the emergence and dynamics of citizenship behavior.

Practical Implications

The current research also provided some practical suggestions for organizations to facilitate employees' adaptability and citizenship behaviors. First, according to our findings, employees' CSE is beneficial in the development of employees' career adaptability, which then leads to an increase in employees' OCB. In rapidly changing organizational situations, the cultivation of employees' adaptabilities and motivation to respond to situations proactively is becoming a critical challenge for management practice (Wang et al., 2017). Organizations could pay attention to the recruitment and selection of newcomers to make sure they have a high level of CSE. These newcomers will adapt to the new environment faster and have more citizenship behaviors.

Second, the finding of the substitutive effect of ethical leadership on the influence of CSE on adaptability and OCB calls for organizations' special attention to the situational factors of employees' adaptability and citizenship behaviors. For instance, organizations could create more supportive environments to help employees develop adaptability in an unpredictable workplace. Moreover, organizations could have leaders engage in training on ethical behavior norms, which in turn, have more leaders act as ethical models and help employees build up adaptability resources, especially for employees with a relatively low level of CSE.

Limitations and Future Directions for Research

There are limitations to this study. First, although we used the two-wave data that measured the predictors and criterion at two times separately, our results do not allow us to conclude the causality among variables. We encourage the longitudinal/cross-lagged design or experiment design to make stronger causal interference for the relationship. Second, the self-reported measures may raise concerns about the common method bias. Our time-lagged design overcomes some problems because the previous levels of the outcome variable were controlled to a certain degree. The CFA results also showed that the constructs could be empirically discriminated. In addition, Siemsen, Roth, and Oliveira (2010) argued that interaction effects would not be exaggerated by common-method bias, which suggests that our hypothesized joint-effect is reliable. We encourage further researchers to provide more valid evidence by using peer-rated or supervisor-rated measures of proactive behaviors. Third, the sample was from a single organization in China, which would limit the generalizability of our findings. Future researchers could survey samples from a broader range of organizations in different cultures to replicate the findings.

Conclusion

Drawing upon the career construction theory (Savickas, 1997, 2013) and the trait activation theory (Judge & Zapata, 2015; Tett & Burnett, 2003; Tett & Guterman, 2000), we first explored the interaction effect between CSE and ethical leadership on career adaptability. Moreover, we also examined the mediating role of career adaptability in the relationship between CSE and OCB and the moderating role of ethical leadership in this mediated relationship. With two-wave data from 156 employees collected in a manufacturing company over a one-month interval, results first revealed that ethical leadership moderated the relationship between CSE and career adaptability. Specifically, the positive relationship between CSE and career adaptability was stronger when ethical leadership was low. Furthermore, career adaptability mediated the relationship between CSE and OCB, and the mediated relationship was stronger when ethical leadership was low. The current study contributes to the literature by demonstrating the interplay of CSE and ethical leadership in promoting the development of career adaptability and further adapting behaviors (e.g., OCB).

Funding

This work was supported by the National Natural Science Foundation of China (grant ID: 71702184).

ORCID

Kun Yu http://orcid.org/0000-0002-9373-8367

References

Aiken, L. S., & West, S. G. (1991). *Multiple regression: Testing and interpreting interactions.* Thousand Oaks, CA: Sage.

Allen, T. D., & Rush, M. (1998). The effects of organizational citizenship behavior on performance judgments: A field study and a laboratory experiment. *Journal of Applied Psychology, 83*(2), 247–260. doi:10.1037/0021-9010.83.2.247

Autin, K. L., Douglass, R. P., Duffy, R. D., England, J. W., & Allan, B. A. (2017). Subjective social status, work volition, and career adaptability: A longitudinal study. *Journal of Vocational Behavior, 99*, 1–10. doi:10.1016/j.jvb.2016.11.007

Babcock-Roberson, M. E., & Strickland, O. J. (2010). The relationship between charismatic leadership, work engagement, and organizational citizenship behaviors. *Journal of Psychology, 144*, 3113–3326. doi: doi:10.1080/00223981003648336

Bandura, A. (1977). *Social learning theory.* Englewood Cliffs, NJ: Prentice Hall.

Bauer, T. N., Bodner, T. E., Erdogan, B., Truxillo, D. M., & Tucker, J. S. (2007). Newcomer adjustment during organizational socialization: A meta-analytic review of antecedents, outcomes, and methods. *Journal of Applied Psychology, 92*(3), 707–721. doi:10.1037/0021-9010.92.3.707

Berry, C. M., Ones, D. S., & Sackett, P. R. (2007). Interpersonal deviance, organizational deviance, and their common correlates: A review and meta-analysis. *Journal of Applied Psychology, 92*(2), 410–424. doi:10.1037/0021-9010.92.2.410

Bolino, M. C., & Turnley, W. H. (2003). Going the extra mile: Cultivating and managing employee citizenship behavior. *Academy of Management Perspectives, 17*, 60–71. doi:10.5465/AME.2003.10954759

Bono, J. E., & Judge, T. A. (2003). Core self-evaluations: A review of the trait and its role in job satisfaction and job performance. *European Journal of Personality, 17*(S1), S5–S18. doi:10.1002/per.481

Borman, W. C., & Motowidlo, S. J. (1997). Task performance and contextual performance: The meaning for personnel selection research. *Human Performance, 10*(2), 99–109.

Bouckenooghe, D., Zafar, A., & Raja, U. (2015). How ethical leadership shapes employees' job performance: The mediating roles of goal congruence and psychological capital. *Journal of Business Ethics, 129*(2), 251–264. doi:10.1007/s10551-014-2162-3

Brislin, R. W. (1980). Translation and content analysis of oral and written material. In H. C. Triandis & J. W. Berry (Eds.), *Handbook of cross-cultural psychology* (Vol. 2, pp. 349–444). Boston, MA: Allyn & Bacon.

Brown, M. E., Treviño, L. K., & Harrison, D. A. (2005). Ethical leadership: A social learning perspective for construct development and testing. *Organizational Behavior and Human Decision Processes, 97*(2), 117–134. doi:10.1016/j.obhdp.2005.03.002

Cai, Z., Guan, Y., Li, H., Shi, W., Guo, K., Liu, Y., … Hua, H. (2015). Self-esteem and proactive personality as predictors of future work self and career adaptability: An examination of mediating and moderating processes. *Journal of Vocational Behavior, 86*, 86–94. doi:10.1016/j.jvb.2014.10.004

Chan, S. H. J., Mai, X., Kuok, O. M. K., & Kong, S. H. (2016). The influence of satisfaction and promotability on the relation between career adaptability and turnover intentions. *Journal of Vocational Behavior, 92*, 167–175. doi:10.1016/j.jvb.2015.12.003

Chang, C.-H. (Daisy), Ferris, D. L., Johnson, R. E., Rosen, C. C., Tan, J. A., & Ferrin, D. L. (2012). Core self-evaluations: A review and evaluation of the literature. *Journal of Management, 38*(1), 81–128. doi:10.1177/0149206311419661

Chen, G., Gully, S. M., & Eden, D. (2001). Validation of a new general self-efficacy scale. *Organizational Research Methods, 4*(1), 62–83. doi:10.1177/109442810141004

Chen, S. Y., & Hou, Y. H. (2016). The effects of ethical leadership, voice behavior and climates for innovation on creativity: A moderated mediation examination. *Leadership Quarterly, 27*(1), 1–13. doi:10.1016/j.leaqua.2015.10.007

Chiu, S.-F., & Tsai, M.-C. (2006). Relationships among burnout, job involvement, and organizational citizenship behavior. *The Journal of Psychology, 140*(6), 517–530. doi:10.3200/JRLP.140.6.517-530

Coetzee, M., & Harry, N. (2014). Emotional intelligence as a predictor of employees' career adaptability. *Journal of Vocational Behavior, 84*(1), 90–97. doi:10.1016/j.jvb.2013.09.001

Cohen, J., Cohen, P., West, S. G., & Aiken, L. (2003). *Applied multiple regression/correlation analysis for the behavioral sciences* (3rd ed.). Hillsdale: NJ: Erlbaum.

Ferris, D. L., Rosen, C. R., Johnson, R. E., Brown, D. J., Risavy, S. D., & Heller, D. (2011). Approach or avoidance (or both?): Integrating core self-evaluations within an approach/avoidance framework. *Personnel Psychology, 64*(1), 137–161. doi:10.1111/j.1744-6570.2010.01204.x

Fiori, M., Bollmann, G., & Rossier, J. (2015). Exploring the path through which career adaptability increases job satisfaction and lowers job stress: The role of affect. *Journal of Vocational Behavior, 91*, 113–121. doi:10.1016/j.jvb.2015.08.010

Gardner, W. L., Avolio, B. J., Luthans, F., May, D. R., & Walumbwa, F. (2005). "Can you see the real me?" A self-based model of authentic leader and follower development. *Leadership Quarterly, 16*(3), 343–372. doi:10.1016/j.leaqua.2005.03.003

Gooty, J., Gavin, M., Johnson, P. D., Frazier, M. L., & Snow, D. B. (2009). In the eyes of the beholder: Transformational leadership, positive psychological capital, and performance. *Journal of Leadership & Organizational Studies, 15*, 353–367. doi:10.1177/1548051809332021

Hayes, A. F. (2013). *Introduction to mediation, moderation, and conditional process analysis: A regression-based approach*. New York, NY: Guilford Press.

Hirschi, A., Herrmann, A., & Keller, A. C. (2015). Career adaptivity, adaptability, and adapting: A conceptual and empirical investigation. *Journal of Vocational Behavior, 87*, 1–10. doi:10.1016/j.jvb.2014.11.008

Hou, Z. J., Leung, S. A., Li, X., Li, X., & Xu, H. (2012). Career Adapt-Abilities Scale-China Form: Construction and initial validation. *Journal of Vocational Behavior, 80*(3), 686–691. doi:10.1016/j.jvb.2012.01.006

Ito, J. K., & Brotheridge, C. M. (2005). Does supporting employees' career adaptability lead to commitment turnover, or both? *Human Resource Management, 44*(1), 5–19. doi:10.1002/hrm.20037

Johnston, C. S. (2018). A systematic review of the career adaptability literature and future outlook. *Journal of Career Assessment, 26*(1), 3–30. doi:10.1177/1069072716679921

Judge, T. A., Erez, A., Bono, J. E., & Thoresen, C. J. (2002). Are measures of self-esteem, neuroticism, locus of control, and generalized self-efficacy indicators of a common core construct? *Journal of Personality and Social Psychology, 83*(3), 693–710. doi:10.1037/0022-3514.83.3.693

Judge, T. A., Erez, A., Bono, J. E., & Thoresen, C. J. (2003). The core self-evaluations scale: Development of a measure. *Personnel Psychology, 56*(2), 303–331. doi:10.1111/j.1744-6570.2003.tb00152.x

Judge, T. A., Locke, E. A., Durham, C. C., & Kluger, A. N. (1998). Dispositional effects on job and life satisfaction: The role of core evaluations. *Journal of Applied Psychology, 83*(1), 17–34. doi:10.1037/0021-9010.83.1.17

Judge, T. A., & Zapata, C. P. (2015). The person-situation debate revisited: Effect of situation strength and trait activation on the validity of the big five personality traits in predicting job performance. *Academy of Management Journal, 58*(4), 1149–1179. doi:10.5465/amj.2010.0837

Kammeyer-Mueller, J. D., Judge, T. A., & Scott, B. A. (2009). The role of core self-evaluations in the coping process. *Journal of Applied Psychology, 94*(1), 177–195. doi:10.1037/a0013214

Kim, Y. J., Van Dyne, L., Kamdar, D., & Johnson, R. E. (2013). Why and when do motives matter? An integrative model of motives, role cognitions, and social support as predictors of OCB. *Organizational Behavior and Human Decision Processes, 121*(2), 231–245. doi:10.1016/j.obhdp.2013.03.004

Lam, C. F., Wan, W., & Roussin, C. (2016). Going the extra mile and feeling energized: An enrichment perspective of organizational citizenship behaviors. *Journal of Applied Psychology, 101*(3), 379–391. doi:10.1037/apl0000071

Lee, K., & Allen, N. J. (2002). Organizational citizenship behavior and workplace deviance: The role of affect and cognitions. *Journal of Applied Psychology, 87*(1), 131–142. doi:10.1037/0021-9010.87.1.131

LePine, J. A., Erez, A., & Johnson, D. E. (2002). The nature and dimensionality of organizational citizenship behavior: A critical review and meta-analysis. *Journal of Applied Psychology, 87*(1), 52–65. doi:10.1037/0021-9010.87.1.52

Levy, P. E. (2003). *Industrial/organizational psychology: Understanding the workplace.* Boston, MA: Houghton Mifflin.

Merino-Tejedor, E., Hontangas, P. M., & Boada-Grau, J. (2016). Career adaptability and its relation to self-regulation, career construction, and academic engagement among Spanish university students. *Journal of Vocational Behavior, 93*, 92–102. doi:10.1016/j.jvb.2016.01.005

Neureiter, M., & Traut-Mattausch, E. (2017). Two sides of the career resources coin: Career adaptability resources and the impostor phenomenon. *Journal of Vocational Behavior, 98*, 56–69. doi:10.1016/j.jvb.2016.10.002

Nilforooshan, P., & Salimi, S. (2016). Career adaptability as a mediator between personality and career engagement. *Journal of Vocational Behavior, 94*, 1–10. doi:10.1016/j.jvb.2016.02.010

Organ, D. W. (1988). Organizational citizenship behavior: The good soldier syndrome. *Administrative Science Quarterly, 41*, 692–703.

Piccolo, R. F., Greenbaum, R., Den Hartog, D. N., & Folger, R. (2010). The relationship between ethical leadership and core job characteristics. *Journal of Organizational Behavior, 278*, 259–278. doi:10.1002/job.627

Ployhart, R. E., & Bliese, P. D. (2006). Individual adaptability (I-ADAPT) theory: Conceptualizing the antecedents, consequences, and measurement of individual differences in adaptability. In C. S. Burke, L. G. Pierce, & E. Salas (Eds.), *Understanding adaptability: A prerequisite for effective performance within complex environments* (pp. 3–39). Amsterdam: Elsevier.

Podsakoff, P. M., MacKenzie, S. B., Paine, J. B., & Bachrach, D. G. (2000). Organizational citizenship behaviors: A critical review of the theoretical and empirical literature and suggestions for future research. *Journal of Management, 26*(3), 513–563. doi:10.1177/014920630002600307

Pulakos, E. D., Arad, S., Donovan, M. A., & Plamondon, K. E. (2000). Adaptability in the workplace: Development of a taxonomy of adaptive performance. *Journal of Applied Psychology, 85*(4), 612–624. doi:10.1037/0021-9010.85.4.612

Rossier, J., Zecca, G., Stauffer, S. D., Maggiori, C., & Dauwalder, J. P. (2012). Career Adapt-Abilities Scale in a French-speaking Swiss sample: Psychometric properties and relationships to personality and work engagement. *Journal of Vocational Behavior, 80*(3), 734–743. doi:10.1016/j.jvb.2012.01.004

Rudolph, C. W., Lavigne, K. N., & Zacher, H. (2017). Career adaptability: A meta-analysis of relationships with measures of adaptivity, adapting responses, and adaptation results. *Journal of Vocational Behavior, 98*, 17–34. doi:10.1016/j.jvb.2016.09.002

Saks, A. M., & Ashforth, B. E. (1997). Organizational socialization: Making sense of the past and present as a prologue for the future. *Journal of Vocational Behavior, 51*(2), 234–279. doi:10.1006/jvbe.1997.1614

Savickas, M. L. (1997). Career adaptability: An integrative construct for Life-span, Life-space Theory. *The Career Development Quarterly*, *45*(3), 247–259. doi:10.1002/j.2161-0045.1997.tb00469.x

Savickas, M. L. (2002). Career construction: A developmental theory of vocational behavior. In D. Brown (Ed.), *Career choice and development* (pp. 149–205). San Francisco, CA: Jossey-Bass.

Savickas, M. L. (2005). The theory and practice of career construction. In S. D. Brown & R. W. Lent (Eds.), Career development and counseling: Putting theory and research to work (pp. 42–70). Hoboken, NJ: Wiley.

Savickas, M.L. (2012). Life design: A paradigm for career intervention in the 21st century. *Journal of Counseling and Development*, *90*, 13–19. doi:10.1111/j.1556-6676.2012.00002.xC

Savickas, M. L. (2013). Career construction theory and practice. In R. W. Lent & S. D. Brown (Eds.), *Career development and counseling: Putting theory and research into work* (2nd ed., pp. 147–183). Hoboken, NJ: Wiley.

Savickas, M. L., & Porfeli, E. J. (2012). Career adapt-abilities scale: Construction, reliability, and measurement equivalence across 13 countries. *Journal of Vocational Behavior*, *80*(3), 661–673. doi:10.1016/j.jvb.2012.01.011

Siemsen, E., Roth, A., & Oliveira, P. (2010). Common method bias in regression models with linear, quadratic, and interaction effects. *Organizational Research Methods*, *13*(3), 456–476. doi: 10.1177/1094428109351241

Spurk, D. M., Kauffeld, S., Meinecke, A. L., & Ebner, K. (2016). Why do adaptable people feel less insecure? Indirect effects of career adaptability on job and career insecurity via two types of perceived marketability. *Journal of Career Assessment*, *24*(2), 289–306. doi:10.1177/1069072715580415

Tang, Y. Y. (2009). Interdependence and organizational citizenship behavior: Exploring the mediating effect of group cohesion in multilevel analysis. *The Journal of Psychology*, *143*, 625–640. doi:10.1080/00223980903218273

Taylor, S. G., & Pattie, M. W. (2014). When does ethical leadership affect workplace incivility? The moderating role of follower personality. *Business Ethics Quarterly*, *24*(4), 595–616. doi: 10.5840/beq201492618

Tett, R. P., & Burnett, D. D. (2003). A personality trait-based interactionist model of job performance. *Journal of Applied Psychology*, *88*(3), 500–517. doi:10.1037/0021-9010.88.3.500

Tett, R. P., & Guterman, H. A. (2000). Situation trait relevance, trait expression, and cross-situational consistency: Testing a principle of trait activation. *Journal of Research in Personality*, *34*(4), 397–423. doi:10.1006/jrpe.2000.2292

Van Dyne, L., Cummings, L. L., & Parks, M. J. (1995). Extra-role behaviors: In pursuit of construct and definitional clarity (a bridge over muddied waters). *Research in Organizational Behavior*, *17*, 215–285.

Walumbwa, F. O., Morrison, E. W., & Christensen, A. L. (2012). Ethical leadership and group in-role performance: The mediating roles of group conscientiousness and group voice. *Leadership Quarterly*, *23*(5), 953–964. doi:10.1016/j.leaqua.2012.06.004

Wang, H. J., Demerouti, E., & Le Blanc, P. (2017). Transformational leadership, adaptability, and job crafting: The moderating role of organizational identification. *Journal of Vocational Behavior*, *100*, 185–195. doi:10.1016/j.jvb.2017.03.009

Zacher, H. (2014). Career adaptability predicts subjective career success above and beyond personality traits and core self-evaluations. *Journal of Vocational Behavior*, *84*(1), 21–30. doi: 10.1016/j.jvb.2013.10.002

Zhao, H., Peng, Z., & Chen, H. (2014). Compulsory citizenship behavior and organizational citizenship behavior: The role of organizational identification and perceived interactional justice. *The Journal of Psychology*, *148*(2), 177–196. doi:10.1080/00223980.2013.768591

Leader–Follower Congruence in MD Propensity and UPB: A Polynomial Regression Analysis

Jun Song, Jin Yang, and Changqing He

ABSTRACT

Drawing on previous work on moral disengagement and balance theory, the (in)congruence effect of leader and follower moral disengagement (MD) propensity on followers' unethical pro-organizational behavior (UPB) was examined in this study. Dyad data were gathered from 185 CEOs and 555 followers from 185 firms located in China. The polynomial regression analysis results suggest that followers in the presence of leader–follower congruence in MD propensity conduct more UPBs. Moreover, followers conduct more UPBs with MD propensity in the presence of congruence. We also found asymmetrical incongruence effects. Followers engage more in UPBs when their MD propensity exceeds their leaders' MD propensity than when their leaders' MD propensity exceeds their own. Overall, the findings emphasize the value of considering followers' and leaders' traits for shedding light on the occurrence of UPBs.

In recent years, unethical pro-organizational behaviors (UPBs), which are unethical behaviors that benefit an organization (e.g. withholding negative information about the organization from the public or deliberately exaggerating facts for the sake of the organization; Umphress et al., 2010), have gained increasing amounts of attention. Previous studies have recognized leader (e.g. Cheng et al., 2019; Kalshoven et al., 2016) and employee (e.g. Ghosh, 2017; Kong, 2016) factors as predictors of UPB. Recent works on business ethics have suggested that follower–leader characteristic (in)congruence is particularly influential in explaining an individual's unethical behavior (Qin et al., 2018, 2019). However, little is known about whether there is a joint effect of leader and follower characteristics on UPB. This scenario is a critical theoretical issue because considering leader and follower factors (i.e. personal traits) simultaneously is believed to provide a more accurate and nuanced picture than considering only the information provided by either party (Qin et al., 2018). To fill this important yet unexplored research gap, the current study aims to explore whether there is a joint effect of leader and follower moral disengagement (MD) propensity on follower UPB.

MD propensity is a kind of personality trait related to ethics that is conceptualized as one's tendency to deal with ethical issues through cognitive disengagement from moral norms (Aquino et al., 2007; Paciello et al., 2008). Individuals with high MD propensity are more inclined to employ morally disengaged tactics that free them from accompanying self-sanctions and guilt when behaving unethically than those with low MD propensity (Fehr et al., 2020; Knoll et al., 2016). An individual's decision to perform unethical behaviors is also influenced by his/her leader's characteristics (e.g. MD propensity; Bonner et al., 2016), implying that leader and follower MD propensity jointly affect the follower's unethical behaviors. Moreover, balance theory (Heider, 1958; Korman,1970) indicates that leader–follower congruence makes the follower perceive a favorable relationship with his/her leader. A high-quality relationship between leaders and followers has been found to stimulate followers to work for leaders and organizations represented by the leaders (Bryant & Merritt, 2019). Therefore, we can infer that leader–follower congruence and MD propensity influence the pro-organizational side and unethical side of behavior independently, which raises the following questions: Does leader–follower MD propensity (in)congruence influence follower UPB? If so, how?

To address this question, we integrate balance theory with the MD literature to investigate how follower UPB is shaped by various combinations of leader–follower (in)congruence in MD propensity by performing polynomial regression and response surface model. Our research contributes to the behavioral ethics and MD literature in three ways. First, in contrast to previous research on UPB that separately but not simultaneously examined the roles played by leaders and followers, this study is among the first to explore how leader and follower factors jointly influence UPB. By adopting a leader--follower congruence approach, our knowledge on the predictors of UPB is enriched. Second, by considering MD propensity held by multiple entities (i.e. leaders and followers) rather than a single entity, our study moves beyond the extant literature on moral disengagement, which has mainly focused on the effect of follower MD propensity on one's unethical decisions (e.g. Dang et al., 2017; Moore et al., 2012; Samnani et al., 2014), thereby providing a comprehensive and nuanced understanding of the complicated process of how MD propensity influences one's unethical behavior. Third, by revealing the positive impact of leader–follower congruence in MD propensity on follower UPB, our study provides evidence for the flip side of leader–follower congruence and further extends the prior research (*et al.*, Kang et al., 2014; Strauss et al., 2001; Zhang et al., 2012) that exclusively highlights the beneficial side of leader–follower congruence.

Theory and Hypotheses

Leader–Follower Congruence in MD Propensity and UPB

The (in)congruence of leader–follower MD propensity has been proposed to explain the causes of UPB. Particularly, the core point of balance theory is that the goal of a human being is to pursue a balanced state (i.e. a harmonious context where the entities can coexist without pressure) (Treadway et al., 2007; Woodside & Chebat, 2001). A balanced state with MD propensity occurs when a follower and leader hold similar values and propensities on ethical issues (i.e. leader–follower congruence in MD propensity). In such a balanced state, the follower feels relaxed when dealing with the leader because both parties are not pressured to change (Wilson et al., 2018). Moreover, given that "we tend to like people who have the same beliefs and attitudes as we have" (Heider, 1958, p. 195), followers who exhibit MD propensity congruence with their leaders tend to perceive a harmonious interpersonal relationship with their leaders. This perception motivates followers to work for their leaders (Bryant & Merritt, 2019). Considering that leaders are often considered as the representative of an organization (Zhang et al., 2014), followers in the presence of leader–follower congruence in MD propensity are willing to serve their organization's interests *via* all means available, including walking into moral gray areas and resorting to unethical acts that favor their organizations (i.e. UPBs) (Umphress & Bingham, 2011).

In the presence of leader–follower incongruence in MD propensity, the two entities may be inclined to disengage morally on ethical issues and follow various moral principles to different extents when making behavioral decisions (Moore et al., 2012). As a result of such inconsistency, interpersonal conflicts between followers and leaders, especially on unethical issues, are exacerbated (Kammeyer-Mueller et al., 2012; Pircher Verdorfer & Peus, 2020; Thorne, 2010). The interpersonal incompatibility caused by MD propensity incongruence plays a powerful role in destroying the interactions between leaders and followers, which in turn creates an imbalance between the two parties. Based on balance theory, which states that negative psychological experiences (e.g. dissatisfaction, disturbance, and tension) are nourished in unbalanced states (Crano & Cooper, 1973; Woodside & Chebat, 2001), followers are likely to show anger, disgust, and dislike directed at leaders in the presence of MD propensity incongruence. These unfavorable feelings derived from interactions with leaders might also reflect their feelings toward the organization because leaders are representatives of organizations in the eyes of followers (Eisenberger et al., 2010; Loi et al., 2014). Consequently, a follower's psychological attachment with the organization is weakened, and he/she is unlikely to feel obligated to abide with the rules of the organization (Eisenberger et al., 2002). Therefore, followers tend to decrease their willingness to work for organizations by crossing moral boundaries (i.e. conducting UPB) when they exhibit incongruent MD propensity with their leaders. Thus, we predict:

> **Hypothesis 1:** There are more UPBs when a leader and a follower are congruent in MD propensity than when they are incongruent.

Distinguishing Two Scenarios of MD Propensity Congruence

Followers and leaders can exhibit congruence at either low or high levels of MD propensity. We contend that follower UPB may differ based on the two types of congruence. On the one hand, leader–follower congruence with high MD propensity promotes favorable mutual interactions between two parties, which is in line with the general logic of person–supervisor fit theory (Kristof-Brown et al., 2005) and balance theory (Heider, 1958). As previously mentioned, positive interactions between followers and leaders provide a balanced and pleasant state for followers, which further strengthens the followers' motivation to conduct pro-organizational behaviors. In addition to an enhanced pro-organizational motivation, the high MD propensity leads to additional unethical elements in a follower's behavior because it protects the follower high in MD propensity against self-sanctions and guilt when he/she is violating moral principles (Moore, 2008). Moreover, when both followers and leaders have a high MD propensity, the leaders are likely to be perceived as unethical behavioral models (Bonner et al., 2016). According to social cognitive theory, followers' behaviors are often influenced by external behavioral models (Bandura, 1973; Hannah et al., 2013), and followers supervised by leaders with high MD propensity are likely to behave with loose moral standards. Based on the above ideas, leader–follower congruence in high MD propensity not only motivates the follower to serve the organization's interests but also reduces the level of morality of their behaviors. Thus, we contend that a follower's willingness to conduct UPB is strengthened in the presence of leader–follower congruence with high MD propensity.

Similarly, a balanced state occurs when a follower and a leader exhibit congruence in the presence of low MD propensity, as they have consistent ethical expectations and thus experience few conflicts and contradictions when facing moral issues. Notably, however, individuals with low MD propensity are more likely to regulate themselves by following moral principles than those with high MD propensity (Fehr et al., 2020). Thus, low–low MD propensity interactions may reduce the level of immorality of followers' behaviors. Consequently, followers in the presence of congruence in low MD propensity prefer to pursue an ethical approach rather than an unethical approach to work for the interests of organizations, leading to a decrease in the likelihood of followers' engagement in UPBs. Thus, we predict:

> **Hypothesis 2:** UPBs are more likely to arise in the presence of high follower–high leader MD propensity than in the presence of low follower–low leader MD propensity.

Distinguishing Two Scenarios of MD Propensity Incongruence

We propose two possible permutations, namely, when a leader possesses a higher level of MD propensity than a follower and when a leader possesses a lower level of MD propensity than a follower. Although an unbalanced status can be caused by personal trait (i.e. MD propensity) misfit, we contend that the possibility of follower UPB is higher in the presence of low leader–high follower MD propensity than in the presence of high leader–low follower MD propensity.

Drawn from the theory of balance, a follower may be placed in a more unbalanced and stressful status when his/her level of MD propensity is low while his/her leader's level of MD propensity is high. Previous studies have shown that individuals with high MD propensity exhibit a greater possibility of using morally disengaged tactics (e.g. reconstructing unethical behaviors to reduce their immorality, distorting or obscuring the consequences of and responsibility for unethical conduct, and minimizing the harm caused by unethical behaviors to the victims) (Kacmar et al., 2019; Lee et al., 2016), which can free individuals from the accompanying self-sanctions and guilt of their unethical behavior (Knoll et al., 2016). Thus, leaders who hold high MD propensity tend to behave in accordance with loose moral norms. Morality is more important to followers with low MD propensity than those with high MD propensity, and accordingly, such people are more likely to behave morally and be attentive to ethical issues (Dang et al., 2017). Once they observe a leader's unethical actions, followers low in MD propensity will have more negative psychological experiences (e.g. discomfort, dissonance, or guilt) (Bandura, 1999; Detert et al., 2008). Consequently, interpersonal conflicts between a leader and a follower are likely to become exacerbated. That is, low follower–high leader MD propensity is likely to cause the follower to be in a relatively unbalanced and unpleasant state, and in this case, followers may feel more disappointed toward their leaders with higher MD propensity than them. These negative feelings toward leaders will be transferred to the organization, as leaders are often regarded as representatives of organizations (Zhang et al., 2014). Finally, followers' willingness to be involved in ethical or unethical pro-organizational behaviors (i.e. UPBs) is weakened in the presence of low follower–high leader MD propensity.

In contrast, followers who hold high MD propensity are more likely to remove self-sanctions and the accompanying guilt when behaving in an unethical manner or observing others' (e.g. leaders') misconduct (Bandura, 1999; Detert et al., 2008). Thus, such followers are more likely to adopt an indifferent attitude toward leaders' behaviors and are less likely to care whether their leaders' behaviors are unethical. Consequently, followers with high MD propensity are unlikely to be influenced by the ethical message delivered by leaders with low MD propensity because MD propensity is a chronic trait (Dang et al., 2017). This kind of indifference can alleviate the intensity of interpersonal conflicts concerning ethical issues caused by MD propensity incongruence, thereby attenuating unbalanced experiences and the accompanying negative effect on followers' motivation to engage in UPBs. Thus, we predict:

> **Hypothesis 3:** UPBs are more in the case of high follower–low leader MD propensity than in the case of low follower–high leader MD propensity.

Method

Sample and Procedure

The data included in this research were collected from chief executive officers (CEOs) and three followers (the managers of the R&D department, the marketing department, and the human resources (HR) & administration department) in eastern China. Online questionnaires were sent out with the help of the local Commissions of Economy and Information Technology. The researchers guaranteed that the information provided by the participants would be anonymous and confidential and would be used for research only. To improve the response rate, the researchers reminded the participants to fill out the questionnaires *via* email or telephone. Of the total 767 firms invited to participate, 492 CEOs (64.15% of the total sample) completed the survey, with an above average response rate for executives in organizational survey research (37%, see meta-analysis by Anseel et al., 2010). Because only the CEOs with all three followers were included in our study, mismatching data from 307 firms were excluded. Our final sample consisted of 185 CEOs and 555 followers from 185 firms. Among the 185 CEOs, 96.2% were male, 27.6% were above the age of 40 years, and 30.8% held a bachelor's degree or above. Among the 555 followers, 86.5% were male, 54.8% were under the age of 40 years, and 36.9% held a bachelor's degree or above.

Measures

All measurements were originally constructed in an English version and were then translated to Chinese. Back translation procedures (Brislin, 1980) were conducted to ensure the equivalence of English-based measures and Chinese-based measures (Song et al., 2017). All the measures adopted in the current research were rated *via* a five-point Likert scale that ranges from 1 (strongly disagree) to 5 (strongly agree).

MD Propensity

Leaders' and followers' levels of MD propensity were rated by adopting the eight-item scale developed by Moore et al. (2012). The participants were asked to score items such as "It is okay to spread rumors to defend those you care about" and "Taking personal credit for ideas that were not yours is no big deal." The values of Cronbach's alpha (α) were .96 for the followers and .96 for the leaders.

Upb

The six-item scale from Umphress et al. (2010) work was adopted to evaluate each follower's UPB. The participants were asked to score items such as "If it would help my organization, I would misrepresent the truth to make my organization look good" and "If needed, I would conceal information from the public that would be damaging to my organization." The value of α was .97.

Control Variables

The dissimilarities between a leader and his or her followers regarding age, education, gender, and tenure influence the followers' attitudes, affects, and behaviors (Bauer & Green, 1996; Tsui & O'reilly, 1989). Tenure, age, education, and gender dissimilarity between leaders and followers were operated as controls in the current study.

Analytical Strategy

Polynomial regression procedures (Jansen & Kristof-Brown, 2005) were adopted to test hypotheses 1, 2, and 3. Response surface modeling (Edwards & Parry, 1993) was employed to accurately present and plot the results. To examine (in)congruence effects on the outcomes, polynomial regression procedures that can generate three-dimensional response surfaces have been suggested by Edwards and Van Harrison (1993) and Edwards and Parry (1993). This method has been applied by Jansen and Kristof-Brown (2005) to account for non-independence among followers who are supervised by the same leader. This method was employed in the present analysis owing to the nested nature of our data. In particular, we regressed the outcome variable (i.e. UPB) as a dependent variable on the controls, the centered follower MD propensity (F), the centered leader MD propensity (L), the follower MD propensity squared (F^2), the follower MD propensity times the leader MD propensity ($F \times L$), and the leader MD propensity squared (L^2). Consistent with previous work on polynomial regressions (e.g. Audenaert et al., 2018; Yang et al., 2017; Zhang et al., 2012), F and L were initially grand-mean centered. On this basis, we calculated the second-order terms (i.e. F^2, $F \times L$, L^2) to improve the interpretability of the results and reduce the possibility of multicollinearity. The simplified regression equation adopted in this study, with the omission of all controls (i.e. age dissimilarity, education dissimilarity, and gender dissimilarity), is expressed as follows:

$$Z = b_0 + b_1F + b_2L + b_3F^2 + b_4F \times L + b_5L^2 + e,$$

where Z represents UPB, F represents the follower's MD propensity, and L represents the leader's MD propensity. The regression coefficients of F and L were used to plot the response surfaces with three dimensions.

After performing polynomial regressions, we conducted additional tests for slope and curvature examinations along the incongruence (i.e. $F = -L$) and congruence (i.e. $F = L$) lines. The shape of the surface along the $F = L$ line was obtained by plugging the formula of the congruence line into the equation of regression. Similarly, the shape of the surface along the $F = -L$ line was obtained by plugging the formula of the incongruence line into the equation of regression.

To test the first hypothesis, we initially assessed whether a significant joint effect exists among F^2, $F \times L$, and L^2. Subsequently, we tested whether a significantly negative curvature (b_3-b_4+b_5) exists along the $F = -L$ line. When these two conditions are satisfied, we can conclude that there is a significant congruence effect, thereby supporting hypothesis 1. We tested the second hypothesis by computing the slope along the $F = L$ line. When a significant and positive slope (b_1+b_2) exists along this line, more UPBs arise when congruence exists in the presence of high MD propensity than in the presence of low MD propensity. To test the third hypothesis, we followed the approach of Edwards and Van Harrison (1993) for computing the lateral shift $((b_1-b_2)/(2\times(b_{11}-b_{12}+b_{22})))$ along the $F = -L$ line, representing this lateral shift's magnitude and direction. Atwater et al. (1998) suggested that a negative value in a concave surface implies sharper changes in the $F < L$ region of the surface than in the $F > L$ region.

Results

(1) Reliability analysis, (2) convergent validity analysis, and (3) discriminant validity analysis were conducted to examine the measurement model's reliability and validity. Cronbach's alpha (α) was first adopted to evaluate the internal consistency of the research model, which can reflect the reliability of the measurement model. All α values in Table 1 exceed the threshold value .70, thereby indicating acceptable reliability for all constructs. Second, the composite reliability (CR) and average variance extracted (AVE) of each construct and loadings of all items were computed to reflect the convergent validity of the measurement model. Table 3 shows the results. Each item's loading is greater than the .70 criterion, CR values for all constructs are above the .70 criterion, and the values of AVEs for all constructs are higher than the .50 criterion. Thus, the convergent validity is satisfactory. Third, we compared the square roots of the AVE values ($\sqrt{AVE}$) with the correlations among the constructs to evaluate the discriminant validity of the measurement model. The values of $\sqrt{AVE}$ for all constructs in Table 2 are greater than the correlations among variables, indicating

Table 1. Descriptive Statistics and Correlations among Variables of This Study[a].

Variables	*M*	*SD*	1	2	3	4	5	6	7
1. Gender dissimilarity	.17	.37							
2. Age dissimilarity	.63	.48	.07						
3. Education dissimilarity	.37	.48	.04	.19***					
4. Tenure dissimilarity	.54	.50	.03	.24***	.10*				
5. UPB	1.50	.92	–.05	–.06	.08	.09*	(.97)		
6. Follower MD propensity	1.51	.88	–.06	–.06	.11*	.13**	.82***	(.96)	
7. Leader MD propensity	1.65	1.01	.01	–.03	.08	.10*	.43***	.45***	(.96)

[a]$N_{Follower}$= 555. Reliabilities (α) are presented along the diagonal in parentheses. When calculating the correlations, the value of the leader-level variable (i.e. leader MD propensity) was disaggregated to the follower level.
* $p< .05$; ** $p< .01$; ***$p< .001$.

Table 2. Loadings, Cronbach's Alpha (α), Composite Reliability (CR), and Average Variance Extracted (AVE).

Variables	N	Loading	α	CR	AVE
UPB	6	.911–.952	.97	.98	.93
Follower MD propensity	8	.765–.946	.96	.97	.89
Leader MD propensity	8	.786–.943	.96	.97	.89

Table 3. Polynomial Regression Results: The Effects of the Congruence/Incongruence of MD Propensity on UPB[a].

Variable	UPB	
Constant	2.85*** (.06)	3.00*** (.07)
Gender Dissimilarity	.00 (.06)	–.00 (.06)
Age Dissimilarity	–.01 (.05)	–.02 (.05)
Education Dissimilarity	–.02 (.05)	–.01 (.05)
Tenure Dissimilarity	–.04 (.05)	–.04 (.05)
Follower MD propensity (FMDP)	.81*** (.03)	.85*** (.04)
Leader MD propensity (LMDP)	.08** (.03)	.19*** (.03)
$FMDP^2$		–.03 (.03)
FMDP * LMDP		.11*** (.02)
$LMDP^2$		–.05* (.02)
Congruence		
(FMDP = LMDP) line		
Slope		1.04***
Curvature		.04
Incongruence		
(FMDP = –LMDP) line		
Slope		.66***
Curvature		–.19***
F for the three quadratic terms		13.02***

Note. [a]$N_{Follower} = 555$, $N_{Leader} = 185$.
*$p < .05$; **$p < .01$; ***$p < .001$.

good discriminant validity. Overall, these findings indicate acceptable reliability and validity.

Hypothesis 1 suggests a positive effect of MD propensity congruence between a leader and a follower on UPB. Table 3 shows the curvatures and slopes along (in)congruence lines, as well as the estimated coefficients for the polynomial regressions in predicting UPB. Figure 1 plots the response surface based on these coefficients. Table 3 reveals a significant joint effect among F^2, $F \times L$, and L^2 (13.02, $p < .001$). Furthermore, a significantly negative curvature of the $F = -L$ line (–.19, $p < .001$) is shown, thereby indicating a curved downward response surface along the $F = -L$ line. Therefore, more UPBs arise

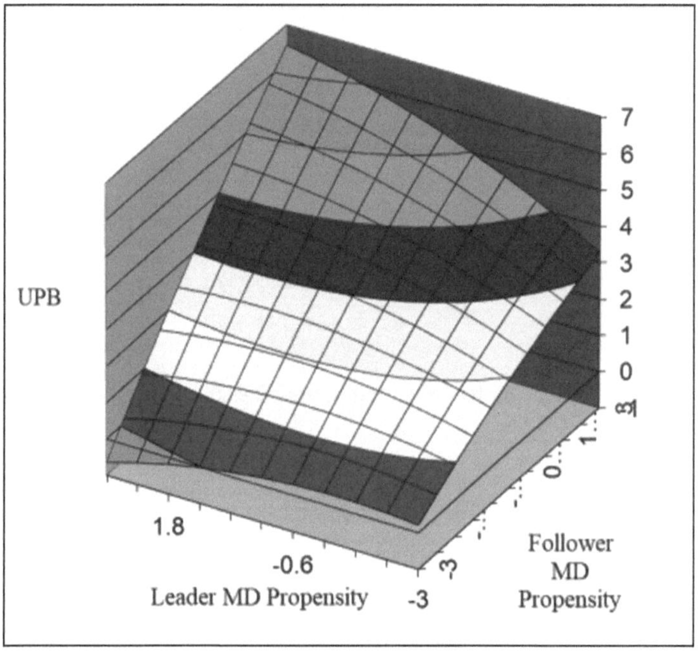

Figure 1. Response surface of the congruence of leader–follower MD propensity and its effect on UPB.

when the MD propensity held by a follower is aligned with that of his or her leader. In addition, any deviation from the $F=L$ line can induce a decrease in UPBs. Hence, Hypothesis 1 is supported.

Hypothesis 2 suggests that more UPBs arise when a follower and his or her leader are aligned at high (vs. low) levels of MD propensity. Table 3 shows a significantly positive slope along the $F=L$ line (1.04, $p < .001$). Therefore, more UPBs exist in the condition of high follower–high leader congruence than in the condition of low follower–low leader congruence in MD propensity. Figure 1 illustrates that fewer UPBs occurs in the presence of low follower–low leader congruence than in the presence of high follower–high leader congruence in MD propensity. Therefore, Hypothesis 2 is supported.

With regard to hypothesis 3, the lateral shift magnitude was significant and negative (-1.75, 95% CI [-11.41, −.51], excluding 0), supporting the asymmetrical assumption about the relationship between the incongruence in leader–follower MD propensity and followers' UPB. When the level of MD propensity held by a follower is lower than that of his or her leader, a sharper decrease is found than in the condition when MD propensity held by a follower is higher than his or her leader. Hence, hypothesis 3 was supported. Figure 1 provides additional support for hypothesis 3. Figure 1 illustrates that a higher UPB value can be found at the A point ($F=2$, $L = -2$) than at the B point ($F = -2$, $L=2$).

Discussion

A growing attention has been paid to the topic of UPB (e.g. Bryant & Merritt, 2019; Shaw et al., 2020; Zhang, 2020), but scholars have not yet uncovered the reasons for an individual's engagement in UPB from the perspective of leader–follower congruence. In this study, we developed a dyadic model to test whether a combination effect of leader and follower MD propensity on follower UPB exists by integrating balance theory with the existing literature on moral disengagement. We found that leader–follower congruence in MD propensity increases the likelihood of follower UPB because MD propensity congruence contributes to a follower's pro-organizational motivation by inducing a balanced state between a leader and a follower. Moreover, this positive effect was stronger in the dyads of high follower–high leader MD propensity congruence than in the dyads of low follower–low leader MD propensity congruence, as high–high MD propensity congruence enhances a follower's pro-organizational motivation and adds additional unethical components into his/her behavior. Furthermore, although a follower's pro-organizational motivation is destroyed by leader–follower misfit, followers will demonstrate different levels of UPB in two scenarios of MD propensity incongruence (i.e. high leader–low follower and low leader–high follower) because high MD propensity makes followers ignore ethical messages from leaders with low MD propensity. Particularly, we demonstrated that more UPBs arise when a follower's MD propensity is higher than their leaders' than when followers' MD propensity is lower than their leaders', suggesting the importance of follower MD propensity in buffering the effect of MD propensity misfit on follower UPB. These findings offer several theoretical and practical implications along with future research directions.

Theoretical Implications

Our study contributes to the existing literature on behavioral ethics, moral disengagement, and congruence in three ways. First, by integrating leader–follower (in)congruence framework as well as moral disengagement literature into the research of UPB, our study extends the existing literature on the antecedents of follower UPB by revealing that leader–follower (in)congruence in MD propensity influences the likelihood for the follower's engagement in UPB. Previous empirical studies have identified leadership (e.g. Cheng et al., 2019; Effelsberg & Solga, 2015; Graham et al., 2015; Kalshoven et al., 2016; Miao et al., 2013) and employee characteristics (e.g. Castille et al., 2018; Graham et al., 2020; Kong, 2016) as predictors of employee UPB. These findings have revealed the influences of leaders and followers separately, but the studies have not investigated how leader and follower factors jointly (i.e. the leader–follower fit in personal characteristics) influence the occurrence of follower UPB, thereby preventing us from gaining a comprehensive understanding of the circumstances in which UPBs occur. The present study demonstrates that the answer to this question is far more complicated than previously thought by showing that follower UPB is related to congruence and incongruence between leaders and followers at different levels of MD propensity. Specifically, our findings indicate that depending on a leader's MD propensity level, a low level of follower MD propensity may not always decrease his/her willingness to conduct UPBs. There is an interesting but counterintuitive result that when both parties hold a low level of MD propensity, the follower may still be involved in UPB. Our findings prove that considering the joint effect of leader and follower characteristics needs to be considered to understand what triggers follower UPB. Moreover, our work extends beyond previous studies, which mainly use social exchange theory (e.g. Umphress & Bingham, 2011), social identity theory (e.g. Kalshoven et al., 2016) and social cognitive theory (e.g. Chen et al., 2016) as the guiding theories for investigating the antecedents of UPB, and provides a new perspective for understanding the causes of UPB by applying person–supervisor fit theory and balance theory into the UPB domain.

Second, this study contributes to the existing literature on moral disengagement by revealing that the influence of followers' or leaders' MD propensity on follower's behavior partly depends on the level of MD propensity of the other party. Nearly all the previous studies on moral disengagement have exclusively focused on the role of MD propensity held by a follower in triggering his/her unethical behaviors (e.g. Fehr et al., 2020; Reynolds et al., 2014) while overlooked the simultaneous effect of leader and follower MD propensity. One exception is Bonner et al. (2016) research, which identified follower MD propensity as a moderator in the relationship between leader MD propensity and perceived ethical leadership. Our research moves beyond previous works on MD propensity by (a) assessing simple effects of leader–follower MD propensity congruence on follower UPB, (b) comparing two scenarios of MD propensity congruence (i.e. high–high MD propensity vs. low–low MD propensity), and (c) comparing two scenarios of MD propensity incongruence (i.e. high–low MD propensity vs. low–high MD propensity). Moreover, in contrast to previous studies that have highlighted the positive effect of MD propensity on individual unethical behavior (e.g. Moore, 2008; Samnani et al., 2014), our study demonstrates that followers with low MD propensity may also engage in a high level of UPB when their leaders hold low MD propensity. This finding implies that considering leader and follower MD propensity simultaneously is necessary for a nuanced understanding of the complicated behavioral consequences of MD propensity. By adopting a trait view and focusing on MD propensity, our study also provides a comprehensive framework for understanding the complex role played by moral disengagement. The existing empirical research has mainly identified moral disengagement as a cognitive state in which self-sanctions are removed when followers behave in an unethical manner (e.g. Duffy et al., 2012) while considerably disregarded the fact that moral disengagement is not only a state but also a personality trait. Moreover, by identifying UPB as the consequence of leader–follower MD propensity (in)congruence, our study also enriches the extant research on the outcomes of MD propensity, including counterproductive workplace behavior (Samnani et al., 2014), unethical behavior (Kouchaki & Smith, 2014), and organizational citizenship behavior (Shin et al., 2017).

Third, our findings provide evidence for the flip side of leader–follower congruence by showing a positive relationship between leader–follower congruence in MD propensity and follower UPB. Our study, therefore, advances the prior research that exclusively highlights the benefits of leader–follower congruence in stimulating superiority on one's work outcomes (e.g. Schaubroeck & Lam, 2002; Strauss et al., 2001; Zhang et al., 2012) and reducing the occurrence of unethical behaviors (Qin et al., 2019). Moreover, the majority of past works on leader–follower congruence have concentrated on the effect of congruence on general outcomes, while only a few studies have explored congruence's effect on ethical or unethical behaviors by adopting the leader–follower congruence approach (e.g. Qin et al., 2018, 2019; Shin et al., 2017). The present study extends this line of research and deepens our understanding of the implications of leader–follower congruence by identifying a specific type of unethical behavior (i.e. UPB) as the outcome of leader–follower congruence.

Managerial Implications

This study provides several implications for managerial practice. Unethical behaviors performed in the name of organizations (i.e. UPB) yield large losses to organizations because such misconduct undermines stakeholders' trust in organizations (Umphress et al., 2010). Consequently, such behaviors can potentially ruin organizations (Chen et al., 2016). Regarding the joint effect of leader and follower MD propensity on UPB, organizations should develop an accurate and comprehensive understanding of a leader's and a follower's tendency to disengage morally with each other.

Although MD propensity is believed to play a vital role in an individual's unethical behavioral decisions, our findings show that followers with low MD propensity may also engage in high levels of UPB when the leader also holds low MD propensity. To counterbalance this congruent effect, organizations should build an organizational culture that highlights social responsibility and ethics. This type of culture will reduce employees' willingness to conduct UPB (May et al., 2015) and reinforce moral consciousness.

Our findings show that a leader low in MD propensity cannot prevent the occurrence of UPBs conducted by a follower high in MD propensity, as MD propensity is a chronic trait and cannot be easily changed. This revelation indicates that the case of low leader–high follower MD propensity may be particularly problematic. Given the above situation, organizations could obtain first-hand information on each employee's MD propensity *via* surveys during the recruiting process, which can help organizations make the right decision. Moreover, organizations should develop ethical training programmes for their in-service staff members. By attending such training programmes, employees can effectively grasp the boundaries between morality and immorality and behave in an ethical manner in the future.

Limitations

Despite these theoretical and managerial implications, our study has certain limitations. First, we fail to conclude a causal relationship because our data were collected *via* a cross-sectional design. Therefore, future research should be conducted with an experimental or longitudinal research design to examine the causal relationship between MD propensity and UPB, thus extending the external validity of this study. Second, our research concentrates on the main effect of leader–follower (in)congruence in MD propensity on UPB but overlooks the underlying mechanisms. Balance theory suggests that leader–follower incongruence in individual characteristics can increase the occurrence of stressful experiences for both parties and thereby influence the follower's work or nonwork outcomes (Tse et al., 2013). Therefore, future research could explore the potential mediators from the perspective of stress. Third, our study assesses the focal employee's intention to conduct UPBs rather than the actual UPBs. Although unethical intentions have been widely adopted to substitute individuals' actual unethical behaviors (e.g. Castille et al., 2018; Effelsberg et al., 2014), measuring actual unethical behaviors is confirmed to reveal more valid conclusions and thus serves as a potential topic for future research. Fourth, all the participants were from a society with a specific culture, China, which may limit the generalizability of our findings. Regarding this issue, a cross-cultural study should be conducted to confirm the generalizability of our findings. Fifth, this study focused on only personality (i.e. MD propensity) and did not address leadership, although leadership has been found to be a powerful driver of follower UPB (e.g. Cheng et al., 2019; Effelsberg & sSolga, 2015; Graham et al., 2015). Thus, examining whether congruence or incongruence between actual leadership exhibited by leaders and leadership perceived by followers has an effect on follower UPB should be addressed in future research.

Conclusion

UPB has gained an increasing amount of attention from scholars. The present study investigates the role of MD propensity in follower UPB by adopting the approach of leader–follower congruence. Our findings support the crucial role of the congruence of leader–follower MD propensity in predicting UPB. Future research can also benefit from considering the approach of leader–follower congruence in other individual differences when exploring the predictors of follower UPB.

Disclosure Statement

The authors declare that they have no conflict of interest.

Funding

This study was funded by National Natural Science Foundation of China (Grant No. 72001100); Ministry of Education Project of Humanities and Social Science (Grant No. 20YJC880026; 20YJC630122); Fundamental Research Funds for the Central Universities (Grant No. NS2020060); Project of Humanities and Social Science of Jiangsu Province (Grant No. 20GLC005); Nanjing University of Finance and Economy (Grant No. gjgfb201925; gigfb201911; gigfb201913).

ORCID

Jun Song http://orcid.org/0000-0002-3849-2544

References

Anseel, F., Lievens, F., Schollaert, E., & Choragwicka, B. (2010). Response rates in organizational science, 1995-2008: A meta-analytic review and guidelines for survey researchers. *Journal of Business and Psychology*, *25*(3), 335–349. https://doi.org/10.1007/s10869-010-9157-6

Aquino, K., Reed, A., II, Thau, S., & Freeman, D. (2007). A grotesque and dark beauty: How moral identity and mechanisms of moral disengagement influence cognitive and emotional reactions to war. *Journal of Experimental Social Psychology*, *43*(3), 385–392. https://doi.org/10.1016/j.jesp.2006.05.013

Atwater, L. E., Ostroff, C., Yammarino, F. J., & Fleenor, J. W. (1998). Self-other agreement: Does it really matter? *Personnel Psychology*, *51*(3), 577–598. https://doi.org/10.1111/j.1744-6570.1998.tb00252.x

Audenaert, M., Carette, P., Shore, L. M., Lange, T., Van Waeyenberg, T., & Decramer, A. (2018). Leader-employee congruence of expected contributions in the employee-organization relationship. *The Leadership Quarterly*, *29*(3), 414–422. https://doi.org/10.1016/j.leaqua.2017.09.003

Bandura, A. (1973). *Aggression: A social learning analysis*. Prentice-Hall.

Bandura, A. (1999). Moral disengagement in the perpetration of inhumanities. *Personality and Social Psychology Review : An Official Journal of the Society for Personality and Social Psychology, Inc*, *3*(3), 193–209. ttps://doi.org/10.1207/s15327957pspr0303_3 https://doi.org/10.1207/s15327957pspr0303_3

Bauer, T. N., & Green, S. G. (1996). Development of leader-member exchange: A longitudinal test. *Academy of Management Journal*, *39*(6), 1538–1567. https://doi.org/10.5465/257068

Bonner, J. M., Greenbaum, R. L., & Mayer, D. M. (2016). My boss is morally disengaged: The role of ethical leadership in explaining the interactive effect of supervisor and employee moral disengagement on employee behaviors. *Journal of Business Ethics*, *137*(4), 731–742. https://doi.org/10.1007/s10551-014-2366-6

Brislin, R. W. (1980). Translation and content analysis of oral and written material. In H. C. Triandis & J. W. Berry (Eds.), *Handbook of Cross-Cultural Psychology*., 2(2), 349–444Allyn & Bacon.

Bryant, W., & Merritt, S. M. (2019). Unethical Pro-organizational Behavior and Positive Leader–Employee Relationships. *Journal of Business Ethics*, Advance online publication. https://doi.org/10.1007/s10551-019-04211-x

Castille, C. M., Buckner, J. E., & Thoroughgood, C. N. (2018). Prosocial citizens without a moral compass? Examining the relationship between Machiavellianism and unethical pro-organizational behavior. *Journal of Business Ethics*, *149*(4), 919–930. https://doi.org/10.1007/s10551-016-3079-9

Chen, M., Chen, C. C., & Sheldon, O. J. (2016). Relaxing moral reasoning to win: How organizational identification relates to unethical pro-organizational behavior. *The Journal of Applied Psychology*, *101*(8), 1082–1096. https://doi.org/10.1037/apl0000111

Cheng, K., Wei, F., & Lin, Y. (2019). The trickle-down effect of responsible leadership on unethical pro-organizational behavior: The moderating role of leader-follower value congruence. *Journal of Business Research*, *102*, 34–43. https://doi.org/10.1016/j.jbusres.2019.04.044

Crano, W. D., & Cooper, R. E. (1973). Examination of Newcomb's extension of structural balance theory. *Journal of Personality and Social Psychology*, *27*(3), 344–353. https://doi.org/10.1037/h0034942

Dang, C. T., Umphress, E. E., & Mitchell, M. S. (2017). Leader social accounts of subordinates' unethical behavior: Examining observer reactions to leader social accounts with moral disengagement language. *The Journal of Applied Psychology*, *102*(10), 1448–1461. https://doi.org/10.1037/apl0000233

Detert, J. R., Treviño, L. K., & Sweitzer, V. L. (2008). Moral disengagement in ethical decision making: A study of antecedents and outcomes. *The Journal of Applied Psychology*, *93*(2), 374–391. https://doi.org/10.1037/0021-9010.93.2.374

Duffy, M. K., Scott, K. L., Shaw, J. D., Tepper, B. J., & Aquino, K. (2012). A social context model of envy and social undermining. *Academy of Management Journal*, *55*(3), 643–666. https://doi.org/10.5465/amj.2009.0804

Edwards, J. R., & Parry, M. E. (1993). On the use of polynomial regression equations as an alternative to difference scores in organizational research. *Academy of Management Journal, 36*(6), 1577–1613. https://doi.org/10.5465/256822

Edwards, J. R., & Van Harrison, R. (1993). Job demands and worker health: Three-dimensional reexamination of the relationship between person-environment fit and strain. *The Journal of Applied Psychology, 78*(4), 628–648. https://doi.org/10.1037/0021-9010.78.4.628

Effelsberg, D., & Solga, M. (2015). Transformational leaders' in-group versus out-group orientation: Testing the link between leaders' organizational identification, their willingness to engage in unethical pro-organizational behavior, and follower-perceived transformational leadership. *Journal of Business Ethics, 126*(4), 581–590. https://doi.org/10.1007/s10551-013-1972-z

Effelsberg, D., Solga, M., & Gurt, J. (2014). Transformational leadership and follower's unethical behavior for the benefit of the company: A two-study investigation. *Journal of Business Ethics, 120*(1), 81–93. https://doi.org/10.1007/s10551-013-1644-z

Eisenberger, R., Karagonlar, G., Stinglhamber, F., Neves, P., Becker, T. E., Gonzalez-Morales, M. G., & Steiger-Mueller, M. (2010). Leader-member exchange and affective organizational commitment: The contribution of supervisor's organizational embodiment. *The Journal of Applied Psychology, 95*(6), 1085–1103. https://doi.org/10.1037/a0020858

Eisenberger, R., Stinglhamber, F., Vandenberghe, C., Sucharski, I. L., & Rhoades, L. (2002). Perceived supervisor support: Contributions to perceived organizational support and employee retention. *The Journal of Applied Psychology, 87*(3), 565–573. https://doi.org/10.1037/0021-9010.87.3.565

Fehr, R., Fulmer, A., & Keng-Highberger, F. T. (2020). How do employees react to leaders' unethical behavior? the role of moral disengagement. *Personnel Psychology, 73*(1), 73–93. https://doi.org/10.1111/peps.12366

Ghosh, S. K. (2017). The direct and interactive effects of job insecurity and job embeddedness on unethical pro-organizational behavior: An empirical examination. *Personnel Review, 46*(6), 1182–1198. https://doi.org/10.1108/PR-05-2015-0126

Graham, K. A., Resick, C. J., Margolis, J. A., Shao, P., Hargis, M. B., & Kiker, J. D. (2020). Egoistic norms, organizational identification, and the perceived ethicality of unethical pro-organizational behavior: A moral maturation perspective. *Human Relations, 73*(9), 1249–1277. https://doi.org/10.1177/0018726719862851

Graham, K. A., Ziegert, J. C., & Capitano, J. (2015). The effect of leadership style, framing, and promotion regulatory focus on unethical pro-organizational behavior. *Journal of Business Ethics, 126*(3), 423–436. https://doi.org/10.1007/s10551-013-1952-3

Hannah, S. T., Schaubroeck, J. M., Peng, A. C., Lord, R. G., Trevino, L. K., Kozlowski, S. W. J., Avolio, B. J., Dimotakis, N., & Doty, J. (2013). Joint influences of individual and work unit abusive supervision on ethical intentions and behaviors: A moderated mediation model. *The Journal of Applied Psychology, 98*(4), 579–592. https://doi.org/10.1037/a0032809

Heider, F. (1958). *Psychology of interpersonal relations*. Wiley.

Jansen, K. J., & Kristof-Brown, A. L. (2005). Marching to the beat of a different drummer: Examining the impact of pacing congruence. *Organizational Behavior and Human Decision Processes, 97*(2), 93–105. https://doi.org/10.1016/j.obhdp.2005.03.005

Kacmar, K. M., Carlson, D. S., Thompson, M., & Zivnuska, S. (2019). But I Still Feel Guilt: A Test of a Moral Disengagement Propensity Model. *Human Performance, 32*(3-4), 165–180. https://doi.org/10.1080/08959285.2019.1646746

Kalshoven, K., van Dijk, H., & Boon, C. (2016). Why and when does ethical leadership evoke unethical follower behavior? *Journal of Managerial Psychology, 31*(2), 500–515. https://doi.org/10.1108/JMP-10-2014-0314

Kammeyer-Mueller, J. D., Simon, L. S., & Rich, B. L. (2012). The psychic cost of doing wrong: Ethical conflict, divestiture socialization, and emotional exhaustion. *Journal of Management, 38*(3), 784–808. https://doi.org/10.1177/0149206310381133

Kang, S. W., Byun, G., & Park, H. J. (2014). Leader-follower value congruence in social responsibility and ethical satisfaction: A polynomial regression analysis. *Psychological Reports, 115*(3), 725–740. https://doi.org/10.2466/01.14.PR0.115c33z9

Knoll, M., Lord, R. G., Petersen, L. E., & Weigelt, O. (2016). Examining the moral grey zone: The role of moral disengagement, authenticity, and situational strength in predicting unethical managerial behavior. *Journal of Applied Social Psychology*, *46*(1), 65–78. https://doi.org/10.1111/jasp.12353

Kong, D. T. (2016). The pathway to unethical pro-organizational behavior: Organizational identification as a joint function of work passion and trait mindfulness. *Personality and Individual Differences*, *93*, 86–91. https://doi.org/10.1016/j.paid.2015.08.035

Korman, A. K. (1970). Toward an hypothesis of work behavior. *Journal of Applied Psychology*, *54*(1, Pt.1), 31–41. https://doi.org/10.1037/h0028656

Kouchaki, M., & Smith, I. H. (2014). The morning morality effect: The influence of time of day on unethical behavior. *Psychological Science*, *25*(1), 95–102. https://doi.org/10.1177/0956797613498099

Kristof-Brown, A. L., Zimmerman, R. D., & Johnson, E. C. (2005). Consequences of individual's fit at work: A meta-analysis of person-job, person-organization, person-group, and person-supervisor fit. *Personnel Psychology*, *58*(2), 281–342. https://doi.org/10.1111/j.1744-6570.2005.00672.x

Lee, K., Kim, E., Bhave, D. P., & Duffy, M. K. (2016). Why victims of undermining at work become perpetrators of undermining: An integrative model. *The Journal of Applied Psychology*, *101*(6), 915–924. https://doi.org/10.1037/apl0000092

Loi, R., Chan, K. W., & Lam, L. W. (2014). Leader–member exchange, organizational identification, and job satisfaction: A social identity perspective. *Journal of Occupational and Organizational Psychology*, *87*(1), 42–61. https://doi.org/10.1111/joop.12028

May, D. R., Chang, Y. K., & Shao, R. (2015). Does ethical membership matter? Moral identification and its organizational implications. *The Journal of Applied Psychology*, *100*(3), 681–694. https://doi.org/10.1037/a0038344

Miao, Q., Newman, A., Yu, J., & Xu, L. (2013). The relationship between ethical leadership and unethical pro-organizational behavior: Linear or curvilinear effects? *Journal of Business Ethics*, *116*(3), 641–653. https://doi.org/10.1007/s10551-012-1504-2

Moore, C. (2008). Moral disengagement in processes of organizational corruption. *Journal of Business Ethics*, *80*(1), 129–139. https://doi.org/10.1007/s10551-007-9447-8

Moore, C., Detert, J. R., Klebe Treviño, L., Baker, V. L., & Mayer, D. M. (2012). Why employees do bad things: Moral disengagement and unethical organizational behavior. *Personnel Psychology*, *65*(1), 1–48. https://doi.org/10.1111/j.1744-6570.2011.01237.x

Paciello, M., Fida, R., Tramontano, C., Lupinetti, C., & Caprara, G. V. (2008). Stability and change of moral disengagement and its impact on aggression and violence in late adolescence. *Child Development*, *79*(5), 1288–1309. https://doi.org/10.1111/j.1467-8624.2008.01189.x

Pircher Verdorfer, A., & Peus, C. (2020). Leading by example: Testing a moderated mediation model of ethical leadership, value congruence, and followers' openness to ethical influence. *Business Ethics: A European Review*, *29*(2), 314–332. https://doi.org/10.1111/beer.12255

Qin, X., Huang, M., Hu, Q., Schminke, M., & Ju, D. (2018). Ethical leadership, but toward whom? How moral identity congruence shapes the ethical treatment of employees. *Human Relations*, *71*(8), 1120–1149. https://doi.org/10.1177/0018726717734905

Qin, X., Liu, X., Brown, J. A., Zheng, X., & Owens, B. P. (2019). Humility Harmonized? Exploring Whether and How Leader and Employee Humility (In) Congruence Influences Employee Citizenship and Deviance Behaviors. *Journal of Business Ethics. Advance Online Publication*, https://doi.org/10.1007/s10551-019-04250-4

Reynolds, S. J., Dang, C. T., Yam, K. C., & Leavitt, K. (2014). The role of moral knowledge in everyday immorality: What does it matter if I know what is right? *Organizational Behavior and Human Decision Processes*, *123*(2), 124–137. https://doi.org/10.1016/j.obhdp.2013.10.008

Samnani, A. K., Salamon, S. D., & Singh, P. (2014). Negative affect and counterproductive workplace behavior: The moderating role of moral disengagement and gender. *Journal of Business Ethics*, *119*(2), 235–244. https://doi.org/10.1007/s10551-013-1635-0

Schaubroeck, J., & Lam, S. S. (2002). How similarity to peers and supervisor influences organizational advancement in different cultures. *Academy of Management Journal*, *45*(6), 1120–1136. https://doi.org/10.5465/3069428

Shaw, K. H., Tang, N., & Liao, H. Y. (2020). Authoritarian-Benevolent Leadership, Moral Disengagement, and Follower Unethical Pro-organizational Behavior: An Investigation of the Effects of Ambidextrous Leadership. *Frontiers in Psychology, 11*, 590–600. https://doi.org/10.3389/fpsyg.2020.00590

Shin, Y., Kim, M. S., Choi, J. N., Kim, M., & Oh, W. K. (2017). Does leader-follower regulatory fit matter? The role of regulatory fit in followers' organizational citizenship behavior. *Journal of Management, 43*(4), 1211–1233. https://doi.org/10.1177/0149206314546867

Song, J., Wu, J., & Gu, J. (2017). Voice behavior and creative performance moderated by stressors. *Journal of Managerial Psychology, 32*(2), 177–192. https://doi.org/10.1108/JMP-03-2016-0078

Strauss, J. P., Barrick, M. R., & Connerley, M. L. (2001). An investigation of personality similarity effects (relational and perceived) on peer and supervisor ratings and the role of familiarity and liking. *Journal of Occupational and Organizational Psychology, 74*(5), 637–657. https://doi.org/10.1348/096317901167569

Thorne, L. (2010). The association between ethical conflict and adverse outcomes. *Journal of Business Ethics, 92*(2), 269–276. https://doi.org/10.1007/s10551-009-0153-6

Treadway, D. C., Ferris, G. R., Duke, A. B., Adams, G. L., & Thatcher, J. B. (2007). The moderating role of subordinate political skill on supervisors' impressions of subordinate ingratiation and ratings of subordinate interpersonal facilitation. *The Journal of Applied Psychology, 92*(3), 848–855. https://doi.org/10.1037/0021-9010.92.3.848

Tse, H. H., Lam, C. K., Lawrence, S. A., & Huang, X. (2013). When my supervisor dislikes you more than me: The effect of dissimilarity in leader-member exchange on coworkers' interpersonal emotion and perceived help. *The Journal of Applied Psychology, 98*(6), 974–988. https://doi.org/10.1037/a0033862

Tsui, A. S., & O'reilly, C. A. (1989). Beyond simple demographic effects: The importance of relational demography in superior-subordinate dyads. *Academy of Management Journal, 32*(2), 402–423. https://doi.org/10.5465/256368

Umphress, E. E., & Bingham, J. B. (2011). When employees do bad things for good reasons: Examining unethical pro-organizational behaviors. *Organization Science, 22*(3), 621–640. https://doi.org/10.1287/orsc.1100.0559

Umphress, E. E., Bingham, J. B., & Mitchell, M. S. (2010). Unethical behavior in the name of the company: The moderating effect of organizational identification and positive reciprocity beliefs on unethical pro-organizational behavior. *The Journal of Applied Psychology, 95*(4), 769–780. https://doi.org/10.1037/a0019214

Wilson, K. S., Baumann, H. M., Matta, F. K., Ilies, R., & Kossek, E. E. (2018). Misery loves company: An investigation of couples' interrole conflict congruence. *Academy of Management Journal, 61*(2), 715–737. https://doi.org/10.5465/amj.2016.0395

Woodside, A. G., & Chebat, J. C. (2001). Updating Heider's balance theory in consumer behavior: A Jewish couple buys a German car and additional buying–consuming transformation stories. *Psychology and Marketing, 18*(5), 475–495. https://doi.org/10.1002/mar.1017

Yang, K., Yan, X., Fan, J., & Luo, Z. (2017). Leader-follower congruence in proactive personality and work engagement: A polynomial regression analysis. *Personality and Individual Differences, 105*, 43–46. https://doi.org/10.1016/j.paid.2016.09.033

Zhang, S. (2020). Workplace spirituality and unethical pro-organizational behavior: The mediating effect of job satisfaction. *Journal of Business Ethics, 161*(3), 687–705. https://doi.org/10.1007/s10551-018-3966-3

Zhang, H., Kwan, H. K., Zhang, X., & Wu, L. Z. (2014). High core self-evaluators maintain creativity: A motivational model of abusive supervision. *Journal of Management, 40*(4), 1151–1174. https://doi.org/10.1177/0149206312460681

Zhang, Z., Wang, M. O., & Shi, J. (2012). Leader-follower congruence in proactive personality and work outcomes: The mediating role of leader-member exchange. *Academy of Management Journal, 55*(1), 111–130. https://doi.org/10.5465/amj.2009.0865

Supervisor Incivility and Employee Job Performance: The Mediating Roles of Job Insecurity and Amotivation

Yuhyung Shin and Won-Moo Hur

ABSTRACT

Despite the increasing body of research on workplace incivility, the relationship between supervisor incivility and employee job performance, as well as its intermediary mechanisms, has received relatively little attention from researchers. Drawing on the transactional model of stress and self-determination theory, we propose employees' job insecurity and amotivation as mediating mechanisms between supervisor incivility and employee job performance. The proposed serial-mediation model was tested through a multilevel analysis of two-wave surveys collected from kindergarten teachers and their principals. Our mediation analysis revealed that incivility perpetrated by kindergarten principals exerted a negative effect on teachers' job performance three months later by shaping job insecurity perceptions and amotivation. These findings have theoretical implications for the workplace incivility literature and managerial implications for practitioners.

Over the last few decades, the mistreatment or harassment of employees in the workplace has received growing attention from researchers. Incivility, known to be the most prevalent form of workplace mistreatment (Cortina, 2008), has increasingly been a topic of research in the literature (e.g., Hur, Moon, & Jun, 2016; Jawahar & Schreurs, 2018; Meier & Gross, 2015; Rhee, Hur, & Kim, 2017). Supervisor incivility refers to uncivil behavior (e.g., sarcasm, rude remarks, hostile stares, gossip, and shunning) instigated by a supervisor (Reio, 2011). It is different from other forms of workplace mistreatment in that it represents low-intensity deviance arising from an ambiguous intention to harm the target (Andersson & Pearson, 1999). The incivility literature suggests that supervisor incivility is more detrimental to targeted employees than coworker incivility because supervisors have the authority to evaluate and reward employees' performance (Cho, Bonn, Han, & Lee, 2016; Hershcovis & Barling, 2010; Schilpzand, De Pater, & Erez, 2016). Yet, only a handful of studies have examined the effect of supervisor incivility on employee outcomes (e.g., Cho et al., 2016; Jawahar & Schreurs, 2018; Kabat-Farr, Cortina, & Marchiondo, 2018; Lim & Lee, 2011; Reio, 2011). Moreover, these studies have mainly focused on emotional reactions (e.g., negative affect and emotional exhaustion) as intermediary processes through which supervisor incivility impairs employee performance (e.g., Cho et al., 2016; Kabat-Farr et al., 2018).

A notable gap in the existing research on supervisor incivility is the negligence of cognitive appraisal as a linking mechanism between supervisor incivility and employee performance. This is a critical omission since supervisors play a determinant role in shaping employees' perceptions of what is going on in their workplace (Colbert, 2004). As supervisors have the power and authority to set work rules and make critical human-resource (HR) decisions, uncivil behavior perpetrated by supervisors should exert a strong effect on employees' cognitive appraisal of their job. Unfortunately, prior research on supervisor incivility has rarely explored this possibility. Drawing on the transactional model of stress (TMS; Lazarus & Folkman, 1984), we propose employees' cognitive appraisal of their job (i.e., job insecurity) as a key mediating mechanism between supervisor incivility and employee performance. TMS advocates that when exposed to a stressor in the workplace, employees go through cognitive processes to cope with the stressor. Because supervisor incivility is a major work stressor (Cho et al., 2016; Hershcovis & Barling, 2010; Schilpzand et al., 2016), it should strongly affect employees' perceptions of job security (Park & Ono, 2017).

Prior research on supervisor incivility is also limited in that it has rarely considered the role of motivation in the relationship between supervisor incivility and employee performance. While supervisor incivility has been found to undermine employee performance by eliciting employees' negative emotions or emotional exhaustion (e.g., Cho et al., 2016; Kabat-Farr et al., 2018), the motivational processes underlying this relationship are unexplored in the literature. Building upon TMS, we postulate that the employees' cognitive appraisal of their job affects their motivation. This proposition is also grounded in self-determination theory (SDT), whose basic premise is that motivation is a key driver of human behavior (Deci & Ryan, 1985). Scholars claim that SDT effectively explains the motivational processes of individuals in job-insecurity situations (Vander Elst, Van den Broeck, De Witte, & De Cuyper, 2012; Vansteenkiste, Lens, De Witte, & Feather, 2005). SDT can elucidate how job insecurity perceptions triggered by supervisor incivility erode employees' motivation. Furthermore, among a variety of motivational theories, SDT offers a relevant framework to understand the effect of supervisor incivility and job insecurity on motivational processes. Distinct from other motivational theories that focus on the intensity or strength of motivation, SDT differentiates between different types of motivation (i.e., autonomous motivation, controlled motivation, and amotivation) and identifies amotivation as a unique type of motivation that is qualitatively different from the other two types (Vansteenkiste et al., 2005). Of the three types of motivation, we attend to amotivation as a motivational state elicited by job insecurity perceptions. Drawing on SDT, we further propose that amotivation damages job performance. As such, the purpose of this study is to examine the mediating roles of job insecurity and amotivation in the supervisor incivility-employee performance relationship.

This study is intended to make a twofold contribution to the workplace incivility literature. First, it is one of the few studies that examine the effect of supervisor incivility on employee outcomes. Although scholars have attended to various forms of incivility, such as coworker and customer incivility, little knowledge has been accumulated with respect to the topic of supervisor incivility despite its potential influence on employee work outcomes. Our research aims to shed light on the role of supervisor incivility as a crucial form of workplace mistreatment. Second, this study is expected to delve into the mediating mechanisms of the supervisor incivility-employee performance relationship through the TMS and SDT perspectives. Complementing prior work that has identified emotional processes as mediators, we offer a novel perspective for understanding supervisor incivility by proposing cognitive (i.e., job insecurity) and motivational (i.e., amotivation) processes as mediating mechanisms, which have hitherto received relatively little attention in the workplace incivility research.

Theoretical Background and Hypothesis Development

Supervisor Incivility and Employee Outcomes

Workplace incivility is defined as "low-intensity deviant workplace behavior with an ambiguous intent to harm" (Andersson & Pearson, 1999, p. 457). Workplace incivility is conceptualized as perceptions of uncivil incidents in the workplace (Sliter, Sliter, & Jex, 2012), which implies that whether or not a specific behavior is considered an uncivil incident depends on the perceptions of the target. Thus, scholars highlight that the target's perspective or subjective experience is pivotal in defining an uncivil behavior (Cortina & Magley, 2009). The workplace incivility literature identifies coworkers, work units, supervisors, and customers as the perpetrators of incivility (Cortina, Kabat-Farr, Magley, & Nelson, 2017; Schilpzand et al., 2016). In the current study, we attend to supervisor-initiated incivility as a crucial form of workplace incivility. Scholars maintain that uncivil supervisors are a major health hazard because of their negative impact on their subordinates' well-being (Hogan & Kaiser, 2005). Uncivil or abusive supervisors incur considerable costs for organizations and society by harming employees' well-being and quality of life (Hogan & Kaiser, 2005). For this reason, researchers have recognized supervisors' uncivil behavior as a key source of managerial failure (Furnham & Taylor, 2004). Indeed, supervisor incivility has been found to be positively associated with negative employee outcomes such as workplace exhaustion, lack of reciprocity, and anger (Blau, 2007; Blau & Andersson, 2005; Cho et al., 2016; Meier, Semmer, & Gross, 2014). At the same time, supervisor incivility is known to have a negative relationship with desirable outcomes, including employees' performance, job satisfaction, work engagement, organizational commitment, and fairness perceptions (Duffy & Ferrier, 2003; Jawahar & Schreurs, 2018; Schilpzand et al., 2016).

Of the various work outcomes, we focus on employees' job performance as the final outcome of supervisor incivility. Job performance refers to the extent to which employees successfully perform their tasks and roles as prescribed in their job descriptions (Williams & Anderson, 1991). Job performance is a crucial work outcome since it reflects the extent to which employees' in-role performance makes a significant contribution to organizational performance (Williams & Anderson, 1991). Furthermore, as job performance serves as a basis for employees' performance evaluation and rewards, we assume job performance to be an outcome variable that is heavily influenced by supervisors' uncivil behavior. Supervisor incivility research has unequivocally demonstrated the negative effect of supervisor incivility on employee performance. For example, Cho et al. (2016) reported that supervisor incivility is negatively associated with employee service performance through emotional exhaustion. In a similar vein, Jawahar and Schreurs (2018) found that supervisor incivility has a negative effect on employees' task and citizenship performance by decreasing their work engagement.

While these studies provide novel insights into how supervisor incivility decreases employee performance, they largely focus on emotional processes as mediating mechanisms. We extend prior research by proposing cognitive and motivational processes as linking mechanisms between supervisor incivility and employee job performance. Drawing on TMS and SDT, we isolate job insecurity and amotivation as cognitive and motivational processes that stem from supervisor incivility, respectively. We propose a double-mediation model in which supervisory incivility negatively affects employee job performance through job insecurity and amotivation. Each path in this model is explained in detail in the following sections.

Relationship Between Supervisor Incivility and Employee Job Insecurity

Job insecurity is defined as "perceived powerlessness to maintain desired continuity in a threatened job situation" (Greenhalgh & Rosenblatt, 1984, p. 468). Manifested in perceptions of potential job loss, job insecurity reflects an employee's cognitive appraisal of his/her job (Greenhalgh & Rosenblatt, 1984; Sverke & Hellgren, 2002). Research on the antecedents of job insecurity has generally identified organizational (e.g., downsizing) and individual factors (e.g., short length of service and external locus of control) as forces causing job insecurity. However, a growing body of research has recognized that interpersonal factors can also be sources of job insecurity (Glambek, Skogstad, & Einarsen, 2018; Shoss, 2017). In line with this stream of research, we assume interpersonal relationships with supervisors to be an important source of job insecurity. This is because supervisors strongly affect employees' perceptions and interpretations of workplace events or phenomena (Colbert, 2004). The organizational justice literature suggests that perceptions of unfair treatment from supervisors (i.e., low interactional justice) influence employees' perceptions about their job, including job insecurity perceptions (Caza & Cortina, 2007). Indeed, research has indicated that perceptions of interactional injustice exerted a negative effect on employees' attitudinal and behavioral reactions (Colquitt, Conlon, Wesson, Porter, & Ng, 2001; Tyler & Blader, 2000). Therefore, how supervisors treat their employees should determine employees' cognitive appraisal of their jobs.

TMS is effective in addressing how employees react to and create meaning from workplace events such as supervisor incivility. Central to TMS is that when exposed to stressors in the workplace, employees go through appraisal processes to determine the significance of the stressors and the seriousness of their consequences (i.e., primary appraisal), and then come up with necessary actions or coping strategies (i.e., secondary appraisal) (Folkman & Moskowitz, 2004; Lazarus & Folkman, 1984). Uncivil behavior instigated by supervisors initiates the primary appraisal processes. In other words, when facing bullying events in the workplace, employees come to interpret the meaning of the events and appraise the seriousness of their consequences (Park & Ono, 2017). We reason that such primary appraisal processes are of particular importance in interactions with supervisors. Because supervisors make important job-related decisions such as performance appraisals and promotion/compensation recommendations, uncivil behavior instigated by a supervisor signals that the supervisor may make a decision that has an adverse impact on the target employee's job. Furthermore, employees experiencing supervisor incivility tend to regard uncivil behavior as isolation and rejection from their supervisors and interpret it as a serious threat to their job security (Park & Ono, 2017). In a similar vein, research has indicated that workplace mistreatment causes employees to feel worthless (Loh, Restubog, & Zagenczyk, 2010) and that repeated workplace bullying incurs a feeling of exclusion from the organization (Hogh, Mikkelsen, & Hansen, 2010). Building on these findings, we reason that supervisor incivility increases employees' concerns about job security by degrading their self-worth in the organization (Park & Ono, 2017).

Although not in the domain of supervisor incivility, the abusive supervision literature suggests that the victims of abusive supervision feel pressured to quit their jobs (Arif, Sindhu, & Urooj, 2017; Haar, de Fluiter, & Brougham, 2016; Mathieu & Babiak, 2016; Xu, Martinez, & Van Hoof, 2018). Abusive or uncivil behavior instigated by supervisors drains employees' psychological resources and deteriorates their ability to cope with work stressors, which in turn leads to increased job-insecurity perceptions (Wang et al., 2019). Analogous to the effect of abusive supervision on job insecurity, we contend that supervisor incivility has a detrimental effect on employees' self-worth, social identity, and social acceptance, thereby eliciting feelings of helplessness and isolation from the organization (Hogh et al., 2010; Loh et al., 2010; Park & Ono, 2017). As a result, the victims of supervisor incivility are likely to perceive their jobs as insecure (Park & Ono, 2017). We therefore put forth the following hypothesis.

Hypothesis 1: Supervisor incivility is positively related to employees' job insecurity.

Relationship Between Job Insecurity and Amotivation

In the job insecurity literature, stress-related factors have often been identified as intermediary mechanisms between job insecurity and job performance. Job insecurity has a negative effect on employee job performance by increasing psychological strains (e.g., Darvishmotevali, Arasli, & Kilic, 2017; Shoss, 2017). Distinct from this line of research, the present study isolates amotivation as a motivational process that transmits the negative effect of job insecurity onto job performance. SDT holds that motivation underlies any human behavior and categorizes work motivation into intrinsic and extrinsic motivation and amotivation (Deci & Ryan, 2000a). Amotivation refers to "a state in which individuals do not associate a behavior with subsequent outcomes, and as such, behaviors are executed for reasons unknown or not executed at all" (Deci & Ryan, 2000b). Amotivation is the state of lacking any intention to initiate an action or expend effort on a task or activity (Deci & Ryan, 2000a; Howard, Gagné, Morin, & Van den Broeck, 2016).

Although researchers have rarely explored the role of motivational processes in the relationship between supervisor incivility and employee performance, TMS and SDT offer an appropriate framework for addressing the cognitive and motivational processes as linking mechanisms between supervisor incivility and employee performance. According to TMS, the primary appraisal of a stressful event leads to a secondary appraisal. In the secondary appraisal processes, individuals determine strategies or interventions to cope with the stressor. Employees experiencing supervisor incivility perform a cognitive appraisal of their job and perceive a high level of job insecurity in the first appraisal stage. When they perceive their job as highly insecure, employees are likely to lose control of their job and feel helpless (Vander Elst, De Cuyper, & De Witte, 2011), which dampens their motivation to take actions to cope with the stressor. We further theorize that amotivation is particularly relevant to the secondary appraisal processes since it pertains to employees' inability to perceive contingencies between a specific outcome and work involvement (Deci & Ryan, 2000a). As job-insecure employees experience a loss of valued job features, they underestimate the meaning of work involvement (Vander Elst et al., 2014), thereby remaining unmotivated in their job. As such, job insecurity perceptions shaped in the primary appraisal stage lead to a lack of motivation for generating coping strategies in the secondary appraisal stage. In particular, the negative spiral of motivation across the primary and secondary appraisal stages is aggravated in encounters with supervisors. If job insecurity perceptions are caused by supervisors' uncivil behavior, employees tend to overestimate the seriousness of its consequences, thereby concluding that they cannot change the situation at all (Park & Ono, 2017). As a result, they tend to lack motivation to come up with any coping strategies.

Empirical findings have documented that job insecurity incurs perceived powerlessness and a lack of control, which in turn attenuate employees' work motivation (De Spiegelaere, Van Gyes, De Witte, Niesen, & Van Hootegen, 2014; Glavin, 2013; Vander Elst et al., 2014). Consistent with these findings, it is generally known that amotivation arises when individuals perceive forces beyond their control (Zigarmi, Galloway, & Roberts, 2018). Taken together, these findings suggest that job insecurity perceptions elicit a state of amotivation as individuals may experience a lack of control over their job. When employees perceive a high level of job insecurity, thereby losing control over their job, they find it wasteful to devote effort and resources to their job (Glavin, 2013). As a result, they become reluctant to mobilize motivation and energy toward their job. On the basis of this theorizing, job insecurity is anticipated to result in amotivation. This argumentation leads to the following hypothesis.

Hypothesis 2: Employees' job insecurity is positively related to their amotivation.

Relationship Between Amotivation and Job Performance

The negative relationship between amotivation and work outcomes is well established in the SDT literature (Deci & Ryan, 2000a; Gorozidis & Papaioannou, 2014; Legault, Green-Demers, & Pelletier, 2006; Mielniczuk & Laguna, 2017; Ryan & Deci, 2017). Given that motivation is an impetus for human behavior and performance (Deci & Ryan, 2000a), a lack of motivation should result in decreased job performance. Individuals with amotivation have several commonalities: (a) they feel incapable of accomplishing their tasks; (b) they are reluctant to exert the sustained effort necessary for performing their tasks; and (c) they are not confident that their effort will lead to desired outcomes (Legault et al., 2006). Therefore, amotivated individuals feel incompetent and behave as if they have no control over their behavior (Deci & Ryan, 2000a).

Furthermore, amotivated employees tend to feel detached from their work and incapable of regulating their behavior toward the attainment of desired outcomes (Howard et al., 2016). As a consequence, they invest less effort or resources in job-related activities, which in turn results in impaired job performance. Amotivation or a lack of motivation has been found to be positively related to negative outcomes such as emotional exhaustion, burnout, stress, and turnover intention, and negatively related to desirable outcomes such as vitality, job satisfaction, commitment, adaptivity, proactivity, and job effort (Gagné et al., 2015; Lion & Burch, 2018; Nie, Chua, Yeung, Ryan, & Chan, 2015; Tremblay, Blanchard, Taylor, Pelletier, & Villeneuve, 2009). On the basis of these findings and SDT, amotivation is expected to impair job performance. Thus, the following hypothesis is proposed.

Hypothesis 3: Employees' amotivation is negatively related to their job performance.

Mediating Effects of Job Insecurity and Amotivation

Combining the aforementioned relationships, we put forth a double-mediation model in which supervisor incivility decreases employees' subsequent job performance through increased job insecurity and amotivation. The overall structure of the proposed model is grounded in TMS and SDT. According to TMS, stressful events in the workplace trigger primary and secondary appraisals of the events, which in turn affect the victim's engagement in coping strategies. SDT postulates that one's motivation determines one's engagement in a behavior (Deci & Ryan, 1985).

Integrating these two theoretical perspectives, we posit that employees' cognitive appraisal of stressors and the resultant motivation function as mediating mechanisms between supervisor incivility and employee job performance. More precisely, when exposed to supervisor incivility, victims initiate a primary appraisal of the incident and interpret the seriousness of its consequences. In this stage, supervisor incivility is likely to form perceptions of job insecurity by signaling that the victims are being negatively evaluated by the supervisor and that they may be rejected by the supervisor. Such perceptions developed in the primary appraisal stage strongly affect the victims' motivation for coping strategies in the secondary appraisal stage. That is, perceptions of job insecurity in the primary appraisal stage are likely to inculcate amotivation in the secondary appraisal stage. If the victims perceive their job security as being threatened, they lose a sense of control and power, and therefore remain passive and unmotivated about coping with the current situation. Amotivation pervasive in the victims dissuades them from expending effort in job-related activities, which in turn leads to decreased job performance.

According to TMS, the effect of cognitive appraisal of workplace events on behavioral outcomes prolongs over time (Park & Ono, 2017). This is because the victims of supervisor incivility undergo the appraisal processes repeatedly as they are constantly exposed to supervisors' uncivil behavior. As this process recurs in their interactions with supervisors, the victims regard the consequences of the uncivil behavior as being serious, which exerts a long-term effect on the victims' behavior. We therefore predict that supervisor incivility has a long-term negative effect on employee job performance through increased job insecurity and amotivation.

Although virtually no research has examined cognitive and motivational processes as linking mechanisms between supervisor incivility and employee performance, similar relationships can be found in the related literature. For example, Park and Ono (2017) reported that exposure to workplace bullying has a negative impact on employees' work engagement and health problems by shaping job insecurity perceptions. Similarly, Glambek et al. (2018) found that workplace bullying significantly predicts employees' job insecurity two years later. Hur et al.'s (2016) findings revealed that coworker and customer incivility is negatively associated with service employee creativity through emotional exhaustion and intrinsic motivation. Taken together, these findings support our argument that job insecurity and motivation are central mediators between supervisor incivility and employee performance. Therefore, we formulate the following double-mediation hypothesis.

> Hypothesis 4: The negative relationship between supervisor incivility and employees' job performance is sequentially mediated by their job insecurity and amotivation.

Methods

Participants and Procedures

We contacted South Korean kindergartens and requested that they administer surveys to their principals and teachers. As recommended in previous research (Elicker, Noppe, Noppe, & Fortner-Wood, 1997; Wells, 2015), we used a snowball sampling method, which is desirable when surveys deal with sensitive issues (e.g., experiences of incivility, verbal aggression, and harassment) (Faugier & Sargeant, 1997). Thus, the kindergarten principals who agreed to participate in our study then referred us to other kindergartens and assisted us in gaining access to them. As a result, 43 kindergartens assented to participate in our study. We then randomly selected teachers from the participating kindergartens, which yielded a sample of approximately ten teachers per kindergarten. There was only one principal per kindergarten.

To mitigate potential common method biases and assess the lagged effect of supervisor incivility on employee performance, we administered two-wave surveys to the principals and teachers of the 43 kindergartens. At Time 1 (T1), the teachers were solicited to report the level of the incivility perpetrated toward them by their principal as well as the levels of their own job insecurity and amotivation. Three months later at Time 2 (T2), we asked the principals of the 43 kindergartens to rate the job performance of the teachers who responded to the T1 surveys. Of the 430 questionnaires distributed at T1, we gathered 321 matched responses from the teachers and their principals across T1 and T2 (response rate = 74.5%). Our data collection procedure is in line with prior multilevel research that collected data from small organizations whose size ranges between five and ten employees (e.g., Chen, Zhu, & Zhou, 2015; Hox & Maas, 2001). On average, seven teachers (Min = 5, Max = 10) per kindergarten participated in our study.

Respondents were assured of the confidentiality of their responses. They were told that their responses would be used for research purposes only. Although the respondents were not required to report their name, we asked them to indicate the name of their kindergarten to match teachers' surveys with those of their principal. Each respondent received a packet containing a cover letter, a self-administered questionnaire, and a stamped pre-addressed envelope. We instructed them to seal the completed survey in the pre-addressed envelope and mail it to the researcher. We gave the respondents a $5 gift card as a reward for their participation.

We used the full-information maximum likelihood (FIML) technique to handle missing data. FIML is "direct model estimation method that deals with missing data and can estimate parameters" (Olinsky, Chen, & Harlow, 2003, p. 56). Because the FIML approach computes a case-wise likelihood function with observed variables for each case (Arbuckle, 1996), it is superior to other imputation techniques that may cause biased results (e.g., listwise deletion) (Asendorpf, Van De Schoot, Denissen, & Hutteman, 2014).

The participants were predominantly women (99.1%). Their average age and average organizational tenure in current organization were 32.2 years ($SD = 8.3$) and 3.1 years ($SD = 3.1$), respectively. Their education levels varied: graduate school (5.3%), four-year university (42.0%), two-year college (48.3%), high school (2.5%), and other (1.9%).

Measures

Following Brislin's (1970) back-translation procedure, we had four bilingual scholars translate the original survey items into Korean and then back-translate them into English. The resulting survey items were equivalent to the original items. Except for supervisor incivility, all other variables were assessed on a Likert-type scale (1 = *strongly disagree*, 5 = *strongly disagree*). The sponsoring kindergartens were concerned about survey length and time since participating in the survey may distract teachers from their work. As kindergarten teachers' primary duty is to take care of children, even a small distraction can result in an accident. For this reason, we had to construct a short survey to minimize the time spent on survey completion. Specifically, we used an abbreviated scale for job performance. Conversely, we retained the full scales for supervisor incivility, job insecurity, and amotivation because those scales consist of a small number of items.

Supervisor Incivility

The four-item scale developed by Sliter et al. (2012) was used to assess how often kindergarten teachers had experienced uncivil behaviors from their principal (e.g., rude, disrespectful, or condescending behaviors toward them) within the past six months. Responses ranged from 1 (*never*) to 5 (*very often*). Sample items included "How often does your principal ignore or exclude you while at work?" and "How often is your principal rude to you at work?" The coefficient alpha for the supervisor-incivility scale was .92, which was higher than its past reliability ($\alpha = .85$; e.g., Abubakar, Namin, Harazneh, Arasli, & Tunç, 2017).

Job Insecurity

In line with prior research (e.g., Schreurs, Van Emmerik, Günter, & Germeys, 2012), job insecurity was measured with De Witte's (2000) four-item scale. One example of such items was "I think that I will lose my job in the near future." The alpha for the job-insecurity scale was .85, which is within the range of its previous reliabilities (e.g., α =.90, Schreurs, Van Emmerik, Notelaers, & De Witte, 2010; α =.81, Shin & Hur, 2019).

Amotivation

We used Gagné et al.'s (2015) three-item scale to measure amotivation. A sample item of amotivation was "I don't know why I'm doing this job, it's pointless work." The alpha for the amotivation scale was .85, which is within the range of its prior reliabilities (e.g., α = .75–.84, Leroy & Bressoux, 2016; α =.74–.87, Howard et al., 2016).

Job Performance

Job performance was assessed through three items adopted from Williams and Anderson's (1991) seven-item in-role performance scale. Those three items were selected because of high factor loadings in prior research (e.g., Way, Sturman, & Raab, 2010). One example includes "This employee adequately completed his/her assigned duties." The alpha for the job-performance scale was .96, which exceeds the range of the reliabilities of abbreviated job-performance scales (e.g., α = .81–.83, Bal, De Lange, Jansen, & Van Der Velde, 2013; α=.90, Chun & Choi, 2014; α = .77, Snape & Redman, 2010).

Control Variables

Demographic characteristics have been found to affect job insecurity (e.g., De Bustillo & De Pedraza, 2010), amotivation (e.g., Nie et al., 2015), and job performance (e.g. Bowen, Swim, & Jacobs, 2000; Shin, Hur, & Oh, 2015; Shin, Hur, & Choi, 2019). Therefore, we controlled for teachers' age, gender, and organizational tenure in all subsequent analyses.

Analytic Strategy

As the data in the present study possessed a multilevel structure in which each principal rated an average of seven teachers, we conducted one-way random-effect analyses of variance (ANOVA) with organizations as the independent variable, and job insecurity, amotivation, and job performance as the dependent variables (Bliese, 2000). The intraclass correlation coefficients ($ICC_{(1)}$) were .17 for job insecurity (F=2.43, $p < .01$), .11 for amotivation (F=1.95, $p < .01$), and .35 for job performance (F=5.20, $p < .01$). Thus, because of the non-independence of endogenous variables, we performed random coefficient modeling (i.e., multilevel path modeling) with M-plus 8.1 software. To account for the nesting effect, we allowed a random intercept. All exogenous variables were group-mean-centered, and endogenous variables were grand-mean-centered, prior to being included in the multilevel analyses.

Table 1. Mean, Standard Deviations, and Correlations Among Variables.

Variables	1	2	3	4	5	6	7
1. Gender	–						
2. Age	−.00	–					
3. Job tenure	−.05	.19**	–				
4. Supervisor incivility	−.06	.07*	−.03	**.72**			
5. Job insecurity	−.04	.04	−.09	.25**	**.61**		
6. Amotivation	.09†	−.06	.02	.24**	.27**	**.68**	
7. Job performance	.03	.05	.15*	−.06	.01	−.12*	**.85**
Mean	.01	32.19	3.10	1.39	1.99	1.67	4.24
SD	.08	8.33	3.09	.57	.81	.71	.76
Cronbach's α	–	–	–	.92	.85	.85	.96
CR	–	–	–	.91	.86	.86	.94

Note. $^{*}p < .05$, $^{**}p < .01$. Bold numbers along the diagonal are AVEs.

Because our research model assumes serial mediation relationships, we performed a re-sampling simulation analysis based on the Monte Carlo method suggested by Preacher, Zyphur, and Zhang (2010), which provides the most robust evidence for the significance and 95% confidence interval (CI) of a serial mediation effect (replication = 20,000; Hayes, 2013; Preacher & Selig, 2012).

Results

Tests of Reliability and Validity

Table 1 presents the descriptive statistics and correlations of the study variables. The reliability coefficients for the scales ranged from .85 to .96, illustrating that the measurement scales displayed acceptable levels of reliability (Nunnally, 1978).

A multilevel confirmatory factor analysis (MCFA) was carried out to test the convergent and discriminant validity of the measurement model. The hypothesized four-factor measurement model (i.e., supervisor incivility, job insecurity, amotivation, and job performance) exhibited a good fit to the data in an absolute sense ($\chi^2_{(142)} = 237.61$, $p <$ .05; Comparative Fit Index (CFI) = .97; Tucker Lewis Index (TLI) = .96; Root Mean Square Error of Approximation (RMSEA) = .05; Standardized Root Mean Square Residual $(SRMR)_{within}$ = .05). Furthermore, all variables demonstrated a sufficient level of reliability, with composite reliabilities (CR_{within}) ranging from .86 to .92 (see Table 1).

We further evaluated the discriminant validity of the measures based on Fornell and Larcker's (1981) procedure. We found that all average variances extracted (AVEs) were greater than the squared correlation between the target variable and any of the others (see Table 1). Taken together, the results of the reliability and validity analyses revealed that our constructs possessed sound measurement properties.

Hypotheses Testing

As presented in Figure 1, Hypothesis 1, which posited a positive relationship between supervisor incivility and employee job insecurity, was supported ($b = .21$, $p < .05$). Hypothesis 2, which proposed a positive relationship between job insecurity and amotivation, was also supported ($b = .23$, $p < .01$). Hypothesis 3, which predicted a negative

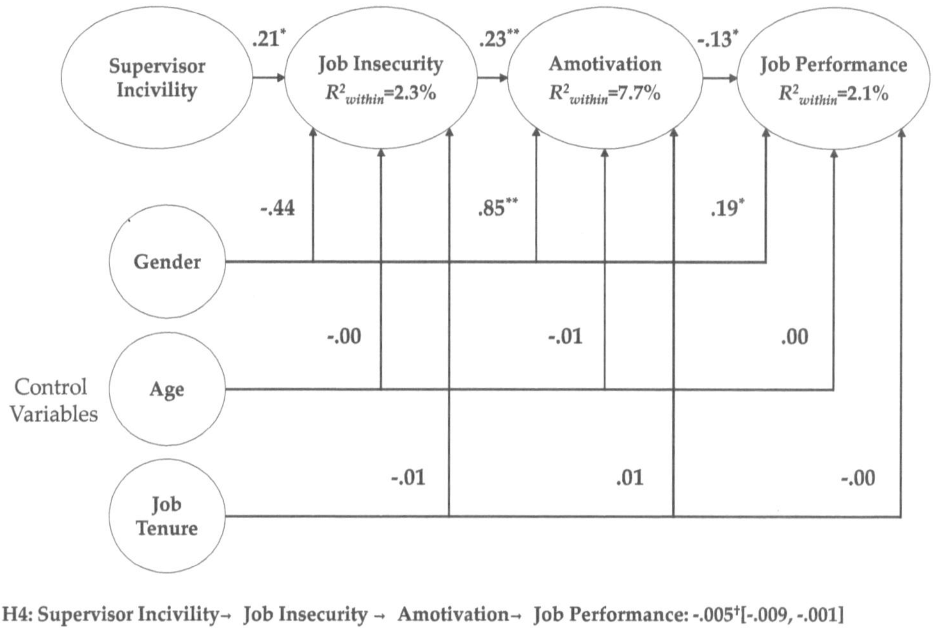

Figure 1. Results of hypotheses test. *Note.* $^{\dagger}p < .10$, $^{*}p < .05$, $^{**}p < .01$.

relationship between amotivation and job performance, was again supported ($b = -.13$, $p < .05$).

Hypothesis 4 postulated a double-mediation relationship in which supervisor incivility negatively predicts T2 job performance through job insecurity and amotivation. More precisely, we specified a three-path mediated effect (Lau & Cheung, 2012; Macho & Ledermann, 2011; Taylor, MacKinnon, & Tein, 2008). This approach allowed us to assess the indirect effects involving both mediators in a proposed double-mediation model. The test of the full model estimated the path coefficients of the direct relationships between supervisor incivility, job insecurity, amotivation, and job performance. To test Hypothesis 4, we estimated three additional paths: supervisor incivility → amotivation, supervisor incivility → job performance, and job insecurity → job performance (Macho & Ledermann, 2011; Taylor et al., 2008). Figure 1 reports the results of this estimation, along with the Monte Carlo confidence intervals for the path estimates (replication = 20,000; Hayes, 2013; Preacher & Selig, 2012). As shown in Figure 1, job insecurity and amotivation sequentially mediated the relationship between supervisor incivility and job performance ($b = -.005$, 90% CI = [−.009, −.001]), thereby lending support to Hypothesis 4.

Discussion

The objective of this study was to explore the cognitive and motivational processes underlying the negative relationship between supervisor incivility and employee job performance. As predicted, we detected positive relationships between supervisor incivility and employees' job insecurity and between employees' job insecurity and their amotivation, as well as a negative relationship between employees' amotivation and their job performance. Employees' job insecurity and amotivation further mediated the relationship between supervisor incivility and employee job performance.

Our findings have important implications for job insecurity research. Prior research on incivility and job insecurity has documented that job insecurity is an antecedent of workplace bullying. More specifically, contrary to De Cuyper, Baillien, and De Witte's (2009) findings that revealed that employees in job-insecure situations tend to engage in more workplace bullying and experience more bullying in the workplace, our study revealed that job insecurity is a cognitive outcome of supervisor incivility. This is consistent with Glambek et al.'s (2018) and Park and Ono's (2017) findings that workplace bullying leads to increased job insecurity perceptions. Based on these findings, it is reasonable to infer a reciprocal relationship between workplace mistreatment and job insecurity, such that while exposure to job insecurity can lead to workplace mistreatment toward others, experiencing mistreatment from supervisors can also be a source of job insecurity perceptions. As such, our study offers a nuanced understanding of the link between workplace mistreatment and job insecurity.

Our findings further advance the job insecurity literature by presenting amotivation as an intermediary process between job insecurity and job performance. Although it has been well documented that job insecurity has a negative effect on work outcomes by decreasing intrinsic motivation (e.g., Hur et al., 2016), the role of amotivation has rarely been explored in the domain of job insecurity. Extending prior work that adopts a motivational perspective, our findings clearly demonstrate that job insecurity decreases job performance by creating a state characterized by the absence of motivation, which suggests that the detrimental effect of job insecurity on employee motivation may be much stronger than has been previously.

The two-wave longitudinal design is one of the strengths of our research. While a number of empirical studies have investigated the relationship between workplace incivility and employee performance, the majority of them relied on a cross-sectional research design, which makes it difficult to ascertain the causal direction between workplace incivility and employee performance. This issue becomes aggravated in the domain of workplace mistreatment because poor performers are vulnerable to workplace mistreatment. For this reason, even though a significant, negative relationship was found between workplace incivility and employee performance, we cannot infer that incivility is a precursor of employee performance. Our research contributes to the resolution of this issue by placing a three-month lag between the measurement of supervisor incivility and that of employee job performance. Our findings indicate that supervisor incivility is strong enough to exert a long-term effect on employee job performance through job insecurity and amotivation.

Theoretical Implications

The present research has important theoretical implications. While mounting research has examined the effect of supervisor incivility on employee outcomes, the majority of this research has focused on health-related or affective outcomes (e.g., work engagement, emotional exhaustion, and negative affect) and has generally adopted affective events theory (AET; Weiss & Cropanzano, 1996) as a theoretical framework that addresses the effect of supervisor incivility. AET holds that workplace events elicit employees' affective responses, which, in turn, influences their behavior. Although the AET research has provided meaningful insights into the emotional paths linking supervisor incivility and employee outcomes, the cognitive or motivational paths underlying those relationships remain unclear.

Our study fills this gap by presenting job insecurity as a cognitive path and amotivation as a motivational path on the basis of the transactional model of stress (TMS) and self-determination theory (SDT). More specifically, the finding that supervisor incivility negatively affects employee job performance through job insecurity and amotivation validates the transactional model of stress (TMS), which proposes that stressful work events have an adverse effect on employee performance through the primary and secondary appraisal processes. Our serial mediation model endorses such a proposition by demonstrating job insecurity as the primary appraisal process and amotivation as the secondary appraisal process. As revealed in our findings, exposure to supervisors' uncivil behavior leads to employees' cognitive evaluation of their job, which in turn stifles their motivation to take any action to change the current situation. Such a lack of motivation results in decreased job performance. As such, by uncovering the cognitive and motivational mechanisms underlying the relationship between supervisor incivility and employee job performance from TMS and SDT perspectives, our study highlights the importance of cognitive and motivational theories in understanding the role of supervisor incivility.

Practical Implications

The findings of the present study also have several implications for organizational leaders and HR professionals. First of all, on the basis of the finding that supervisor incivility has a long-term negative effect on employee job performance by eliciting job insecurity perceptions and amotivation, organizations need to devise interventions to prevent or reduce supervisors' uncivil behavior. In doing so, it is critical to select and retain supervisors who possess the requisite interpersonal and communication skills (Cho et al., 2016). Organizational scholars have recommended programs or meetings for supervisors and subordinates to clarify supervisors' expectations for subordinates and facilitate communication between the two parties (Cho et al., 2016). In addition, supervisor incivility can be prevented and mitigated by training programs designed to establish a code of conduct for supervisors and heighten the awareness of the negative impact of supervisor incivility. It is also important to provide supervisors with regular feedback regarding the degree to which they display uncivil behavior toward their subordinates (Cho et al., 2016).

Given that job insecurity and amotivation are channels through which supervisor incivility has a harmful effect on employee job performance, decreasing job insecurity perceptions and amotivation can be a potential solution in preventing employees who face supervisor incivility from reducing their work effort. Thus, organizational leaders and HR professionals need to assure employees that their jobs are secure (Park & Ono, 2017). Because employees are likely to be more motivated if they perceive a high level of job security, organizational leaders would be advised to adopt a motivational approach that imbues employees with a sense of safety rather than a sense of crisis. Moreover, organizational leaders and HR professionals can decrease employees' job insecurity perceptions and promote their motivation by offering them the necessary resources to cope with job insecurity threats (Bakker & Demerouti, 2007; Hobfoll & Shirom, 2001). A safe work environment and a supportive work climate would be examples of such resources (Park & Ono, 2017).

Limitations and Directions for Future Research

Despite its theoretical and practical implications, our study has some limitations that need to be addressed in future research. First, although we employed a two-wave longitudinal design, the independent variable and the mediators were measured simultaneously; this may leave the causality between supervisor incivility and job insecurity and amotivation questionable. In particular, given that the primary appraisal processes precede the secondary appraisal processes in TMS, a longitudinal or time-lagged design is desirable in order to rigorously test the relationship between job insecurity and amotivation. Furthermore, as noted earlier, considering the empirical evidence for the causal direction going from job insecurity to workplace mistreatment, the causal relationship between supervisor incivility, job insecurity, and job performance can be better determined in research that uses a four-wave longitudinal design.

Second, while we uncovered the cognitive and motivational paths linking supervisor incivility and employee job performance, we did not examine the sequence or interplay between cognitive and motivational paths and emotional paths. In light of the cognitive-motivational-relational theory of emotions (Smith & Lazarus, 1990), which predicts that the cognitive appraisal of a work stressor shapes emotional reactions to it, cognitive and motivational processes involving workplace incivility are inseparable from emotional processes. Therefore, future research needs to take a more integrative approach to the understanding of the consequences of supervisor incivility by taking both cognitive/motivational and emotional processes into account.

Third, the understanding of mediating mechanisms between supervisor incivility and employee outcomes may be incomplete without the examination of moderators affecting the mediating relationships. For instance, Taylor, Bedeian, and Kluemper (2012) findings revealed that the indirect effect of workplace incivility on citizenship performance through affective commitment was stronger for individuals with high conscientiousness than those with low conscientiousness. Chen et al. (2013) reported that the indirect effect of workplace incivility on task performance through work engagement was more pronounced for narcissistic people than for less narcissistic ones. These findings suggest that there can be potential moderators that strengthen or weaken the mediating relationships proposed in our research. We call for future research that explores such moderators to secure a more refined understanding of the mediating processes between workplace incivility and employee outcomes.

Fourth, our sampling procedure may limit the generalizability of the present findings. Because our research deals with sensitive issues (e.g., supervisor incivility and job insecurity), we recruited participating kindergartens via snowball sampling. However, snowball sampling is vulnerable to sampling biases such as self-selection, underrepresentation of the population, and generation of an unbalanced sample (Sadler, Lee, Lim, &

Fullerton, 2010). For instance, the principals who agreed to participate in our study may be more cooperative than those who declined. Cooperative leaders are unlikely to commit uncivil behavior, as indicated by the low mean for supervisor incivility ($M = 1.47$, SD = .54). Thus, probability sampling is desirable in workplace incivility research. Another sampling issue is that 99% of our sample comprised female teachers. Given that women are more relationship-oriented than men (Eagly & Wood, 1999), mistreatment from the principal may have exerted a strong effect on female teachers, which raises the possibility that male employees react to supervisor incivility differently than female employees. We recommend that future research validate the present findings in more diverse, gender-balanced samples.

Finally, the cultural context of the current study may have affected the study findings. Because harmonious interpersonal relationships are valued in collectivistic societies such as Korea (Hofstede, 1980), the detrimental effect of mistreatment from supervisors may be more pronounced in Korean samples. Another cultural characteristic, power distance, may have also influenced the present findings. In the Korean culture characterized by high power distance, employee-supervisor relationships are hierarchical, and authority figures have a strong influence on employee behavior (Hofstede, 1980). Thus, the effect of supervisor incivility on employee outcomes may have been inflated in the context of the Korean culture. Given this, the results of the current research need to be replicated in different cultures.

Conclusion

This study contributes to the workplace mistreatment literature by attending to the role of supervisor incivility as a crucial form of workplace incivility that has a negative effect on employee job performance. Complementing prior research that has identified affective processes as linking mechanisms between workplace incivility and employee performance, our findings reveal job insecurity and amotivation as key mediators underlying the negative relationship between supervisor incivility and employee job performance. We hope that our work inspires follow-up investigations into various forms of workplace incivility as well as their mediators and moderators at different organizational levels.

ORCID

Won-Moo Hur http://orcid.org/0000-0002-8042-2603

References

Abubakar, A. M., Namin, B. H., Harazneh, I., Arasli, H., & Tunç, T. (2017). Does gender moderates the relationship between favoritism/nepotism, supervisor incivility, cynicism and workplace withdrawal: A neural network and SEM approach. *Tourism Management Perspectives*, *23*, 129–139. doi:10.1016/j.tmp.2017.06.001

Andersson, L., & Pearson, C. (1999). Tit for tat? The spiraling effect of incivility in the workplace. *The Academy of Management Review*, *24*(3), 452–471. doi:10.2307/259136

Arbuckle, J. L. (1996). Full information estimation in the presence of incomplete data. In G. A. Marcoulides & R. E. Schumacker (Eds.), *Advanced structural equation modeling* (pp. 243–277). Mahwah, NJ: Lawrence Erlbaum Associates, Inc.

Arif, M., Sindhu, M. I., & Urooj, S. F. (2017). Impact of abusive supervision on turnover intention through future work self-salience and organization-based self-esteem. *International Journal of Organizational Leadership*, *6*(4), 481–490.

Asendorpf, J. B., Van De Schoot, R., Denissen, J. J., & Hutteman, R. (2014). Reducing bias due to systematic attrition in longitudinal studies: The benefits of multiple imputation. *International Journal of Behavioral Development*, *38*(5), 453–460. doi:10.1177/0165025414542713

Bakker, A. B., & Demerouti, E. (2007). The job demands-resources model: State of the art. *Journal of Managerial Psychology*, *22*(3), 309–328. doi:10.1108/02683940710733115

Bal, P. M., De Lange, A. H., Jansen, P. G., & Van Der Velde, M. E. (2013). A longitudinal study of age-related differences in reactions to psychological contract breach. *Applied Psychology*, *62*(1), 157–181. doi:10.1111/j.1464-0597.2012.00524.x

Blau, G. (2007). Partially testing a process model for understanding victim responses to an anticipated worksite closure. *Journal of Vocational Behavior*, *71*(3), 401–428. doi:10.1016/j.jvb.2007.08.005

Blau, G., & Andersson, L. (2005). Testing a measure of instigated workplace incivility. *Journal of Occupational and Organizational Psychology*, *78*, 595–614. doi:10.1348/096317905X26822

Bliese, P. D. (2000). Within-group agreement, non-independent and reliability: Implications for data aggregation and analysis. In K. J. Klein & S. W. J. Kozlowski (Eds.), *Multilevel theory, research, and methods in organizations: Foundations, extensions, and new directions* (pp. 349–381). San Francisco, CA: Jossey-Bass.

Bowen, C. C., Swim, J. K., & Jacobs, R. R. (2000). Evaluating gender biases on actual job performance of real people: A meta-analysis. *Journal of Applied Social Psychology*, *30*(10), 2194–2215. doi:10.1111/j.1559-1816.2000.tb02432.x

Brislin, R. W. (1970). Back-translation for cross-cultural research. *Journal of Cross-Cultural Psychology*, *1*(3), 185–216. doi:10.1177/135910457000100301

Caza, B. B., & Cortina, L. M. (2007). From insult to injury: Explaining the impact of incivility. *Basic and Applied Social Psychology*, *29*(4), 335–350. doi:10.1080/01973530701665108

Chen, Y., Ferris, D. L., Kwan, H. K., Yan, M., Zhou, M., & Hong, Y. (2013). Self-love's lost labor: A self-enhancement model of workplace incivility. *Academy of Management Journal*, *56*(4), 1199–1219. doi:10.5465/amj.2010.0906

Chen, Z., Zhu, J., & Zhou, M. (2015). How does a servant leader fuel the service fire? A multilevel model of servant leadership, individual self-identity, group competition climate, and customer service performance. *Journal of Applied Psychology*, *100*(2), 511–521. doi:10.1037/a0038036

Cho, M., Bonn, M. A., Han, S. J., & Lee, K. H. (2016). Workplace incivility and its effect upon restaurant frontline service employee emotions and service performance. *International Journal of Contemporary Hospitality Management*, *28*(12), 2888–2912. doi:10.1108/IJCHM-04-2015-0205

Chun, J. S., & Choi, J. N. (2014). Members' needs, intragroup conflict, and group performance. *Journal of Applied Psychology*, *99*(3), 437–450. doi:10.1037/a0036363

Colbert, A. E. (2004). *Understanding the effects of transformational leadership: The mediating role of leader-follower value congruence* (Unpublished doctoral dissertation). University of Iowa, Iowa City, IA.

Colquitt, J. A., Conlon, D. E., Wesson, M. J., Porter, C., & Ng, K. Y. (2001). Justice at the millennium: A meta-analysis review of 25 years of organizational justice research. *Journal of Applied Psychology*, *86*(3), 425–445. doi:10.1037/0021-9010.86.3.425

Cortina, L. M. (2008). Unseen injustice: Incivility as modern discrimination in organizations. *Academy of Management Review*, *33*(1), 55–75. doi:10.5465/amr.2008.27745097

Cortina, L. M., Kabat-Farr, D., Magley, V. J., & Nelson, K. (2017). Researching rudeness: The past, present, and future of the science of incivility. *Journal of Occupational Health Psychology*, *22*(3), 299–313. doi:10.1037/ocp0000089

Cortina, L. M., & Magley, V. J. (2009). Patterns and profiles of response to incivility in the workplace. *Journal of Occupational Health Psychology*, *14*(3), 272–288. doi:10.1037/a0014934

Darvishmotevali, M., Arasli, H., & Kilic, H. (2017). Effect of job insecurity on frontline employee's performing looking through the lens of psychological strains and leverages. *International Journal of Contemporary Hospitality Management*, *29*(6), 1724–1744. doi:10.1108/IJCHM-12-2015-0683

De Bustillo, M. R., & De Pedraza, P. (2010). Determinants of job insecurity in five European countries. *European Journal of Industrial Relations*, *16*, 5–20. doi:10.1177/0959680109355306

Deci, E. L., & Ryan, R. M. (1985). *Intrinsic motivation and self-determination in human behavior.* New York, NY: Plenum.

Deci, E. L., & Ryan, R. (2000a). Intrinsic and extrinsic motivations: Classic definitions and new directions. *Contemporary Educational Psychology*, *25*, 54–67. doi:10.1006/ceps.1999.1020

Deci, E. L., & Ryan, R. M. (2000b). Self-determination theory and the facilitation of intrinsic motivation, social development, and well-being. *American Psychologist*, *55*, 68–78. doi:10.1037//0003-066X.55.1.68

De Cuyper, N., Baillien, E., & De Witte, H. (2009). Job insecurity, perceived employability, and targets' and perpetrators' experiences of workplace bullying. *Work & Stress*, *23*, 206–224. doi:10.1080/02678370903257578

De Spiegelaere, S., Van Gyes, G., De Witte, H., Niesen, W., & Van Hootegen, G. (2014). On the relation of job insecurity, job autonomy, innovative work behavior and the mediating effect of work engagement. *Creativity and Innovation Management*, *23*(3), 318–330. doi:10.1111/caim.12079

De Witte, H. (2000). Arbeidsethos en jobonzekerheid: Meting en gevolgen voor welzijn, tevredenheid en inzet op het werk [Work ethic and job insecurity: Measurement and consequences for well-being, satisfaction and performance]. In R. Bouwen, K. De Witte, H. De Witte, & T. Taillieu (Eds.), *Van groep naar gemeenschap [From group to community]. Liber Amicorum Prof. Dr. Leo Lagrou* (pp. 325–350). Leuven, Belgium: Garant.

Duffy, M. K., Ferrier, W. J. (2003). Birds of a feather … ? How supervisor-subordinate dissimilarity moderates the influence of supervisor behaviors on workplace attitudes. *Group and Organization Management*, *28*(2), 217–248.

Eagly, A. H., & Wood, W. (1999). The origins of sex differences in human behavior: Evolved dispositions versus social roles. *American Psychologist*, *54*(6), 408–423. doi:10.1037//0003-066X.54.6.408

Elicker, J., Noppe, I. C., Noppe, L. D., & Fortner-Wood, C. (1997). The parent–caregiver relationship scale: Rounding out the relationship system in infant childcare. *Early Education & Development*, *8*(1), 83–100. doi:10.1207/s15566935eed0801_7

Faugier, J., & Sargeant, M. (1997). Sampling hard to reach populations. *Journal of Advanced Nursing*, *26*(4), 790–797.

Folkman, S., & Moskowitz, J. T. (2004). Coping: Pitfalls and promise. *Annual Review of Psychology*, *55*, 745–774. doi:10.1146/annurev.psych.55.090902.141456

Fornell, C., & Larcker, D. F. (1981). Evaluating structural equation models with unobservable variables and measurement error. *Journal of Marketing Research*, *18*(1), 39–50. doi:10.2307/3151312

Furnham, A., & Taylor, J. (2004). *The dark side of behavior at work: Understanding and avoiding employees leaving, thieving, and deceiving.* Basingstoke, UK: Palgrave Macmillan.

Gagné, M., Forest, J., Vansteenkiste, M., Crevier-Braud, L., van den Broeck, A., Aspeli, A. K., … Westbye, C. (2015). The multidimensional work motivation scale: Validation evidence in seven languages and nine countries. *European Journal of Work and Organizational Psychology*, *24*(2), 178–196. doi:10.1080/1359432X.2013.877892

Glambek, M., Skogstad, A., & Einarsen, S. (2018). Workplace bullying, the development of job insecurity and the role of laissez-faire leadership: A two-wave moderated mediation study. *Work & Stress*, *32*, 297–312. doi:10.1080/02678373.2018.1427815

Glavin, P. (2013). The impact of job insecurity and job degradation on the sense of personal control. *Work and Occupations*, *40*(2), 115–142. doi:10.1177/0730888413481031

Gorozidis, G., & Papaioannou, A. (2014). Teachers, motivation to participate in training and to implement innovations. *Teaching and Teacher Education*, *39*, 1–11. doi:10.1016/j.tate.2013.12.001

Greenhalgh, L., & Rosenblatt, Z. (1984). Job insecurity: Toward conceptual clarity. *The Academy of Management Review*, *9*(3), 438–448. doi:10.2307/258284

Haar, J. M., de Fluiter, A., & Brougham, D. (2016). Abusive supervision and turnover intentions: The mediating role of perceived organizational support. *Journal of Management & Organization*, *22*, 139–153. doi:10.1017/jmo.2015.34

Hayes, A. F. (2013). *Introduction to mediation, moderation, and conditional process analysis: A regression-based approach*. New York, NY: Guilford.

Hershcovis, M. S., & Barling, J. (2010). Towards a multi-foci approach to workplace aggression: A meta-analytic review of outcomes from different perpetrators. *Journal of Organizational Behavior*, *31*(1), 24–44. doi:10.1002/job.621

Hobfoll, S. E., & Shirom, A. (2001). Conservation of resource theory: Applications to stress and management in the workplace. In R. T. Golenbiewski (Ed.), *Handbook of organizational behavior* (2nd ed.) (pp. 57–80). New York, NY: Marcel Dekker.

Hofstede, G. (1980). *Culture's consequences: International differences in work-related values*. Beverly Hills, CA: Sage.

Hogan, R., & Kaiser, R. B. (2005). What we know about leadership. *Review of General Psychology*, *9*(2), 169–180. doi:10.1037/1089-2680.9.2.169

Hogh, A., Mikkelsen, E. G., & Hansen, A. M. (2010). Individual consequences of workplace bullying/mobbing. In S. Einarsen, H. Hoel, D. Zapf, & C. Cooper (Eds.), *Bullying and harassment in the workplace: Developments in theory, research, and practice* (pp. 107–128). Boca Raton, FL: CRC Press.

Howard, J., Gagné, M., Morin, A. J., & Van den Broeck, A. (2016). Motivation profiles at work: A self-determination theory approach. *Journal of Vocational Behavior*, *95*, 74–89. doi:10.1016/j.jvb.2016.07.004

Hox, J. J., & Maas, C. J. (2001). The accuracy of multilevel structural equation modeling with pseudo-balanced groups and small samples. *Structural Equation Modeling: A Multidisciplinary Journal*, *8*(2), 157–174. doi:10.1207/S15328007SEM0802_1

Hur, W., Moon, T., & Jun, T. (2016). The effect of workplace incivility on service employee creativity: The mediating role of emotional exhaustion and intrinsic motivation. *Journal of Services Marketing*, *30*(3), 302–315. doi:10.1108/JSM-10-2014-0342

Jawahar, I. M., & Schreurs, B. (2018). Supervisor incivility and how it affects subordinates' performance: A matter of trust. *Personnel Review*, *47*(3), 709–726. doi:10.1108/PR-01-2017-0022

Kabat-Farr, D., Cortina, L. M., & Marchiondo, L. A. (2018). The emotional aftermath of incivility: Anger, guilt, and the role of organizational commitment. *International Journal of Stress Management*, *25*(2), 109–128. doi:10.1037/str0000045

Lau, R. S., & Cheung, G. W. (2012). Estimating and comparing specific mediation effects in complex latent variable models. *Organizational Research Methods*, *15*(1), 3–16. doi:10.1177/1094428110391673

Lazarus, R. S., & Folkman, S. (1984). *Stress, appraisal, and coping*. New York, NY: Springer.

Legault, L., Green-Demers, I., & Pelletier, L. (2006). Why do high school students lack motivation in the classroom? Towards an understanding of academic amotivation and the role of social support. *Journal of Educational Psychology*, *98*(3), 567–582. doi:10.1037/0022-0663.98.3.567

Leroy, N., & Bressoux, P. (2016). Does amotivation matter more than motivation in predicting mathematics learning gains? A longitudinal study of sixth-grade students in France. *Contemporary Educational Psychology, 44*, 41–53. doi:10.1016/j.cedpsych.2016.02.001

Lim, S., & Lee, A. (2011). Work and nonwork outcomes of workplace incivility: Does family support help? *Journal of Occupational Health Psychology, 16*(1), 95–111. doi:10.1037/a0021726

Lion, R. W., & Burch, T. (2018). When feelings matter: Affect as a mediator between motivational regulation and work intentions. *Advances in Developing Human Resources, 20*(2), 214–226. doi:10.1177/1523422318756645

Loh, J., Restubog, S. L. D., & Zagenczyk, T. J. (2010). Consequences of workplace bullying on employee identification and satisfaction among Australians and Singaporeans. *Journal of Cross-Cultural Psychology, 41*(2), 236–252. doi:10.1177/0022022109354641

Macho, S., & Ledermann, T. (2011). Estimating, testing, and comparing specific effects in structural equation models: The phantom model approach. *Psychological Methods, 16*(1), 34–43. doi:10.1037/a0021763

Mathieu, C., & Babiak, P. (2016). Corporate psychopathy and abusive supervision: Their influence on employees' job satisfaction and turnover intentions. *Personality and Individual Differences, 91*, 102–106. doi:10.1016/j.paid.2015.12.002

Meier, L. L., & Gross, S. (2015). Episodes of incivility between subordinates and supervisors: Examining the role of self-control and time with an interaction record diary study. *Journal of Organizational Behavior, 36*(8), 1096–1113. doi:10.1002/job.2013

Meier, L., Semmer, N. K., & Gross, S. (2014). The effect of conflict at work on well-being: Depressive symptoms as a vulnerability factor. *Work & Stress, 28*, 31–48. doi:10.1080/02678373.2013.876691

Mielniczuk, E., & Laguna, M. (2017). Motivation and training initiation: Evidence from Poland. *Journal of Workplace Learning, 29*(1), 24–36. doi:10.1108/JWL-01-2016-0002

Nie, Y., Chua, B. L., Yeung, A. S., Ryan, R. M., & Chan, W. Y. (2015). The importance of autonomy support and the mediating role of work motivation for well-being: Testing self-determination theory in a Chinese work organization. *International Journal of Psychology, 50*(4), 245–255. doi:10.1002/ijop.12110

Nunnally, J. C. (1978). *Psychometric theory* (2nd ed.). New York, NY: McGraw-Hill.

Olinsky, A., Chen, S., & Harlow, L. (2003). The comparative efficacy of imputation methods for missing data in structural equation modeling. *European Journal of Operational Research, 151*(1), 53–79. doi:10.1016/S0377-2217(02)00578-7

Park, J., & Ono, M. (2017). Effects of workplace bullying on work engagement and health: The mediating role of job insecurity. *The International Journal of Human Resource Management, 28*(22), 3202–3225. doi:10.1080/09585192.2016.1155164

Preacher, K. J., & Selig, J. P. (2012). Advantages of Monte Carlo confidence intervals for indirect effects. *Communication Methods and Measures, 6*(2), 77–98. doi:10.1080/19312458.2012.679848

Preacher, K. J., Zyphur, M. J., & Zhang, Z. (2010). A general multilevel SEM framework for assessing multilevel mediation. *Psychological Methods, 15*(3), 209–233. doi:10.1037/a0020141

Reio, T. G., Jr. (2011). Supervisor and coworker incivility: Testing the work frustration-aggression model. *Advances in Developing Human Resources, 13*(1), 54–68. doi:10.1177/1523422311410648

Rhee, S., Hur, W., & Kim, M. (2017). The relationship of coworker incivility to job performance and the moderating role of self-efficacy and compassion at work: The job demands-resources approach. *Journal of Business and Psychology, 32*(6), 711–726. doi:10.1007/s10869-016-9469-2

Ryan, R. M., & Deci, E. L. (2017). *Self-determination theory: Basic psychological needs in motivation, development, and wellness.* New York, NY: Guilford Press.

Sadler, G. R., Lee, H., Lim, R. S., & Fullerton, J. (2010). Recruitment of hard-to-reach population subgroups via adaptations of the snowball sampling strategy. *Nursing & Health Sciences, 12*, 369–374. doi:10.1111/j.1442-2018.2010.00541.x

Schilpzand, P., De Pater, I. E., & Erez, A. (2016). Workplace incivility: A review of the literature and agenda for future research. *Journal of Organizational Behavior, 37*, S57–S88. doi:10.1002/job.1976

Schreurs, B. H. J., Van Emmerik, I. J. H., Günter, H., & Germeys, F. (2012). A weekly diary study on the buffering role of social support in the relationship between job insecurity and employee performance. *Human Resource Management, 51*(2), 259–280. doi:10.1002/hrm.21465

Schreurs, B., Van Emmerik, H., Notelaers, G., & De Witte, H. (2010). Job insecurity and employee health: The buffering potential of job control and job self-efficacy. *Work & Stress, 24*, 56–72. doi:10.1080/02678371003718733

Shin, I., Hur, W. M., & Oh, H. (2015). Essential precursors and effects of employee creativity in a service context: Emotional labor strategies and official job performance. *Career Development International, 20*(7), 733–752. doi:10.1108/CDI-10-2014-0137

Shin, Y., & Hur, W. M. (2019). When do service employees suffer more from job insecurity? The moderating role of coworker and customer incivility. *International Journal of Environmental Research and Public Health, 16*(7), 1298. doi:10.3390/ijerph16071298

Shin, Y., Hur, W. M., & Choi, W. H. (2019). Coworker support as a double-edged sword: A moderated mediation model of job crafting, work engagement, and job performance. *The International Journal of Human Resource Management*, 1–22. doi:10.1080/09585192.2017.1407352

Shoss, M. K. (2017). Job insecurity: An integrative view and agenda for future research. *Journal of Management, 43*(6), 1911–1939. doi:10.1177/0149206317691574

Sliter, M. T., Sliter, K. A., & Jex, S. M. (2012). The employee as a punching bag: The effect of multiple sources of incivility on employee withdrawal behavior and sales performance. *Journal of Organizational Behavior, 33*(1), 121–139. doi:10.1002/job.767

Smith, C. A., & Lazarus, R. S. (1990). Appraisal components, core relational themes, and the emotions. *Cognition & Emotion, 7*, 233–269. doi:10.1080/02699939308409189

Snape, E., & Redman, T. (2010). HRM practices, organizational citizenship behaviour, and performance: A multi-level analysis. *Journal of Management Studies, 47*, 1219–1247. doi:10.1111/j.1467-6486.2010.00911.x

Sverke, M., & Hellgren, J. (2002). The nature of job insecurity: Understanding employment uncertainty on the brink of a new millennium. *Applied Psychology, 51*(1), 23–42. doi:10.1111/1464-0597.0077z

Taylor, A. B., MacKinnon, D. P., & Tein, J. (2008). Tests of the three-path mediated effect. *Organizational Research Methods, 11*(2), 241–269. doi:10.1177/1094428107300344

Taylor, S. G., Bedeian, A. G., & Kluemper, D. H. (2012). Linking workplace incivility to citizenship performance: The combined effects of affective commitment and conscientiousness. *Journal of Organizational Behavior, 33*(7), 878–893. doi:10.1002/job.773

Tremblay, M. A., Blanchard, C. M., Taylor, S., Pelletier, L. G., & Villeneuve, M. (2009). Work extrinsic and intrinsic motivation scale: Its value for organizational psychology research. *Canadian Journal of Behavioural Science, 41*(4), 213–226. doi:10.1037/a0015167

Tyler, T. R., & Blader, S. (2000). *Cooperation in groups: Procedural justice, social identity, and behavioral engagement.* Philadelphia, PA: Psychology Press.

Vander Elst, T., De Cuyper, N., & De Witte, H. (2011). The role of perceived control in the relationship between job insecurity and psychosocial outcomes: Moderator or mediator?. *Stress and Health, 27*(3), e215–227. doi:10.1002/smi.1371

Vander Elst, T., Richter, A., Sverke, M., Näswall, K., De Cuyper, N., & De Witte, H. (2014). Threats of losing valued job features: The role of perceived control in mediating the effect of qualitative job insecurity on job strain and psychological withdrawal. *Work & Stress, 28*, 143–164. doi:10.1080/02678373.2014.899651

Vander Elst, T., Van den Broeck, A., De Witte, H., & De Cuyper, N. (2012). The mediating role of frustration of psychological needs in the relationship between job insecurity and work-related well-being. *Work & Stress, 26*, 252–271. doi:10.1080/02678373.2012.703900

Vansteenkiste, V., Lens, W., De Witte, H., & Feather, N. T. (2005). Understanding unemployed people's job research behavior, unemployment experience and well-being: A comparison of expectancy-value theory and self-determination theory. *British Journal of Social Psychology, 44*(2), 269–287. doi:10.1348/014466604X17641

Wang, D., Li, X., Zhou, M., Maguire, P., Zong, Z., & Hu, Y. (2019). Effects of abusive supervision on employees' innovative behavior: The role of job insecurity and locus of control. *Scandinavian Journal of Psychology, 60*(2), 152–159. doi:10.1111/sjop.12510

Way, S. A., Sturman, M. C., & Raab, C. (2010). What matters more? Contrasting the effects of job satisfaction and service climate on hotel food and beverage managers' job performance. *Cornell Hospitality Quarterly, 51*(3), 379–397.

Weiss, H. M., & Cropanzano, R. (1996). Affective events theory: A theoretical discussion of the structure, causes, and consequences of affective experiences at work. In B. M. Staw & L. L. Cummings (Eds.), *Research in organizational behavior* (Vol. 18, pp. 1–74). Greenwich, CT: JAI Press.

Wells, M. B. (2015). Predicting preschool teacher retention and turnover in newly hired head start teachers across the first half of the school year. *Early Childhood Research Quarterly, 30*, 152–159. doi:10.1016/j.ecresq.2014.10.003

Williams, L. J., & Anderson, S. E. (1991). Job satisfaction and organizational commitment as predictors of organizational citizenship and in-role behaviors. *Journal of Management, 17*(3), 601–617. doi:10.1177/014920639101700305

Xu, S., Martinez, L. R., & Van Hoof, H. (2018). The impact of abusive supervision and co-worker support on hospitality and tourism student employees' turnover intentions in Ecuador. *Current Issues in Tourism, 21*(7), 775–790. doi:10.1080/13683500.2015.1076771

Zigarmi, D., Galloway, F. J., & Roberts, T. P. (2018). Work locus of control, motivational regulation, employee work passion, and work intentions: An empirical investigation of an appraisal model. *Journal of Happiness Studies, 19*(1), 231–256. doi:10.1007/s10902-016-9813-2

Inclusive Leadership and Innovative Work Behavior: Examination of LMX Perspective in Small Capitalized Textile Firms

Basharat Javed, Abdul Karim Khan, and Samina Quratulain

ABSTRACT

The purpose of this paper is to explore the relationship between inclusive leadership, Leader-Member Exchange (LMX) and innovative work behavior (IWB) in employees of small capitalized textile firms of Pakistan. We hypothesized that LMX mediates the relationship between inclusive leadership and IWB. We collected data from 150 supervisors–subordinate dyads to test our hypotheses. We selected small capitalized firms because they are more innovative and change-oriented in order to enhance their innovativeness. Moreover, these firms enjoy the benefits of lack of bureaucracy and low resistance to change. Therefore, employees are better able to experience a close relationship with entrepreneurial leaders who tend to be inclusive, in order to facilitate the process of innovation. In line with these facts, our results also suggest that inclusive leadership is positively related with IWB and LMX partially mediates this relationship. The theoretical and practical implications of our findings are also discussed.

Innovative Work Behavior (IWB) is crucial for the successful functioning of organizations due to its continuous attention on organizational improvement (Fuller, Marler, & Hester, 2006, p. 50). Many researchers have therefore focused their attention on employees' IWB across organizational settings (Banu Goktan & Miles, 2011; Parker, Williams, & Turner, 2006; Unsworth & Clegg, 2010; Xu & Rickards, 2007). IWB involves non-routine behavior that incorporates idea generation and promotion, as well as implementation (Baregheh, Rowley & Sambrook, 2009; Basadur, 2004; De Jong & Den Hartog, 2007). This implies that employees who exhibit IWB take steps to go beyond the standard operating procedures and challenge their leaders, therefore, they need a supportive organizational work environment to do so (Javed, Bashir, Rawwas, & Arjoon, 2017a; Javed, Khan, Bashir, & Arjoon, 2017b). When employees are supported by their leadership, they feel more encouraged to display IWB (Amabile, 1996; De Jong & Den Hartog, 2007; Zhang & Zhou, 2014).

Realizing the importance of leadership as a trigger to IWB, various studies examined the effect of different leadership behaviors (for instance, influence-based leadership, transformational leadership, charismatic leadership, transactional leadership, authentic leadership, and ethical leadership) on employees' IWB (Černe, Jaklič, & Škerlavaj, 2013; Krause, 2004; Michaelis, Stegmaier, & Sonntag, 2009; Pieterse, Van Knippenberg, Schippers, & Stam, 2009; Reuvers, Van Engen, Vinkenburg, & Wilson-Evered, 2008; Yidong & Xinxin, 2013). However, the focus of these studies remained on a leader-centric approach which highlights the importance of leaders' traits such as character and charisma in promoting IWB. This view, however, neglects the role of essential leader-follower relationship in promoting IWB (Day & Harrison, 2007). Our goal in the current study is to address this shortcoming in earlier works and examine the relationship between Inclusive Leadership (IL) and IWB. We also aim to explore the mediating mechanism between IL and IWB relationship. Nembhard and Edmondson (2006) defined IL as "words and deeds by a leader or leaders that indicate an invitation and appreciation for others' contributions" (p. 947). It also refers to "leaders who exhibit openness, accessibility, and availability in their interactions with followers" (Carmeli, Reiter-Palmon, & Ziv, 2010, p. 250).

It is important to move beyond leader-centric leadership approach because complex changes are attracting organizations to move beyond the mechanistic structure associated with the leader-centric approach (Drath, 2001; Heifetz, 1994; Kahane, 2004). Directing employees to carry out particular tasks is a reductionist view for leaders to achieve the desired objectives. Success in the attainment of the desired objectives is also connected by workplace ties between leaders and employees to create a collective as well as connected leadership in the work setting (Berger, 2014; Brown & Gioia, 2002; Cox, Pearce, & Perry, 2003; Lipman-Blumen, 2000). Given this phenomenon of connected leadership, we believe that IL is an approach that provides an opportunity to facilitate connected leadership in organizations.

We invoked arguments discussed in IL and Leader-Member Exchange (LMX) literatures to answer our research questions. We argued that IL fosters a mature relationship with employees in which both leaders and employees trust and work as a team to support each other. This relationship is characterized by open communication with a high level of confidence, consideration, mutual obligation, and maintenance of a long-term relationship (Dienesch & Liden, 1986; Maslyn & Uhl-Bien, 2001; Sullivan, Bretschneider, & McCausland, 2003). These interactions are based on exchanges where quality relationships are promoted based on trust between leaders and employees (Lavelle, Rupp, & Brockner, 2007; Yin, 2013; Zhang, Wang, & Shi, 2012). Based on LMX theory, we argued that Inclusive leaders develop a strong relationship with employees, and as such, this results in a higher quality LMX relationship (Graen & Scandura, 1987). Within the context of IL, leaders develop a close relationship with employees where inclusive leaders put questions to employees, for instance: "Could we do this in a better way?" (Hollander, 2009, p. 4). This indicates that employees experience a mutual understanding with inclusive leaders (Carmeli et al., 2010; Fletcher, 2004, 2007) and consequently a higher quality LMX occurs in the organizations (Yin, 2003). Further, the quality of LMX which is based on social exchange; encourages employees to display IWB (Basu & Green, 1997; Schermuly, Meyer, & Dämmer, 2013). These findings show that LMX, in the presence of IL, enhances IWB. Therefore, we examine the direct effect of IL on IWB and also propose that IL indirectly affects employees' IWB

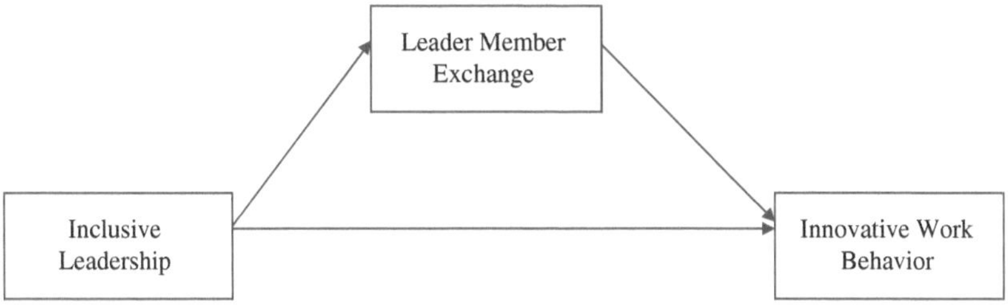

Figure 1. Hypothesized model.

through the mediating mechanism of LMX. The hypothesized model is shown in Figure 1.

Literature Review and Hypotheses Development

IL and IWB

The concept of IL was first coined by Nembhard and Edmondson (2006) who stated that inclusive leaders shape a situation where one can see the state of status or power distance which values the others point of view, for instance, "voices are genuinely valued" (p. 948). Leaders who display participative behavior provide employees with an encouraging context where they can voice their opinions as opposed to when they face the controlling behavior of leaders (Nembhard & Edmondson, 2006). Inclusive leaders place an emphasis on recognition, respect, responsiveness, and responsibility which legitimize and approve the followers' actions with leadership (Hollander, 2009).

IL is associated with leaders' coaching conduct where they primarily facilitate and offer clarifications (Edmondson, 1999), and develop participative leadership where they share authority with employees to decide their work activities (Portugal & Yukl, 1994). Furthermore, IL deals directly with situations where leaders work with employees and acknowledge and value their opinions and views (Nembhard & Edmondson, 2006). Moreover, it was found that different employees favor different leadership styles (Choi, Tran, & Park, 2015). In this regard, IL can be argued as the best approach to manage the diverse work values through inviting all employees in the decision-making process (Nembhard & Edmondson, 2006; Shuck & Herd, 2012). Employees who have input in decisions and deliberations would be able to execute innovative thoughts (De Jong & Den Hartog, 2010; Dorenbosch, Engen, & Verhagen, 2005; Edmondson, 2004; Nembhard & Edmondson, 2006).

IWB consists of different behaviors occurring in different stages: employees first start with idea explorations and idea generation to try to avail new opportunities (Amabile, Conti, Coon, Lazenby, & Herron, 1996). The next stage covers idea championing where employees promote ideas to get other's support (Dorenbosch et al., 2005). The final stage covers idea implementation where employees implement the novel ideas which benefit the organization in practical terms (De Jong & Den Hartog, 2010). After implementation of new ideas, there is no guarantee that the organization will always achieve the desired objectives, because many times new ideas fail because of lack of support and resources from leadership. Thus, while showing IWB, employees step beyond the define concrete paths; therefore, IWB is highly complex and ambiguous in nature (Kriegesmann, Kley & Schwering, 2007).

Employees show IWB only when they are supported and rewarded (Clegg, Unsworth, Epitropaki & Parker, 2002; Janssen, 2005). In the context of Small Capitalized Firms (SCFs) of the Textile Industry, McAdam and McClelland (2002) stated that innovation enhancing values help employees of SCFs to innovatively meet the changing needs of customers. Consequently, in order to successfully meet the new changes through employees' IWB, the leaders of SCFs, instead of nepotism and autocratic control, emphasize innovative supportive values including empowering employees with effective inter-personal communication in order to help employees to innovate new ideas (Bailey, Bellandi, Caloffi & Propris, 2010; McAdam, McConvery, & Armstrong, 2004; Mosey, Clare, & Woodcock, 2002; Taştan & Güçel, 2014; Zhou, Yim & Tse, 2005). By demonstrating the characteristics of inclusive leadership such as openness, availability and accessibility, leaders in SCFs promote the employees' IWB at work setting (Javed et al., 2017c). Inclusive leaders are able to show their support and accessibility (Janakiraman, 2011; Ryan, 2006) which encourage employees to exhibit IWB (Altunoğlu & Gürel, 2015; Basu & Green, 1997; Carmeli et al., 2010).

Many researches have investigated the association between IL and IWB. For instance, Choi, Tran, and Kang (2017) examined the impact of IL on IWB with the mediation of person-job fit of employees in the telecommunication industry; they found an enhancing role of IL on IWB. Javed et al. (2017c) studied the impact of IL on IWB under the mediation of Psychological Safety (PS) in the small textile firms of Pakistan; they found a positive relationship between IL and IWB. Therefore, considering these studies, we hypothesize the following relationship:

Hypothesis 1: IL is positively related to IWB

Mediating Role of LMX

Our study defines LMX as "following" which characterizes the relationship between employees and their immediate supervisor. Liden and Maslyn (1998, p. 50) found that LMX has four conditions: *loyalty* (consistent faithfulness), *affect* (mutual liking), *contribution* (amount of activity toward the shared goals), and *specialized admiration* (perception of reputation). The quality of a leader-follower relationship is shaped by information, physical and mental effort, material resources, with the most important determinant being the social supports in a leader-followers relationship (Liden, Sparrowe, & Wayne, 1997). Employees consequently experience a high level of confidence and consideration from their leader and therefore experience a social exchange relationship with the leader (Wayne, Shore, & Liden, 1997).

The SCF's are characterized by a high level of control exerted by the owners over their business (Goffee & Scase, 2015). Similarly, the internal dynamics of a typical SCF are described by frequent informal communication, lack of formal systems, informality among owners, managers, and employees and unpredictability in decision making (Haugh & McKee 2004; Rainnie, 1989). The owner-dependent, informal and autocratic decision-making as contextual realities of SCFs, make the role of leadership an important component in fostering employees' IWB. Building on these arguments, we argue that employees have to indulge in frequent informal interactions and exchanges with the owners of the SCF which may lead us to conclude that LMX is an important factor in the context of SCF to foster IWB.

IL considers input from all employees with open communication which shows care and concern for them. This consideration of the leader helps employees to be actively involved in different work processes and so helps overcome leader-follower communication gaps (Carmeli et al., 2010). Consequently, the quality of LMX increases with leader's inclusiveness. IL, with its relational style, comprises differentiation and belongingness (Brewer, 1991; Shore et al., 2011) which enhance the followers' identification (Salib, 2014) and therefore contributes to a higher quality LMX (Farmer, Van Dyne & Kamdar, 2015; Hornsey & Jetten, 2004). Moreover, in such a case, employees tend to be more prone to develop trust, identity, and mutual respect (Graen & Uhl-Bien, 1995; Van Dyne, Kamdar & Joireman, 2008). Because inclusive leaders respond to employees' opinions and value their contributions, such leaders gain employees' trust and commitment (Hsiung, 2012) which contributes to a higher quality LMX (Nahrgang, Morgeson & Ilies, 2009).

In this relationship, employees can gain access to more work-related information, as well as time and high emotional support (Liden et al., 1997). Therefore, employees achieve high trust and respect from the leader and consequently spend more time on non-routine tasks (Graen & Cashman, 1975). In performing a non-routine task, employees are more likely to generate new ideas, and because of autonomy, they experience more opportunities to implement new ideas (Sparrowe & Liden, 2005). In addition, employees can experience the availability attribute of inclusive leaders; this facilitates the development of new ideas with constructive feedback from the leader, which further motivates employees to develop IWB (Schermuly et al., 2013).

Numerous researchers found that in a high quality LMX, employees experience high autonomy to show discretionary behavior such as IWB in the organization. For instance, Pelz and Andrews (1966) found a positive relationship between LMX and employees' innovation. Scott and Bruce (1994) studied different antecedents of IWB along with LMX and found a positive relationship between LMX and employees' IWB; Basu and Green (1997) found a positive influence of LMX on IWB; Janssen and Van Yperen (2004) also found a positive relationship between quality LMX and employees' IWB. Taştan and Davoudi (2015) examined the relationship between LMX and IWB with the moderation of trust in the leader and found a positive relationship between LMX and IWB.

Wang, Fang, Qureshi, and Janssen (2015) integrated the LMX and social network to understand the employee innovative behavior in a high tech firm in China and found a positive association between LMX and IWB. Schermuly et al. (2013) found a substantial association between LMX and innovative behavior while considering mediation of psychological empowerment. Following this line of research findings, we hypothesis the following relationship:

Hypothesis 2: LMX mediates the relationship between IL and IWB

Method

Sample and Procedure

The sample population of this study was employees of the textile industry in Pakistan. The textile industry was selected because of new changes in the advancement of technology due to innovative ideas through Research and Development (R&D) efforts; which are critical for an organization's survival in the textile industry (Laursen & Foss, 2003; Marcati, Guido, & Peluso, 2008; McAdam & McClelland, 2002). SCFs were selected because they pay sufficient attention to innovation activities. SCFs are more innovative and change-oriented in order to enhance their innovativeness (Brunswicker & Vanhaverbeke, 2015; Hotho & Champion, 2011).

SCFs require an innovative entrepreneur and SCFs identify, explore, and acquire new work means and new equipment which all can be seen as an necessity of innovation (Gibb, 2000). Therefore, SFCs of the Textile Industry have a special interest in leveraging employees' capabilities to generate and execute innovative thoughts in employees, to enhance production standards (Brunswicker & Vanhaverbeke, 2015; Enkel & Gassmann, 2010; Hotho & Champion, 2011). Furthermore, when considering leadership support in settings of SCFs, Vossen (1998) and Gray and Allan (2002) found that such firms enjoy the benefits of lack of bureaucracy and low resistance to change. Therefore, employees are better able to experience a close relationship with entrepreneurial leaders who tend to be inclusive, in order to facilitate the process of innovation. Employees were approached by following a procedure; such as visiting the various work sites and precisely explaining the subject matter to the Directors of the Human Resource Departments in order to clarify the purpose of the data collection exercise. Subsequently, the authors committed to present the outcomes of the study, as required.

Accordingly, the authors visited different SCFs in different cities in Pakistan, and distributed questionnaires with a cover letter to employees in their natural job setting. In each department, employees were taken in confidence to fill questionnaires at two points in time, with a lag of two months (Time 1 and Time 2). The questionnaires were filled by the respondents on-site during their scheduled work time sessions. In order to correlate the same respondent who filled the questionnaires from Time 1 and Time 2, and to preserve the respondent's anonymity, employees were briefed to specify the names of their maternal grandparents. The author apprized that the maternal grandparents' names were required to attain the additional survey after two months; this same method was used in the study of Carmeli et al. (2010). Moreover, to ensure supervisors filled the questionnaires regarding their particular employees, on each questionnaire the letter A, B, C, D with their particular desk numbers was noted. Following the methodology used by previous researchers (Carmeli et al., 2010; Chughtai, Byrne, & Flood, 2015; Namasivayam, Guchait, & Lei, 2014), data regarding the independent variable (IL) was collected in Time 1, and data regarding the mediator variable (LMX) and dependent variable (IWB) was collected at Time 2. As our study was time-lagged, and moreover data collection was both from supervisors and employees, the data collection was free from social desirable bias (Arnold & Feldman, 1981; Davis, Thake, & Vilhena, 2010). Out of 250 questionnaires, 150 were completely filled by the employees and their line managers, which yielded a response rate of 60%. The ratio was 1:1, which means

Table 1. Demographic Profile of Respondents.

Characteristic	Percentage
Gender	
Male	68
Female	32
Age (years)	
18–25	22.7
26–33	50
34–41	21.3
42–49	2.7
≥50	3.3
Qualification	
Bachelors	68
Masters	28
Mphil	4
Experience (years)	
<1	16
1–5	59.3
6–11	20
12–17	2
≥18	2.7
Time spent with leader (years)	
<1	26.7
1–5	64
6–11	6.7
12–17	2
≥18	.7
Tenure (years)	
<1	27.3
1–5	66
6–11	4.7
12–17	2

one supervisor rated only one employee. Table 1 shows the demographic characteristics of employees.

Measurements

Responses were obtained by using a 5-point Likert-type scale with 1 = strongly disagree, 2 = disagree, 3 = neither agree nor disagree, 4 = agree, and 5 = strongly agree for IL and LMX. The responses regarding IWB were obtained on 5-point Likert-type scale with 1 = never, 2 = rarely, 3 = occasionally, 4 = very frequently, and 5 = always. In order to eliminate the effect of same source bias, employees received questionnaires related to IL and LMX. Finally, the responses regarding IWB were collected from leaders who were immediate supervisors;

IL measurement was based on 9-items developed by Carmeli et al. (2010), Questionnaires were filled by employee respondents. Sample items are "The manager is open to hearing new ideas" (openness), "The manager encourages me to access him/her on emerging issues" (accessibility) and "The manager is ready to listen to my requests" (availability). Cronbach alpha for IL was 0.94 andthe same scale was used in other studies which reported its high reliability (Choi et al., 2015, 2017; Hirak, Peng, Carmeli, & Schaubroeck, 2012).

LMX was measured using a 7-items scale developed by Liden and Maslyn (1998). Sample items are: "I always know how satisfied my supervisor is with what I do", "My supervisor understands my problems and needs well enough," and "My supervisor would personally use his/her power to solve my work problems." Cronbach alpha for this measure was 0.84 and numerous studies which used this LMX scale; reported good reliability (Maslyn & Uhl-Bien, 2001; Yin, 2013).

IWB was measured using 10-items of De Jong and Den Hartog (2010) scale. Cronbach alpha for this measure was greater than 0.70. Sample items are: "How often does this employee, pay attention to issues that are not part of his/her daily work?" (Ideas exploration), "How often does this employee, generate original solutions for problems?" (idea generation), "How often does this employee, make important organizational members enthusiastic for innovative ideas?" (idea championing), and "How often does this employee, contribute to the implementation of new ideas?" (idea implementation). This same scale, used in other studies, also reported high reliability (De Spiegelaere, Van Gyes, De Witte, Niesen, & Van Hootegem, 2014; De Spiegelaere, Van Gyes, & Hootegem, 2012).

Covariates

The literature shows that numerous factors like, gender, age, experience, education, time spent with the leader, R&D tenure, and task types, affect employees' IWB (Janssen, 2000; Keller, 1992; Scott & Bruce, 1994; Shin & Zhou, 2003). Therefore, gender, age, experience, education, time spent with the leader, R&D tenure, and task types were used as a control variable in our study.

Results

Measurement Model

Table 2 shows the degree of association across the variables. Confirmatory Factor Analysis (CFA) was used to justify and confirm measurement model (Anderson & Gerbing, 1988) which consisted of three (3) latent variables: IL, LMX, and IWB. The combination of different fit indices: Model Chi-square, Tucker-Lewis index (TLI), Comparative Fit Index (CFI), and Root Mean Square Error of Approximation (RMSEA) were used to assess the model fit. The measurement model provided an exceptional fit to the data: $\chi^2/\mathrm{df} = 1.78$, IFI = 0.92; TLI = 91; CFI = 92; RMSEA = 0.05) sown in Table 3. The factor loading of the items which were loaded in their respective latent construct is shown in Table 4.

Composite Reliability and Average Variance Extracted (AVE)

Convergent and discriminant validities were established through Composite reliability and AVE (Fornell & Larcker, 1981). Convergent validity confirmed when the value of

Table 2. Means, Standard Deviations, Coefficient Alpha Reliabilities, and Intercorrelations.

Variables	Mean	SD	1	2	3
1 Inclusive leadership	3.94	.55	(.86)		
2 Leader member exchange	3.48	.77	.22**	(.86)	
3 Innovative work behavior	3.77	.64	.30**	.20**	(.90)

Note. **$p < .01$.

Table 3. Comparison of Measurement Model.

Models	Factors	χ^2	df	$\Delta\chi^2$	RMSEA	IFI	TLI	CFI
Baseline model	Three factors	368.77	207		.06	.92	.91	.92
Model 1	Two factors: Inclusive leadership and innovative Work behavior combined into one factor	613.97	209	245.2	.11	.82	.77	.81
Model 2	Two factors: Inclusive leadership and leader Member exchange combined into one factor	840.19	209	471.42	.14	.72	.65	.71
Model 3	Two factors: Leader member exchange And innovative work behavior combined into one factor	829.94	209	461.17	.14	.72	.66	.71
Model 9	One factor: All variables combined into one factor	1071.89	210	703.12	.16	.61	.53	.61

Table 4. Correlations Among Latent Variables, Composite Reliability (CR) and Average Variance Extracted (AVE).

Variables	1	2	3
1. Inclusive leadership	1		
2. Leader member exchange	.28	1	
3. Innovative work behavior	.20	.15	1
CR	.89	.91	.92
AVE	.50	.68	.60

Table 5. Factor Loadings.

Item	Item label	Factor loading
IL1	The manager is open to hearing new ideas	.80
IL2	The manager is attentive to new opportunities to improve work processes	.75
IL3	The manager is open to discuss the desired goals and new ways to achieve them	.61
IL4	The manager is available for consultation on problems	.55
IL5	The manager is an ongoing 'presence' in this team-someone who is readily available	.79
IL6	The manager is available for professional questions I would like to confirm with him/her	.77
IL7	The manager is ready to listen to my requests	.70
IL8	The manager encourages me to access him/her on emerging issues	.72
IL9	The manager is accessible for discussing emerging problems	.58
LMX1	I always know how satisfied my supervisor is with what I do	.78
LMX2	My supervisor understands my problems and needs well enough	.57
LMX3	My supervisor recognizes my potentials	.90
LMX4	My supervisor would personally use his/her power to me solves my work problems	.92
LMX5	I have enough confidence in my supervisor to defend and justify my decisions when I am not present to do so	.90
IWB2	How often does this employee wonder how things can be improved?	.63
IWB3	How often does this employee search out new working methods, techniques or instruments?	.83
IWB4	How often does this employee generate original solutions for problems?	.57
IWB5	How often does this employee find new approaches to execute tasks?	.80
IWB6	How often does this employee make important organizational members enthusiastic for innovative ideas?	.81
IWB7	How often does this employee attempt to convince people to support an innovative idea?	.79
IWB8	How often does this employee systematically introduce innovative ideas into work practices?	.83
IWB9	How often does this employee contribute to the implementation of new ideas?	.89

composite reliability is greater than .6 and value of AVE is greater than .5 (Bagozzi & Yi, 1988). Result shown in Table 4 indicate that convergent validity is established because composite reliability of three latent variables (IL, LMX, and IWB) ranged from .89 to .90 and moreover AVE of these latent variables ranged from .50 to .68. In addition, discriminant validity is established when square root of AVE of a construct is more than the correlation of that construct shared with other constructs in the model (Fornell & Larcker, 1981). Results in the Table 5 shows that discriminant validity is

Table 6. Path Coefficients in the Baseline Model.

Structural path	Path coefficients
Inclusive leadership → Innovative work behavior	.18*
Inclusive leadership → Leader member exchange	.16*
Leader member exchange → Innovative work behavior	.12*

Note. *$p < .05$.

Table 7. Results on the Mediating Roles of Creative Self Efficacy with Inclusive Leadership and Innovative Work Behavior.

	Indirect effects	BC (95% CI)
Bootstrapping		
Inclusive leadership → Leader member exchange → Innovative work behavior	.14*	(.08, .26)

BC means bias corrected, 2,000-bootstrap samples, CI confidence interval.
Note. *$p < .05$.

established, as AVE with square root of each latent construct is greater than the correlations involving that construct.

Intraclass Correlation

We calculated Intraclass correlation for average measure of IWB using one-way random effect model and it was 0.86.

Tests of Hypotheses

For hypotheses testing, we used seven control variables (gender, age, experience, education, time spent with the leader, research and development tenure (R&D) tenure, and task types) in the analyses while testing for hypotheses 1 and 2. The results are shown in Tables 6 and 7. Hypothesis1 stated that inclusive leadership (IL) is positively related to IWB (IWB). The regression coefficient and significant level supported this relationship ($\beta = 0.18$, $p < .05$). Hypothesis 2 stated that LMX mediates the association among IL and IWB. When IWB was regressed mutually on IL and LMX, the preceding regression coefficient between IL and IWB reduced in size ($\beta = 0.14$, $p < .01$). This showed that LMX partially mediates the association between IL and IWB (CI values between 0.08 and 0.26). Therefore, Hypothesis 2 was partially supported.

Discussion

The rationale of the research was to investigate the association between IL and IWB with the mediating role of LMX. The results showed that IL was significantly related to IWB. These findings are aligned with previous studies which found a positive influence of IL on IWB (Choi et al., 2017; Javed et al., 2017c). Moreover, the results confirmed the mediating role of LMX in the association between IL and IWB. IWB involves some sort of non-routine risky performance wherein employees avoid conventional work activities and voice their own views for new work techniques. This indicates that employees challenge the existing work standards and disagree with the leader and the *status quo*. Therefore, employees need a quality relationship with the leader to challenge the existing standard operating procedures (Janssen, 2005). Employees, in this regard, exhibit a strong quality relationship with the leader to attain creative freedom. Therefore, a leader-follower relationship which is based on social exchange instead of economic exchange is seen to boost employees' IWB.

Inclusive leaders send a signal to employees that they can openly share their views and can avoid traditional work means (Carmeli et al., 2010). Therefore a quality communication environment increases the quality of LMX (Nishii & Mayer, 2009). Consequently, employees freely communicate with the leader about work-related problems and, when necessary, share other technical ways to solve problems via ideation, promotion, and implementation of technical ideas (Agarwal, Datta, Blake-Beard, & Bhargava, 2012; Choi et al., 2015). Moreover, when a leader openly communicates with employees, in the innovation context, leaders share important knowledge which helps employees to generate, endorse, and execute useful thoughts (Yeoh & Mahmood, 2013). Inclusive leaders also focus on morality via encouraging participation of employees in decision making (Hollander, 2009), therefore their trustworthiness is enhanced in the eyes of subordinates (Brown, Treviño, & Harrison, 2005; Treviño, Brown, & Hartman, 2003) and employees perceive the leader as caring and committed to their needs (Walumbwa et al., 2011). Therefore, a quality LMX occurs which comprises mutual support, emotional connection, and loyalty (Erdogan, Liden, & Kraimer, 2006; Wayne, Shore, Bommer, & Tetrick, 2002), and as such, employees show IWB (Basu & Green, 1997). Therefore, IL through its strong emphasizes on building quality LMX, shapes employees' IWB.

Implications

Theoretical Implications

The current study has several theoretically implications. First, this study supports the notion that situational factors enhance IWB (Tett & Guterman, 2000), by examining the effect of IL on IWB. Moreover, this study supported the leader's process view, where IL processes the quality LMX which engendered the employees' IWB. In this study, this process view was supported through the mediating role of LMX in the association among IL and IWB, which is novel in the literature of IWB. This later process view, also supported the social exchange view provided by Blau (1964) which explains that, when employees find leadership in terms of quality relationship, then they show extra-role behaviors (e.g., IWB).

Practical Implications

The outcomes of this research have various implications for managers working in SCFs of the Textile Industry in Pakistan. Numerous studies stated that innovation is vital for the growth and survival of SCFs (Ohashi, 2007; Soriano & Dobon, 2009). The SCFs have small market capitalization, therefore they focus attention on innovation to compete in the market and to improve their overall market capitalization (Kaufmann & Tödtling, 2002; Rosenbusch, Brinckmann, & Bausch, 2011). Consequently, in order to effectively convene innovative modifications and to improve the product and services, our study provides several managerial implications for SCFs.

First, our findings suggest that an inclusive leadership style facilitates employees' IWB. Therefore, managers in SCFs need to adapt inclusive leadership styles by emphasizing on attributes like being available and accessible for employees, and more importantly to promote open communication with employees. More specifically, we reiterate here the suggestions of Ryan (2006) on how to become inclusive leaders. First, they must show respect to employees and recognize their contributions. Second, managers should listen conscientiously to employees' suggestions. Third, managers should give productive feedback to employees on their performance. Fourth, the approach of managers should be futuristic instead of considering and evaluating past performance. Fifth, managers can empower employees to independently decide their work activities. The final way to become an IL is to encourage open communication that can have a positive impact on employees' loyalty and trust. In the presence of such characteristics of leadership, employees would be more encouraged to exhibit innovation related behaviors (Choi et al., 2017).

Second, our findings suggest that IL affects employees' IWB through the intervening mechanism of LMX. This highlights that managers must initiate a quality relationship with employees, which is not only based on economic exchange but also on social exchange as advocated by LMX theory. This is because researchers found that leader-followers relationship, which is based on social exchange, motivates employees to show extra role behavior such as IWB (Ilies, Nahrgang, & Morgeson, 2007; Schermuly et al., 2013). IWB is a risky behavior which entails higher chances of failure. New ideas don't have a guarantee for successful achievement of the desired goal since most ideas failed (Hammond, Neff, Farr, Schwall, & Zhao, 2011). Therefore, employees should seek a valued relationship with the leader where they experience the beneficial resources, challenging tasks, recognition and support when taking risks; and leaders should maintain their expectations for high performance which would encourage employees to exhibit IWB (De Jong & Den Hartog, 2007; Janssen & Van Yperen, 2004). Managers displaying an IL style can encourage employees' IWB via a quality relationship, specifically, through LMX. Inclusive leaders enhance LMX by empowering employees through delegating authority and control (Nishii & Mayer, 2009). Therefore, employees have high trust with inclusive leaders, which in turn motivates them to display IWB.

Strengths, Limitations, and Future Directions

The current research entails several strengths that augment the outcomes' confidentiality. First, separate sources were used to collect data for IL, LMX and IWB. Moreover, the data was collected in two time lags. In time 1, the IL data was collected, while in time 2 after two months, the data for LMX and IWB was collected. This method reduces the biases effects in data due to a single source and common method biases. Despite these strengths, there are some limitations which also need attention. First, the sample size was small, therefore a larger sample is needed including other sectors to generalize the findings. Moreover, in the current study, results found a partial mediation among IL and IWB, which suggest the role of other intervening mechanisms in the IL-IWB relationship. Therefore, we suggest some potential mediating mechanisms for future research, like psychological empowerment, creative self-efficacy and climate for innovation for the association among IL and IWB.

Disclosure Statement

The authors declare that they have no conflict of interest.

References

Agarwal, U. A., Datta, S., Blake-Beard, S., & Bhargava, S. (2012). Linking LMX, innovative work behaviour and turnover intentions: The mediating role of work engagement. *Career Development International*, *17*(3), 208–230.

Altunoğlu, A. E., & Gürel, E. B. B. (2015). Effects of leader–member exchange and perceived organizational support on organizational innovation: The case of Denizli Technopark. *Procedia-Social and Behavioral Sciences*, *207*, 175–181.

Amabile, T. M. (1996). *Creativity in context: Update to "the social psychology of creativity"*. Boulder, CO: *Westview Press*.

Amabile, T. M., Conti, R., Coon, H., Lazenby, J., & Herron, M. (1996). Assessing the work environment for creativity. *Academy of Management Journal*, *39*(5), 1154–1184.

Anderson, J. C., & Gerbing, D. W. (1988). Structural equation modeling in practice: A review and recommended two-step approach. *Psychological Bulletin*, *103*(3), 411.

Arnold, H. J., & Feldman, D. C. (1981). Social desirability response bias in self-report choice situations. *Academy of Management Journal*, *24*(2), 377–385.

Bagozzi, R. P., & Yi, Y. (1988). On the evaluation of structural equation models. *Journal of the Academy of Marketing Science*, *16*(1), 74–94.

Bailey, D., Bellandi, M., Caloffi, A., D., & Propris, L. (2010). Place-renewing leadership: Trajectories of change for mature manufacturing regions in Europe. *Policy Studies*, *31*(4), 457–474.

Banu Goktan, A., & Miles, G. (2011). Innovation speed and radicalness: Are they inversely related? *Management Decision*, *49*(4), 533–547.

Baregheh, A., Rowley, J., & Sambrook, S. (2009). Towards a multidisciplinary definition of innovation. *Management Decision*, *47*(8), 1323–1339.

Basadur, M. (2004). Leading others to think innovatively together: Creative leadership. *The Leadership Quarterly*, *15*(1), 103–121.

Basu, R., & Green, S. G. (1997). Leader-member exchange and transformational leadership: An empirical examination of innovative behaviors in leader-member dyads. *Journal of Applied Social Psychology*, *27*(6), 477–499.

Berger, J. B. (2014). *Leadership: A concise conceptual overview*. Boston, MA: Center for International Education Faculty Publications.

Blau, P. M. (1964). *Exchange and power in social life*. Camden, NJ: Transaction Publishers, Rutgers University.

Brewer, M. B. (1991). The social self: On being the same and different at the same time. *Personality and Social Psychology Bulletin*, *17*(5), 475–482.

Brown, M. E., & Gioia, D. A. (2002). Making things click: Distributive leadership in an online division of an offline organization. *The Leadership Quarterly, 13*(4), 397–419.

Brown, M. E., Treviño, L. K., & Harrison, D. A. (2005). Ethical leadership: A social learning perspective for construct development and testing. *Organizational Behavior and Human Decision Processes, 97*(2), 117–134.

Brunswicker, S., & Vanhaverbeke, W. (2015). Open innovation in small and medium-sized enterprises (SMEs): External knowledge sourcing strategies and internal organizational facilitators. *Journal of Small Business Management, 53*(4), 1241–1263.

Carmeli, A., Reiter-Palmon, R., & Ziv, E. (2010). Inclusive leadership and employee involvement in creative tasks in the workplace: The mediating role of psychological safety. *Creativity Research Journal, 22*(3), 250–260.

Černe, M., Jaklič, M., & Škerlavaj, M. (2013). Authentic leadership, creativity, and innovation: A multilevel perspective. *Leadership, 9*(1), 63–85.

Choi, S. B., Tran, T. B. H., & Kang, S.-W. (2017). Inclusive leadership and employee well-being: The mediating role of person-job fit. *Journal of Happiness Studies, 18*(6), 1877–1901.

Choi, S. B., Tran, T. B. H., & Park, B. I. (2015). Inclusive leadership and work engagement: Mediating roles of affective organizational commitment and creativity. *Social Behavior and Personality: An International Journal, 43*(6), 931–943.

Chughtai, A., Byrne, M., & Flood, B. (2015). Linking ethical leadership to employee well-being: The role of trust in supervisor. *Journal of Business Ethics, 128*(3), 653–663.

Clegg, C., Unsworth, K., Epitropaki, O., & Parker, G. (2002). Implicating trust in the innovation process. *Journal of Occupational and Organizational Psychology, 75*(4), 409–422.

Cox, J. F., Pearce, C. L., & Perry, M. L. (2003). *Toward a model of shared leadership and distributed influence in the innovation process: How shared leadership can enhance new product development team dynamics and effectiveness* (p. 4876). Thousand Oaks, CA: Shared Leadership: Reframing the Hows and Whys of Leadership.

Davis, C. G., Thake, J., & Vilhena, N. (2010). Social desirability biases in self-reported alcohol consumption and harms. *Addictive Behaviors, 35*(4), 302–311.

Day, D. V., & Harrison, M. M. (2007). A multilevel, identity-based approach to leadership development. *Human Resource Management Review, 17*(4), 360–373.

De Jong, J., & Den Hartog, D. (2010). Measuring innovative work behaviour. *Creativity and Innovation Management, 19*(1), 23–36.

De Jong, J., & Den Hartog, D. N. (2007). How leaders influence employees' innovative behaviour. *European Journal of Innovation Management, 10*(1), 41–64.

De Spiegelaere, S., Van Gyes, G., De Witte, H., Niesen, W., & Van Hootegem, G. (2014). On the relation of job insecurity, job autonomy, innovative work behaviour and the mediating effect of work engagement. *Creativity and Innovation Management, 23*(3), 318–330.

De Spiegelaere, S., Van Gyes, G., & Hootegem, G. V. (2012). Job design and innovative work behavior: One size does not fit all types of employees. *Journal of Entrepreneurship, Management and Innovation, 8*(4), 5–20.

Dienesch, R. M., & Liden, R. C. (1986). Leader-member exchange model of leadership: A critique and further development. *Academy of Management Review, 11*(3), 618–634.

Dorenbosch, L., Engen, M. L V., & Verhagen, M. (2005). On-the-job innovation: The impact of job design and human resource management through production ownership. *Creativity and Innovation Management, 14*(2), 129–141.

Drath, W. H. (2001). *The deep Blue Sea: Rethinking the source of leadership: Jossey-Bass* San Francisco, CA: Jossey-Bass.

Edmondson, A. (1999). Psychological safety and learning behavior in work teams. *Administrative Science Quarterly, 44*(2), 350–383.

Edmondson, A. (2004). Psychological safety, trust, and learning in organizations: A group-level lens. *Trust and Distrust in Organizations: Dilemmas and Approaches, 12*, 239–272.

Enkel, E., & Gassmann, O. (2010). Creative imitation: Exploring the case of cross-industry innovation. *R&D Management, 40*(3), 256–270.

Erdogan, B., Liden, R. C., & Kraimer, M. L. (2006). Justice and leader-member exchange: The moderating role of organizational culture. *Academy of Management Journal, 49*(2), 395–406.
Farmer, S. M., Van Dyne, L., & Kamdar, D. (2015). The contextualized self: How team-member exchange leads to coworker identification and helping OCB. *The Journal of Applied Psychology, 100*(2), 583
Fletcher, J. K. (2004). The paradox of postheroic leadership: An essay on gender, power, and transformational change. *The Leadership Quarterly, 15*(5), 647–661.
Fletcher, J. K. (2007). Leadership, power, and positive relationships. In J. E. Dutton & B. R. Ragins (Eds.), *Exploring positive relationships at work: Building a theoretical and research foundation* (pp. 347–371). Mahwah, NJ: Lawrence Erlbaum Associates Publishers.
Fornell, C., & Larcker, D. F. (1981). Evaluating structural equation models with unobservable variables and measurement error: Algebra and statistics. *Journal of Marketing Research, 18*, 382–388.
Fuller, J. B., Marler, L. E., & Hester, K. (2006). Promoting felt responsibility for constructive change and proactive behavior: Exploring aspects of an elaborated model of work design. *Journal of Organizational Behavior, 27*(8), 1089–1120.
Gibb, A. A. (2000). SME policy, academic research and the growth of ignorance, mythical concepts, myths, assumptions, rituals and confusions. *International Small Business Journal, 18*(3), 13–35.
Goffee, R., & Scase, R. (2015). *The real world of the small business owner (Routledge Revivals)*. New York, NY: Routledge.
Graen, G. B., & Cashman, J. F. (1975). A role-making model of leadership in formal organizations: A developmental approach. In J. G. Hunt & L. L. Larson (Eds.), *Leadership Frontiers* (pp. 143–165). Kent, OH: Kent State.
Graen, G. B., & Scandura, T. A. (1987). Toward a psychology of dyadic organizing. *Research in Organizational Behavior, 9*, 175–208.
Graen, G. B., & Uhl-Bien, M. (1995). Relationship-based approach to leadership: Development of leader-member exchange (LMX) theory of leadership over 25 years: Applying a multi-level multi-domain perspective. *The Leadership Quarterly, 6*(2), 219–247.
Gray, C., & Allan, J. (2002). Role of management education in developing capacity for innovation in small firms. *International Journal of Entrepreneurship and Innovation Management, 2*(4/5), 373–389.
Hammond, M. M., Neff, N. L., Farr, J. L., Schwall, A. R., & Zhao, X. (2011). Predictors of individual-level innovation at work: A meta-analysis. *Psychology of Aesthetics, Creativity, and the Arts, 5*(1), 90–105.
Haugh, H., & McKee, L. (2004). The cultural paradigm of the smaller firm. *Journal of Small Business Management, 42*(4), 377–394.
Heifetz, R. A. (1994). *Leadership without easy answers* (Vol. 465). Cambridge, MA: Harvard University Press.
Hirak, R., Peng, A. C., Carmeli, A., & Schaubroeck, J. M. (2012). Linking leader inclusiveness to work unit performance: The importance of psychological safety and learning from failures. *The Leadership Quarterly, 23*(1), 107–117.
Hollander, E. (2009). *Inclusive leadership: The essential leader-follower relationship*. New York, NY: Routledge.
Hornsey, M. J., & Jetten, J. (2004). The individual within the group: Balancing the need to belong with the need to be different. *Personality and Social Psychology Review, 8*(3), 248–264.
Hotho, S., & Champion, K. (2011). Small businesses in the new creative industries: Innovation as a people management challenge. *Management Decision, 49*(1), 29–54.
Hsiung, H.-H. (2012). Authentic leadership and employee voice behavior: A multi-level psychological process. *Journal of Business Ethics, 107*(3), 349–361.
Ilies, R., Nahrgang, J. D., & Morgeson, F. P. (2007). Leader-member exchange and citizenship behaviors: A meta-analysis. *The Journal of Applied Psychology, 92*(1), 269–277.

Janakiraman, M. (2011). Inclusive leadership: Critical for a competitive advantage. *Berlitz Cultural Insight Series*, 1-6. https://www.berlitz.com/SiteData/docs/BerlitzWPI/2b6dd531f5ed23d1/BerlitzWP_InclusiveLeadershipFinal.pdf

Janssen, O. (2000). Job demands, perceptions of effort-reward fairness and innovative work behaviour. *Journal of Occupational and Organizational Psychology, 73*(3), 287–302.

Janssen, O. (2005). The joint impact of perceived influence and supervisor supportiveness on employee innovative behaviour. *Journal of Occupational and Organizational Psychology, 78*(4), 573–579.

Janssen, O., & Van Yperen, N. W. (2004). Employees' goal orientations, the quality of leader-member exchange, and the outcomes of job performance and job satisfaction. *Academy of Management Journal, 47*(3), 368–384.

Javed, B., Bashir, S., Rawwas, M. Y., & Arjoon, S. (2017a). Islamic Work Ethic, innovative work behaviour, and adaptive performance: The mediating mechanism and an interacting effect. *Current Issues in Tourism, 20*(6), 647. doi:10.1080/13683500.2016.1171830

Javed, B., Khan, A. A., Bashir, S., & Arjoon, S. (2017b). Impact of ethical leadership on creativity: The role of psychological empowerment. *Current Issues in Tourism, 20*(8), 839–813.

Javed, B., Naqvi, S. M. M. R., Khan, A. K., Arjoon, S., & Tayyeb, H. H. (2017c). Impact of inclusive leadership on innovative work behavior: The role of psychological safety. *Journal of Management & Organization, 23*, 1–20. doi:10.1017/jmo.2017.17

Kahane, A. (2004). *Solving tough problems: An open way of talking, listening, and creating new realities*. San Francisco, CA: Berrett-Koehler Publishers.

Kaufmann, A., & Tödtling, F. (2002). How effective is innovation support for SMEs? An analysis of the region of Upper Austria. *Technovation, 22*(3), 147–159.

Keller, R. T. (1992). Transformational leadership and the performance of research and development project groups. *Journal of Management, 18*(3), 489–501.

Krause, D. E. (2004). Influence-based leadership as a determinant of the inclination to innovate and of innovation-related behaviors: An empirical investigation. *The Leadership Quarterly, 15*(1), 79–102.

Kriegesmann, B., Kley, T., & Schwering, M. G. (2007). Making organizational learning happen: The value of "creative failures". *Business Strategy Series, 8*(4), 270–276.

Laursen, K., & Foss, N. J. (2003). New human resource management practices, complementarities and the impact on innovation performance. *Cambridge Journal of Economics, 27*(2), 243–263.

Lavelle, J. J., Rupp, D. E., & Brockner, J. (2007). Taking a multifoci approach to the study of justice, social exchange, and citizenship behavior: The target similarity model. *Journal of Management, 33*(6), 841–866.

Liden, R. C., & Maslyn, J. M. (1998). Multidimensionality of leader-member exchange: An empirical assessment through scale development. *Journal of Management, 24*(1), 43–72.

Liden, R. C., Sparrowe, R. T., & Wayne, S. J. (1997). *Leader-member exchange theory: The past and potential for the future*. In *Research in Personnel and Human Resources Management* (Vol. 15, pp. 47–120). Greenwich, CT: JAI Press.

Lipman-Blumen, J. (2000). *Connective leadership: Managing in a changing world*. Oxford, UK: Oxford University Press.

Marcati, A., Guido, G., & Peluso, A. M. (2008). The role of SME entrepreneurs' innovativeness and personality in the adoption of innovations. *Research Policy, 37*(9), 1579–1590.

Maslyn, J. M., & Uhl-Bien, M. (2001). Leader–member exchange and its dimensions: Effects of self-effort and other's effort on relationship quality. *Journal of Applied Psychology, 86*(4), 697.

McAdam, R., & McClelland, J. (2002). Sources of new product ideas and creativity practices in the UK textile industry. *Technovation, 22*(2), 113–121.

McAdam, R., McConvery, T., & Armstrong, G. (2004). Barriers to innovation within small firms in a peripheral location. *International Journal of Entrepreneurial Behavior & Research, 10*(3), 206–221.

Michaelis, B., Stegmaier, R., & Sonntag, K. (2009). Affective commitment to change and innovation implementation behavior: The role of charismatic leadership and employees' trust in top management. *Journal of Change Management, 9*(4), 399–417.

Mosey, S., Clare, J. N., & Woodcock, D. J. (2002). Innovation decision making in British manufacturing SMEs. *Integrated Manufacturing Systems, 13*(3), 176–184.

Nahrgang, J. D., Morgeson, F. P., & Ilies, R. (2009). The development of leader–member exchanges: Exploring how personality and performance influence leader and member relationships over time. *Organizational Behavior and Human Decision Processes, 108*(2), 256–266.

Namasivayam, K., Guchait, P., & Lei, P. (2014). The influence of leader empowering behaviors and employee psychological empowerment on customer satisfaction. *International Journal of Contemporary Hospitality Management, 26*(1), 69–84.

Nembhard, I. M., & Edmondson, A. C. (2006). Making it safe: The effects of leader inclusiveness and professional status on psychological safety and improvement efforts in health care teams. *Journal of Organizational Behavior, 27*(7), 941–966.

Nishii, L. H., & Mayer, D. M. (2009). Do inclusive leaders help to reduce turnover in diverse groups? The moderating role of leader-member exchange in the diversity to turnover relationship. *Journal of Applied Psychology, 94*(6), 1412.

Ohashi, H. (2007). *How to Measure the Outcome of Innovations: Application to Product Innovations.* Paper presented at the Conference Paper. Towards Global Innovation Ecosystem beyond National Innovation. Faculty of Economics, University of Tokyo, and National Institute of Science and Technology Policy.

Parker, S. K., Williams, H. M., & Turner, N. (2006). Modeling the antecedents of proactive behavior at work. *The Journal of Applied Psychology, 91*(3), 636.

Pelz, D. C., & Andrews, F. M. (1966). Autonomy, coordination, and stimulation, in relation to scientific achievement. *Systems Research and Behavioral Science, 11*(2), 89–97.

Pieterse, A. N., Van Knippenberg, D., Schippers, M., & Stam, D. (2009). Transformational and transactional leadership and innovative behavior: The moderating role of psychological empowerment. *Journal of Organizational Behavior, 31*(4), 609–623.

Portugal, E., & Yukl, G. (1994). Perspectives on environmental leadership. *The Leadership Quarterly, 5*(3–4), 271–276.

Rainnie, A. (1989). *Industrial relations in small firms: Small isn't beautiful.* London: Routledge

Reuvers, M., Van Engen, M. L., Vinkenburg, C. J., & Wilson-Evered, E. (2008). Transformational leadership and innovative work behaviour: Exploring the relevance of gender differences. *Creativity and Innovation Management, 17*(3), 227–244.

Rosenbusch, N., Brinckmann, J., & Bausch, A. (2011). Is innovation always beneficial? A meta-analysis of the relationship between innovation and performance in SMEs. *Journal of Business Venturing, 26*(4), 441–457.

Ryan, J. (2006). Inclusive leadership and social justice for schools. *Leadership and Policy in Schools, 5*(1), 3–17.

Salib, E. R. (2014). *A model of inclusion and inclusive leadership in the US.* New Brunswick: Rutgers University-Graduate School.

Schermuly, C. C., Meyer, B., & Dämmer, L. (2013). Leader-member exchange and innovative behavior. *Journal of Personnel Psychology, 12*(3), 132–142.

Scott, S. G., & Bruce, R. A. (1994). Determinants of innovative behavior: A path model of individual innovation in the workplace. *Academy of Management Journal, 37*(3), 580–607.

Shin, S. J., & Zhou, J. (2003). Transformational leadership, conservation, and creativity: Evidence from Korea. *Academy of Management Journal, 46*(6), 703–714.

Shore, L. M., Randel, A. E., Chung, B. G., Dean, M. A., Holcombe Ehrhart, K., & Singh, G. (2011). Inclusion and diversity in work groups: A review and model for future research. *Journal of Management, 37*(4), 1262–1289.

Shuck, B., & Herd, A. M. (2012). Employee engagement and leadership: Exploring the convergence of two frameworks and implications for leadership development in HRD. *Human Resource Development Review, 11*(2), 156–181.

Soriano, D. R., & Dobon, S. R. (2009). Linking globalization of entrepreneurship in small organizations. *Small Business Economics, 32*(3), 233–239.

Sparrowe, R. T., & Liden, R. C. (2005). Two routes to influence: Integrating leader-member exchange and social network perspectives. *Administrative Science Quarterly, 50*(4), 505–535.

Sullivan, J., Bretschneider, J., & McCausland, M. P. (2003). Designing a leadership development program for nurse managers: An evidence-driven approach. *Journal of Nursing Administration, 33*(10), 544–549.

Taştan, S. B., & Davoudi, S. M. M. (2015). An examination of the relationship between leader-member exchange and innovative work behavior with the moderating role of trust in leader: A study in the Turkish context. *Procedia-Social and Behavioral Sciences, 181*, 23–32.

Taştan, S. B., & Güçel, C. (2014). Explaining intrapreneurial behaviors of employees with perceived organizational climate and testing the mediating role of organizational identification: A research study among employees of Turkish innovative firms. *Procedia-Social and Behavioral Sciences, 150*, 862–871.

Tett, R. P., & Guterman, H. A. (2000). Situation trait relevance, trait expression, and cross-situational consistency: Testing a principle of trait activation. *Journal of Research in Personality, 34*(4), 397–423.

Treviño, L. K., Brown, M. E., & Hartman, L. P. (2003). A qualitative investigation of perceived executive ethical leadership: Perceptions from inside and outside the executive suite. *Human Relations, 56*(1), 5–37.

Unsworth, K. L., & Clegg, C. W. (2010). Why do employees undertake creative action? *Journal of Occupational and Organizational Psychology, 83*(1), 77–99.

Van Dyne, L., Kamdar, D., & Joireman, J. (2008). In-role perceptions buffer the negative impact of low LMX on helping and enhance the positive impact of high LMX on voice. *The Journal of Applied Psychology, 93*(6), 1195.

Vossen, R. W. (1998). Relative strengths and weaknesses of small firms in innovation. *International Small Business Journal, 16*(3), 88–94.

Walumbwa, F. O., Mayer, D. M., Wang, P., Wang, H., Workman, K., & Christensen, A. L. (2011). Linking ethical leadership to employee performance: The roles of leader–member exchange, self-efficacy, and organizational identification. *Organizational Behavior and Human Decision Processes, 115*(2), 204–213.

Wang, X. H. F., Fang, Y., Qureshi, I., & Janssen, O. (2015). Understanding employee innovative behavior: Integrating the social network and leader–member exchange perspectives. *Journal of Organizational Behavior, 36*(3), 403–420.

Wayne, S. J., Shore, L. M., Bommer, W. H., & Tetrick, L. E. (2002). The role of fair treatment and rewards in perceptions of organizational support and leader-member exchange. *Journal of Applied Psychology, 87*(3), 590.

Wayne, S. J., Shore, L. M., & Liden, R. C. (1997). Perceived organizational support and leader-member exchange: A social exchange perspective. *Academy of Management Journal, 40*(1), 82–111.

Xu, F., & Rickards, T. (2007). Creative management: A predicted development from research into creativity and management. *Creativity and Innovation Management, 16*(3), 216–228.

Yeoh, K. K., & Mahmood, R. (2013). The relationship between pro-innovation organizational climate, leader-member exchange and innovative work behavior: A study among the knowledge workers of the knowledge intensive business services in Malaysia. *Business Management Dynamics, 2*(8), 15–30.

Yidong, T., & Xinxin, L. (2013). How ethical leadership influence employees' innovative work behavior: A perspective of intrinsic motivation. *Journal of Business Ethics, 116*(2), 441–455.

Yin, L. W. (2013). Inclusive Leadership and Employee Voice: Mediating Roles of Psychological Safety and Leader member Exchange (Unpublished undergraduate thesis). Hong Kong Baptist University.

Yin, R. K. (2003). *Case study research: Design and methods, Applied social research methods series.* Thousand Oaks, CA: Sage Publications, Inc.

Zhang, Z., Wang, M., & Shi, J. (2012). Leader-follower congruence in proactive personality and work outcomes: The mediating role of leader-member exchange. *Academy of Management Journal, 55*(1), 111–130.

Zhang, X., & Zhou, J. (2014). Empowering leadership, uncertainty avoidance, trust, and employee creativity: Interaction effects and a mediating mechanism. *Organizational Behavior and Human Decision Processes, 124*(2), 150–164.

Zhou, K. Z., Yim, C. K., & Tse, D. K. (2005). The effects of strategic orientations on technology- and market-based breakthrough innovations. *Journal of Marketing, 69*(2), 42–60.

Trust in Supervisor and Job Engagement: Mediating Effects of Psychological Safety and Felt Obligation

Ameer A. Basit

ABSTRACT
In the social context of job engagement, the role of trust in supervisor in predicting engagement of employees has received attention in research. Very limited research, however, has investigated the mechanisms mediating this dynamic relationship. To address this important gap in knowledge, the aim of this study was to examine psychological safety and felt obligation as two psychological mechanisms mediating the effect of trust in supervisor on job engagement. Drawing from job engagement and social exchange theories, the mediating roles of psychological safety and felt obligation in the trust-engagement relationship were empirically investigated in the Malaysian context. Using self-report questionnaires, data were collected from 337 nurses employed in a public hospital located near Kuala Lumpur, Malaysia. Results fully supported the proposed serial multiple mediator model. Trust in supervisor was indirectly related to job engagement via psychological safety followed by felt obligation. This study provides empirical evidence that trust in supervisor makes employees feel psychologically safe to employ and express their selves in their job roles. This satisfaction of the psychological safety need is interpreted by employees as an important socioemotional benefit that, in turn, makes them feel obligated to pay back to their organization through their enhanced level of job engagement. Implications for theory and practice were discussed.

One way of making organizations meaningful is to focus on creating work environments that can aid in engaging employees fully and allow them to maximize their potential. Evidence shows that organizations across the globe are largely unsuccessful in keeping their employees engaged. For instance, in the *Global Workforce Study* (Towers Watson, 2014), analysts reported that only 40% of employees were highly engaged at their work around the globe and the remaining 60% of them were either disengaged or feel detached and unsupported. This implies that more than half of the employees who are disengaged, detached, and unsupported at the workplace lack meaningfulness in their work lives, thus, pose a serious threat to the success of their organizations in today's competitive global business environment.

An impressive amount of research has investigated the antecedents and consequences of job engagement since the landmark qualitative study of Kahn (1990), accompanied by several integrative literature reviews (e.g., Albrecht, Bakker, Gruman, Macey, & Saks, 2015; Carasco-Saul, Kim, & Kim, 2015; Kim, Kolb, & Kim, 2012; Lee, Kown, Kim, & Cho, 2016; Saks & Gruman, 2014) and quantitative meta analyses (e.g., Christian, Garza, & Slaughter, 2011; Crawford, Lepine, & Rich, 2010; Halbesleben, 2010; Mackay, Allen, & Landis, 2016). These reviews show that the antecedents of job engagement consist of leadership (e.g., transformational and empowering leadership), work conditions (e.g., job resources and job demands), individual differences (e.g., conscientiousness, core self-evaluations, and positive affect), personal resources (e.g., self-efficacy, optimism, and self-esteem), and HRM practices (e.g., recruitment and selection, performance management, training, and career development). Furthermore, these reviews also demonstrate that engaged employees bring various benefits to their personal and organizational lives. For instance, at the personal level, employees benefit from their engagement in terms of improved job performance and health (Byrne, Peters, & Weston, 2016; Christian et al., 2011; Halbesleben, 2010; Kim et al., 2012). At the organizational level, organizations benefit from their engaged human capital in terms of improved organizational commitment, enhanced citizenship behavior, reduced workplace accidents, and improved bottom-line gains, such as customer satisfaction, productivity, and profitability (Halbesleben, 2010; Harter, Schmidt, & Hayes, 2002; Macey, Schneider, & Barbera, 2009).

The Present Study

Despite considerable research on the antecedents and consequences of job engagement, the extant theory and evidence about job engagement is greatly skewed to one particular conceptualization and measurement of engagement that is rooted in burnout research (i.e., Schaufeli, Salanova, González-Romá, & Bakker, 2002), and limited research has focused on Kahn's (1990) construct of engagement that is grounded in motivation theories and has its own compelling merits (Byrne et al., 2016; Saks & Gruman, 2014). Moreover, the leadership context in which the job engagement of employees occurs has not been widely investigated (Carasco-Saul et al., 2015). Thus, the present study aims to address the following four gaps in the job engagement research:

Firstly, the meaning of job engagement has lacked consensus from the beginning and research has, thus, advanced in two distinct streams (Saks & Gruman, 2014). The first stream is rooted in job burnout and employee well-being research and conceptualizes engagement as positive and fulfilling state of mind that is characterized by vigor, dedication, and absorption in work (Schaufeli et al., 2002, p. 74). The other stream, which has received relatively less attention, is based on Kahn's (1990) work on engagement that is grounded in role, motivation, and work-design theories. In this view, engagement is the investment of one's cognitive (i.e., focus and attention), emotional (i.e., high pleasantness and activation) and physical (i.e., work intensity) energies in work in simultaneous and holistic manner (Kahn, 1990, p. 694). At present, engagement research is greatly skewed to the Schaufeli et al.'s (2002) vigor-dedication-absorption conceptualization.

Recently, Saks and Gruman (2014) and Byrne et al. (2016) have compared the engagement constructs of Schaufeli et al. (2002) and Kahn (1990). Saks and Gruman (2014), have noted that although Kahn (1990) and Schaufeli et al. (2002) view engagement as a motivational state, Kahn's (1990) conceptualization of engagement is relatively more precise and grounded in theory. These authors conclude that Kahn's (1990) conceptualization of engagement is much deeper and substantial than the one proposed by Schaufeli et al. (2002).

In a similar vein, Byrne et al. (2016) have compared the two measures of engagement across five field samples and noted substantial differences between the Utrecht Work Engagement Scale (UWES) that is based on Schaufeli et al.'s (2002) work and the Job Engagement Scale (JES) that is based on Kahn's (1990) work. The authors noted that the UWES assessed a broader affective-cognitive state without focusing on any specific job, individual, or behavior as compared with the JES that assessed a more concentrated state focused on the job role. Because of this difference in focus, their result showed that the UWES correlated relatively higher with most variables in the nomological network of engagement than did the JES and these correlations were statistically different from one another, such as stress (UWES: $r = -.493$, JES: $r = -.255$), job performance (UWES: $r = .588$, JES: $r = .468$), physical strains (UWES: $r = -.296$, JES: $r = -.116$), organizational commitment (UWES: $r = .755$, JES: $r = .588$), job commitment (UWES: $r = .704$, JES: $r = .286$), and burnout (UWES: $r = -.586$, JES: $r = -.340$). The authors concluded that despite capturing some common meaning of engagement, these two engagement measures were not interchangeable and therefore they recommended using the JES in research. Byrne et al. (2016) stated:

> When the aim is to extract and delineate between concepts, such as in research settings, we recommend the JES for assessing engagement. Our findings show the JES has less overlap with associated attitudes than the UWES, making it potentially more useful in identifying the edges of engagement's construct domain. (p. 1218).

This study, thus, responds to the call of Byrne et al. (2016) for utilizing the JES to advance research on job engagement.

Secondly, researchers have highlighted that trust in leadership is a central issue in the social context of work that shapes employee attitudes and behavior, including their engagement in work (Dirks & Ferrin, 2002; Schneider, Macey, Barbera, & Young, 2010). Very limited empirical research, however, has tested the effect of trust in leader on job engagement, and most of those studies have utilized Schaufeli et al.'s (2002) definition of work engagement (e.g., Chughtai & Buckley, 2009; 2011; Ugwu, Onyishi, & Rodríguez-Sánchez, 2014). On the other hand, researchers following Kahn's (1990) work on engagement have largely focused on the antecedents related to social support and leadership, such as supportive supervisor relations, leadership, co-worker relations and norms, and perceived organizational support (e.g., May, Gilson, & Harter, 2004; Rich, Lepine, & Crawford, 2010; Saks, 2006; Shuck, Reio, & Rocco, 2011; Xu & Thomas, 2011). To date, no empirical study has considered the role of trust in supervisor in predicting job engagement grounded in Kahn's (1990) work.

Thirdly, Kahn (1990) developed a model to explain the effects of work, social, and personal factors on job engagement through psychological conditions of meaningfulness, safety, and availability. Kahn (1990) argues that the social environment of employees makes them feel psychologically safe (or unsafe) and that, in turn, influences their willingness to invest their cognitive, emotional, and physical energies in work. To date, only May and associates (2004) have tested this model and have found rewarding coworker relations and supportive supervisor relations to be positively related to psychological safety that, in turn, predicted job engagement. Thus, the present study will contribute to our knowledge by providing empirical examination of the mediating role of psychological safety in the relationship between trust in supervisor and job engagement.

Finally, although earlier research has theoretically explained the trust-engagement link using Kahn's (1990) engagement model and Blau's (1964) social exchange theory (SET), it is not explicit how these two perspectives fit together in explaining the trust-engagement link. Is job engagement a reaction to a psychological safety need which is met as a result of trust in supervisor? Or, is job engagement an act of reciprocation that occurs when one feels obligated as a result of working under a trustworthy supervisor? Are these two explanations competing or do they fit together in some order? Apparently, it looks like that the reciprocity based explanation of the trust-engagement relationship competes with the satisfaction of psychological safety-based explanation. In the present study, it is contended that these explanations are not competing, but occur in a sequential manner in the relationship between trust in supervisor and job engagement.

The above argument of serial causation in the trust-engagement link is supported by Saks (2006) who was the first one to suggest that the effect of psychological conditions (i.e., meaningfulness, safety, availability) on job engagement in Kahn's (1990) engagement model can be better understood in the light of SET. Saks (2006) argued that the satisfaction of these psychological conditions can be considered as valued benefits that are reciprocated by employees through their level of job engagement. In order to empirically test this assertion of serial causation, the present study proposes that the effect of psychological safety on job engagement goes through felt obligation, which represents an all-encompassing sense of reciprocation (Colquitt, Lepine, Piccolo, & Zapata, 2012). It is expected that in the relationship between trust in supervisor and job engagement, psychological safety occurs first as a distal variable followed by a more proximal variable of felt obligation in a sequential manner. Thus, this study will be the first to extend Kahn's (1990) model of engagement by introducing felt obligation as a social exchange based mediating mechanism following psychological safety in the trust-engagement relationship.

In sum, it is contended that trust in supervisor would increase psychological safety of employees, which would in turn promote their felt obligation to give back to their organization, which in turn would translate into their enhanced job engagement. The proposed serial multiple mediator model of the trust-engagement relationship is illustrated in Figure 1.

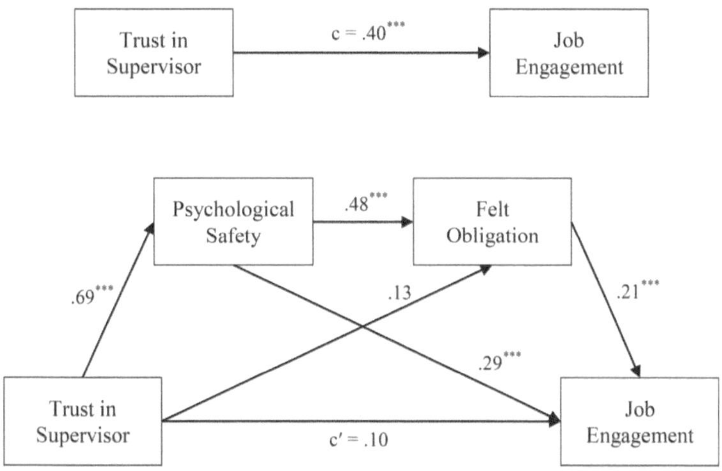

Figure 1. Structural path estimates of the serial multiple mediator model. *Note.* χ^2 (48) = 89.55, $p < .001$; TLI = .98; CFI = .98; RMSEA = .05; SRMR = .04.

Theory and Hypotheses

Kahn's Construct and Model of Job Engagement

Job engagement refers to the employment and expression of employees' real selves into their work roles cognitively, emotionally, and physically (Kahn, 1990, p. 694). Employees are regarded as engaged at work when they are cognitively vigilant, emotionally connected, and physically involved in their jobs. This description of engagement is rooted in the need-based theories of motivation, which states that people have inherent needs to employ and express themselves in their lives. Kahn's (1990) construct of engagement is motivational in that it broadly represents one's simultaneous allocation of cognitive, emotional, and physical resources to the job and refers to intense and persistent application of these resources (Rich et al., 2010). In organizations, for example, the phenomenon of engagement can be observed when employees are focused on their tasks, show care about completing them effectively, work hard for best results, give ideas with confidence, and use their thoughts, feelings, hunches, and experiences in performing their tasks as best as they can (Kahn, 2010).

As noted above, in addition to proposing the construct of job engagement, Kahn (1990) also proposed a model according to which factors related to work design, social environment, and personal characteristics influence one's engagement in work via influencing underlying psychological conditions of meaningfulness, safety, and availability, respectively. *Psychological meaningfulness* is a feeling that one is receiving a return on investment of one's self in a currency of physical, cognitive, or emotional energy (Kahn, 1990, p. 704). *Psychological safety* is feeling able to express one's self without fear of negative consequences to self-image, status, or career (Kahn, 1990, p. 708). Finally, *psychological availability* is the sense of having the physical, emotional, or psychological resources to personally engage in work (Kahn, 1990, p. 714). Kahn (1990) argued that meaningfulness mediates the relationship between work elements (i.e., tasks, roles, interactions) and engagement, safety mediates the relationship between social systems (i.e., relationships, group dynamics, norms) and engagement, whereas availability mediates the relationship between individual characteristics (i.e., energy, outside life, ambivalences) and engagement.

Trust in Supervisor

The central role of trust in leadership has been recognized for many decades in organizational behavior research (e.g., Bachmann & Zaheer, 2006; Dirks & Ferrin, 2002). Trust is commonly defined as "a psychological state comprising the intention to accept vulnerability based upon positive expectations of the intentions or behavior of another" (Rousseau, Sitkin, Burt, & Camerer, 1998, p. 395). The extant trust literature delineates trust into character-based and relationship-based trust, where the former is cognitive in nature that captures the competence and reliability aspects of the trustee, and the latter is affective in nature that captures the benevolence aspects of the trustee (Dirks & Ferrin, 2002; McAllister, 1995).

In the context of supervisor-supervisee relationships, trust in supervisor refers to a supervisee's positive expectations of competence, reliability, and benevolence of the supervisor (Dirks & Ferrin, 2002; McAllister, 1995). Supervisors are perceived as competent when they demonstrate abilities, skills, and knowledge necessary to perform work (Nooteboom, 2002). They are perceived reliable when their future behavior is predictable and when they demonstrate consistency between their words and deeds over time and across situations (Whitener,

Brodt, Korsgaard, & Werner, 1998). Finally, supervisors are considered as benevolent when they demonstrate care and concern for the welfare of the supervisees through their words and actions (McAllister, 1995).

The Relationship Between Trust in Supervisor and Job Engagement

Although the importance of trust in supervisor in promoting employee job engagement has been recognized at the theoretical level in earlier studies of engagement (e.g., Kahn, 1990; Macey et al., 2009), very few studies have directly examined this relationship at the empirical level (e.g., Chughtai & Buckley, 2009; 2011; Ugwa et al., 2014). In these empirical studies, researchers have explained the relationship between trust in supervisor and job engagement using Kahn's (1990) work on engagement or SET (Blau, 1964). For instance, Chughtai and Buckley (2009) examined the mediating role of work engagement and organizational identification in the relationship between trust in school principal and different outcomes (i.e., in-role job performance, organizational citizenship behavior, learning goal orientation) among high school teachers in Pakistan. They found that work engagement significantly mediated the trust-outcomes relationships. Drawing from Kahn's (1990) view, the authors argued that trust in principal eliminated worries among teachers about negative consequences as a result of actions taken by the principal.

In another study, Chughtai and Buckley (2011) found that trust in supervisor was significantly related to work engagement among scientists in Irish research centers. They argued that the character-based aspect of trust (concerns about ability, dependability, and integrity) in supervisor promoted engagement of scientists, because it reduced vulnerability and enhanced their motivation and commitment by assuring efficient and impartial treatment by their supervisors. Drawing from SET (Blau, 1964), which states that people tend to reciprocate in equally positive ways on receiving valued benefits from others, the authors further argued that the relationship-based aspect of trust in supervisor made scientists feel obligated to reciprocate with their level of engagement in work.

In a similar vein and at the more general level, Ugwa et al. (2014) recently viewed the trust-engagement relationship in the light of SET and investigated the effect of organizational trust on engagement, by also including items to measure trust in supervisor, among employees of banks and pharmaceutical companies in Nigeria. The authors found that organizational trust was significantly related to engagement and psychological empowerment (perception of having meaning, self-determination, competence, and impact) moderated this relationship. Thus, on the basis of above theoretical logic and empirical evidence, the following hypothesis is proposed:

Hypothesis 1: Trust in supervisor is positively related to job engagement.

The Mediating Role of Psychological Safety

Psychological safety is an affect-laden cognitive state that refers to the feeling that one is able to exhibit and employ oneself in work without fearing negative consequences to one's self-image, status, or career (Kahn, 1990, p. 708). It represents employees' perceptions towards the consequences of taking interpersonal risks (speaking up with ideas, questions, and concerns) while performing their work (Edmondson & Lei, 2014). Because supervisors possess legitimate power to influence decisions about performance appraisals, promotions, rewards, and career growth of their subordinates, it becomes a central concern of the subordinates to be vigilant about cues associated with trust in their supervisors. Kahn (1990) notes that subordinates feel psychologically safe in situations where they trust that they would not suffer for their engagement in work.

According to Kahn's (1990) engagement model, the social context of work influences one's psychological safety that ultimately determines the extent to which one is willing to invest cognitive, emotional, and physical energies in role performance. It is proposed that trust in supervisor is an important characteristic of employees' social context and is likely to promote job engagement of employees by satisfying their psychological safety need. Specifically, it can be argued that the character-based trust reflected by trust in competence and reliability of the supervisor promotes employees' psychological safety because it introduces clarity and predictability in work situations (e.g., Kahn, 1990; Schaubroeck, Lam, & Peng, 2011), reduces worries about negative outcomes (e.g., Kahn, 1990; Skinner & Searle, 2011), enables employees to judge situations in a favorable light (e.g., Hon & Lu, 2010; Yang, Mossholder, & Peng, 2009), encourages employees to take risks (e.g., Dirks & Ferrin, 2002; Kahn, 1990), and allows employees to take instructions from supervisors without fear (e.g., Hon & Lu, 2010).

In a related vein, it is contended that being rooted in concerns for care, the relationship-based aspect of trust in supervisor enhances employees' psychological safety by signaling to them that their interests are protected from threats (e.g., Colquitt et al., 2012; Kahn, 1990; May et al., 2004; McAllister, 1995). In addition, the relationship-based trust in supervisor mitigates the unrelated sources of confusion and anxiety in performing work roles (e.g., Colquitt et al., 2012; Schaubroeck et al., 2011).

As for the relationship between psychological safety and job engagement, one can argue that psychological safety promotes job engagement because engagement of self in work is an act of risk that makes employees feel vulnerable to negative consequences, and it becomes their central concern about how safe it would be to engage in work (Kahn, 1990; Schneider et al., 2010). Psychological safety not only alleviates anxiety about the negative consequences as a result of engagement (e.g., Edmondson, 1999; May et al., 2004), but also provides energy and physiological resourcefulness necessary for engagement (e.g., Heaphy & Dutton, 2008; Kark & Carmeli, 2009; Quinn, 2007). Thus, it is proposed that:

> *Hypothesis 2*: Psychological safety mediates the relationship between trust in supervisor and job engagement.

The Mediating Role of Felt Obligation

SET (Blau, 1964) provides another conceptual lens to understand the phenomenon of job engagement (Saks, 2006). According to SET, one party makes a move by supplying benefits to the other party and as a result of receiving valued benefits, the other party feels obligated to respond in kind. Once social exchange is in motion, a consequence of each exchange activates the next exchange that leads the whole series of interactions to the development of high-quality relationships characterized by trust and social support (Dutton & Heaphy, 2003). In light of SET, one can argue that when employees receive valued benefits from their organization, they feel obligated to return to their organization.

Felt obligation refers to a "prescriptive belief regarding whether one should care about the organization's well-being and should help the organization reach its goals" (Eisenberger,

Armeli, Rexwinkel, Lynch, & Rhoades, 2001, p. 42). Employees feel obligated when they receive economic benefits from their organization which meet their financial needs and when they receive socioemotional benefits which meet their psychological needs (Cropanzano & Mitchell, 2005). Felt obligation is based on a culturally universal social norm of reciprocity according to which people tend to reciprocate the help they receive from their helpers (Gouldner, 1960; Perugini, Gallucci, Presaghi, & Ercolani, 2003). Colquitt et al. (2012) have noted that the construct of felt obligation provides an all-encompassing sense of reciprocity compared with other social exchange constructs that capture limited aspects of it, such as affective commitment, normative commitment, and psychological contract fulfillment (Meyer & Herscovitch, 2001; Robinson & Rousseau, 1994).

Kahn (2010) argues that employees make some internal calculus to demonstrate engagement of their authentic selves in performing work roles consciously or unconsciously in different degrees and dimensions. Viewing the trust-engagement relationship through the lens of SET, it can be argued that the sense of feeling obligated to reciprocate is one such internal calculus that employees make when their positive expectation of trust in their supervisors are sufficiently met. Moreover, employees who feel obligated to help their organization to reach its objectives have identified with the personal importance of job engagement for their organization and have accepted its regulation as their own (Ryan & Deci, 2000). There is evidence that positive interpersonal relationships between supervisors and supervisees are governed by reciprocity that influences positive attitudes and behaviors of the supervisees (e.g., Coyle-Shapiro, Morrow, & Kessler, 2006; Liang, Farh, & Farh, 2012; Zapata, Olsen, & Martins, 2013).

In their meta-analysis of trust in leadership, Dirks and Ferrin (2002) argued that social exchange process exists in the leader-follower relationship in that both parties operate on the basis of trust and the perception of mutual obligation, and where care and consideration play a central role. It can be assumed that trust in supervisor is perceived by the employees as a valuable socioemotional reward by the organization that makes them feel obligated to help their organization to reach its objectives with their positive attitudes and behaviors.

More specifically, it can be argued that when supervisors demonstrate competence in their work and adhere to moral principles, they signal to their subordinates that they are dependable and reliable, which makes reciprocity more customary for the supervisees (Colquitt et al., 2012). Likewise, when employees see their supervisors expressing genuine care and concern for their welfare, they view these acts of benevolence as valued benefits from the organization that may obligate them to reciprocate with a higher level of job engagement. Thus, based on the above reasoning, it is proposed that:

> *Hypothesis 3*: Felt obligation mediates the relationship between trust in supervisor and job engagement.

Although researchers have used SET (Blau, 1964) and Kahn's (1990) model of engagement in explaining the trust-engagement relationship, these explanations remained independent of each other and no link was developed between the two. It can be contended that trust in supervisor might not generate the sense of felt obligation directly among employees. Felt obligation rather occurs when the satisfaction of psychological safety need under the trustworthy supervisor is sufficiently met. In other words, the relationship between trust in supervisor and job engagement is mediated by psychological safety and felt obligation in a sequence. Thus, in order to test this serial multiple mediation in the trust-engagement relationship, it is proposed that:

Hypothesis 4: The relationship between trust in supervisor and job engagement is sequentially mediated by psychological safety and felt obligation.

Method

The conceptual model of the study was tested in a cross-sectional field study of nurses employed in a large public hospital located in Kuala Lumpur, Malaysia. There were two main reasons for selecting nurses in this study. First, nurses experience difficult and stressful work situations that are also demanding, therefore their cognitive, emotional, and physical engagement with patient care greatly depends on their supervisors who are responsible for providing them with enough resources and opportunities to cope with such work conditions effectively (Othman & Nasurdin, 2013). Second, the motivation and engagement of nurses in serving patients deteriorate when they do not experience good relationships with their supervisors (Trinchero, Brunetto, & Borgonovi, 2013). Moreover, there is evidence that healthy supervisor-nurse relationship has a strong association with engagement of nurses in hospitals (Brunetto et al., 2013).

Sample and Procedure

After obtaining approval from the Research and Ethics Committee of the hospital, questionnaires were distributed among nurses in all major 26 wards of the hospital ($n = 600$). A research assistant was recruited from the hospital to brief the participants in each ward about the scope of the study and their rights to participate in this research. Although the respondents were not required to reveal their identity, they were further assured that their responses would be kept in strict confidentiality and that their participation would be voluntary. A total of 471 questionnaires were returned after three weeks, yielding an overall response rate of 79 percent. As a result of preliminary analyses, 125 cases were found to be largely incomplete and 9 cases were identified as outliers because their standardized values exceeded ±3.29 (Tabachnick & Fidell, 2007). Thus, these 134 cases were deleted from the dataset and the remaining 337 cases were retained for the main analysis.

Analysis of demographic data of the respondents showed that the majority of respondents were female (97%), married (63%), and belonged to the Malay ethnic group (98%). Most of the respondents had earned a three-year diploma in nursing education (89%). An average respondent was 29 years old ($SD = 4.51$) and had worked for the hospital for 7 years ($SD = 4.31$).

Measures

Variables in this study were measured using self-reported items. Respondents indicated the extent of their agreement with each item on a five-point Likert scale ranging from *strongly disagree* (1) to *strongly agree* (5).

Job Engagement

Employee job engagement was measured using the 18-item JES developed by Rich et al. (2010). Because Kahn's (1990) construct of engagement is multidimensional, this scale consists of three 6-item subscales to measure physical engagement (e.g., "I work with intensity on my job"), emotional engagement (e.g., "I am enthusiastic in my job"), and cognitive engagement (e.g., "At work, my mind is focused on my job"). In this study, reliability coefficients for physical, emotional, and cognitive subscales were .90, .90, and .91, respectively. The reliability coefficient for the overall job engagement scale was .94. These values of reliabilities are consistent with earlier research using the JES in diverse samples, ranged from .88 to .96 (e.g., Alfes, Shantz, Trust, & Soane, 2012; Basit & Arshad, 2016; Byrne et al., 2016; Chen, Yen, & Tsai, 2014; He, Zhu, & Zheng, 2014; Rich et al., 2010; Shuck, Twyford, Reio, & Shuck, 2014).

Trust in Supervisor

In order to measure trust in supervisor, McAllister's (1995) trust scale was used. This 11-item scale comprised of six items to assess employees' perceptions of supervisor's competence and reliability (e.g., "My supervisor approaches his/her job with dedication"). The other five items assessed employees' perceptions of supervisor's benevolence (e.g., "My supervisor responds caringly when I share my problems"). The reliability coefficients for cognitive trust, affective trust, and overall trust in supervisor were .84, .85, and .89, respectively. These reliability values were consistent with past research ranged from .82 to .93 (e.g., Conchie, Taylor, & Donald, 2012; McAllister, 1995; Schaubroeck et al., 2011).

Psychological Safety

Liang et al.'s (2012) scale was used to assess psychological safety. This scale captured the extent to which the employees perceived it to be safe to express their thoughts and feelings in their work units. It comprised of five items (e.g., "In my work unit, I can freely express my thoughts"). The reliability coefficient for this scale was .81, which was slightly higher than Liang et al.'s (2012) reliability coefficients of .72 (time 1) and .75 (time 2)

Felt Obligation

The scale developed by Eisenberger et al. (2001) was used to assess felt obligation. This scale comprised of seven items (e.g., "I feel a personal obligation to do whatever I can to help my organization achieve its goals") and captured the extent to which an employee feels obligated to give back to his/her organization as a result of receiving valued benefits. The reliability coefficient for this scale was .88, which was consistent with past research ranged from .86 to .92 (e.g., Coyle-Shapiro et al., 2006; Eisenberger et al., 2001)

Results

Descriptive Statistics and Correlations

Table 1 presents the means, standard deviations, and correlations among the study variables. It can be noted that trust in supervisor is positively correlated with the mediating variables of psychological safety ($r = .62, p < .001$) and felt obligation ($r = .46, p < .001$). Furthermore, trust in supervisor is also positively correlated with the outcome variable of job engagement ($r = .49, p < .001$). In addition, psychological safety is positively correlated with felt obligation ($r = .52, p < .001$) and job engagement ($r = .54, p < .001$). Felt obligation is also positively correlated with job engagement ($r = .52, p < .001$). In general, strong correlations were observed among the main study variables. Moreover, due to the homogeneous

Table 1. Descriptive Statistics, Correlations, and Scale Reliabilities.

	Variable	*M*	*SD*	1	2	3	4	5	6	7
1	Job engagement	4.32	.38	(.94)						
2	Physical engagement	4.43	.42	.85***	(.90)					
3	Emotional engagement	4.35	.45	.89***	.66***	(.90)				
4	Cognitive engagement	4.18	.46	.86***	.56***	.64***	(.91)			
5	Trust in supervisor	3.72	.49	.49***	.35***	.42***	.50***	(.89)		
6	Psychological safety	3.73	.52	.54***	.38***	.50***	.52***	.62***	(.81)	
7	Felt obligation	4.02	.48	.52***	.46***	.43***	.45***	.46***	.52***	(.88)

Note. $N = 337$; reliability coefficients are reported along the diagonal.
$^{***}p < .001$.

nature of the respondents, none of the demographic variables showed significant correlations with the main variables and, thus, were not included as control variables in this study.

Confirmatory Factor Analysis

In the first step of data analysis, confirmatory factor analysis (CFA) was performed to establish convergent and discriminant validity of the proposed model using Amos 20 software. In order to reduce complexity of the measurement model, the total number of indicators of each construct was reduced to three. The first indicator was created by averaging items having highest and lowest factor loading values. The same method was applied on the remaining items for creating the second and third indicators. In Structural Equation Modeling, this method is recommended to maintain favorable parameter to sample size ratio and develop just-identified measurement model (e.g., Bandalos, 2002; Landis, Beal, & Tesluk, 2000; Little, Rhemtulla, Gibson, & Schoemann, 2013). In job engagement literature, use of this practice can be seen in the recent study of Chughtai (2016).

The CFA results showed that measurement model achieved a good model fit (χ^2 (48) = 89.55, $p < .001$; TLI = .98; CFI = .98; RMSEA = .05; SRMR = .04). Further, factor loadings of all indicators on their respective constructs were above .70 (.75–.90), alpha reliabilities (.81–.94) and construct reliabilities (.81–.90) were above .70, and average variances extracted (.60–.75) were above .50. These results provided evidence that the measurement model achieved convergent validity.

Discriminant validity was assessed by comparing the original four-factor model with various alternative models that were constrained by setting the covariance between the constructs to the value of 1. Table 2 shows that the hypothesized four-factor model is superior to all other models, because the values of the Chi-square difference test for these models are significant. Further, values of average variance extracted (.60–.75) were greater than the squared correlations between the related constructs (.17–.59), showing that the hypothesized

Table 2. Discriminant Validity with Comparison of Alternative Measurement Models.

Model	χ^2	*df*	$\Delta\chi^2$	Δdf	RMSEA	SRMR	TLI	CFI
Hypothesized four-factor	89.55	48	—		.05	.04	.98	.98
Three-factor (merged TIS & PS)	473.41	51	348***	3	.15	.23	.79	.84
Two-factor (merged TIS, PS, & FO)	944.88	54	855***	6	.22	.31	.55	.63
Single-factor (merged TIS, PS, FO, & JE)	1185.35	58	1096***	10	.24	.36	.47	.54

Note. TIS = trust in supervisor; PS = psychological safety; FO = felt obligation; JE = job engagement.
$^{***}p < .001$.

four-factor model was the best among other models, evidencing that discriminant validity was sufficiently achieved.

In addition, a separate CFA was performed on the JES to examine how well the data supported the three-dimensional structure of Kahn's (1990) engagement construct. Initial results with 18-items showed that model fit indices were slightly away from their cutoff points (χ^2 (132) = 649.89, $p < .001$; TLI = .87; CFI = .88; RMSEA = .10; SRMR = .07). Due to poor factor loadings or high covariance between error terms, one item from physical engagement ("I exert a lot of energy on my job"), one item from cognitive engagement ("At work, my mind is focused on my job"), and two items from emotional engagement ("I am interested in my job" and "I am proud of my job") were removed. As a result, a good model fit was achieved (χ^2 (74) = 261.99, $p < .001$; TLI = .93; CFI = .95; RMSEA = .08; SRMR = .05). Factor loadings of indicators of physical (.70–.89), emotional (.70–.85), and cognitive (.75–.87) dimensions ranged from .70 to 89. Moreover, the three-factor model was compared with one-factor model (χ^2 (80) = 1317.40, $p < .001$; TLI = .58; CFI = .63; RMSEA = .22; SRMR = .32), whose fit to the data was found to be poor. Results revealed that the three-factor model was superior to the one-factor model because value of the Chi-square different test was significant ($\Delta\chi^2$ = 1055.40, $p < .001$). Thus, it can be concluded that the data supported the Kahn's (1990) three-dimensional construct of engagement.

Common Method Bias Test

During the design and execution stages of this study, several procedural remedies were followed to increase the accuracy of responses as suggested by Podsakoff, MacKenzie, and Podsakoff (2012). Despite taking these precautions, the use of self-reported items in this cross-sectional study might raise the possibility of common method bias. Thus, Harman's single-factor test was performed (Podsakoff, MacKenzie, Lee, & Podsakoff, 2003). All items of the four constructs were forced to load on a single un-rotated factor that extracted only 37% of the variance, indicating that much of the variance was not captured by this single factor. Furthermore, factor analysis using the principle component method yielded six factors that accounted for 67% of the variance together, where the first factor extracted only 12% of the variance. In addition to these results, a one-factor model in Table 2 showed poor fit to the data. All these results together led to the conclusion that the common method bias did not influence the findings presented in this study.

Test of Hypotheses

In order to test the serial multiple mediator model proposed in this study, path estimates of the structural model (χ^2 (48) = 89.55, $p < .001$; TLI = .98; CFI = .98; RMSEA = .05; SRMR = .04) were computed using the Maximum Likelihood estimation method. However, indirect effects were computed using Model 6 of the Process procedure in SPSS software developed by Preacher and Hays (2008) for the serial multiple-mediation. Using the bias-corrected bootstrapping method, 10,000 bootstrap samples were generated to calculate indirect effects at 95% level of confidence for confidence intervals. The combined results of these two statistical procedures are presented in Table 3.

Table 3. Structural Path Coefficients and Indirect Effects for Mediation Models.

	Path Coefficients			Indirect Effects	
	Psychological Safety	Felt Obligation	Job Engagement	Estimates	Bias-corrected 95% CI
Trust in Supervisor	.69*** (.06)	.13 (.08)	.10 (.06)		
Psychological Safety	—	.48*** (.09)	.29*** (.07)		
Felt Obligation	—	—	.21*** (.05)		
TIS → PS → JE				.13 (.03)	.08, .19
TIS → FO → JE				.05 (.02)	.02, .08
TIS → PS → FO → JE				.05 (.01)	.03, .08

Note. $N = 337$. TIS = trust in supervisor; PS = psychological safety; JE = job engagement; FO = felt obligation. CI = confidence interval. Bootstrap confidence intervals were constructed using 10,000 resamples. Total effect (T → JE) = 0.40 (.05). Standard error is shown in parentheses.
$^{***}p < .001$.

Hypothesis 1 proposed a positive relationship between trust in supervisor and job engagement. Results showed that the total effect of trust in supervisor on job engagement was significant ($b = .40, p < .001$), thus lending support to Hypothesis 1.

In Hypothesis 2, it was proposed that psychological safety would mediate the relationship between trust in supervisor and job engagement. It was found that psychological safety significantly mediated this relationship (effect size = .13, CI[.08, .19]), because its 95% confidence interval did not contain zero (Preacher & Hayes, 2008). Thus, Hypothesis 2 was supported. Further examination of these results revealed that the direct effect of trust in supervisor on felt obligation was not significant ($b = .13, p > .05$), which indicated that psychological safety fully mediated the effect of trust in supervisor on felt obligation.

In a similar vein, Hypothesis 3 proposed that felt obligation would mediate the relationship between trust in supervisor and job engagement. Results revealed that the mediating role of felt obligation was significant (effect size = .05, CI[.02, .08]) since its 95% confidence interval did not contain zero. Thus, Hypothesis 3 was supported. Further examination of these results revealed that the direct effect of psychological safety on job engagement remained significant ($b = .29, p < .001$) in the model, which indicated that felt obligation partially mediated the effect of psychological safety on job engagement.

Finally, Hypothesis 4 proposed that the relationship between trust in supervisor and job engagement would be mediated by psychological safety and felt obligation in a sequence. Results showed that these mediators significantly mediated the effect of trust in supervisor on job engagement in a sequence (effect size = .05, CI[.03, .08]) since 95% confidence interval of their combined indirect effect did not contain zero. Thus, Hypothesis 4 also found support. Moreover, the direct effect of trust in supervisor on job engagement became nonsignificant ($b = .10, p > .05$) in the presence of psychological safety and felt obligation. It can be concluded from this finding that psychological safety and felt obligation together fully mediated the effect of trust in supervisor on job engagement.

Discussion

This study examined the effect of trust in supervisor on job engagement via the mediating roles of psychological safety and felt obligation in a sequence. Although trust is a reciprocal and dynamic construct that continually evolves in relationships, this study captured a snapshot in time within this dynamic trust-engagement relationship among 337 nurses employed in a Malaysian public hospital. Results revealed that trust in supervisor was a strong predictor of job engagement. Furthermore, analysis of the serial multiple mediator model of the study showed that the effect of trust in supervisor was fully mediated by psychological safety and felt obligation together in a sequence.

Theoretical Contribution

This study contributes to the literature in three ways. First, this study has advanced research on Kahn's (1990) motivational construct of engagement measured by the JES (Rich et al., 2010). The CFA results of the JES confirmed that Kahn's (1990) conceptualization of engagement in the forms of physical, emotional, and cognitive engagement is supported well by data obtained from a Malaysian sample. This finding suggests that use of the JES is equally suitable for the non-Western samples, which greatly extends boundaries of job engagement research to other geographical regions.

Second, as noted earlier, most of the empirical studies following Kahn's (1990) work on engagement in the social context of job engagement have largely focused on the antecedents related to social support and leadership. This study is the first that has empirically examined and found support for the role of trust in supervisor in predicting job engagement grounded in Kahn's (1990) engagement model.

Third, one of the salient contributions of this study is that it has shed light on the psychological mechanisms that govern the relationship between trust in supervisor and job engagement. The study provides empirical evidence that the effect of trust in supervisor on job engagement goes sequentially through psychological safety and felt obligation. This finding confirms that the satisfaction of psychological safety need and the sense of felt obligation have causal associations in the trust-engagement relationship rather than being competing. In this manner, the study extends Kahn's engagement model by introducing felt obligation in the relationship between psychological safety and job engagement. Moreover, the study provides empirical support to Saks' (2006) assertion that the relationship between psychological safety and job engagement involves mechanism of social exchange.

Managerial Implications

The study has some important implications for organizations. First, the effect of trust in supervisor on job engagement observed in this study highlights the importance of managing trust in organizations and reinforces the practical value of sensitizing supervisors to the concerns of their subordinates pertaining to trust in supervisor. The use of effective selection methods at the time of hiring supervisors can serve as the first step to manage trust in organizations. The aspects of trust in supervisor related to competence, reliability, and benevolence can be measured in advance through widely used selection tools, such as cognitive ability, integrity, and personality tests (Klotz, Da Motta Veiga, Buckley, & Gavin, 2013).

A cognitive ability test measures one's general ability to perform a job and is well-known for predicting job performance and job-related learning (Klotz et al., 2013; Schmidt & Hunter, 1998; Van Iddekinge & Ployhart, 2008). Researchers recommend that a cognitive ability test can be used as a proxy for the competence component of trust because of its high association with performance and learning outcomes (Klotz et al., 2013). Integrity tests measure the reliability and honesty of employees and scores of these tests are negatively associated with counterproductive work behaviors (Klotz et al., 2013; Schmidt & Hunter, 1998). According to Klotz et al. (2013), integrity tests can be used to identify potential supervisors who are reliable in performing their supervisory roles by assessing perceptions of their own trustworthiness (i.e., honesty image) and by measuring their beliefs concerning how often others behave dishonestly (i.e., norms of general dishonesty). Finally, personality tests provide employers with information pertaining to various personality traits of the applicants including agreeableness that reflects trustfulness, cooperation, friendliness, and compliance (Barrick, Mount, & Judge, 2001). Having aspects of trustworthiness, agreeableness can also be used as a proxy for the benevolence component of trust during the selection process of supervisors (Klotz et al., 2013; Schmidt & Hunter, 1998). In fact, Byle and Holtgraves (2008) have noted that applicants who score high in agreeableness tend to answer integrity tests more truthfully than those who score low in agreeableness. Moreover, individuals high in agreeableness perform well in jobs that require teamwork, particularly, in the healthcare professions (Barrick et al., 2001).

Second, managerial training is another important tool for organizations to improve the trustworthiness of their supervisors. Effectiveness of managerial training in organizations has long been acknowledged in meta-analytic studies (e.g., Arthur, Bennett, Edens, & Bell, 2003; Salas, Tannenbaum, Kraiger, & Simth-Jentsch, 2012). It is well established that supervisors can be successfully trained to demonstrate competence, reliability, and benevolence in their supervisory activities (Colquitt et al., 2012). Because supervisors can exercise the greatest degree of control over their actions relative to their subordinates' perceptions, training programs should be focused at developing supervisory behaviors that form these trust perceptions (Whitener et al., 1998). Providing training using different methods, such as lectures, discussions, and behavioral modeling can improve competence, reliability, and benevolence of supervisors which, in turn, can enhance employees' trust in them (Arthur et al., 2003; Colquitt et al., 2012; Salas et al., 2012).

Third, communication among supervisors and their subordinates that is frequent, transparent, and honest is an important factor for the development of trust in supervisors (Kam, Morin, Meyer, & Topolnytsky, 2013). In the context of nursing, McCabe and Sambrook (2013) noted that nurses are more likely to trust supervisors who have open styles of communication. Thus, supervisors can enhance psychological safety and felt obligation and, in turn, job engagement by considering this important role of communication in developing trust and the sense of safety and obligation while interacting with their subordinates.

Fourth, this study also informs that low trust in supervisor leads to low employee job engagement. Supervisors become untrustworthy in the eyes of their subordinates when they exploit their subordinates' dependency on them or neglect to fulfill their expectations (Kim, Dirks, & Cooper, 2009). As a consequence, subordinates feel unsafe under such supervisors and feel less obligated to reciprocate with their level of job engagement. The effects of low trust in supervisor can be so severe that employees may even start to think about quitting their jobs (Dirks & Ferrin, 2002). Furthermore, recent developments in trust research have revealed that trust can be repaired through various tactics, such as apologies, promises, denials, penance, regulation, and reparation (Kim et al., 2009). The use of these tactics to repair trust can help supervisors improve their trustworthiness among their subordinates and can motivate them to demonstrate enhanced engagement with work.

Finally, in addition to using various above-mentioned methods for enhancing trust in supervisors, organizations may also consider enhancing job engagement by focusing on other sources of felt obligation. For instance, use of various human resource practices, such as job security, favorable pay, promotion, and better work conditions can generate felt obligation among employees that can make them reciprocate these benefits through their level of job engagement (Yu & Frenkel, 2013).

Limitations and Future Research

This study has some limitations that offer opportunities for future research. First, the use of cross-sectional data made it difficult to infer causality among variables with absolute certainty (Shadish, Cook, & Campbell, 2002, p. 18). Alternatively, it is possible that the positive experiences of job engagement might lead employees to evaluate trust in their supervisors in a more positive manner due to the social exchange mechanism in this relationship that strengthens trust over time (Blau, 1964; Cropanzano & Mitchell, 2005). Thus, a longitudinal design could better clarify the direction of relationship with more certainty and highlight possible variations in job engagement over time.

Second, although all target respondents were encouraged to complete the questionnaire, their participation was voluntary. Considering the relatively high mean score (4.32) of job engagement measure in this study, it is possible that engaged respondents were more likely to participate in the survey than those who had less motivation for engagement with work. In order to have more objective picture of the respondents' level of job engagement in future research, it is suggested to measure job engagement from sources other than the same respondents, such as colleagues who work closely with the target respondents (Rich et al., 2010).

Third, the study sample was very homogeneous. For instance, there were only 3% of male nurses in the sample because of the profession being dominated by females (Barnett, Namasivayam, & Narudin, 2010). It was, therefore, not possible to compare males with females in this study. Research shows that female employees reporting to male supervisors have higher levels of trust than female employees reporting to female supervisors (Jeanquart-Barone & Sekaran, 1994). It would be informative to examine the trust-engagement relationship from gender perspective in future research.

Finally, this study focused only on the mediating mechanisms while examining the trust-engagement relationship. Future research may also consider the moderating conditions of this relationship. For instance, employees who have the disposition of high trust propensity might perceive their supervisors as more trustworthy, feel safer, and feel more obligated to give back to their organization with enhanced job engagement. Furthermore, limited studies to date have focused on job engagement from the organizational justice perspective (e.g., Ghosh, Rai, & Sinha, 2014; He et al., 2014; Saks, 2006). It is recommended to examine the moderating roles of distributive, procedural, and interactional types of organizational justice (Colquitt, Greenberg, & Zapata-Phelan, 2005) in the trust-engagement relationship between supervisors and employees.

Conclusion

The present study provides evidence for the perspectives of Kahn's (1990) engagement view and SET (Blau, 1964) on the relationship between trust in supervisor and job engagement. In doing so, this study contributes to the literature on leadership trust and job engagement by modeling psychological safety and felt obligation as mediating mechanisms. This study illustrates the importance of trust in supervisor in promoting employee job engagement in organizations, and the importance of a theory-based approach to understanding the trust-engagement relationship between supervisors and employees.

ORCID

Ameer A. Basit http://orcid.org/0000-0002-2540-1631

References

Arthur, W., Bennett, W., Edens, P. S., & Bell, S. T. (2003). Effectiveness of training in organizations: A meta-analysis of design and evaluation features. *Journal of Applied Psychology*, *88*, 234–245. https://doi.org/10.1037/0021-9010.88.2.234

Albrecht, S. L., Bakker, A. B., Gruman, J. A., Macey, W. H., & Saks, A. M. (2015). Employee engagement, human resource management practices and competitive advantage: An integrated approach. *Journal of Organizational Effectiveness: People and Performance*, *2*, 7–35. https://doi.org/10.1108/JOEPP-08-2014-0042

Alfes, K., Shantz, A. D., Truss, C., & Soane, E. C. (2012). The link between perceived human resource management practices, engagement and employee behaviour: A moderated mediation model. *The International Journal of Human Resource Management*, *24*, 330–351. https://doi.org/10.1080/09585192.2012.679950

Bachmann, R., & Zaheer, A. (2006). *Handbook of trust research*. Cheltenham, PA: Edward Elgar.

Bandalos, D. L. (2002). The effects of item parceling on goodness-of-fit and parameter estimate bias in structural equation modeling. *Structural Equation Modeling*, *9*, 78–102. https://doi.org/10.1207/S15328007SEM0901_5

Barnett, T., Namasivayam, P., & Narudin, D. A. A. (2010). A critical review of the nursing shortage in Malaysia. *International Nursing Review*, *57*, 32–39. https://doi.org/10.1111/j.1466-7657.2009.00784.x

Barrick, M. R., Mount, M. K., & Judge, T. A. (2001). Personality and performance at the beginning of the new millennium: What do we know and where do we go next? *International Journal of Selection & Assessment*, *9*, 9–30. https://doi.org/10.1111/1468-2389.00160

Basit, A. A., & Arshad, R. (2016). The role of needs-supplies fit and job satisfaction in predicting employee engagement. *Jurnal Pengurusan*, *47*, 3–12. https://doi.org/10.17576/pengurusan-2016-47-01

Blau, P. M. (1964). *Exchange and power in social life*. New York, NY:Wiley.

Brunetto, Y., Xerri, M., Shriberg, A., Farr-Wharton, R., Shacklock, K., Newman, S., & Dienger, J. (2013). The impact of workplace relationships on engagement, well-being, commitment and turnover for nurses in Australia and the USA. *Journal of Advanced Nursing*, *69*, 2786–2799. https://doi.org/10.1111/jan.12165

Byle, K., & Holtgraves, T. (2008). Integrity testing, personality, and design: Interpreting the personnel reaction blank. *Journal of Business & Psychology*, *22*, 287–295. https://doi.org/10.1007/s10869-008-9059-z

Byrne, Z. S., Peters, J. M., & Weston, J. W. (2016). The struggle with employee engagement: Measures and construct clarification using five samples. *Journal of Applied Psychology*, *101*, 201–1227. https://doi.org/10.1037/apl0000124

Carasco-Saul, M., Kim, W., & Kim, T. (2015). Leadership and employee engagement: Proposing research agendas through a review of literature. *Human Resource Development Review*, *14*, 38–63. https://doi.org/10.1177/1534484314560406

Chen, C., Yen, C., & Tsai, F. C. (2014). Job crafting and job engagement: The mediating role of person-job fit. *International Journal of Hospitality Management*, *37*, 21–28. https://doi.org/10.1016/j.ijhm.2013.10.006

Christian, M. S., Garza, A. S., & Slaughter, J. E. (2011). Work engagement: A quantitative review and test of its relations with task and contextual performance. *Personnel Psychology*, *64*, 89–136. https://doi.org/10.1111/j.1744-6570.2010.01203.x

Chughtai, A. A. (2016). Servant leadership and follower outcomes: Mediating effects of organizational identification and psychological safety. *The Journal of Psychology*, *150*, 866–880. https://doi.org/10.1080/00223980.2016.1170657

Chughtai, A. A., & Buckley, F. (2009). Linking trust in the principal to school outcomes: The mediating role of organizational identification and work engagement. *International Journal of Educational Management*, *23*, 574–589.

Chughtai, A. A., & Buckley, F. (2011). Work engagement: Antecedents, the mediating role of learning goal orientation and job performance. *Career Development International*, *16*, 684–705. https://doi.org/10.1108/13620431111187290

Colquitt, J. A., Greenberg, J., & Zapata-Phelan, C. P. (2005). What is organizational justice? A historical overview. In J. Greenberg & J. A. Colquitt (Eds.), *The handbook of organizational justice* (pp. 3–56). Mahwah, NJ: Erlbaum.

Colquitt, J. A., Lepine, J. A., Piccolo, R. F., & Zapata, C. P. (2012). Explaining the justice-performance relationship: Trust as exchange deepener or trust as uncertainty reducer? *Journal of Applied Psychology*, *97*, 1–15. https://doi.org/10.1037/a0025208

Conchie, S. M., Taylor, P. J., & Donald, I. J. (2012). Promoting safety voice with safety-specific transformational leadership: The mediating role of two dimensions of trust. *Journal of Occupational Health Psychology*, *17*, 105–115. https://doi.org/10.1037/a0025101

Coyle-Shapiro, J., Morrow, P. C., & Kessler, I. (2006). Serving two organizations: Exploring the employment relationship of contracted employees. *Human Resource Management*, *45*, 561–583. https://doi.org/10.1002/hrm.20132

Crawford, E. R., LePine, J. A., & Rich, B. L. (2010). Linking job demands and resources to employee engagement and burnout: A theoretical extension and meta-analytic test. *Journal of Applied Psychology*, *95*, 834–848. https://doi.org/10.1037/a0019364

Cropanzano, R., & Mitchell, M. S. (2005). Social exchange theory: An interdisciplinary review. *Journal of Management*, *31*, 874–900. https://doi.org/10.1177/0149206305279602

Dirks, K. T., & Ferrin, D. L. (2002). Trust in leadership: Meta-analytic findings and implications for research and practice. *Journal of Applied Psychology*, *87*, 611–628. https://doi.org/10.1037/0021-9010.87.4.611

Dutton, J. E., & Heaphy, E. D. (2003). The power of high-quality connections. In K. S. Cameron, J. E. Dutton, & R. E. Quinn (Eds.), *Positive organizational scholarship: Foundations of a new discipline*. San Francisco, CA: Berrett-Koehler.

Edmondson, A. (1999). Psychological safety and learning behavior in work teams. *Administrative Science Quarterly*, *44*, 350–383. https://doi.org/10.2307/2666999

Edmondson, A., & Lei, Z. (2014). Psychological safety: The history, renaissance, and future of an interpersonal construct. *Annual Review of Organizational Psychology and Organizational Behavior*, *1*, 23–43. https://doi.org/10.1146/annurev-orgpsych-031413-091305

Eisenberger, R., Armeli, S., Rexwinkel, B., Lynch, P. D., & Rhoades, L. (2001). Reciprocation of perceived organizational support. *Journal of Applied Psychology*, *86*, 42–51. https://doi.org/10.1037/0021-9010.86.1.42

Ghosh, P., Rai, A., & Sinha, A. (2014).Organizational justice and employee engagement: Exploring the linkage in public sector banks in India. *Personnel Review*, *43*, 628–652. https://doi.org/10.1108/PR-08-2013-0148

Gouldner, A. W. (1960). The norm of reciprocity: A preliminary statement. *American Sociological Review*, *25*, 161–178. https://doi.org/10.2307/2092623

Halbesleben, J. R. B. (2010). A meta-analysis of work engagement: Relationships with burnout, demands, resources, and consequences. In A. B. Bakker & M. P. Leiter (Eds.), *Work engagement: A handbook of essential theory and research*: 102–117. New York, NY: Psychology Press.

Harter, J. K., Schmidt, F. L., & Hayes, T. L. (2002). Business-unit-level relationship between employee satisfaction, employee engagement, and business outcomes: A meta-analysis. *Journal of Applied Psychology, 87*, 268–279. https://doi.org/10.1037/0021-9010.87.2.268

He, H., Zhu, W., & Zheng, X. (2014). Procedural justice and employee engagement: Roles of organizational identification and moral identity centrality. *Journal of Business Ethics, 122*, 681–695. https://doi.org/10.1007/s10551-013-1774-3

Heaphy, E. D., & Dutton, J. E. (2008). Positive social interactions and the human body at work: Linking organizations and physiology. *Academy of Management Review, 33*, 137–162. https://doi.org/10.5465/AMR.2008.27749365

Hon, A. H. Y., & Lu, L. (2010). The mediating role of trust between expatriate procedural justice and employee outcomes in Chinese hotel industry. *International Journal of Hospitality Management, 29*, 669–676. https://doi.org/10.1016/j.ijhm.2010.01.002

Jeanquart-Barone, S., & Sekaran, U. (1994). Effect of supervisor's gender on American women's trust. *Journal of Social Psychology, 134*, 253–255. https://doi.org/10.1080/00224545.1994.9711391

Kahn, W. A. (1990). Psychological conditions of personal engagement and disengagement at work. *Academy of Management Journal, 33*, 692–724. https://doi.org/10.2307/256287

Kahn, W. A. (2010). The essence of engagement: Lessons from the field. In S. L. Albrecht (Eds.), *Handbook of employee engagement: Perspectives, issues, research and practice.* Cheltenham, PA: Edward Elgar.

Kam, C., Morin, A. J. S., Meyer, J. P., & Topolnytsky, L. (2016). Are commitment profiles stable and predictable? A latent transition analysis. *Journal of Management, 42*, 1462–1490. https://doi.org/10.1177/0149206313503010

Kark, R., & Carmeli, A. (2009). Alive and creating: The mediating role of vitality and aliveness in the relationship between psychological safety and creative work involvement. *Journal of Organizational Behavior, 30*, 785–804. https://doi.org/10.1002/job.571

Kim, P. H., Dirks, K. T., & Cooper, C. D. (2009). The repair of trust: A dynamic bilateral perspective and multilevel conceptualizaiton. *Academy of Management Review, 34*, 401–422. https://doi.org/10.5465/AMR.2009.40631887

Kim, W., Kolb, J. A., & Kim, T. (2012). The relationship between work engagement and performance: A review of empirical literature and a proposed research agenda. *Human Resource Development Review, 12*, 248–276. https://doi.org/10.1177/1534484312461635

Klotz, A. C., Da Motta Veiga, S. P., Buckley, M. R., & Gavin, M. B. (2013). The role of trustworthiness in recruitment and selection: A review and guide for future research. *Journal of Organizational Behavior, 34*, 104–119. https://doi.org/10.1002/job.1891

Landis, R. S., Beal, D. J., & Tesluk, P. E. (2000). A comparison of approaches to forming composite measures in structural equation models. *Organizational Research Methods, 3*, 186–207. https://doi.org/10.1177/109442810032003

Lee, Y., Kown, K., & Kim, W., & Cho, D. (2016). Work engagement and career: Proposing research agendas through a review of literature. *Human Resource Development Review, 15*, 29–54. https://doi.org/10.1177/1534484316628356

Liang, J., Farh, C. I. C., & Farh, J. (2012). Psychological antecedents of promotive and prohibitive voice: A Two-wave examination. *Academy of Management Journal, 55*, 71–73. https://doi.org/10.5465/amj.2010.0176

Little, T. D., Rhemtulla, M., Gibson, K., & Schoemann, A. M. (2013). Why the items versus parcels controversy needn't be one. *Psychological Methods, 18*, 285–300. https://doi.org/10.1037/a0033266

Macey, W. H., Schneider, B., Barbera, K. M., & Young, S. A. (2009). *Employee engagement: Tools for analysis, practice, and competitive advantage.* Chichester, UK: Blackwell Publishing. https://doi.org/10.1002/9781444306538

Mackay, M. M., Allen, J. A., & Landis, R. S. (2016). Investigating the incremental validity of employee engagement in the prediction of employee effectiveness: A meta-analytic path analysis. *Human Resource Management Review*, *27*, 108–120. https://doi.org/10.1016/j.hrmr.2016.03.002

May, D. R., Gilson, R. L., & Harter, L. M. (2004). The psychological conditions of meaningfulness, safety and availability and the engagement of the human spirit at work. *Journal of Occupational and Organizational Psychology*, *77*, 11–37. https://doi.org/10.1348/096317904322915892

McAllister, D. J. (1995). Affect- and cognition-based trust as foundations for interpersonal cooperation in organizations. *Academy of Management Journal*, *38*, 24–59. https://doi.org/10.2307/256727

McCabe, T. J., & Sambrook, S. (2013). The antecedents, attributes and consequences of trust among nurses and nurse managers: A concept analysis. *International Journal of Nursing Studies*, *51*, 815–827. https://doi.org/10.1016/j.ijnurstu.2013.10.003

Meyer, J. P., & Herscovitch, L. (2001). Commitment in the workplace: Toward a general model. *Human Resource Management Review*, *11*, 299–326. https://doi.org/10.1016/S1053-4822(00)00053-X

Nooteboom, B. (2002). *Trust: Forms, foundations, functions, failures, and figures*. Cheltenham, PA: Edward Elgar.

Othman, N., & Nasurdin, A. M. (2013). Social support and work engagement: A study of Malaysian nurses. *Journal of Nursing Management*, *21*, 1083–1090. https://doi.org/10.1111/j.1365-2834.2012.01448.x

Perugini, M., Gallucci, M., Presaghi, F., & Ercolani, A. P. (2003). The personal norm of reciprocity. *European Journal of Personality*, *17*, 251–283. https://doi.org/10.1002/per.474

Podsakoff, P. M., MacKenzie, S. B., & Podsakoff, N. P. (2012). Sources of method bias in social science research and recommendations on how to control it. *Annual Review of Psychology*, *63*, 539–569. https://doi.org/10.1146/annurev-psych-120710-100452

Podsakoff, P. M., MacKenzie, S. B., Lee, J. -Y., & Podsakoff, N. P. (2003). Common method biases in behavioral research: A critical review of the literature and recommended remedies. *Journal of Applied Psychology*, *88*, 879–903. https://doi.org/10.1037/0021-9010.88.5.879

Preacher, K. J., & Hayes, A. F. (2008). Asymptotic and resampling strategies for assessing and comparing indirect effects in multiple mediator models. *Behavior Research Methods*, *40*, 879–891. https://doi.org/10.3758/BRM.40.3.879

Quinn, R. W. (2007). Energizing others in work connections. In J. E. Dutton & B. R. Ragins & (Eds.), *Exploring positive relationships at work: Building a theoretical and research foundation*. Mahwah, NJ: Lawrence Erlbaum.

Rich, B. L., Lepine, J. A., & Crawford, E. R. (2010). Job engagement: Antecedents and effects on job performance. *Academy of Management Journal*, *53*, 617–635. https://doi.org/10.5465/AMJ.2010.51468988

Robinson, S. L., & Rousseau, D. M. (1994). Violating the psychological contract: Not the exception but the norm. *Journal of Organizational Behavior*, *15*, 245–259. https://doi.org/10.1002/job.4030150306

Rousseau, D. M., Sitkin, S. B., Burt, R. S., & Camerer, C. (1998). Not so different after all: A cross-discipline view of trust. *Academy of Management Review*, *23*, 393–404. https://doi.org/10.5465/AMR.1998.926617

Ryan, R. M., & Deci, E. L. (2000). Intrinsic and extrinsic motivations: Classic definitions and new directions. *Contemporary Educational Psychology*, *25*, 54–67. https://doi.org/10.1006/ceps.1999.1020

Saks, A. M. (2006). Antecedents and consequences of employee engagement. *Journal of Managerial Psychology*, *21*, 600–619. https://doi.org/10.1108/02683940610690169

Saks, A. M., & Gruman, J. A. (2014). What do we really know about employee engagement? *Human Resource Development Quarterly*, *25*, 155–182. https://doi.org/10.1002/hrdq.21187

Salas, E., Tannenbaum, S. I., Kraiger, K., & Simth-Jentsch, K. A. (2012). The science of training and development in organizations: What matters in practice. *Psychological Science in the Public Interest*, *13*, 74–101. https://doi.org/10.1177/1529100612436661

Schaubroeck, J. M., Lam, S. S. K., & Peng, A. C. (2011). Cognition-based and affect-based trust as mediators of leader behavior influences on team performance. *Journal of Applied Psychology, 96*, 863–871. https://doi.org/10.1037/a0022625

Schaufeli, W. B., Salanova, M., González-Romá, V., & Bakker, A. B. (2002). The measurement of engagement and burnout: A two sample confirmatory factor analytic approach. *Journal of Happiness Studies, 3*, 71–92. https://doi.org/10.1023/A:1015630930326

Schmidt, F. L., & Hunter, J. E. (1998). The validity and utility of selection methods in personnel psychology: Practical and theoretical implications of 85 years of research findings. *Psychological Bulletin, 124*, 262–274. https://doi.org/10.1037/0033-2909.124.2.262

Schneider, B., Macey, W. H., Barbera, K. M., & Young, S. A. (2010). The role of employee trust in understanding employee engagement. In S. L. Albrecht (Eds.), *Handbook of employee engagement: Perspectives, issues, research and practice*. Cheltenham, PA: Edward Elgar.

Shadish, W. R., Cook, T. D., & Campbell, D. T. (2002). *Experimental and quasi-experimental designs for generalized causal inference*. Boston, MA: Houghton Mifflin.

Shuck, M. B., Reio, T. G., & Rocco, T. S. (2011). Employee engagement: An examination of antecedent and outcome variables. *Human Resource Development International, 14*, 427–445. https://doi.org/10.1080/13678868.2011.601587

Shuck, M. B., Twyford, D., Reio, T. G., & Shuck, A. (2014). Human resource development practices and employee engagement: Examining the connection with employee turnover intentions. *Human Resource Development Quarterly, 25*, 239–270. https://doi.org/10.1002/hrdq.21190

Skinner, D., & Searle, R. H. (2011). Trust in the context of performance appraisal. In R. H. Searle & D. Skinner & (Eds.), *Trust and human resource management*. Cheltenham, PA: Edward Elgar.

Tabachnick, B. G., & Fidell, L. S. (2007). *Using multivariate statistics*. Boston, MA: Pearson Education.

Towers Watson. (2014). *The 2014 global workforce study*. Retrieved from https://www.towerswatson.com/en/Insights/IC-Types/Survey-Research-Results/2014/08/the-2014-global-workforce-study

Trinchero, E., Brunetto, Y., & Borgonovi, E. (2013). Examining the antecedents of engaged nurses in Italy: Perceived Organisational Support (POS); satisfaction with training and development; discretionary power. *Journal of Nursing Management, 21*, 805–816. https://doi.org/10.1111/jonm.12143

Ugwu, F. O., Onyishi, I. E., & Rodríguez-Sánchez, A. M. (2014)., Linking organizational trust with employee engagement: The role of psychological empowerment, *Personnel Review, 43*, 377–400. https://doi.org/10.1108/PR-11-2012-0198

Van Iddekinge, C. H., & Ployhart, R. E. (2008). Developments in the criterion-related validation of selection procedures: A critical review and recommendations for practice. *Personnel Psychology, 61*, 871–925. https://doi.org/10.1111/j.1744-6570.2008.00133.x

Whitener, E. M., Brodt, S. E., Korsgaard, M. A., & Werner, J. M. (1998). Managers as initiators of trust: An exchange relationship framework for understanding managerial trustworthy behavior. *Academy of Management Review, 23*, 513–530.

Xu, J., & Thomas, H. C. (2011). How can leaders achieve high employee engagement? *Leadership & Organization Development Journal, 32*, 399–416. https://doi.org/10.1108/01437731111134661

Yang, J., Mossholder, K. W., & Peng, T. K. (2009). Supervisory procedural justice effects: The mediating roles of cognitive and affective trust. *The Leadership Quarterly, 20*, 143–154. https://doi.org/10.1016/j.leaqua.2009.01.009

Yu, C., & Frenkel, S. J. (2013). Explaining task performance and creativity from perceived organizational support theory: Which mechanisms are more important? *Journal of Organizational Behavior, 34*, 1165–1181. https://doi.org/10.1002/job.1844

Zapata, C. P., Olsen, J. E., & Martins, L. L. (2013). Social exchange from the supervisor's perspective: Employee trustworthiness as a predictor of interpersonal and informational justice. *Organizational Behavior and Human Decision Processes, 121*, 1–12. https://doi.org/10.1016/j.obhdp.2012.11.001

Work Engagement: Investigating the Role of Transformational Leadership, Job Resources, and Recovery

Amy J. Hawkes, Amanda Biggs, and Erin Hegerty

ABSTRACT

While the relationship between job resources and engagement has been well established, a greater understanding of the upstream factors that shape job resources is required to develop strategies to promote work engagement. The current study addresses this need by exploring transformational leadership as an upstream job resource, and the moderating role of recovery experiences. It was hypothesized that job resources would mediate the relationship between transformational leadership and engagement. Recovery experiences were expected to moderate the relationship between resources and engagement. A sample of 277 employees from a variety of organizations and industries was obtained. Analysis showed direct relationships between: transformational leadership and engagement, and transformational leadership and job resources. Mediation analysis using bootstrapping found a significant indirect path between transformational leadership and engagement via job resources. Recovery experiences did not significantly moderate the relationship between job resources and engagement. To date, the majority of published literature on recovery has focused on job demands; hence the nonsignificant result offers insight of a potentially more complex relationship for recovery with resources and engagement. Overall, the current study extends the JD-R model and provides evidence for broadening the model to include upstream organizational variables such as transformational leadership.

Creating and supporting an engaged workforce has become a central issue in contemporary organizational psychology. The personal and organizational benefits linked to engagement are well documented, as are the theoretical conceptualizations underlying work engagement (Bakker & Leiter, 2010). To date, engagement research has primarily focused on proximal antecedents such as control, supervisor and colleague support, feedback or recognition (Brough et al., 2013; Hakanen & Roodt, 2010; Siu et al., 2010). Several recent reviews have noted the need to expand our understanding of engagement to include distal antecedents, or upstream resources, such as leadership, culture, climate, and broader organizational resources (Albrecht, Bakker, Gruman, Macey, & Saks, 2015; Dollard & Bakker, 2010; Hakanen & Roodt, 2010). These broader antecedents help promote environments conducive to positive job resources (Macey & Schneider, 2008). Leadership is responsible for affecting almost all workplace experiences (Hentrich et al., 2017), hence positive leadership styles such as transformational leadership offer a useful perspective as an organizational resource. Transformational leadership has a substantial evidence-base, and has been linked individually to some job resources and even proposed as an intervention for improving job resources (Albrecht et al., 2015). Remarkably, leadership is yet to be operationalized as an upstream resource within the JD-R framework and these associations are far from being well understood (Hentrich et al., 2017). Finally, recent developments in the JD-R model have identified the potential for experiences outside of the workplace to influence outcomes (Albrecht et al., 2015; Demerouti, Bakker, Geurts, & Taris, 2009). In particular, the current study will explore the role of recovery experiences.

The current study aims to contribute to the existing JD-R literature by taking a broader perspective on engagement, incorporating transformational leadership and factors external to the workplace (recovery). It is argued that transformational leadership fosters job resources, which are subsequently related to increased work engagement. This aspect of the research contributes to our understanding of the JD-R model by examining the upstream factors (i.e., leadership) that influence job-related characteristics. While the relationship between resources and work engagement is well established, less is known about how these resources are developed (Albrecht et al., 2015) and transformational leadership is a particularly promising explanatory upstream factor due to its demonstrated effect on work characteristics and individual/organizational outcomes.

Furthermore, it is expected that an employees' experiences outside of work, namely recovery experiences, will moderate the relationship between job resources and engagement. Recovery experiences have been investigated primarily within the energy process of the JD-R model, and less is known about their effect on the motivational process. Recovery experiences are expected to strengthen the relationship between job resources and engagement, due to their capacity to develop personal resources and increase individual's openness and receptiveness to job resources that enable employees to fully engage in their job. This research contributes to our understanding of the role of recovery in the JD-R's motivational process, as well as the role of both work and non-work factors more broadly.

Theoretical Framework

The concept of engagement gained attention two decades ago as an extension of burnout research, and has since become popular with practitioners and researchers alike (Bakker, Schaufeli, Leiter, & Taris, 2008; Wollard & Shuck, 2011). Contemporary conceptualizations consider engagement to be a separate construct that is negatively associated with burnout. Engagement, therefore, exists and develops as a discrete entity, and describes employees who are motivated, self-efficacious, and positively connected to their work (Bakker et al., 2008). The benefit of this approach is that engagement can be understood as more than just the absence of burnout.

Engagement is most often conceptualized as "a positive, fulfilling, work-related state of mind that is characterized by vigor, dedication, and absorption" (Schaufeli, Salanova, González-Romá, & Bakker, 2002, p. 74). Vigor describes the high levels of energy that employees show as well as a propensity to invest effort into work. Dedication is characterized by strong identification with work, and a sense of pride and achievement in the work. Lastly, absorption refers to the experience of being completely engrossed in one's work, so that concentration can be maintained easily and time passes quickly (Schaufeli et al., 2002). Engagement is thus representative of a positive, energetic and engrossed state of being at work. Indeed, engaged employees report increased enthusiasm for their work, take initiative, and feel as though time at work flies by, instead of the exhaustion and antipathy for work reported by disengaged employees (Bakker et al., 2008).

To date, research has shown engagement to significantly reduce turnover intentions, increase productivity, job performance, occupational success, and employee organizational commitment (Rana, Arcdichvili, & Tkachenko, 2014; Schaufeli et al., 2002). Arguably, however, the most important organizational benefit of engaged staff is organizational growth and financial success (Xanthopoulou, Bakker, Demerouti, & Schaufeli, 2009). Additionally, engaged employees report work-family enrichment (Siu et al., 2010); improved physical health, mental health, and well-being (Robertson & Cooper, 2010); reduced burnout and psychological strain (Biggs, 2011); and improved meaningfulness and sense of purpose in work (Robertson & Cooper, 2010). Hence, engagement has benefits for both the organization and the individual employee.

Currently, the best understanding of the precursors of engagement is provided by the job demands-resources model (JDR; Bakker & Demerouti, 2007). At its core is the assumption that all workplace specific characteristics can be categorized as either demands (i.e., stress risk factors) or resources (i.e., protective factors; Demerouti, Bakker, Nachreiner, & Schaufeli, 2001). A key benefit of the JD-R model is that its broad categorizations allow it to be applied to any organizational context. Job demands are characterized as aspects of a job that require sustained mental (cognitive or affective) and/or physical effort. While job demands may not automatically increase stress, if demands are high or prolonged they can become stressors (Bakker & Demerouti, 2007). In contrast, resources (both within the workplace and personal resources) are linked to increased engagement and occupational health. Bakker and Demerouti (2007) focus specifically on job resources and explain that these are work features that can (a) aid goal achievement, (b) reduce associated costs of job demands, or (c) facilitate employee growth and development. Importantly, the JD-R model proposes that job resources are positively related to increased work engagement (Bakker & Demerouti, 2007). Work resources that enhance engagement include social support from supervisors and/or colleagues, supervisory coaching, and performance feedback (Bakker, Demerouti, & Schaufeli, 2003; Schaufeli & Bakker, 2004); and control, autonomy, and opportunities for personal development (Xanthopoulou, Bakker, Demerouti, & Schaufeli, 2007). The JD-R offers a parsimonious model for combining a range of resources to understand engagement, irrespective of work context (Demerouti et al., 2001).

However, within the JD-R framework, there is little research on the processes that precede job resources and, therefore, engagement. In an effort to address this gap, attention has turned to upstream organizational resources, such as leadership and psychosocial safety climate, to explore how job resources can be developed (Dollard & Bakker, 2010). Albrecht et al. (2015) recently proposed an extended model of the JD-R that included Human Resource policies and practices, and psychosocial safety climate as distal organization level antecedents. Further, this review included transformational leadership as one intervention for Human Resource departments to create a positive environment and boost job resources. However, there is a need for more empirical research connecting transformational leadership to a JD-R model (Hentrich et al., 2017). This study will explore the relationships between transformational leadership, job resources, and engagement.

Transformational Leadership

Leadership has been positioned as one of the most crucial factors in building work engagement (Buckingham & Coffman, 1999). Importantly, we now understand it is also the quality and type of leadership experienced by employees that plays the critical role. There have been a number of conceptualizations of transformational leadership (e.g., Carless, Wearing, & Leon, 2000; Wang & Howell, 2010), although two are more commonly used. The first includes four behavioral components: idealized influence, inspirational motivation, intellectual stimulation, and individualized consideration (Avolio & Bass, 1991; Avolio, Bass, & Jung, 1999). The other widely-used conceptualization presents six transformational dimensions: conveying vision, providing appropriate modelling, motivating followers to accept team goals, communicating high performance expectations, individualized consideration, and intellectual stimulation (Podsakoff, MacKenzie, Moorman, & Fetter, 1990). Both definitions conform to the basic underlying theory of transformational leadership and provide well established scales.

Transformational leaders expect more from their followers, positively challenging them, and studies have found these leaders typically see greater motivation, performance, and improved organizational outcomes as a result (Bass & Riggio, 2006; Katou, 2015). In essence, transformational leaders are more effective leaders than those adopting transactional approaches because their behavior provides additional support, guidance, and recognition (Breevaart et al., 2014). Overall, it is accepted that transformational leadership encapsulates core behaviors of providing direction and meaning; motivating followers to identify with, and achieve, goals; and encouraging followers to adopt creative approaches to problems (Breevaart et al., 2014).

Empirical investigation has supported the theorized benefits of transformational leadership. Transformational leadership behaviors are linked to improved performance, occupational citizenship behaviors, and employee well-being (Bass & Riggio, 2006; Braun, Peus, Weisweiler, & Frey, 2013). While it is clear that transformational leadership is associated with positive organizational outcomes, leadership has been theorized to play a vital role in the development of engagement (Schmitt, Den Hartog, & Belschak, 2016).

Conceptualizations of transformational leadership have described a number of ways through which leadership might influence engagement. Shamir, House, and Arthur (1993) discussed how transformational and charismatic leaders role model positive work behaviors, which enhance employees' commitment to the organization's espoused mission and values, creating more engaged followers. Similarly, Ghadi, Fernando, and Caputi (2013) proposed that transformational leaders strengthen engagement through offering individualized consideration to followers. Intellectual stimulation may also play a role through encouraging employees to develop creative and innovative solutions to problems (Bass & Bass, 2008). Furthermore, transformational leadership has been linked to key motivational processes, such as empowerment, for decades (Parker & Griffin, 2011). Given the clear theoretical links between transformational leadership and engagement, Bakker, Albrecht, and Leiter (2011) argued for more in depth analysis of the leadership-engagement relationship, and Parker and Griffin (2011) agree that the "field could benefit from specific studies of engagement" (p. 64).

Of the studies that have investigated the transformational leadership-engagement link empirically, results have been positive. In a South Korean cross-sectional study, engagement mediated the relationship between transformational leadership and organizational knowledge creation (Song, Kolb, Lee, & Kim, 2012). Engagement has also been found to mediate the relationship between transformational leadership and proactive behavior (Schmitt et al., 2016) and intention to leave (Wefald, Reichard, & Serrano, 2011). Tims, Bakker, and Xanthopoulou (2011) showed that employee daily ratings of transformational leadership behaviors were significantly associated with higher engagement the subsequent day. Similarly, transformational leadership was found to help build follower engagement over time, even when controlling for prior levels of engagement (Breevaart et al., 2014). Such longitudinal studies offer sound evidence for transformational leadership being an effective antecedent of engagement. Encouragingly, this relationship has been found across diverse cultures including the Netherlands (Tims et al., 2011), Iran (Hayati, Charkhabi, & Naami, 2014), and Australia (Ghadi et al., 2013).

Despite this recent work on transformational leadership and engagement Schmitt et al. (2016) stated that "While there is some research supporting this proposed linkage between transformational leadership and work engagement ... the available body of empirical evidence is still relatively limited" (p. 592). Based on the extant literature, and the call for more research, this study proposes that transformational leadership is related to increased engagement.

***Hypothesis 1**: Transformational leadership will be positively related to work engagement.*

To date, most of the leadership research has focused on how leaders achieve improved organizational outcomes via engagement. Separately, there is an established literature on job related factors that contribute to engagement (Liaw, Chi, & Chuang, 2010). Hence, a key contribution of this study will be to extend upon this literature by combining both approaches, to explore how leaders may contribute to these job resources and in-turn increase engagement.

The Mediating Role of Job Resources

In trying to understand the processes through which transformational leadership increases engagement, a number of mechanisms have been examined (Tims et al., 2011; Zhu, Avolio, & Walumbwa, 2009). However, few studies have examined the mediating role of job resources in this relationship, despite the emphasis on upstream organizational resources influencing job resources (Dollard & Bakker, 2010), and the JD-R model specifying that job resources are a key determinant of engagement (Bakker & Demerouti, 2007).

As detailed above, job resources have a motivating potential that leads to increased engagement (Bakker, Demerouti, & Euwema, 2005). The JD-R model specifies that this is due to job resources helping meet employee needs while also intrinsically motivating employees through aiding the achievement of goals; strong support has been received for this model (Bakker & Demerouti, 2007). By changing employee cognitions when presented with demands and helping to reduce the strength of stress responses, job resources have also been found to buffer against the effects of job demands (Bakker & Demerouti, 2007; Bakker et al., 2005). This motivational pathway has been well established in the literature (Bakker & Demerouti, 2007). Therefore, job resources are important mechanisms in their own right, through which employees can be supported and inspired at work.

***Hypothesis 2**: Job resources will be positively related to engagement.*

However, research has only recently begun to investigate the precursors that help build job resources, with most studies only measuring the presence of job resources alone. Broadening our understanding of this process is vital, as knowing how perceived job resources are developed is necessary to effectively facilitate them. Recently, researchers have attempted to fill this gap by arguing that leaders fundamentally influence the work environment through their actions (Yukl, 2010). This theory has been supported by numerous empirical studies demonstrating transformational leadership builds job resources (Bryant, 2003; Pejtersen, Kristensen, Borg, & Bjorner, 2010). Importantly, research has examined how transformational leadership builds positive factors, such as empowerment (Jung, Chow, & Wu, 2003) and support (Liaw et al., 2010), which are resources positively associated with engagement (Bass & Riggio, 2006). While these studies were not explicitly testing the JDR conceptualization as a constellation of resources, they do assess resource components that help to justify the proposed relationship between transformational leadership and job resources. In one of the few studies to integrate transformational leadership with a JDR approach, using a cross-sectional survey design, transformational leadership was linked to improved self-efficacy (a personal resource), which mediated the relationship with ill-health (Hentrich et al., 2017). This study presents an integration of leadership and the JDR, something that has been called for over many years (Biggs, Brough, & Barbour, 2014). The current study aims to contribute to this area by investigating a set of job resources, rather than personal resources, in the context of engagement rather than ill-health.

This research draws upon the extended JD-R theory to examine how transformational leadership impacts work engagement, via the indirect influence of job resources. Although the JD-R model presents a wide range of potential job resources (see Schaufeli & Taris, 2014), three are of particular interest within a leadership to engagement framework: influence at work, supervisor support, and recognition (Pejtersen et al., 2010). *Influence* over work environments and the ability to manage priorities is argued to be an important condition for employees to maintain engagement with their work (Tims & Bakker, 2010). *Supervisor support* is reflected in followers' general belief that their leader values their well-being and contributions (Kottke & Sharafinski, 1988), and has been shown to play a role in promoting engagement, through reducing employee experiences of stress and burnout (Skakon, Nielsen, Borg, & Guzman, 2010), satisfying intrinsic need for belonging (Van den Broeck, Vansteenkiste, De Witte, & Lens, 2008), promoting self-esteem and companionship, and providing practical and informational support (Cohen & Willis, 1985). Finally, the importance of *recognition* as an influential motivating factor is well established, dating back to Herzberg's (1968) theory of motivation. A sense of recognition, and feeling appreciated and respected, has been empirically linked to increased engagement (Bakker et al., 2008; Breevaart et al., 2014; Koyuncu, Burke, & Fiksenbaum, 2006).

In order to increase employees' sense of influence, support, and recognition, and ultimately improve engagement, it is important to understand the upstream factors that shape these job resources. Transformational leadership behaviors have been associated with an increased sense of influence in employees, through involving followers in decision making and stimulating them to think independently (Breevaart et al., 2014). Transformational leaders build a sense of influence through providing opportunities and involvement, and encouraging employee growth and creativity through support and recognition (Zhu, May, & Avolio, 2004). Other research has demonstrated the link between transformational leadership and influence as part of the broader psychological empowerment construct (Avolio,

Zhu, Koh, & Bhatia, 2004; Jung et al., 2003). Empowered employees report a sense of intrinsic motivation that includes confidence in their abilities to complete a task, a sense of purpose, influence, and meaning (Spreitzer, 1996; Thomas & Velthouse, 1990).

Additionally, transformational leaders have repeatedly been shown to provide employees with high levels of perceived support and recognition due to an emphasis on individualized consideration (Bass & Riggio, 2006). Through providing regular feedback and recognition, followers' display increased sense of professional efficacy, and thus reduced burnout and increased engagement (Maslach, Schaufeli, & Leiter, 2001). Moreover, leaders are a core component of an employee's social environment, which necessarily influences judgments of the work environment (Yukl, 2010). Consequently, transformational leaders who attend to employee concerns are more likely to engender a sense of support and recognition in followers. Furthermore, followers who feel supported are more likely to display increased commitment and action towards a leader's vision (Liaw et al., 2010). Thus, transformational leadership can be conceptualized as a precursor to increased job resources, and in line with the JD-R model, may aid the development of engagement (Biggs et al., 2014).

However, there is a noticeable gap in the literature when it comes to empirically studying the mediating role of job resources together within the leadership-engagement relationship. Indeed, only one study was identified as having empirically examined the role of job resources within a leadership-engagement relationship (Breevaart et al., 2014). This study explored social support and autonomy as resources. It is worth noting that autonomy and influence are both considered types of control an individual may have over their work, with autonomy focused on personal control an individual has to complete tasks in their own way (Jung et al., 2003) and influence focused on the ability to control strategic and operating outcomes at work (Spreitzer, 1996). Breevaart et al. (2014) found that both autonomy and social support significantly and positively mediated the effects of transformational leadership on engagement in naval cadets. Yet, one study is not sufficient for confident conclusions to be drawn, particularly as Breevaart et al. (2014) only looked at these effects within a specific sub-section of the population. Further, only one study exploring transformational leadership has tested both job demands and resources in relation to ill-health (Hentrich et al., 2017). However, some of these relationships have been well established outside of the JDR model when explored as separate constructs (e.g. social support) or as mediators of different outcomes (e.g. autonomy, Jung et al., 2003; Liaw et al., 2010). Hence, it is logical to draw a link between transformational leadership and engagement, as mediated by job resources, but more research is needed to support these statements (Schmitt et al., 2016).

> ***Hypothesis 3***: *Job resources will mediate* the *relationship between transformational leadership and work engagement.*

The Moderating Role of Recovery

It is well established that work conditions have a profound impact on engagement (Bakker & Leiter, 2010). However, what is not yet understood is how non-work experiences might influence this relationship. Non-work experiences generally describe activities undertaken during an individual's leisure time and are linked to both psychological and occupational outcomes (Mojza, Sonnentag, & Bornemann, 2011). In particular, one non-work experience that has been related to engagement is recovery (Moreno-Jiménez, Rodríguez-Muñoz, Sanz-Vergel, & Garrosa, 2012).

Recovery is the daily process of re-building personal resources lost due to job demands and is associated with a number of well-being outcomes, not least being engagement (Demerouti et al., 2009). Four specific restorative experiences have been identified as facilitating effective recovery: psychological detachment, relaxation, mastery, and control (Sonnentag, Binnewies, & Mojza, 2008). Taken together, recovery experiences have been shown to promote the development of personal resources and help individuals feel capable of meeting new demands at work (Bakker, Demerouti, Oerlemans, & Sonnentag, 2013).

Not surprisingly, recovery has been positioned as a key moderator in the relationship between work characteristics and employee well-being (Sonnentag, Binnewies, & Mojza, 2010). Most recovery literature has discussed how recovery works to attenuate the relationship between job demands and low engagement by reducing stressful activation systems and replenishing resources (Kinnunen, Mauno, & Siltaloppi, 2010; Moreno-Jiménez et al., 2012). Yet, research that has explored recovery as a moderator has produced mixed results. Sonnentag et al. (2010) found that psychological detachment, the most investigated recovery experience, moderated the relationship between job demands and engagement. Additionally, Kinnunen et al. (2010) showed that psychological detachment reduced the strength of the negative relationship between job insecurity (a job demand) and employee vigor (a key dimension of engagement). In contrast, an earlier study found that while certain recovery experiences moderated the effects of job demands on employee well-being, similar interaction effects were not found for engagement (Siltaloppi, Kinnunen, & Feldt, 2009). However, this study used a modified measure of engagement, which did not assess all three defined dimensions, which may have influenced the findings.

This research will focus on the moderating effect of recovery on the resources to engagement pathway. Drawing on conservation of resources (COR) theory (Hobfoll, 2001), employees are motivated to build and protect personal and job-related resources, as the accumulation of resources reduces their vulnerability to future stressors and enables the investment of resources to maintain positive psychological states, such as engagement. Within COR theory, Hobfoll (2001) elaborated on the existence of resource caravans, in which access to an enriched work environment facilitates the accrual of further personal and job-related resources, demonstrating resources do not exist in isolation but work together to maintain positive psychological states. Recovery time outside of work is essential for recharging personal resources, which in turn allows an employee to be more receptive to job resources and, therefore, more engaged at work. Schaufeli and Taris (2014) argued that personal resources can act as either mediators or moderators of engagement. While recovery experiences have been implicated in the development and maintenance of personal resources (such as personal initiative; Sonnentag, 2003). In the current study, it is the experience of recovery specifically that will be examined in the context of transformational leadership and job resources, not the resulting personal resources. This interaction between experiences at work and experiences at home influencing well-being and engagement has been well established in the work-life conflict literature (Demerouti, Taris, & Bakker, 2007). For instance, home-work interference combined with a lack of recovery at home resulted in a negative spiral that impacted work performance (Demerouti et al., 2007). It is argued that the relationship between resources and engagement will be stronger if personal resources are replenished when away from work via recovery experiences, thus creating a gain spiral (Salanova, Schaufeli, Xanthopoulou, & Bakker, 2010).

Reviewing the literature shows there is substantive theoretical justification for combining job resources with recovery. However, the moderating effects of recovery have focused

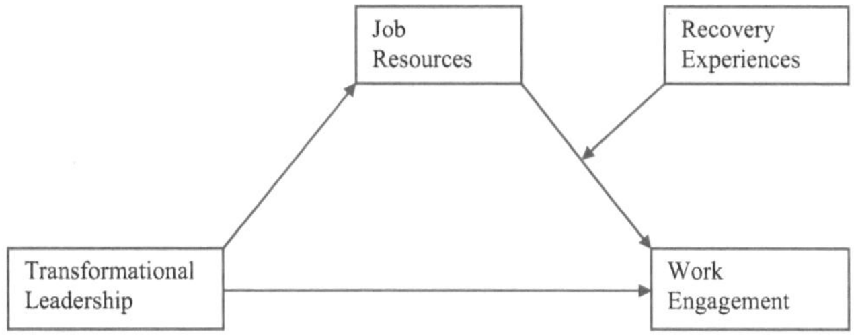

Figure 1. Proposed research model.

primarily on job demands; and these findings are limited by the selective use of construct subscales. Thus, less is known about the ability of recovery to interact with job resources to positively build engagement at work. Logically, recovery should work to strengthen the relationship between job resources and engagement. This is through helping to restore personal resources, which not only aid employees to cope more effectively with adverse workplace conditions (Xanthopoulou et al., 2007) but also interact with job resources to enable the employee to fully engage (Salanova et al., 2010). Thus it is proposed that recovery outside of work may moderate the relationship between job resources and work engagement.

> ***Hypothesis 4***: *Recovery experiences will moderate the relationship between job resources and engagement. Specifically, it is hypothesized that the relationship between job resources and engagement will be stronger for those who experience high levels of recovery, than for those who experience lower levels of recovery.*

To summarize, engagement plays a vital role in promoting organizational outcomes and employee well-being, and as such, developing a clear understanding of its antecedents is an important endeavor. The JD-R model specifies that both job resources and personal resources contribute to increased engagement (Bakker & Demerouti, 2007; Bakker et al., 2008), although less is known about the development of these resources (Albrecht et al., 2015). To this end, transformational leadership has been posed as a key, distal, factor in the development of engagement by helping to increase perceived job resources (Breevaart et al., 2014). Drawing on COR theory it is expected that recovery experiences outside of work will enable employees to be more open and receptive to job resources. Hence, recovery experiences are proposed to interact with job resources in explaining variance in engagement. The model being tested has been detailed in Figure 1. By investigating these relationships, the current study aims to not only confirm and strengthen previous findings, but also to expand on the existing literature. This study contributes to the literature through positioning transformational leadership in the JD-R framework as an upstream variable. The addition of recovery provides a more comprehensive investigation of engagement through consideration of work and leisure contexts.

Method

Participants and Procedure

Participants working in Australia were recruited through personal contacts, social-networks, approaching individuals, advertising (posters) within workplaces, and through staff email distribution lists. A total sample of 277 surveys was collated. Due to the nature of the data collection, forwarded on behalf of researchers to staff email lists and shared through social-media sites, it is not possible to calculate an accurate response rate. Participants reported working in a variety of industries including engineering, health, community and public services, retail, and sales. Participant age ranged from 18 to 65 years ($M = 35.05$, $SD = 11.70$), of which 54.58% were female ($n = 143$). The majority of participants reported working full-time ($n = 184$), and the remaining were part-time ($n = 5$), casual ($n = 35$), or unspecified ($n = 53$). Mean tenure reported was 4.78 years ($SD = 5.96$), ranging from one month to 37 years (16 participants did not provide tenure information). Participants reported a range of working hours per week from five to 80 hours, with 17 participants not reporting any working hours ($M = 35.81$, $SD = 14.84$).

Measures

Engagement

The Utrecht Work Engagement Scale (UWES-9) was used to measure work engagement (Schaufeli, Bakker, & Salanova, 2006). The scale consists of nine items, assessing the three underlying dimensions of vigor, dedication and absorption. An example question is "When I get up in the morning, I feel like going to work." Each item was scored on a seven-point scale ranging from zero (*never*) to six (*always*).

Transformational Leadership

Transformational leadership was assessed using the leadership behavior scale (Podsakoff et al., 1990). The scale consists of twenty-three items assessing six transformational leadership dimensions. The subscale, high performance expectations, was removed from the total transformational leadership scale due to poor fit and inconsistent correlations[1]. An example item is "[my leader] inspires others with his/her plans for the future." Responses are scored on a seven-point scale ranging from one (*strongly disagree*) to seven (*strongly agree*).

Job Resources

Measures of job resources were taken from the second version of the Copenhagen Psychosocial Questionnaire (COPSOQ II, Pejtersen et al., 2010). The three resources measured were influence at work, supervisor support and recognition. Influence at work was assessed by four items (e.g., "Do you have a large degree of influence concerning your work?"). Supervisor support was assessed using three items (e.g., "How often do you get help and support from your nearest supervisor?"). Recognition at work was assessed by three items (e.g., "Is your work recognized and appreciated by the management?"). Influence and supervisor support were measured on five-point scales ranging from one (*never/hardly ever*) to five (*always*); recognition was also scored on a five-point scale, ranging from one (*To a very small extent*) to five (*To a very large extent*). For the current study a total job resources score was calculated using all three sub-scales, as is consistent with previous job resources literature (Sonnentag et al., 2010).

[1] Please contact the authors for supporting materials, including detail of subscale inter-correlations across all measures.

Recovery Experiences

Recovery was measured by the recovery experience questionnaire (Sonnentag & Fritz, 2007), which consists of 16 items, with four items assessing each of the four recovery experience dimensions. An example item is "I use the time to relax." It is scored on a five-point scale, ranging from one (*I do not agree at all*) to five (*I fully agree*).

Demographics

Based on empirical and theoretical reasoning, two variables, age and the number of hours worked per week, were identified as appropriate control variables and were included in the survey (Becker, 2005).

Statistical Analysis

Zero-order correlations were conducted to examine the bivariate relationship between the variables. After removing respondents with greater than 10% missing data on a single measure ($n = 15$), maximum likelihood estimation with the expectation-maximization algorithm was employed to impute the remaining missing values. A hierarchical multiple regression analysis was conducted to examine the relationships between transformational leadership, job resources, and engagement (Hypotheses 1 and 2). A bootstrapped mediation analysis was conducted to investigate the indirect effects of transformational leadership on engagement via job resources (Hypothesis 3; Preacher & Hayes, 2008). To test the moderating effects of recovery on the relationship between job resources and engagement (Hypothesis 4), a moderated hierarchical multiple regression analysis was conducted, with main and interaction effects entered.

Results

Confirmatory Factor Analysis

Two competing measurement models were assessed to demonstrate validity of the hypothesized multifactor structure: a one-factor model with all indicators loading on a single variable compared with a six-factor model, with separate indicators reflecting influence, supervisor support, recognition, transformational leadership, recovery, and engagement. The one-factor model produced poor fit statistics (Model 1, Table 1), while the six-factor model demonstrated acceptable model-fit (Model 2, Table 1). The CFA results indicated that the squared multiple correlations for one subscale of the transformational leadership measure (performance expectations) was less than .30 (i.e., .01) and this subscale was deleted from the measure. The fit statistics for the refined six-factor model were also acceptable (Model 3, Table 1). Overall, the hypothesized multi-factor structure was valid, and indicated that the research variables were empirically distinct. The refined six-factor model was run with and without a common method latent factor (Podsakoff, MacKenzie, Lee, & Podsakoff, 2003). The standardized regression weights were compared across the two models and the

Table 1. Confirmatory factor analysis.

CFA model		χ^2	*df*	SRMR	TLI	CFI	PCFI	RMSEA	AIC
1.	One-factor model	1625.69	229	.13	.54	.59	.53	.15	1719
2.	Six-factor model	482.73	213	.06	.91	.92	.78	.07	608
3.	Refined six-factor model	393.89	192	.05	.93	.94	.78	.06	515

difference in weights were small (<.1), indicating common method bias did not have a substantial impact on the results.

Correlations

All means, standard deviations, zero-order correlations and internal consistencies are presented in Table 2. Internal consistencies for all measures were good, with Cronbach's α ranging from .85 to .96, and inspection of means indicated no floor or ceiling effects. Significant positive correlations were found between engagement and transformational leadership, engagement and job resources, and between engagement and recovery, consistent with Hypotheses 1 and 2. Resources were not significantly correlated with recovery. In contrast, transformational leadership and resources were strongly correlated ($r = .63$). Finally, participants' age and working hours had significant zero-order correlations with engagement; all analyses were run both with, and without, the selected control variables (Becker, 2005). The results were essentially identical in terms of interpretation, indicating the control variables contributed little explanatory power to the findings. For parsimony, all further analyses are therefore reported without controls included.

Regression Analysis

Multiple hierarchical regressions were conducted to further investigate the relationship between transformational leadership, resources, engagement, and explore the moderating role of recovery. Transformational leadership was entered into the first step of the model with resources entered as the second step. Results of the hierarchical regression are presented in Table 3. The initial model (Step 1) found transformational leadership to predict engagement as the obtained R^2 was significantly different from zero, $F\ (1, 260) = 72.76, p < .001$, 95%. Independently, transformational leadership was found to account for 22% of the variance in engagement [CI: .36, .62], supporting Hypothesis 1. In the subsequent model (Step 2), the addition of resources resulted in a significant incremental change to the R^2, $F_{inc}\ (1,259) = 29.56, p < .001$, 95%. Job resources were significantly related to engagement, accounting for 8% of the unique variance in engagement [CI .44, .95], supporting Hypothesis 2.

Table 2. Means, standard deviations, zero-order correlations and internal consistencies for the independent, dependent, mediating, moderating and proposed control variables.

	M	*SD*	1	2	3	4	5	6	7	8	9
1. Engagement[a]	4.09	1.267	(.93)								
2. Transformational Leadership[a]	4.79	1.18	.47***	(.96)							
3. Job Resources[a]	3.14	.66	.52***	.63***	(.85)						
4. Influence[a]	2.71	.78	.36***	.26***	.75***	(.77)					
5. Supervisor Support[a]	3.36	.93	.39***	.62***	.76***	.26**	(.83)				
6. Recognition[a]	3.50	.88	.46***	.63***	.82***	.42**	.54***	(.86)			
7. Recovery[a]	3.42	.74	.18***	.18***	.09	−.05	.11	.17***	(.91)		
8. Age[b]	35.05	11.70	.18***	.03	.11	.17**	.05	.03	−.14*	—	
9. Employment Hours[c]	35.81	14.84	.17***	.07	.13*	.27**	.02	.03	−.15*	.27***	—

Note. Cronbach's α is provided on the diagonal.
[a]$n = 262$, [b]$n = 255$, [c]$n = 259$.
*$p < .05$, **$p < .01$, ***$p < .001$

Table 3. Results of hierarchical multiple regression analysis of transformational leadership, job resources, recovery, and interaction term on engagement.

	Model 1				Model 2				Model 3			
	B	*(SE)*	*β*	*sr²*	*B*	*(SE)*	*β*	*sr²*	*B*	*(SE)*	*β*	*sr²*
Step 1.												
Transformational Leadership	.50	.06*	.49***	.22	.25	.07	.24***	.03	.23	.07	.21**	.03
Step 2.												
Job Resources					.70	.13	.37***	.08	1.20	.43	.63**	.02
Step 3												
Recovery									.60	.37	.35	.01
Resources x Recovery									−.14	.12	−.38	.004
ΔR^2							.08***				.02	
R^2			.22***				.29***				.30***	

Note. n = 262.
$^{**}p < .01$, $^{***}p < .001$, (SE): standard error, sr^2: squared semipartial correlation.

Step 3 (Table 3) includes recovery and the product term (job resources x recovery). Overall, the regression model was significant, $R^2 = .30$, $F(4,257) = 29.34$, $p < .001$. In the final model, transformational leadership and job resources were significant, while recovery was not significantly related to engagement [CI: −.12, 1.33]. However, it should be noted that these effects are conditional in the presence of the product term. The test of moderation, which is the interaction between job resources and recovery, was not significant, $b = -0.14$, $t(257) = -1.18$, CI [−.38, .10], $p = .24$. Therefore, Hypothesis 4 is not supported.

For the completed hierarchical model, the obtained R^2 remained significantly different from zero, $F(4, 257) = 29.34$, $p < .001$, explaining 30% of the variance in engagement within the current sample. Despite the added explanatory power of resources, transformational leadership remains a significant predictor in the final model, and continues to account for 2.66% of the total variance in engagement.

Mediation

Mediation was tested with the PROCESS function in SPSS (version 2.16; Hayes, 2012). Bootstrapping involves resampling with replacement to create a hypothetical normal distribution from which an accurate estimate of standard error can be drawn. The significance of any mediation can then be established dependent on whether the confidence interval does, or does not, span zero. The results of the bootstrapped analysis with 10,000 resamples are reported in Table 4.

The total mediation model was found to be significant, with transformational leadership and resources together accounting for 29.87% of the variance seen in engagement, $F(2, 259) = 55.15$, $p < .001$. The 95% confidence interval for the indirect effect of transformational leadership on engagement, through resources, did not cross zero (*ab* path = 0.25, bootstrap $SE = 0.05$, 95% CI [.15 to .36]. As such the indirect effect of job resources can be considered significant ($p < .05$), and this finding is consistent with Hypothesis 3.

Based upon the ratio of indirect to direct effect, the indirect effect of resources is shown to be positive, and accounts for 25% of the direct effect of transformational

Table 4. Bootstrap analysis of the mediation model of transformational leadership on engagement through job resources.

				95% Confidence Intervals	
	B	*(SE)*	*p*	Lower	Upper
Engagement[a]					
Transformational Leadership	.25	.07	<.001	.11	.39
Resources	.70	.13	<.001	.44	.95
Resources[b]					
Transformational Leadership	.35	.03	<.001	.30	.41

Note. [a]Regression with Engagement as outcome. [b]Regression with Resources as outcome. SE: standard error.

leadership on engagement. Furthermore, when controlling for mediation effects the relationship between transformational leadership and engagement was weaker (c path = 0.50, c' path = 0.25). A visual summary of the mediation model is presented in Figure 2.

As detailed above the moderation effect of recovery and resources on engagement was not significant. To confirm this, the conditional indirect effects of resources on engagement at different levels of recovery was checked using moderated mediation (Model 14) in PROCESS. These results were consistent with the hierarchical regression: for the interaction term $b = -.14$, $t(260) = -1.18$, $p = .24$ [−.38, .10]. At different levels of recovery, the conditional indirect effect remained significant. Overall, the index of moderated mediation was −0.05, SE(Boot) = .04, [CI: −.14, .03]. Thus confirming the previous conclusion that Hypothesis 4 was not supported.

Discussion

The aim of the current study was to contribute to the literature by expanding our knowledge of both the proximal and distal variables explaining variance in work engagement. Transformational leadership and job resources were explored as key factors in understanding engagement. The study also investigated the under-examined role of job resources as a mediator between transformational leadership and engagement. Finally, the study aimed to test the effects of non-work experiences, by examining the role of recovery experiences in moderating the relationship between job resources and engagement.

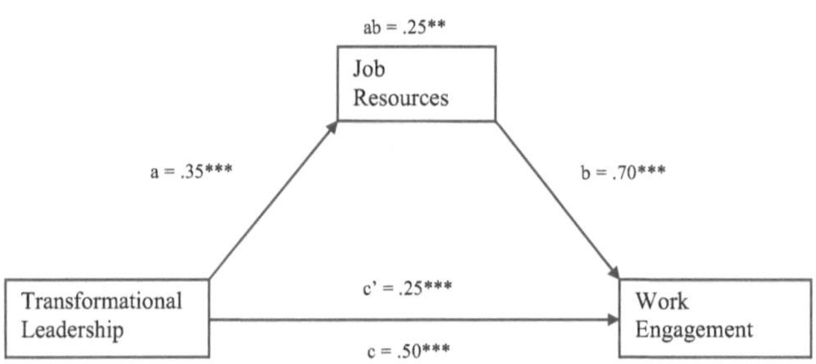

Figure 2. Regression derived *a* path, *b* path, *c* path and *c′* path b-weights, and bootstrap derived *ab* path b-weight for the mediation model of transformational leadership on engagement. Note. $^{**}p < .01$, $^{***}p < .001$ $n = 262$.

Summary of Results

Transformational Leadership

The results supported Hypothesis 1; transformational leadership behaviors were associated with higher engagement. Importantly, transformational leadership was not only directly linked to engagement, but a significant relationship was present even when job resources were included in the model. These findings show that employees who rated their leaders as demonstrating more transformational behaviors were more likely to report feeling engaged at work. Transformational leadership has long been theorized to play a vital role in engagement (Buckingham & Coffman, 1999) and there have been continued calls for further empirical examination of the leadership-engagement relationship (Blomme, Kodden, & Beasley-Suffolk, 2015; Schmitt et al., 2016). The results of the present study are consistent with other literature that has found a relationship between transformational leadership and engagement (Hayati et al., 2014; Tims et al., 2011). This paper also addresses the need for more research on upstream organizational factors in the JD-R model predicting engagement. Transformational leadership is a particularly promising upstream factor due to the long history of research linking this leadership style to various organizational and personal outcomes.

Job Resources

Job resources were significantly related to reported engagement, consistent with the established JD-R literature and providing support for Hypothesis 2. In addition to the direct relationship, the current study also found that job resources are, in part, one of the mechanisms that explain the relationship between transformational leadership and engagement. That is, the results show a significant positive indirect effect of transformational leadership on engagement, through job resources, and thus Hypothesis 3 was also supported. This implies that participants whose leaders exhibited more transformational behaviors also experienced greater perceived job resources, which in turn was linked to increased feelings of engagement at work.

These results provide support for two central streams of research. Firstly, consistent with the established JD-R literature, job resources play a key role in the development of engagement (Bakker & Demerouti, 2007). Secondly, transformational leadership behaviors can fundamentally influence working environments (Yukl, 2010) and thus affect the perception of job resources. Notably, the current study provides valuable support for the role of transformational leadership as an upstream organizational factor related to increased job resources and increased engagement. Similar to the findings by Breevaart et al. (2014), job resources were found to mediate this relationship; however, unlike previous research, this pattern was not limited to a specific population but was found across a broad cross-section of roles and industries. This is an area in which there has been limited empirical investigation of transformational leadership as part of the JD-R model (with only one prior study identified; Breevaart et al., 2014); therefore these findings provide a valuable contribution to the JD-R literature. The job resources in the current study (supervisor support, recognition and influence) only explained part of the variance in the relationship between transformational leadership and engagement. Hence, further research could investigate additional job resources (for instance, goal clarity, fairness or trust) as well as personal resources (for instance, psychological capital or intrinsic motivation) as additional mediators.

Recovery

The current study also investigated the role of recovery in moderating the relationship between job resources and engagement (Hypotheses 4). Unexpectedly, recovery did not significantly influence the relationship between the two, as job resources were significantly linked to engagement at all levels of recovery. The lack of moderating effects for recovery could be due to several factors. One possible explanation is the role of recovery in the motivational process of the JD-R theory may be more complex than in the strain process. Although it is expected there will be an overall positive effect of recovery on the motivation process, some recent studies have identified highly engaged employees potentially have trouble balancing work and non-work commitments, as they become engrossed in their work (Halbesleben, Harvey, & Bolino, 2009). So, while recovery is likely to be important for maintaining engagement, there may be a temptation for highly engaged employees to become engrossed in their work. Hence, there could be mixed roles of recovery in the motivation process, depending on an individual's current level of engagement.

Additionally, moderator effects are notoriously difficult to detect in non-experimental research (Siltaloppi et al., 2009). Even when moderation effects have been identified, explanation rates are often low and theorists have proposed that effects are still valuable when explaining as little as 1% of the total variance in a model (Evans, 1985). This may be another reason for the mixed results seen in the literature regarding the moderating role of recovery with job demands. To date, recovery (or a subscale of recovery) has been found to moderate the effects of job demands on engagement in some instances (Kinnunen et al., 2010; Sonnentag et al., 2010), but not in others (Siltaloppi et al., 2009). However, there is little research exploring the moderating role of recovery with job resources. The lack of literature on this relationship may not be due to a lack of interest but rather a bias towards publishing significant results (Ferguson & Heene, 2012). There is strong theoretical and empirical evidence for the positive effects of resource caravans on engagement, and recovery should fit within this approach through building personal resources. Furthermore, the work-life balance literature recognizes the interplay between events at home and outcomes at work, and vice versa (Demerouti et al., 2007). However, most leadership and JD-R research largely ignores what occurs outside of the workplace. Thus, despite the null results found in the current study, it is clear that further investigation is warranted to better understand the effects of recovery for both job demands and job resources at various levels of engagement.

Limitations and Future Directions

As with all psychological research, the study was not without certain limitations. A cross-sectional design was used and thus only association, not causality, can be inferred from the results (Mitchell & Jolley, 2007). However, while a reverse interpretation is possible, it is not theoretically justified with strong empirical evidence existing for the directional relationships between the studied constructs (Bakker & Demerouti, 2007; Breevaart et al., 2014). Nevertheless, to ascertain causality, future research could expand upon the findings of the current study by adopting longitudinal and/or experimental designs. Such designs would also assist in the further investigation of potential gain spirals between job resources and personal resources.

Another limitation of the study was the use of self-report measures, which may increase the risk of common method bias (Podsakoff et al., 2003). However, the nature of the variables measured: an individual's perception of their leader, perception of their job resources, and personal ratings of engagement as a psychological state, necessitated a self-report approach. Conway and Lance (2010) propose that the use of self-report measures is still appropriate if researchers take precautions to reduce bias. To this end, all measures utilized in the current study were shown to have appropriate construct validity. Furthermore, studies where a mix of significant and non-significant results are found, as in the case of the current study, are unlikely to be affected by overarching biases as this would be expected to inflate all variables measured, not just certain relationships (Spector, 2006). Finally, CFA demonstrated a good fit for the multi-factor model, indicating variables were empirically distinct. Even so, incorporating additional features designed to reduce bias, such as counterbalancing or sourcing predictor and dependent variable ratings on separate occasions, should be considered in future research.

One final limitation of the study concerns the conceptualization of job resources, and reflects a broader criticism of the JD-R literature. Specifically, no clear, empirically supported list of job resources exists. While the JD-R model definition of job resources, and demands, is necessarily vague to allow for differences in working environment (Bakker & Demerouti, 2007), this flexibility does result in a lack of consistency. Of the studies examined, few looked at the same set of resources, and while the resources selected were justified in most cases, and certainly in the case of the present study, it does make it difficult to accurately compare results across studies (Mitchell & Jolley, 2007). It is outside the scope of this study to detail a specific list of job resources. However, it is suggested that the Copenhagen Psychosocial Questionnaire (Pejtersen et al., 2010) might provide a suitable preliminary list. Of course, further investigation is necessary to determine the appropriateness of the COPSOQ II for this purpose, and the value of a resources list more generally.

Theoretical and Practical Implications

The results of the study offer a number of implications for both practice and theory. Importantly, the study provides further support for the development of transformational behaviors in organizational leaders. A growing body of research has shown that promoting transformational leadership is linked to a number of organizational benefits, not least of which is highly engaged employees (Breevaart et al., 2014; Tims et al., 2011). Essentially, developing transformational leaders is one method whereby organizations may gain a competitive advantage. Notably, this study helps to elucidate the process through which this happens, which may be of benefit to practitioners when communicating the value of leadership training to organizations.

In addition to furthering the support for practical leadership training, the current study also works to advance transformational leadership theory. By examining the indirect effect of job resources, this study has helped develop an understanding of the processes underlying the influence of leadership behaviors on follower outcomes. This not only supports the theorized mechanisms proposed by a number of leadership researchers (Bass & Bass, 2008; Ghadi et al., 2013), but also supports the recent findings that transformational leadership is positively related to engagement. Importantly, the study gives weight to the core assumption of leadership theory; which is that leaders can fundamentally influence the perceived working environment (Yukl, 2010).

Similarly, the current study provides further support for the JD-R model and helps to extend the theory as well. Traditionally, most JD-R research has started with the measurement of job resources and has neglected to consider the upstream organizational factors that work to create these resources (Skakon et al., 2010; Tims & Bakker, 2010). By showing that transformational leadership behaviors are related to increased perceptions of job resources, the current study helps researchers better understand the process through which job resources are facilitated. While the current study failed to find a moderating effect of recovery, the construct shows promise and practitioners and researchers should continue working to understand how recovery experiences may interact with experiences on the job. Thus the current study provides a more rounded, working model of the antecedents of job resources and engagement. Practically, this means that the JD-R model of engagement, and its proponents, can no longer overlook the role of upstream variables such as leadership.

Summary

In summary, this study provides further evidence for the importance of transformational leadership and job resources in promoting work engagement. The study also helps shed light on the process through which this happens, by showing that job resources significantly mediate the relationship between transformational leadership and engagement. Future research should look at replicating these findings longitudinally to substantiate causality. Additionally, future research into the structure of transformational leadership measures is also warranted, as is the development of a specific list of job resources, to ensure consistency across the literature. Overall, it is hoped that by developing a holistic understanding of the antecedents of engagement, organizations can better facilitate engagement in employees. Thus improving the well-being of employees generally, and promoting organizational success.

Funding

This research was supported by the Behavioural Basis of Health at Griffith University.

References

Avolio, B. J., & Bass, B. M. (1991). *The full range leadership development programs: Basic and advanced manuals*. New York, NY: Bass & Avolio Associates.

Avolio, B. J., Bass, B. M., & Jung, D. I. (1999). Re-examining the components of transformational and transactional leadership using the Multifactor Leadership Questionnaire. *Journal of Occupational and Organizational Psychology*, *72*(4), 441–462. doi:10.1348/096317999166789

Albrecht, S. L., Bakker, A. B., Gruman, J. A., Macey, W. H., & Saks, A. M. (2015). Employee engagement, human resource management practices and competitive advantage. *Journal of Organizational Effectivenes*, *2*(1), 7–35. doi:10.1108/JOEPP-08-2014-0042

Avolio, B. J., Zhu, W., Koh, W., & Bhatia, P. (2004). Transformational leadership and organizational commitment: Mediating role of psychological empowerment and moderating role of structural distance. *Journal of Organizational Behavior*, *25*, 951–968. doi:10.1002/job.283

Bakker, A. B., Albrecht, S. L., & Leiter, M. P. (2011). Work engagement: Further reflections on the state of play. *European Journal of Work and Organizational Psychology*, *20*(1), 74–88. doi:10.1080/1359432X.2010.546711

Bakker, A. B., & Demerouti, E. (2007). The Job Demands-Resources model: State of the art. *Journal of Managerial Psychology*, *22*(3), 309–328. doi:10.1108/02683940710733115

Bakker, A. B., Demerouti, E., & Euwema, M. C. (2005). Job resources buffer the impact of job demands on burnout. *Journal of Occupational Health Psychology*, *10*(2), 170–180. doi:10.1037/1076-8998.10.2.170

Bakker, A. B., Demerouti, E., Oerlemans, W., & Sonnentag, S. (2013). Workaholism and daily recovery: A day reconstruction study of leisure activities. *Journal of Organizational Behavior*, *34*, 87–107. doi:10.1002/job.1796

Bakker, A. B., Demerouti, E., & Schaufeli, W. B. (2003). Dual processes at work in a call centre: An application of the job demands-resources model. *European Journal of Work and Organizational Psychology*, *12*(4), 393–417. doi:10.1080/13594320344000165

Bakker, A. B., & Leiter, M. P. (2010). *Work engagement: A handbook of essential theory and research*. New York: Taylor & Francis.

Bakker, A. B., Schaufeli, W. B., Leiter, M. P., & Taris, W. (2008). Work engagement: An emerging concept in occupational health psychology. *Work & Stress*, *22*(3), 187–200. doi:10.1080/02678370802393649

Bass, B. M., & Bass, R. (2008). The *bass handbook of leadership*: Theory, *research, and managerial applications*. New York: The Free Press.

Bass, B. M., & Riggio, R. E. (2006). Transformational leadership. Mahwah, NJ: Lawrence Erlbarum Associates, Inc.

Becker, T. E. (2005). Potential problems in the statistical control of variables in organizational research: A qualitative analysis with recommendations. *Organizational Research Methods*, *8*, 274–289. doi:10.1177/1094428105278021

Biggs, A. (2011). *A longitudinal evaluation of strain, work engagement, and intervention strategies to address the health of high-risk employees (Doctoral Thesis)*. Brisbane, Australia: Griffith University.

Biggs, A., Brough, P., & Barbour, J. P. (2014). Enhancing work-related attitudes and work engagement: A quasi-experimental study of the impact of an organizational intervention. *International Journal of Stress Management*, *21*(1), 43–68. doi:10.1037/a0034508

Blomme, R. J., Kodden, B., & Beasley-Suffolk, A. (2015). Leadership theories and the concept of work engagement: Creating a conceptual framework for management implications and research. *Journal of Management & Organization*, *21*(2), 125–144. doi:10.1017/jmo.2014.71

Braun, S., Peus, C., Weisweiler, S., & Frey, D. (2013). Transformational leadership, job satisfaction, and team performance: A multilevel mediation model of trust. *The Leadership Quarterly*, *24*, 270–283. doi:10.1016/j.leaqua.2012.11.006

Breevaart, K., Bakker, A. B., Hetland, J., Demerouti, E., Olsen, O. K., & Espevik, R. (2014). Daily transactional and transformational leadership and daily employee engagement. *Journal of Occupational and Organizational Psychology*, *87*, 138–157. doi:10.1111/joop.12041

Brough, P., Timms, C., Siu, O., Kalliath, T., O'Driscoll, M., Sit, C., … Lu, C. (2013). Validation of the Job Demands-Resources model in cross-national samples: Cross-sectional and longitudinal predictions of psychological strain and work engagement. *Human Relations*, *66*(10), 1311–1335. doi:10.1177/0018726712472915

Bryant, S. E. (2003). The role of transformational and transactional leadership in creating, sharing and exploiting organizational knowledge. *Journal of Leadership & Organizational Studies*, *9*(4), 32–44. doi:10.1177/107179190300900403

Buckingham, M., & Coffman, C. (1999). *First, break all of the rules. What the worlds greatest managers do differently*. New York, NY: Simon & Schuster.

Carless, S. A., Wearing, A. J., & Leon, M. (2000). A short measure of transformational leadership. *Journal of Business and Psychology*, *14*(3), 389–405. doi:10.1023/A:1022991115523

Cohen, S., & Willis, T. A. (1985). Stress, social support, and the buffering hypothesis. *Psychological Bulletin*, *98*, 310–357. doi:10.1037/0033-2909.98.2.310

Conway, J. M., & Lance, C. E. (2010). What reviewers should expect from authors regarding common method bias in organizational research. *Journal of Business Psychology*, 25, 325–334. doi:10.1007/s10869-010-9181-6

Demerouti, E., Bakker, A. B., Geurts, S. A. E., & Taris, T. W. (2009). Daily recovery from work-related effort during non-work time. In S. Sonnentag, P. L. Perrewe, & D. C. Ganster (Eds.), *Current perspectives on job-stress recovery (Research in occupational stress and well-being)* (Vol. 7, pp. 85–123): Emerald Group Publishing Limited.

Demerouti, E., Bakker, A. B., Nachreiner, F., & Schaufeli, W. B. (2001). The job demands-resources model of burnout. *Journal of Applied Psychology*, *86*(3), 499–512. doi:10.1037/0021-9010.86.3.499

Demerouti, E., Taris, T. W., & Bakker, A. B. (2007). Need for recovery, home–work interference and performance: Is lack of concentration the link? *Journal of Vocational Behavior*, *71*(2), 204–220. doi:10.1016/j.jvb.2007.06.002

Dollard, M. F., & Bakker, A. B. (2010). Psychosocial safety climate as a precursor to conducive work environments, psychological health problems, and employee engagement. *Journal of Occupational and Organizational Psychology*, *83*(3), 579–599. doi:10.1348/096317909X470690

Evans, M. G. (1985). A Monte Carlo study of the effects of correlated method variance in moderated multiple regression analysis. *Organizational Behavior and Human Decision Processes*, *36*(3), 305–323. doi:10.1016/0749-5978(85)90002-0

Ferguson, C. J., & Heene, M. (2012). A vast graveyard of undead theories publication bias and psychological science's aversion to the null. *Perspectives on Psychological Science*, *7*(6), 555–561. doi:10.1177/1745691612459059

Ghadi, M. Y., Fernando, M., & Caputi, P. (2013). Transformational leadership and work engagement: The mediating effect of meaning in work. *Leadership & Organization Development Journal*, *34*(6), 535–550

Hakanen, J. J., & Roodt, G. (2010). Using the job demands-resources model to predict engagement: Analysing a conceptual model. *Work engagement: A handbook of essential theory and research* (pp. 85–101). East Sussex, UK: Psychology Press.

Halbesleben, J. R. B., Harvey, J., & Bolino, M. C. (2009). Too engaged? A conservation of resources view of the relationship between work engagement and work interference with family. *Journal of Applied Psychology*, *94*(6), 1452–1465. doi:10.1037/a0017595

Hayati, D., Charkhabi, M., & Naami, A. Z. (2014). The relationship between transformational leadership and work engagement in governmental hospitals nurses: A survey study. *SpringerPlus*, *3*(1), 1–7. doi:10.1186/2193-1801-3-25

Hayes, A. F. (2012). PROCESS: A versatile computational tool for observed variable mediation, moderation, and conditional process modeling [White paper] Retrieved from http://www.afhayes.com/public/process2012.pdf

Hentrich, S., Zimber, A., Garbade, S. F., Gregersen, S., Nienhaus, A., & Petermann, F. (2017). Relationships between transformational leadership and health: The mediating role of perceived job demands and occupational self-efficacy. *International Journal of Stress Management*, *24*(1), 34–61. doi: 10.1037/str0000027

Herzberg, F. (1968). *One more time: How do you motivate employees* (pp. 46–57). Boston, MA: Harvard Business Review

Hobfoll, S. E. (2001). The influence of culture, community and the nested-self in the stress process: Advancing the Conservation of Resources theory. *Applied Psychology: An International Review, 50*, 337–421. doi:10.1111/1464-0597.00062

Jung, D. I., Chow, C., & Wu, A. (2003). The role of transformational leadership in enhancing organizational innovation: Hypotheses and some preliminary findings. *The Leadership Quarterly, 14*, 525–544. doi:10.1016/S1048-9843(03)00050-X

Katou, A. A. (2015). Transformational leadership and organisational performance: Three serially mediating mechanisms. *Employee Relations, 37*(3), 329–353. doi:10.1108/ER-05-2014-0056

Kinnunen, U., Mauno, S., & Siltaloppi, M. (2010). Job insecurity, recovery and well-being at work: Recovery experiences as moderators. *Economic and Industrial Democracy, 31*(2), 179–194. doi:10.1177/0143831X09358366

Kottke, J. L., & Sharafinski, C. E. (1988). Measuring perceived supervisory and organizational support. *Educational and Psychological Measurement, 48*, 1075–1079. doi:10.1177/0013164488484024

Koyuncu, M., Burke, R. J., & Fiksenbaum, L. (2006). Work engagement among women managers and professionals in a Turkish bank. *Equal Opportunities International, 25*(4), 299–310. doi:10.1108/02610150610706276

Liaw, Y. J., Chi, N. W., & Chuang, A. (2010). Examining the Mechanisms Linking Transformational Leadership, Employee Customer Orientation, and Service Performance: The Mediating Roles of Perceived Supervisor and Coworker Support. *Journal of Business and Psychology, 25*(3), 477–492. doi:10.1007/s10869-009-9145-x

Macey, W. H., & Schneider, B. (2008). The meaning of employee engagement. *Industrial and Organizational Psychology, 1*(1), 3–30. doi:10.1111/j.1754-9434.2007.0002.x

Maslach, C., Schaufeli, W. B., & Leiter, M. P. (2001). Job burnout. *Annual Review of Psychology, 52*(1), 397–422. doi:10.1146/annurev.psych.52.1.397

Mitchell, M. L., & Jolley, J. M. (2007). *Research design explained* (6th ed.). Belmont, CA: Thomson Wadsworth

Mojza, E. J., Sonnentag, S., & Bornemann, C. (2011). Volunteer work as a valuable leisure-time activity: A day-level study on volunteer work, non-work experiences, and well-being at work. *Journal of Occupational and Organizational Psychology, 84*, 123–152. doi:10.1348/096317910X485737

Moreno-Jiménez, B., Rodríguez-Muñoz, A., Sanz-Vergel, A. I., & Garrosa, E. (2012). Elucidating the role of recovery experiences in the job demands-resources model. *The Spanish Journal of Psychology, 15*(2), 659–669. doi:10.5209/rev_SJOP.2012.v15.n2.38877

Parker, S. K., & Griffin, M. A. (2011). Understanding active psychological states: Embedding engagement in a wider nomological net and closer attention to performance. *European Journal of Work and Organizational Psychology, 20*(1), 60–67. doi:10.1080/1359432X.2010.532869

Pejtersen, J. H., Kristensen, T. S., Borg, V., & Bjorner, J. B. (2010). The second version of the Copenhagen psychosocial questionnaire. *Scandinavian Journal of Public Health, 38*(3), 8–24. doi:10.1177/1403494809349858

Podsakoff, P. M., MacKenzie, S. B., Lee, J., & Podsakoff, N. P. (2003). Common method biases in behavioral research: A critical review of the literature and recommended remedies. *Journal of Applied Psychology, 88*(5), 879–903. doi:10.1037/0021-9010.88.5.879

Podsakoff, P. M., MacKenzie, S. B., Moorman, R. H., & Fetter, R. (1990). Transformational leader behaviors and their effects on followers' trust in leader, satisfaction, and organizational citizenship behaviors. *Leadership Quarterly, 1*(2), 107–142. doi:10.1016/1048-9843(90)90009-7

Preacher, K. J., & Hayes, A. F. (2008). Asymptotic and resampling strategies for assessing and comparing indirect effects in multiple mediator models. *Behavior Research Methods, 40*(3), 879–891. doi:10.3758/BRM.40.3.879

Rana, A., Arcdichvili, A., & Tkachenko, O. (2014). A theoretical model of the antecedents and outcomes of employee engagement. *Journal of Workplace Learning, 26*(3/4), 249–266. doi:10.1108/JWL-09-2013-0063

Robertson, I. T., & Cooper, C. L. (2010). Full engagement: The integration of employee engagement and psychological well-being. *Leadership & Organization Development Journal, 31*(4), 324–336. doi:10.1108/01437731011043348

Salanova, M., Schaufeli, W. B., Xanthopoulou, D., & Bakker, A. B. (2010). The gain spiral of resources and work engagement: Sustaining a positive worklife. In A. B. Bakker and M. P. Leiter (Eds). *Work engagement: A handbook of essential theory and research* (pp. 118–131). East Sussex, UK: Psychology Press.

Schaufeli, W. B., & Bakker, A. B. (2004). Job demands, job resources, and their relationship with burnout and engagement: A multi-sample study. *Journal of Organizational Behavior and Human Decision Processes, 25*(3), 293–315. doi:10.1002/job.248

Schaufeli, W. B., Bakker, A. B., & Salanova, M. (2006). The measurement of work engagement with a short questionnaire: A cross-national study. *Educational and Psychological Measurement, 66*(4), 701–716. doi:10.1177/0013164405282471

Schaufeli, W. B., Salanova, M., González-Romá, V., & Bakker, A. B. (2002). The measurement of engagement and burnout: A two sample confirmatory factor analytic approach. *Journal of Happiness Studies, 3*(1), 71–92. doi:10.1023/A:1015630930326

Schaufeli, W. B., & Taris, T. W. (2014). A critical review of the job demands-resources model: Implications for improving work and health. In G. F. Bauer & O. Hämmig (Eds.), *Bridging occupational, organizational and public health: 43A Transdisciplinary approach.* (pp. 43–68), Netherlands: Springer.

Schmitt, A., Den Hartog, D. N., & Belschak, F. D. (2016). Transformational leadership and proactive work behaviour: A moderated mediation model including work engagement and job strain. *Journal of Occupational and Organizational Psychology, 89*(3), 588–610. doi:10.1111/joop.12143

Shamir, B., House, R. J., & Arthur, M. B. (1993). The motivational effects of charismatic leadership: A self-concept based theory. *Organization Science, 4*(4), 577–594. doi:10.1287/orsc.4.4.577

Siltaloppi, M., Kinnunen, U., & Feldt, T. (2009). Recovery experiences as moderators between psychosocial work characteristics and occupational well-being. *Work & Stress, 23*(4), 330–348. doi:10.1080/02678370903415572

Siu, O., Lu, J., Brough, P., Lu, C., Bakker, A. B., Kalliath, T., … Shi, K. (2010). Role resources and work-family enrichment: The role of work engagement. *Journal of Vocational Behavior, 77*(3), 470–480. doi:10.1016/j.jvb.2010.06.007

Skakon, J., Nielsen, K., Borg, V., & Guzman, J. (2010). Are leaders' well-being, behaviours, and style associated with the affective well-being of their employees? A systematic review of three decades of research. *Work & Stress, 24*(2), 107–139. doi:10.1080/02678373.2010.495262

Song, J. H., Kolb, J. A., Lee, U. H., & Kim, H. K. (2012). Role of transformational leadership in effective organizational knowledge creation practices: Mediating effects of employees' work engagement. *Human Resource Development Quarterly, 23*, 65–101. 790 doi:10.1002/hrdq.21120

Sonnentag, S. (2003). Recovery, work engagement, and proactive behavior: A new look at the interface between nonwork and work. *Journal of Applied Psychology, 88*(3), 518.doi:10.1037/0021-9010.88.3.518

Sonnentag, S., Binnewies, C., & Mojza, E. J. (2008). Did you have a nice evening? A day-level study on recovery experiences, sleep, and affect. *Journal of Applied Psychology, 93*, 674–684. doi:10.1037/0021-9010.93.3.674

Sonnentag, S., Binnewies, C., & Mojza, E. J. (2010). Staying well and engaged when demands are high: The role of psychological detachment. *Journal of Applied Psychology, 95*(5), 965–976. doi:10.1037/a0020032

Sonnentag, S., & Fritz, C. (2007). The recovery experience questionnaire: Development and validation of a measure for assessing recuperation and unwinding from work. *Journal of Occupational Health Psychology, 12*(3), 204–221. doi:10.1037/1076-8998.12.3.204

Spector, P. E. (2006). Method variance in organizational research: Truth or urban legend? *Organizational Research Methods, 9*, 221–232. doi:10.1177/1094428105284955

Spreitzer, G. M. (1996). Social structural characteristics of psychological empowerment. *Academy of Management Journal, 39*(2), 483–504. doi:10.2307/256789

Thomas, K. W., & Velthouse, B. A. (1990). Cognitive elements of empowerment: An "interpretive" model of intrinsic task motivation. *Academy of Management Review, 15*(4), 666–681.

Tims, M., & Bakker, A. B. (2010). Job crafting: Towards a new model of job redesign. *South African Journal of Industrial Psychology, 36*, 1–9

Tims, M., Bakker, A. B., & Xanthopoulou, D. (2011). Do transformational leaders enhance their followers' daily work engagement? *The Leadership Quarterly, 22*, 121–131. doi:10.1016/j.leaqua.2010.12.011

Van den Broeck, A., Vansteenkiste, M., De Witte, H., & Lens, W. (2008). Explaining the relationships between job characteristics, burnout, and engagement: The role of basic psychological need satisfaction. *Work & Stress, 22*, 277–294. doi:10.1080/02678370802393672

Wang, X.-H., & Howell, J. M. (2010). Exploring the dual-level effects of transformational leadership on followers. *Journal of Applied Psychology, 95*(6), 1134–1144. doi:10.1037/a0020754

Wefald, A. J., Reichard, R. J., & Serrano, S. A. (2011). Fitting engagement into a nomological network: The relationship of engagement to leadership and personality. *Journal of Leadership & Organizational Studies, 18*(4), 522–537. doi:10.1177/1548051811404890

Wollard, K. K., & Shuck, B. (2011). Antecendents to employee engagement: A structured review of the literature. *Advances in Developing Human Resources, 13*(4), 429–446. doi:10.1177/1523422311431220

Xanthopoulou, D., Bakker, A. B., Demerouti, E., & Schaufeli, W. B. (2007). The role of personal resources in the job demands-resources model. *International Journal of Stress Management, 14*(2), 121–141. doi:10.1037/1072-5245.14.2.121

Xanthopoulou, D., Bakker, A. B., Demerouti, E., & Schaufeli, W. B. (2009). Reciprocal relationships between job resources, personal resources, and work engagement. *Journal of Vocational Behavior, 74*, 235–244. doi:10.1016/j.jvb.2008.11.003

Yukl, G. (2010). *Leadership in organizations* (7th ed.). Englewood Cliffs, NJ: Prentice Hall.

Zhu, W., Avolio, B. J., & Walumbwa, F. O. (2009). Moderating role of follower characteristics with transformational leadership and follower work engagement. *Group and Organizational Management, 34*(5), 590–619. doi:10.1177/1059601108331242

Zhu, W., May, D. R., & Avolio, B. J. (2004). The impact of ethical leadership behavior on employee outcomes: The roles of psychological empowerment and authenticity. *Journal of Leadership & Organizational Studies, 11*(1), 16–26. doi:10.1177/107179190401100104

What Does Leaders' Character Add to Transformational Leadership?

Patrick Liborius

ABSTRACT
The influence of leaders' character (e.g., integrity, humility/forgiveness) has rarely been examined in leadership research. The current investigation focused on the impact of integrity and humility/forgiveness on both followers' perceptions of leaders' worthiness of being followed (WBF) and stress. Results from a scenario experiment ($n = 347$) and a field study ($n = 110$) indicated that these aspects incrementally predict WBF above and beyond the impact of transformational leadership. Similar results were found concerning followers' stress with the exception of leader integrity in the field study. According to relative importance analyses, integrity and transformational leadership predict WBF equally well. The results have conceivable implications for human resources (personnel selection and development). Future research should examine additional outcome variables that are affected by certain leader characteristics as well as potential negative effects of the examined character aspects.

Prior to investigating any individual aspect of leadership character and virtue (e.g., integrity, humility/forgiveness), several leadership constructs that contain one or more such aspects have been shown to be positively related to desired outcome variables (e.g., performance, trust, satisfaction). These leadership constructs include Ethical Leadership (Brown & Treviño, 2006), Servant Leadership (Greenleaf, 1977), Authentic Leadership (George, 2003; Avolio & Gardner, 2005), Spiritual Leadership (Fry, 2003), and Worthy Leadership (Thompson, Grahek, Phillips, & Fay, 2008). In recent years, researchers have (e.g., Palanski & Yammarino, 2011) begun to focus more on specific character aspects as well as the empirical examination of their specific impact on certain outcome variables. In empirical leadership research, the aspect of integrity is the one most frequently addressed. Still, Moorman, Darnold, and Priesemuth (2013) found it fair to question whether this amount of research is enough to support the idea that integrity is an axiomatic characteristic of effective leadership. Humility is another aspect of leadership character that has received some attention in the research literature. However, the first empirical examination of the effect of humility on followers was not conducted until 2013 (Owens, Johnson, & Mitchell, 2013). Today, the importance of humility has been captured by several scholars (e.g., Sousa & van Dierendonck,

2015), and calls to further examine this aspect are made, for example by Owens et al. (2013) who call for research examining the relationship between leader humility and followers' psychological and physical health.

Simons, Palanski, and Treviño (2013) posed the question whether integrity is able to predict outcomes above and beyond existing constructs (i.e., transformational leadership). The aim of the present study is to begin to answer this question, for two aspects of character—integrity and humility/forgiveness—on two important outcomes (i.e., followers' perception of their leader as worthy of being followed, and stress). In order to understand the role of leader character, we have to examine the incremental validity of these character aspects above and beyond the impact of already well-studied leadership concepts (i.e., transformational leadership). If leadership character does not have an additional positive influence on outcome variables, future research may not be worthwhile. The transformational leadership concept is most suitable to answer this research question because it has dominated current thinking about leadership as indicated by the fact that more studies on transformational leadership were published in the last three decades than on all other popular theories of leadership combined (Judge & Piccolo, 2004; Kovjanic, Schuh, Jonas, van Quaquebeke, & Dick, 2012; Zhu, Newman, Miao, & Hooke, 2013). Another reason is that positive effects of transformational leadership on both followers and organizations have been demonstrated in numerous studies worldwide (Judge & Piccolo, 2004; Wang, Oh, Courtright, & Colbert, 2011).

The purpose of the current study was to provide new information concerning the impact of leadership character (i.e., integrity, humility/forgiveness) above and beyond the impact of transformational leadership (measured by a German translation of the 4 Is of the MLQ; Bass & Avolio, 1990; Geyer & Steyrer, 1998) on two important outcomes: leaders' worthiness of being followed (WBF) and followers' perceived stress. These variables were chosen based on past empirical research of transformational leadership, integrity, and humility, and the call for research presented above.

Transformational Leadership

Transformational leadership consists of four components: idealized influence, inspirational motivation, intellectual stimulation, and individual consideration (Bass, 1998). Idealized influence refers to leaders who serve as role models by acting in a manner that is admired by many people. These leaders communicate a sense of purpose for all employees and articulate high expectations regarding company or group goals. They are able and willing to pursue these goals with self-sacrificing behavior (Bass & Avolio, 1994). Inspirational motivation implies communicating a clear vision, obtaining commitment to this vision from subordinates, and generating optimism that this vision can be achieved (Avolio, 1999). Intellectual stimulation involves encouraging followers to look at problems in a new and different way. It also stimulates creativity in followers by encouraging them to think innovatively and independently. Leaders ask their followers to question common ways of working and develop even better ways. In addition, they view their subordinates as a source of work-related ideas (Bass & Avolio, 1994). Individualized consideration includes the attention to followers' needs as well as acting as a mentor. Leaders show a genuine concern for their followers' well-being (Judge & Piccolo, 2004).

Transformational Leadership and Integrity

Transformational leadership by original definition (Bass, 1985) did not include integrity. Subsequently, Bass and Steidlmeier (1999) revised the concept with the supposition that authentic transformational leaders are by definition ethical, whereas pseudo-transformational leaders lack integrity. They aimed to create a moral version of transformational leadership, knowing that transformational leadership can be used in an egoistic manner, which they called pseudo-transformational leadership. Bass and Steidlmeier stated that authentic transformational leaders differ in that they have virtues of integrity, truthfulness, and credibility. Based on the definitions of George (2003) and Palanski and Yammarino (2007), leaders' integrity refers to the consistency of an acting leader's words and actions, which includes reliable, honest, and promise-keeping behavior. Still, leaders with transformational attributes described above can lack integrity, although their impact on followers may be questionable as a result. Nevertheless, transformational leadership is conceptually related to integrity although empirical evidence is modest. Some researchers have found positive relations between transformational leadership and perceived leader integrity (Engelbrecht, van Aswegen, & Theron, 2005; Parry & Proctor-Thomson, 2002; Tracey & Hinkin, 1994). MLQ items (which have also been used in the present study) also relate positively to integrity (Parry & Proctor-Thomson, 2002). Still, although perceptions of leaders' integrity are closely related to transformational leadership, transformational leaders do not necessarily display the full range of integrity. In addition, measures of transformational leadership do not capture the concept in its entirety. Likewise, Palanski and Yammarino (2007), as well as Leroy, Palanski, and Simons (2012) stated that despite similarities and high correlations between authentic leadership and behavioral integrity, they are not the same. In other words, transformational leadership and integrity are distinct concepts with both shared and unique aspects. Thus, integrity is suggested to explain leadership outcomes above and beyond the impact of transformational leadership.

Transformational Leadership and Humility

Giampetro-Meyer, Brown, Browne, and Kubasek (1998) suggested that transformational leaders may be overly narcissistic and self-centered, attributes that are both opponents of humility. The origin of the word humility is based on the Latin word humilis, which literally means "on the ground." This grounded view has nothing to do with inferiority. Rather, it enables individuals to see themselves and others more accurately in terms of their respective strengths and weaknesses (Owens, Rowatt, & Wilkins, 2011; Weick, 2011). Thus, humble leaders hold neither inappropriately grandiose nor self-deprecating views of themselves. Instead, they possess a realistic vision of who they are as well as which abilities they do and do not possess (Nielsen, Marrone, & Slay, 2010). Some empirical evidence comes from Khoo and Burch (2008), who found moderately large correlations between attributed idealized influence and the Hogan Development survey (HDS; Hogan, 1997) theme "bold," which includes feelings of grandiosity and overestimation of one's abilities—i.e., the opposite of humility. On the other hand, humility most closely resembles the transformational leadership concept of individualized consideration—i.e., non-egocentric behavior toward one's subordinates in the form of individualized guiding and coaching. Basford, Offermann, and Behrend (2014) argued that a leader who does not communicate humility does not demonstrate individualized consideration and is instead self-focused, caring only little about followers' well-being. However, humility is more than merely caring for someone. Rather, it also includes a passive component of being open, supportive, and encouraging, by receiving everything gratefully and not placing oneself at the center of attention, in addition to knowing one's own limitations. Empirical evidence came from a study by Owens et al. (2011) in which 1,500 employee ratings of their leaders indicated that humility is conceptually distinct from transformational leadership.

Humility, knowing oneself to be imperfect and being aware of one's weaknesses and failures, is mandatory to practice forgiveness. Grenberg (2005, in Sousa & van Dierendonck, 2015) suggests that humility is a kind of meta-virtue that forms the foundation of other virtues such as forgiveness. Thus, humility and forgiveness will merge in practice, both will be treated as a single combined construct—humility/forgiveness—in the current study. Forgiveness means engaging in constructive responses following an interpersonal offense instead of allowing destructive thoughts, feelings, and behaviors (Owens & Hekman, 2012). For Peterson and Seligman (2004), forgiveness is a behavior that is manifested in granting pardon to those who mistreated us. Based on these attributes, the definition of leaders' humility and forgiveness from Grahek, Thompson, and Toliver (2010) is applied. They combined humility and forgiveness as effectively handling oneself in a non-egocentric, positive, and offense-resistant manner. Thus, it is suggested that leaders' humility/forgiveness is more than described and measured within the "4 Is" of transformational leadership and therefore explains leadership outcomes above and beyond the impact of transformational leadership.

Worthiness of Being Followed

Chiu, Huang, and Hung (2012) stated that "leaders should allow subordinates to be willing to follow leaders" (p. 132). In addition, Jenkins (2011) argued that researchers should examine whom followers will follow. This is exactly what the WBF concept does. It measures followers' willingness to follow a leader (i.e., followers' perception of their leader as worthy of being followed). The concept of WBF is defined as employees' perception of their leader as worthy of being followed and is based on subordinates' feelings of loyalty toward their leader as well as their perception of their leader as a competent leader and role model (Liborius, 2014). Basford et al. (2014) found a positive relation between transformational leadership and subordinate loyalty. Transformational leaders inspire their followers and are viewed as a role model because they communicate sense-giving missions and encourage commitment to those missions in their followers. Thus, it is hypothesized that transformational leaders will be perceived as worthy of being followed.

Hypothesis 1: Transformational leadership is positively related to WBF.

Integrity has been shown to be one of the most important aspects to engender followers' respect (Reave, 2005), which leaders receive from their subordinates when they are viewed as worthy of being followed. Honesty, another sub-construct of integrity, is a character attribute that nearly 90% of survey participants (Kouzes & Posner, 2004) look for in leaders whom they will willingly follow. Thus, followers perceive leaders with integrity as worthy of being followed.

Hypothesis 2a: Leaders' integrity is positively related to WBF.

Dotlich and Cairo (2003) showed that many of the complaints subordinates have about their leaders concern arrogant behavior—i.e., the opposite of humility. Thus, arrogant leaders will not be seen as being worthy of being followed by their employees. Instead, subordinates distrust such leaders and are not motivated to behave loyally. Sousa and van Dierendonck (2015) and Nielsen et al. (2010) argued that employees' perception of leaders' humility is related to perceived leader competence and subordinate loyalty toward their leader. In addition, Exline and Geyer (2004, in Nielsen et al., 2010) found a positive association between humility and leadership ability. Consequently, the following is suggested:

Hypothesis 2b: Leaders' humility/forgiveness is positively related to WBF.

As stated above, integrity and humility/forgiveness are suggested to have an impact on WBF above and beyond the impact of transformational leadership. Thus, the following hypotheses were derived:

Hypothesis 3a: Leaders' integrity is positively related to WBF above and beyond the effect of transformational leadership.

Hypothesis 3b: Leaders' humility/forgiveness is positively related to WBF above and beyond the effect of transformational leadership.

Followers' Perceived Stress Level

Perceived stress can be viewed as an outcome variable measuring the experienced level of stress as a function of objective stressful events, coping processes, and personality factors (Cohen, Kamarck, & Mermelstein, 1983). Cohen et al.'s perceived stress scale items were designed to assess the degree to which individuals perceive their lives to be unpredictable, uncontrollable, and overloading. These aspects represent central components of individuals' stress experience (Cohen et al., 1983). In the present study, this definition and operationalization were adopted. It is assumed that transformational leadership, integrity, and humility/forgiveness each have the potential to reduce (the emergence of) subordinates' stress level. Transformational leaders have the potential to encourage their followers through individual consideration. Moreover, transformational leaders' intellectual stimulation can change negative thoughts into constructive ones and, as a result, reduce subordinates' stress levels. In addition, leaders' intellectual stimulation may help followers solve problems that may have otherwise acted as stressors. Through inspirational motivation and idealized influence, transformational leaders help their subordinates to transcend their self-interests and work in the interest of the group or company. As a result, subordinates perceive greater meaning in their work, which is an aspect that may increase satisfaction and thus lower stress levels (Bass, 1999). Gill, Flaschner, and Shachar (2006) found a significant negative relationship between job stress and transformational leadership. Arnold, Turner, Barling, Kelloway, and McKee (2007) showed that transformational leadership was positively related to affective well-being and mental health, which can both be considered at the opposite end of the spectrum as compared to perceived stress. Thus, the following is hypothesized.

Hypothesis 4: Transformational leadership is negatively related to followers' perception of stress.

High behavioral integrity on the part of a leader is a strong indicator that the leader's word can be trusted. This provides a sense of certainty and enables followers to make sense of situations (Simons, Friedman, Liu, & McLean Parks, 2007). Leaders with behavioral integrity provide their followers with a kind of control concerning their work. Control is a major theme in the literature on stress (Ganster & Murphy, 2000). Moreover, leader integrity should lead to lower perceived stress and uncertainty in the workplace, as it provides a sense of safety, in that it is perceived as trustworthiness, morality, and consistency between the leader's words and actions. Finally, by reducing uncertainty, stress will also be reduced (Greco & Roger, 2003). The study of Andrews, Kacmar, and Kacmar (2015) revealed a negative relation between behavioral integrity and job tension after controlling for other variables (i.e., hours of work, organizational tenure, and gender). Thus, the following is hypothesized.

Hypothesis 5a: Leaders' integrity is negatively related to followers' perception of stress.

Leaders' lack of appreciation and unfair behavior cause followers to experience stress. Leaders with humility understand the need to respect others (Chiu et al., 2012). Leaders' correct understanding of their followers is also important for them to be able to correctly assess how much their followers can successfully bear. Moreover, humble leaders are proposed to be supportive (Morris, Brotheridge, & Urbanski, 2005), which is one potential aspect to reduce stress. Other aspects include an interest in, understanding of, and caring for employees, which leaders acting with humility will display. Owens and Hekman (2012) further proposed that a leader's humble behaviors can increase the sense of personal freedom and engagement among followers by legitimizing their developmental journey, which takes pressure away from the followers and, thus, reduces their stress levels. In addition, leaders who are aware of their own shortcomings show followers that they can understand their own mistakes (Owens & Hekman, 2012). This means that making mistakes in front of the leader is not necessarily stress inducing. In contrast, when non-humble leaders appear to have all the answers themselves (Owens & Hekman, 2012), followers easily feel like they cannot do anything well enough to please their leader, which can also result in an increased stress level. In addition, forgiveness is a great way to handle interpersonal conflict, which has been shown to be significantly linked to health problems within a longitudinal study of several thousands of Finnish and Swedish employees (Hyde, Jappinen, Theorell, & Oxenstierna, 2006). Consequently, the following is hypothesized.

Hypothesis 5b: Leaders' humility/forgiveness is negatively related to followers' perception of stress.

As stated above, integrity and humility/forgiveness are suggested to have an impact on followers' perceived stress above and beyond the impact of transformational leadership. Thus, the following hypotheses were derived:

Hypothesis 6a: Leaders' integrity is negatively related to followers' perception of stress above and beyond the effect of transformational leadership.

Hypothesis 6b: Leaders' humility/forgiveness is negatively related to followers' perception of stress above and beyond the effect of transformational leadership.

All hypotheses were tested in two studies—the first using an experimental design in two scenario studies to test for causality (Study 1); the second using a field study (Study 2) to provide external validity. The concepts of both studies and their results are described in the following sections.

Study 1 Method

Participants and Procedures

Prior to conducting field research, the effects of transformational leadership, integrity, and humility/forgiveness must first be examined by means of scenario experiments (cf. Avolio, Mahtre, Norman, & Lester, 2009a; Liborius, 2014; Palanski & Yammarino, 2011) to provide evidence of causal effects on followers' perceived stress and perceptions of WBF. Neither effect has been previously tested in this manner.

Therefore, an e-mail was distributed with an invitation to take part in a leadership study to various contacts through personal, professional, and online networks. Participants were asked to read a scenario and complete the target survey and had the chance to win one of six 50-Euro gift certificates for a well-known online retailer. A sample of 347 German participants took part in the online survey. After following the link in the invitation e-mail, participants were randomly assigned to one of eight different experimental conditions (transformational leadership high vs. low combined with integrity high vs. low, and transformational leadership high vs. low combined with humility/forgiveness high vs. low). At the first page, they read the explanation of the purpose of the study, and it was emphasized that participation is voluntary and confidential and that the completion will take about 10 minutes. They then read a scenario involving a fictitious supervisor who showed behavior either related to transformational leadership and integrity or transformational leadership and humility/forgiveness, depending on condition. Each scenario (copies from the scenario can be obtained from the author) was written in a manner so that participants were directly confronted with the behavior of their supervisor. After reading the scenario, participants responded to manipulation check items as well as items assessing the dependent variables and demographic information. Participants were assured that there are no right or wrong answers, rather only answers that fit their true impressions and anticipated reactions.

A total of 347 people completed the survey (61.8% female). On average, participants were 27.74 ($SD = 9.87$) years old and had an average work experience of 5.95 years ($SD = 8.49$). Twenty-five percent of participants currently held leadership positions.

Measures

For purposes of brevity, only a small number of items were selected to measure each variable (cf. Meierhans, Rietmann, & Jonas, 2008). All items were answered on a six-point scale ranging from 1 (strongly disagree) to 6 (strongly agree). Higher scores indicate higher levels of the respective variable.

Transformational Leadership

The appropriateness of the transformational leadership manipulation was checked using three items for each of the four aspects (12 items) of the Multifactor Leadership Questionnaire (MLQ; Bass & Avolio, 1990; German translation by Geyer & Steyrer, 1998). As in previous studies (e.g., Gilmore, Wei, Tetrick, & Zaccaro, 2013), the four dimensions of transformational leadership, although conceptually distinct, were viewed as parts of a higher order construct.

Integrity

The items for the integrity manipulation check were orientated on the above-given definition ("My supervisor does what he says.", "My supervisor's words and deeds fit together.", "My supervisor is honest.", "I can rely on my supervisor.") and were already used by Liborius (2014).

Humility/Forgiveness

The successful manipulation of humility/forgiveness was tested with four items—two concerning humility ("My supervisor is humble" & "My supervisor considers himself as something better (inverted)") and two concerning forgiveness ("My supervisor tends to hold grudges (inverted)", "My supervisor shows himself as indulgent") and were also already used by Liborius (2014).

Worthiness of Being Followed (WBF)

Based on the concept of WBF (Liborius, 2014), the scale combines items measuring loyalty (Rich, 1997, e.g., "I feel a strong loyalty towards my supervisor."), competence (Mayer & Davis, 1999, e.g., "My supervisor is very capable of performing his/her job."), and role modeling (Rich, 1997, e.g., "My supervisor provides a good model for me to follow."). WBF was operationalized as the mean of these three constructs, which were measured with two items each.

Stress

Three items from the Perceived Stress Scale (Cohen & Williamson, 1988) were used to measure job specific stress as well as stress that participants perceive in their everyday lives as a result of leaders' behavior (e.g., "In the last month, I have often felt nervous and stressed.").

Adaptation of Item Formulation To Fit the Scenario

The items of the dependent variables (i.e., WBF and stress) were formulated with an additional conditional clause to fit the experiment scenario. For example, the item "In the last month, I have often felt nervous and stressed." was rephrased to "Based on the situations that I experienced with my supervisor in the scenario, I can imagine that I often felt nervous or stressed within the last month."

Neuroticism

Followers' perceived stress has been shown to correlate with their neuroticism (Denney & Frisch, 1981), which is defined as a predisposition to experience negative affect (McCrae, 1990). For this reason, neuroticism was included as a control variable when analyzing stress in this study. Neuroticism was measured using three items from the BFI-K (Rammstedt & John, 2005)—e. g., "I feel depressed and dejected easily.").

Demographics

Participants gender (female/male), age (in years), work experience (in years), if participants are subordinated to a leader now (yes/no), and if yes for how long (in years), were also assessed. Finally, participants were asked if they are in a leadership position themselves (yes/no), and if yes for how long (in years).

Study 1 Results

Confirmatory Factor Analysis

The validity of the measurement model of the dependent variables was tested by means of confirmatory factor analysis. Kelloway (1998) noted that the quality of a measurement model is based on two aspects. First, it provides a good fit to the data. Second, it fits the data better than alternative models. The results demonstrated that the hypothesized 2-factor model of WBF and stress fit the model well ($\chi^2 = 44.70$; $df = 24$; RMSEA = .05, CFI = .99, TLI = .99, SRMR = .02). Within this model, two loyalty items from the WBF scale as well as two competence items were allowed to covary due to their similar wording (see Moorman et al., 2013). The model was compared against two alternative models: one combining all items in a single factor; and one containing four separate constructs, three of which represented each of the WBF sub-scales. The hypothesized model demonstrates superior fit to both alternative models, indicating the validity of the measurement model of the dependent variables.

Descriptive Statistics

Table 1 presents the means, standard deviations, internal consistency, and intercorrelations of all variables in the study for the transformational leadership plus integrity manipulation ($N = 175$) and the transformational plus humility/forgiveness manipulation ($N = 172$).

Manipulation Checks

Several analyses of variance (ANOVAs) were conducted to demonstrate that the transformational leadership, integrity, and humility/forgiveness manipulations were successful. Results indicated the manipulations for transformational leadership ($F(1, 172) = 211.5, \eta 2 = .55, p = .00, M_{low} = 2.16, M_{high} = 4.13$; $F(1, 170) = 192.4, \eta 2 = .53, p = .00, M_{low} = 2.14, M_{high} = 4.08$), integrity ($F(1, 172) = 181.7, \eta 2 = .51, p = .00, M_{low} = 1.95, M_{high} = 4.24$), and humility/forgiveness ($F(1, 170) = 206.8, \eta 2 = .55, p = .00, M_{low} = 2.86, M_{high} = 4.00$) were successful.

In addition, discriminant and convergent validity of the manipulation for character and transformational leadership were checked; whether the character manipulations were each influencing the intended aspect of the leader in the scenario and not the perception of transformational leadership, and vice versa. Results show high correlations between the manipulation and the

Table 1. Correlations and reliabilities from the transformational leadership + integrity and transformational leadership + humility/forgiveness scenarios.

	Variable	M	SD	1	2	3	4	5
1	Transformational leadership	–	–	–	–	.67	−.23	.10
2	Integrity/humility/forgiveness	–	–	–	–	.43	−.31	.10
3	Worthiness of being followed (WBF)	3.03/3.04	1.51/1.46	.59	.43	(.96/.96)	−.45	.03
4	Stress	3.62/3.69	1.01/1.13	−.36	−.23	−.53	(.70/.83)	.14
5	Neuroticism	3.21/3.22	0.97/1.04	−.08	.07	−.01	.20	(.77/.81)

Note. Correlations in study 1 (N = 175) are presented below the diagonal, and correlations in study 2 (N = 172) are presented above the diagonal. Reliabilities are presented in the diagonal, whereas the first number belongs to study 1 and the second to study 2; the same is true for means and standard deviations of the dependent variables. Transformational leadership, integrity, and humility/forgiveness have been manipulated (and therefore coded 0/1); so mean and standard deviation have been omitted.

associated manipulation-check items ($r = .72–.74$) and low correlations only between the manipulation and the manipulation-check items of the other manipulated aspect ($r = .25–.38$).

Hypothesis Testing

The hypotheses were first tested separately for each of the two scenarios using one-way multivariate analyses of variance (MANOVA): 1) transformational leadership + integrity, 2) transformational leadership + humility/forgiveness on WBF and stress, respectively. For each scenario, a 2 × 2 MANOVA was performed to help protect against inflating the Type 1 error rate in the follow-up ANOVAs.

First, all hypotheses were tested by means of multivariate MANOVA, whereby the transformational leadership (high vs. low) and the leadership character (high vs. low) manipulation were used as the two factor variables, and WBF and stress were set as the dependent variables. Multivariate statistics indicated that in the first scenario, both transformational leadership ($F(2, 171) = 63.85$, $p = .00$; Wilk's $\Lambda = .57$) and integrity ($F(2, 171) = 32.18$, $p = .00$; Wilk's $\Lambda = .73$) influenced participants' WBF and stress, and that in the second scenario, both transformational leadership ($F(2, 168) = 101.25$, $p = .00$; Wilk's $\Lambda = .45$) and humility/forgiveness ($F(2, 168) = 44.37$, $p = .00$; Wilk's $\Lambda = .65$)influenced participants' WBF and stress. Means for WBF and stress within each experimental combination of transformational leadership and character are displayed in Table 2.

Next, univariate statistics were considered to test each hypothesis separately, in order to gain insights on the impact on each of the two dependent variables and on the amount of incremental impact the character aspects have above and beyond the impact of transformational leadership on WBF and stress. Please refer to Table 3 for an overview of tested hypotheses and related statistics.

In summary, all hypotheses were supported. Thus, it appears that transformational leadership, integrity, and humility/forgiveness, on their own, influence WBF and followers' perceived stress level, such that WBF is higher when transformational leadership, leaders' integrity, and leaders' humility/forgiveness is high rather than low. In addition, integrity and humility/forgiveness also had an effect on both WBF and followers' perceived stress level above and beyond that of transformational leadership alone. Transformational leadership influences the perception of followers' perceived stress level, such that employees having a leader high in transformational leadership, anticipate less stress than employees' with a

Table 2. Means for WBF and stress within each experimental condition.

Group means in the TL+Int scenario		
	WBF	stress
TL low/Int low	1.67	4.12
TL low/Int high	2.61	3.85
TL high/Int low	3.12	3.57
TL high/Int high	4.72	2.94
group means in the TL+H&F scenario		
TL low/H&F low	1.56	4.30
TL low/H&F high	2.59	3.59
TL high/H&F low	3.26	3.76
TL high/H&F high	4.76	3.10

Note. TL = transformational leadership manipulation. Int = integrity manipulation. H&F = humility/forgiveness manipulation.

Table 3. Study 1—Overview of tested hypotheses and statistics.

	Hypothesis	statistic	*p*
1	Transformational leadership is positively related to WBF.	1) $\eta^2 = .34$ 2) $\eta^2 = .44$	.00
2a	Leaders' integrity is positively related to WBF.	$\eta^2 = .18$	.00
2b	Leaders' humility/forgiveness is positively related to WBF.	$\eta^2 = .19$	.00
3a	Leaders' integrity is positively related to WBF above and beyond the effect of transformational leadership.	$\Delta\eta^2 = .18$	.00
3b	Leaders' humility/forgiveness is positively related to WBF above and beyond the effect of transformational leadership.	$\Delta\eta^2 = .19$	.00
4	Transformational leadership is negatively related to followers' perception of stress.	1) $\eta^2 = .13$ 2) $\eta^2 = .05$	.00
5a	Leaders' integrity is negatively related to followers' perception of stress.	$\eta^2 = .05$	.00
5b	Leaders' humility/forgiveness is negatively related to followers' perception of stress.	$\eta^2 = .09$	.00
6a	Leaders' integrity is negatively related to followers' perception of stress above and beyond the effect of transformational leadership.	$\Delta\eta^2 = .05$	.00
6b	Leaders' humility/forgiveness is negatively related to followers' perception of stress above and beyond the effect of transformational leadership.	$\Delta\eta^2 = .09$	.00

Note. Hypotheses 1, 2, 4, and 5 were examined by means of ANOVA. Since both factors (transformational leadership and integrity or humility/forgiveness) are uncorrelated, the statistics of hypothesis 2 (η^2) and 3 ($\Delta\eta^2$), as well as for hypothesis 5 (η^2) and 6 ($\Delta\eta^2$) are identical. For hypotheses 1 and 4, two samples were available: 1) Transformational leadership + integrity, 2) transformational leadership + humility/forgiveness.

leader low in transformational leadership. Both integrity and humility/forgiveness had an additional impact on followers' perception of stress, such that employees with leaders high in integrity and humility/forgiveness, anticipate less stress than employees' with a leader low in integrity and humility/forgiveness, respectively.

Study 2 Method

Participants and Procedures

Study 2 was utilized to validate the effects observed in study 1 using field data. To do so, an online survey was conducted in which initial contacts and their social networks were invited to participate in an online survey on leadership. The initial contacts included in this sample did not participate in study 1. In order to participate in the study, participants had to be at least 18 years of age, working with their current supervisor for at least 3 months and have at least a 16-hour work week. Once they followed the invitation link, participants read the explanation of the purpose of the study first, and it was emphasized that participation is voluntary and confidential and that the completion will take about 10 minutes. Participants were then asked to think about their current supervisor and their work under his or her supervision while completing the online questionnaire.

One hundred ten employees (60.9% female) ranging in age from 18 to 60 years (M = 29.13, SD = 10.24) participated in the study after receiving an invitation e-mail with a link to the questionnaire. Participants were employees from a wide range of organizations in Germany from different sectors. Time at current job ranged from 3 months to 18 years (M = 3.32 years, SD = 3.04 years). All participants had at least some secondary education. Fifty-nine participants worked full time. Twenty-nine participants held leadership positions.

The described method of data collection is similar to recruiting participants via e-mail, newspaper, and flyer (Dalal, Baysinger, Brummel, & LeBreton, 2012). It results in an independent sample including participants working for diverse companies and supervisors.

Measures

To ensure consistency across both studies, participants' perceptions of their supervisors' transformational leadership, integrity, humility/forgiveness, and WBF as well as participants' perceived stress levels were measured using the same items as in Study 1. All items were measured on a six-point scale ranging from 1 (strongly disagree) to 6 (strongly agree). Demographic questions such as gender, age, work and leader experience, as well as the question for how long participants have worked under their current supervisor were included at the end of the survey.

Study 2 Results

Descriptive Statistics

Table 4 displays the means, standard deviations, internal consistencies, and intercorrelations of all variables in the study.

Confirmatory Factor Analysis

As displayed in Table 4, relatively high correlations were found between transformational leadership, integrity, humility/forgiveness, and WBF, which may indicate the presence of common method bias. Thus, the hypothesized measurement model was tested against alternative models in which items from these constructs loaded on to the same factor. First, Harmon's single-factor test (Podsakoff & Organ, 1986) was used, which checks whether variance can be largely attributed to a single factor. The hypothesized model was superior to the alternative model. The hypothesized model was also tested against a two-factor model (one factor for all predictors and one factor for all dependent variables) and a three-factor model (a predictor factor and two dependent variables factors). Finally, it was tested whether a six-factor model (humility and forgiveness separated) may fit the data better, which was also not the case. Thus, the hypothesized five-factor model adequately fit the data ($\chi^2 = 282.92$; $df = 178$; RMSEA $= .08$, CFI $= .94$, TLI $= .93$, SRMR $= .05$).

Table 4. Correlations and reliabilities for study 2.

	Variable	M	SD	1	2	3	4	5	6
1	Transformational leadership	4.02	1.08	(.92)					
2	Integrity	4.57	1.12	.82	(.89)				
3	Humility/forgiveness	4.15	1.05	.64	.58	(.70)			
4	Worthiness of being followed	4.24	1.37	.87	.86	.65	(.95)		
5	Stress	3.05	1.28	−.13	−.15	−.27	−.16	(.75)	
6	Neuroticism	3.21	1.13	−.25	−.25	−.25	−.24	.47	(.79)

Note. N = 110.

Table 5. Study 2—Overview of tested hypotheses and statistics.

Hypothesis		statistic	*p*
1	Transformational leadership is positively related to WBF.	$\beta = .88$	.00
2a	Leaders' integrity is positively related to WBF.	$\beta = .86$	.00
2b	Leaders' humility/forgiveness is positively related to WBF.	$\beta = .64$	.00
3a	Leaders' integrity is positively related to WBF above and beyond the effect of transformational leadership.	$\Delta R^2 = .06$	.00
3b	Leaders' humility/forgiveness is positively related to WBF above and beyond the effect of transformational leadership.	$\Delta R^2 = .01$	.03
4	Transformational leadership is negatively related to followers' perception of stress.	$\beta = -.13$	.19
5a	Leaders' integrity is negatively related to followers' perception of stress.	$\beta = -.15$	.11
5b	Leaders' humility/forgiveness is negatively related to followers' perception of stress.	$\beta = -.26$	.01
6a	Leaders' integrity is negatively related to followers' perception of stress above and beyond the effect of transformational leadership.	$\Delta R^2 = .00$	.54
6b	Leaders' humility/forgiveness is negatively related to followers' perception of stress above and beyond the effect of transformational leadership.	$\Delta R^2 = .03$	.02

Note. N = 110. WBF = Worthiness of being followed. Hypotheses 1, 2, 4, and 5 were examined by means of regression analyses. Hypotheses 3 and 6 were examined by means of hierarchical regression analyses. The statistics in the rows of hypothesis 3 and 6 are the increased explanation of variance by adding integrity and humility/forgiveness, respectively.

Hypothesis Testing

Regression analyses were applied to test hypotheses 1–2 and 4–5. For hypotheses 3 and 6, the incremental effects of integrity and humility/forgiveness were analyzed by means of hierarchical regression analyses. Therefore, first transformational leadership was entered as the predictor variable, and subsequently, integrity and humility/forgiveness were added, respectively, to the regression model. Whether the explanation of variance in the depended variable increases was tested by adding integrity and humility/forgiveness, respectively. Please refer to Table 5 for an overview of tested hypotheses and related statistics. In summary, except for hypotheses 4, 5a, and 6a, all other hypotheses yielded statistical support. Transformational leadership and leaders' integrity did not relate to employees' perception of stress.

Because of the strong correlations between the independent and dependent variables, variance inflation factor (VIF; O'Brien, 2007) was calculated for the regression models testing hypotheses 3 and 6. VIF values were all under four, indicating that collinearity was not a serious problem.

In addition, relative importance of each predictor has been assessed on each of the two outcome variables using relative weight analysis (Johnson, 2000), which has been shown to be the preferred method over the more common analysis of multiple regression weights (Tonidandel & LeBreton, 2011). Even so the analysis of relative importance is theory driven, it lacks specific hypotheses. Instead, the goal is to obtain a general idea of the degree to which the character aspects contribute to the regression on WBF and followers' perceived stress as compared to transformational leadership. Based on the analysis, integrity had the same strong relation on WBF as transformational leadership. Both integrity and transformational leadership had a stronger relation to WBF than humility/forgiveness. The only predictor that had a relation to followers' perceived stress—in addition to neuroticism—was humility/forgiveness. Even though the relation on stress was statistically significant in the hypothesized direction, the relation of followers' neuroticism was almost four times greater.

Discussion

The present study examined the impact of transformational leadership, integrity, and humility/forgiveness on two important outcome variables (WBF & stress), as well as the incremental impact of integrity and humility/forgiveness above and beyond the impact of transformational leadership. Whereas all hypotheses were supported by the data in the first study, in the second study, hypothesis 4 (transformational leadership relates to followers' perceived stress) and hypothesis 5a (leaders' integrity relates to followers' perceived stress), as well as hypothesis 6a (leaders' integrity relates to followers' perceived stress above and beyond the effect of transformational leadership) could not yield support. Reasons therefore are discussed below.

Theoretical Implications

In the scenario study, transformational leadership had a strong impact on WBF and a small to moderate impact on followers' perceived stress. In the field study, transformational leadership explained even more variance in WBF, but none in terms of followers' perceived stress. In comparison to the relation between transformational leadership and stress in the study from Gill et al. (2006), which found a R^2 of .13 to .18, the relation found in the current study is much smaller. This difference may be caused by a different operationalization of stress. While Gill et al. (2006) examined job-specific stress, the present study examined stress in general, i.e., stress experienced by employees in their daily lives, which is much farther reaching than job-specific stress. Therefore, it is obvious that the influence beyond the job environment is weaker. The difference between the relation of transformational leadership and stress in the scenario study compared to the non-significant relation in the field study may be due to different types of mindsets when answering the measurement items. In the first study, participants had to anticipate their stress as a result of the leader's hypothetical action, whereas in the second study—where no relation could be found—more general stress was measured.

Both integrity and humility/forgiveness had a great impact on WBF and a moderate impact on followers' perceived stress in the scenario study. In the field study, integrity failed to explain variance in employees' stress levels. This might also be due to the conceptualization of stress within this study. It is also possible that integrity truly does not have an impact on employees' stress perception in natural environments. This question should be addressed in future research examining job-specific stress. However, humility/forgiveness has found to be moderately related to employees' stress level.

The three predictor variables transformational leadership, integrity, and humility/forgiveness were all highly correlated with both each other and WBF. This is in line with previous research. For example, in the study of Basford et al. (2014), the correlation between humility and satisfaction (which is related to the WBF concept) was $r = .75$, whereas the correlation between humility and transformational leadership was $r = .86$. However, in the study of Parry and Proctor-Thomson (2002), the correlation between integrity and transformational leadership was only moderate ($r = .44$). Thus, high correlations were also observed in past research among these variables. This raises the question whether the three variables (i.e., transformational leadership, integrity, and humility/forgiveness) may have similar antecedents.

When examining the incremental validity of integrity and humility/forgiveness, both variables had an additional high impact on WBF and a small to moderate impact on stress in the scenario study. The additional explained variance of the two character aspects in the field study, however, was much lower. Integrity yielded moderate incremental validity for WBF, whereas the relation of humility/forgiveness was only small, though significant. Nevertheless, this is an important contribution to the literature. In comparison, Judge and Piccolo (2004) found in their meta-analysis an incremental validity of $R^2 = .14$ on follower satisfaction with the leader beyond the impact of transformational leadership for all three aspects of transactional and laissez-faire leadership combined. Thus, integrity and humility/forgiveness both lead to greater incremental validity in a very similar outcome variable than transactional leadership and laissez fair combined.

Furthermore, followers' health and well-being (i.e., followers' perception of stress) is a relatively under-examined outcome variable within transformational leadership and leadership character research. No study could be found in the literature comparing the incremental effect on stress above and beyond that of transformational leadership. Leaders' humility/forgiveness explained an additional three percent of variance above the influence of employees' neuroticism. Again, some of the observed effect sizes are small but still worth noting because of their clear contribution to the leadership literature regarding the impact of leaders' character.

Finally, the second study was additionally used to test the relative importance of the predictors (transformational leadership and the two character aspects), which lead to additional insights. In order to explain variance in WBF, integrity and transformational leadership are equally important. Humility/forgiveness has been found to be only half as important as integrity and transformational leadership. Thus, the different aspects of leadership differ significantly concerning their contribution in explaining variance in WBF. Furthermore, in terms of explaining stress variance between individuals, neuroticism is more than three times more important than the only other significant predictor—humility/forgiveness. Still, humility/forgiveness dominated over one well-known positive leadership concept (i.e., transformational leadership) as well as another positive character aspect (i.e., integrity) in terms of predicting employees' perceived stress.

The fact that integrity and humility/forgiveness had only small to moderate incremental effects above transformational leadership in the field study contrasts with the high incremental effects observed in the scenario study. This contrast may be since all variables (i.e., transformational leadership, integrity, humility/forgiveness) were clearly manipulated in the scenario study and non-related to each other. Unlike in the field, in which these variables are obviously related to each other, which is why the incremental effect of another variable is much smaller. To generalize the effects found in the present study to actual work behavior, one might be cautious to make a judgment about the real incremental effect of humility/forgiveness to early. What appears clear, however, is that the incremental effect of integrity and humility/forgiveness varies on diverse outcome variables.

Practical Implications

The findings of the two studies have clear implications for leadership practice. Based on the positive impact of integrity and humility/forgiveness on WBF and followers' perceived stress, both leaders and companies are well advised to ensure that leadership behavior displays integrity and humility/forgiveness above and beyond the well-known impact of transformational leadership. First and foremost, it is important for leaders to have subordinates who willingly follow and, thus, work for them. Second, reduced stress is at least equally important for companies that want to reduce health problems and their associated costs. Gill et al. (2006) showed that job stress is significantly related to burnout, which is always associated with high costs for the affected companies. Therefore, not only researchers, but also companies should have a keen interest in the health of their employees—at the very least because they are required to pay for every sick day. Thus, strategies to reduce employees' level of stress are in great demand. Zellars, Perrewé, and Brees (2003), for example, discussed a loss of billions of dollars due to stress-related absenteeism and depression. Integrity has become more popular in recent years and found its way into leadership practice. However, humility/forgiveness, although already addressed in leadership research, has not yet reached the attention of the working society. This is likely due to the perception that such characteristics are not competitively advantageous. The results of this study, together with the results of previous research, indicate that this perception may be false. Beyond the positive impact on WBF and stress, humility/forgiveness has the potential to give birth to an organization with a courteous, self-reflecting, understanding, and harmonious culture (Chiu et al., 2012). Thus, it may be necessary to change the way in which today's leaders are educated. Sarros, Cooper, and Hartican (2006) measured seven character aspects in a sample of 238 Australian managers—humility was associated with the lowest value among the seven aspects, especially for managers in the upper echelon. This indicates that the aspect of humility is in most need of development. Research has shown that transformational leadership is trainable, but is this also the case for integrity and humility/forgiveness? Humility has not only been seen as a character aspect (Thompson et al., 2008) but also as a trait, orientation, and meta-attitude (Owens et al., 2011). Regardless of the way in which it is categorized, humility is supposed to be something that can be developed (Owens et al., 2011). Crossan, Mazutis, and Seijts (2013) discussed the question of humility's trainability. Vera and Rodriguez-Lopez (2004) argued that humility can be learned just like any other virtues, although it is a long process. The same applies for integrity. Further investigations are needed to develop effective trainings based on the current body of research regarding integrity and humility/forgiveness. Gentry et al. (2013) suggest that character can be developed through interventions using mentors or coaches who demonstrate when and how integrity and humility/forgiveness affect their work and the work of others as well as how they as leaders are perceived by their subordinates (e.g., reality-based feedback). Brown & Treviño (2006) described an intervention to enhance transformational leadership (Barling, Weber, & Kelloway, 1996). The training consisted of a 1-day group session and four individual sessions in which participants received coaching and were taught about the basic elements of transformational leadership and how to apply them in the workplace. Similar interventions are possible for integrity as well as humility/forgiveness. Another possibility to develop these aspects is through role modeling (i.e., top-down process within the company). The opportunity to learn from role models can also be implemented within training interventions (Owens et al., 2011). Because the development of these aspects is a long process, companies are well advised to include such criteria in their selection processes—for example, by including personality tests covering important characteristics such as integrity and humility/forgiveness in their recruitment processes (Nichols & Cottrell, 2014).

Limitations

Although this research makes several contributions to research regarding leaders' character and its impact on important outcome variables, several limitations should be noted. The strength of this study lies in the combination of experimental and field data, although both research methods alone are subject to various weaknesses. The scenario experiment, which used a vignette in which participants assumed the role of the subordinate, may not have provided sufficient information for participants to obtain a clear idea of how it is to be in the described situation. As a result, their answers might be too hypothetical. Nevertheless, the scenario experiment allows for causality interpretations, which is an important contribution to this relatively new area of research.

Another clear limitation in both studies is the use of self-report data only. Otherwise, in the first study, experimental manipulation was used to assess transformational leadership, integrity, and humility/forgiveness. Moreover, the two outcome variables in both studies are most accurately measured by self-report. Because both studies are interested in followers' subjective perceptions, self-report measures in this specific research context are appropriate. As for integrity, Palanski & Yammarino (2011) remind us that integrity is typically in the eye of the beholder. Nevertheless, for the measurement of integrity in the field study, data may have been more accurate if the leaders have been rated by their superiors instead of being rated by their respective followers—at the very least to avoid common source bias. However, leadership character is only influential in the sense that it is perceived by followers. Thus, it is a valid method to allow followers rate their perceptions of their leaders' integrity and humility/forgiveness. Another issue is the use of non-validated measures for integrity and humility/forgiveness, respectively. The measures were only used once in the study of Liborius (2014). Thus, we cannot clearly assume what these items really measure. Although the items were obviously orientated on the definitions given above, both constructs were measured by only a few items. Thus, future research may use more established measurement methods—e.g., Moorman et al.'s (2013) integrity measure and Owens et al.'s (2013) humility measure.

A further issue is related to the high correlation of the leadership variables. This high correlation could be seen as indicating common-method variance. Yet, there are two reasons that speak against it. First, there are other studies in which similar leadership aspects were also highly correlated (e.g., Basford et al., 2014; Sousa & van Dierendonck, 2015). Second, Harmon's single factor test was utilized, which revealed that no single or general factor emerged to account for all the variance. In addition, also other possible alternative measurement models were tested, whereas the hypothesized model remained superior. Still, the presence of common-method variance cannot completely be ruled out.

Future Research Directions

This specific field of research is in its infancy. Therefore, there are many directions for future research—two of them will be briefly presented. First, little is known about the factors that may foster or hinder the occurrence of integrity and humility/forgiveness as well as other character aspects. Thus, the antecedents of certain character aspects remain unclear. As they are highly correlated with each other, it is quite possible that transformational leadership, integrity, and humility/forgiveness might have similar antecedents. Another possibility is that humility/forgiveness and integrity act as antecedents of certain leadership styles. Peus, Wesche, Streicher, Braun, and Frey (2012), for example, showed that self-knowledge and self-consistency are antecedents of authentic leadership, which are both close to integrity (i.e., self-consistency) and humility (i.e., self-knowledge). Second, leadership scholars have not yet examined the conditions under which the aspects of leadership character that are now known to be positively related to desired outcome variables might become obstacles for leaders. Nielsen et al. (2010) posited that humility might have a negative impact for transactional leaders, as they use power to influence their followers, meaning that demonstrated weakness could be detrimental. In addition, Owens et al. (2011) raise the question whether humble leaders might not be assertive enough in their groups to excel. Research on the negative effects of humility will be able to answer these questions and gain the bigger picture.

The current study aims to arouse interest and invite researchers to investigate in these and further related research questions.

Conclusion

In the last decade, a keen interest has developed in examining the impact of leadership character on followers' attitudes and behavior. The present research explored the impact of leadership character (i.e., integrity and humility/forgiveness) on two important outcome variables (i.e., WBF and stress) based on two complementary studies (a scenario experiment and an open field study). This study contributes to leadership studies by being the first to examine the effects of integrity and humility/forgiveness on these two important outcome variables above and beyond the effect of transformational leadership. Finally, this research revealed the relative importance of the two character aspects in predicting WBF and stress as compared to transformational leadership.

References

Andrews, M. C., Kacmar, K. M., & Kacmar, C. (2015). The interactive effects of behavioral integrity and procedural justice on employee job tension. *Journal of Business Ethics, 126*(3), 371–379. doi:10.1007/s10551-013-1951-4

Arnold, K. A., Turner, N., Barling, J., Kelloway, E. K., & McKee, M. C. (2007). Transformational leadership and psychological well-being: the mediating role of meaningful work. *Journal of Occupational Health Psychology, 12*(3), 193. doi:10.1037/1076-8998.12.3.193

Avolio, B. J. (1999). *Full leadership development: Building the vital forces in organizations*. Thousand Oaks, CA: Sage.

Avolio, B. J., & Gardner, W. L. (2005). Authentic leadership development: Getting to the root of positive forms of leadership. *The Leadership Quarterly, 16*(3), 315–338. doi:10.1016/j.leaqua.2005.03.001

Avolio, B. J., Mahtre, K., Norman, S. M., & Lester, P. (2009a). The moderating effect of gender on leadership intervention impact. *Journal of Leadership and Organizational Studies, 15*, 325–341. 10.1177/1548051809333194

Barling, J., Weber, T., & Kelloway, E. K. (1996). Effects of transformational leadership training on attitudinal and financial outcomes: A field experiment. *Journal of Applied Psychology, 81*, 827–832. doi:10.1037/0021-9010.81.6.827

Basford, T. E., Offermann, L. R., & Behrend, T. S. (2014). Please accept my sincerest apologies: Examining follower reactions to leader apology. *Journal of Business Ethics, 119*(1), 99–117. 10.1007/s10551-012-1613-y

Bass, B. M. (1985). *Leadership and performance beyond expectation*. En Murillo, FJ: Nueva York, Free Press.

Bass, B. M. (1998), *Transformational leadership: Industrial, military, and educational impact*. Mahwah, NJ: Lawrence Erlbaum.

Bass, B. M. (1999). Two decades of research and development in transformational leadership. *European Journal of Work and Organizational Psychology, 8*(1), 9–32. doi:10.1080/135943299398410

Bass, B. M. & Avolio, B. J. (1990): *Transformational leadership development: Manual for the multifactor leadership questionnaire*. Palo Alto: Consulting Psychologists Press.

Bass, B. M., & Avolio, B. J. (1994). *Improving organizational effectiveness through transformational leadership*. Thousand Oaks, CA: Sage.

Bass, B. M., & Steidlmeier, P. (1999). Ethics, character, and authentic transformational leadership behavior. *The Leadership Quarterly, 10*(2), 181–217. doi:10.1016/S1048-9843(99)00016-8

Brown, M. E., & Treviño, L. K. (2006). Ethical leadership: A review and future directions. *The Leadership Quarterly, 17*(6), 595–616. doi:10.1016/j.leaqua.2006.10.004

Chiu, T. C. S., Huang, H. J., & Hung, Y. (2012). The influence of humility on leadership: A Chinese and western review. *International Proceedings of Economics Development and Research, 29*, 129–133.

Cohen, S., Kamarck, T., & Mermelstein, R. (1983). A global measure of perceived stress. *Journal of Health and Social Behavior, 4*, 385–396. doi:10.2307/2136404

Cohen, S., & Williamson, G. (1988). Perceived stress in a probability sample of the United States. In S. Cohen & S. L. Syme (Eds.), *Social support and health* (pp. 3–22). San Francisco: Academic Press.

Crossan, M., Mazutis, D., & Seijts, G. (2013). In search of virtue: The role of virtues, values and character strengths in ethical decision making. *Journal of Business Ethics, 113*(4), 567–581. doi:10.1007/s10551-013-1680-8

Dalal, R. S., Baysinger, M., Brummel, B. J., & LeBreton, J. M. (2012). The relative importance of employee engagement, other job attitudes, and trait affect as predictors of job performance. *Journal of Applied Social Psychology, 42*, 295–325. doi: 10.1111/j.15591816.2012.01017.x

Denney, D. R., & Frisch, M. B. (1981). The role of neuroticism in relation to life stress and illness. *Journal of Psychosomatic Research, 25*(4), 303–307. doi:10.1016/0022-3999(81)90007-6

Dotlich, D. L., Cairo, P. C. (2003). *Why CEOs fail: The 11 behaviors that can derail your climb to the top-and how to manage them*. San Francisco: Jossey-Bass.

Engelbrecht, A. S., Van Aswegen, A. S., & Theron, C. C. (2005). The effect of ethical values on transformational leadership and ethical climate in organisations. *South African Journal of Business Management, 36*(2).

Exline, J. J., & Geyer, A. L. (2004). Perceptions of humility: A preliminary study. *Self and Identity, 3*(2), 95–114. doi:10.1080/13576500342000077

Fry, L. W. (2003). Toward a theory of spiritual leadership. *The Leadership Quarterly, 14*(6), 693–727. doi:10.1016/j.leaqua.2003.09.001

Ganster, D. C., & Murphy, L. (2000). Workplace interventions to prevent stress-related illness: Lessons from research and practice. In C. L. Cooper & E. A. Locke (Eds.), *Industrial and organizational psychology: Linking theory with practice* (pp. 34–51). Oxford, United Kingdom: Blackwell.

Gentry, W. A., Cullen, K. L., Sosik, J. J., Chun, J. U., Leupold, C. R., & Tonidandel, S. (2013). Integrity's place among the character strengths of middle-level managers and top-level executives. *The Leadership Quarterly, 24*(3), 395–404. doi: 10.1016/j.leaqua.2012.11.009

George, B. (2003). *Authentic leadership: Rediscovering the secrets to creating lasting value*. San Francisco: Jossey-Bass.

Geyer, A., & Steyrer, J. (1998). Messung und Erfolgswirksamkeit transformationaler Führung. *German Journal of Human Resource Management: Zeitschrift für Personalforschung, 12*(4), 377–401. doi: 10.1177/239700229801200401

Giampetro-Meyer, A., Brown, S. T., Browne, M. N., & Kubasek, N. (1998). Do we really want more leaders in business? *Journal of Business Ethics, 17*(15), 1727–1736. DOI: 10.1023/A:1006092107644

Gill, A. S., Flaschner, A. B., & Shachar, M. (2006). Mitigating stress and burnout by implementing transformational-leadership. *International Journal of Contemporary Hospitality Management, 18* (40), pp. 469–481. doi:10.1108/09596110610681511

Gilmore, P. L., Hu, X., Wei, F., Tetrick, L. E., & Zaccaro, S. J. (2013). Positive affectivity neutralizes transformational leadership's influence on creative performance and organizational citizenship behaviors. *Journal of Organizational Behavior, 34*(8), 1061–1075. doi: 10.1002/job.1833

Grahek, M. S., Thompson, A. D., & Toliver, A. (2010). The character to lead: A closer look at character in leadership. *Consulting Psychology Journal: Practice and Research, 62*(4), 270–290. doi:10.1037/a0022385

Greco, V., & Roger, D. (2003). Uncertainty, stress, and health. *Personality and Individual Differences, 34*(6), 1057–1068. doi:10.1016/S0191-8869(02)00091-0

Greenleaf, R. K. (1977). *Servant leadership: A journey into the nature of legitimate power and greatness.* Mahwah, NJ: Paulist Press.

Grenberg, J. (2005). *Kant and the ethics of humility: A story of dependence, corruption and virtue.* Cambridge, UK: Cambridge University Press.

Hogan, R. (1997). *Hogan development survey manual.* Tulsa, OK: Hogan Assessment Systems.

Hyde, M., Jappinen, P., Theorell, T., & Oxenstierna, G. (2006). Workplace conflict resolution and the health of employees in the Swedish and Finnish units of an industrial company. Social Science and Medicine, *63*(8), 2218–2227. doi:10.1016/j.socscimed.2006.05.002

Jenkins, S. (2011, December 1). *Tim Tebow shows that in sports, there's no faking leadership (and Bruce Boudreau and Randy Edsall could take note).* The Washington Post. Retrieved from https://www.washingtonpost.com/sports/in-sports-theres-no-faking-leadership/2011/11/30/gIQAnoksGO_story.html?utm_term=.6014ed0e24ef

Johnson, J. W. (2000). A heuristic method for estimating the relative weight of predictor variables in multiple regression. *Multivariate Behavioral Research, 35*(1), 1–19. doi:10.1207/S15327906MBR3501_1

Judge, T. A., & Piccolo, R. F. (2004). Transformational and transactional leadership: a meta-analytic test of their relative validity. *Journal of Applied Psychology, 89*(5), 755. doi:10.1037/0021-9010.89.5.755

Kelloway, E. K. (1998). *Using LISREL for structural equation modeling: A researcher's guide.* Thousand Oaks, CA: Sage.

Khoo, H. S., & Burch, G. S. J. (2008). The 'dark side' of leadership personality and transformational leadership: An exploratory study. *Personality and Individual Differences, 44*(1), 86–97. doi:10.1016/j.paid.2007.07.018

Kouzes, J. M., & Posner, B. Z. (2004). Follower-oriented leadership. In J. M. Burns, G. R. Goethals, & G. J. Sorenson (Eds.), *Encyclopedia of leadership* (pp. 494–499). Thousand Oaks, CA: Berkshire Publishing Group.

Kovjanic, S., Schuh, S. C., Jonas, K., van Quaquebeke, N., & Dick, R. (2012). How do transformational leaders foster positive employee outcomes? A self-determination-based analysis of employees' needs as mediating links. *Journal of Organizational Behavior, 33*(8), 1031–1052. doi:10.1002/job.1771

Leroy, H., Palanski, M. E., & Simons, T. (2012). Authentic leadership and behavioral integrity as drivers of follower commitment and performance. *Journal of Business Ethics, 107*(3), 255–264. doi:10.1007/s10551-011-1036-1

Liborius, P. (2014). Who is worthy of being followed? The impact of leaders' character and the moderating role of followers' personality. *The Journal of Psychology, 148*(3), 347–385. doi:10.1080/00223980.2013.801335

Mayer, C. G., & Davis, J. H. (1999). The effect of the performance appraisal system on trust for management: A field quasi-experiment. *Journal of Applied Psychology, 84*(1), 123–136. doi: 10.1037/0021-9010.84.1.123

McCrae, R. R. (1990). Controlling neuroticism in the measurement of stress. *Stress Medicine, 6*(3), 237–241. doi:10.1002/smi.2460060309

Meierhans, D., Rietmann, B., & Jonas, K. (2008). Influence of fair and supportive leadership behavior on commitment and organizational citizenship behavior. *Swiss Journal of Psychology/Schweizerische Zeitschrift Für Psychologie/Revue Suisse De Psychologie, 67*(3), 131. doi:10.1024/1421-0185.67.3.131

Moorman, R. H., Darnold, T. C., & Priesemuth, M. (2013). Perceived leader integrity: Supporting the construct validity and utility of a multi-dimensional measure in two samples. *The Leadership Quarterly, 24*(3), 427–444. doi:10.1016/j.leaqua.2013.02.003

Morris, J. A., Brotheridge, C. M., & Urbanski, J. C. (2005). Bringing humility to leadership: Antecedents and consequences of leader humility. *Human Relations, 58*, 1323–1350. doi:10.1177/0018726705059929

Nichols, A. L., & Cottrell, C. A. (2014). What do people desire in their leaders? The role of leadership level on trait desirability. *The Leadership Quarterly, 25*(4), 711–729. doi:10.1016/j.leaqua.2014.04.001

Nielsen, R., Marrone, J. A., & Slay, H. S. (2010). A new look at humility: Exploring the humility concept and its role in socialized charismatic leadership. *Journal of Leadership and Organizational Studies, 17*(1), 33–43. doi:10.1177/1548051809350892

O'Brien, R. M. (2007). A caution regarding rules of thumb for variance inflation factors. *Quality and Quantity, 41*, 673–690. doi:10.1007/s11135-006-9018-6

Owens, B., & Hekman, D. (2012). Modeling how to grow: An inductive examination of humble leader behaviors, contingencies, and outcomes. *Academy of Management Journal, 55*(4), 787–817. doi:10.5465/amj.2010.0441

Owens, B. P., Johnson, M. D., & Mitchell, T. R. (2013). Expressed humility in organizations: Implications for performance, teams, and leadership. *Organization Science, 24*(5), 1517–1538. doi:10.1287/orsc.1120.0795

Owens, B. P., Rowatt, W. C., & Wilkins, A. L. (2011). Exploring the relevance and implications of humility in organizations. In K. S. Cameron & G. S. Spreitzer (Eds.), *Handbook of positive organizational scholarship* (pp. 260–272). Oxford, UK: Oxford University Press.

Palanski, M. E., & Yammarino, F. J. (2007). Integrity and Leadership: Clearing the Conceptual Confusion. *European Management Journal, 25*(3), 171–184. doi:10.1016/j.emj.2007.04.006

Palanski, M. E., & Yammarino, F. J. (2011). Impact of behavioral integrity on follower job performance: A three-study examination. *The Leadership Quarterly, 22*(4), 765–786. doi:10.1016/j.leaqua.2011.05.014

Parry, K. W., & Proctor-Thomson, S. B. (2002). Perceived integrity of transformational leaders in organisational settings. *Journal of Business Ethics, 35*(2), 75–96. doi: 10.1023/A:1013077109223

Peterson, C., & Seligman, M. E. P. (2004). *Character strengths and virtues: A handbook and classification*. New York: Oxford/American Psychological Association.

Peus, C., Wesche, J. S., Streicher, B., Braun, S., & Frey, D. (2012). Authentic leadership: An empirical test of its antecedents, consequences, and mediating mechanisms. *Journal of Business Ethics, 107* (3), 331–348. doi:10.1007/s10551-011-1042-3

Podsakoff, P. M., & Organ, D. W. (1986). Self-reports in organizational research: Problems and prospects. *Journal of Management, 12*(4), 531–544. doi:10.1177/014920638601200408

Rammstedt, B., & John, O. P. (2005). Kurzversion des Big Five Inventory (BFI-K). *Diagnostica, 51*(4), 195–206. doi:10.1026/0012-1924.51.4.195

Reave, L. (2005). Spiritual values and practices related to leadership effectiveness. *The Leadership Quarterly, 16*(5), 655–687. doi:10.1016/j.leaqua.2005.07.003

Rich, G. A. (1997). The sales manager as a role model: Effects on trust, job satisfaction, and performance of salespeople. *Journal of the Academy of Marketing Science, 25*(4), 319–328. doi: 10.1177/0092070397254004

Sarros, J. C., Cooper, B. K., & Hartican, A. M. (2006). Leadership and character. *Leadership and Organization Development Journal, 27*(8), 682–699. doi:10.1108/01437730610709291

Simons, T., Friedman, R., Liu, L. A., & McLean Parks, J. (2007). Racial differences in sensitivity to behavioral integrity: attitudinal consequences, in-group effects, and "trickle down" among black and non-black employees. *Journal of Applied Psychology, 92*(3), 650. doi:10.1037/0021-9010.92.3.650

Simons, T., Palanski, M., & Treviño, L. (2013). Toward a broader—but still rigorous—definition of leader integrity: Commentary. *The Leadership Quarterly, 24*(3), 391–394. doi:10.1016/j.leaqua.2013.03.002

Sousa, M., & van Dierendonck, D. (2015). Servant leadership and the effect of the interaction between humility, action, and hierarchical power on follower engagement. *Journal of Business Ethics*, 1–13. doi:10.1007/s10551-015-2725-y

Thompson, A. D., Grahek, M., Phillips, R. E., & Fay, C. L. (2008). The search for worthy leadership. *Consulting Psychology Journal: Practice and Research, 60*, 366–382. doi: 10.1037/1065-9293.60.4.366

Tonidandel, S., & LeBreton, J. M. (2011). Relative importance analysis: A useful supplement to regression analysis. *Journal of Business and Psychology, 26*(1), 1–9. doi:10.1007/s10869-010-9204-3

Tracey, J. B., & Hinkin, T. R. (1994). Transformational leaders in the hospitality industry. *Cornell Hotel and Restaurant and Administration Quarterly, 35*, 18–24. doi:10.1016/0010-8804(94)90014-0

Vera, D., & Rodriguez-Lopez, A. 2004. Humility as a source of competitive advantage. *Organizational Dynamics, 33*, 393–408.

Wang, G., Oh, I. S., Courtright, S. H., & Colbert, A. E. (2011). Transformational leadership and performance across criteria and levels: A meta-analytic review of 25 years of research. *Group and Organization Management, 36*(2), 223–270. doi:10.1177/1059601111401017

Weick, K. E. 2001. Leadership as the legitimization of doubt. In W. Bennis, G. M. Spreitzer, & T. G. Cummings (Eds.), *The future of leadership: Today's top leadership thinkers speak to tomorrow's leaders*, 91–102. San Francisco: Jossey-Bass.

Zellars, K. L., & Perrewe, K. L. (2003). The role of spirituality in occupational stress and well-being. In R. A. Giacalone, & C.L. Jurkiewicz (Eds.), *Handbook of workplace spirituality and organizational performance* (pp. 300–313). New York: M.E. Sharpe.

Zhu, W., Newman, A., Miao, Q., & Hooke, A. (2013). Revisiting the mediating role of trust in transformational leadership effects: Do different types of trust make a difference? *The Leadership Quarterly, 24*(1), 94–105. doi:10.1016/j.leaqua.2012.08.004

Is Charismatic Leadership Effective When Workers Are Pressured To Be Good Citizens?

DEWAYNNA HORN

CHRISTOPHER J. MATHIS

SAMMIE L. ROBINSON

NATASHA RANDLE

ABSTRACT. Prior research has explored how employees' perceptions of their leaders impact their work attitudes and behaviors. Studies have shown that charismatic leaders motivate individuals to be more engaged and to exhibit more organizational citizenship behaviors. This study considers how a moderator, citizenship pressure, affects how charismatic leaders might inspire their followers to go above and beyond and be more engaged in their work. Using a sample of 243 workers, this study's findings show that charismatic leadership has a stronger positive effect on job engagement when employees perceive less citizenship pressure. Citizenship pressure did not moderate the relationship between charismatic leadership and organizational citizenship behavior. Implications of this study include an examination of the moderating influence of citizenship pressure, a relatively new construct. Practically, the implications may shed some light on leadership factors that encourage increased effort from employees and greater employee engagement. More specifically, findings suggest that persons are motivated to exhibit more OCBs to meet high expectations of charismatic leaders. However, when seeking engagement, feeling pressure to perform these OCBs has a reverse effect as more job engagement results with less citizenship pressure. Future research suggestions and limitations are discussed.

CHARISMATIC LEADERS ARE PASSIONATE, DRIVEN INDIVIDUALS who are able to paint a compelling vision of the future, generate high levels of excitement and initiative, and build strong emotional attachments among followers (Hughes, Ginnett, & Curphy, 2009). They "cause followers to become highly committed to their mission, to make significant personal sacrifices in the interest of the mission, and to perform above and beyond the call of duty" (Shamir, House, & Arthur, 1993, p. 577). We seek to examine charismatic leaders' impact on organizational citizenship behavior and job engagement. In a business environment characterized by uncertainty, global competition, and diversity, exceptional leaders who have extraordinary effects on their followers are considered to be a resource to manage far-reaching challenges in the workplace. One of the biggest challenges for leaders is encouraging employee engagement and motivating employees to go above and beyond in contributing their knowledge and experience to the organization (Vlachoutsicos, 2011).

Empirical research has yielded findings concerning a positive effect of charismatic leadership on organizational citizenship behavior (OCB) (Babcock-Roberson & Strickland, 2010; Bettencourt, 2004; De Cremer & Van Knippenberg, 2002; Deluga, 1995; Den Hartog, De Hoogh, & Keegan, 2007; Shamir, Zakay, Breinin, & Popper, 1998) and job engagement (Babcock-Roberson & Strickland). However, there are few examinations of specific variables that may reduce or enhance the influence of charismatic leaders on employees' OCB and job engagement (Boerner, Dütschke, & Wied, 2008; Den Hartog et al.).

The purpose of this study is to examine a moderator, citizenship pressure, to account for boundary conditions in which charismatic leaders will inspire others to go above and beyond or be more fully immersed in their jobs. Citizenship pressure, a concept that has recently been introduced in the OCB literature stream, is defined as a specific job demand in which an individual feels pressured to perform extra-role job duties that are above and beyond those specified in the job description (Bolino, Turnley, Gilstrap, & Suazo, 2010). Citizenship pressure occurs when employees perceive an implicit expectation to engage in discretionary activities. At first glance, one might presume only negative consequences of citizenship pressure; however, studies have also yielded a positive relationship regarding the effects of citizenship pressure on job engagement (Cates, Mathis, & Randle, 2010) and OCB (Bolino et al.). Building on the job demands-resources model, this study specifically focuses on citizenship pressure as a job demand, which reduces the influence of a charismatic leader.

First, we examine the previously studied links between charismatic leadership and OCBs and charismatic leadership and job engagement (Babcock-Roberson & Strickland, 2010) for our sample. Second, we extend the understanding of this link by exploring the potential moderating influence of citizenship pressure. We feel that citizenship pressure is an important boundary to study in the context of this relationship because citizenship pressure represents the notion that OCBs are often informally encouraged and rewarded. Thus there appears to be a blurred line between motivating an employee (as with charismatic leadership) versus pressuring an employee (as with citizenship pressure). What happens to a charismatic leader's influence when an individual feels pressured? Furthermore, several researchers have called for more studies to examine moderators of the relationship between charismatic leadership and its observed outcomes (Boerner et al., 2008; Kark, Shamir, & Chen, 2003; Porter & McLaughlin, 2006; Shamir et al., 1993). Researchers have called for more research to understand the factors such as social support, organizational support, or supportive colleagues and teammates that might lessen the negative effects of citizenship pressure (Bolino et al., 2010). Accordingly, in this study, we examine the interaction of citizenship pressure and charismatic leadership with both OCB and job engagement. To our knowledge, this interaction has not been tested.

Literature Review

Charismatic Leadership, OCB, and Job Engagement

Charismatic leadership is a theory of leadership that asserts that leaders transform the needs, values, preferences, and aspirations of followers, causing followers to become highly committed to the leader's mission, and to perform above and beyond the call of duty (Shamir et al., 1993, 1998). Empirical examinations of charismatic leaders espouse behavioral and psychological attributes, which include vision, an ability to inspire, dominance, articulation ability, a need for influence, and unconventional and/or counter normative behavior (Conger & Kanungo, 1987). One of the most important attributes of charismatic leaders is their ability to be highly motivational. They are motivational in that they increase the intrinsic value of followers' efforts; enhance followers' self-esteem, self-worth, and self-efficacy beliefs; increase the intrinsic value of followers' goal accomplishment; instill faith in a better future; and cause followers to be more committed (Shamir et al., 1993). Charismatic leaders are able to motivate by functioning as an observable, ideal point of reference and by engaging in clear communications processes that mobilize followers to action. They provide clarity when the situation is unclear (Babcock-Roberson & Strickland, 2010) and convince followers to sacrifice in an effort to achieve the leader's goals and realize their vision (Galvin, Balkundi, & Waldman, 2010). By communicating high performance expectations (Babcock-Roberson & Strickland), charismatic leaders have a profound and extraordinary effect on followers (Conger & Kanungo, 1987; House & Baetz, 1979; Shamir et al., 1993).

Equally relevant to this study is OCB, which Organ (1988) defines as "individual behavior that is discretionary, not directly or explicitly recognized by the formal reward system, and that in aggregate, promotes the effective functioning of the organization" (p. 4). An important assessment of OCB, its nature, antecedents, and consequences has been advanced that supports the premise that OCB improves organizational effectiveness. Thus, organizations should manage, support, and encourage ways to promote such behavior (Organ, Podsakoff, & MacKenzie, 2006). We examine a specific type of OCB, individual initiative, in which employees "engage in task-related behaviors at a level that is so far beyond minimally required or generally expected levels that it takes on a voluntary flavor" (Podsakoff, MacKenzie, Paine, & Bachrach, 2000, p. 524). Examples of individual initiative include going into the office outside of and in addition to normal work hours, taking work home although it is not required, answering work calls at home, and volunteering for special projects in addition to one's normal job duties. On the one hand, individual initiative is similar, but distinct from personal initiative. Individual initiative, in contrast, describes job-related behaviors that are at a level that far exceeds minimum requirements and standards of normally accepted practice. On the other hand, personal initiative is conceptually similar to proactive personality (Crant, 2000) since it describes the extent to which employees act without having to be told, look for opportunities to serve and problems to solve, and persist in overcoming barriers (Frese & Fay, 2001).

Empirical studies reveal a positive relationship exists between charismatic leadership and OCB (Babcock-Roberson & Strickland, 2010; Bettencourt, 2004; De Cremer & Van Knippenberg, 2002; Deluga, 1995; Den Hartog et al., 2007; Shamir et al., 1998). Leaders who possess charisma get their followers to go above and beyond by enhancing follower's self- efficacy, intrinsic motivation, and trust (Shamir et al., 1993). In addition, leaders who possess charisma are credited with increasing job engagement among followers (Babcock-Roberson & Strickland). Following previous empirical examinations, we propose a positive relationship between charismatic leadership and OCB for our sample.

> *Hypothesis 1:* Charismatic leadership will be positively related to employee's OCBs.

Job engagement refers to an individual's psychological presence in role activities and may be an important ingredient for effective role performance. It is defined as "the simultaneous employment and expression of a person's 'preferred self' in task behaviors that promote connections to work and to others' personal presence (physical, cognitive, and emotional), and active full performances" (W. A. Kahn, 1990, p. 700). Further, W. A. Kahn explains that when people are engaged, they are more fully immersed in and obligated to the role that they are performing. Individuals become physically involved in tasks, cognitively attentive, and thoughtfully connected to others in ways that display true thoughts, feelings, and creative expression. Moreover, they demonstrate fundamental beliefs and values, as well as personal connections to others.

Theoretically, social exchange theory, which has been used in previous literature as a rationale to explain the antecedents and consequences of job engagement, asserts that "obligations are generated through a series of interactions between parties who are in a state of reciprocal interdependence" (Saks, 2006, p. 603). Considering W. A. Kahn's (1990) definition of engagement, employees may feel obliged to bring themselves more deeply into their role performances as repayment for the profound and extraordinary effect of a charismatic leader.

Leader behavior has been empirically linked to job engagement. Tims, Bakker, and Xanthopoulou (2010) revealed that a transformational leadership style, of which charismatic leadership is a component, enhances employees' work engagement. Babcock-Roberson and Strickland (2010) found a significant positive relationship between charismatic leadership and job engagement. We propose a positive relationship exists between charismatic leadership and job engagement.

> *Hypothesis 2:* Charismatic leadership will be positively related to employee's job engagement.

Moderating Role of Citizenship Pressure

While Organ's (1988) definition of OCB implies that discretionary behavior will have a positive impact on the organization, researchers have begun to realize that there may be negative implications of OCB. Specifically, higher levels of OCB are associated with pressure to perform such discretionary behaviors. Citizenship pressure is defined in consideration of Schaufeli and Bakker's (2004) conceptualization of job demands, as a "specific job demand in which an employee feels pressured to perform OCBs" (Bolino et al., 2010, p. 836). Employees may feel obligated to perform OCBs rather than experience the discretionary desire to impress managers in order to receive favorable outcomes (e.g., higher performance evaluations, pay increases, promotions, or even to maintain employment in volatile or uncertain environments). Managers may use OCBs, as opposed to prescribed job duties, as a basis to differentiate between high and low performing employees. Further, there are positive and negative effects of citizenship pressure. Bolino et al. quantitatively examined and found a positive relationship between citizenship pressure and the actual occurrence of OCB. However, these findings also indicate that citizenship pressure affects workers by making their jobs stressful. In addition, employees working in the same organizational environment and even for the same supervisor could experience differing levels of citizenship pressure, which means an employee's response to this pressure may be unique and individual.

Similarly, Vigoda-Gadot (2006, 2007) proposed a different look at OCB which focused on the exploitative and abusive tendency of some supervisors and managers to impose a requirement of extra-role activities in the workplace. This research argued that such behaviors are a substantial deviation from the original meaning of OCB and thus should be recognized and analyzed separately. A total of 206 teachers were examined and results revealed that a substantial majority, 75%, reported feeling strong pressure to engage in what we usually define as OCB. The study revealed negative outcomes stemming from this forced behavior, such as higher levels of job stress and job burnout; stronger perceptions of organizational politics; greater intentions to leave the organization; and lower levels of job satisfaction, innovation, and in-role performance.

We posit the impact of charismatic leadership on subordinates' OCB varies with subordinates' perceived levels of citizenship pressure. To support our hypotheses, we look to the job demands-resources perspective given it suggests that there are two classifications of job-related factors: job demands and job resources (Conger, Kanungo, & Menon, 2000). Job demands refer to aspects of the job that require sustained physical and/or psychological effort as well as associated physiological and/or psychological costs. Job resources represent aspects of the job that promote growth, goal attainment, and wellbeing. Bolino et al. (2010) specifically defined citizenship pressure as a job demand. Based on the job demands-resources perspective and Bolino et al.'s definition of citizenship pressure, citizenship pressure may be viewed as a job demand and charismatic leadership may be viewed as a job resource. One of the major propositions of the job demands-resources model is job demands may reduce the influence of job resources (Bakker & Demerouti, 2006).

In this case, the moderating variable, citizenship pressure, "can reduce *or enhance* the tendency of *individual or* organizational properties to generate specific stressors *or motivators*, alter the perceptions and cognitions evoked by such stressors *or motivators*, moderate responses that follow the appraisal process, or reduce*/enhance the effects* of such responses" (R. L. Kahn & Byosiere, 1992, p. 622). Along these lines, a perceived implicit requirement to perform duties that are above and beyond the basic job description (citizenship pressure) reduces the charismatic leader's effect (i.e., inspiration and motivation; expressions of value toward followers' contributions; recognition of follower's talents; instilling hope in followers that they will attain their professional goals; and communication of clear expectations for high performance). Essentially, individuals who benefit from the efforts of a charismatic leader and simultaneously perceive there is a requirement, not a choice, to work outside and above their actual job description, actually exhibit less OCBs. In such instances, high levels of citizenship pressure, combined with the leader's charisma, decreases the level and frequency of discretionary behaviors exhibited. According to previous empirical findings, citizenship pressure affects workers by generating feelings of stress (Bolino et al., 2010). Thus, a charismatic leader may communicate clear expectations for high performance, further stimulating workers who are more likely to exhibit OCBs, but when this motivation and inspiration is coupled with the stress that citizenship pressure presents, the result is a reduction in OCBs exhibited. Based on this reasoning and the job demands resources perspective, citizenship pressure, viewed as a job demand, reduces the charismatic leader's motivational effect and the charismatic leader's ability to motivate their followers to perform above and beyond at work may be reduced when employees perceive citizenship pressure.

> *Hypothesis 3:* Citizenship pressure will moderate the relationship between charismatic leadership and OCB such that charismatic leaders will have a stronger influence on the OCBs of employees who perceive less citizenship pressure.

Although research has yielded a positive relationship between charismatic leadership and job engagement (Babcock-Roberson & Strickland, 2010), to our knowledge, little is known about specific contextual factors that impact this relationship. Citizenship pressure, an added job demand (Bolino et al., 2010), could change the nature of this relationship. The presence of job demands, as suggested in the job demands-resources model, may have significant psychological costs and has been linked to increased employee burnout and decreased job engagement (Crawford, LePine, & Rich, 2010; Demerouti, Bakker, DeJonge, Janssen, & Schaufeli, 2001; Nahrgang, Morgeson, & Hofmann, 2010; Schaufeli, Bakker, & Van Rhenen, 2009).

Research on the relationship of job demands to engagement suggests that there are challenge demands and hindrance demands (Crawford et al., 2010). Challenge demands promote mastery, personal growth, or future gains, and employees view these demands as opportunities to learn, achieve, and demonstrate competence. However, hindrance demands, which include role conflict, role ambiguity, and role overload, are more salient in this study. They have been found to impede personal growth, learning, and goal attainment and are generally seen by employees as constraints, barriers, or roadblocks that hinder progress toward goals and effective performance. Further, hindrance demands are negatively correlated to job engagement (Crawford et al., 2010). In the explication of role conflict theory, R. L. Kahn, Wolfe, Quinn, Snoek, and Rosenthal (1964) explained, "there is the possibility that coping with the pressures of the work will involve the formation of affective or physiological symptoms" (p. 29).

Although job demands are not necessarily negative, they may become job stressors when meeting those demands requires high effort from an employee (Schaufeli et al., 2009). Drawing again upon the job demands–resources model, we view citizenship pressure as a hindrance job demand that may reduce the charismatic leader's effects on followers, thus, obstructing job engagement. For example, on the one hand, a charismatic leader could affect an individual by instilling the hope of attaining a professional goal, such as a promotion, causing the individual to be more actively engaged in his or her prescribed job responsibilities. On the other hand, if this feeling of job engagement, as a result of the charismatic leader's efforts, is coupled with perceptions of pressure in the environment to perform above and beyond his or her prescribed job description, the stress that results from perceptions citizenship pressure (Bolino et al., 2010) may act as a hindrance to impede goal attainment. The individual may view the additional pressure as a distraction from being fully immersed or engaged in the job. Charismatic leaders' ability to motivate their followers to be engaged in their work may be limited when employees perceive more citizenship pressure.

> *Hypothesis 4:* Citizenship pressure will moderate the relationship between charismatic leadership and job engagement such that charismatic leaders will have a stronger influence on the job engagement of employees who perceive less citizenship pressure.

Methods

Participants and Procedures

Study participants were obtained via snowball sampling. Snowball sampling is a respondent-driven sampling technique where participants recruit their acquaintances to complete surveys (Goodman, 2011). Social science scholars have obtained information from specific industries, organizations, and communities using this sampling technique (Eddleston, Veiga, & Powell, 2006; Martins, Eddleston, & Veiga, 2002). We targeted individuals who (1) work full-time professional or clerical positions, (2) work away from home (as opposed to working in-home in a telecommuting arrangement), and (3) live with a spouse, partner, or significant other (hereafter referred to as mates). To reach individuals who met the criteria for inclusion, MBA students from four universities were asked to participate. These participants were asked to provide names and email addresses of persons who they thought would meet the study criteria.

Once the sample was identified, data was collected online after an e-mail invitation was sent to explain the purpose of the study and provide a link to complete the web-based survey. Qualified participants (hereafter referred to as workers) were requested to complete the survey. Workers were emailed a survey for their mate with instructions to forward the message to their mates' email address. Throughout the data collection process, there were sequential steps to ensure matched worker–mate surveys. The steps were as follows: (1) send and receive completed worker survey, (2) send and receive completed mate survey, and (3) match all surveys. We confirmed that we received completed surveys at each step. The worker and mates were informed that their responses would be kept confidential. Workers did not receive a copy of the mate's response; rather, all surveys for workers and mates were submitted directly to the investigators.

The survey for the worker contained measures for charismatic leadership, citizenship pressure, job engagement, and demographic information (e.g., gender, age, education, marital status). The mates' survey included a measure for Organizational Citizenship Behavior (OCB)-individual initiative.

In designing the study, it was deemed essential to give close attention to the factors, such as how and when data were collected, that may affect external validity. For this reason, data were collected from both employees *and* their mates in order to obtain corroborating evidence of specific variables under investigation by using more than one source. Collecting data from more than a single source is a procedural remedy to minimize common method variance (Podsakoff, MacKenzie,

Lee, & Podsakoff, 2003). In addition, it provides a unique perspective on the occurrence of an event (Scandura & Williams, 2000).

> The advantage of this procedure is that it makes it impossible for the mindset of the source or rater to bias the observed relationship between the predictor and criterion variable, thus eliminating the effects of consistency motifs, implicit theories, social desirability tendencies, dispositional and transient mood states, and any tendencies on the part of the rater to acquiesce or respond in a lenient manner. (Podsakoff et al., 2003, p. 887)

E-mail invitations were sent to 557 workers; 392 responded. Adjusting for incomplete surveys and unqualified participants, 317 workers completed the survey, for an approximate 57 percent response rate. These 317 workers forwarded the survey to their mates. Of this number, 243 responded. After matching all completed responses received from the worker–mate pairs, the overall response rate was approximately 44% or 243 matched surveys.

Demographically, most respondents, 61.7%, were between the ages of 28 and 46. Sixty-three percent were female and the same percentage were African American (63%); of these 77.4% were married and living with their spouse. Respondents reported organizational tenure as follows: one to five years (37.4%) and six to 10 years (25.5%) and an average workweek of 44.82 hours. In addition, respondents reported household annual salaries as follows: less than $50,000 (11.1%), $50,000 to $80,000 (21.8%), and greater than $80,000 (63.4%). Means, standard deviations, and correlations among the study variables are presented in Table 1.

Measures

For this study, the exogenous variables are charismatic leadership, citizenship pressure, while the endogenous variables are OCB-individual initiative and job engagement. Some control variables are included. All variables had reliability greater than 0.70 as suggested by Nunnally (1978), and are provided and presented in Table 1.

Charismatic Leadership

After reviewing the literature, we chose to use the Multifactor Leadership Questionnaire (MLQ) to measure charismatic leadership, because it is the most widely used measure and the most dominant framework guiding research on transformational and charismatic leadership (van Knippenberga & Sitkin, 2013). The MLQ contains the charismatic leadership subscale, which is of specific interest in this study. It measures the extent to which the participants perceive their superior as possessing charismatic characteristics (Avolio, Bass, & Jung, 1999). Other measures have been espoused in the literature (Conger & Kanungo, 1994; Podsakoff, MacKenzie, Moorman, & Fetter, 1990; Rafferty & Griffin, 2004; Shamir et al.,

TABLE 1. Means, Standard Deviations, and Zero-Order Correlations[a]

VAR[b]	AGE	INCOME	CL	OCBII	JE	CP
Income	.259[c]					
Charismatic Leadership	.003	−.077				
OCBII	−.161	.167	.171			
Job Engagement	−.238	.124	.377	.210		
Citizenship Pressure	.048	.089	.041	.258	.096	
Mean			3.657	2.653	4.220	2.080
SD			1.009	0.889	0.661	0.818

Note. VAR = Variables; INCOME = total household income; CL = Charismatic Leadership; JE = Job Engagement; OCBII = Partner's Perception of the Individual's Organizational Citizenship Behavior – Individual Initiative; CP = Citizenship Pressure.

[a]$n = 243$. Correlations with absolute values of .126 or greater are significant at the $p < .05$ level or better.

[b]Coding was as follows: Age: 1 = Older than 65, 2 = 60–65, 3 = 54–59, 4 = 47–53, 5 = 41–46, 6 = 37–40, 7 = 33–36, 8 = 28–32; Income: 1 = Less than $10,000, 2 = $10,000–$19,999, 3 = $20,000–$29,999, 4 = $30,000–$39,999, 5 = $40,000–$49,999, 6 = $50,000–$59,999, 7 = $60,000–$69,999, 8 = $70,000–$79,999, 9 = $80,000–$89,999, 10 = $90,000–$99,999, 11 = $100,000–$109,999, 12 = $110,000–$119,999, 13 = $120,000–$129,999, 14 = $130,000–$139,999, 15 = $140,000–$149,999, 16 = $150,000 or greater.

[c]Given age and income are categorical variables, Cramer's *V* was used to calculate the correlation ($V = .259$, $p = .084$), which means that the strength of association between the two categorical variables are weak.

1998), but these measures, although they appear to be different with regard to conceptualization, they share a lot of operational overlap with the MLQ measure (van Knippenberga & Sitkin). Specifically, one study examined the convergent, divergent, and criterion validity between the MLQ and the Conger-Kanungo measure and found a high intercorrelation ($r = 0.88$) (Rowold & Heinitz, 2007).

Charismatic leadership was measured using three subscales (idealized attributes, idealized behaviors, and inspirational motivation), each with four questions, totaling 12 items from the MLQ (Avolio et al., 1999). We aggregated each of the averages for idealized attributes, idealized behaviors, and inspirational motivation items to form an average composite scale of charismatic leadership based upon the description in the MLQ. Responses for the charismatic subscale were measured on a 5-point scale ranging from 1 = not at all to 5 = frequently. An example of idealized attributes, idealized behaviors, and inspirational motivation, respectively, is "Goes beyond self-interest for the good of the group," "Considers the moral and ethical consequences of decisions," and "Talks enthusiastically about what needs to be accomplished." These 12 items were averaged to yield a charismatic leadership score, in which respondents indicated their perception of their leader as charismatic ($\alpha = .945$; 95% CI = .934 to .955).

Citizenship Pressure

Citizenship pressure is a relatively new construct in the literature. Thus, we felt it was important to use the existing measure based on previously validated scores. Citizenship pressure was measured using Bolino et al.'s (2010) 34-item scale, which includes three dimensions of OCB: 14 items assessing helping (Settoon & Mossholder, 2002), 15 items assessing individual initiative (Bolino & Turnley, 2005), and 5 items assessing loyalty (Moorman & Blakely, 1995). Sample items for each of the dimensions are as follows: "Cheer up coworkers who are having a bad day" (helping); "Bring things home to work on" (individual initiative); and "Show pride when representing the organization in public" (loyalty). Respondents were asked to indicate how often they felt pressured to perform certain duties, which were consistent with the three forms of OCB, using a 5-point scale ranging from 1 = never feel pressured to 5 = always feel pressured.

While several forms of citizenship behaviors exist, we chose to examine only helping, individual initiative, and loyalty as these comprehensively reflect behaviors that are both (a) salient among professional employees and (b) beneficial to most organizations. In addition, we aggregated the three dimensions into an overall measure of citizenship pressure consistent with the Bolino et al. (2010) study, which reported an acceptable alpha value of .97 for the aggregated dimensions, and averaged each result to yield a citizenship pressure score ($\alpha = .959$; 95% CI = .951 to .966). We deemed this appropriate because overall citizenship pressure was important to this study and we expected no differences in the outcomes related to the different dimensions.

Organizational Citizenship Behavior (OCB)-Individual Initiative

Given that existing measures of individual initiative focused on blue-collar workers (e.g., Niehoff & Moorman, 1993), we chose to use Bolino and Turnley's (2005) scale because it focuses on behaviors that are most relevant among our targeted sample of white-collar employees. Research has demonstrated that persons who take individual initiative tend to come into work early or stay late, communicate with their job while on vacation, check email or voicemail while away from work (i.e., either from home or while on vacation), take work home, and take on additional responsibilities that are not a part of their job descriptions (e.g., Coleman & Borman, 2000; Podsakoff, MacKenzie, & Hui, 1993). Bolino and Turnley (2005) developed a 15-item scale for individual initiative that measures the extent to which employees engaged in these types of behaviors. Despite the infancy of their scale, these researchers have established its suitability for measuring individual initiative among professional employees.

Of the other OCB types that exist, including helping behavior, sportsmanship, organizational loyalty, organizational compliance, civic virtue, and self-development (Podsakoff et al., 2000), we used only individual initiative. In designing the study, we were interested in reducing common method variance by collecting ratings from another source, mates. To eliminate common method variance (Podsakoff et al., 2003), researchers tend to collect ratings of citizenship behaviors from the employee's supervisor or peers. As many of the behaviors under investigation take place outside of normal working hours, the collection of supervisor or peer ratings for Individual Initiative was deemed not to be appropriate in this study. Mates are not able to attest to the other types of OCB, as those behaviors are not likely to occur at home. Therefore, we collected ratings from their mates about the worker's individual initiative in order to test the extent to which the workers and their mates viewed OCB-individual initiative in the same manner. In addition, workers were asked for their responses to the same questions in order to provide some evidence of the measure's validity. The correlation between the worker ratings and the mate ratings on individual initiative was .544 ($p < .001$).

Although citizenship behavior was rated by two sources, LePine, Erez, and Johnson (2002) suggest that theory and reasoning should determine who should be the person rating citizenship behavior. The citizenship behaviors investigated in this particular study are ones we feel that the worker's mates are qualified to evaluate. That is, we believe employees' mates are in a position to report the work behaviors of their mates as it relates to performing job related tasks outside the workplace. In order to avoid single-source bias, we used only the mates' responses in testing the hypotheses. As reported in the "Participants and Procedures" section, citizenship behavior was measured utilizing the 15-item individual initiative scale developed by Bolino and Turnley (2005), the mates were instructed to report the extent to which they believe the worker perform certain job related tasks. Responses for the 15-item scale were made on a 5-point scale ranging from 1 (never) to 5 (always). These 15 items were averaged to yield an OCB-individual initiative score ($\alpha = .927$; 95% CI = .913 to .940).

It should be noted that citizenship pressure was measured by a 34-item scale in which 15 items were also used to measure OCB-individual initiative. In order to ensure that the two variables were distinct, we collected data for the two measures at separate points in time. We presented the instructions for each measure differently. In addition, we compared the fit of a two-factor model and a one-factor model. OCB-individual initiative and Citizenship Pressure-individual initiative were represented by 15 items each. Conducting a confirmatory factor analysis with maximum likelihood estimation, the two-factor solution provided significant improvement over the one-factor solution ($\Delta\chi^2 = 860.961$, $\Delta df = 1, p < .001$). This indicates there is a distinct difference between the two measures.

Job Engagement

Job engagement was measured with an 18-item scale developed by Rich (2006). The scale captured six items in each of the three dimensions: physical, emotional, and cognitive. An example of each dimension is as follows: "I devote a lot of energy to my job" (physical); "I am enthusiastic about my job" (emotional); and "At work, my mind is focused on my job" (cognitive). Responses were made on a 5-point scale ranging from 1 = strongly disagree to 5 = strongly agree. These 18 items were averaged to yield a job engagement score (α = .940; 95% CI = .928 to .950).

Furr and Bacharach (2014) argue that an important advantage of the confirmatory factor analysis over correlation (and many alternative analytic strategies) is that "researchers can evaluate validity evidence in terms of the estimated correlation between a scale and criterion, while accounting for measurement error in both the scale and the criterion" (p. 353). To check the convergent and discriminant validity among all variables, we conducted a series of confirmatory factor analyses with maximum likelihood estimation. OCBII was represented by composite parcels of items, as outlined by Bagozzi and Heatherton (1994) for scales with five or more items. For this study, OCBII items were systematically assigned to parcels using the following procedure: items with the highest and lowest loadings on this factor were assigned to the first parcel, the second-highest and -lowest items to the second parcel, the third-highest and -lowest items to the third parcel, and so on. Charismatic leadership was represented by the idealized attributes, idealized behaviors, and inspirational motivation scales; job engagement by physical, emotional, and cognitive scales; and citizenship pressure by helping, individual initiative, and loyalty scales. Specifically, we compared the fit of a four-factor model with the fit of four alternatives (a one-factor model; a two-factor model in which citizenship pressure, OCBII, and job engagement items loaded onto the same factor; a three-factor model in which OCBII and job engagement loaded onto the same factor; a three-factor model in which OCBII and citizenship pressure loaded onto the same factor). Using maximum likelihood estimation, the four-factor solution provided reasonable fit for the data [$\chi 2$ = 248.063(113), $p < .001$, normed $\chi 2$ = 2.195, GFI = .891, CFI = .943, RMSEA = .070, SRMR = .064], GFI and CFI are acceptable (Bentler, 1990; Byrne, 2001); a value below 5 for normed χ^2 (Schumacker & Lomax, 2004); RMSEA meets the cut-off value of .07 (Steiger, 2007); SRMR value is less than .08 (Hu & Bentler, 1999); and each indicator's loading is significant ($p < .001$) on the appropriate latent construct. However, all other alternative models did not yield as good a fit (e.g., one-factor model: $\chi 2$ = 1,191.384(119), $p < .001$, normed $\chi 2$ = 10.012, GFI = .637, CFI = .547, RMSEA = .193, SRMR = .161; two-factor model: $\chi 2$ = 578.176(118), $p < .001$, normed $\chi 2$ = 4.900, GFI = .778, CFI = .806, RMSEA = .127, SRMR = .117; three-factor model (same factor = OCBII and job engagement): $\chi 2$ = 438.252(116), $p < .001$, normed $\chi 2$ = 3.778, GFI = .823, CFI = .864, RMSEA = .107, SRMR = .106; three-factor model (same factor = OCBII and citizenship pressure): $\chi 2 = 389.104(116)$, $p < .001$, normed $\chi 2 = 3.353$, GFI = .838, CFI = .885, RMSEA = .099, SRMR = .082]. In every instance, the four-factor model provided significantly better fit than the four alternatives.

Control Variables

Our analyses include demographic factors (i.e., age, income). Results of past research examining citizenship behavior has demonstrated that age (Bolino & Turnley, 2005) should be used as a control variable. Although findings by Bolino and others (Bolino & Turnley, 2005; Bolino et al., 2010) found that salary should be included as a control variable, we believe that the total household income may possibly affect individuals' on-the-job engagement and their decisions to perform above and beyond the call of duty at work. These persons may believe that the level of household income is sufficient motivation for deciding how hard they will work on their job. For this reason, we considered total household income as a possible or potential explanatory factor for some of the variance in the endogenous variables. Income was measured as the approximate total household income.

Results

Data Analysis and Hypothesized Relationships

Path analysis was used to test the hypothesized model using the analysis of moment structures (AMOS) computer program (Arbuckle, 2010). Figure 1 presents the standardized estimates of the hypothesized model that depicts citizenship pressure moderating the relationships between charismatic leadership and OCBII, and between charismatic leadership and job engagement. The hypothesized model fit the data well [χ^2 (9, $n = 243$) = 12.167, $p = .204$; normed $\chi^2 = 1.352$; GFI = .986; CFI = .972; RMSEA = .038 (90% CI = .000 to .087); SRMR = .039]. After establishing satisfactory model fit, the structural coefficients were interpreted.

In order to minimize Type 1 error or false discoveries, we used the Benjamini and Hochberg (1995) approach. After selecting five control variables (i.e., age, data collection site, organizational tenure, sex, total household income), we determined the incidence of Type 1 error increased due to the inclusion of too many variables. Thus, we deleted the three control variables (i.e., data collection site, organizational tenure, sex) that were not significant to the model in order to reduce the Type 1 error. Once these were eliminated, we used two remaining control variables, age and total household income, to test the four hypotheses. In support of Hypothesis 1, charismatic leadership is positively related to OCBII (.169, $p = .005$, *adj* $p = .013$). In support of Hypothesis 2, charismatic leadership is positively related to a worker's job engagement (.360, $p < .001$, *adj* $p < .001$).

To test for moderation, the coefficient of the interaction term should be significant. If significant, then the interaction should be graphed to allow for proper

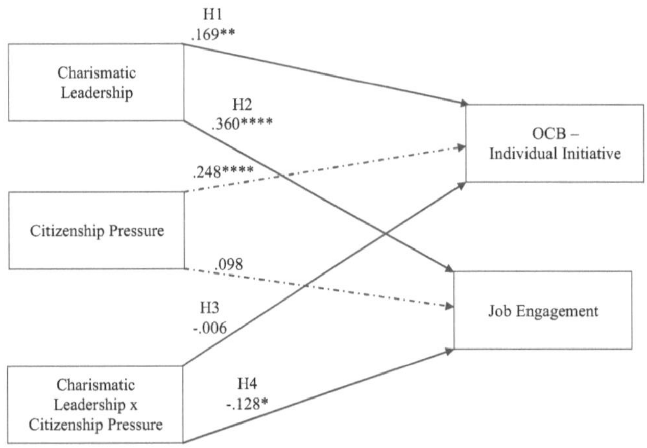

FIGURE 1. Standardized solution for final path analysis model. n = 243. Standardized coefficients are provided for each path in the model tested (except for paths from the two control variables, which are not shown for presentation purposes). $^{*}p < 0.05$. $^{**}p < 0.01$. $^{****}p < 0.001$.

interpretation (Cohen & Cohen, 1975). Citizenship pressure was examined as a moderator of the relationship between charismatic leadership and OCBII (Hypothesis 3). The interaction term, charismatic leadership and citizenship pressure, was not significant, as it relates to OCBII (−.006, $p = .919$, *adj* $p = .919$). Therefore, Hypothesis 3 is not supported for our sample. Lastly, in support for Hypothesis 4, the interaction term, charismatic leadership and citizenship pressure, was significant (−.128, $p = .025$, *adj* $p = .042$), as it relates to job engagement. As shown in Figure 2, the positive relationship was stronger for individuals who felt less pressured. Further, citizenship pressure was positively related to OCBII (.248, $p < .001$, *adj* $p < .001$).

The effects of control variables in the final model are not depicted in Figure 1 to simplify the illustration. Only one variable was significant. In our findings, age was negatively related to OCBII (−.142, $p = .022$, *adj* $p = .042$) and job engagement (−.212, $p < .001$, *adj* $p < .001$).

Treatment of Common Method Variance (CMV)

Since a majority of our data were collected from the same source, we employed several procedural and statistical remedies for controlling common method biases as offered by Podsakoff et al. (2003). Procedurally, we presented detailed information about the precautions taken to ensure the confidentiality of their responses, and all participants were assured that there were no right or wrong

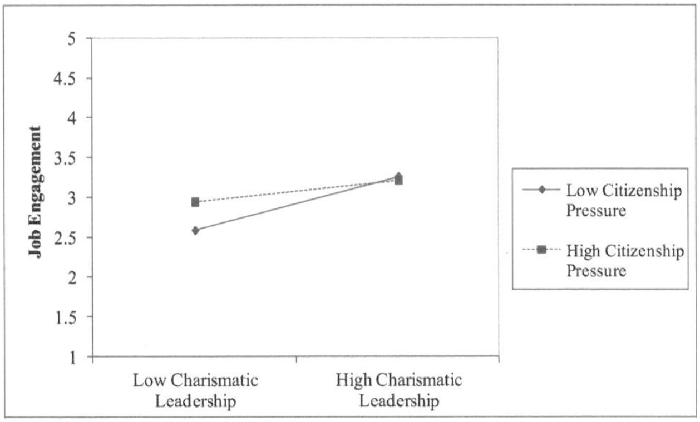

FIGURE 2. Moderation of citizenship pressure on the relationship between charismatic leadership and job engagement.

answers. All variables in this study contained multiple indicators and the reliability of the variables was acceptable. In addition, we used existing measures from the published literature that had already undergone reliability and validity testing. Lastly, for OCB, we collected OCB from a different source (i.e., mate). This ultimately minimized the potential impact of CMV. These procedures were conducted in order to decrease socially desirable responses, to increase the number of honest responses, since, for most variables, no other source was used to corroborate answers to survey questions, and to reduce evaluation apprehension.

We employed remedies to address common method variance in our analyses. Using AMOS, we estimated a full measurement model, which included a factor for each of the three variables measuring charismatic leadership, citizenship pressure, and job engagement. Next, we estimated a model that included a fourth latent variable to represent a method factor and allowed the nine dimensions to load on this uncorrelated factor (Podsakoff et al., 2003). If the fit of the measurement model significantly improves with the addition of the uncorrelated method factor, then CMV may be an issue (Williams, Cote, & Buckley, 1989). The fit statistics for the one-factor model [χ^2 (27, n = 243) = 379.530, $p < .001$; normed $\chi^2 = 14.057$; CFI = .667; NFI = .653; SRMR = .172] indicate that the data did not fit the model. The fit statistics for the three-factor measurement model [χ^2 (24, n = 243) = 84.078, $p < .001$; normed $\chi^2 = 3.503$; CFI = .943; NFI = .923; SRMR = .078] indicate that the model fit the data well. After adding an uncorrelated method factor, the fit statistics significantly improved [χ^2 (15, n = 243) = 24.594, $p = .056$; normed $\chi^2 = 1.640$; CFI = .991; NFI = .978; SRMR = .040]. The χ^2 difference test between the one-factor model and the three-factor model [χ^2_{diff} (3, n = 243) = 295.452, $p < .001$] was significant; the

χ^2 difference test between the one-factor model and the method factor model was significant [χ^2_{diff} (12, $n = 243$) = 354.936, $p < .001$]; as was the χ^2 difference test between the three-factor model and the method factor model [χ^2_{diff} (9, $n = 243$) = 59.484, $p < .001$]. These results indicate that while the three-factor measurement model is a better depiction of the data than a one-factor model, adding a method factor improves the measurement model.

In order to determine the extent of the influence of CMV, we calculated the variance explained by using the sum of the squared loadings to index the total amount of variation due to the method factor. Given our model, CMV accounted for 14.80%, which is less than the 25% as observed by Williams et al. (1989). These results suggest that our model did benefit from the addition of the method factor with a small gain in fit; however, and, more importantly, the method factor appears to account for little variation in the data. Therefore, we believe that the procedural and statistical precautions that were used in our study to control common method variance were effective. Based upon these findings, we believe that CMV is not an invasive problem in our study and that the relationships observed represent substantive rather than diminutive effects.

Discussion

This study answers a call by researchers to examine moderators of the relationship between charismatic leadership and its observed outcomes (Boerner et al., 2008; Kark et al., 2003; Porter & McLaughlin, 2006; Shamir et al., 1993). Thus, our results add to literature on charismatic leadership by documenting empirical support of the moderating role of citizenship pressure. First, as confirmed in previous studies (Babcock-Roberson & Strickland, 2010; Bettencourt, 2004; De Cremer & Van Knippenberg, 2002; Deluga, 1995; Den Hartog et al., 2007; Shamir et al., 1998), we expected charismatic leadership to be positively related to OCB. This hypothesis was supported for our sample. In addition, consistent with previous research (Babcock-Roberson & Strickland, 2010), charismatic leadership was positively related to job engagement.

The results did not support our argument that citizenship pressure moderates the relationship between charismatic leadership and OCB. Specifically, the findings indicate that a charismatic leader's effect on the performance of OCBs is not reduced when followers perceive citizenship pressure. This is consistent with the common and traditional view that OCBs are a matter of good will even in the face of environmental and social pressures (Organ, 1988). This supports Bolino et al.'s (2010) finding that employees who feel pressured to perform OCBs actually do perform OCBs. Conversely, the results revealed a moderating role of citizenship pressure in the relationship between charismatic leadership and job engagement. As expected, charismatic leadership has a stronger effect on job engagement when the employees perceive less citizenship pressure, thus citizenship pressure reduces the charismatic leader's ability to motivate followers to be engaged in their jobs. This adds to recent findings that indicate that the actual performance of OCB is associated with personal costs and the relatively new concept in the OCB literature, citizenship pressure, has negative implications for employees (Bolino et al., 2010).

Beyond the theoretical implications this study has for the future development of the variables under investigation, it may also have interesting practical implications. The overall empirical evidence of a moderating role of citizenship pressure indicates that when followers perceive their leader to be charismatic, this leader engages workers, causing them to be more fully immersed in their job duties in order to align themselves with the leader's clear, high expectations, but they do so under conditions where less citizenship pressure is present. In consideration of this result, managers should note that although higher levels of citizenship pressure may, at times, produce positive outcomes (Cates et al., 2010), research reveals there are also negative outcomes of this subtle forced behavior, such as more ambiguous jobs (Bolino et al., 2010). Communication of high performance expectations should be more explicit and clear, rather than implicit and vague, as may be the case when more citizenship pressure is perceived. Also, employees should feel more confident about the potential positive impact of meeting a charismatic leader's high performance expectations. Managers should focus on communicating how their employees' personal aspirations and expectations are aligned with opportunities within the organization, thus providing individuals with challenging and stimulating work and offering meaningful feedback and recognition (Conger et al., 2000). Individuals should not be put in a position of assuming they are required to do whatever it takes and feeling pressured to involuntarily work outside their prescribed duties to meet high performance expectations or be left to guess about the future outcome of these added demands. Thus, the leader must be a resource to individuals and display supportive behaviors, such as expressions of overall concern about the employee (i.e., emotional support) and tangible assistance to enhance employee wellbeing (instrumental support) (Kossek, Pichler, Bodner, & Hammer, 2011).

Limitations and Future Research Suggestions

The results of this study should be considered in light of its limitations. We relied mainly on self-report measures, presenting the potential problem of common method bias. Given our cross sectional data, issues of causality cannot be inferred or suggested between the exogenous variables and job engagement. Even though Podsakoff et al. (2003) suggests collecting data from other perspectives (e.g., spouse, coworkers), we contend that some personal evaluations are essential. Therefore, all of the measures except OCB were based on self-reported measures. Scholars may assume that the use of self-reports automatically implies that observed relationships among variables are inflated. However, Conway and Lance

(2010) argue against these misconceptions, proposing instead that they are not necessarily true, and that it is acceptable to use self-reports as long as four specific conditions are met. First, authors should justify their reasoning why self-reports are more appropriate. In this study, it was a logical choice for a majority of the measures to be self-reported compared to using other sources because the study variables involved internal processes that would be best suited if answered by the individual. In particular, it would be difficult for a coworker to approximate truthfully the extent to which an individual was engaging in their job because the nature of this approach is unknown. In addition, coworker estimates may contain employee citizenship pressure and job engagement; however, self-reports of these variables ultimately provides measurements that are more accurate. Second, consistent with Conway and Lance's recommendations, it is acceptable to use self-reports if the measures used have construct validity. For this study, we carefully selected and used existing measures based on previously validated scores that had already been tested and validated. Third, self-reports are acceptable to use as long as there is no substantial overlap in item content between measures. Based upon the descriptions and definitions of our study measures and the sample items within these measures, OCB and job engagement appear to be the only ones where the possibility of overlap is present. For that reason, we checked for discriminant validity, which confirmed that the two variables were distinct, as previously discussed. Lastly, we took necessary precautions during data collection to proactively deal with common method bias by ensuring the respondents' confidentiality and informing them that there were no right or wrong answers.

Although it is logical to collect self-report measures of job attitudes and perceptions, supervisors often provide ratings of OCB. In contrast, both self-reported and live-in spouse or significant other or partner ratings of individual initiative (OCB) were collected here. The ratings of the mates were used to analyze the data. It is not clear how the OCB ratings might correlate with supervisor ratings. Ideally, we would have collected ratings of OCB from other sources, including peers, supervisors, and archival records in order to minimize the common source bias.

The sample of workers used in this study may not be representative of the general population. It should be noted 64% of the respondents were African American. Also, 63% of the respondents reported household income greater than $80,000 per year. Thus, the occurrence of OCB may be quite different in other samples of employees. In particular, given that the respondents here were well paid, they may be more willing to do whatever is necessary to help their organizations. Considering this, the results could be different with other populations.

For future research, it would be interesting to determine whether the source of the citizenship pressure makes a difference in the leader's ability to affect followers. Identifying the source of citizenship pressure is important because the source could influence the ways in which employees interpret and react to such pressure (Bolino et al., 2010). For instance, are the results different if the pressures stemmed from either internal (e.g., dispositional) or external (e.g., group norms, role perceptions, desire for advancement) forces? In addition, other studies have examined leader effects on OCB across cultures. Thus, it may be interesting to examine these variables among different cultures (Soo, 2012). Also future studies could examine other organizational outcomes. (e.g., job satisfaction, turnover intent). In addition, future research should investigate the moderating role of personal and situational variables. More specifically, it would be interesting to examine the current findings in relation to occupational type and stage of employment (i.e., newly hired, close to retirement) as those in more autonomous roles and/or closer to retirement may be more immune to organizational expectations considered to be citizenship pressure. Thus, they may be less affected by this pressure. Future research should examine longitudinal data. The result is likely to inform our understanding of whether or not length of service alters these relationships. It will also offer insights on the effects of charismatic leadership on job engagement and OCB as employees evolve and as environmental factors shift the organizational landscape. All of these future research directions can have a positive impact on the practice of management and leadership as companies seek to understand just what motivates the productivity and retention of one of the most significant organizational resources, human capital.

REFERENCES

Arbuckle, J. L. (2010). *IBM SPSS Amos 19 user's guide*. Crawfordville, FL: Amos Development Corporation.

Avolio, B. J., Bass, B. M., & Jung, D. I. (1999). Re-examining the components of transformational and transactional leadership using the multifactor leadership questionnaire. *Journal of Occupational and Organizational Psychology*, *72*(4), 441–462. doi: 10.1348/096317999166789

Babcock-Roberson, M. E., & Strickland, O. J. (2010). The relationship between charismatic leadership, work engagement, and organizational citizenship behaviors. *The Journal of Psychology, 144*(3), 313–356. doi: 10.1080/00223981003648336

Bagozzi, R. P., & Heatherton, T. F. (1994). A general approach for representing multifaceted personality constructs: Application to state self-esteem. *Structural Equation Modeling, 1*(1), 35–67. doi: 10.1080/10705519409539961

Bakker, A. B., & Demerouti, E. (2006). The job demands-resources model: State of the art. *Journal of Managerial Psychology, 22*(3), 309–328. doi: 10.1108/02683940710733115

Benjamini, Y., & Hochberg, Y. (1995). Controlling the false discovery rate: A practical and powerful approach to multiple testing. *Journal of the Royal Statistical Society. Series B (Methodological), 57*(1), 289–300. doi: 10.2307/2346101

Bentler, P. M. (1990). Comparative fit indexes in structural models. *Psychological Bulletin, 107*(2), 238–246. doi: 10.1037/0033-2909.107.2.238

Bettencourt, L. A. (2004). Change-oriented organizational citizenship behavors: The direct and moderating influence of goal orientation. *Journal of Retailing, 80*(3), 165–180. doi: 10.1016/j.jretai.2003.12.001

Boerner, S., Dütschke, E., & Wied, S. (2008). Charismatic leadership and organizational citizenship behaviour: Examining the role of stressors and strain. *Human Resource Development International, 11*(5), 507–521. doi: 10.1080/13678860802417643

Bolino, M. C., & Turnley, W. H. (2005). The personal costs of citizenship behavior: The relationship between individual initiative and role overload, job stress, and work–family conflict. *Journal of Applied Psychology, 90*(4), 740–748. doi: 10.1037/0021-9010.90.4.740

Bolino, M. C., Turnley, W. H., Gilstrap, J. B., & Suazo, M. M. (2010). Citizenship under pressure: What's a "good soldier" to do? *Journal of Organizational Behavior, 31*(6), 835–855. doi: 10.1002/job.635

Byrne, B. M. (2001). *Structural equation modeling with Amos: Basic concepts, applications and programming*. Mahwah, NJ: Laurence Erlbaum.

Cates, D. A., Mathis, C. J., & Randle, N. W. (2010). A positive perspective of citizenship pressure among working adults. *Journal of Managerial Issues, 22*(3), 330–344.

Cohen, J., & Cohen, P. (1975). *Applied multivariate regression/correlation analysis for the behavioral sciences*. Hillsdale, NJ: Lawrence Erlbaum.

Coleman, V. I., & Borman, W. C. (2000). Investigating the underlying structure of the citizenship performance domain. *Human Resource Management Review, 10*(1), 25–44 .doi: 10.1016/S1053-4822(99)00037-6

Conger, J. A., & Kanungo, R. N. (1987). Toward a behavioral theory of charismatic leadership in organizational settings. *Academy of Management Review, 12*(4), 637–647. doi: 10.5465/AMR.1987.4306715

Conger, J. A., & Kanungo, R. N. (1994). Charismatic leadership in organizations: Perceived behavioral attributes and their measurement. *Journal of Organizational Behavior, 15*(5), 439–452. doi: 10.1002/job.4030150505

Conger, J. A., Kanungo, R. N., & Menon, S. T. (2000). Charismatic leadership and follower effects. *Journal of Organizational Behavior, 21*(7), 747–767. doi: 10.1002/1099-1379(200011)21:7<747::AID-JOB46>3.0.CO;2-J

Conway, J., & Lance, C. E. (2010). What reviewers should expect from authors regarding common method bias in organizational research. *Journal of Business and Psychology, 25*(3), 325–334. doi: 10.1007/s10869-010-9181-6

Crant, J. M. (2000). Proactive behavior in organizations. *Journal of Management, 26*(3), 435–462. doi: 10.1177/014920630002600304

Crawford, E. R., LePine, J. A., & Rich, B. L. (2010). Linking job demands and resources to employee engagement and burnout: A theoretical extension and meta-analytic test. *Journal of Applied Psychology, 95*(5), 834–848. doi: 10.1037/a0019364

De Cremer, D., & Van Knippenberg, D. (2002). How do leaders promote cooperation? The effects of charisma and procedural fairness. *Journal of Applied Psychology*, *87*(5), 858–866. doi: 10.1037//0021-9010.87.5.858
Deluga, R. J. (1995). The relationshp between attributional charismatic leadership and organizational citizenship behaviour. *Journal of Applied Social Psychology*, *25*(18), 1652–1669. doi: 10.1111/j.1559-1816.1995.tb02638.x
Demerouti, E., Bakker, A. B., DeJonge, J., Janssen, P. P. M., & Schaufeli, W. B. (2001). Burnout and engagement at work as a function of demands and control. *Scandinavian Journal of Work, Enviroment & Health*, *27*, 279–286.
Den Hartog, D. N., De Hoogh, A. H. B., & Keegan, A. E. (2007). The interactive effects of belongingness and charisma on helping and compliance. *Journal of Applied Psychology*, *92*(4), 1131–1139. doi: 10.1037/0021-9010.92.4.1131
Eddleston, K. A., Veiga, J. F., & Powell, G. N. (2006). Explaining sex differences in managerial career satisfier preferences: The role of gender self-schema. *Journal of Applied Psychology*, *91*(2), 437–445. doi: 10.1037/0021-9010.91.2.437
Frese, M., & Fay, D. (2001). Personal initiative (PI): An active performance concept for work in the 21st century. In B. M. Staw & R. M. Sutton (Eds.), *Research in organizational behavior* (Vol. 23, pp. 133–187). Amsterdam: Elsevier Science.
Furr, R. M., & Bacharach, V. R. (2014). *Psychometrics: An introduction* (2nd ed.). Los Angeles, CA: Sage.
Galvin, B. M., Balkundi, P., & Waldman, D. A. (2010). Spreading the word: The role of surrogates in charismatic leadership processes. *Academy of Management Review*, *35*(3), 477–494. doi: 10.5465/AMR.2010.51142542
Goodman, L. A. (2011). Comment: On respondent-driven sampling and snowball sampling in hard-to-reach populations and snowball sampling not in hard-to-reach populations. *Sociological Methodology*, *41*(1), 347–353. doi: 10.1111/j.1467-9531.2011.01242.x
House, R. J., & Baetz, M. L. (1979). Leadership: Some empirical generalizations and new research directions. *Research in Organizational Behavior*, *1*, 399–401.
Hu, L. T., & Bentler, P. M. (1999). Cutoff criteria for fit indices in covariance structural analysis: Conventional criteria versus new alternatives. *Structural Equation Modeling*, *6*(1), 1–55. doi: 10.1080/10705519909540118
Hughes, R. L., Ginnett, R. C., & Curphy, G. J. (2009). *Leadership: Enhancing the lessons of experience* (6th ed.). New York, NY: McGraw-Hill/Irwin.
Kahn, R. L., & Byosiere, P. (1992). Stress in organizations. In M. D. Dunnette & L. M. Hough (Eds.), *Handbook of industrial and organizational psychology* (2nd ed., Vol. 3, pp. 571–650). Palo Alto, CA: Consulting Psychologists Press.
Kahn, R. L., Wolfe, D. M., Quinn, R., Snoek, J. D., & Rosenthal, R. A. (1964). *Organizational stress: Studies in role conflict and ambiguity*. Malabar: Robert E. Krieger Publishing Company, Inc.
Kahn, W. A. (1990). Psychological conditions of personal engagement and disengagement at work. *Academy of Management Journal*, *33*(44), 692–724. doi: 10.2307/256287
Kark, R., Shamir, B., & Chen, G. (2003). The two faces of transformational leadership: Empowerment and dependency. *Journal of Applied Psychology*, *88*(2), 246–255. doi: 10.1037/0021-9010.88.2.24
Kossek, E. E., Pichler, S., Bodner, T., & Hammer, L. B. (2011). Workplace social support and work–family conflict: A meta-analysis clarifying the influence of general and work–family specific supervisor and organizational support. *Personnel Psychology*, *64*(2), 289–313. doi: 10.1111/j.1744-6570.2011.01211.x
LePine, J. A., Erez, A., & Johnson, D. E. (2002). The nature and dimensionality of organizational citizenship behavior: A critical review and meta-analysis. *Journal of Applied Psychology*, *87*(1), 52–65. doi: 10.1037/0021-9010.87.1.52

Martins, L. L., Eddleston, K. A., & Veiga, J. F. (2002). Moderators of the relationship between work–family conflict and career satisfaction. *Academy of Management Journal, 45*(2), 399–409. doi: 10.2307/3069354
Moorman, R. H., & Blakely, G. L. (1995). Individualism collectivism as an individual difference predictor of organizational citizenship behavior. *Journal of Organizational Behavior, 16*(2), 127–142. doi: 10.1002/job.4030160204
Nahrgang, J. D., Morgeson, F. P., & Hofmann, D. A. (2010). Safety at work: A meta-analytic investigation of the link between job demands, job resources, burnout, engagement, and safety outcomes. *Journal of Applied Psychology, 96*(1), 71–94. doi: 10.1037/a0021484
Niehoff, B. P., & Moorman, R. H. (1993). Justice as a mediator of the relationship between methods of monitoring and organizational citizenship behavior. *Academy of Management Journal, 36*(3), 527–556. doi: 10.2307/256591
Nunnally, J. C. (1978). *Psychometric theory*. New York, NY: McGraw-Hill.
Organ, D. W. (1988). *Organizational citizenship behavior: The good soldier syndrome*. Lexington, MA: Lexington Books.
Organ, D. W., Podsakoff, P. M., & MacKenzie, S. B. (2006). *Organizational citizenship behavior: Its nature, antecedents, and consequences*. Thousand Oaks, CA: Sage Publications.
Podsakoff, P. M., MacKenzie, S. B., & Hui, C. (1993). Organizational citizenship behaviors and managerial evaluations of employee performance: A review and suggestions for future research. In G. R. Ferris & K. M. Rowland (Eds.), *Research in personnel and human resources management* (Vol. 11, pp. 1–40). Greenwich, CT: JAI Press.
Podsakoff, P. M., MacKenzie, S. B., Lee, J. Y., & Podsakoff, N. P. (2003). Common method biases in behavioral research: A critical review of the literature and recommended remedies. *Journal of Applied Psychology, 88*(5), 879–903. doi: 10.1037/0021-9010.88.5.879
Podsakoff, P. M., MacKenzie, S. B., Moorman, R. H., & Fetter, R. (1990). Transformational leader behaviors and their effects on followers' trust in leader, satisfaction, and organizational citizenship behaviors. *The Leadership Quarterly, 1*(2), 107–142. doi: 10.1016/1048-9843(90)90009-
Podsakoff, P. M., MacKenzie, S. B., Paine, J. B., & Bachrach, D. G. (2000). Organizational citizenship behaviors: A critical review of the theoretical and empirical literature and suggestions for future research. *Journal of Management, 26*(3), 513–563. doi: 10.1177/014920630002600307
Porter, L. W., & McLaughlin, G. B. (2006). Leadership and the organizational context: Like the weather?. *Leadership Quarterly, 17*(6), 559–576. doi: 10.1016/j.leaqua.2006.10.002
Rafferty, A. E., & Griffin, M. A. (2004). Dimensions of transformational leadership: Conceptual and empirical extensions. *The Leadership Quarterly, 15*(3), 329–354. doi: 10.1016/j.leaqua.2004.02.009
Rich, B. L. (2006). *Job engagement: Construct validation and relationships with job satisfaction, job involvement, and intrinsic motivation*. Doctor of Philosophy doctoral dissertation, University of Florida.
Rowold, J., & Heinitz, K. (2007). Transformational and charismatic leadership: Assessing the convergent, divergent, and criterion validity of the mlq and the cks. *The Leadership Quarterly, 18*(2), 121–133. doi: 10.1016/j.leaqua.2007.01.003
Saks, A. M. (2006). Antecedents and consequences of employee engagement. *Journal of Managerial Psychology, 21*(7), 600–619. doi: 10.1108/02683940610690169
Scandura, T. A., & Williams, E. A. (2000). Research methodology in management: Current practices, trends, and implications for future research. *Academy of Management Journal, 43*(6), 1248–1264. doi: 10.2307/1556348
Schaufeli, W. B., & Bakker, A. B. (2004). Job demands, job resources, and their relationship with burnout and engagement: A multi-sample study. *Journal of Organizational Behavior, 25*(3), 293–315. doi: 10.1002/job.248

Schaufeli, W. B., Bakker, A. B., & Van Rhenen, W. (2009). How changes in job demands and resources predict burnout, work engagement, and sickness absenteeism. *Journal of Organizational Behavior*, *30*, 893–917. doi: 10.1002/job.595

Schumacker, R. E., & Lomax, R. G. (2004). *A beginner's guide to structural equation modeling* (2nd ed.). Mahwah, NJ: Lawrence Erlbaum Associates.

Settoon, R. P., & Mossholder, K. W. (2002). Relationship quality and relationship context as antecedents of person- and task-focused interpersonal citizenship behavior. *Journal of Applied Psychology*, *87*(2), 255–267. doi: 10.1037//0021-9010.87.2.255

Shamir, B., House, R. J., & Arthur, M. B. (1993). The motivational effects of charismatic leadership: A self-concept based theory. *Organization Science*, *4*(4), 577–594. doi: 10.1287/orsc.4.4.577

Shamir, B., Zakay, E., Breinin, E., & Popper, M. (1998). Correlates of charismatic leader behavior in militariy units: Subordinates' attitutes, unit characteristics, and superiors' appraisals of leader performance. *Academy of Management Journal*, *41*(4), 387–409. doi: 10.2307/257080

Soo, H. S. (2012). *The mediation and moderation effects of stress and social support on leadership–organizational citizenship behavior relationship: A study among bank employees in malaysia*. Ph.D., Universiti Utara Malaysia.

Steiger, J. H. (2007). Understanding the limitations of global fit assessment in structural equation modeling. *Personality and Individual Differences*, *42*(5), 893–898. doi: 10.1016/j.paid.2006.09.017

Tims, M., Bakker, A. B., & Xanthopoulou, D. (2010). Do transformational leaders enhance their followers' daily work engagement? *The Leadership Quarterly*, *22*(1), 121–131. doi: 10.1016/j.leaqua.2010.12.011

van Knippenberga, D., & Sitkin, S. B. (2013). A critical assessment of charismatic–transformational leadership research: Back to the drawing board? *The Academy of Management Annals*, *7*(1), 1–60. doi: 10.1080/19416520.2013.759433

Vigoda-Gadot, E. (2006). Compulsory citizenship behavior in organizations: Theorizing some dark sides of the good soldier syndrome. *Journal for the Theory of Social Behavior*, *36*(1), 77–93. doi: 10.1111/j.1468-5914.2006.00297.x

Vigoda-Gadot, E. (2007). Redrawing the boundaries of OCB? An empirical examination of compulsory extra-role behavior in the workplace. *Journal of Business and Psychology*, *21*(3), 377–405. doi: 10.1007/s10869-006-9034-5

Vlachoutsicos, C. (2011). How to cultivate engaged employees. *Harvard Business Review*, *89*(9), 123–126.

Williams, L. J., Cote, J. A., & Buckley, M. R. (1989). Lack of method variance in self-reported affect and perceptions at work: Reality or artifact? *Journal of Applied Psychology*, *74*(3), 462–468.

Original manuscript received April 11, 2014
Final version accepted October 15, 2014

Part III

Organizational Culture

Mitigating the Harmful Effect of Perceived Organizational Compliance on Trust in Top Management: Buffering Roles of Employees' Personal Resources

Dirk De Clercq and Dave Bouckenooghe

ABSTRACT

This study considers how employees' POC—defined as their beliefs that the organizational climate stifles change and values compliance with the status quo—reduce their trust in top management, as well as how this negative relationship might be buffered by access to two personal resources that support organizational change: openness to experience and affective commitment to change. Data from a sample of Pakistan-based organizations reveal that POC reduce trust in top management, but this effect is weaker at higher levels of openness to experience and affective commitment to change. These findings are significant in that they indicate that employees who operate in organizational climates marked by "yea-saying" can counter the difficulty of improving their job situation by drawing from adequate personal resources.

Organizational scholarship acknowledges the importance of developing trusting relationships between employees and organizational authorities (Clapp-Smith, Vogelgesang, & Avey, 2009; Zhang, Tsui, Song, Li, & Jia, 2008). In particular, employees' high levels of trust in top management—defined herein as the extent to which they believe that their organization's senior decision makers are dependable and open in their communication and thus care for their well-being (Bouckenooghe, 2012; Bouckenooghe & Menguc, 2018; Lee, Kim, Kim, Kwon, & Cho, 2013)—is a significant manifestation of how they feel about their employment situation (Kramer, 1999; Mahajan, Bishop, & Scott, 2012). For example, when employees express high levels of trust in top management, their organizational commitment (Mahajan et al., 2012) and work engagement (Chughtai & Buckley, 2013) increase, and they are more likely to engage in productive behaviors such as innovation (Michaelis, Stegmaier, & Sonntag, 2009) and to pursue their organization's goals (Thomas, Zolin, & Hartman, 2009). In contrast, a lack of trust in top management contributes to increased feelings of burnout, stress, and job dissatisfaction (Lambert, Hogan, Barton-Bellessa, & Jiang, 2012). Organizations thus have a critical need to understand which factors might inhibit the development of trust between employees and top management.

Previous research mostly emphasizes how positive contextual forces shape employees' trust in top management, such as leader–membership exchanges (van Dam, Oreg, & Schyns, 2008), perceived organizational support (Webber, Bishop, & O'Neill, 2012), perceived justice (Colquitt & Rodell, 2011; Wu, Huang, Li, & Liu, 2012), acceptable performance appraisal systems (Mayer & Davis, 1999), or the possibility to voice opinions about the organization's internal functioning (Holland, Cooper, Pyman, & Teicher, 2012). To extend research beyond these facilitators of trust, we investigate how dysfunctional political climates—that is, organizational climates that discourage change and personal initiative, and thereby curtail opportunities for learning and personal development (Byrne, 2005; Kacmar & Baron, 1999)—might *diminish* trust in top management, as well as how personal resources might mitigate this effect. Doing so reflects our acknowledgment that employee–top management relationships are inherently asymmetric, and employees might experience significant stress if the organizational climate limits their ability to alter or improve their current job situations (Barry & Wilkinson, 2016; Grimland, Vigoda-Gadot, & Baruch, 2012; Hurley, 2006; Kacmar & Baron, 1999).

Although an organizational climate that focuses on a strict adherence to the status quo might not always be negative, previous research emphasizes the dysfunctional character of organizational climates that reflect a "go-along-to-get-ahead" (i.e., GATGA) mentality. A climate anchored in a GATGA mentality embraces *covert* political behaviors that cause employees to become overly dependent on existing power structures (Byrne, 2005; O'Connor & Morrison, 2001). In a "yea-saying" climate, employees often feel discouraged from speaking up about potential improvements in their work environment, even if doing so would benefit their performance outcomes and career development (Hochwarter, Witt, & Kacmar, 2000). Perceptions of the presence of an organizational climate that values strong compliance with the status quo—for parsimony, we use the term "perceptions of organizational compliance" (POC)—are a significant source of stress for employees, because such beliefs prevent them from improving their job situation and thwart their personal growth (Byrne, 2005; Grimland et al., 2012; Magner & Staley, 2014).

To substantiate our arguments about the relationship between employees' POC and their trust in top management, as well as identify conditions in which POC might be less harmful, we draw from the job demands–resources (JD-R) model (Bakker & Demerouti, 2007). This model proposes that stressful work conditions steer employees away from positive attitudes toward their employer, but access to relevant resources can buffer or mitigate this process (Bakker & Demerouti, 2007; Crawford, LePine, & Rich, 2010; Hakanen, Schaufeli, & Ahola, 2008). Accordingly, when employees believe that the organizational climate favors compliance over personal initiative, they might become so concerned about their limited ability to improve their job situation that they perceive their organization's senior leadership as untrustworthy and not interested in their well-being (Byrne, 2005; Kacmar & Baron, 1999).

Moreover, we argue that this negative process may be less prominent to the extent that employees can rely on two critical personal resources that stimulate organizational change: their openness to experience and affective commitment to change. Openness to experience is a personality trait that reflects the tendency of employees to seek out new, varied experiences (McCrae & Costa, 1997). Among the Big Five personality traits, this one speaks most directly to employees' ability to come up with *novel* ideas and solutions to address constraining organizational climates that discourage personal initiative (Baer & Oldham, 2006; McCrae, 1994). Affective commitment to change instead captures employees' beliefs about the intrinsic value of organizational change (Herscovitch & Meyer, 2002) and the positive emotions that employees might experience in response to changes to the organizational status quo (Kabanoff, Waldersee, & Cohen, 1995). Although employees marked by high levels of affective commitment to change might feel some frustration in organizational climates that stifle initiative, the argument advanced in this article, as informed by the JD-R model (Bakker & Demerouti, 2007), is that the positive change-related energy that gets generated by this personal resource (Choi, 2011) might help employees *overcome* the stress invoked by such climates, such that they maintain some level of trust in top management. Further, in contrast with previous studies that examine how openness to experience might influence employees' attitudes toward change, and particularly reduce their resistance to it (Saksvik & Hetland, 2009), we focus on the *concurrent* roles of their openness to experience and affective commitment to change in shaping their reactions to POC.

These two personal resources, conceptualized as moderators in our proposed model, align with the logic of the JD-R model, according to which access to relevant resources provides employees with the energy needed to maintain positive work attitudes, despite the presence of workplace adversity (Bakker & Demerouti, 2007; Pooja, De Clercq, & Belausteguigoitia, 2016). In particular, the glue that binds the two resources is that they both instill positive change-related energy in employees, such that they increase the ability to mitigate the stress that comes with organizational environments that stifle employee initiative and critical thinking (Quinn, Spreitzer, & Lam, 2012). They both might help employees overcome the limitations that surround an organizational climate that thwarts change and supports a GATGA mentality. Moreover, both resources complement each other: openness to experience is a personality trait that captures employees' natural tendency and associated cognitive ability to try new things and find creative ways to deal with adverse work situations (McCrae & Costa, 1997), and affective commitment to change is an individual state-like characteristic that reflects the intrinsic value that employees assign to organizational changes (Choi, 2011).[1] The combined consideration of these two contingency factors therefore provides a consistent, comprehensive approach to determine how employees' resource access may buffer against the likelihood of distrust in top management when rigid organizational climates discourage change (Bakker & Demerouti, 2007).

The contribution of this study is multifold. First, extant research has paid little attention to how employees' trust in top management might be hampered by perceptions of covert political behaviors that thwart personal initiative and change. Instead, organizational change studies typically focus on *outcomes*, highlighting, for example, how trust in top management can stimulate employees' support for change (Michaelis et al., 2009; van

[1]The affective dimension of commitment to change contrasts with its normative and continuance counterparts, which reflect a sense of obligation to support organizational change and a recognition of the potential costs when the change is not supported, respectively (Herscovitch & Meyer, 2002).

Dam et al., 2008). We propose that perceptions about whether the organizational climate supports change in themselves might be significant drivers of trust in top management. Second, previous research has not considered how the translation of dysfunctional organizational politics into lower trust in top management may be mitigated by employees' access to personal resources (Byrne, 2005). This significant oversight prevents organizations from fully understanding how negative reactions (i.e., reduced trust in top management) to climates that prioritize compliance over speaking up might be contained by relevant individual characteristics. By studying the contingent factors of openness to experience and affective commitment to change, we consider how employees' access to two relevant personal resources can buffer or diminish the likelihood that they experience negative feelings about their employer in response to a compliance-oriented climate (Schaufeli & Bakker, 2004), and we also respond to calls to apply contingency approaches to study the outcomes of destructive political behaviors (Chang, Rosen, Siemieniec, & Johnson, 2012; Chen & Fang, 2008; Miller, Rutherford, & Kolodinsky, 2008). Third, the JD-R framework is useful for investigating the negative impact of adverse work conditions on employees' feelings about their organization (e.g., Crawford et al., 2010; Pooja et al., 2016). However, to the best of our knowledge, it has not been applied to important questions about how and when a compliance-oriented organizational climate might dampen employees' trust in top management. Thus, with this study, we extend the scope of the JD-R framework. The proposed theoretical framework is summarized in Figure 1.

Theoretical background

Previous research extensively considers the question of why some employees express more or less trust in other organizational members (e.g., Colquitt, Scott, & Lepine, 2007; Nienaber, Romeike, Searle, & Schewe, 2015; Schoorman, Mayer, & Davis, 2007). Trust has been conceptualized in various ways, including employees' willingness to be vulnerable to the actions of others (Colquitt et al., 2007; Rousseau, Sitkin, Burt, & Camerer, 1998) or their belief that others will make good faith efforts to meet their commitments (Cummings & Bromily, 1996). A critical aspect that binds these conceptualizations is the positive expectations that employees have, namely, that other members

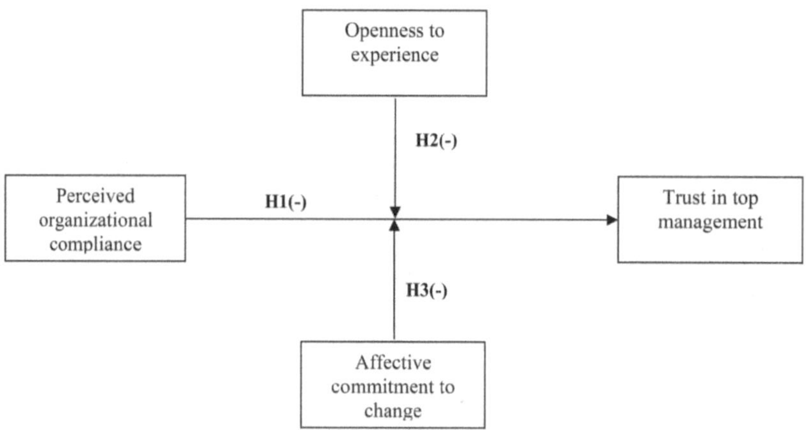

Figure 1. Conceptual model.

will act in reliable and consistent ways and are concerned about their well-being (Lewicki, Tomlinson, & Gillespie, 2006; Nienaber et al., 2015).

With this study, we focus on employees' trust in *top management*, or the group of senior decision makers who operate at the top of the organizational chart (McCauley & Kuhnert, 1992). The level of trust that employees have in organizational authorities influences other attitudes, such as their work engagement (Chughtai & Buckley, 2013), and their behaviors, such as their innovative activities (Michaelis et al., 2009). Such elements in turn have direct implications for organizational performance. Consistent with previous research (Bouckenooghe, 2012; Korsgaard, Schweiger, & Sapienza, 1995; Lee et al., 2013; Schoorman et al., 2007), we conceptualize trust in top management as the belief that the organization's senior leadership is consistent in its decision making, fulfills previously made promises, and adopts open communication practices—all features that reflect top management's benevolence or the extent to which it has employees' best interests at heart (Mayer, Davis, & Schoorman, 1995; Schoorman et al., 2007).

Previous research indicates that the trust that employees have in top management is mostly informed by their assessments of organization-wide processes and procedures, instead of characteristics of their interpersonal relationships with specific organizational members (McCauley & Kuhnert, 1992; cf. Costigan, Insinga, Berman, Kranas, & Kureshov, 2011). As we noted previously, extant studies of contextual influences highlight the enabling roles of positive factors, such as perceived organizational support (Webber et al., 2012), leader–member exchanges (van Dam et al., 2008), performance appraisals (Mayer & Davis, 1999), and job involvement (Mahajan et al., 2012) in shaping employees' trust in top management. In turn, relatively little attention has been devoted to the harmful effects that negative factors might play in inhibiting such trust, including the presence of an organizational climate that embraces destructive political behaviors (Chen & Indartono, 2011; Nienaber et al., 2015). Yet such political behaviors constitute important realities that challenge effective organizational functioning (Blass, Brouer, Perrewe, & Ferris, 2007; Grimland et al., 2012; Vredenburgh & Shea-VanFossen, 2010). For example, dysfunctional political climates can lead to enhanced job stress and burnout (Valle & Perrewe, 2000), reduce organizational commitment (Vigoda, 2000) and job satisfaction (Zhou & Ferris, 1995), and increase uncertainty about whether work efforts generate positive performance outcomes (Cropanzano, Howes, Grandey, & Toth, 1997). Destructive organizational politics also can inhibit positive organizational change, as manifested in fewer opportunities to voice opinions about how the organizational status quo can be improved (Li, Wu, Liu, Kwan, & Liu, 2014), as well as lower creativity (Rosen, Ferris, Brown, Chen, & Yan, 2014) and innovation (Frost & Egri, 1991).

Notably, dysfunctional, politically oriented climates can take different forms. They are not restricted to overt, self-serving political behaviors, such as blatantly spreading negative rumors to achieve direct personal gains. Rather, they might entail obscure or hidden behaviors, such as when employees feel forced to align their opinions with those of senior decision makers (Byrne, 2005). We focus on this type of dysfunction and acknowledge that a significant manifestation of *covert* politics takes place when the organizational climate promotes strict compliance with the status quo (Kacmar & Carlson, 1997). Such a climate can be stressful for employees, because it limits their ability to improve their job situation and learn from their efforts, thereby undermining their personal development (Li et al., 2014; Parker, Dipboye, & Jackson, 1995). An organizational climate that supports GATGA behavior thus might be frustrating for employees, because it indicates that adherence to the status quo takes precedence over individual employee initiative or well-being (Espedal, 2017; Kacmar & Baron, 1999).

To anchor our theoretical arguments about the negative relationship between POC and trust in top management, we draw from the JD-R model (Bakker & Demerouti, 2007). It predicts that adverse work conditions generate significant stress among employees, which can translate into negative attitudes toward the organization (Pooja et al., 2016). Furthermore, it postulates that workplace adversity has less harmful effects to the extent that employees have access to relevant resources, including those that they hold individually (Schaufeli & Bakker, 2004; Schmitz & Ganesan, 2014). That is, in the presence of relevant personal resources, stressful work conditions are less likely to turn into negative work attitudes, because the resources protect or *buffer* against this impact (Bakker & Demerouti, 2007; Van Emmerik, Bakker, & Euwema, 2009).

First, we argue that POC is a stressor that directly informs employees' negative attitudes toward their organization's senior leadership. According to the JD-R model, job demands—such as unfavorable physical work conditions, excessive workloads, or unsupportive organizational climates—are energy draining and generate psychological costs for employees (Bakker & Demerouti, 2007). Similarly, perceptions that it would be difficult to improve the current organizational situation, in response to an organizational climate that stifles personal initiative and focuses on the status quo, may be a significant source of stress that undermines employees' ability to find ways to meet their job requirements (Byrne, 2005; Kacmar & Baron, 1999).

Second, we apply the buffering argument of the JD-R model (Bakker & Demerouti, 2007) by predicting a mitigating effect of openness to experience and affective commitment to change on the negative influence of POC on trust in top management. Openness to experience, one of the Big Five personality traits (Barrick & Mount, 1991), should have a beneficial effect in situations in which employees face constraining, initiative-thwarting work situations, by enabling them to try new methodologies and approaches (Keller & Weibler, 2015). Affective commitment to change in turn captures employees' emotional buy-in and adherence to the idea that change is instrumental for improving the organization, even if the organizational climate might obstruct change (Herscovitch & Meyer, 2002). The JD-R model thus offers a theoretical framework that advances not only our understanding of the negative outcomes of POC on trust in top management but also the buffering roles of these critical personal resources in this process, as we detail in the Hypotheses section.

Hypotheses

Perceptions of Organizational Compliance and Trust in Top Management

We predict a negative relationship between employees' POC and their trust in top management. According to the JD-R model, adverse work situations are stressful and can lead to negative feelings toward the organization, because the situations deplete employees' positive energy reservoirs as they try to cope with the adversity (Hakanen et al., 2008; Pooja et al., 2016; Schaufeli & Bakker, 2004). Similarly, when employees are convinced that the organizational climate favors compliance rather than personal initiative, they may experience significant frustration, because they feel constrained and fear that the climate will compromise their ability to improve their own job situation (Kacmar & Ferris, 1991; Li et al., 2014). This fear then may lead to negative attitudes toward their organization's senior leadership, as reflected in low trust in top management, because employees are preoccupied with negative feelings of anxiety and worry about their organizational functioning (Bakker & Demerouti, 2007; Mahajan et al., 2012). For example, an organizational climate that prefers yea-saying over speaking up may give employees the impression that top management is filtering out important information, because the climate discourages "rocking the boat" or speaking up about problem areas. These employees likely believe top management is not open to their communication, withholds crucial development opportunities, or undermines their ability to perform and develop themselves through their active contributions to organizational improvement (Byrne, 2005; Grimland et al., 2012; Kacmar & Baron, 1999; Li et al., 2014; Rosen et al., 2014). Similarly, previous research on trust in top management shows that when employees are not allowed to be involved in their organization's decision-making process, their trust gets compromised, because they believe their organization's senior leadership does not value their opinions or care for their well-being (Mahajan et al., 2012). If instead they experience a climate that discourages blind compliance, employees should feel less stressed and believe that their organization can be counted on to support their endeavors to improve their current job situation, which leads to positive feelings of trust in their organization's senior leadership (Bakker & Demerouti, 2007; Mahajan et al., 2012).

A climate that focuses on compliance with the status quo instead of personal initiative also might reduce trust in top management, because it can be interpreted as insensitive and disrespectful (Chang, Rosen, & Levy, 2009; Ferris & Kacmar, 1992). When employees experience stressful work conditions that discourage their attempts to take on existing power structures or question organizational malfunctions, they may experience strong animosity, or even anger, toward organizational authorities, because the organization's features undermine their ability to perform well or advance (Bakker & Demerouti, 2007; Grimland et al., 2012; Kacmar & Ferris, 1993). We therefore anticipate less trust in top management when employees have strong negative views about the organizational climate. Explicitly, if they perceive that the organizational climate emphasizes compliance with the status quo and discourages personal initiative, they may predict destructive managerial decision making (Bouckenooghe, 2012; Eisenhardt & Bourgeois, 1988) and regard the setting as counterproductive or offensive. Ultimately, they would exhibit little trust that top management cares about their well-being.

Hypothesis 1: There is a negative relationship between employees' perceptions of organizational compliance and their trust in top management.

Moderating Role of Openness to Experience

We predict a buffering effect of employees' openness to experience on this negative relationship between their POC and trust in top management. According to the JD-R model, the harmful effect of work stressors diminishes when employees can draw from personal resources that help them undo the accompanying stress (Bakker & Demerouti, 2007; van Doorn & Hülsheger, 2015). Openness to experience means that employees are motivated to find creative ways to deal with negative organizational climates, such as those that do not grant them room to take personal initiative (McCrae & Costa, 1997). This motivation may reduce or buffer the stress that stems from the adverse situation and diminish their propensity to distrust management (Bakker, Demerouti, & Euwema, 2005). For example, suggestions about how to improve the current job situation may encounter great resistance from top management in a yea-saying climate, particularly if those suggestions undermine their personal turf (Chen, Liu, & Tjosvold, 2005; Van Dyne, Ang, & Botero, 2003). But employees with greater openness to experience are more likely to pursue novel ways to reduce such resistance and should be highly involved in such activities (George & Zhou, 2001; McCrae & Costa, 1997). Therefore, they might maintain some trust in top management, even in a compliance-oriented climate (Mahajan et al., 2012). Previous research similarly indicates that employees high on openness to experience express more curiosity about novel ways to deal with stressful work situations, which mitigates the uncertainty that arises in such situations (Baer & Oldham, 2006).

Moreover, employees who score high on openness to experience may feel positively energized when confronted with work situations that run counter to their natural tendencies. In response, they may feel compelled to tackle these challenging situations, and executing job tasks in a compliance-oriented climate may provide some personal fulfillment (Keller & Weibler, 2015; McCrae, 1987). In this sense, the personal resource of openness to experience might stimulate not just employees' ability to address the negative consequences of covert political behavior but also the personal joy that they derive from this process (McCrae & Costa, 1997), which ultimately should diminish the harm to their trust in top management (Mahajan et al., 2012). Conversely, employees who are not open to experience generally have less motivation to find novel solutions to challenging situations (Keller & Weibler, 2015), so they allocate less energy to improving their job situation or personal development in a climate that emphasizes strict compliance with the status quo, which should diminish their trust in top management.

Hypothesis 2: The negative relationship between employees' perceptions of organizational compliance and their trust in top management is moderated by their openness to experience, such that the relationship is weaker at higher levels of openness to experience.

Moderating Role of Affective Commitment to Change

We predict a similar buffering role of affective commitment to change; employees who believe in the value of change should be better able to protect themselves against the stress that comes with an organizational climate that favors the status quo over personal initiative. Employees who exhibit a strong belief in the value of change are more likely to reach out to peers and ask for their advice about how to improve their job situation in a climate that focuses on strict compliance with the status quo (Choi, 2011; Herscovitch & Meyer, 2002). Consistent with the JD-R model, this advice might serve as a buffer that mitigates the frustration that results from such a climate (Bakker & Demerouti, 2007; Byrne, 2005; Cohen &

Wills, 1985) and prevents employees from believing that their organization is withholding critical information from them. Enhanced information sharing with peers also can generate new insights into *why* the organizational climate might encourage yea-saying over personal initiative (Wanberg & Banas, 2000). These insights then can help employees cope with the stress that comes with a constraining, compliance-oriented climate and maintain some trust in top management (Bakker & Demerouti, 2007). Similarly, previous research indicates that access to adequate information is beneficial for the development of trust in top management (Thomas et al., 2009). Thus, a strong affective commitment to change should mitigate the likelihood that POC translate into lower trust in top management, because the organizational environment is perceived as less harmful.

The frustration that employees feel when encountering an organizational compliance climate also might be contained more easily if they feel passionate about changing the situation, because they enjoy the challenge of finding solutions (Baum & Locke, 2004; Choi, 2011). Affective commitment to change thus may attenuate the potency with which POC reduces trust in top management, because it increases the attractiveness of speaking out against such a climate (Rosen et al., 2014). Employees who feel committed to change also have a strong intrinsic motivation to exploit their skill set to deal with stressful work situations (Meyer & Herscovitch, 2001; Neves & Caetano, 2009), so positive feelings of accomplishment when they succeed in these endeavors may diminish the belief that top management is withholding critical information from them. Conversely, when employees are unconvinced of the value of change, they likely feel less excited or energized about opportunities to overcome a compliance-oriented climate (Wanberg & Banas, 2000), so they may develop less positive feelings toward their organization's senior leadership.

> *Hypothesis 3: The negative relationship between employees' perceptions of organizational compliance and their trust in top management is moderated by their affective commitment to change, such that the relationship is weaker at higher levels of affective commitment to change.*

Research Method

Sample and Data Collection

We collected data for this study from two companies that participated in an executive training program at a leading business school in Lahore, Pakistan: a nonprofit organization active in the educational sector and a for-profit company in the textile sector. The data collection process involved two surveys, distributed in two waves with a time lag of 2 weeks, consistent with previous research (Bouckenooghe, De Clercq, & Deprez, 2014; De Clercq, Haq, & Azeem, 2018). The use of a time lag between the measurement of the dependent variable and independent variables is a standard procedure that alleviates potential common method variance (Podsakoff, MacKenzie, Lee, & Podsakoff, 2003). Furthermore, the time lag was long enough to reduce concerns about reverse causality (e.g., high levels of trust in top management might generate positive feelings in employees about their organizational climate) but not so long that significant organizational events could have occurred during the research period.

The two surveys contained unique identification numbers, so we could match responses collected in each wave. A cover letter explained the purpose of the study and assured participants of the complete confidentiality of their responses, noting that the responses would be accessible only to the research team, no information at the individual level would ever be made public, and only aggregate data would be used in the research. Moreover, the surveys contained reassurances that there were no correct or incorrect answers, and we asked the respondents to answer the questions as honestly as possible. These measures helped diminish social desirability or acquiescence biases (Spector, 2006). The first survey assessed employees' POC, openness to new experiences, and opinions about change in the organization. The second survey then asked these same respondents to assess their trust in the organization's top management. Of the 350 surveys distributed, we received 164 completed pairs of surveys across the two data collection points, 112 for the educational organization and 52 for the textile company, resulting in an overall response rate of 47%. The respondents were on average 39.62 years old and had worked for their organization for 9.85 years.[2]

Measures

The measures of the focal constructs used items from previous research, with five-point Likert scales ranging from 1 ("strongly disagree") to 5 ("strongly agree"). To assess how much trust employees have in their organization's top management, we applied a four-item scale borrowed from previous research that emphasizes the importance of consistency and open communication (Bouckenooghe, 2012). Two example items are "Top management fulfills its promises" and "Top management keeps all departments informed about its decisions" (Cronbach's alpha = .73). This measure captures the content domain of our conceptualization of trust in top management, namely, the extent to which employees believe that top management is dependable and transparent in its communication. It has robust psychometric properties (Bouckenooghe, Devos, & Van den Broeck, 2009) and has been applied previously to study perceived organizational politics (Bouckenooghe, 2012).

We used the six-item go-along-to-get-ahead (GATGA) scale by Kacmar and Carlson (1997) to measure POC. Previous research indicates that such perceptions can be treated as distinctive features of dysfunctional organizational politics, separate from the direct political behaviors that people use blatantly to advance themselves by tearing others down, as well as from political games played to earn pay or promotion benefits (Byrne, 2005; Kacmar & Carlson, 1997). For example, items indicated, "It is best not to rock the boat in this organization" and "Sometimes it is easier to remain quiet than to fight the system" (Cronbach's alpha = .70).

For the moderators, we measured openness to experience with nine items from the Big Five personality traits inventory (John, Donahue, & Kentle, 1991; Watson, Suls, & Haig, 2002), such as, "I see myself as someone who is original" and "I see myself as someone

[2]An independent-samples *t*-test, which compared the respondents in the educational organization and textile company, indicated that there were no significant differences in employees' trust in top management (3.81 versus 3.93, respectively, *ns*) and affective commitment to change (4.10 versus 4.02, *ns*). Yet there were significant differences in employees' POC (2.75 versus 3.09, $p < .01$), openness to experience (4.16 versus 3.90, $p < .01$), age (43.85 versus 30.42 years, $p < .001$), and organizational tenure (12.64 versus 3.77 years, $p < .001$). In light of these differences in sample means for some variables, we included a dummy variable for organization type in the regression analyses.

who is curious about many different things" (Cronbach's alpha = .71).[3] To measure affective commitment to change, we used a six-item scale based on Herscovitch and Meyer (2002), capturing employees' perceptions of the intrinsic value of change. For example, the respondents indicated whether "I believe in the value of change" and "Change serves an important purpose" (Cronbach's alpha = .72). Consistent with previous research (Macky & Boxall, 2007; Shen, Tang, & D'Netto, 2014), we controlled for age and organizational tenure. We also controlled for organization type (1 = textile company; see Footnote 2).

Results

Preliminary Analyses

Before testing the hypotheses, we checked the appropriateness of the data for the analyses. First, because the responses included some missing data, we performed Little's test of whether data are missing completely at random (Little & Rubin, 1989; Schafer, 1997); they were for our sample ($\Delta\chi^2_{(467)} = 439.75$, $p = .81$). Moreover, the percentage of missing data equaled 1.50%, below the 5% cutoff that marks inconsequential missing data (Schafer, 1999). We also replaced the missing values by applying the expectation maximization algorithm (Dempster, Laird, & Rubin, 1977), which is an appropriate method for treating missing data, because the estimated parameters are consistent with missing-at-random conditions (Dempster et al., 1977; Little & Schenker, 1995).

Second, we checked for multivariate normality with the standard normality test in AMOS, notwithstanding the argument that deviations from multivariate normality do not automatically affect the analysis results. For example, Arbuckle (1997, p. 239) argues that "a departure from normality that is big enough to be significant could still be small enough to be harmless." For our study, the critical ratios for the skewness and kurtosis of the openness to experience and affective commitment to change constructs were greater than the benchmark of ±2.0, yet the value for the multivariate omnibus test was less than 2.0. According to the Mahalanobis d-squared values, 5 of the 164 observations were potentially problematic outliers that caused non-normality in our data. After removing these outliers, the critical ratios were lower than 2.0 in absolute value for each construct. Therefore, we tested the hypotheses using 159 responses, after excluding these outliers. An advantage of deleting the outliers, rather than an alternative approach of transforming the data, is that it retains the assumption of linearity (Gao, Mokhtarian, & Johnston, 2008).

Third, we estimated a four-factor measurement model with confirmatory factor analysis (Anderson & Gerbing, 1988). Although global fit indices such as the goodness-of-fit index and adjusted goodness-fit-index often serve to assess model fit, they also have been criticized (Hu & Bentler, 1998). Instead, Hu and Bentler (1998) recommend the use of the incremental and confirmatory fit indices (IFI and CFI) or residual fit indices (e.g., standardized root mean residual [SRMR]) (Bentler, 1995; Joreskog & Sorbom, 1986). Monte Carlo studies reveal that

[3]We deleted one (reverse-coded) item from the ten-item scale, because the alpha value was below .70 (Nunnally, 1978) when we included it. This particular item had a corrected item-to-total correlation of .03, suggesting very little variance in common with the other items. A robustness check with a composite measure that included all 10 items generated results that were completely consistent with those reported in Table 2. The omission of unreliable items from scales measuring the Big Five inventory is consistent with previous research (e.g., Leung, Wong, Chan, & Lam, 2013; Raja & Johns, 2010; Spence, Owens, & Goodyer, 2012).

these fit indices offer more robust measures than their global fit counterparts (e.g., Fan, Thompson & Wang, 1999; Hu & Bentler, 1998; Jackson, 2007; Marsh, Balla, & Hau, 1996). Moreover, the root mean square error of approximation (RMSEA) performs well in terms of providing an adequate model specification without being dependent on sample size (Jackson, Gillaspy, & Purc-Stephenson, 2009). Our measurement model yielded an adequate fit, according to these preferred fit indices ($\chi^2_{(261)} = 347.19$, $\chi^2/df = 1.33$, IFI = .91, CFI = .90, SRMR = .07, RMSEA = .05; Bentler & Bonett, 1980; Yuan, 2005).[4] Moreover, we found support for discriminant validity, because in each construct pair, there were significant differences between the chi-square values of the constrained models in which the correlations between the two constructs were set to equal 1 and their unconstrained counterparts in which the correlations were set free ($\Delta\chi^2_{(1)} > 3.84$; Anderson & Gerbing, 1988).

Fourth, we performed two tests to check for common method bias. In Harman's single-factor test (Podsakoff & Organ, 1986), if common method bias exists, a single factor would account for most of the variance in the data. Our exploratory factor analysis instead indicated that the first factor accounted for only 16% of the variance. Next, the confirmatory factor analysis of a model in which we let each measurement item load on a single factor generated significantly worse fit than the fit of the four-factor model. The difference in the chi-square values of these two models was strongly significant ($\Delta\chi^2_{(38)} = 489.43$, $p < .01$). This finding further alleviates concerns about common method bias. Previous research also shows that the risk of common method bias is substantially lower for theoretical models that include moderating effects, because it is more difficult for respondents to identify those effects (Brockner, Siegel, Daly, Tyler, & Martin, 1997; Simons & Peterson, 2000).

Hypothesis Tests

In Table 1, we present the zero-order correlations and descriptive statistics; in Table 2, we provide the regression results. Model 1 included the control variables, Model 2 added POC, and Model 3 added the two moderators of openness to experience and affective commitment to change. In Models 4 and 5, we added the POC × openness to experience and POC × affective commitment to change interaction terms, respectively. Previous research affirms that it is appropriate to add multiple interaction terms separately, because the simultaneous inclusion of multiple interaction terms into a single model can mask the true moderating effects (Aiken & West, 1991; De Clercq, Bouckenooghe, Raja, & Matsyborska, 2014; Zahra & Hayton 2008). We mean-centered the variables before calculating the interaction terms (Aiken & West, 1991).

In support of our baseline prediction in Hypothesis 1, that employees' perceptions of a climate that favors compliance with the status quo generate negative feelings toward the employer, Model 2 reveals that POC relates negatively to trust in top management ($\beta = -.46$, $p < .001$). Although not part of our theoretical framework, Model 3 also indicates a direct positive relationship between affective commitment to change and trust in top management ($\beta = .25$, $p < .05$), whereas the link between openness to experience and trust in top management is not significant ($\beta = .11$, *ns*).

[4]Despite the relatively small sample size, the participant-to-item ratio met the rule of five (159/26 = 6.12) (Bryant & Yarnold, 1995).

Table 1. Descriptive Statistics and Correlations.

	Mean	SD	1	2	3	4	5	6
1. Trust in top management	3.84	.71						
2. Perceived organizational compliance	2.86	.64	−.38**					
3. Openness to experience	4.08	.49	.10	−.10				
4. Affective commitment to change	4.07	.53	.24**	−.14	.18*			
5. Age	39.62	9.81	.00	−.26**	.24**	.08		
6. Organizational tenure	9.85	7.09	−.07	−.17*	.15	.03	.81**	
7. Organization type (1 = textile)	.31	.47	.08	.25**	−.25**	−.07	−.64**	−.58**

Notes: $N = 159$.
**$p < .05$; **$p < .01$.

Table 2. Regression Results (Dependent Variable: Trust in Top Management).

	Model 1	Model 2	Model 3	Model 4	Model 5
Age	.02[a]	.01	.00	−.00	.01
Organizational tenure	−.02	−.01	−.01	−.01	−.01
Organization type (1 = textile)	.18	.28+	.31*	.30*	.32*
H_1: perceived organizational compliance (POC)		−.46***	−.43***	−.45***	−.50***
Openness to experience			.11	.07	.10
Affective commitment to change			.25*	.24*	.24*
H_2: POC × openness to experience				.40*	
H_3: POC × affective commitment to change					.51***
R^2	.02	.18	.22	.25	.27
R^2 change		.16***	.04*	.03*	.05***

Notes: $N = 159$; unstandardized coefficients (two-tailed p-values).
***$p < .001$; **$p < .01$; *$p < .05$.

Models 4 and 5 support the hypothesized buffering effects of openness to experience ($\beta = .40$, $p < .05$) and affective commitment to change ($\beta = .51$, $p < .001$) on the relationship between POC and trust in top management. That is, increasing the levels of POC has a smaller likelihood of diminishing trust in top management when employees are more open to trying new, varied experiences (Hypothesis 2) or express stronger beliefs about the intrinsic value of change for their organization (Hypothesis 3). To clarify the nature of these interactions, we plotted the effects of POC on trust in top management at high and low levels of the two moderators (Figures 2 and 3), combined with a simple slope analysis for each (Aiken & West, 1991). The results of the simple slope analyses indicate that the relationship between POC and trust in top management is significant at low levels of both openness to experience ($\beta = -.84$, $p < .001$) and affective commitment to change ($\beta = -1.01$, $p < .001$) but *not* significant at high levels of these moderators ($\beta = -.05$, *ns*; $\beta = .02$, *ns*, respectively), in further support of Hypotheses 2 and 3.

In addition to assessing the statistical significance of the hypothesized effects, we checked their practical significance by calculating the corresponding semi-partial correlation coefficients (Aloe & Becker, 2012). We found a semi-partial correlation coefficient of .40 for the main effect of POC in Model 2, then semi-partial correlation coefficients of .17 and .23 for the interaction effects of POC × openness to experience and POP × affective commitment to change in Models 4 and 5, respectively. These correlation coefficients indicate relatively low values for the amount of unique variance explained by these three factors—the value of .40 corresponds with 16% explained variance, the value of .17 with 3% explained variance, and the value of .23 with 5%

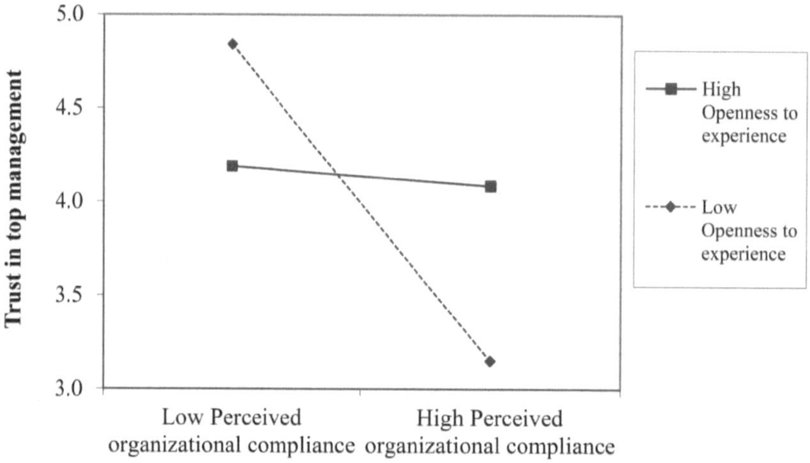

Figure 2. Moderating effect of openness to experience on the POC–trust in top management relationship.

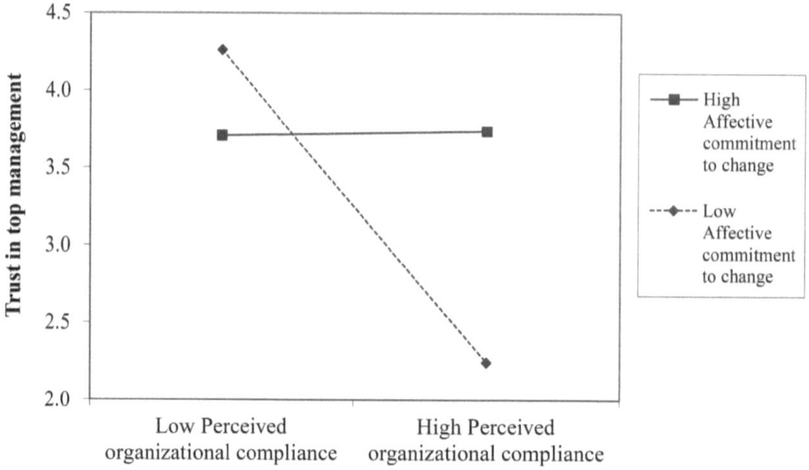

Figure 3. Moderating effect of affective commitment to change on the POC–trust in top management relationship.

explained variance—yet they still are higher than the median correlational effect size of .16 that Bosco, Aguinis, Singh, Field, and Pierce (2015) found in their analysis of effect sizes in applied psychology research, so they can be considered medium in size.[5] Moreover, in light of the critical importance of employees' trust in top management,

[5]With data from 1,660 articles published in *Journal of Applied Psychology and Personnel Psychology*, Bosco et al. (2015) identified a median effect size—which they defined as the absolute value of the corresponding correlation coefficients—of .16 across 147,328 correlational effect sizes. They accordingly argued that correlational effect sizes that fall within the range from .10 to .39 are medium in size and generally acceptable. For correlational effects pertaining to relationships among attitudes specifically, as in our study, the interval that defines a medium effect size according to Bosco et al. (2015) was [.18, .39]. This interval encompasses the correlational effect sizes we found, with the slight exception of the .17 value for the POC × openness to experience interaction term, which is just below the lower bound of the interval. Overall, the effect sizes in this study, though somewhat relatively weak, therefore are not exceptionally low.

which deeply informs the extent to which they undertake positive work behaviors that add to organizational effectiveness (e.g., Michaelis et al., 2009; Thomas et al., 2009), even small effects still could have substantial practical relevance for organizations.

Even though the conceptual focus of this study is on the *concurrent* interplay of POC, openness to experience, and affective commitment to change in predicting trust in top management, we undertook a post hoc analysis that accounted for possible interdependencies among these constructs, such as the possibility that employees' affective commitment to change might be influenced by their POC and their openness to experience. Accordingly, we ran two path models, corresponding with the two regression Models 4–5 in Table 2, that included covariances among POC, openness to experience, and commitment to change. The hypothesized effects were consistent with the results obtained from the regression analysis (Table 2); the main effect of POC and the moderating effects of openness to experience and affective commitment to change remained robust even after accounting for their possible causal interdependencies (De Clercq, Thongpapanl, & Dimov, 2009). Finally, we checked an alternative model in which affective commitment to change served as a potential mediating variable, but we failed to find empirical support for this model, because bootstrapping generated a confidence interval for the indirect effect of POC on trust through affective commitment to change that included 0 ([–.853; .001], Preacher & Hayes, 2004).

Discussion

Explaining why some employees are more likely than others to perceive their organization's senior leadership as trustworthy is an important endeavor, because such perceptions inform positive employee behaviors such as organizational goal accomplishment (Colquitt et al., 2007; Thomas et al., 2009) and innovation implementation efforts (Michaelis et al., 2009). This study contributes to extant research by elaborating on how employees' POC might lead to lower levels of trust in top management, as well as how their personal resources may function as buffers in this process. The relatively limited attention to this issue is surprising, in light of the argument that frustration with dysfunctional political climates might be countered by access to relevant resources (Abbas, Raja, Darr, & Bouckenooghe, 2014; Bouckenooghe, 2012). Consistent with the JD-R model, we theorize that openness to experience and affective commitment to change, as personal resources, mitigate the likelihood that employees respond to POC with reduced trust in top management. Our findings support these theoretical arguments. This study thereby offers significant insights for organizational research and practice, by highlighting an important challenge associated with maintaining positive relationships between employees and organizational authorities, as well as identifying ways that this challenge can be resolved.

The direct negative effect of employees' POC on trust mirrors findings from previous research about the harmful effects of destructive political maneuvers on positive work attitudes and behaviors (Crawford et al., 2010; Rosen et al., 2014; Vigoda, 2000; Zhou & Ferris, 1995). This negative relationship seemingly arises because employees interpret compliance-oriented climates as counterproductive and disrespectful (Ferris & Kacmar, 1992). Even if strict compliance with the current organizational situation might not be harmful automatically, such as when organizations operate in stable external environments (Jiao, Alon, Koo, & Cui, 2013), perceptions that the status quo is preferred over personal initiative tend to be counterproductive, in that they undermine employees' beliefs that they have the discretion to improve their current job situations or learn from their work efforts (Grimland et al., 2012; Kramer, 1999). In addition, negative feelings of frustration or anger that emerge in response to political decision making that thwarts employee initiative (Chang et al., 2009; Kacmar & Ferris, 1993) may fuel beliefs that top management is withholding critical information and does not have the best interests of employees at heart.

Yet this negative effect of POC on trust can be mitigated by employees' tendency to search for and engage in new experiences (McCrae & Costa, 1997), as well as by the value that they attribute to change for effective organizational functioning (Herscovitch & Meyer, 2002). These two personal resources enhance the likelihood that employees can find creative ways to deal with an organizational climate in which personal initiative is curtailed by a preference for the status quo, which in turn mitigates the stress resulting from such an unfavorable work situation (Bakker et al., 2005; Kacmar & Ferris, 1993). Ultimately, their propensity to express reduced trust in top management then may diminish. Moreover, these resources can fuel the joy that employees experience when they seek to improve their current job situation. Employees who score high on openness to experience or affective commitment to change may feel energized when they encounter and overcome an adverse situation, such as one that promotes covert politics (McCrae & Costa, 1997; Meyer & Herscovitch, 2001). Consistent with the JD-R model, this feeling reduces the likelihood that they develop negative feelings toward top management (Bakker & Demerouti, 2007; Pooja et al., 2016).

Interestingly, Table 1 indicates non-significant correlation coefficients between the independent variable (POC) and the two moderators (openness to experience and affective commitment change), which mitigates concerns about the presence of multicollinearity or high shared variances among these variables. Moreover, the lack of a significant correlation and relationship between employees' openness to experience and trust in top management shows that a personality trait such as openness does not directly influence employees' attitudes toward their organization's top management but rather plays a more indirect role by influencing their attitudinal responses to adverse organizational climates. Notably, our theoretical focus on the buffering roles of both openness to experience and affective commitment to change revolves around the *incremental* role of POC in reducing trust. We thus offer organizations better insights into the conditions in which a culture marked by yea-saying is less likely to reduce trust in top management. Empirically, these buffering roles are supported by the *slope* differences that appear at different levels of the moderators. The interaction plots in Figures 2 and 3, and the corresponding simple slope analyses, indicate that increasing levels of POC do *not* contribute significantly to lowered trust in top management when employees are curious and seek out new experiences or believe in the intrinsic value of change for their organization. Thus, the belief that the organization favors strict compliance over personal initiative harms employees' trust in top management only when those employees have limited access to these personal resources.

The theoretical focus of this study was on assessing slope differences at different levels of the study's moderators—as informed by the JD-R logic regarding the buffering effects of personal resources on how employees react to stress-inducing organizational climates (Bakker & Demerouti, 2007)—not on comparing the actual values of employees' trust in top management at different levels of the independent and moderating variables. Nonetheless, one could argue for the likely presence of higher trust levels when workplace adversity is minimal (i.e., low organizational compliance) and personal resources are abundant (i.e., high openness to experience and high affective commitment to change). Yet the patterns in Figures 2 and 3 indicate a far more complex dynamic. First, when POC is *low*, trust in top management seems to be higher among employees who score low on openness to experience and affective commitment to change. A possible explanation is that when personal initiative is encouraged by the organization *and* employees tend to be complacent with regard to change (i.e., have a low natural tendency to experiment or do not see value in organizational change), they might over-rely on top management to tell them what to do. Second, Figures 2 and 3 indicate that when POC is *high*, trust in top management is higher among employees with high levels of openness to experience and affective commitment to change. Perhaps employees *need* to be able to draw from a minimum level of positive energy—derived from their personality or general attitudes toward change—that makes them confident that they can alter the status quo and maintain some trust in top management when their organization makes it challenging to take personal initiative. These post hoc explanations are highly speculative though; further studies might theorize, for example, how the relative usefulness of energy-enhancing personal resources, such as the ones studied herein, influence employees' attitudes toward top management, depending on their perceptions of their surrounding organizational environment.

Managerial Implications

This study also has important practical implications. The belief that the organizational climate discourages employees from rocking the boat can be a significant source of stress. In response, organizations should seek strategies to diminish the occurrence of POC. Some employees may be hesitant to report cases in which their personal opinions have been ignored in such cultures, to avoid potential negative repercussions from powerful others (Barry & Wilkinson, 2016). Organizations therefore must be proactive in identifying and resolving situations that prevent employees from speaking up about how to improve the status quo. For example, to the extent that the organization's historical functioning has created a culture that encourages covert political behaviors that favor the status quo, targeted development programs should stimulate employees to speak out frankly about organizational malfunctioning, even if these efforts challenge current power structures (Vredenburgh & Shea-VanFossen, 2010). In the absence of such measures, the frustration that employees experience about not being able to improve their job situation may translate into negative feelings and ultimately lead them to distrust top management.

Employees' openness to experience is another tool that organizational decision makers can leverage to mitigate frustration with a culture that thwarts personal initiative.

Organizations marked by compliance-based climates can benefit from recruiting employees who score high on openness to experience and feel motivated to learn about new experiences and who are likely to come up with novel solutions to improve the organizational status quo *despite* strong resistance (McCrae & Costa, 1997). Moreover, affective commitment to change is another lever for organizations that seek to mitigate problems associated with a political culture that focuses on the status quo. Organizations marked by compliance and yea-saying can benefit from hiring employees who believe that organizational change serves an important purpose and is key to the organization's long-term success. Notably, employees' affective commitment to change is not set in stone; it can be developed through targeted initiatives. For example, employees might grow more motivated to support change in their organization to the extent that they enjoy higher levels of job security (Chawla & Kelloway, 2004) or perceive less conflict among their different job roles (Iverson, 1996).

Limitations and Future Research

Some shortcomings of this study suggest research opportunities. First, our theoretical arguments about the negative relationship between employees' perceptions about a climate that values strict compliance with the status quo and their trust in top management is based on the assumption that an organization-wide adherence to existing power structures is inherently dysfunctional. Although it might not be the case in all organizations, especially if their industrial context is stable and predictable (Jiao et al., 2013), political climates that stifle employee input about possible job improvements, even if incremental, tend to be perceived as counterproductive by employees, because such climates hamper their personal growth and career advancement (Byrne, 2005; Grimland et al., 2012). Nonetheless, future research might test our proposed framework across a wider set of organizations, to address the potential variance in the perceived usefulness of personal initiative, according to external competitive influences. Such research could also collect informative employee data about the actual or perceived need for change.

Second, we considered two specific contingency factors but ignored alternative potential buffers of the negative relationship between POC and trust in top management. For example, other personal characteristics could function as buffers too, such as employees' creative self-efficacy (Tierney & Farmer, 2002) or resilience, which reflects their ability to bounce back from adverse situations that constrain their personal initiative (Youssef & Luthans, 2007). Additional contextual factors also could influence the likelihood that a compliance-based climate leads to reduced levels of trust in top management, such as whether employees believe they are fairly rewarded for their job efforts (Colquitt, Conlon, Wesson, Porter, & Ng, 2001) or whether they share their employer's goals (Nahapiet & Ghoshal, 1998).

Third, an empirical limitation of this study pertains to our reliance on students of an executive education program, who represent only a small proportion of the total workforce and may possess better-than-average personal resources, as suggested by their relatively high scores on the openness to experience and affective commitment to change constructs. Although these restricted response ranges actually provide a more conservative statistical test of the theoretical relationships (i.e., we find significant moderating effect relationships *despite* this restriction), additional studies should include a more diverse set of employees to assess the generalizability of the reported findings.

Fourth, another empirical limitation pertains to our focus on organizations that are based in one specific country (Pakistan); cultural factors cannot be excluded. Our theoretical arguments are not country specific, but Pakistani culture tends to be more risk averse than that of many Western countries (Hofstede, 2001), so employees may be hesitant to go out of their way to change or improve their job situation in the presence of an organizational climate that focuses on the status quo. In turn, the usefulness of change-supportive resources for reducing the negative effects of a compliance-oriented climate on trust in top management might be more salient in our study context than it would be in more risk-prone countries. Moreover, Pakistan reveals an intermediate score on the power distance construct, or general attitudes about whether members of societies can be unequal (Hofstede, 2001). This cultural dimension may influence the extent to which employees experience a compliance-oriented organizational climate as appropriate or stressful. Cross-country studies therefore might compare the relative importance of POC, in terms of defining how employees feel about top management and the potency of the underlying moderators, across different cultural contexts. Moreover, future studies could compare the role of relevant cultural values, such as power distance, at the *individual* level (Daniels & Greguras, 2014) to investigate their potential role as moderators of the relationship between POC and trust in top management.

Finally, an important empirical limitation pertains to the reliability values for the focal constructs. Their Cronbach's alpha values range between .70 and .73, such that they meet or exceed the well-established cutoff of .70 (Nunnally, 1978), yet they admittedly are relatively low. McCrae, Kurtz, Yamagata, and Terracciano (2011) recommend interpreting Cronbach's alpha values in relation to values found in similar empirical settings. For example, previous cross-cultural studies indicate that the reliability of scales that measure the Big Five personality traits and affective commitment to change tend to be lowest in developing countries (Allik & McCrae, 2004; Bouckenooghe, 2012; Kwantes, 2003; Schmitt, Allik, McCrae, & Benet-Martinez, 2007; Yilmaz, Ozer, & Gunluk, 2014).[6] Notably, low reliabilities tend to attenuate the estimates of relationships between variables in regression analysis (Schmitt, 1996). That is, in the presence of lower reliabilities, any relationships between a focal variable and other variables may be underestimated because of the relative high random measurement error, which may lead to a failure to find true significant effects. Accordingly, studies that find significant effects, *despite* the relatively low reliabilities, arguably provide a more conservative statistical test of hypothesized relationships. Nonetheless, we consider the low reliabilities a potential weakness of this study, which suggests the need to establish the replicability of the results, which may reflect some "random noise" in the measurement scales. In particular, continued studies might replicate our test of the conceptual framework in

[6]The Cronbach's alpha values in our study are comparable with those reported in previous studies that took place in similar contexts. For example, trust in management evokes reliability values ranging between .76 and .79 (Bouckenooghe, 2012; Bouckenooghe et al., 2009); perceptions of organizational politics reveal reliability values ranging between .67 and .73 (Byrne, 2005; Samad, 2011; Yilmaz et al., 2014); openness to experience scores an average reliability value of .76 across 56 countries, with several values below .60 (Schmitt et al., 2007); and affective commitment has reliability values of .73 in Bhatnagar (2007) and .75 in Kwantes (2003).

contexts that are similar to and different from the context we study, to determine if the low reliabilities might be due to a specific country setting, sample size, or limited number of scale items. Another option could be to apply scales that may be less prone to random measurement error (Lattin, Carroll, & Green, 2003; Warner, 2013).

Conclusion

This study has investigated how employees' perceptions of organizational climates that favor strict compliance over personal initiative spur negative feelings toward top management, in the form of reduced trust. The likelihood that POC leads to lower trust in top management decreases when employees can draw from the personal resources of openness to experience or affective commitment to change. These resources reduce employees' frustration with the limited opportunities for improving their job situation in a compliance-oriented climate, because they are more likely to go out of their way to pursue positive organizational change. Overall, this study introduces a platform for further investigations of how organizations can mitigate the challenges that result from constraining political climates that promote the status quo, such that they can better avoid the development of negative feelings in their employee bases.

References

Abbas, M., Raja, U., Darr, W., & Bouckenooghe, D. (2014). Combined effects of perceived politics and psychological capital on job satisfaction, turnover intentions, and performance. *Journal of Management*, *40*(7), 1813–1830.

Aiken, L. S., & West, S. G. (1991). *Multiple regression: Testing and interpreting interactions.* Newbury Park, CA: Sage.

Aloe, A. M., & Becker, B. J. (2012). An effect size for regression predictors in meta-analysis. *Journal of Educational and Behavioral Statistics*, *37*(2), 278–297.

Allik, J., & McCrae, R. R. (2004). Towards a geography of personality traits: Patterns of profiles across 36 cultures. *Journal of Cross-Cultural Psychology*, *35*(1), 13–28.

Anderson, J. C., & Gerbing, D. W. (1988). Structural equation modeling in practice: A review and recommended two-step approach. *Psychology Bulletin*, *103*(3), 411–423.

Arbuckle, J. (1997). *Amos users' guide, version 3.6*, Chicago IL: Smallwaters Corporation.

Baer, M., & Oldham, G. R. (2006). The curvilinear relation between experienced creative time pressure and creativity: Moderating effects of openness to experience and support for creativity. *Journal of Applied Psychology*, *91*(4), 963–970.

Bakker, A. B., & Demerouti, E. (2007). The job demands-resources model: State of the art. *Journal of Managerial Psychology*, *22*(3), 309–328.

Bakker, A. B., Demerouti, E., & Euwema, M. C. (2005). Job resources buffer the impact of job demands on burnout. *Journal of Occupational Health Psychology, 10*(2), 170–180.

Barrick, M. R., & Mount, M. K. (1991). The big five personality dimensions and job performance: A meta-analysis. *Personnel Psychology, 44*(1), 1–26.

Barry, M., & Wilkinson, A. (2016). Pro-social or pro-management? A critique of the conception of employee voice as a pro-social behaviour within organizational behaviour. *British Journal of Industrial Relations, 54*(2), 261–284.

Baum, J. R., & Locke, E. A. (2004). The relationship of entrepreneurial traits, skill, and motivation to subsequent venture growth. *Journal of Applied Psychology, 89*(4), 587–598.

Bentler, P. M. (1995). *EQS structural equations program manual.* Encino, CA: Multivariate Software.

Bentler, P. M., & Bonett, D. G. (1980). Significance tests and goodness of fit in the analysis of covariance structures. *Psychological Bulletin, 88*(3), 588–606.

Bhatnagar, J. (2007). Predictors of organizational commitment in India: Strategic HR roles, organizational learning capability and psychological empowerment. *International Journal of Cross Cultural Management, 18*(10), 1782–1811.

Blass, F. R., Brouer, R. L., Perrewe, P. L., & Ferris, G. R. (2007). Politics understanding and networking ability as a function of mentoring: The roles of gender and race. *Journal of Leadership & Organizational Studies, 14*(2), 93–105.

Bosco, F. A., Aguinis, H., Singh, K., Field, J. G., & Pierce, C. A. (2015). Correlational effect size benchmarks. *The Journal of Applied Psychology, 100*(2), 431–449.

Bouckenooghe, D. (2012). The role of organizational politics, contextual resources, and formal communication on change recipients' affective commitment to change: a multilevel study. *European Journal of Work and Organizational Psychology, 21*(4), 575–602.

Bouckenooghe, D., De Clercq, D., & Deprez, J. (2014). Interpersonal justice, relational conflict, and commitment to change: The moderating role of social interaction. *Applied Psychology: An International Review, 63*(3), 509–540.

Bouckenooghe, D., Devos, G., & Van den Broeck, H. (2009). Organizational change questionnaire – Climate of change, processes, and readiness: Development of a new instrument. *The Journal of Psychology, 143*, 559–599.

Bouckenooghe, D., & Menguc, B. (2018). Understanding the dynamics between supervisor-follower social capital, work engagement, and employees' creative work involvement. *Canadian Journal ofAdministrative Sciences*, 35(2), 238–251.

Brockner, J., Siegel, P. A., Daly, J. P., Tyler, T., & Martin, C. (1997). When trust matters: The moderating effect of outcome favorability. *Administrative Science Quarterly, 42*(3), 558–583.

Bryant, F. B., & Yarnold, P. R. (1995). Principal component analysis and exploratory and confirmatory factor analysis. In L.G. Grimm, & R.R. Yarnold (Eds.), *Reading and understanding multivariate statistics* (pp. 99–136). Washington DC: American Psychological Association.

Byrne, Z. S. (2005). Fairness reduces the negative effects of organizational politics on turnover intentions, citizenship behavior and job performance. *Journal of Business and Psychology, 20*(2), 175–200.

Chang, C.-H., Rosen, C. C., & Levy, P. E. (2009). The relationship between perceptions of organizational politics and employee attitudes, strain, and behavior: A meta-analytic examination. *Academy of Management Journal, 52*(4), 779–801.

Chang, C.-H., Rosen, C. C., Siemieniec, G. M., & Johnson, R. E. (2012). Perceptions of organizational politics and employee citizenship behaviors: Conscientiousness and self-monitoring as moderators. *Journal of Business and Psychology, 27*(4), 395–406.

Chawla, A., & Kelloway, K. (2004). Predicting openness and affective commitment to change. *Leadership and Leadership & Organization Development Journal, 25*(6), 485–498.

Chen, C.-H. V., & Indartono, S. (2011). Study of commitment antecedents: The dynamic point of view. *Journal of Business Ethics, 103*(4), 529–541.

Chen, G., Liu, C., & Tjosvold, D. (2005). Conflict management for effective top management teams and innovation in China. *Journal of Management Studies, 42*(2), 277–300.

Chen, Y.-Y., & Fang, W. (2008). The moderating effect of impression management on the organizational politics–performance relationship. *Journal of Business Ethics, 79*(3), 263–277.

Choi, M. (2011). Employees' attitudes toward organizational change: A literature review. *Human Resource Management, 50*(4), 479–500.

Chughtai, A. A., & Buckley, F. (2013). Exploring the impact of trust on research scientists' work engagement. *Personnel Review, 42*(4), 396–421.

Clapp-Smith, R., Vogelgesang, G. R., & Avey, J. B. (2009). Authentic leadership and positive psychological capital: The mediating role of trust at the group level of analysis. *Journal of Leadership & Organizational Studies, 15*(3), 227–239.

Cohen, S., & Wills, T. A. (1985). Stress, social support, and the buffering hypothesis. *Psychological Bulletin, 98*(2), 310–357.

Colquitt, J. A., Conlon, D. E., Wesson, M. J., Porter, C. O. L. H., & Ng, K. Y. (2001). Justice at the millennium: A meta-analytic review of 25 years of organizational justice research. *Journal of Applied Psychology, 86*(3), 425–445.

Colquitt, J. A., & Rodell, J. B. (2011). Justice, trust, and trustworthiness: A longitudinal analysis integrating three theoretical perspectives. *Academy of Management Journal, 54*(6), 1183–1206.

Colquitt, J. A., Scott, B. A., & Lepine, J. A. (2007). Trust, trustworthiness, and trust propensity: A meta-analytic test of their unique relationships with risk taking and job performance. *Journal of Applied Psychology, 92*(4), 909–927.

Costigan, R. D., Insinga, R. C., Berman, J. J., Kranas, G., & Kureshov, V. A. (2011). Revisiting the relationship of supervisor trust and CEO trust to turnover intentions: A three-country comparative study. *Journal of World Business, 46*(1), 74–83.

Crawford, E. R., LePine, J. A., & Rich, B. L. (2010). Linking job demands and resources to employee engagement and burnout: A theoretical extension and meta-analytic test. *Journal of Applied Psychology, 95*(5), 834–848.

Cropanzano, R., Howes, J. C., Grandey, A. A., & Toth, P. (1997). The relationship of organizational politics and support to work behaviors, attitudes, and stress. *Journal of Organizational Behavior, 18*(2), 159–180.

Cummings, L. L., & Bromily, P. (1996). The organizational trust inventory (OTI): Development & validation. In Kramer, R. and Tyler, T. (Eds.), *Trust in organizations* (pp. 302–330). Thousand Oaks, CA: Sage.

Daniels, M. A., & Greguras, G. J. (2014). Exploring the nature of power distance: Implications for micro- and macro-level theories, processes, and outcomes. *Journal of Management, 40*(5), 1202–1229.

De Clercq, D., Bouckenooghe, D., Raja, U., & Matsyborska, G. (2014). Servant leadership and work engagement: The contingency effects of leader-follower social capital. *Human Resource Development Quarterly, 25*(2), 183–212.

De Clercq, D., Haq, I. U., & Azeem, M. U. (2018). Self-efficacy to spur job performance: Roles of job-related anxiety and perceived workplace incivility. *Management Decision, 56*(4), 891–907.

De Clercq, D., Thongpapanl, N., & Dimov, D. (2009). When good conflict gets better and bad conflict becomes worse: The role of social capital in the conflict–innovation relationship. *Journal of the Academy of Marketing Science, 37*(3), 283–297.

Dempster, A. P., Laird, N. M., & Rubin, D. B. (1977). Maximum likelihood estimation from incomplete data via the EM algorithm. *Journal of the Royal Statistical Society Series B, 39*, 1–38.

Eisenhardt, K. M., & Bourgeois, L. J. (1988). Politics of strategic decision making in high-velocity environments. *Academy of Management Journal, 32*, 543–576.

Espedal, B. (2017). Understanding how balancing autonomy and power might occur in leading organizational change. *European Management Journal, 35*(2), 155–163.

Fan, X., Thompson, B., & Wang, L. (1999). The effects of sample size, estimation methods, and model specification on SEM fit indices. *Structural Equation Modeling: A Multidisciplinary Journal, 6*(1), 56–83.

Ferris, G. R., & Kacmar, K. M. (1992). Perceptions of organizational politics. *Journal of Management, 18*(1), 93–116.

Frost, P. J., & Egri, C. P. (1991). The political process of innovation. In B.M. Staw & L.L. Cummings (Eds.), *Research in organizational behavior*. Vol. *13* (pp. 229–295), Greenwich, CT: JAI Press.

Gao, S., Mokhtarian, P., & Johnston, R. (2008). Nonnormality of data in structural equation models. *Transportation Research Record: Journal of the Transportation Research Board, 2082*(1), 116–124.

George, J. M., & Zhou, J. (2001). When openness to experience and conscientiousness are related to creative behavior: An interactional approach. *The Journal of Applied Psychology, 86*(3), 513–524.

Grimland, S., Vigoda-Gadot, E., & Baruch, Y. (2012). Career attitudes and success of managers: The impact of chance event, protean, and traditional careers. *International Journal of Human Resource Management, 23*(6), 1074–1094.

Hakanen, J. J., Schaufeli, W. B., & Ahola, K. (2008). The job demands-resources model: A three-year cross-lagged study of burnout, depression, commitment, and work engagement. *Work & Stress, 22*(3), 224–241.

Herscovitch, L., & Meyer, J. P. (2002). Commitment to organizational change: Extension of a three component model. *Journal of Applied Psychology, 87*(3), 474–487.

Hochwarter, W. A., Witt, L. A., & Kacmar, K. M. (2000). Perceptions of organizational politics as a moderator of the relationship between conscientiousness and job performance. *Journal of Applied Psychology, 85*(3), 472–478.

Hofstede, G. (2001). *Culture's consequences: Comparing values, behaviors, institutions and organizations across nations* (2nd ed.). Thousand Oaks, CA: Sage Publications.

Holland, P., Cooper, B. K., Pyman, A., & Teicher, J. (2012). Trust in management: the role of employee voice arrangements and perceived managerial opposition to unions. *Human Resource Management Journal, 22*(4), 377–391.

Hu, L. T., & Bentler, P. M. (1998). Fit indices in covariance structure modeling: Sensitivity to underparameterized model misspecification. *Psychological Methods, 3*(4), 424–453.

Hurley, R. F. (2006). The decision to trust. *Harvard Business Review, 84*(9), 55–62.

Iverson, R. D. (1996). Employee acceptance of organizational change: The role of organizational commitment. *International Journal of Human Resource Management, 7*(1), 122–149.

Jackson, D. L. (2007). The effect of the number of observations per parameter in misspecified confirmatory factor analytic models. *Structural Equation Modeling, 14*(1), 48–76.

Jackson, D. L., Gillaspy, J. A., & Purc-Stephenson, R. (2009). Reporting practices in confirmatory factor analysis: An overview and some recommendations. *Psychological Methods, 14*(1), 6–23.

Jiao, H., Alon, I., Koo, C. K., & Cui, Y. (2013). When should organizational change be implemented? The moderating effect of environmental dynamism between dynamic capabilities and new venture performance. *Journal of Engineering and Technology Management, 30*(2), 188–205.

John, O. P., Donahue, E. M., & Kentle, R. L. (1991). *The "Big Five" inventory—versions 4a and 5a*. Berkley, CA: Institute of Personality and Social Research, University of California.

Joreskog, K. G., & Sorbom, D. (1986). *LISREL VI: Analysis of linear structural relationships by maximum likelihood and least squares methods*. Mooresville, IN: Scientific Software.

Kabanoff, B., Waldersee, R., & Cohen, M. (1995). Espoused values and organizational change themes. *Academy of Management Journal, 38*(4), 1075–1104.

Kacmar, K. M., & Baron, R. A. (1999). Organizational politics: The state of the field, links to related processes, and an agenda for future research. In G.R. Ferris (Ed.), *Research in personnel and human resources management* (pp. 1–40). Stamford, CT: JAI Press.

Kacmar, K. M., & Carlson, D. S. (1997). Further validation of the perceptions of politics scale (POPS): A multiple sample investigation. *Journal of Management, 23*(5), 627–658.

Kacmar, K. M., & Ferris, G. R. (1991). Perceptions of organizational politics scale (POPS): Development and construct validation. *Educational and Psychological Measurement, 51*(1), 193–205.

Kacmar, K. M., & Ferris, G. R. (1993). Politics at work: Sharpening the focus of political behavior in organizations. *Business Horizons, 36*(4), 70–74.

Keller, T., & Weibler, J. (2015). What it takes and costs to be an ambidextrous manager: Linking leadership and cognitive strain to balancing exploration and exploitation. *Journal of Leadership & Organizational Studies, 22*(1), 54–71.

Korsgaard, M. A., Schweiger, D. M., & Sapienza, H. J. (1995). Building commitment, attachment, and trust in strategic decision-making teams: The role of procedural justice. *Academy of Management Journal, 38*(1), 60–84.

Kramer, R. M. (1999). Trust and distrust in organizations: Emerging perspectives, enduring questions. *Annual Review of Psychology, 50*(1), 569–598.

Kwantes, C. T. (2003). Organizational citizenship and withdrawal behaviors in the USA and India: Does commitment make. *International Journal of Cross Cultural Management, 3*(1), 5–26.

Lambert, E. G., Hogan, N. L., Barton-Bellessa, S. M., & Jiang, S. (2012). Examining the relationship between supervisor and management trust and job burnout among correctional staff. *Criminal Justice and Behavior, 39*(7), 938–957.

Lattin, J. M., Carroll, J. D., & Green, P. E. (2003). *Analyzing multivariate data.* Belmont, CA: Thomson Brooks/Cole.

Lee, D., Kim, K., Kim, T. G., Kwon, S., & Cho, B. (2013). How and when organizational integration efforts matter in South Korea: A psychological process perspective on the post-merger integration. *International Journal of Human Resource Management, 24*(5), 944–965.

Leung, D., Wong, E., Chan, S., & Lam, T. H. (2013). Psychometric properties of the Big Five Inventory in a Chinese sample of smokers receiving cessation treatment: A validation study. *Journal of Nursing Education and Practice, 3*(6), 1–10.

Lewicki, R. J., Tomlinson, E. C., & Gillespie, N. (2006). Models of interpersonal trust development: Theoretical approaches, empirical evidence and future directions. *Journal of Management, 32*(6), 991–1022.

Li, J., Wu, L.-Z., Liu, D., Kwan, H. K., & Liu, J. (2014). Insiders maintain voice: A psychological safety model of organizational politics. *Asia Pacific Journal of Management, 31*(3), 853–874.

Little, R. J. A., & Rubin, D. B. (1989). The analysis of social science data with missing values. *Sociological Methods and Research, 18*(2–3), 292–326.

Little, R. J. A., & Schenker, N. (1995). Missing data. In G. Arminger, C. Clogg, & M. Sobel (Eds.), *Handbook of statistical modeling for the social and behavioral sciences* (pp. 39–75). New York, NY: Plenum Press.

Liu, J., Siu, O. L., & Shi, K. (2009). Transformational leadership and employee well-being: The mediating role of trust in the leader and self-efficacy. *Applied Psychology, 59*(3), 454–479.

Macky, K., & Boxall, P. (2007). The relationship between 'high-performance work practices' and employee attitudes: An investigation of additive and interaction effects. *International Journal of Human Resource Management, 18*(4), 537–567.

Magner, N., & Staley, A. B. (2014). Roles of instrumental and noninstrumental voice in members' reactions toward interorganizational committees. *International Journal of Organization Theory and Behavior, 17*(3), 311–334.

Mahajan, A., Bishop, J. W., & Scott, D. (2012). Does trust in top management mediate top management communication. *Employee Involvement and Organizational Commitment Relationships? Journal of Managerial Issues, 24*, 173–190.

Marsh, H. W., Balla, J. R., & Hau, K. T. (1996). An evaluation of incremental fit indices: A clarification of mathematical and empirical properties. In G.A. Marcoulides & R.E. Schumacker, (Eds.), *Advanced structural equation modeling: Issues and techniques.* Mahwah, NJ: Erlbaum.

Mayer, R. C., & Davis, J. H. (1999). The effect of performance appraisal system on trust for management: A field quasi-experiment. *Journal of Applied Psychology, 84*(1), 123–136.

Mayer, R. C., Davis, J. H., & Schoorman, F. D. (1995). An integrative model of organizational trust. *Academy of Management Review, 20*(3), 709–734.

McCauley, D. P., & Kuhnert, K. W. (1992). A theoretical review and empirical investigation of employee trust in management. *Public Administration Quarterly, 16*, 265–282.

McCrae, R. R. (1987). Creativity, divergent thinking, and openness to experience. *Journal of Personality and Social Psychology, 52*(6), 1258–1265.

McCrae, R. R. (1994). Openness to experience: Expanding the boundaries of Factor V. *European Journal of Personality, 8*(4), 251–272.
McCrae, R. R., & Costa, P. T. (1997). Conceptions and correlates of openness to experience. In R. Hogan, J. Johnson, & S. Briggs (Eds.), *Handbook of personality psychology* (pp. 825–847). San Diego, CA: Academic Press.
McCrae, R., Kurtz, J. E., Yamagata, S., & Terracciano, A. (2011). Internal consistency, retest reliability, and their implications for personality scale validity. *Personality and Social Psychology Review, 15*(1), 28–50.
Meyer, J. P., & Herscovitch, L. (2001). Commitment in the workplace: Toward a general model. *Human Resource Management Review, 11*(3), 299–326.
Michaelis, B., Stegmaier, R., & Sonntag, K. (2009). Affective commitment to change and innovation implementation behavior: The role of charismatic leadership and employees' trust in top management. *Journal of Change Management, 9*, 399–417.
Miller, B. K., Rutherford, M. A., & Kolodinsky, R. W. (2008). Perceptions of organizational politics: A meta-analysis of outcomes. *Journal of Business and Psychology, 22*(3), 209–222.
Nahapiet, J., & Ghoshal, S. (1998). Social capital, intellectual capital, and the organizational advantage. *Academy of Management Review, 23*(2), 242–268.
Neves, P., & Caetano, A. (2009). Affective commitment to change: Contributions to trust in the supervisor and work outcomes. *Group & Organization Management, 34*(6), 623–644.
Nienaber, A.-M., Romeike, P. D., Searle, R., & Schewe, G. (2015). A qualitative meta-analysis of trust in supervisor-subordinate relationships. *Journal of Managerial Psychology, 30*(5), 507–534.
Nunnally, J. C. (1978). *Psychometric theory* (2nd ed.). New York, NY: McGraw-Hill.
O'Connor, W. E., & Morrison, T. G. (2001). A comparison of situational and dispositional predictors of perceptions of organizational politics. *The Journal of Psychology, 135*(3), 301–312.
Parker, C. P., Dipboye, R. L., & Jackson, S. L. (1995). Perceptions of organizational politics: An investigation of antecedents and consequences. *Journal of Management, 21*(5), 891–912.
Podsakoff, P., MacKenzie, S., Lee, J., & Podsakoff, N. (2003). Common method biases in behavioral research: A critical review of the literature and recommended remedies. *Journal of Applied Psychology, 88*(5), 879–903.
Podsakoff, P. M., & Organ, D. W. (1986). Self-reports in organization research: Problems and prospects. *Journal of Management, 12*(4), 531–544.
Pooja, A. A., De Clercq, D., & Belausteguigoitia, I. (2016). Job stressors and organizational citizenship behavior: The roles of organizational commitment and social interaction. *Human Resource Development Quarterly, 27*(3), 373–405.
Preacher, K. J., & Hayes, A. F. (2004). SPSS and SAS procedures for estimating indirect effects in simple mediation models. *Behavior Research Methods, Instruments, & Computers, 36*(4), 717–731.
Quinn, R. W., Spreitzer, G. M., & Lam, C. F. (2012). Building a sustainable model of human energy in organizations: Exploring the critical role of resources. *Academy of Management Annals, 6*(1), 337–396. Vol.
Raja, U., & Johns, G. (2010). The joint effects of personality and job scope on in-role performance, citizenship behaviors, and creativity. *Human Relations, 63*(7), 981–1005.
Rosen, C. C., Ferris, D. L., Brown, D. J., Chen, Y., & Yan, M. (2014). Perceptions of organizational politics: A need satisfaction paradigm. *Organization Science, 25*(4), 1026–1055.
Rousseau, D. M., Sitkin, S. B., Burt, R. S., & Camerer, C. (1998). Not so different after all: A cross-discipline view of trust. *Academy of Management Review, 23*(3), 393–404.
Saksvik, I. B., & Hetland, H. (2009). Exploring dispositional resistance to change. *Journal of Leadership & Organizational Studies, 16*(2), 175–183.
Samad, S. (2011). Examining the effects of emotional intelligence on the relationship between organizational politics and job performance. *International Journal of Business and Social Science, 2*, 119–126.
Schafer, J. (1997). *Analysis of incomplete multivariate data*. London: Chapman & Hall.
Schafer, J. L. (1999). Multiple imputation: A primer. *Statistical Methods in Medical Research, 8*(1), 3–15.

Schaufeli, W. B., & Bakker, A. B. (2004). Job demands, job resources, and their relationship with burnout and engagement: A multi-sample study. *Journal of Organizational Behavior, 25*(3), 293–315.

Schmitt, N. (1996). Uses and abuses of coefficient alpha. *Psychological Assessment, 8*(4), 350–353.

Schmitt, D. P., Allik, J., McCrae, R. R., & Benet-Martinez, V. (2007). The geographic distribution of Big Five personality traits: Patterns and profiles of human self-description across 56 nations. *Journal of Cross Cultural Psychology, 38*(2), 173–212.

Schmitz, C., & Ganesan, S. (2014). Managing customer and organizational complexity in sales organizations. *Journal of Marketing, 78*(6), 59–77.

Schoorman, D. F., Mayer, R. C., & Davis, J. M. (2007). An integrative model of organizational trust: past, present and future. *Academy of Management Review, 32*(2), 344–354.

Shen, J., Tang, N., & D'Netto, B. (2014). A multilevel analysis of the effects of HR diversity management on employee knowledge sharing: The case of Chinese employees. *International Journal of Human Resource Management, 25*(12), 1720–1738.

Simons, T., & Peterson, R. S. (2000). Task conflict and relationship conflict in top management teams: The pivotal role of intragroup trust. *Journal of Applied Psychology, 85*(1), 102–111.

Spector, P. E. (2006). Method variance in organizational research: Truth or urban legend? *Organizational Research Methods, 9*(2), 221–232.

Spence, R., Owens, M., & Goodyer, I. (2012). Item response theory and validity of the NEO-FFI in adolescents. *Personality and Individual Differences, 53*(6-4), 801–807.

Thomas, G. F., Zolin, R., & Hartman, J. L. (2009). The central role of communication in developing trust and its effect on employee involvement. *Journal of Business Communication, 46*(3), 287–310.

Tierney, P., & Farmer, S. M. (2002). Creative self-efficacy: Potential antecedents and relationship to creative performance. *Academy of Management Journal, 45*(6), 1137–1148.

Valle, M., & Perrewe, P. L. (2000). Do politics perception related to political behavior? *Human Relations, 53*(3), 359–386.

Van Dam, K., Oreg, S., & Schyns, B. (2008). Daily work contexts and resistance to organisational change: The role of leader-member exchange, development climate, and change process characteristics. *Applied Psychology: An International Review, 57*(2), 313–334.

Van Doorn, R. R. A., & Hülsheger, U. R. (2015). What makes employees resilient to job demands? The role of core self-evaluations in the relationship between job demands and strain reactions. *European Journal of Work and Organizational Psychology, 24*(1), 76–87.

Van Dyne, L., Ang, S., & Botero, I. C. (2003). Conceptualizing employee silence and employee voice as multidimensional constructs. *Journal of Management Studies, 40*(6), 1359–1392.

van Emmerik, I. J. H., Bakker, A. B., & Euwema, M. C. (2009). Explaining employees' evaluations of organizational change with the job demands-resources model. *Career Development International, 14*(6), 594–613.

Vigoda, E. (2000). Organizational politics, job attitudes, and work outcomes: Exploration and implications for the public sector. *Journal of Vocational Behavior, 57*(3), 326–347.

Vredenburgh, D., & Shea-VanFossen, R. (2010). Human nature, organizational politics, and human resource development. *Human Resource Development Review, 9*(1), 26–47.

Wanberg, C. R., & Banas, J. T. (2000). Predictors and outcomes of openness to changes in a reorganizing workplace. *The Journal of Applied Psychology, 85*(1), 132–142.

Warner, R. M. (2013). *Applied statistics* (2nd ed.). Thousand Oaks, CA: Sage.

Watson, D., Suls, J., & Haig, J. (2002). Global self-esteem in relation to structural models of personality and affectivity. *Journal of Personality and Social Psychology, 83*(1), 185–197.

Webber, S., Bishop, K., & O'Neill, R. (2012). Trust repair: The impact of perceived organizational support and issue-selling. *Journal of Management Development, 31*(7), 724–737.

Wu, M., Huang, X., Li, C., & Liu, W. (2012). Perceived interactional justice and trust-in-supervisor as mediators for paternalistic leadership. *Management and Organization Review, 8*(01), 97–121.

Yilmaz, E., Ozer, G., & Gunluk, M. (2014). Do organizational politics and organizational commitment affect the budgetary slack creation in publication organizations. *Procedia - Social and Behavioral Sciences, 150*, 241–250.

Youssef, C. M., & Luthans, F. (2007). Positive organizational behavior in the workplace: The impact of hope, optimism, and resiliency. *Journal of Management, 33*(5), 774–800.

Yuan, K.-H. (2005). Fit indices versus test statistics. *Multivariate Behavioral Research, 40*(1), 115–148.

Zahra, S., & Hayton, J. C. (2008). The effect of international venturing on firm performance: The moderating influence of absorptive capacity. *Journal of Business Venturing, 23*(2), 195–220.

Zhang, A. Y., Tsui, A. S., Song, L. J., Li, C., & Jia, L. (2008). How do I trust thee? The employee-organization relationship, supervisory support, and middle manager trust in the organization. *Human Resource Management, 47*(1), 111–132.

Zhou, J., & Ferris, G. R. (1995). The dimensions and consequences of organizational politics perceptions: A confirmatory analysis. *Journal of Applied Social Psychology, 25*, 1747–1764.

Bouncing Back from Setbacks: On the Mediating Role of Team Resilience in the Relationship Between Transformational Leadership and Team Effectiveness

Isabel Dórdio Dimas, Teresa Rebelo, Paulo Renato Lourenço, and Carina Isabel Pereira Pessoa

ABSTRACT

The purpose of this study was to clarify the role of team resilience on different facets of effectiveness (team viability and quality of the group experience). Moreover, given the importance of team resilience for the organizational context, it was also our aim to contribute to the study of the conditions that promote team resilience, analyzing the role of transformational leadership. Finally, we examined whether the relationship between transformational leadership and team resilience stimulates positive team outcomes. Ninety teams (445 employees from 40 companies) were surveyed and path analysis was used in the test of the hypotheses. The results showed a positive direct effect of team resilience on both team viability and the quality of the group experience. Moreover, a positive relationship was also identified between transformational leadership and team resilience. Finally, support was found for the mediated effect of team resilience on the relationship between transformational leadership and the dimensions of team effectiveness considered. The findings of this study highlight the role of team resilience as an intervening process between transformational leadership and team effectiveness. Supervisors should promote team resilience, adopting transformational leadership behaviors, in order to contribute to increase team viability and the quality of the group experience.

Organizations worldwide in a complex and ever-changing environment have to continually face a range of risks, challenges and setbacks that threaten their functioning and viability (Powley, 2009). In this context, the capacity of employees and organizations to generate a specific response to crises has become particularly relevant, emerging as a competitive asset. As a result, in recent years, significant attention has been paid to individual resilience. In a general sense, resilience is the ability to bounce back from challenges and stressful experiences (Alliger, Cerasoli, Tannenbaum, & Vessey, 2015). Previous studies highlighted that resilient employees are better prepared to overcome difficulties and stressful events and are able to find a positive meaning in negative circumstances, becoming more adaptive and successful over time (Tugade & Fredrickson, 2004; Youssef & Luthans, 2007).

Although much of the research on resilience has been conducted at the individual level of analysis (Carmeli, Friedman, & Tishler, 2013; Meneghel, Salanova, & Martínez, 2016a), with the widespread use of teams in the organizational setting (Mathieu, Tannenbaum, Donsbach, & Alliger, 2014), understanding the way teams face challenges and difficulties in order to be effective emerges as a fundamental topic of study. Since bringing together a set of resilient employees will not necessarily generate a resilient team, it is important to explore resilience as a team construct (Alliger et al., 2015; Meneghel et al., 2016a). Team resilience is the ability of a team to withstand and recover from challenges, stressful events or any other threat to well-being (Alliger et al., 2015; West, Patera, & Carsten, 2009). It is a process of adaptation in the face of difficulties that enable the team to better manage uncertainty and pressure without threatening cohesion and performance (Sutcliffe & Vogus, 2003).

Despite the importance of team resilience, little research has been conducted in this area. Specifically, further research is needed on the effects of this process for team and organizational outcomes (Carmeli et al., 2013). The few studies developed on team resilience have already highlighted the relevance of this variable for team performance (e.g., Meneghel et al., 2016a; Meneghel, Martínez, & Salanova, 2016b). However, because team effectiveness is more than performance (Aubé & Rousseau, 2005) it is important to expand on previous studies considering the role of team resilience in other team outcomes. Accordingly, in the present research, two different criteria of team effectiveness will be considered, which are in line with two of the dimensions of Hackman's effectiveness approach (1987, 2012): team viability, which can be conceived as the extent to which team members are able to continue to work together in the future (Hackman, 1987; Rousseau & Aubé, 2010) and the quality of the group experience, which relates to the quality of the social climate within the team (Aubé & Rousseau, 2005; McGrath, 1991).

Moreover, given the relevance that team resilience has in the organizational context, it is also extremely important to study the variables that contribute to building this team capacity (Carmeli et al., 2013). Due to the crucial influence that the leader has on the functioning and dynamics of a team (Rousseau, Aubé, & Tremblay, 2013), leadership behaviors become a central variable to be studied. Hence, in the present research, it is also our aim to contribute to the study of the conditions that promote team resilience, analyzing the role of leadership, specifically, transformational leadership behaviors, on the development of team resilience. Transformational leadership is a leadership style that is characterized by giving support to individuals, helping them to overcome their limitations and difficulties, transcending, in this way, what they originally expected (Bass, 1999). By guiding team members, inspiring them and being supportive, transformational leaders can influence the team's ability to face challenging situations.

Finally, we examine whether the relationship between transformational leadership and team resilience stimulates positive team outcomes. Specifically, the present study aims to understand how transformational leadership behaviors drive positive psychological resources (i.e., resilience) among teams, in order to achieve higher levels of team effectiveness.

The present study expands on previous research in different ways. First, to the best of our knowledge, this is one of the first studies that considers the role of team leader behaviors, namely transformational behaviors, in promoting resilience within the team. Due to the characteristics of the transformational leadership style and also the centrality of the leader in the team context, studying how those behaviors promote the capacity of the team to face challenges is an important path to pursue. Second, effectiveness is conceptualized as a multidimensional construct and the impact of both transformational leadership and resilience on different dimensions is considered, covering a broader spectrum of team-level outcomes. Third, effectiveness ratings are obtained both by team members and supervisors, thus leading to a more accurate assessment of team effectiveness and, at the same time, contributing to reducing the impact of method bias (Conway & Lance, 2010).

Literature Review

Transformational Leadership and Team Resilience

Among the various leadership theories, the transformational leadership theory has been the most widely studied over the last three decades (Judge & Piccolo, 2004). Transformational leadership can be defined as an adaptable and flexible leadership style that mobilizes individuals to go beyond their individual interests in order to achieve a common goal (Bass, 1985; Bass & Riggio, 2006; Bass, Avolio, Jung, & Berson, 2003). A transformational leader energizes followers to perform beyond expectations, broadening and changing their interests and leading to conscientiousness and acceptance of the group's purposes (Bass, 1999).

Podsakoff, MacKenzie, Moorman, and Fetter (1990), through a literature review about transformational leadership, concluded that the concept can be summarized in six fundamental behaviors: identifying and articulating a vision; providing an appropriate model; promoting the acceptance of group goals; developing high performance expectations; giving individual support; and providing intellectual stimulation to staff. Inspired by this model, Carless, Wearing, and Mann (2000), described transformational leaders as those who exhibit the following seven behaviors: they (1) communicate a vision (developing an image of the future of the organization and communicating it); (2) develop staff (diagnosing the needs and capacities of each employee and expressing an individual interest in each one); (3) provide support for them to work towards their objectives through coordinated teamwork; (4) empower staff, giving them authority to implement policies and supporting their decisions); (5) are innovative, using non-conventional strategies to achieve their goals; (6) lead by example (adopting behaviors that are congruent with the attitudes and values they support); (7) are charismatic (inspiring employees to transcend their personal interests and limitations, developing an awareness of the collective interests and guiding them to achieve extraordinary goals).

The leader has a central role in the team context, influencing team functioning in a decisive way (Dimas, Rebelo, & Lourenço, 2016; Volmer, 2012). The team leader can set the tone for his or her team, stimulating or hindering the development of resilient behaviors among team members (Alliger et al., 2015). A transformational leadership style contributes to increased self-efficacy by empowerment and positive feedback in such a way that when facing setbacks, team members are more likely to persist (Michaelis, Stegmaier, & Sonntag, 2009; Salanova, Llorens, & Schaufeli, 2011). Moreover, transformational leaders provide support to team members and in a supportive environment, followers are more likely to overcome difficulties (Bandura, 1986; Michaelis et al., 2009). Besides, transformational leaders contribute to establishing positive relationships among team members and to building up a positive energy and climate (Cameron, Mora, Leutscher, & Calarco, 2011; López, Alonso, Morales, & León, 2015), which might facilitate information sharing and the development of adaptive solutions to problems, promoting resilience (Carmeli et al., 2013; Stephens, Heaphy, Carmeli, Spreitzer, & Dutton, 2013). We therefore expect that:

> Hypothesis 1: Transformational leadership will be positively related to team resilience.

Resilience and Team Effectiveness

Resilience is considered as the process of persevering and responding positively in the face of challenges. There are numerous challenges that can impact team functioning which can be broadly distinguished as chronic and acute: chronic challenges are ongoing or long-lasting and even if they are not particularly intense, they are damaging because their impact accumulates over time (e.g., ambiguous team roles; lack of clarity about roles played by each one of the team members); acute challenges are short-lived but generally more intense than chronic challenges (e.g., radical loss of resources; sudden increase in workload) (Alliger et al., 2015). Resilience helps teams to be better prepared to deal with the stressor, no matter its type. A resilient team has the ability to absorb, preserve and improve functioning while encountering adversities and complexities, in such a way that it might even become stronger after overcoming the setback (Carmeli et al., 2013; Sutcliffe & Vogus, 2003).

Previous evidence revealed that team resilience is positively related to team cohesion, cooperation and coordination (West et al., 2009) as well as to team performance (Meneghel et al., 2016a; Salanova, Llorens, Cifre, & Martínez, 2012). Since resilient teams tend to be creative and adaptive to change and adversity, they are more prepared to deal with challenges and difficulties, which might translate into higher levels of performance (Luthans, Avolio, Walumbwa, & Li, 2005; Meneghel et al., 2016b). Moreover, team resilience is a process of adaptation and adjustment to changing conditions (Sutcliffe & Vogus, 2003). Being embedded in an organizational context, organizational teams continually have to cope with stressful events along their lifetime, such as changing conditions in terms of membership, technology and operating conditions (Argote & McGrath, 1993). A high level of team resilience means that the team has the capacity to withstand, overcome and bounce back from stressful events, which might lead to an increase in its ability to persist over time, that is, its on-going viability (Alliger et al., 2015; Carmeli et al., 2013). Thus, we expect a positive relationship between team resilience and team viability. Moreover, we argue that team resilience will have a positive relationship with the quality of the group experience. Previous research found that positive organizational behavior capacities (such as team resilience) drive the within-team experience, promoting favorable reactions among team members (Luthans, 2002; West et al., 2009). The ability of resilient teams to succeed in face of adversity may increase the sense of belonging and the social ties between team members, influencing the emergence of a better social climate. Therefore, we predict that:

> Hypothesis 2: Team resilience will have a positive relationship with team viability (2a) and the quality of the group experience (2b).

Finally, building on the functional perspective of leadership (e.g., Morgeson, DeRue, & Karam, 2010), we examine team resilience as an intervening variable through which transformational leadership may exercise a positive effect on team effectiveness. Although there is little research that directly assesses the mediational processes through which team leadership affects team outcomes, an increasing number of studies suggest that a large part of the influence that transformational leadership can generate is tangible but indirect (e.g., Boies &

Howell, 2009; Moynihan, Pandey, & Wright, 2012; Weng, Huang, Chen, & Chang, 2015). More than acting directly on team results, leaders can promote the conditions for success by shaping key mediating variables. Hence, transformational leaders may contribute to higher levels of team effectiveness through their influence on the team capacity to persist in the face of adversity and threats. Therefore, we predict that:

> Hypothesis 3: Team resilience will mediate the relationship between transformational leadership and team viability (3a) and the quality of the group experience (3b).

Method

Sample and Procedure

In order to collect the data, we previously contacted the key stakeholders in each organization (CEOs or human resources managers) to explain the purpose and requirements of the study. When the organization agreed to participate in our study, the selection of teams to survey was based in the following criteria (Cohen & Bailey, 1997; Schein, 1980): teams must be composed of at least three members (1), perceived by themselves and others as a team (2), that interact regularly, in an interdependent way, to accomplish a common goal (3), and who have a formal supervisor who is responsible for the actions of the team (4).

Data was collected following two strategies. In the majority of the organizations, the questionnaires were administered by a member of the research team or by a person with authority at the organization and with a strategic relationship with the employees (and who had been previously instructed by a research team member). However, when it was not possible to implement this strategy, the questionnaires were filled in online via an electronic platform, with the link being provided to the participants. In both cases, the participation in the study was voluntary and it was clarified on the front page of the survey that only aggregated data would be reported and that all identifying information would be removed.

After eliminating from the sample the questionnaires where at least 10% of the answers were missing (Bryman & Cramer, 2005) and also the teams with a team member response rate below 60%, the remaining sample had a total of 445 employees nested in 90 teams from 40 Portuguese companies (18.5%, were large, 47% were medium, 34.5% were small). The most representative organizational sector was the services sector (34.2%), followed by industry (17.1%). The teams' size ranged from 3 to 27 employees, with an average of 6.66 (SD = 5.16). Of the team members (N = 445), 52.9% were female, 36.2% had completed secondary education and 37.3% had a higher education background. The mean age was approximately 35 years (SD = 10.03). The average job tenure in the organization was approximately 9 years (SD = 8.46) and in the team approximately 5 years (SD = 5.71). Regarding team leaders (N = 90), 66.3% were male, the mean age was about 40 years (SD = 9.91) and 48.8% had completed secondary education whereas 45.2% had a higher education background. Leaders had, on average, about 14 years of experience in the organization (SD = 7.76) and about 8 years of experience in the function (SD = 6.96).

Measures

To reduce common method variance (Podsakoff, MacKenzie, Lee, & Podsakoff, 2003), we collected data from two sources, namely the team members and their supervisors. Team members were surveyed about transformational leadership, team resilience and quality of group experience, whereas team leaders provided data concerning the viability of the team.

All variables were measured with previously validated scales that were adapted to the Portuguese language following the procedure proposed by DeVellis (2003). The measures were answered on a 5-point Likert scale ranging from (1) *almost doesn't apply* to (5) *almost totally applies* (with the exception of the quality of group experience, which was also measured on a 5-point Likert scale but ranging from (1) *strongly disagree* to (5) *strongly agree*). Team members were asked to refer to the team in which they work and team leaders to the team that they supervise while completing the questionnaire. In order to avoid errors concerning the level of analysis, each item explicitly referred to the team.

Transformational Leadership

Transformational leadership was measured with the Global Transformational Leadership scale developed by Carless et al. (2000). This scale is composed of seven items based on the seven behaviors of transformational leadership defined by the authors. A sample item is "My team leader gives encouragement and recognition to staff".

Team Resilience

Team resilience was measured with the 3-item scale developed by Stephens et al. (2013). A sample item is "This team knows how to cope with challenges."

Quality of Group Experience

The quality of group experience was measured through the scale developed by Aubé and Rousseau (2005). This scale integrates three items concerning the quality of intrateam social climate. A sample item is "In our team, relationships are harmonious."

Team Viability

Team viability was assessed using the scale developed by Aubé and Rousseau (2005). This scale contains four items that measure the team's capability to adapt to a changing environment, to solve problems, to integrate new members and to keep working as a whole in the future. A sample item is "The members of this team could work a long time together."

Control Variables

Because various studies have shown that team size has an influence on the functioning and outputs of teams (e.g., Brewer & Kramer, 1986), we included it as a control variable. Team size was obtained by asking team leaders about the number of members of their team.

Validity of the Measures

Since transformational leadership, team resilience and quality of group experience were obtained from team members, convergent and discriminant validity of these constructs were tested through Confirmatory Factor Analysis (CFA) using the maximum likelihood estimation method (covariance matrix as input) with AMOS. Concerning team viability, since it was obtained from team leaders, a separate CFA was run. To evaluate the level of adjustment of the models, the following indicators were considered: χ^2 Goodness-of-Fit Statistic, Root Mean Square Error of Approximation (RMSEA), and the Comparative Fit Index (CFI).

Values below .08 for RMSEA indicate a good fit (Browne & Cudeck, 1993). For CFI, values greater than .90 indicate a good fit, whereas values greater than .95 indicate superior fit (Hu & Bentler, 1999).

Concerning the team members' constructs (N = 445), the goodness of fit of the expected three-factor model presented good values (χ^2 (62) = 176.64, p < .000, CFI = .98, RMSEA = .06, 90% confidence interval .05–.07, p = .016), substantially better than the fit of a one-factor solution, where all items loaded in the same factor (χ^2 (65) = 1802.87, p < .000, CFI = .71, RMSEA = .25, 90% confidence interval .24–.25, p <.000). All the indicator loadings were above .85, indicating convergent validity, and the correlations between factors were not excessively high (between .57 and .58), indicating discriminant validity (Kline, 2005).

Concerning team viability, assessed by team leaders (N = 90), the results of the one-factor solution were: χ^2 (2) = 3.472, p = .176; CFI = .98; RMSEA = .09, 90% confidence interval of .00–.25, p = .24. Although the RMSEA value exceed the .08 cut-off value generally accepted, Hu and Bentler (1999) found that small samples tend to produce larger RMSEA values, rejecting too often the true model. Moreover, all other indexes indicate a good fit of the model, any model modification was suggested by the analyses, and all the indicators loaded acceptably on the factor (above .58). So, all in all, the results support an acceptable fit of this expected one-factor solution to the data.

Results

In this study, the unit of analysis was the group rather than the individual and as a result, members' responses were aggregated to the team level. To justify aggregation, we computed the average deviation index (ADM Index) developed by Burke, Finkelstein, and Dusig (1999). Following the authors' recommendations, we used the criterion ADM $\leq$ 0.83 to aggregate individual responses to the team level with confidence. The average ADM values obtained for transformational leadership (M = 0.50, SD = 0.28), team resilience (M = 0.41, SD = 0.22) and the quality of the group experience (M = 0.40, SD = 0.27) were below the upper-limit criterion of 0.83, revealing that the level of within-team agreement was sufficient to aggregate team members' scores. Additionally, to check whether aggregation was justified, we also computed the intraclass coefficients ICC(1) and ICC(2) (Bliese, 2000). The ICC(1) values for transformational leadership, team resilience and quality of the group experience were .33, .19 and .22, respectively. The ICC(2) values obtained for the same variables were, .71, .54 and .58, respectively. Overall, the values gave support to the aggregation of data to the team level (Bliese, 2000; Klein & Kozlowski, 2000).

To evaluate the model of relationships proposed we used structural equation modelling (SEM). We had to keep the model under test parsimonious due to the size of the sample. Thus, we chose to run a path analysis, a technique for analyzing structural models with observed variables (Kline, 2005). Thus, in this model, the indicators (or observed variables) are the score of the items of each variable. As the distributions of the variables were approximately normal, we chose the ML (Maximum Likelihood) estimation method. Finally, in order to test the mediation effect, Baron and Kenny's (1986) recommendations were followed. According to Kenny (2016), bootstrapping was used for testing the statistical significance of the indirect effects.

Table 1. Descriptive Statistics, Intercorrelations among Indicator Variables and Scale Reliabilities.

	M	*SD*	1	2	3	4
1.Transformational leadership	3.94	0.66	(.98)			
2. Team resilience	3.98	0.50	.62***	(.93)		
3. Quality of group experience	4.06	0.56	.61***	.67***	(.96)	
4. Team viability	4.05	0.57	.35**	.37***	.35**	(.75)
5. Team size	6.46	5.00	−.34**	−.23*	−.32**	−.08

*$p < .05$, **$p < .01$, ***$p < .001$; Scale reliabilities are presented in the diagonal.

Table 1 presents the descriptive statistics, the intercorrelations between the variables, and the scale reliabilities. The pattern of correlations supported the hypothesized relationships. Team size is significantly correlated with team resilience and quality of group experience, which justify its inclusion as control variable in the path model under study. Moreover, team size is significantly correlated with transformational leadership so this correlation will be also estimated in the path analysis. According to Kline (2005) the estimation of the correlation between the independent variables considered in a path analysis is a frequent procedure.

In line with Baron and Kenny's (1986) recommendations for testing a mediation effect, the direct effect should be estimated along with the indirect effects in the same model. Thus, although not stated as hypotheses, this model also estimates the direct effects of transformational leadership on team viability and on quality of group experience (cf. Figure 1). The path analysis results showed a good adjustment between the model and the data (χ^2 (2) = 1.31, p = .519; CFI = 1.00; RMSEA = .00, 90% confidence interval of .00–.19, p = .590).

When examining the coefficients between variables, transformational leadership is positively related to team resilience, supporting the first hypothesis, and team resilience has a positive relationship with team viability and the quality of the group experience, supporting the second hypothesis. The third hypothesis, which states a mediation effect of team resilience on the relationship between transformational leadership and team viability and quality of the group experience, is also supported. Actually, a full mediation effect of team resilience occurs on the relationship between transformational leadership and team viability, whereas a partial mediation effect emerges on the relationship with quality of group experience (Baron & Kenny, 1986).

For testing the statistical significance of the indirect effect of transformational leadership on team viability and quality of group experience via team resilience, the bootstrapping

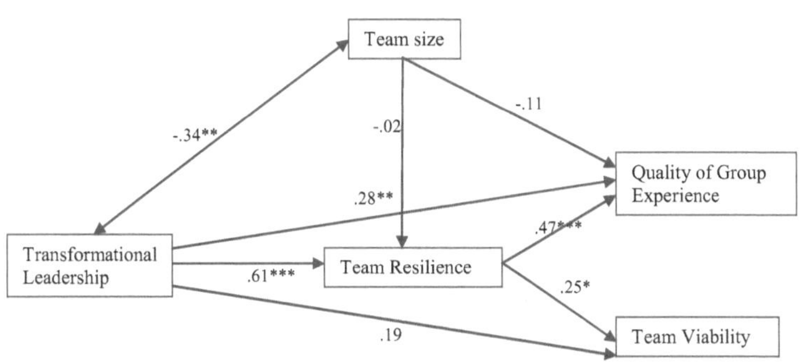

Figure 1. A path analysis of the mediation effect of team resilience on the relationship of transformational leadership with quality of group experience and team viability. *$p < .05$, **$p < .01$, ***$p < .001$.

method was used. By means of a bootstrap approximation obtained by constructing a two-side, bias-corrected 90% confidence interval with 2000 samples, a statistically significant standardized indirect (mediated) effect of transformational leadership on team viability and on quality of group experience was estimated ($p = .03$ and $p < .001$, respectively).

Discussion

Teams embedded in the organizational setting have to face constant challenges and difficulties that may jeopardize the ability to accomplish goals. In consequence, almost any business team can benefit from greater resilience (Alliger et al., 2015). With the present study, we intended to contribute to the study of team resilience, analyzing the direct and indirect relationships between transformational leadership, team resilience and team outcomes.

The first hypothesis predicted that transformational leadership behaviors would contribute to develop the levels of resilience of the team. Results gave support to this expected positive relationship. Hence, a transformational leadership style is characterized by giving feedback and support to team members, behaviors that contribute to fostering the levels of confidence of the team, leading to a greater ability to face situations of adversity. Further, transformational leaders positively influence the quality of the relationships between team members and positive relationships are crucial to the development of resilience (Gittel, Cameron, Lim, & Rivas, 2006).

Moreover, transformational leaders lead by example, acting in consonance with what they preach. In this way, they boost the levels of team resilience not only through the way they communicate with the team, but also through their own behaviors. In fact, since individuals learn by observing salient others and tend to reproduce behaviors that have positive results (Bandura, 1977), team members will witness the way the leader overcomes difficulties and setbacks and will reproduce those kinds of behaviors.

Our study gave also support to the importance of team resilience for team effectiveness. Our results extend the findings from previous studies that stressed the importance of team resilience for team performance (e.g., Meneghel et al., 2016a), and highlighted that team resilience is also relevant for other two, and no less important, criteria of effectiveness: viability and quality of the group experience (Hackman, 1987, 2012). To the extent that resilient teams have the ability to overcome difficulties and setbacks, they are better prepared to face the challenges of today's business setting, namely the need to adapt to changes, enhancing, in consequence, their ability to persist over time. Moreover, the shared belief that together team members are able to overcome challenges induces a "we are in it together" attitude within the team (Aubé & Rousseau, 2005). This sense of belonging incites team members to build and maintain positive relationships within the team, promoting, in consequence, the quality of the group experience.

Finally, this study reveals that the relationship between transformational leadership and team viability is indirect since team resilience completely mediated the relationship between transformational leadership and team viability. These results suggest that transformational leadership behaviors promote the levels of team resilience, which in turn may increase the levels of team viability. Concerning the quality of the group experience, a partial mediation of team resilience was identified. This means that transformational leadership presents both a direct and an indirect relationship with the quality of the group experience. Therefore, if the actions of the leader *per se* contribute directly to increasing the social climate and the sense of well-being in the team, he/she also contributes to increasing the levels of the quality of the team experience through its influence on team resilience.

Final Conclusions, Limitations and Further Research

The present study contributes to the literature in many different ways. First, our study contributes to the emerging field of research that focuses on resilience as a team level variable (e.g., Meneghel et al., 2016a; Salanova et al., 2012; West et al., 2009). Nowadays, organizations have to face continuous challenges and difficulties that may undermine the achievement of organizational aims and objectives. To survive in this competitive context, organizations, and in consequence their teams, have to face these difficulties, overcoming barriers and setbacks. Our study extends previous studies (e.g., Meneghel et al., 2016a; Salanova et al., 2012) and highlights that the impact of team resilience on team results goes beyond performance, also influencing the quality of the group experience and the viability of the group.

Second, to the best of our knowledge, this is the first attempt to empirically examine the role of leadership in promoting team resilience. Clarifying the antecedents of team resilience is a fundamental path to pursue in order to better prepare teams to respond to challenges and setbacks. Our findings reveal that the adoption of transformational leadership behaviors by the leader could promote the ability of the team to recover from difficulties.

Finally, our study contributes not only to research on team resilience but also to the body of knowledge of transformational leadership by examining one of the team processes (i.e., team resilience) underlying the relationships between transformational leadership and team outcomes. Hence, our results contribute to clarifying the importance of leadership behaviors in shaping the way the team interacts and reacts to situations, which in turn leads to team effectiveness. If we focus our attention only on the direct effects of transformational leadership on team results, this may lead us to underestimate its relative importance in affecting other factors that influence team outcomes (Moynihan et al., 2012). These results are in line with previous studies that highlight the indirect relationships of leadership behaviors with team outcomes (e.g., Dimas et al., 2016; Moynihan et al., 2012), revealing team resilience as an intervening mechanism in this relationship.

In addition to the above-mentioned theoretical contributions, the results of this study also have significant implications for practice. By clearly highlighting the importance of transformational leadership behaviors in developing the capacity of teams to face crises and challenges, our findings suggest a promising direction for interventions. Accordingly, in order to increase team resilience and improve effectiveness in the team context, organizations should implement training programs focused on developing transformational leadership behaviors. Transformational leaders motivate, give support and guidance to their teams, promoting a positive social environment, enhancing the quality of the relationships between team members and developing team adaptive competencies. In this kind of context, team members learn to look at challenges and risks as opportunities to learn and grow, instead of avoiding them. In the complex environment that characterizes modern organizations, training in transformational leadership behaviors emerges as a fundamental strategy to be implemented in order to better prepare individuals and teams to respond to changes, increasing the sustainability of the team and the organization in the future. Indeed, the literature shows that resilient teams are better prepared to deal with unsuccessful and/or stressful experiences as a collective unit (West et al., 2009). In addition, organizations may also implement strategies to promote the development of problem-solving behaviors in the work setting, such as developing training sessions on this topic, creating focus groups or implementing suggestion schemes. When problem-solving behaviors are part of everyday organizational life, employees are better prepared to respond to setbacks and crises when they happen.

While it is hoped that our research findings contribute both to the literature and to the practice in several ways, it is worth noting the particular limitations that our research design entails. One of the limitations of the present study is its cross-sectional design, which makes it impossible to draw conclusions about the causality of relationships. In fact, although the direction of the relationships hypothesized is well supported in the literature, the reverse direction might also be possible. Therefore, the present findings need to be tested, in the future, by other studies, namely with a longitudinal design (Maxwell & Cole, 2007). Another shortcoming of our research is the fact that the relationships between transformational leadership, team resilience and the quality of the group experience may be affected by common source bias, because these constructs were rated by the same source, i.e., team members (Conway & Lance, 2010; Podsakoff, Mackenzie, & Podsakoff, 2012; Spector, 2006). Yet, it is important to note that these variables were aggregated to the team level, a strategy that can contribute to diminishing the effects of that threat (Conway & Lance, 2010). Besides, team viability was assessed by another source, i.e., the leader, and the results went in the same direction as the quality of the group experience, which may suggest that the findings were not affected by this problem. Moreover, as stated by Spector (2006), the use of a common method to measure variables does not necessarily affect results or conclusions. A final limitation of the present research is the convenience nature of the sample that hinders the generalization of the results. Future research should replicate the present study in different and broader settings. Moreover, in the future, it would be interesting to expand the results of the present research, analyzing the effect of transformational leadership and team resilience on other outcomes, such as team innovation. Because team resilience is a process of adaptation and adjustment to changing conditions (Sutcliffe & Vogus, 2003), resilient teams may be more aware of opportunities and more competent in applying problem-solving strategies in order to improve team processes and outcomes. Since team resilience concerns the ability of the team to face adverse situations, future research should explore the impact of the level of adversity on the development of resilience. Finally, team resilience has been presented as one of the four positive psychological capital characteristics, the other three being hope, optimism and efficacy (Luthans, 2002). In the future, it would be interesting to study the four characteristics together since the effect of team resilience on team outcomes might be influenced by the presence of the other capacities.

ORCID

Isabel Dórdio Dimas http://orcid.org/0000-0003-4481-2644
Teresa Rebelo http://orcid.org/0000-0003-3380-0840
Paulo Renato Lourenço http://orcid.org/0000-0003-1405-3835
Carina Isabel Pereira Pessoa http://orcid.org/0000-0002-6789-733X

References

Alliger, G. M., Cerasoli, C. P., Tannenbaum, S. I., & Vessey, W. B. (2015). Team resilience: How teams flourish under pressure. *Organizational Dynamics*, *44*(3), 176–184. doi:10.1016/j.orgdyn.2015.05.003

Argote, L., & McGrath, J. E. (1993). Group processes in organizations: Continuity and change. In C. L. Cooper & I. T. Robertson (Eds.), *International review of industrial and organizational psychology* (Vol. *8*, pp. 333–389). New York, NY: John Wiley.

Aubé, C., & Rousseau, V. (2005). Team goal commitment and team effectiveness: The role of task interdependence and supportive behaviors. *Group Dynamics: Theory, Research, and Practice*, *9*(3), 189–204. doi:10.1037/1089-2699.9.3.189

Bandura, A. (1977). Self-efficacy: Toward a unifying theory of behavioral change. *Psychological Review*, *84*, 191–215. doi:10.1037/0033295X.84.2.191

Bandura, A. (1986). *Social foundation of thought and action: A social cognitive theory*. Englewood Cliffs, NJ: Prentice Hall.

Baron, R. M., & Kenny, D. A. (1986). The moderator-mediator variable distinction in social psychological research: Conceptual, strategic, and statistical considerations. *Journal of Personality and Social Psychology*, *51*, 1173–1182. doi:10.1037/0022-3514.51.6.1173

Bass, B. M. (1985). *Leadership and performance beyond expectations*. New York: Free Press Collier Macmillan.

Bass, B. M. (1999). Two decades of research and development in transformational leadership. European. *Journal of Work and Organizational Psychology*, *8*(1), 9–32. doi:10.1080/135943299398410

Bass, B. M., Avolio, B. J., Jung, D. I., & Berson, Y. (2003). Predicting unit performance by assessing transformational and transactional leadership. *Journal of Applied Psychology*, *88*(2), 207–218. doi:10.1037/0021-9010.88.2.207

Bass, B. M., & Riggio, R. E. (2006). *Transformational leadership* (3rd ed.). Mahwah, N.J: Lawrence Erlbaum Associates.

Bliese, P. D. (2000). Within-group agreement, non-independence, and reliability: Implications for data aggregation and analysis. In K. J. Klein & S. W. J. Kozlowski (Eds.), *Multilevel theory, research, and methods in organizations* (pp. 349–381). San Francisco, CA: Jossey-Bass.

Boies, K., & Howell, J. M. (2009). Leading military teams to think and feel: Exploring the relations between leadership, soldiers' cognitive and affective processes, and team effectiveness. *Military Psychology, 21*(2), 216–232. doi:10.1080/08995600902768743

Brewer, M. B., & Kramer, R. M. (1986). Social identity and cooperation in social dilemmas. *Rationality and Society, 18*(4), 443–470. doi:10.1177/1043463106066381

Browne, M. W. & Cudeck, R. (1993). Alternative ways of assessing model fit. In K. A. Bollen, & J. S. Long (Eds.), *Testing structural equation models* (pp. 136–162). Newbury Park, CA: Sage.

Bryman, A., & Cramer, D. (2005). Quantitative Data Analysis with SPSS 12 and 13: A guide for Social Scientists. East Sussex, UK: Routledge.

Burke, M. J., Finkelstein, L. M., & Dusig, M. S. (1999). On average deviation indices for estimating interrater agreement. *Organizational Research Methods, 2*(1), 49–68. doi:10.1177/109442819921004

Cameron, K., Mora, C., Leutscher, T., & Calarco, M. (2011). Effects of positive practices on organizational effectiveness. *Journal of Applied Behavioral Science, 47*, 266–308. doi:10.1177/0021886310395514

Carmeli, A., Friedman, Y., & Tishler, A. (2013). Cultivating a resilient top management team: The importance of relational connections and strategic decision comprehensiveness. *Safety Science, 51* (1), 148–159. doi:10.1016/j.ssci.2012.06.002

Carless, S., Wearing, L., & Mann, L. (2000). A short measure of transformational leadership. *Journal of Business and Psychology, 14*(3), 389–405. doi:10.2307/25077344

Cohen, S. G., & Bailey, D. E. (1997). What makes teams work: Group effectiveness research from the shop floor to the executive suite. *Journal of Management, 23*(3), 239–290. doi:10.1177/014920639702300303

Conway, J. M., & Lance, C. E. (2010). What reviewers should expect from authors regarding common method bias in organizational research. *Journal of Business and Psychology, 25*, 325–334. doi:10.1007/s10869-010-9181-6

DeVellis, R. (2003). *Scale Development: Theory and Applications* (2nd Ed). Thousand Oaks: Sage.

Dimas, I. D., Rebelo, T. R., & Lourenço, P. R. (2016). Team coaching: One more clue for fostering team effectiveness. *European Review of Applied Psychology, 66*(5), 233–242. doi:10.1016/j.erap.2016.05.003

Gittel, J. H., Cameron, K., Lim, S., & Rivas, V. (2006). Relationship, layoff, and organizational resilience. Airline industry responses to September 11. *The Journal of Applied Behavioral Science, 42*(3), 300–329. doi:10.1177/0021886306286466

Hackman, J. R. (1987). The design of work teams. In J. Lorsch (Eds.), *Handbook of organizational behavior* (pp. 315–342). Englewood Cliffs, NJ: Prentice–Hall.

Hackman, J. R. (2012). From causes to conditions in group research. *Journal of Organizational Behavior, 33*, 428–444. doi:10.1002/job.1774

Hu, L., & Bentler, P. M. (1999). Cutoff criteria for fit indexes in covariance structure analysis: Conventional criteria versus new alternatives. *Structural Equation Modeling, 6*, 1–55. doi:10.1080/10705519909540118

Judge, T. A., & Piccolo, R. F. (2004). Transformational and transactional leadership: A meta-analytic test of their relative validity. *Journal of Applied Psychology, 89*(5), 755. doi:10.1037/0021-9010.89.5.755

Klein, K. J., & Kozlowski, S. W. J. (2000). (Eds.), *Multilevel theory, research, and methods in organizations: Foundations, extensions, and new directions*. San Francisco, CA: Jossey-Bass.

Kenny, D. (2016). Mediation. Retrieved January, 2017, from http://davidakenny.net/cm/mediate.htm

Kline, R. B. (2005). *Principles and practice of structural equation modelling* (2nd ed.). New York, NY: The Guilford Press.

López, C. G., Alonso, F. M., Morales, M. M., & León, J. A. M. L. (2015). Authentic leadership, group cohesion and group identification in security and emergency teams. *Psicothema, 27*(1), 59–64. doi:10.7334/psicothema2014.161

Luthans, F. (2002). Positive organizational behavior: Developing and managing psychological strengths. *Academy of Management Executive, 16*, 57–72. doi:10.5465/AME.2002.6640181

Luthans, F., Avolio, B. J., Walumbwa, F. O., & Li, W. (2005). The psychological capital of Chinese workers: Exploring the relationship with performance. *Management and Organization Review, 1* (2), 247–269. doi:10.1111/j.1740-8784.2005.00011.x

Mathieu, J. E., Tannenbaum, S. I., Donsbach, J. S., & Alliger, G. M. (2014). A review and Integration of team composition models moving toward a dynamic and temporal framework. *Journal of Management, 40*(1), 130–160. doi:10.1177/0149206313503014

Maxwell, S. E., & Cole, D. A. (2007). Bias in cross-sectional analyses of longitudinal mediation. *Psychological Methods, 12*(1), 23–44. doi:10.1037/1082-989x.12.1.23

McGrath, J. E. (1991). Time, interaction, and performance (TIP): A theory of groups. *Small Group Research, 22*, 147–174. doi:10.1177/1046496491222001

Meneghel, I., Salanova, M., & Martínez, I. M. (2016a). Feeling good makes Us stronger: How team resilience mediates the effect of positive emotions on team performance. *Journal of Happiness Studies, 17*(1), 239–255. doi:10.1007/s10902-014-9592-6

Meneghel, I., Martínez, I. M., & Salanova, M. (2016b). Job-related antecedents of team resilience and improved team performance. *Personnel Review, 45*(3), 505–522. doi:10.1108/PR-04-2014-0094

Michaelis, B., Stegmaier, R., & Sonntag, K. (2009). Affective commitment to change and innovation implementation behavior: The role of charismatic leadership and employees' trust in top management. *Journal of Change Management, 9*(4), 399–417. doi:10.1080/14697010903360608

Morgeson, F. P., DeRue, D. S., & Karam, E. P. (2010). Leadership in teams: A functional approach to understanding leadership structures and processes. *Journal of Management, 36*(1), 5–39. doi:10.1177/0149206309347376

Moynihan, D. P., Pandey, S. K., & Wright, B. E. (2012). Setting the table: How transformational leadership fosters performance information use. *Journal of Public Administration Research and Theory, 22*(1), 143–164. doi:10.1093/jopart/mur024

Podsakoff, P., MacKenzie, S., Moorman, S., & Fetter, R. (1990). Transformational leader behaviors and their effects on followers' trust in leader, satisfaction, and organizational citizenship behaviors. *Leadership Quarterly, 1*, 107–142. doi:10.1016/1048-9843(90)90009-7

Podsakoff, P. M., MacKenzie, S. B., Lee, J-Y, & Podsakoff, N. (2003). Common method biases in behavioral research: A critical review of the literature and recommended remedies. *Journal of Applied Psychology, 88*(5), 879–903. doi:10.1037/0021-9010.88.5.879

Podsakoff, P., Mackenzie, S., & Podsakoff, N. (2012). Sources of method bias in social science research and recommendations on how to control it. *Annual Review of Psychology, 63*, 539–569. doi:10.1146/annurev-psych-120710-100452

Powley, E. H. (2009). Reclaiming resilience and safety: Resilience activation in the critical period of crisis. *Human Relations, 6*, 1289–1326. doi:10.1177/0018726709334881

Rousseau, V., & Aubé, C. (2010). Team self-managing behaviors and team effectiveness: The moderating effect of task routineness. *Group & Organization Management, 35*(6), 751–781. doi:10.1177/1059601110390835

Rousseau, V., Aubé, C., & Tremblay, S. (2013). Team coaching and innovation in work teams: An examination of the motivational and behavioral intervening mechanisms". *Leadership & Organization Development Journal, 34*, 344–364. doi:10.1108/LODJ-08-2011-0073

Salanova, M., Llorens, S., & Schaufeli, W. B. (2011). "Yes, I can, I feel good, and I just do it!" on gain cycles and spirals of efficacy beliefs, affect, and engagement. *Applied Psychology: An International Review, 60*(2), 255–285. doi:10.1111/j.1464-0597.2010.00435.x

Salanova, M., Llorens, S., Cifre, E., & Martínez, I. M. (2012). We need a hero! Toward a validation of the Healthy and Resilient Organization (HERO) model. *Group and Organization Management, 37* (6), 785–822. doi:10.1177/1059601112470405

Schein, E. H. (1980). *Organizational psychology*. Englewood Cliffs, NJ: Prentice Hall.

Spector, P. E. (2006). Method variance in organizational research: Truth or urban legend? *Organizational Research Methods, 9*(2), 221–232. doi:10.1177/1094428105284955

Stephens, J. P., Heaphy, E. D., Carmeli, A., Spreitzer, G. M., & Dutton, J. E. (2013). Relationship quality and virtuousness: Emotional carrying capacity as a source of individual and team resilience. *The Journal of Applied Behavioral Science, 49*(1), 13–41. doi:10.1177/0021886312471193

Sutcliffe, K. M., & Vogus, T. (2003). Organizing for resilience. In K. Cameron, J. E. Dutton, & R. Quinn (Eds.), *Positive organizational scholarship* (pp. 94–121). San Francisco, CA: Berrett-Koehler.

Tugade, M. M., & Fredrickson, B. L. (2004). Resilient individuals use positive emotions to bounce back from negative emotional experiences. *Journal of Personality and Social Psychology*, *86*(2), 320–333. doi:10.1037/0022-3514.86.2.320

Volmer, J. (2012). Catching leaders' mood: Contagion effects in teams. *Administrative Sciences*, *2*(3), 203–220. doi:10.3390/admsci2030203

Weng, R. H., Huang, C. Y., Chen, L. M., & Chang, L. Y. (2015). Exploring the impact of transformational leadership on nurse innovation behaviour: A cross—sectional study. *Journal of nursing management*, *23*(4), 427–439. doi:10.1111/jonm.12149

West, B. J., Patera, J. L., & Carsten, M. K. (2009). Team level positivity: Investigating positive psychological capacities and team level outcomes. *Journal of Organizational Behavior*, *30*(2), 249–267. doi:10.1002/job.593

Youssef, C. M., & Luthans, F. (2007). Positive organizational behavior in the workplace: The Impact of hope, optimism, and resilience. *Journal of Management*, *33*(5), 774–800. doi:10.1177/0149206307305562

Psychological Capital, Team Resources and Organizational Citizenship Behavior

Ronit Bogler and Anit Somech

ABSTRACT
The study aimed to examine the impact of team resources – learning values and team leader optimism – as moderating variables affecting the relationship between team psychological capital (PsyCap) and organizational citizenship behavior (OCB), measured as a team outcome. Eighty-two management teams involving 395 participants from educational organizations responded to a quantitative questionnaire. Hierarchical regression analyses confirmed interactive effects of both moderating variables, which serve as positive resources for the team by enhancing the impact of team PsyCap on the willingness of the team to engage in OCB. Team PsyCap functioned as a positive team resource that brings about an environment that induces exhibition of high levels of OCB. This relationship is strengthened when both team learning and team leader's optimism are high. The findings provide support for the relevance of contingency theories by emphasizing the necessity of certain situational features existing in order to have an impact on organization outcomes. Theoretical and practical implications of the findings are discussed.

The phenomenon of people who are willing to perform "beyond the call of duty" or "go the extra mile" has had a long history, though the term Organizational Citizenship Behavior (OCB) was coined only in the 1980s (Organ, 2018). Since then, the research on OCB has shown an impressive rapid growth in the interest of researchers to study it, applying it in various disciplines and, consequently, in different types of organizations (MacKenzie, Podsakoff, & Podsakoff, 2018). The importance of investigating this citizenship behavior lies in its positive effect on the individual-level and organizational level (MacKenzie et al., 2018) outcomes. Thus, it is not surprising that researchers aim at examining the antecedents of OCB, including the mediating and moderating variables that affect the relationship between the antecedents and OCB. OCB can be examined on the individual level, which is frequently the case (e.g., Bogler & Somech, 2005; Lilly, Virick, & Wipawayangkool, 2015) or at the team level, which is beyond the sum of individual levels of OCBs (e.g., Ehrhart & Naumann, 2004; Heled, Somech, & Waters, 2016). The goal of the current study is to examine team OCB as affected by team resources. The first, team psychological capital (PsyCap) – a positive psychological state of development (Luthans, Avey, Avolio, Norman, & Combs, 2006) – is the antecedent of OCB that is moderated by team learning values – a team climate characteristic – and the team leader's optimism – a statelike construct. Hence, we offer a situational model, where two team-level variables serve as moderators in the relationship between team PsyCap and team OCB.

Theoretical Framework

Organizational Citizenship Behavior

Organizational citizenship behaviors (OCBs) are voluntary activities that are important and moreover crucial for organizations' survival and success (e.g., Organ, 1997; Somech & Oplatka, 2014). OCBs are essential because formal in-role job descriptions cannot cover the entire array of behaviors needed for achieving schools' objectives (Bogler & Somech, 2005). OCBs contribute to organizational effectiveness in various ways, such as freeing up resources for more productive purposes and enabling teachers to adapt more effectively to environmental changes (DiPaola & Hoy, 2005; Podsakoff, MacKenzie, Paine, & Bachrach, 2000).

The common approach to understanding OCB in organizations is to identify it as an individual phenomenon. However, this approach seems to fall short of its purpose. The research on OCB as a team or organizational-level concept has grown in recent years (e.g., Ehrhart & Naumann, 2004; Heled et al., 2016; Rego et al., 2017, 2019; Vigoda-Gadot, 2007). It seems that an individual member of a team will exhibit more OCBs when his/her team members show high level of OCB (e.g., George, 1990). However, team OCB is above and beyond the sum of individual levels of OCBs. Team OCB represents the team's "shared understanding of the typical and normative level of OCB" that contains "functions of norms, such as influencing social identity and regulating social interaction" that differentiate its OCB at the individual level (Nohe & Michaelis, 2016, p. 885). Hence, team OCB is defined as the "extra efforts performed by the whole team, that are above and beyond what is required, and contribute to the effective functioning of the organization" (Lau & Lam, 2008, p. 142). This multidimensional construct is defined in the current study according to Williams and Anderson's conceptualization (1991): team OCBI that represents behaviors directed to the individual, and team OCBO that refers to behaviors directed to the organization. The contribution of the current study is in its focus on team resources that affect team OCB. Team PsyCap functions as a positive team resource that brings about an environment that induces exhibition of high levels of OCB.

Team Psychological Capital – An Antecedent of OCB

Psychological capital is a concept developed within the field of positive psychology. PsyCap, "a statelike positive core construct" (Avey, Luthans, & Youssef, 2010, p. 434), is defined as "an individual's positive psychological state of development" (Luthans et al., 2006, p. 388) that is depicted by four dimensions: (1) self-efficacy, one's confidence to take on and invest the effort needed to overcome complex tasks; (2) optimism, one's positive attitude about succeeding in actions one takes in the present and in the future; (3) hope, one's perseverance regarding achieving goals and, when needed, reconsidering paths to these goals; and (4) resilience, one's coping with difficulties and hardship by "sustaining and bouncing back and even beyond" to fulfill accomplishments (Luthans, Youssef, & Avolio, 2007, p. 3, 2015). PsyCap is perceived as "a core confidence higher-order construct" that comprises four overlapping components, which implies that "the four constructs share a common confidence core that exists at a higher level of abstraction" (Stajkovic, 2006, p. 1212). As indicated by Stajkovic (2006), although the four constructs have been researched extensively in the literature, they have not been examined "as a part of a common core" (p. 1209). In the past decade, this notion is supported also by others (e.g., Avey, Reichard, Luthans, & Mhatre, 2011; Dawkins, Martin, Scott, & Sanderson, 2013; Luthans, Avolio, Avey, & Norman, 2007; Rego et al., 2017, 2019).

PsyCap is examined in this study as a collective structure at the team level that is defined as "a collective psychological state that is characterized by self-efficacy, hope, optimism, and resilience" (Heled et al., 2016, p. 305). Justification for considering PsyCap as a team-level phenomenon can be drawn from situation-specific models (Ehrhart & Naumann, 2004). Research has shown that teams, who interact within the same environment, have a major influence on the perceptions, beliefs, and attitudes of their members (Mohammed, Ferzandi, & Hamilton, 2010). Put it differently, team members who work in the same context, develop shared mental models. They tend to organize their knowledge about tasks, goals, and capabilities in a similar manner; a mechanism that might lead to develop a collective PsyCap (Lim & Klein, 2006). Indeed, the studies of Heled et al., 2016, and Mathe-Soulek, Scott-Halsell, Kim, & Krawczyk (2017) supported the notion that PsyCap grows in a context and can be treated as a collective construct.

To understand the significance of PsyCap as a resource to the team members, we use the Conservation of Resources (COR) theory (Hobfoll, 1989, 2001; Hobfoll, Halbesleben, Neveu, & Westman, 2018), which argues that individuals strive to attain, preserve and extend their personal resources. When they are confronted with a threat or a loss of their resources, their tension goes up. Therefore, the more they maintain an extra supply of resources the more they will be able as individuals or as a team to replace the loss of their own resources or their team. Consequently, being equipped with resources such as favorable organizational conditions will increase the chances of the team performing at higher levels of team OCB.

Team Psychological Capital and Team OCB

PsyCap is a team resource that generates a team climate that encourages the team to engage in prosocial behaviors of assistance and willingness to go above and beyond (George, 1996). It is described as a motivational inclination (Luthans et al., 2007) that may bring about desirable employee attitudes (Avey et al., 2011). Hence, teams that are characterized by optimism and positive mood will tend to demonstrate social behaviors that preserve their positive emotional state (Williams & Shiaw, 1999). Furthermore, team PsyCap enables team members to experience success that emphasizes the positive emotional state, which in turn encourages positive gestures (West, Patera, & Carsten, 2009). Research shows that team members who are optimistic and resilient create more positive relationships with others partly because of their belief that others will grant them the assistance they need (Srivastava, McGonigal, Richards, Butler, & Gross, 2006). Indeed, the relationship between PsyCap and OCB at the team level has been studied elsewhere (Heled et al., 2016).

In the current study, we aim to focus on the situational conditions that may strengthen this relationship. Specifically, we will examine team resources that may amplify the PsyCap-OCB relationship at the team level. The question that arises is what are the conditions under which team PsyCap-team OCB relationship will be enhanced, as there is no sole management model that will fit all contexts in all organizations. As contingency theories assert, there are certain situational features that affect the organization effectiveness, such as the organizational climate and characteristics of the task and leader's traits (Jago, 1982; Vroom & Jago, 1998). Though it is possible to suggest various potential variables that might moderate the relationship between team PsyCap and team OCB (e.g., demographic variables or team leader's leadership style), our goal in the present study was to demonstrate how two different team measures, vital components of team's working context, impact the relationship between team PsyCap and team OCBs. To better understand OCB in teams, we should examine concurrently the resources of the team members and those of the context within which they operate. Team members' characteristic of PsyCap will promote team OCB depending on the contextual factors within which the team members act, i.e., team learning values and team leader's optimism. Using the contingency perspective as a theoretical framework and applying COR theory, we propose that teams characterized by a higher level of PsyCap, whose favorable team resources include learning values that fit the team's mission and team leader's optimism, will enhance the team's likelihood of performing high levels of OCBs.

Testing a research model that explores the impact of team resources on this relationship has not been investigated yet, as far as we know. We refer to the COR theory (Hobfoll, 1989) that asserts that individuals are driven to attain, preserve and increase their personal resources for the sake of coping with challenges and hardships in their work. Thus, the greater the resource reservoir, the more likely the team will be able to replace the loss of a resource with other resources. Consequently, being equipped with resources such as favorable organizational conditions will increase the chances that the team will perform higher levels of team OCB. Therefore, testing the impact of resources that are vital to team functioning, such as learning values and team leader optimism, is indispensable to understanding the power of team resources in explaining the team PsyCap-team OCB relationship of management teams.

Team Learning Values as a Moderating Variable Affecting the Relation Between Team Psychological Capital and Team OCB

Learning values (LV) is a critical dimension of the learning climate, which represents a set of perceptions that may help or deter the learning of team members (Mikkelsen, Saksvik, & Ursin, 1998). According to Popper and Lipshitz (2000), LV is comprised of four sub-categories: valid information, transparency, issue orientation and accountability. Valid information, a critical factor for learning, entails a call for complete, accurate and verified information. Transparency refers to the disclosing of thoughts or actions to others for the sake of getting feedback. When transparency prevails, openness among individuals exists and they feel confident to deal with criticism in order to enhance their performance. Issue orientation denotes evaluation of the information relevant only to the issue, disregarding irrelevant aspects such as the characteristics of the source of the information or its recipient. Accountability, the fourth dimension of LV, refers to one's responsibility for actions and the implications of one's deeds, including being able to draw conclusions from these inferences (Somech & Drach-Zahavy, 2004).

In the current study, we focus on team values in relation to learning as they encompass all aspects that are inherent to the learning climate of the team, enabling continuous and ongoing learning. Learning values promote open discussion and reflection, as well as establish an environment that is based on trust and reliability (Heled et al., 2016). This environment may have great impact on the connection between PsyCap of the team members and their OCBs because the four sub-categories of LV correspond to the PsyCap construct identified by the four positive psychological resources. A team based on LV values that advocates openness and trust to promote a supportive environment, and whose team members are equipped with positive resources embedded in their PsyCap, will have a significant impact on the team members to perform beyond their call of duty. Going back to contingency theory, the learning values shared by the team represent an organizational climate characteristic that may play a critical role in enhancing the impact of team PsyCap on team OCB.

We suggest that team members, who are influenced by and act according to their team LV, will have an effect on the team PsyCap-team OCB relationship. In other words, we propose that LV can be viewed as the input, which provides working circumstances that enable the team to translate its PsyCap resources to citizenship behaviors; namely, when team LV are high, team PsyCap is expected to be more positively related to team OCB. Thus, we hypothesize that:

> *Hypothesis 1*: Team LV will moderate the relationship between team PsyCap and team OCB, such that the relationship between the two will be more positive under higher than lower levels of team LV.

Team Leader's Optimism as a Moderating Variable Affecting the Relation Between Team Psychological Capital and Team OCB

Optimism, defined as "a cognitive disposition to expect positive outcomes" (Srivastava et al., 2006, p. 143), represents a positive individual psychological state of development (Heled et al., 2016; Luthans et al., 2006). Hence, optimists are individuals who tend to be "favorable in their outlook" and expect good outcomes (Scheier & Carver, 1985, p. 219). They are conceived as optimistic by and large, and their positive expectations are not restricted to a specific behavioral area or setting. Optimists view obstacles as challenges to be overcome, thus, impediments that arise during their daily activities are expected to be less disrupting and have fewer problematical consequences for them (Scheier & Carver, 1985).

As a generalized positive viewpoint that produces overall positive expectations (Luthans & Frey, 2017), optimism is based on realistic assessment "of what one can accomplish in a specific situation, given the available resources at that time" (Luthans, Norman, Avolio, &

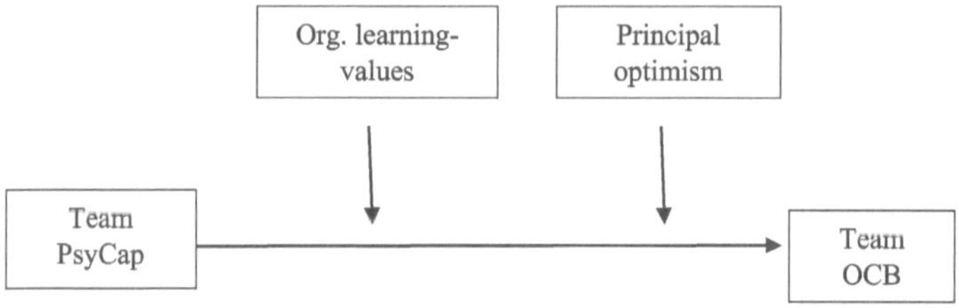

Figure 1. Research model.
PsyCap, Psychological Capital; OCB, Organizational Citizenship Behavior

Avey, 2008, p. 222). We, therefore, suggest that team leaders, who have a realistic assessment of the organizational goals that can be achieved with the existing resources, and who maintain a favorable outlook of reality with the expectations for favorable outcomes, will have a positive impact on the relationship between team PsyCap and team OCB. Relying on social contagion theory (Brett & Stroh, 2003; Levy & Nail, 1993) that refers to one's behavior in accord with others' states, we assert that team members, characterized by self-efficacy, hope, optimism and resilience, who view their leader as optimistic, may take on the optimistic view of their leader and act in unison with these states (Luthans, Norman, & Hughes, 2006). According to this theory, people change their behaviors because of their social interaction with others. Furthermore, the contagion effect has an impact on ensuing group dynamics among the group members also at the group level (Barsade, 2002). Therefore, an optimistic team leader will have an impact on team members who will adhere to his or her perspective that will further encourage them to perform OCBs. Another explanation for the potential impact of the team leader's optimism on the above relationship is derived from Seligman's (2004) interpretation of optimism. In his book on authentic happiness, Seligman presents two fundamental dimensions of one's interpretation of positive and negative events: permanence (relates to time) and pervasiveness (refers to space). Considering permanence, optimists interpret negative events as temporary, while pessimists regard them as being permanent. The opposite is true with regard to positive events: optimists refer to them with permanence, while pessimists attach to them temporariness. When referring to pervasiveness, optimists attach specific ascriptions to negative events, while pessimists make universal attributions to them, and vice versa for positive events. We, therefore, claim that when a team leader's optimism is high, team PsyCap is expected to be more positively related to team OCB (see Figure 1 for the research model).

Hence, we hypothesize that:

> *Hypothesis 2*: A team leader's optimism will moderate the relationship between team PsyCap and team OCB, such that the relationship between the two will be more positive under higher than lower optimism of the team leader.

The study was carried out in Israel, a Western-oriented society with culture characteristics that are similar to those in Western Europe and in the United States (Abu-saad & Isralowitz, 1997; Ben-Shem & Avi-Itzhak, 1991). Based on the general resemblance between Israeli society and societies in Western Europe and the United States, we expected to find similar patterns of attitudes among management teams regarding their perceptions of the impact of team resources on the relationship between team PsyCap and OCB.

Method

Sample: Eighty-two management teams in educational organizations were included in the current research (a total of 395 participants, of whom 82 were principals and 313 were school staff members, such as assistant principals and educational counselors). The average team size was 3.84 (SD = 1.20), and they met once a week on average. Of the 313 management team members, 274 were women (87.5%). The demographic characteristics of the participants were: age ($M = 42.53$, SD = 8.02); years in present management role ($M = 10.43$ years, SD = 8.45); bachelor's degree ($N = 172$, 55%); master's degree ($N = 141$, 45%). Among the 82 principals, who also served as heads of the management teams, 62 were women (76%). Their average age was 49 (SD = 6.25), and they had an average of 9.41 years of management experience in their current schools (SD = 8.39). Nineteen of the principals had a bachelor's degree (23%), 61 had a master's degree (74%) and two had a PhD (2%).

To avoid single-source bias, data were collected from two sources. The management team members evaluated LV and the team's PsyCap; team leaders (i.e., the school principals) evaluated their own level of optimism and the team's OCB. With regard to the latter measure, team leaders were asked to indicate the degree to which they agree with each of the statements on team OCB.

Following the approval from the Chief Scientist of the Israel Ministry of Education to conduct the research, school principals in various school districts were contacted to obtain their consent to conduct the research in their school's site. Anonymity and confidentiality were assured to encourage the participants' cooperation in filling out the questionnaires that were returned to the researchers by mail.

Measures

A quantitative questionnaire using a 6-point Likert scale ranging from 1 (strongly disagree) to 6 (strongly agree) was employed. The questionnaire was the basis for data analysis in a previous publication (Heled et al., 2016).

Team psychological capital was measured by the revised PsyCap questionnaire, designed to evaluate the team's collective PsyCap (Mathe-Soulek et al., 2017). In a previous study (Heled et al., 2016), the eight-item scale provided a better fit than the eleven-item scale, and therefore, it was adopted (p. 308). The scale has four dimensions: self-efficacy (two items) ("Members of this team confidently contribute to discussions about the team's strategy"); hope (two items) ("Members of this team think of many ways to attain work goals"); resilience ("Members of this team usually take stressful things at work in stride"); and optimism (two items) ("Members of this team are optimistic about what will happen to them in the future as it pertains to work"). Cronbach's α for the whole scale was .78.

Learning values were measured by 18 items (Ellis, Caridi, Lipshitz, & Popper, 1999) that were comprised of four factors: transparency (six items) ("Management team members customarily discuss mistakes made during work"); accountability (four items) ("Management team members take personal responsibility for failure even if they acted as part of a group or team"); issue orientation ("Management team members refer to the mistake itself, not to the person who made it"); and valid information (four items)

("Management team members tell the truth about their performance even when it might harm them"). Cronbach's α for the whole scale was .81.

Principal's optimism was measured by a scale of six items (Luthans et al., 2007) with $\alpha = .74$ ("I always look on the bright side of things regarding my job").

OCB was measured using Williams and Anderson's questionnaire (1991), with 13 items measuring OCBI that is directed toward the individual in the organization (six items) with $\alpha = .74$ ("Management team members help other employees who were absent"), and OCBO that is directed toward the organization as a whole (seven items) with $\alpha = .82$ ("Management team members give notice when they are unable to come to work"). Cronbach's α of team OCB scale, reported by team leaders, was .80. *Control variable.* The frequency of team meetings served as a control variable in the current study. Research has demonstrated the impact of frequency of team's meetings on team members' performance, their commitment to the organization (Harbin, Ringwalt, & Bastita, 1998; Schwartz, 1994) as well as their willingness to exhibit OCB (Somech, 2005). The number of team meetings per week was measured based on the report of the principal.

Levels of Analysis

OCB was measured at the team level and was evaluated by each of the school principals for his or her team. Team PsyCap and team LV were measured as team-level constructs and were evaluated by each of the management team members. Prior to aggregation, the degree of agreement among team members was determined. Two measures were examined: r_{wg} (within-group interrater agreement) and ICC (intra-class correlation). A value of .70 or above is conceived as a "good" extent of within-group interrater agreement (Dunlap, Burke, & Smith-Crowe, 2003; James, Demaree, & Wolf, 1993). All scales exceeded this criterion: average scores were .95 for LV and .93 for team PsyCap. The measures of ICC(1) and ICC(2) usually range from 0 to .50 with a median of .12 (Bliese, 2000), but there are no unequivocal rules for defining acceptable values. The values for ICC(1) and ICC(2) were .45 and .76 for LV, and .25 and .61 for team PsyCap. The above values were comparable to the median or to recommended ICC values; therefore, the scores of both variables were aggregated to the team-level.

Results

Means, standard deviations, and intercorrelations for the study variables are shown in Table 1. Team PsyCap was positively correlated with team LV ($r = 0.54$, $p < .001$) and with team OCB ($r = .32$, $p < .01$). Team LV had positive correlation with team OCB ($r = 0.51$, $p < .001$). Team PsyCap and team OCB had positive correlations with team's weekly meetings ($r = .26$, $p < .05$; $r = .25$, $p < .05$, respectively).

To test the study hypotheses, a hierarchical regression analyses for predicting team OCB were conducted. To avoid a possible problem of high multicollinearity with the interaction terms, and to facilitate interpretation of the results, the variables were centered and the interaction terms between team PsyCap and team LV and between PsyCap and principal optimism were created (Aiken & West, 1991). The control

Table 1. Means, Standard Deviations and Zero-Order Correlations Among Study Variables ($N = 82$).

Variable	Mean	s.d.	2	3	4	5
1. Team PsyCap	4.93	.36	.54***	.09	.32**	.26*
2. Team LV	4.08	.34		.16	.51***	.09
3. Principal optimism	5.28	.63			.15	−0.2
4. Team OCB	4.27	.39				.25*
5. MeetWeek	1.43	1.12				

*$p < .05$.
**$p < .01$.
***$p < .001$.
PsyCap, Psychological Capital; LV, Learning Values; OCB, Organizational Citizenship Behavior; MeetWeek, Frequency of team's weekly meetings.

Table 2. Results of Hierarchical Regression Analyses for Predicting Team OCB ($N = 82$).

Step variables	*B*	*SE*	*T*	ΔR^2	ΔF
Step 1: Control variable				.06	5.37*
MeetWeek	.09	.04	2.32*		
Step 2: Main effects				.25	9.29***
MeetWeek	.08	.03	2.21*		
Team PsyCap	−.01	.13	−.01		
Team LV	.55	.13	4.25***		
Principal optimism	.06	.06	.92		
Step 3: Interaction effects				.12	7.90***
MeetWeek	.08	.03	2.32*		
Team PsyCap	.001	.12	.01		
Team LV	.57	.12	4.80***		
Principal optimism	.10	.06	1.77†		
Team PsyCap X Team LV	.68	.29	2.39*		
Team PsyCap X Principal optimism	.37	.16	2.41*		

†$p < .10$.
*$p < .05$.
**$p < .01$.
***$p < .001$.
OCB, Organizational Citizenship Behavior; MeetWeek, Frequency of team's weekly meetings; PsyCap, Psychological Capital; LV, Learning Values. Unstandardized regression coefficients are shown.

variable (frequency of the team's weekly meetings) was entered in Step 1. The main effect terms of team PsyCap, team LV, and principal optimism were entered in Step 2, and the interaction effect terms in Step 3. Team OCB served as the dependent variable. The results of the hierarchical regression analyses are presented in Table 2.

As shown in Table 2, the control variable, the frequency of the team's weekly meetings, accounted for a small percentage of the variance in team OCB, 6%, but it was significant, $p < .05$. The main effect of team PsyCap, team LV and principal optimism accounted for 25%, $\Delta F = 9.29$, $p < .001$, of the variance in team OCB. Specifically, team LV was positively and significantly associated with team OCB, $b = .55$, $p < .001$. Neither team PsyCap nor principal optimism was significantly associated with team OCB.

The second-order interaction effects between team PsyCap and team LV, and between team PsyCap and principal optimism, entered in Step 3, accounted for an additional 12% of the variance of team OCB, $\Delta F = 7.90$, $p < .001$. In line with *Hypothesis 1*, the interaction effect between team PsyCap and team LV on team OCB was statistically significant, $B = .68$, $p < .05$.

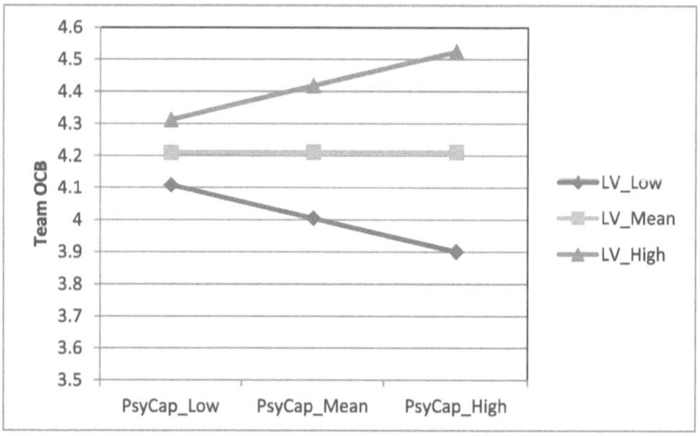

Figure 2. Interaction effect of team learning values on team PsyCap – team OCB relationship. PsyCap, Psychological Capital; LV, Learning Values; OCB, Organizational Citizenship Behavior

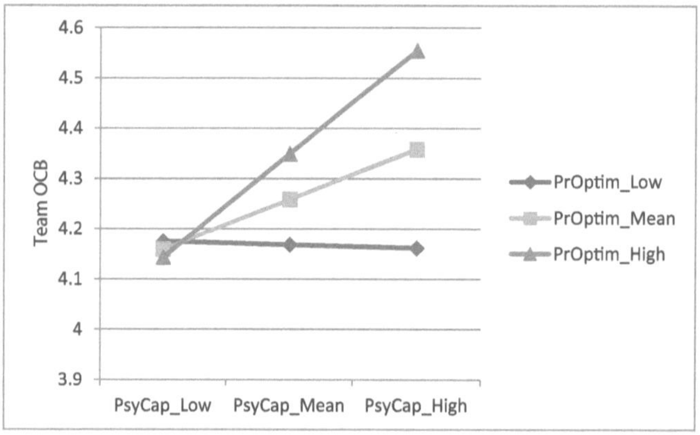

Figure 3. Interaction effect of principal optimism on team PsyCap – team OCB relationship. PsyCap, Psychological Capital; PrOptim, Principal Optimism; OCB, Organizational Citizenship Behavior

To better understand the interaction patterns, we plotted the high (+1SD) and low (-1SD) levels of the moderators, team LV and principal optimism, using the unstandardized regression coefficients (*B*) from the regression equation (Aiken & West, 1991; Hayes & Matthes, 2009). This procedure is aimed at providing less biased regression coefficients for measuring the moderating effects. Examination of the interaction plots regarding the effect of team LV on team PsyCap-team OCB relationship is shown in Figure 2.

The simple slope analysis indicated that when team LV was high (1 SD above the mean), team PsyCap was significantly and positively related to team OCB, $B = 0.38$, $t = 2.46$, $p < .05$. When team LV was low (1 SD below the mean), team PsyCap was negatively related to team OCB, $B = -0.26$, $t = -1.70$, $p < .10$. These results indicate, in line with *Hypothesis 1*, that the positive association between team PsyCap and team OCB is stronger when the level of team LV is high.

In line with *Hypothesis 2*, the interaction effect between team PsyCap and principal optimism on team OCB was significant, $B = .37$, $p < .05$. Examination of the interaction plots regarding the effect of principal optimism on team PsyCap-team OCB relationship is shown in Figure 3.

When referring to principal optimism, the simple slope analysis indicated that when the optimism was high (1 SD above the mean), team PsyCap was significantly and positively related to team OCB, $B = 0.62$, $t = 3.81$, $p < .001$. When principal optimism was low (1 SD below the mean), team PsyCap was unrelated to team OCB, $B = 0.08$, $t = 0.50$, $p > .05$. These results indicate, in line with *Hypothesis 2*, that the positive association between team PsyCap and team OCB is stronger when the level of principal optimism is high.

Discussion

The study explored the OCB as a context-related phenomenon, namely, as a team phenomenon. This means that team members who perform or fail to perform OCBs do not do so in a vacuum, but rather the team or the organizational context most likely serves to encourage or discourage them (Somech & Drach-Zahavy, 2004). Studying OCB as a team phenomenon has gained a growing attention in recent years (Lau & Lam, 2008; Nohe & Michaelis, 2016; Rego et al., 2017). In the present study, we aimed to examine the impact of team resources – team learning values and team leader optimism – on the relationship between PsyCap and OCB at the team level. The study findings confirmed both hypotheses, indicating that the positive association between team PsyCap and team OCB was stronger under the conditions of high level of team LV and high level of principal optimism. In other words, the impact of team PsyCap on the citizenship behavior of the team members was salient when PsyCap was related to additional team resources – team LV and leader's optimism.

PsyCap has a key role to play in promoting favorable stances and behaviors among team members exhibiting team citizenship behaviors. The results indicated that when members are characterized by optimism, self-efficacy, hope and resilience, they tend to view others in a more favorable perspective. This team resource may lead them to behave in a way that benefits the team members and/or contributes to the organizational outcomes (Somech & Khotaba, 2017). These positive behaviors are attributed to the positive emotions that are likely to be experienced by individuals high in PsyCap who use broader thought-action repertoires to solve problems.

Both study moderators, which provide team members with valuable resources to cope successfully with challenges at work, increased the impact of team PsyCap by enhancing its influence on the willingness of the team members to engage in OCB. Learning values that promote valid information, transparency, issue orientation and accountability shared by team members was found to serve as a significant resource for the creation of a positive team climate that emphasizes ongoing learning. Alternatively, one could state that under conditions of team learning climate where team members make use of their abilities and mobilize their cognitive resources toward successfully fulfilling their tasks, they create a better condition for the use of team PsyCap that affects team members in going the extra mile in their job as a team. Team leader optimism, that was also revealed as a significant resource that invigorates team climate, creates a group affective tone where team members are induced to engage in prosocial behaviors (George, 1996).

Leaders who are high in optimism tend to anticipate positive expectancies that drive them toward achieving high goals and facing challenging circumstances successfully (Gillham, Shatte, Reivich, & Seligman, 2001). For team members, characterized by a higher level of team PsyCap that induces them to exhibit OCB, team leader optimism functions as another motivational resource under which the relationship between team PsyCap and team OCB is more powerful.

Both team LV and team leader optimism that affected the team PsyCap – team OCB relationship provide support to COR theory by stressing the importance of investing in expanding the resource reservoir, and thus protecting against any future resource loss at times of hardship. According to the theory, it seems that the two moderators may represent the energy resources that are characterized by "their value in aiding the acquisition of other kinds of resources" (Hobfoll, 1989, p. 517). Team learning values and team leader's optimism seem to fit the definition of energy resources as they aid in elevating the impact of team PsyCap in affecting team OCB. In addition, according to COR theory, individuals strive to protect their present resources (conservation) and acquire new ones (acquisition) (Hobfoll, 1989; Hobfoll et al., 2018). Two main principles emerge from the theory: *primacy of resource loss*, when loss of resources is disproportionately more critical to individuals than earning resources, and *resource investment*, that stresses the necessity of individuals to invest resources "to protect against resource loss, recover from losses, and gain resources" (Hobfoll, 2011, p. 117). These two principles are relevant to team members as well. Thus, the greater the reservoir of resources the team members maintain, the more likely it is that they will be able to substitute the loss of a resource with other resources. Teams equipped with resources, such as favorable team circumstances, therefore, will increase the chances of exhibiting higher levels of team OCB.

The present study contributes to the knowledge about team PsyCap in organizations. As stated by Avey et al. (2011), "PsyCap seems to have a stronger impact on service work, which relies on more social interactions that require emotional norms favoring the expression of positive affect" (p. 146). Exploring the role of team PsyCap contributes to understanding the collective facet of the phenomenon, which represents the variety of resources that are beyond the individual member, and are used to face challenges and overcome failures (Rego, 2019). Though a positive relationship between team PsyCap and team OCB has been revealed in previous studies (e.g., Gooty, Gavin, Johnson, Frazier, & Snow, 2009; Heled et al., 2016; Somech & Khotaba, 2017), the impact of team working context, as reflected by team LV and the optimistic view of the team leader, has not been scrutinized up until now. The importance of studying these two moderators lies in the significance of climate in this context. Under positive team climate, team resources that are brought to the group by team members are expected to be fully utilized for the good of the collective goals (Kearney & Gebert, 2009), thus encouraging greater team OCB. Leaders are assumed to take a key role in enabling this process for the sake of team members (Hogan & Kaiser, 2005). Therefore, team leaders exhibiting optimism are better equipped with the resource needed for inducing team OCB to members possessing PsyCap.

It should be noted, however, that under low levels of both moderators the relationship between team PsyCap and team OCB revealed different patterns. When team LV is low, team PsyCap shows a negative effect on team OCB. That is, the more the team attained the positive resource of PsyCap, the less it had an impact on team OCB. This surprising finding may be a result of a reality where positive resources, such as team PsyCap, are not supported by a positive climate as measured by team LV. When values that promote valid information, transparency, issue orientation and accountability are not shared by team members, a supportive team climate cannot be established. Therefore, enhancing the positive psychological states of team members in this climate negatively affect team members' motivation to exhibit OCBs. This may imply that positive resources can be materialized only within a supportive organization where learning climate is recognized. Regarding team leader optimism, we reveal that when team members do not perceive their leader as an optimistic person, their PsyCap has no effect on their OCB. These findings stress the importance of adopting moderating research models that allow refined investigation of the relationships among the study variables (Cohen, Cohen, West, & Aiken, 2003; MacKinnon, 2011). Such examination allows us to conclude that the power of team resources explains the PsyCap–OCB relationship of management teams, but this conclusion is generalizable only under one condition - high levels of the moderating variables. This conclusion also provides support for the relevance of contingency theories by emphasizing the necessity of certain situational features existing in order to have an impact on organization outcomes (Vroom & Jago, 1998).

Limitations

Our study is not without limitations. First, one should be cautious regarding causality. Due to the cross-sectional nature of the data, theoretically, reverse causality is plausible, thus hypothesizing whether team resources, team LV and principal optimism are the antecedents of team PsyCap. To better comprehend the nature of relationship among the study variables, a longitudinal type of research method needs to be utilized. Second, other team resources may play a vital role in moderating the relationship between team PsyCap and team OCB, such as team leader leadership style or the leader Big Five personality traits (Chiaburu, Oh, Berry, Li, & Gardner, 2011). Future research should expand this examination to additional moderating factors that may affect this relationship. Third limitation refers to the principals' evaluation of team OCB. Though this choice was adopted to avoid single-source bias, principals may not have as intimate a knowledge of team members' behaviors as they may think. Therefore, their evaluations of team OCB may not match what the team members may have rated OCB. The fourth limitation of the study relates to team PsyCap measure. We have shown agreement for this measure among the team members, but this consent may be for the behavioral expression of psychological capital. PsyCap is a statelike characteristic rather than a personality trait; therefore, it is influenced by the context. Nevertheless, from a functionalist perspective, "individuals differ in the way that they choose/shape, respond to and are shaped by their environment" (Perugini, Costantini, Hughes, & De Houwer, 2016, p. 36), and their response may depend on the degree to which each of them finds the behavioral tendency desirable or valuable (Wood & Denissen, 2015, p. 102). Thus, the team shared PsyCap may represent a more behavioral facet of PsyCap. Lastly, we call attention to the sample of the study and the generalizability of its findings. Data were collected from elementary schools in Israel. To be able to generalize the patterns revealed in the current study, and hence reflect the perceptions of team leaders and members of other levels of schools or organizations, one would need to conduct the research in other settings and examine the applicability of the current findings in other Western countries. As indicated above, Israel's culture orientation is similar to that of Western societies but differences with regard to cultural dimensions such as individualism-collectivism and power distance do exist (Hofstede, 1980, 1991). Therefore, such a study may provide different findings and suggest explanations related to the unique characteristics of each country. We therefore recommend that future research should take this viewpoint into account to be able to generalize or refute generalization of the current findings.

Practical Implications

The current study also has practical implications, and most importantly is the message for leaders and policy makers regarding the power of teams and positive resources to establish a supportive team environment for its members that will result in promoting team OCB. Team members will strive to "go the extra mile" when acting in a team climate that is typified by resources that induce the impact of their psychological capital on their willingness to exhibit citizenship behavior. Working together enriches each individual's resources, thus supporting the saying that "the whole is greater than the sum of its parts." Leaders should encourage and promote the situational conditions within which teams' work could mostly benefit from the team members' psychological capital and the LV of their group work. In addition, employees' perception of their leader's level of optimism is another significant resource that should be fully appreciated by the leaders if they aim at increasing OCBs in their organization. The concepts examined in this study are often scrutinized at the individual level. The present study highlights the importance of a common confidence core (Stajkovic, 2006) shared by team members that affect their shared norms of behavior. This relationship was especially strong when team members had high levels of agreement about their shared learning values and a view of their leader as an optimistic person. Organizational leaders and team management leaders should strive to establish such a team climate that will strengthen the relationship between teams' PsyCap and their OCBs for the benefit of the team and the organization. Investing in such resources would benefit members of the organization, while disregarding them has shown to harm the willingness of members to invest further efforts for the sake of the organization. Furthermore, active support for the teams by offering them professional development programs that correspond to their needs and interests may enhance their willingness to become active agents in their organization, where they will make use of their PsyCap for greater OCB.

Conclusion

We found that team psychological capital creates an environment that encourages team members to exhibit high levels of OCB. This relationship is strengthened when team learning values prevail. Thus, the relationship between team PsyCap and team OCB is stronger when valid information, transparency, issue orientation and accountability are high rather than low. This is also true when principal optimism prevails. We found that principal optimism serves as a positive resource for the team by enhancing the impact of team PsyCap on the willingness of the team to engage in citizenship behaviors.

ORCID

Ronit Bogler https://orcid.org/0000-0001-9484-974X

References

Abu-Saad, I., & Isralowitz, R. E. (1997). Gender as a determinant of work values among university students in Israel. *The Journal of Social Psychology, 137*(6), 749–763. doi:10.1080/00224549709595496

Aiken, L. S., & West, S. G. (1991). *Multiple regression: Testing and interpreting interactions.* Newbury Park, CA: Sage.

Avey, J. B., Luthans, F., & Youssef, C. M. (2010). The additive value of positive psychological capital in predicting work attitudes and behaviors. *Journal of Management, 36*(2), 430–452. doi:10.1177/0149206308329961

Avey, J. B., Reichard, R. J., Luthans, F., & Mhatre, K. H. (2011). Meta-analysis of the impact of positive psychological capital on employee attitudes, behaviors, and performance. *Human Resource Development Quarterly, 22*(2), 127–152. doi:10.1002/hrdq.20070

Barsade, S. G. (2002). The ripple effect: Emotional contagion and its influence on group behavior. *Administrative Science Quarterly, 47*(4), 644–675. doi:10.2307/3094912

Ben-Shem, I., & Avi-Itzhak, T. E. (1991). On work values and career choice in freshmen students: The case of helping vs. other professions. *Journal of Vocational Behavior, 39*(3), 369–379. doi:10.1016/0001-8791(91)90045-N

Bliese, P. D. (2000). Within group agreement, non independence, and reliability. In K. Klein, & S. W. J. Kozlovski (Eds.), *Multi-level theory, research and methods in organizations* (pp. 349–381). San Francisco, CA: Jossey-Bass.

Bogler, R., & Somech, A. (2005). Organizational citizenship behavior in school: How does it relate to participation in decision-making?. *Journal of Educational Administration, 43*(5), 420–438. doi:10.1108/09578230510615215

Brett, J. M., & Stroh, L. K. (2003). Working 61 plus hours a week: Why do managers do it?. *Journal of Applied Psychology, 88*(1), 67–78. doi:10.1037/0021-9010.88.1.67

Chiaburu, D. S., Oh, I. S., Berry, C. M., Li, N., & Gardner, R. G. (2011). The five-factor model of personality traits and organizational citizenship behaviors: A meta-analysis. *Journal of Applied Psychology, 96*(6), 1140–1166. doi:10.1037/a0024004

Cohen, J., Cohen, P., West, S. G., & Aiken, L. S. (2003). *Applied multiple regression/correlation analysis for the behavioral sciences* (3rd ed.). Mahwah, NJ: Erlbaum.
Dawkins, S., Martin, A., Scott, J., & Sanderson, K. (2013). Building on the positives: A psychometric review and critical analysis of the construct of psychological capital. *Journal of Occupational and Organizational Psychology, 86*(3), 348–370. doi:10.1111/joop.12007
DiPaola, M. F., & Hoy, W. K. (2005). School characteristics that foster organizational citizenship behavior. *Journal of School Leadership, 15*(4), 387–406. doi:10.1177/105268460501500402
Dunlap, W. P., Burke, M. J., & Smith-Crowe, K. (2003). Accurate tests of statistical significance for rWG and average deviation interrater agreement indexes. *Journal of Applied Psychology, 88*(2), 356. doi:10.1037/0021-9010.88.2.356
Ehrhart, M. G., & Naumann, S. E. (2004). Organizational citizenship behavior in work groups: A group norms approach. *Journal of Applied Psychology, 89*(6), 960–974. doi:10.1037/0021-9010.89.6.960
Ellis, S., Caridi, O., Lipshitz, R., & Popper, M. (1999). Perceived error criticality and organizational learning: An empirical investigation. *Knowledge and Process Management, 6*(3), 166–175. doi:10.1002/(SICI)1099-1441(199909)6:3 < 166::AID-KPM65 > 3.0.CO;2-S
George, J. M. (1990). Personality, affect and behavior in groups. *Journal of Applied Psychology, 75*(2), 107–116. doi:10.1037/0021-9010.75.2.107
George, J. M. (1996). Group affective tone. In A. M. West (Ed.), *Handbook of work group psychology* (pp. 77–93). Chichester, UK: John Wiley & Sons Ltd.
Gillham, J. E., Shatte, A. J., Reivich, K. J., & Seligman, M. E. (2001). Optimism, pessimism, and explanatory style. In E.C. Chang (Ed.), *Optimism and pessimism: Implications for theory, research, and practice* (pp. 53–75). Washington, DC: APA.
Gooty, J., Gavin, M., Johnson, P., Frazier, L., & Snow, D. (2009). In the eyes of the beholder: Transformational leadership, positive psychological capital and performance. *Journal of Leadership and Organization Studies, 15*(4), 353–357. doi:10.1177/1548051809332021
Harbin, G., Ringwalt, S., & Bastita, L. (1998). *Local interagency coordination councils: Purpose, characteristics, and level of functioning.* Chapel Hill: North Carolina University.
Hayes, A. F., & Matthes, J. (2009). Computational procedures for probing interactions in OLS and logistic regression: SPSS and SAS implementations. *Behavior Research Methods, 41*(3), 924–936. doi:10.3758/BRM.41.3.924
Heled, E., Somech, A., & Waters, L. (2016). Psychological capital as a team phenomenon: Mediating the relationship between learning climate and outcomes at the individual and team levels. *The Journal of Positive Psychology, 11*(3), 303–314. doi:10.1080/17439760.2015.1058971
Hobfoll, S. E. (1989). Conservation of resources: A new attempt at conceptualizing stress. *American Psychologist, 44*(3), 513–524. doi:10.1037/0003-066X.44.3.513
Hobfoll, S. E. (2001). The influence of culture, community, and the nested-self in the stress process: advancing conservation of resources theory. *Applied Psychology, 50*(3), 337–421. doi: 10.1111/1464-0597.00062
Hobfoll, S. E. (2011). Conservation of resource caravans and engaged settings. *Journal of Occupational and Organizational Psychology, 84*(1), 116–122. doi:10.1111/j.2044-8325.2010.02016.x
Hobfoll, S. E., Halbesleben, J., Neveu, J. P., & Westman, M. (2018). Conservation of resources in the organizational context: The reality of resources and their consequences. *Annual Review of Organizational Psychology and Organizational Behavior, 5*(1), 103–128. doi:10.1146/annurev-orgpsych-032117-104640
Hofstede, G. (1991). *Cultures and organizations: Software of the mind.* London: McGraw-Hill.
Hofstede, G. (1980). Motivation, leadership, and organizations: Do American theories apply abroad?. *Organizational Dynamics, 8*, 42–63. doi:10.1016/0090-2616(80)90013-3
Hogan, R., & Kaiser, R. B. (2005). What we know about leadership. *Review of General Psychology, 9*(2), 169–180. doi:10.1037/1089-2680.9.2.169
Jago, A. G. (1982). Leadership: Perspectives in theory and research. *Management Science, 28*(3), 315–336. doi:10.1287/mnsc.28.3.315

James, L. R., Demaree, R. G., & Wolf, G. (1993). *rWG*: An assessment of within-group interrater agreement. *Journal of Applied Psychology, 78*(2), 306–309. doi:10.1037/0021-9010.78.2.306
Kearney, E., & Gebert, D. (2009). Managing diversity and enhancing team outcomes: The promise of transformational leadership. *Journal of Applied Psychology, 94*(1), 77–89. doi:10.1037/a0013077
Lau, D. C., & Lam, L. W. (2008). Effects of trusting and being trusted on team citizenship behaviours in chain stores. *Asian Journal of Social Psychology, 11*(2), 141–149. doi:10.1111/j.1467-839X.2008.00251.x
Levy, D. A., & Nail, P. R. (1993). Contagion: A theoretical and empirical review and reconceptualization. *Genetic, Social, and General Psychology Monographs, 119*(2), 233–284.
Lilly, J., Virick, M., & Wipawayangkool, K. (2015). Regency effects in justice and organizational citizenship behavior: The impact of coping style. *Journal of Business Strategies, 32*(2), 71–109.
Lim, B. C., & Klein, K. J. (2006). Team mental models and team performance: A field study of the effects of team mental model similarity and accuracy. *Journal of Organizational Behavior, 27*(4), 403–418. doi:10.1002/job.387
Luthans, F., Avey, J. B., Avolio, B. J., Norman, S. M., & Combs, G. (2006). Psychological capital development: Toward a micro-intervention. *Journal of Organizational Behavior, 27*(3), 387–393. doi:10.1002/job.373
Luthans, F., Avolio, B., Avey, J. B., & Norman, S. M. (2007). Psychological capital: Measurement and relationship with performance and job satisfaction. *Personnel Psychology, 60*(3), 541–572. doi:10.1111/j.1744-6570.2007.00083.x
Luthans, F., & Frey, R. (2017). Positive psychology in the workplace: The important role of psychological capital (PsyCap). In D.S. Dunn (Ed.), *Positive psychology: Established and emerging issues. Series: Frontiers of social psychology* (pp. 171–196). New York, NY: Routledge.
Luthans, F., Norman, S. M., Avolio, B. J., & Avey, J. B. (2008). The mediating role of psychological capital in the supportive organizational climate-employee performance relationship. *Journal of Organizational Behavior, 29*(2), 219–238. doi:10.1002/job.507
Luthans, F., Norman, S., & Hughes, L. (2006). Authentic leadership. In R.J. Burke and C.L. Cooper (Eds.), *Inspiring leaders* (pp. 84–104). New York, NY: Routledge.
Luthans, F., Youssef, C. M., & Avolio, B. J. (2007). *Psychological capital: Developing the human competitive edge.* Oxford, UK: Oxford University Press.
Luthans, F., Youssef, C. M., & Avolio, B. J. (2015). *Psychological capital and beyond.* New York, NY: Oxford University Press.
MacKinnon, D. P. (2011). Integrating mediators and moderators in research design. *Research on Social Work Practice, 21*(6), 675–681. doi:10.1177/1049731511414148
Mathe-Soulek, K., Scott-Halsell, S., Kim, S., & Krawczyk, M. (2017). Psychological capital in the quick service restaurant industry: A study of unit-level performance. *Journal of Hospitality & Tourism Research, 41*(7), 823–845. doi:10.1177/1096348014550923
MacKenzie, S. B., Podsakoff, N. P., & Podsakoff, P. M. (2018). Individual- and organizational-level consequences of organizational citizenship behaviors. In P.M. Podsakoff, S.B. MacKenzie and N.P. Podsakoff (Eds.), *The oxford handbook of organizational citizenship behavior* (pp. 105–148). Oxford, UK: Oxford University Press.
Mikkelsen, A., Saksvik, P., & Ursin, H. (1998). Job stress and organizational learning climate. *International Journal of Stress Management, 5*(4), 197–209. doi:10.1023/A:1022965727976
Mohammed, S., Ferzandi, L., & Hamilton, K. (2010). Metaphor no more: A 15-year review of the team mental model construct. *Journal of Management, 36*(4), 876–910. doi:10.1177/0149206309356804
Nohe, C., & Michaelis, B. (2016). Team OCB, leader charisma, and organizational change: A multilevel study. *The Leadership Quarterly, 27*(6), 883–895. doi:10.1016/j.leaqua.2016.05.006
Organ, D. W. (1997). Organizational citizenship behavior: It's construct clean-up time. *Human Performance, 10*(2), 85–97. doi:10.1207/s15327043hup1002_2
Organ, D. W. (2018). The roots of organizational citizenship behavior. In P.M. Podsakoff, S.B. MacKenzie and N.P. Podsakoff (Eds.), *The Oxford Handbook of Organizational Citizenship Behavior* (pp. 7–18). Oxford, UK: Oxford University Press.

Perugini, M., Costantini, G., Hughes, S., & De Houwer, J. (2016). A functional perspective on personality. *International Journal of Psychology, 51*(1), 33–39. doi:10.1002/ijop.12175

Podsakoff, P. M., MacKenzie, S. B., Paine, J. B., & Bachrach, D. G. (2000). Organizational citizenship behaviors: A critical review of the theoretical and empirical literature and suggestions for future research. *Journal of Management, 26*(3), 513–563. doi:10.1177/014920630002600307

Popper, M., & Lipshitz, R. (2000). Installing mechanisms and instilling values: The role of leaders in organizational learning. *The Learning Organization, 7*(3), 135–145. doi:10.1108/09696470010335854

Rego, A., Owens, B., Leal, S., Melo, A. I., e Cunha, M. P., Gonçalves, L., & Ribeiro, P. (2017). How leader humility helps teams to be humbler, psychologically stronger, and more effective: A moderated mediation model. *The Leadership Quarterly, 28*(5), 639–658. doi:10.1016/j.leaqua.2017.02.002

Rego, A., Owens, B., Yam, K. C., Bluhm, D., Cunha, M. P. E., Silard, A., … & Liu, W. (2019). Leader humility and team performance: Exploring the mediating mechanisms of team PsyCap and task allocation effectiveness. *Journal of Management, 45*(3), 1009–1033. doi:10.1177/0149206316688941

Scheier, M. F., & Carver, C. S. (1985). Optimism, coping, and health: Assessment and implications of generalized outcome expectancies. *Health Psychology, 4*(3), 219–247. doi:10.1037/0278-6133.4.3.219

Schwartz, M. P. (1994). *Results of a national survey of theological school board characteristics, policies and practices.* Washington, DC: Association of Governing Boards of Universities and Colleges.

Seligman, M. E. (2004). *Authentic happiness: Using the new positive psychology to realize your potential for lasting fulfillment.* New York, NY: Simon and Schuster.

Somech, A. (2005). Teachers' personal and team empowerment and their relations to organizational outcomes: contradictory or compatible constructs?. *Educational Administration Quarterly, 41*(2), 237–266. doi:10.1177/0013161X04269592

Somech, A., & Drach-Zahavy, A. (2004). Exploring organizational citizenship behavior from an organizational perspective: The relationship between organizational learning and organizational citizenship behavior. *Journal of Occupational and Organizational Psychology, 77*(3), 281–298. doi:10.1348/0963179041752709

Somech, A., & Khotaba, S. (2017). An integrative model for understanding team organizational citizenship behavior: Its antecedents and consequences for educational teams. *Journal of Educational Administration, 55*(6), 671–685. doi:10.1108/JEA-09-2016-0104

Somech, A., & Oplatka, I. (2014). *Organizational citizenship behavior in schools: Examining the impact and opportunities within educational systems.* London: Routledge.

Srivastava, S., McGonigal, K. M., Richards, J. M., Butler, E. A., & Gross, J. J. (2006). Optimism in close relationships: How seeing things in a positive light makes them so. *Journal of Personality and Social Psychology, 91*(1), 143–153. doi:10.1037/0022-3514.91.1.143

Stajkovic, A. D. (2006). Development of a core confidence higher-order construct. *Journal of Applied Psychology, 91*(6), 1208–1224. doi:10.1037/0021-9010.91.6.1208

Vigoda-Gadot, E. (2007). Leadership style, organizational politics, and employees' performance: An empirical examination of two competing models. *Personnel Review, 36*(5), 661–683. doi: 10.1108/00483480710773981

Vroom, V. H., & Jago, A. G. (1998). Situation effects and levels of analysis in the study of leader participation. In F. Dansereau & F. J. Yammarino (Eds.), *Leadership: The multilevel approach* (pp. 145–159). Greenwich, CT: JAI.

West, B. J., Patera, J. L., & Carsten, M. K. (2009). Team level positivity: Investigating positive psychological capacities and team level outcomes. *Journal of Organizational Behavior, 30*(2), 249–267. doi:10.1002/job.593

Williams, L., & Anderson, S. (1991). Job satisfaction and organizational commitment as predictor of organization citizenship and in-role behavior. *Journal of Management, 17*(3), 601–617. doi: 10.1177/014920639101700305

Williams, S., & Shiaw, W. T. (1999). Mood and organizational citizenship behavior: The effects of positive affect on employee organizational citizenship behavior intentions. *Journal of Psychology, 133*(6), 656–668. doi:10.1080/00223989909599771

Wood, D., & Denissen, J. J. (2015). A functional perspective on personality trait development. In K.J., and N.R. Branscombe (Eds.), *Psychology of change: Life contexts, experiences, and identities* (pp. 97–115). New York, NY: Psychology Press.

Servant Leadership and Follower Outcomes: Mediating Effects of Organizational Identification and Psychological Safety

Aamir Ali Chughtai

ABSTRACT

This study investigated the mediating role of organizational identification and psychological safety in the relationship between servant leadership and two employee outcomes: employee voice and negative feedback seeking behavior. The sample for this study comprised of 174 full-time employees drawn from a large food company based in Pakistan. Results showed that organizational identification and psychological safety partially mediated the effects of servant leadership on voice and negative feedback seeking behavior. The theoretical and practical implications of this research are discussed.

Introduction

It is now widely recognized that people are the most important asset of an organization (Pfeffer & Veiga, 1999). An organization might have access to latest technology and may possess state of the art production facilities, but without a high quality workforce it is unlikely to create a sustainable competitive advantage (Greer, 2001). Thus, organizations need to invest heavily in the development of their human resources if they intend to compete effectively in today's business environment.

Because of these reasons, the concept of servant leadership has assumed increased significance over the last ten years or so. Servant leaders "go beyond self-interest" (Van Dierendonck, 2011, p. 1231) and exclusively focus on addressing the needs of their followers. Specifically, these leaders strive to create conditions that help employees to grow and realize their full potential. Previous research has shown that servant leaders, through their actions, manage to develop a strong and highly engaged workforce, which can be a considerable source of competitive advantage for their organizations (Walumbwa, Hartnell & Oke, 2010; Liden et al., 2015). However, research on servant leadership is in a "relatively early stage" (Van Dierendonck, Stam, Boersma, Windt, & Alkema, 2014, p. 544) and, therefore, empirical evidence on the outcomes of this leadership style is relatively scarce (Avolio, Walumbwa, & Weber, 2009). Moreover, not much is known about the psychological mechanisms through that servant leadership wields its influence on various follower outcomes (Walumbwa et al., 2010; Van Dierendonck et al., 2014).

The present study attempts to address these gaps by the examining the impact of servant leadership on two employee outcomes that can have important implications for organizations: employee voice and negative feedback seeking behavior. No previous study to the best of my knowledge has empirically explored the effects of servant leadership on these two work outcomes.

This research focused on examining the effects of servant leadership on voice and negative feedback seeking behavior because past studies have shown that employees' tendency to engage in these behaviors can yield significant benefits for organizations. For instance, research evidence indicates that employees' inclination to seek critical feedback is likely to have a positive effect on individual and organizational learning and performance (Edmondson, 1999, 2004). Likewise, voice behaviors, which aim to challenge the status quo and attempt to bring about a constructive change within the work unit, can facilitate the effective functioning of the organization (LePine & Van Dyne, 2001; Detert & Burris, 2007). By providing a first examination of the relationship between servant leadership and these valued outcomes, this study not only provides new theoretical insights into this concept but also seeks to reaffirm its importance as a critical driver of organizational success.

Furthermore, this study sought to identify the underlying processes through which servant leadership relates to voice and negative feedback seeking behavior. Research has demonstrated that exhibition of servant leadership behaviors can increase employees' sense of psychological safety (Schaubroeck, Lam, & Peng, 2011) and strengthen their identification with the organization (Zhang, Kwan, Everett, & Jian, 2012). A high sense of psychological safety (e.g., Edmondson, 2004; Detert & Burris, 2007) coupled with strong organizational identification (e.g., Chughtai & Buckley, 2010; Tangirala & Ramanujam, 2008), in turn, can inspire employees to seek negative feedback and engage in voice behavior. Thus, it is proposed that the effect of servant leadership on voice and negative feedback seeking behavior will be mediated by psychological safety and organizational identification. The conceptual model showing the proposed relationships is depicted in Figure 1.

Literature review and hypotheses development

The concept of servant leadership

Although Greenleaf (1970) introduced the idea of servant leadership nearly 45 years ago, there is still no consensus among scholars and researchers about the precise definition of this construct (Barbuto & Wheeler, 2006; Liden, Wayne, Zhao, & Henderson, 2008; Van Dierendonck, 2011). However, recently Van Dierendonck (2011) conducted a thorough

Figure 1. Hypothesised model.

review of literature and identified six core characteristics of servant leadership. Specifically, servant leaders empower and develop their followers; demonstrate humility; are authentic; accept people for who they are; provide guidance and direction; and are stewards who work for the betterment of the whole society.

The concept of servant leadership has received some critical review on the grounds that it overlaps with other leadership styles such as, transformational leadership, authentic leadership and ethical leadership. However, servant leadership is theoretically distinct from these related constructs in several important ways. For instance, while servant leaders are mainly concerned with creating conditions that enhance the growth and well-being of their followers, transformational leaders are more directed toward organizational goals (Walumbwa et al., 2010; Van Dierendonck, 2011). In addition, servant leadership focuses on authenticity, humility and empathy, none of which are explicit components of transformational leadership (Van Dierendonck, 2011). Similarly, servant leadership has a moral component, which is comparable to that of ethical and authentic leadership (Brown, Trevino, & Harrison, 2005; Neubert, Kacmar, Carlson, Chonko & Roberts, 2008). However, unlike ethical and authentic leadership, servant leadership is uniquely concerned with the success of all organizational stakeholders (Walumbwa et al., 2010; Hunter et al., 2013).

Finally, several studies have empirically demonstrated that servant leadership explains additional variance in follower outcomes beyond that predicted by other leadership styles (Ehrhart, 2004; Liden et al., 2008). Taken together, all this evidence seems to suggest that "servant leadership is a unique leadership theory that can extend researchers' knowledge about leadership processes and outcomes" (Walumbwa et al., 2010, p. 518).

Servant leadership and organizational identification

The concept of organizational identification is based on the social identity theory. This theory has its conceptual origins in research by Henri Tajfel on social factors in perception (e.g., Tajfel, 1959) and on cognitive and social belief aspects of prejudice, discrimination and racism (e.g., Tajfel, 1969). However, the social identity theory was refined and fully developed in the mid and late 1970s by Tajfel and his colleague John Turner (e.g., Tajfel & Turner, 1979).

The main premise of the social identity theory is that group memberships are self-definitional (Van Knippenberg & Sleebos, 2006). Specifically, this theory suggests that individuals not only define themselves in terms of distinctive individual characteristics but also in terms of the unique features and qualities of the groups to which they belong (Tajfel & Turner, 1986). The former refers to their personal identity; whereas the later reflects their social identity.

Organizational identification can be considered as a special type of social identification that leads employees to describe themselves in terms of their organizational membership (Mael & Ashforth, 1992; Dutton, Dukerich, & Harquail, 1994). Specifically, it refers to the "perception of oneness with or belongingness to the organization" (Ashforth & Mael, 1989, p. 22) or "the degree to which a member defines him or herself by the same attributes that he or she believes define the organization" (Dutton et al., 1994, p. 239). Previous studies have demonstrated that organizational identification can deliver important outcomes such as, greater job satisfaction, lower turnover and absenteeism rates, improved health and well-being, and superior job performance (Van Dick, Wagner, Stellmacher, Christ, & Tissington, 2005).

Research evidence indicates that factors, which increase the perceived attractiveness of the organization (Van Knippenberg, Van Dick, & Tavares, 2007) and factors that boost employees' feelings of self-worth (Mael & Ashforth, 1992) have the potential to foster organizational identification.

Servant leaders empower their followers (e.g., by giving followers a say in decision making), focus on satisfying their needs, provide them opportunities for personal growth and development and acknowledge their contributions (Liden et al., 2008; Van Dierendonck, 2011; Hunter et al., 2013). Such positive behaviors on part of the leader might lead employees to believe that they are valued members of the organization, which, in turn, may enhance their feelings of self-worth and as a result increase organizational identification (Fuller et al., 2006). In addition, these behaviors can create a safe and resourceful work environment, which may make the organization a more attractive place to work for (Schaubroeck et al., 2011). In other words, servant leadership might enhance the perceived attractiveness of the organization and consequently amplify organizational identification (Barbuto & Wheeler, 2006). Previous research provides supportive empirical evidence that servant leadership can augment employees' identification with their organization (Zhang et al., 2012). Thus, it is hypothesized:

Hypothesis 1: Servant leadership is positively related to organizational identification.

Servant leadership and psychological safety

Psychological safety refers to the extent to which individuals believe that they would not be punished or rejected for taking well intentioned interpersonal risks such as, seeking feedback, admitting mistakes or speaking up about concerns (Edmondson, 1999; Edmondson, Bohmer, & Pisano, 2001).

In the present study, it is speculated that servant leadership will augment employees' sense of psychological safety. For instance, Edmondson (1999) argued that if the leader is helpful, coaching-oriented and shows non-defensive responses to questions and challenges, employees are likely to infer that their organization or team constitutes a psychologically safe environment. Previous research has shown that servant leaders tend to exhibit all these behaviors (e.g., Liden et al., 2008) and therefore, it is reasonable to assume that such leaders will play a key role in enhancing employees' feelings of psychological safety. Schaubroeck et al. (2011) in their study empirically demonstrated that servant leadership was positively associated with psychological safety. In view of this evidence, it is predicted:

Hypothesis 2: Servant leadership is positively related to psychological safety.

Organizational identification, voice, and negative feedback seeking behavior

Negative feedback seeking behavior refers to employees' desire to obtain information about inadequacies in their work behavior and work performance (Ashford & Tsui, 1991; Chen, Lam, & Zhong, 2007). The importance of negative feedback seeking behavior stems from the fact that it can enable employees to correct weaknesses in performance and consequently help them to achieve their goals (Ashford, Blatt, & VandeWalle, 2003). Previous research has shown that this type of behavior can lead to improved individual (Chen et al., 2007) and team (Edmondson, 2004) performance.

Employee voice is defined as "promotive behavior that emphasizes expression of constructive challenge intended to improve rather than merely criticize" (Van Dyne & LePine, 1998, p.

109). Voice behaviors are categorized as extra-role behaviors, which are not part of employees' formal job description but are necessary for enhancing the efficiency and effectiveness of the organization (Van Dyne, Ang, & Botero, 2003). Although the concept of voice is grounded in the organizational citizenship literature (Botero & Van Dyne, 2009), it is distinct from cooperative forms of citizenship behavior (LePine & Van Dyne, 1998). Specifically, cooperative behavior (e.g., helping) is geared towards preserving or improving relationships, while voice is challenging and therefore, may disrupt interpersonal relationships (Liang, Farh, & Farh, 2012). Specific examples of voice behavior include: making suggestions for improvement; emphasizing the need for change and persuading others to accept ideas and opinions. Previous research indicates that constructive voice behavior can prove beneficial for organizations because it can identify problems and solutions to problems and highlight other ideas that may improve organizational performance (Van Dyne & LePine, 1998).

However, in spite of the potential benefits, the act of seeking negative feedback and the tendency to engage in voice behavior can entail high costs for the concerned individual (VandeWalle, 2003; Liang et al., 2012). For instance, by seeking critical feedback, employees face the risk of being regarded as incompetent, which, in turn, can have a devastating effect on their self-esteem (Ashford et al., 2003). Likewise, when individuals suggest an unorthodox idea or challenge the status quo, they may be perceived as disruptive, which, subsequently can lead to demotion or termination (Detert & Burris, 2007). Thus, individuals will only seek negative feedback or speak up about concerns if they believe that benefits of engaging in these interpersonally risky behaviors outweigh the costs.

In this study, it is proposed that a strong identification with the organization will inspire employees to engage in voice and negative feedback seeking behavior. Research has shown that highly identified employees strive hard to make the organization successful (Mael & Ashforth, 1992; Van Knippenberg, 2000). Thus, it is speculated that employees who strongly identify with their organization, will be more inclined to seek critical feedback because this would allow them to improve their competence and as a result make them better equipped to help the organization achieve its goals (Chughtai & Buckley, 2010). Similarly, high identifiers are also more likely to engage in voice behaviors such as, suggesting improvements in work procedures and proposing creative solutions to problems because these behaviors can positively contribute towards the success of the organization (Fuller et al., 2006). In other words, the motivation to further the interest of the organization might lead these individuals to focus more on the benefits rather than the costs associated with such risky behaviors.

The available empirical evidence indicates that organizational identification has the capacity to fuel voice (Fuller et al., 2006; Tangirala & Ramanujam, 2008) and negative feedback seeking behavior (Chughtai & Buckley, 2010). Therefore, the following hypotheses are stated:

Hypothesis 3: Organizational identification is positively related to negative feedback seeking behavior.

Hypothesis 4: Organizational identification is positively related to voice behavior.

Psychological safety, voice and negative feedback seeking behavior

Psychological safety is also expected to promote voice and negative feedback seeking behavior. Research has shown that in a psychologically safe environment employees are more likely to engage in interpersonally risky behaviors such as, seeking feedback, reporting errors and expressing opinions about work related issues because they feel confident that they will not be ridiculed or penalized for doing so (Edmondson, 1999, 2004). Put differently, a climate of psychological safety can encourage employees to speak up about concerns or seek negative feedback on performance by reducing the costs associated with these behaviors. Several studies have revealed that psychological safety is positively linked to both voice (Walumbwa & Schaubroeck, 2009; Liang et al., 2012) and negative feedback seeking behavior (Edmondson, 1999, 2004). Hence, it is speculated:

Hypothesis 5: Psychological safety is positively related to negative feedback seeking behavior.

Hypothesis 6: Psychological safety is positively related to voice behavior.

The mediating effects of organizational identification and psychological safety

The core elements of servant leadership such as developing people, creating an environment of trust, seeking input from followers and tolerating mistakes can have a profound impact on employees' desire to seek critical feedback and on their willingness to engage in voice behavior (Edmondson, 2004; Detert & Burris, 2007).

However, in this research it is proposed that the direct effect of servant leadership on voice and negative feedback seeking behavior will be mediated by organizational identification and psychological safety. That is, servant leadership will enhance organizational identification (*Hypothesis 1*) and promote feelings of psychological safety (*Hypothesis 2*), which in turn is likely to stimulate negative feedback seeking behavior (*Hypotheses 3 & 5*) and facilitate voice behavior (*Hypotheses 4 and 6*). Hence, the following hypothesis is stated:

Hypothesis 7: Organizational identification and psychological safety will mediate the effects of servant leadership on voice and negative feedback seeking behavior.

Method

Sample and procedure

The sample for this study comprised of full-time employees who were drawn from a large food company located in Pakistan. These employees were working in different departments such as, marketing, finance, production, human resources and quality control. The total number of employees in this company was 205.

Data for this study were collected by administering a paper and pencil questionnaire to all the 205 employees. Before commencing the data collection procedure, the author held a meeting with the human resource manager of the company in order to explain the purpose of the research and seek approval for data collection. After receiving the approval, the author handed over the required number of questionnaires along with a cover letter assuring confidentiality to the human resource manager for distribution to each participant. Participation in this study was completely voluntary. The respondents completed the questionnaire anonymously and returned it to the human resource department. Subsequently, the author collected the completed questionnaires from this department at a mutually agreed time. It took about two months to collect this data.

Of the 205 questionnaires that were distributed, 174 useable questionnaires were received thereby yielding a response rate of 84.9%. Following the recommendations of Newman (2009), the missing data (only 4.01% of the data were missing) were imputed by using the expectation maximization (EM) algorithm. About 88% of the participants were male. The average age of the responding individuals was 30.3 years ($SD = 6.14$), while the average organizational tenure was 3.2 years ($SD = 2.37$). As far as the education level was concerned, approximately 45% of the participants held a Master's degree, while the remaining 55% held a Bachelors level qualification.

Measures

Standardized questionnaires were used to measure all the study variables. All variables were measured on a 5-point Likert-type scale ranging from 1 (*strongly disagree*) to 5 (*strongly agree*).

Servant leadership

Servant leadership was measured by the seven item scale (SL-7) developed by Liden et al. (2015). A sample item includes: "My boss makes my career development a priority." The coefficient alpha for this scale was .85.

Organizational identification

Mael and Ashforth's (1992) six-item scale was used to assess organizational identification. A sample item includes: "When someone criticizes my organization, it feels like a personal insult." The alpha reliability for this scale was .89.

Psychological safety

The three item scale developed by Detert and Burris (2007) was utilized to measure psychological safety. A sample item includes: "In this organization, it is safe for me to make suggestions." The coefficient alpha for this scale was .84.

Voice Behavior

Voice behavior was assessed with the five item promotive voice behavior scale developed by Liang et al. (2012). A sample item includes: "I proactively develop and make suggestions for issues that may influence my organization." The alpha reliability for this scale was .87.

Negative feedback seeking behavior

Negative feedback seeking behavior was measured by two items developed by Ashford and Tsui (1991). A sample item includes: "I ask my boss to be critical when he/she gives me his/her feedback". To assess the reliability of a two item scale, it is recommended that researchers should use the Spearman-Brown reliability coefficient (Eisinga, Grotenhuis, & Pelzer, 2013). Based on this suggestion, the reliability of the two item negative feedback seeking behavior scale was assessed by using this statistic. The value of the Spearman-Brown reliability coefficient for this two item measure was .72, which is considered adequate (Kline, 2005).

Control variables

To rule out the possibility that observed relationships might be influenced by respondents' demographic characteristics, it was decided to control for gender, age and tenure. Age and tenure were self-reported in years, while gender (1 = male; 0 = female) was measured through a dummy variable.

Data analysis

Collectively Hypotheses 1–7 suggest a mediational model, which proposes that the effect of servant leadership on voice and negative feedback seeking behavior will be indirectly transmitted through organizational identification and psychological safety. In this study the mediation hypotheses (Hypotheses 1–7) were tested by using the bootstrapping procedure advocated by Preacher and Hayes (2008). Research has shown that this is one of the most valid and powerful method for testing intervening variable effects (Hayes, 2009; Zhao, Lynch, & Chen, 2010).

Specifically, in order to establish mediation, 95% bias-corrected bootstrap confidence intervals (CI) for the indirect effects were constructed from 1,000 bootstrap samples. A significant mediated effect is demonstrated if the upper and lower bounds of the 95% bias-corrected CI do not include a "zero" (Hayes, 2009). These analyses were conducted by using the SPSS macro developed by Preacher and Hayes (2008). This macro not only generates the 95% bias corrected CIs but also provides estimates of the unstandardized regression coefficients for paths linking the study variables. In addition, the Preacher-Hayes macro allows researchers to include the control variables as covariates. Thus, the three control variables included in this study, that is, gender, age and tenure were entered as covariates in the analysis.

Results

Descriptive Statistics

The means, standard deviations, and correlations among the study variables are presented in Table 1. Results reported in Table 1 showed that servant leadership was positively associated with both organizational identification ($r = .56, p < .01$) and psychological safety ($r = .62, p < .01$). Furthermore, it was found that organizational identification was positively linked to employee voice ($r = .59, p < .01$) and negative feedback seeking behavior ($r = .53, p < .01$). Similarly, results revealed that as expected, psychological safety was also positively and significantly correlated with both voice ($r = .49, p < .01$) and negative feedback seeking behavior ($r = .58, p < .01$).

Table 1. Descriptive Statistics, Correlations, and Scale Reliabilities.

Variable	Mean	*SD*	1	2	3	4	5	6	7	8
1. Gender	.89	.32	**NA**							
2. Age	30.3	6.14	.30**	**NA**						
3. Tenure	3.2	2.37	.10	.440**	**NA**					
4. Servant leadership	3.55	.73	.15	.130	−.10	**.85**				
5. Organizational identification	3.66	.87	.17*	.100	−.09	.56**	**.89**			
6. Psychological safety	3.47	.94	.12	.009	−.03	.62**	.42**	**.84**		
7. Voice behavior	3.46	.87	.18*	.060	−.16*	.61**	.59**	.49**	**.87**	
8. NFSB	3.46	.95	.19*	.120	.04	.59**	.53**	.58**	.45**	[a]**72**

Note. NFSB = Negative feedback seeking behavior. Cronbach alpha reliabilities for observed variables are in bold in the diagonal. [a]This value represents the Spearman-Brown reliability coefficient. *$p < .05$ **$p < .01$.

Confirmatory factor analysis

Prior to testing the research hypotheses, a confirmatory factor analysis (CFA) was conducted through LISREL 8.80 (Joreskog & Sorbom, 2006), to establish discriminant validity among the five multi-item measures. In order to maintain favorable indicator to sample size ratios, three indicators each were created for servant leadership, organizational identification, and voice behavior. Specifically, the items with the highest and lowest factor loadings were combined by averaging them until there were three indicators for each construct (e.g., Hui, Law, & Chen, 1999). Psychological safety (3 items) and negative feedback seeking behavior (2 items) on the contrary were modelled by their respective items.

Results showed that the hypothesised 5-factor measurement model provided a good fit to the data: χ^2 (67) = 69.59, $p > .05$; CFI = 1.0; RMSEA = .02; SRMR = .04. All the indicators loaded significantly on their respective latent factors, with factor loadings ranging from .72 to .93. Next, the fit of this five factor model was compared with fit of several alternative nested models. Results reported in Table 2 revealed that the hypothesised model exhibited a better fit than all the alternative models. These results provided support for the distinctiveness of the five measures used in this research.

Hypothesis testing

The results of the regression analysis provided by the Preacher-Hayes macro are presented in Table 3. Hypothesis 1 stated that servant leadership is positively associated with organizational identification. Results revealed that the unstandardized regression coefficient between servant leadership and organizational identification was significant thereby, corroborating this hypothesis ($B = .64, p < .01$). In support of Hypothesis 2, it was found that servant leadership was positively linked to psychological safety ($B = .81, p < .01$). Similarly, Hypotheses 3 and 4, which predicted that organizational identification was positively related to negative feedback seeking behavior ($B = .28, p < .01$) and voice behavior ($B = .33, p < .01$), respectively, were also substantiated. Results also provided support for Hypotheses 5 and 6, which proposed that psychological safety was positively associated with negative feedback seeking behavior ($B = .32, p < .01$) and voice behavior ($B = .14, p < .05$) respectively. Finally, it was found that none of the control variables were significantly related to the two outcome variables.

Hypothesis 7 predicted that organizational identification and psychological safety will mediate the effects of servant leadership on voice and negative feedback seeking behavior.

Table 2. Comparison of Measurement Models.

Model	Factors	χ^2	df	$\Delta\chi^2$	Δ df	CFI	RMSEA	SRMR
Hypothesized Model	**Five Factors**	69.59 ($p > .05$)	67	—	—	1.0	.02	.04
Model 1	**Four Factors** (OID & PS merged into one factor)	262.60**	71	193.01**	4	.94	.13	.09
Model 2	**Four Factors** (VB & NFSB merged into one factor)	131.63**	71	62.04**	4	.98	.07	.07
Model 3	**Four Factors** (SL & PS merged into one factor)	128.77**	71	59.18**	4	.98	.07	.05
Model 4	**Four Factors** (SL & OID merged into one factor)	188.01**	71	118.42**	4	.96	.10	.08
Model 5	**One Factor** (All items forced to load on a single factor)	310.94**	77	241.35**	10	.93	.13	.09

Note. ** p < .01; SL = Servant leadership; OID = Organizational identification; PS = Psychological safety; VB = Voice behavior; NFSB = Negative feedback seeking behavior.

Table 3. Regression Results for Mediation (Based on Output Provided by the Preacher-Hayes Macro).

	Organizational identification	Psychological safety	Voice behavior	NFSB
Servant leadership	[a]0.64**	0.81**	0.38**	0.33**
Organizational identification			0.33**	0.28**
Psychological safety			0.14*	0.32**
Gender			0.18	0.18
Age			0.001	0.00
Tenure			−0.04	0.04
Equation R^2			**0.49**	**0.47**

Note. NFSB = Negative feedback seeking behavior. [a]These numbers represent the unstandardized regression coefficients.
$^*p < .05$. $^{**}p < .01$.

The output generated by the Preacher-Hayes macro showed that the indirect effect of servant leadership on voice behavior (via organizational identification and psychological safety) was 0.32 and the 95% bias corrected CI for this indirect effect was [.20, .50]. Furthermore, it was found that the indirect effect of servant leadership on negative feedback seeking behavior (via organizational identification and psychological safety) was 0.44 and the 95% bias corrected CI for this indirect effect was [.28, .64]. Since, these CIs did not include 'zero';, it can be concluded that the indirect effect of servant leadership on voice and negative feedback seeking behavior was significant (Hayes, 2009; Zhao et al., 2010).

However, the results reported in Table 3 revealed that the direct effect of servant leadership on voice ($B = 0.38$, $p < .01$) and negative feedback seeking behavior ($B = 0.33$, $p < .01$), after controlling for the effects of the two mediators, was significant. These findings suggest that organizational identification and psychological safety partially mediated the effects of servant leadership on the two employee outcomes (Zhao et al., 2010). Thus, Hypothesis 7 was partly supported.

Discussion

The central aim of study was to explore the mediating role of organizational identification and psychological safety in the relationship between servant leadership and the two employee outcomes: employee voice and negative feedback seeking behavior. Results showed that organizational identification and psychological safety partially mediated the effects of servant leadership on voice and negative feedback seeking behavior. The implications of these findings and the limitations of this research are discussed in the following sections.

Theoretical implications

The present study extends the literature on servant leadership in three ways. First, as mentioned earlier, the research on servant leadership is still in its early stages and therefore, relatively few studies have examined its effects on follower outcomes (e.g., Avolio et al., 2009). Thus, by linking servant leadership to voice and negative feedback seeking behavior for the first time, this research not only offers a new perspective on this concept but also provides evidence about how and why this leadership style can prove beneficial for organizations.

Second, although a small number of studies have explored the effects of servant leadership on follower outcomes, not much is known about the underlying processes through which it influences these outcomes. Thus, by examining the mediating role of organizational identification and psychological safety, this study provides useful insights into what servant leaders can actually do to improve the attitudes and behaviors of their followers.

However, the findings of this study revealed that organizational identification and psychological safety partially mediated the effects of servant leadership on voice and negative feedback seeking behavior. These results suggest that there may be other mediation mechanisms involved in addition to organizational identification and psychological safety. Thus, future research may consider other variables that may act as mediators in the relationship between servant leadership and the two employee outcomes included in this study. For example, it is possible that leader–member exchange and employee engagement may serve as additional potential intervening variables in explaining the effect of servant leadership on voice and negative feedback seeking behavior.

Finally, to the best of my knowledge, this is the first study that has examined the consequences of servant leadership in a Pakistani context. Pakistan is a country, which is high on power distance (Hofstede, 2007) and in recent years has been ravaged by terrorism. The results of this research suggest that the exhibition of servant leadership behaviors can produce favourable outcomes even in this unique context. These findings are important because they tend to dispel the widely held notion that servant leadership is likely to prove more effective in societies which are low on power distance (Van Dierendonck, 2011). In fact, the results of this study seem to indicate that servant leadership can yield rich benefits across a variety of cultures.

Practical implications

The findings of this research can have important implications for organizations. Specifically, results indicate that servant leadership behaviors can inspire employees to proactively seek feedback, express constructive suggestions for change and raise concerns about work-related issues. All these behaviors subsequently can have a positive effect on team and organizational performance (Edmondson, 1999; LePine & Van Dyne, 2001). So how can organizations develop servant leaders? The firms can use two strategies to achieve this objective. Previous research has shown that people, who are high on agreeableness, possess a strong desire to serve others and have high ethical and moral standards are more likely to emerge as servant leaders (Van Dierendonck, 2011; Hunter et al., 2013). Thus, by using appropriate personality and integrity tests, organizations should attempt to identify and hire leaders who possess these characteristics.

Furthermore, by using suitable training programs, organizations should encourage their managers to exhibit servant leadership behaviors. Specifically, these programs can focus on highlighting the importance of empowering employees, fulfilling their growth needs, and treating them with respect and dignity. Managers are more likely to be perceived as servant leaders if they consistently display such behaviors in the workplace.

Limitations and future research directions

In interpreting the results of this study, it is important to keep several issues in mind. First, using a sample of Pakistani employees drawn from a single organization restricts the generalizability of the results to other work contexts. Future studies should seek to evaluate the research model developed in this paper in other work contexts to enhance the external validity of this study.

Second, the cross-sectional design of this study does not allow us to make inferences about causality. In order to have a better idea about causality, future studies can replicate this research with a longitudinal research design.

Third, in this research all variables were measured through self-report surveys and as a result there is a possibility that the findings may have been influenced by common method variance (Podsakoff, MacKenzie, Lee, & Podsakoff, 2003). However, research evidence indicates that the common method variance problem is over stated and does not automatically magnify correlations between self-reported variables (Spector, 2006).

To empirically assess the effects of common method variance, Harman's single factor test was performed (Podsakoff et al., 2003). Specifically, the fit of the hypothesised five factor model was compared to the fit of a one factor model in which all indicators were forced to load on to a single factor (see Table 2). Results revealed that compared to the five factor model, the one factor model provided a poor fit to the data: $\Delta\chi 2$ (10) = 241.35, $p < .01$; CFI = .93; RMSEA = .13; SRMR = .09. These findings indicate that common method variance was not a major problem in this study (Jones, 2009).

To further evaluate the effects of common method variance, the fit of the hypothesized 5-factor model was compared to the fit of an alternative model, which controlled for the effects of an unmeasured latent methods factor (Podsakoff et al., 2003). Results showed that the model with the method factor provided a significantly better fit than the hypothesised model ($\Delta\chi 2$ (14) = 25.49, $p < .05$). However, all the observed indicators loaded significantly and in the expected direction on their corresponding latent factor. In addition, the partitioning of the variance indicated that the method factor accounted for only 3.31% of the total variance, which was considerably lower than the threshold value of 25% recommended by Williams, Cote, and Buckley (1989). Taken together, these results also suggest that common method variance did not pose a serious threat in this study. Nevertheless, to minimize the adverse effects associated with this problem, it is proposed that future research should attempt to acquire data from different sources.

Finally, Van Dierendonck (2011) in his recent review suggests that servant leadership is likely to have a stronger effect on follower outcomes in cultures, which are characterized by a strong humane orientation and are low on power distance. Therefore, an interesting avenue for future research is to investigate if these two cultural dimensions moderate the relationship between servant leadership and employee voice and the relationship between servant leadership and negative feedback seeking behavior. That is, future studies can explore if the relationship between servant leadership and these two employee outcomes is stronger if the society has a strong humane orientation and is low on power distance.

Conclusion

This study highlights the role of servant leadership in promoting employee voice and negative feedback seeking behavior. Specifically, results showed that servant leadership can deliver these positive outcomes by increasing employees' sense of psychological safety and by strengthening their identification with the organization. It is, therefore, hoped that the findings of this study will inspire organizations to take steps that enable them to develop servant leaders.

References

Ashford, S. J., Blatt, R., & Vande Walle, D. (2003). Reflections on the looking glass: A review of research on feedback-seeking behaviour in organizations. *Journal of Management, 29*, 773–799.

Ashford, S. J., & Tsui, A. S. (1991). Self-regulation for managerial effectiveness: The role of active feedback seeking. *Academy of Management Journal, 34*, 251–280.

Ashforth, B. E., & Mael, F. (1989). Social identity theory and the organization. *Academy of Management Review, 14*, 20–39.

Avolio, B. J., Walumbwa, F. O., & Weber, T. J. (2009). Leadership: Current theories, research, and future directions. *Annual Review of Psychology, 60*, 421–449.

Barbuto, J. E., Jr., & Wheeler, D. W. (2006). Scale development and construct clarification of servant leadership. *Group and Organizational Management, 31*, 300–326.

Botero, I. C., & Van Dyne, L. (2009). Employee voice behaviour: Interactive effects of LMX and power distance in the United States and Columbia. *Management Communication Quarterly, 23*, 84–104.

Brown, M. E., Trevino, L. K., & Harrison, D. A. (2005). Ethical leadership: A social learning perspective for construct development and testing. *Organizational Behaviour and Human Decision Processes, 97*, 117–134.

Chen, Z., Lam, W., & Zhong, J. A. (2007). Leader-member exchange and member performance: A new look at individual-level negative feedback seeking behaviour and team-level empowerment climate. *Journal of Applied Psychology, 92*, 202–212.

Chughtai, A. A., & Buckley, F. (2010). Assessing the effects of organizational identification on in-role job performance and learning behaviour – The mediating role of learning goal orientation. *Personnel Review, 39*, 242–258.

Detert, J. R., & Burris, E. R. (2007). Leadership behaviour and employee voice: Is the door really open? *Academy of Management Journal, 50*, 869–884

Dutton, J. E., Dukerich, J. M., & Harquail, C. V. (1994). Organizational images and member identification. *Administrative Science Quarterly, 39*, 239–263.

Edmondson, A. (1999). Psychological safety and learning behaviours in work teams. *Administrative Science Quarterly, 44*, 350–383.

Edmondson, A. (2004). Psychological safety, trust and learning in organizations: A group level lens. In R. M Kramer, & K. S. Cook (Eds.), *Trust and distrust in organizations: Dilemmas and approaches* 239–272. New York, NY: Russell Sage Foundation.

Edmondson, A. C., Bohmer, R. M., & Pisano, G. P. (2001). Disrupted routines: Team learning and new technology implementation in hospitals. *Administrative Science Quarterly, 46*, 685–716.

Ehrhart, M. G. (2004). Leadership and procedural justice climate as antecedents of unit-level organizational citizenship behaviour. *Personnel Psychology, 57*, 61–94.

Eisinga, R., Grotenhuis, M. T., & Pelzer, B. (2013). The reliability of a two-item scale: Pearson, Cronbach, or Spearman-Brown? *International Journal of Public Health, 58*, 637–642.

Fuller, B. J., Hester, K., Barnett, T., Frey, L., Relyea, C., & Beu, D. (2006). Perceived external prestige and internal respect: New insights into the organizational identification process. *Human Relations, 59*, 815–846.

Greenleaf, R. K. (1970). *The servant as a leader* Indianapolis, IN: Greenleaf Centre.

Greer, C. R. (2001). *Strategic human resource management: A general managerial approach* New Delhi, India: Pearson Education.

Hayes, A. F. (2009). Beyond Baron and Kenny: Statistical mediation analysis in the new millennium. *Communication Monographs, 76*, 408–420.

Hofstede, G. (2007). Asian management in the 21st century. *Asia Pacific Journal of Management, 24*, 411–420.
Hui, C., Law, K. S., & Chen, Z. X. (1999). A structural equation model of the effects of negative affectivity, leader-member exchange, and perceived job mobility on in-role and extra-role performance: A Chinese Case. *Organizational Behaviour and Human Decision Processes, 77*, 3–21.
Hunter, E. M., Neubert, M. J., Perry, S. J., Witt, L. A., Penney, L. M., & Weinberger, E. (2013). Servant leaders inspire servant followers: Antecedents and outcomes for employees and the organization. *Leadership Quarterly, 24*, 316–331.
Jones, D. A. (2009). Getting even with one's supervisor and one's organization: Relationships among types of injustice, desires for revenge and counterproductive work behaviours. *Journal of Organizational Behaviour, 30*, 525–542.
Joreskog, K. G., & Sorbom, D. (2006). *Lisrel for windows*. Chicago, IL: Scientific Software.
Kline, R. B. (2005). *Principles and practice of structural equation modelling* New York, NY: Guilford Press.
LePine, J. A., & Van Dyne, L. (1998). Predicting voice behaviour in work groups. *Journal of Applied Psychology, 83*, 853–868.
LePine, J. A., & Van Dyne, L. (2001). Voice and cooperative behaviour as contrasting forms of contextual performance: Evidence of differential relationships with Big Five personality characteristics and cognitive ability. *Journal of Applied Psychology, 86*, 326–336.
Liang, J., Farh, C. I. C., & Farh, J. L. (2012). Psychological antecedents of promotive and prohibitive voice: A two wave examination. *Academy of Management Journal, 55*, 71–92.
Liden, R. C., Wayne, S. J., Meuser, J. D., Hu, J., Wu, J., & Liao, C. (2015). Servant leadership: Validation of a short form of SL-28. *Leadership Quarterly, 26*, 254–269.
Liden, R. C., Wayne, S. J., Zhao, H., & Henderson, D. (2008). Servant leadership: Development of a multidimensional measure and multi-level assessment. *Leadership Quarterly, 19*, 161–177.
Mael, F., & Ashforth, B. E. (1992). Alumni and their alma mater: A partial test of the reformulated model of organizational identification. *Journal of Organizational Behaviour, 13*, 103–123.
Neubert, M. J., Kacmar, K. M., Carlson, D. S., Chonko, L. B., & Roberts, J. A. (2008). Regulatory focus as a mediator of the influence of initiating structure and servant leadership on employee behaviour. *Journal of Applied Psychology, 93*, 1220–1233.
Newman, D. A. (2009). Missing data techniques and low response rates: The role of systematic nonresponse parameters. In C. E. Lance & R. J. Vandenberg (Eds.), *Statistical and methodological myths and urban legends* (pp. 7–36). New York, NY: Taylor and Francis.
Pfeffer, J., & Veiga, J. F. (1999). Putting people first for organizational success. *Academy of Management Perspectives, 13*, 37–48.
Podsakoff, P. M., Mackenzie, S. B., Lee, J. L., & Podsakoff, N. P. (2003). Common method biases in behavioural research: A critical review of the literature and recommended remedies. *Journal of Applied Psychology, 88*, 879–903.
Preacher, K. P., and Hayes, A. F. (2008). Asymptotic and resampling strategies for assessing and comparing indirect effects in multiple mediator models. *Behavior Research Methods, 40*, 879–891.
Schaubroeck, J., Lam, S. S. K., & Peng, A. C. (2011). Cognition-based and affect-based trust as mediators of leader behaviour influences on team performance. *Journal of Applied Psychology, 96*, 863–871.
Spector, P. E. (2006). Method variance in organizational research: Truth or urban legend. *Organizational Research Methods, 9*, 221–232.
Tajfel, H. (1959). Quantitative judgement in social perception. *British Journal of Psychology, 50*, 16–29.
Tajfel, H. (1969). Cognitive aspects of prejudice. *Journal of Social Issues, 25*, 79–97
Tajfel, H., & Turner, J. C. (1979). An integrative theory of intergroup conflict. In W. G. Austin & S. Worchel (Eds.), *The social psychology of intergroup relations* (pp. 33–47). Monterey, CA: Brooks/Cole.
Tajfel, H., & Turner, J. C. (1986). The social identity theory of intergroup behaviour. In S. Worchel, & W. G. Austin (Eds.), *Psychology of Intergroup Relations* (pp. 7–24). Chicago, IL: Nelson Hall.
Tangirala, S., & Ramanujam, R. (2008). Exploring nonlinearity in employee voice: The effects of personal control and organizational identification. *Academy of Management Journal, 51*, 1189–1203.

VandeWalle, D. (2003). A goal orientation model of feedback seeking behaviour. *Human Resource Management Review, 13*, 581–604.

Van Dick, R., Wagner, U., Stellmacher, J., Christ, O., & Tissington, P. A. (2005). To be (long) or not to be (long): Social identification in organizational contexts. *Genetic, Social, and General Psychology Monographs, 131*, 189–218.

Van Dierendonck, D. (2011). Servant leadership: A review and synthesis. Journal of Management, *37*, 1228–1261.

Van Dierendonck, D., Stam, D., Boersma, P., de Windt, N., & Alkema, J. (2014). Same difference? Exploring the differential mechanisms linking servant leadership and transformational leadership to follower outcomes. *Leadership Quarterly, 25*, 544–562.

Van Dyne, L., Ang, S., & Botero, I. C. (2003). Conceptualizing employee silence and employee voice as multidimensional constructs. *Journal of Management Studies, 40*, 1359–1392.

Van Dyne, L., & LePine, J. A. (1998). Helping and voice extra-role behaviours: Evidence of construct and predictive validity. *Academy of Management Journal, 41*, 108–119.

Van Knippenberg, D. (2000). Work motivation and performance: A social identity perspective. *Applied Psychology: An International Review, 49*, 357–371.

Van Knippenberg, D., & Sleebos, E. (2006). Organizational identification versus organizational commitment: Self-definition, social exchange and job attitudes. *Journal of Organizational Behaviour, 27*, 571–584.

Van Knippenberg, D., Van Dick, R., & Tavares, S. (2007). Social identity and social exchange: Identification, support and withdrawal from the job. *Journal of Applied Social Psychology, 37*, 457–477.

Walumbwa, F. O., Hartnell, C. A., & Oke, A. (2010). Servant leadership, procedural justice climate, service climate, employee attitudes, and organizational citizenship behaviour: A cross-level investigation. *Journal of Applied Psychology, 95*, 517–529.

Walumbwa, F. O., & Schaubroeck, J. (2009). Leader personality traits and employee voice behaviour: Mediating roles of ethical leadership and work group psychological safety. *Journal of Applied Psychology, 94*, 1275–1286.

Williams, L. J., Cote, J. A., & Buckley, M. R. (1989). Lack of method variance in self-reported affect and perceptions at work: Reality or artefact? *Journal of Applied Psychology, 74*, 462–468.

Zhang, H., Kwan, H. K., Everett, A. M., & Jian, Z. (2012). Servant leadership, organizational identification, and work-to-family enrichment: The moderating role of work climate for sharing family concerns. *Human Resource Management, 51*, 747–767.

Zhao, X., Lynch, J. G., & Chen, Q. (2010). Reconsidering Baron and Kenny: Myths and truths about mediation analysis. *Journal of Consumer Research, 37*, 197–206.

When Supervisors Perceive Non-Work Support: Test of a Trickle-Down Model

TSUNG-YU WU
SHAO-JEN LEE

CHANGYA HU

CHUN-CHI YANG

ABSTRACT. Using the trickle-down model as the theoretical foundation, we explored whether subordinates' perceived supervisory non-work support (subordinates' PSNS) mediates the relationship between supervisors' perception of higher-level managers' non-work support (supervisors' PSNS) and subordinates' organizational citizenship behaviors. Using dyadic data collected from 132 employees and their immediate supervisors, we found support for the aforementioned mediation process. Furthermore, supervisors' perceived in-group/out-group membership of subordinates moderated the aforementioned supervisors' PSNS-subordinates' PSNS relationship, such that this relationship is stronger for out-group subordinates. Theoretical and practical implications and future research directions are discussed.

POSITIVE ORGANIZATIONAL BEHAVIOR HAS RECEIVED increasing attention from researchers with the burgeoning of positive psychology. Many positive constructs, such as positive personalities (e.g., positive affectivity), attitudes (e.g., job satisfaction), and behaviors (e.g., supervisory support) have regained popularity. Because supervisors have more power than subordinates in an organization and they can provide subordinates with valuable resources that coworkers cannot provide (Ng & Sorensen, 2008), supervisory support has been found to influence employees' psychological well-being, job attitude, and job performance more than other sources of social support (Chen & Chiu, 2008; Ng & Sorensen, 2008; Sullivan, 1989; Yoon & Thye, 2000). Accordingly, our study tries to explore how higher-level supervisors' support transmits to employees and elicits their positive behavior at work.

The existing research on supervisory support has focused mostly on employees' perceived supervisory work support (PSWS) (e.g., Greenhaus, Parasuraman, & Wormley, 1990; Yoon & Thye, 2000) rather than on perceived supervisory non-work support (PSNS). In fact, work support and non-work support constitute two important types of social support (Halbesleben, 2006). In addition to work support, supervisors may also provide non-work support to their subordinates (Farh & Cheng, 2000). According to Pellegrini and Scandura (2008), a leader may play a parent-like role and provide protection and care for his or her subordinate not only in work area but also outside work area. Examples of supervisory non-work support include helping subordinates solve personal problems, caring about subordinates' daily life, and taking care of subordinates as if they were family members (Farh & Cheng, 2000; Pellegrini & Scandura, 2008). Furthermore, empirical studies found that when supervisors show benevolent leadership behaviors in daily or non-work life, subordinates will show a higher level of identification, compliance, and gratitude (Cheng, Chou, Wu, Huang, & Farh, 2004; Cheng, Huang, Chou, Farh, & Peng, 2003), which in turn increases subordinates' organizational citizenship behaviors (OCB) (Hsu, Hu, Ling, Cheng, & Chou, 2004). However, this line of literature generally focuses on the relationship between subordinates' PSNS and their job attitude and performance (Hsu et al., 2004) rather than on factors that may lead supervisors to provide non-work support to subordinates, which limits the practical implication. To address this gap, we identify one potential antecedent of supervisors' provision of non-work support, that is, supervisors' PSNS from their direct supervisor, and examine the potential subordinates' outcomes of PSNS. Specifically, we would like to know whether supervisors who perceive more non-work support from their direct supervisors treat subordinates more supportively in the non-work area. Given that previous researchers have proposed *trickle-down model* to describe the process whereby higher-level manager's behaviors and attitudes transmit down to supervisors, which in turn elicits subordinate's relevant reactions (Shanock & Eisenberger, 2006; Tangirala, Green, & Ramanujam, 2007), the first purpose of our study is to apply the trickle-down model to the context of PSNS. In summary, we intended to explore whether supervisors who perceive non-work support from higher-level supervisors would also provide more non-work support to their subordinates, which would further facilitate subordinates' OCB.

A second purpose of this study is to investigate whether supervisors' social categorization of subordinates moderates the relationship between supervisors' PSNS and subordinates' PSNS in the trickle-down flow. According to leader–member exchange theory (LMX) (Gerstner & Day, 1997; Graen & Scandura, 1987; Graen & Uhl-Bien, 1995; Schriesheim, Castro, & Cogliser, 1999), supervisors categorize their employees into either in-group members or out-group

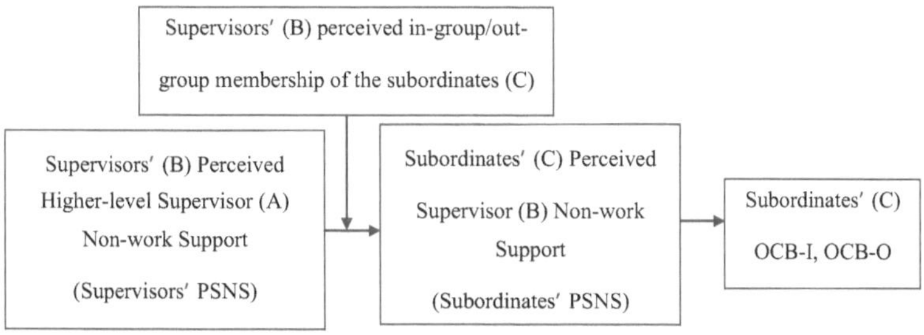

FIGURE 1. Conceptual framework of the current study. Our study involves three different hierarchical roles, the supervisor's supervisor (the higher-level supervisor) (A), the supervisor (the lower-level supervisor) (B), and the subordinates (C).

members. Compared with out-group members, supervisors tend to give in-group members more consideration, caring, and resources, including PSNS. Many previous studies have examined the influence of LMX on subordinates' work attitudes, such as job satisfaction and organizational commitment (Gerstner & Day, 1997), and job performance, such as task performance and OCB (Wang, Law, Hackett, Wang, & Chen, 2005). Relatively little research attention has been given to the role of social categorization, the determinant of LMX, in supervisors' supportive behaviors in non-work area. Accordingly, we investigated whether supervisors' perceived in-group/out-group membership of a subordinate moderates the relationship between the supervisors' PSNS and the subordinates' PSNS. Figure 1 delineates the conceptual framework of our study.

Our study contributes to the existing literature in three ways. First, most available studies on supervisory support focused on PSWS. However, supervisory support of subordinates can go beyond the working context and extend to non-work and life area (Farh & Cheng, 2000). By focusing on PSNS, we fill in the literature gap on supervisory support. Second, many studies have applied the trickle down model to examine the process by which higher-level management influences subordinate behaviors through subordinates' direct supervisors (Aryee, Chen, Sun, & Debrah, 2007; Mayer, Kuenzi, Greenbaum, Bardes, & Salvador, 2009; Shanock & Eisenberger, 2006). We extend this line of research by applying the trickle down model to PSNS. Last, our study incorporates leader–member exchange theory into the trickle-down model in order to examine whether supervisors' social categorization of subordinates moderates the relation between supervisors' PSNS and subordinates' PSNS. This attempt to integrate different theories (Wagner & Berger, 1985) can provide some theoretical contribution to literature on the trickle-down model and leader–member-exchange theory.

In summary, our study goes beyond PSWS and extends to PSNS. We applied *trickle-down model* to PSNS and explored whether supervisors' PSNS will affect subordinates' PSNS, which would in turn transmit to subordinates' OCB. We also investigated whether supervisors' perceived in-group/out-group membership of the subordinates moderates the effect of supervisors' PSNS on subordinates' PSNS.

Literature Review and Hypotheses

Trickle-Down Model and Its Theoretical Bases

Trickle-down model states that employees' perceptions, attitudes, and behaviors are passed from supervisors to subordinates (Bordia, Restubog, Bordia, & Tang, 2010). Through trickle-down process, higher organizational level's behaviors and attitudes will flow down and elicit reactions at the lower organizational level (Aryee et al., 2007). Although trickle-down model provides a framework, which links higher-level manager, supervisors, subordinates, it cannot precisely explain the mechanism behind this top-down flow process. Therefore, past researchers applied at least three lines of theoretical perspectives to explain why trickle-down effect occurs, that is, justice theory, social exchange theory, and social learning theory.

Justice theory argues that justice perception will pass its effect from higher organizational level to lower organizational level. Masterson (2001) proposed the original idea of applying justice theory to trickle-down model. She was also the first scholar to propose trickle-down model in the business context. In her study, Masterson tried to explicate how frontline employees' justice perception influences customers' fairness perception. The results showed that employees who perceived higher organizational justice showed greater organizational commitment, exerted greater effort, and displayed more prosocial behaviors toward customers. Customers, in turn, felt treated fairly by the employees and thus had more positive reactions towards the employees. Afterward, trickle-down model has been extended to describe how supervisors' justice perception influences their leadership behaviors and further affects employees' justice perception and subsequent responses. For example, Tepper and Taylor (2003) reported that supervisors' perception of procedural justice influenced their OCB in the form of mentoring behaviors, and such behaviors further led to subordinates' OCB through subordinates' procedural justice perceptions. In addition, supervisors' OCB role definitions moderated the relation of supervisors' procedural justice perception with supervisors' OCB, while subordinates' OCB role definitions moderated the relationship between subordinate's procedural justice perception and subordinate's OCB. Another example is Aryee et al.'s (2007) study, which showed that supervisors' perception of interactional injustice elicits greater abusive supervision, specifically when supervisors have high level of authoritarian leadership style. Subordinates then perceived less interactional justice, which in turn negatively influenced subordinates' OCB-O, OCB-I, and affective commitment.

Social exchange theory states that more benevolent treatment of higher-level managers toward the supervisors (e.g., supportive behavior) will lead to supervisors' obligated feeling to reciprocate, eliciting supervisors' benevolent treatment of subordinates. Furthermore, the subordinates will increase in-role or extra-role performance or decrease deviant behaviors in response to the supervisors' benevolence. This "chain of social exchanges" constitutes the basis of trickle-down process of benevolent behaviors. For example, Shanock and Eisenberger (2006) reported that supervisors' perceived organizational support is positively related to subordinates' perceived supervisory support, which increased subordinates' in-role and extra-role performance to reciprocate the supervisory support. Mayer et al. (2009) also applied social exchange theory to explain how supervisors' ethical leadership relates to group's behaviors. They proposed that ethical leadership creates positive exchanges, which elicit group's obligation to reciprocate by performing more positive and less negative behaviors. The results showed that supervisors' ethical leadership related positively to group OCB but negatively to group deviance.

Social learning theory states the higher management level often serves as a role model for low management level. For example, Bass, Waldman, Avolio, and Bebb (1987) used role-modeling process as one of the theoretical perspectives and predicted that transformation leadership at a higher level management will also appear at the lower level. The results demonstrated that two levels of managements' transformational leadership correlated positively. Mayer et al. (2009) also used social learning theory to propose that the followers of top-level management will learn and reproduce its ethical leadership. The results revealed that top-level managements' ethical leadership correlated positively with supervisors' ethical leadership.

Taken together, our study adopted trickle-down model as an overarching framework to bridge each part of the top-down flow process. In line with past literature, we also drew on social learning theory, social exchange theory, and justice theory to supplement trickle-down model and to explain the mechanism behind the process.

Relationship Between Supervisors' PSNS and Subordinates' PSNS: The Application of the Theoretical Bases of Trickle-Down Model

Perspective of Justice Perception

From the perspective of justice perception, lower-level supervisors will perceive fair or unfair treatment from the higher-level management. When supervisors obtain upper-level managers' non-work support, they may feel that the benevolent treatment they receive (output) well compensates for the effort they take for the supervision work (input), which increases the possibility of perceived equity and thus results in the *perception of distributive injustice*. In addition, supervisors who receive upper-level managers' non-work treatment may feel that the organization encourages benevolent climate and protects the welfare of the employees, thus leading to *the perception of procedural justice*. Moreover, upper-level managers' non-work support makes supervisors feel treated with respect, consideration, and recognition, thus resulting in the *perception of interactional justice*. All three forms of justice perception will affect the way in which supervisors treat their subordinates (Aryee et al., 2007; Tepper, 2000; Tepper & Taylor, 2003). As mentioned previously, Tepper and Taylor found that the more procedural justice the supervisor perceived, the more OCB in the form of mentoring the supervisor provided. In contrast, Aryee and his colleagues (2007) found that supervisors who perceived interpersonal injustice from higher level of organization are more likely to provide abusive supervision to their subordinates. Accordingly, when lower-level supervisors perceived more non-work support from their higher-level supervisors, they tended to perceive fair treatment and therefore provide more non-work support to their subordinates.

Perspective of Social Learning Theory

Bass et al. (1987) used the "cascading effect of leadership" to describe the flow through which leaders' behaviors or attitudes affect their followers who may develop similar behavior or attitude patterns. Social learning theory (Bandura, 1977, 1986) can explain this effect. According to social learning theory, individuals learn from observing other people's behaviors, especially those behaviors performed by significant others. In work places, supervisors have higher social power and status, and they tend to be regarded as the role model for subordinates. Through the social learning process, when higher-level supervisors offer non-work support to lower-level supervisors, these lower-level supervisors may imitate this behavior and offer non-work support to file-and-rank employees. One important aspect of the social learning theory is that it distinguishes acquisition from performance, such that an individual needs to be motivated in order to perform the learned behavior. When lower-level supervisors learn the provision of non-work support from higher-level supervisors, they are willing to act similarly towards their direct subordinates for the following three reasons. First, higher-level supervisors have higher position and, therefore, it is more likely for lower-level managers to perceive them as role models of career success. Therefore, when lower-level supervisors observe that higher-level supervisors offer non-work support, they may believe that such behaviors lead to career success. In order to increase the opportunity for future promotion, the lower-level managers may imitate this behavior of offering non-work support to subordinates. Second, given that higher-level supervisors are often perceived as being in charge of a work unit, the behaviors of higher-level management may influence the entire work unit and even become norms of work collaboration. Therefore, when higher-level management provides non-work support to their subordinates, it may create a work norm, encouraging supervisors to offer non-work support to their subordinates, which can then influence lower-level supervisors to offer non-work support to subordinates (Mayer et al., 2009). Last, Bolino, Varela, Bande, and Turnley (2006) indicated that by performing impression management in front of supervisors, one can receive higher rating on OCB from the supervisors. This rating of OCB relates positively to supervisors' liking and performance rating. Therefore, when lower-level supervisors observe that higher-level supervisors offer non-work support, the lower-level supervisors may infer that higher-level supervisors prefer subordinates who demonstrate such behavior. Consequently, the lower-level supervisors may imitate and intentionally perform such behavior of providing non-work support to their subordinates for the sake of impressing the management.

Perspective of Social Exchange Theory

The social exchange theory (Blau, 1964; Cropanzano & Mitchell, 2005), which emphasizes the role of reciprocity, can also explain the flow from supervisors' PSNS to subordinates' PSNS. That is, when individual A does something favorable to individual B, individual B feels obligated to return the favor. The aforementioned exchange manifests reciprocal exchange (Gouldner, 1960). Therefore, when a supervisor offers a non-work support to subordinate, the subordinate will do the same favor to the supervisor. However, because there are many targets of interpersonal interaction in an organization, the target of reciprocal exchange may become ambiguous and complicated. In other words, when an individual A does a favor to individual B, individual B may return the favor by doing favor to individual C. For example, when a manager (A) in marketing department helps another manager (B) in the financial department, this financial manager (B) may provide an employee (C) who belongs to marketing department more budgets in return. Therefore, lower-level supervisors may provide non-work support to their subordinates in return for non-work support they received from higher-level supervisors.

> *Hypothesis 1:* Supervisors' PSNS will be positively associated with subordinates' PSNS.

The Moderating Effect of Supervisors' Perceived In-Group/Out-Group Membership of the Subordinate

Leader-member exchange theory suggests that leaders develop differential dyadic relationships with their subordinates through continuous social exchanges (Dansereau, Graen, & Haga, 1975). Because leaders have many work responsibilities and time constraints, they cannot provide all subordinates with equal support and resources. Consequently, leaders may categorize subordinates into in-group or out-groups and treat them differently based on the quality of exchange relationship (Graen & Uhl-Bien, 1995).

One important factor that can explain how someone becomes part of in-group or out-group is the similarity between two parties. Similarity can be divided into surface-level similarity and deep-level similarity (van Emmerik & Brenninkmeijer, 2009). Surface-level similarity refers to similarities among members in overt demographic characteristics (Milliken & Martins, 1996; van Emmerik & Brenninkmeijer, 2009), which are often visible (Riordan, 2000). Such characteristics include age, gender, and race/ethnicity, which can be easily reflected in physical features. Most people use these characteristics to roughly compare themselves to others (Jackson, May, & Whitney, 1995). On the other side, deep-level similarity refers to similarities among team members' psychological characteristics, including personalities, values, and attitudes (van Emmerik & Brenninkmeijer, 2009), which form underlying differences in their attitudes, values, and personalities (Harrison, Price, Gavin, & Florey, 2002).

Although some studies showed that the quality of exchange relationship between managers and employees is associated more with deep-level similarity but less with surface-level similarity (Bauer & Green, 1996), similarity-attraction paradigm states that similarity, including both surface-level and deep-level similarity, facilitates interpersonal attraction and may further increase frequency of interaction and the amount of social integration (van Emmerik & Brenninkmeijer, 2009). In addition, based on social categorization perspective (Shapcott, Carron, Burke, Bradshaw, & Estabrooks, 2006), supervisors tend to categorize subordinates into certain social categories. When a subordinate is perceived similar to the supervisors, the supervisors will categorize this subordinate into the same category as them (i.e., in-group). In contrast, when a subordinate is perceived as different from the supervisors, the supervisors will categorize this subordinate into the category that is different from them (i.e., out-group) (Cheng, 1995).

In-group subordinates may have higher quality exchange relationship with supervisors. Supervisors may give in-group subordinates more challenging assignments to develop their competency, provide subordinates with more resources and information to help them accomplish their tasks, and provide work support when subordinates encounter high pressure situations (work support) (Graen & Scandura, 1987; Schriesheim, Neider, & Scandura, 1998). Supervisors may also extend their care to subordinates' non-work life area and demonstrate more benevolent behaviors (non-work support) (Cheng, 1995). Such non-work support would be given to in-group subordinates due to the high quality relationship between the supervisors and the subordinates, regardless of whether the supervisors have witnessed and learned the same support behaviors from their higher-level supervisors through the social learning process, and regardless of whether the higher-level supervisor established the "norms of non-work support." In addition, for in-group subordinates, their high quality LMX relationship with supervisors creates mutual trust and sense of obligation (Dienesch & Liden, 1986). That is, not only subordinates but also supervisors perceive a sense of mutual obligation in their relationship. Therefore, the supervisors will offer non-work support to subordinates because of their mutual reciprocal relationship, regardless of whether they feel obligated to repay the higher-level supervisors' non-work support in the social exchange process. Therefore, for in-group subordinates, the relationship between supervisors' PSNS and subordinates' PSNS is *weaker*.

Unlike in-group subordinates, out-group subordinates have low quality relationship with their supervisors. Supervisors may interact with out-group subordinates transactionally and impersonally (Furst & Cable, 2008) and thus provide less non-work support. Consequently, the degree to which supervisors provide non-work support to out-group subordinates will not depend on the high-quality relationship and mutual reciprocity between the supervisors and their subordinates; instead, it will depend on the social learning and social exchange process, which occurs in the relationship between the supervisors and their higher-level supervisors. Specifically, such behavior (supervisors' provision of non-work support to subordinates) is associated with supervisors' social learning process through which they observe the non-work supportive behaviors displayed by higher-level supervisors or follow the "norms of non-work support" established by higher-level supervisors. Such behavior is also associated with the extent to which the supervisors feel obligated to reciprocate the higher-level supervisors' non-work support. Therefore, for out-group subordinates, the relationship between supervisors' PSNS and subordinates' PSNS is *stronger*.

Taken together, whether the cascading effect from supervisors' PSNS to subordinates' PSNS is strengthened or weakened will depend on the subordinates' in-group/out-group status. Specifically, such cascading effect is weaker for in-group subordinates compared to out-group subordinates.

> *Hypothesis 2:* Supervisors' perceived in-group/out-group membership of subordinates will moderate the relationship between supervisors' PSNS and subordinates' PSNS, such that this relationship will be weaker for in-group subordinates compared to out-group subordinates.

Relationship of Subordinates' PSNS With Subordinates' OCB-I and OCB-O

Organ (1988) defined OCB as "the behavior that is discretionary, not directly or explicitly recognized by the formal reward system, and in the aggregate promotes the effective functioning of the organization" (p. 4). Much research has suggested that subordinates' perceived supervisory support leads to subordinates' positive extra-role behaviors (Shanock & Eisenberger, 2006; Smith, Organ, & Near, 1983; Zellars & Tepper, 2003), including OCB toward specific individuals (OCB-I) and OCB toward organization in general (OCB-O) (Williams & Anderson, 1991).

According to social exchange theory, when subordinates receive positive treatments from the supervisor (including PSNS), the subordinates will reciprocate the supervisor's benevolence with extra-role behaviors (Shanock & Eisenberger, 2006), including behaviors similar to OCB-I and OCB-O (Podsakoff, MacKenzie,

Paine, & Bachrach, 2000). Although PSNS relates to both OCB-I and OCB-O, the mechanisms behind PSNS- OCB-I relationship and PSNS- OCB-O relationship may be different. We adopted two forms of social exchange rules, *restricted social exchange* and *generalized social exchange*, to clarify such differential mechanisms.

Restricted social exchange means that two parties exchange favors with each other directly. For example, when the supervisor offers support to the subordinate and the subordinate also provide support to the supervisor in return, this form of exchange refers to *restricted social exchange*. Generalized social exchange means that the exchange occurs among at least three parties without direct reciprocity between the two parties. For example, when the supervisor offers support to the subordinate and the subordinate provide support to other coworkers (third party) as a way of reciprocating the supervisor's support, this form of exchange refers to *generalized social exchange* (Ekeh, 1974; Levi-Strauss, 1969; Molm, Collett, & Schaefer, 2007).

We proposed that restricted social exchange could explain the mechanism behind PSNS-OCB-O relationship. Given that supervisors are regarded as the organizational agents (Eisenberger, Stinglhamber, Vandenberghe, Sucharshki, & Rhoades, 2002; Levinson, 1965), supervisors' support to subordinates will also be considered the organizational support (Shanock & Eisenberger, 2006; Sousa-Lima, Michel, & Caetano, 2013). Therefore, the subordinates who receive supervisory non-work support may reciprocate with extra-role behaviors that benefit their organization (Eisenberger et al., 2002). These behaviors are similar to OCB-O. In this case, the supervisor is equivalent to the organization, and thus only two parties (the organization and the subordinate) are involved in the exchange process.

We also propose that generalized social exchange could explain the mechanism behind PSNS- OCB-I relationship. In generalized social exchange, subordinates' obligations to one party (e.g., the supervisor) may be transferred to another party or to the whole group (e.g., the coworkers) (Das & Teng, 2002). Accordingly, when subordinates receive positive treatments from their supervisors, they may feel obligated to return and reciprocate the supervisors' benevolence by engaging in extra-role prosocial behaviors toward coworkers (e.g., helping coworker who have been absent, orienting new coworkers even though it is not required). Such extra-role prosocial behaviors toward coworkers corresponds to OCB-I. In this case, three parties (the supervisor, the subordinate, and other coworkers) are involved in the exchange process, and the support provider (the supervisor) and the receiver (the subordinate) will not reciprocate with each other. Previous empirical research supported the argument that generalized social exchange (among the supervisor, the subordinate, and other coworkers) can explain the mechanism behind subordinates' PSNS- OCB-I relationship. For example, Liu, Zhu, and Yang (2010) found that supervisors' positive leadership behaviors (i.e., transformational leadership) will elicit the subordinates' positive extra-role behaviors toward their coworkers (i.e., affiliative extra-role behavior toward the peers) in return. Shanock and Eisenberger (2006) revealed that when subordinates feel supported from their supervisors, these subordinates engaged in extra-role behaviors, including helping coworkers, to reciprocate supervisors' support. Chen and Chiu (2008) also reported that subordinates' perceived supervisor support is positively correlated with their OCB-I.

Taken together, based on the rule of restricted social exchange, subordinate's PSNS may increase OCB-O. According to the rule of generalized social exchange, subordinate's PSNS may increase OCB-I.

> *Hypothesis 3:* Subordinates' PSNS will be positively associated with their OCB-I and OCB-O.

Mediating Effect of Subordinates' PSNS: The Trickle-Down Model

Trickle-down model can explain the mediating effect of subordinates' PSNS on the relationship between supervisors' PSNS and subordinates' OCB-I and OCB-O. As noted previously, when supervisors receive non-work support from higher-level managers (antecedent), the supervisors will also offer non-work support to the subordinates (mediator). Their non-work support further facilitates subordinates' OCB (consequence). Past empirical studies have applied trickle-down model to illustrate the mediating effect of top-down chain process. For example, Shanock and Eisenberger (2006) showed that supervisors' perceived organizational support leads to subordinates' in-role and extra-role performance via the mediator of subordinates' perceived supervisory support. Mayer et al. (2009) revealed that ethical leadership flows from top-management to subordinates' behaviors (increased OCB and decreased deviance) at the group level through the mediating process of immediate supervisors' ethical leadership. Mayer et al. (2009) suggested that top-management has a broad influence on organization in general and that both immediate supervisors and subordinates are under the influence of top-management. However, compared with the distal relationships between top-management and lower-level employees, immediate supervisor have clearly more proximal and direct relationships with employees. Therefore, it is reasonable to predict that higher-level supervisors' leadership behaviors will influence lower-level employees' behaviors through the subordinates' direct supervisors. In line with trickle-down effect and the above empirical studies, we propose that subordinates' PSNS will mediate the relationship of supervisors' PSNS with subordinates' OCB-I and OCB-O.

> *Hypothesis 4:* Subordinates' PSNS will mediate the relationship of supervisors' PSNS with subordinates' OCB-I and OCB-O.

Method

Participants and Procedure

We used the questionnaire survey to collect data from EMBA students of a private university located in North Taiwan. These EMBA students were full-time employees who had both a direct and a second-line supervisor. They participated in the study voluntarily. We distributed survey packages to the EMBA students who were willing to enroll in the study. Each survey package contained a subordinate questionnaire set (a cover letter, a subordinate questionnaire with a printed matching code) and a supervisor questionnaire set (a cover letter, a supervisor questionnaire with a printed matching code, and a return envelope). By using the dyad data from the supervisors and the subordinate, our design reduces the possibility of common method variance (CMV) problem (Podsakoff, MacKenzie, Lee, & Podsakoff, 2003).

Prior to the survey, we used 10-minutes to introduce the procedure of the study. The EMBA students who participated in the study were assured confidentiality. During the survey, the EMBA students picked up the subordinate questionnaire set, read the instructions, and completed the subordinate questionnaire in a classroom at the university. When they completed the survey, they returned the subordinate questionnaire directly to the researchers and picked up the supervisor questionnaire set, which they took back to their workplace. Afterward, the EMBA students distributed the supervisor questionnaire set to their immediate supervisor, informing them to complete the survey independently and mail the survey directly to the researchers using a return envelope with prepaid postage, not via their subordinates.

Overall, 200 survey packages were distributed and 184 subordinate questionnaires and 135 supervisor questionnaires were returned. After discarding surveys that contained either missing data or when subordinate surveys could not be matched with supervisor forms using the matching codes, the number of valid dyads for analyses was 132. To ensure that the same individual (the EMBA student) did not complete both surveys, we followed Grandey's (2003) practice to assess the handwriting on both subordinate and supervisor survey. The results of our examination revealed that no respondents completed both surveys.

Subordinates' average age was 36.20 ($SD = 6.22$), average tenure in their current organization was 7.26 years ($SD = 6.08$), and 66 (50%) were men. Supervisors' average age was 42.53 ($SD = 9.31$), average tenure in their current organization was 10.42 years ($SD = 8.04$), average working relationship with the subordinate was 4.39 years ($SD = 3.99$), and 82 (62.1%) were men. The industries for which the participants worked included information technology and communication (12.9%), service (6.8%), finance and insurance (33.3%), manufacturing (10.6%), high-tech and electronics (14.4%), civil service (7.6%), education (3.0%), military service (3.0%), and others (8.6%).

Measures

Because Traditional Chinese was the native language for all respondents, all English items were translated into Traditional Chinese with the back-translation approach suggested by Brislin (1980). One author (the first author) first translated items into Chinese, and then the other author (the third author) who is bilingual back translated the Chinese into English. Unless otherwise specified, all items were measured on a 7-point Likert-type scale ranging from 1 (very disagree) to 7 (very agree).

Perceived Supervisory Non-Work Support (PSNS)

Both supervisors and subordinates responded to five items measuring non-work and life support adopted from Cheng, Chou, and Farh (2000) to measure PSNS. Originally, Cheng et al. (2000) developed 11 items to measure benevolent leadership behaviors, 5 of which measure the non-work support of leadership. Therefore, we used these 5 items to measure PSNS. These five items are, "Beyond work relations, my supervisor expresses concern about my daily life," "My supervisor ordinarily shows a kind concern for my comfort," "My supervisor takes very thoughtful care of me," "My supervisor meets my needs according to my personal requests," and "My supervisor handles what is difficult to do or manage in everyday life for me." In Cheng, Chou, and Farh's (2000) study, the Cronbach's alpha coefficient (business samples) of the full 11-item scale was .93. In our study, the Cronbach's alpha coefficients of 5-item scale were .94 for subordinates and .93 for supervisors.

Supervisors' Perceived In-Group/Out-Group Membership of Subordinate

Previous studies on supervisors' social categorization of subordinates often asked supervisors to pick subordinates from different social categorizations (i.e., in-group vs. out-group) and to rate these subordinates separately on different dimensions, such as expectations and performance (e.g., Chu, 2000; Hsu, 2004). However, such evaluation may lead supervisors to evaluate subordinates based on the image of a typical in-group or our-group rather than on subordinates' actual behavior. To prevent such problem, we asked the subordinates to distribute the surveys to the supervisors and asked the supervisors to indicate whether the subordinates are in-group members (coded as 1) or out-group members (coded as 2). In addition, to prevent possible contamination due to social categorization, we presented the OCB-I and OCB-O questions *before* we asked supervisors to make the in-group/out-group judgment.

OCB-I and OCB-O

Supervisors rated subordinates' OCB by responding to 8 items measuring OCB-I and 8 items measuring OCB-O. These items were adopted from Lee and Allen's (2002) scale. Example items were, "This subordinate helps others who have been absent" for OCB-I, and "This subordinate attends functions that are not required but help the organizational image" for OCB-O. In Lee and Allen's (2002) study, the Cronbach's alpha coefficients were .83 for OCB-I and .88 for OCB-O. In our study, the Cronbach's alpha coefficients were .94 for OCB-I and .94 for OCB-O.

Control Variables

Previous research suggested that individuals' demographic background (e.g., gender, organizational tenure, position) and the length of working relationship between supervisor and subordinate could be significantly related to prosocial organizational behaviors, including both in-role and extra-role behaviors (e.g., OCB) (e.g., Brief & Motowidle, 1986; Podsakoff et al., 2000; Rafaeli & Sutton, 1989). Regarding *gender*, Kidder (2002) demonstrated that females are more likely to report performing OCB-altruism compared to males, whereas males are more likely to report performing OCB-civic virtue behaviors. Furthermore, Derlega, Barbee, and Winstead (1994) reported that gender difference plays a significant role in perceiving and providing social support. Regarding *position*, employees in a higher position often have greater access to social resources that they can utilize, control, and allocate (Lin, Ensel, & Vaughn, 1981), which may affect the display of supportive behavior or extra-role behaviors. Regarding *tenure*, organizational tenure, representing the duration of subordinates' relationship with the organization, is positively related to perceived organizational support, while dyad tenure, representing the duration of subordinates' relationship with the supervisor, is positively related to leader-member exchange relationship. Therefore, Wayne et al. (1997) suggested that organizational tenure could be regarded as a control variable for perceived organizational support and dyad tenure as a control variable for the relationship quality between supervisor and subordinate. In our study, perceived organizational support is similar to PSNS, and LMX is similar to in-group/out-group. In addition, past literature also showed that tenure in organization correlated positively with supervisors' benevolent behavior (including non-work support) and extra-role behavior (e.g., Cheng, Shieh, & Chou, 2002). Taken together, when testing the hypothesis concerning subordinates' OCB, we controlled for background variables, including subordinates' gender, position, tenure in the current organization, and tenure with the current supervisor. We conducted the regression analyses to predicting supervisors' non-work support while controlling for supervisors' gender, position, tenure in the current organization, and length of working relationship with the subordinate.

We should note that subordinates' position has four categories (i.e., staff, low-level manager, mid-level manager, and high-level manager), and supervisors' position has three categories (i.e., low-level manager, mid-level manager, and high-level manager). Given that both subordinates position and supervisors' position are categorical variables, we should create dummy variables for further analysis. In our study, we transformed subordinates' position into three dummy variables (i.e., subordinate low-level manager, subordinate mid-level manager, and subordinate high-level manager), with staff as the referent category. Also, we transformed supervisors' position into two dummy variables (i.e., supervisor mid-level manager and supervisor high-level manager), with low-level manager as the referent category.

In addition to demographic variables, we controlled for *supervisors' positive affect* in the regression analyses when predicting supervisors' non-work support, because positive affect may affect one's supportive behavior (e.g., George, 1991; Williams & Shiaw, 1999). We also controlled for *subordinates' positive affect* in the regression analyses when predicting supervisors' OCB, because positive affect makes employees define job role broader and in turn leads to more OCB (Morrison, 1994). Regarding the positive affect measure, we used Wu and Hu's (2009) short four-item version of the positive affect scale (enthusiastic, determined, excited, and interested). The scale items are measured on a 4-point scale ranging from never (1) to strongly (4). The short version of this scale was adapted from Watson, Clark, and Tellegen's (1988) original 10-item scale. In Wu and Hu's study, the Cronbach's alpha coefficient of short-version positive affect scale was .83. In our study, the Cronbach's alpha coefficients were .77 for subordinates and .82 for supervisors.

Analysis

To ensure the construct validity of the studied variables, we first undertook a series of confirmatory factor analyses (CFA) to evaluate the convergent and discriminant validities (Anderson & Gerbing, 1988) of the major study variables of this research. We then used hierarchal regression analyses to test all hypotheses according to Baron and Kenny's (1986) suggestions. To avoid the collinearity problem, we centered the antecedent variables while testing hypotheses (Aiken & West, 1991).

Results

Results of Measurement Model

We conducted CFA of the four study variables, supervisors' PSNS, subordinates' PSNS, OCB-I, and OCB-O. Because we measured supervisors' perceived in-group/out-group membership of subordinates by using a single dichotomous item, we did not include this variable in CFA. The results are shown in Table 1. According to the criteria suggested by Hu and Bentler (1999), the fitting index of baseline four-factor model (Model 1) was acceptable ($\chi^2_{(293)} = 429.09$, $df = 293$, RMSEA = .06, SRMR = .05, NNFI = .97, CFI = .98). All items had significant factor loadings on the factors identified a priori at a significance level of .05 and therefore provided evidence for convergent validity of the four-factor model (Anderson & Gerbing, 1988).

We also examined the discriminant validity by testing three alternative models. The three-factor model where OCB-I and OCB-O were combined into one factor (Model 2), the two-factor model where OCB-I, OCB-O, and subordinates' PSNS were combined into one factor (Model 3), and the one-factor model where all research variables were combined into one factor (Model 4). The results showed that the baseline four-factor model fits the data better compared to the alternative

TABLE 1. Comparison of Measurement Models for Study Variables

Model	Description	χ^2	*df*	$\Delta\chi^2$	RMSEA	SRMR	TLI	CFI
Model 1 (Baseline)	Four factors: OCB-O, OCB-I, subordinates' PSNS, and supervisors' PSNS.	429.09**	293	—	.06	.05	.97	.98
Model 2	Three-factors: OCB-I and OCB-O were combined into one factor.	576.07**	294	146.98**	.09	.06	.96	.97
Model 3	Two factors: OCB-I, OCB-O, and subordinates' PSNS were combined into one factor.	1840.55**	298	1411.46**	.20	.33	.84	.85
Model 4	One factor: all variables were combined into one factor.	2017.65**	299	1588.56**	.21	.33	.84	.85

$^{**}p < .01$, two-tailed test.

models (Model 1 vs. Model 2: $\Delta\chi^2_{(1)} = 146.98$, $p < .01$; Model 1 vs. Model 3: $\Delta\chi^2_{(5)} = 1411.46$, $p < .01$; Model 1 vs. Model 4: $\Delta\chi^2_{(6)} = 1588.56$, $p < .01$). This result implied that supervisors' PSNS, subordinates' PSNS, OCB-I, and OCB-O were distinct constructs in our study, supporting the discriminant validity of these variables.

Descriptive Statistics and Correlations

Table 2 shows the descriptive statistics, Cronbach's alpha coefficients, and intercorrelations among study variables. As can be seen in Table 2, the mean of supervisors' PSNS is 4.23 ($SD = 1.20$), and the mean of subordinates' PSNS is 4.10 ($SD = 1.30$). The means of subordinates' OCB-I and OCB-O are 5.79 ($SD = .84$) and 5.76 ($SD = .80$) respectively. Regarding the correlation coefficients, the supervisors' PSNS is positively correlated with subordinates' PSNS ($r = .35$, $p < .01$). The subordinates' PSNS is positive correlated with subordinate OCB-I ($r = .35$, $p < .01$) and OCB-O was ($r = .34$, $p < .01$), respectively.

TABLE 2. Descriptive Statistics and Correlation Matrix

Variables	Descriptive Statistics			Correlation Matrix																
	N	Mean	SD	1	2	3	4	5	6	7	8	9	10	11	12	13	14	15	16	17
Control Variables																				
1. Subordinate Gender[a]	132	—	—	—																
2. Subordinate low-level manager[b]	132	—	—	.20*	—															
3. Subordinate mid-level manager[b]	132	—	—	–.25**	–.29**	—														
4. Subordinate high-level manager[b]	132	—	—	–.19*	–.16	–.16	—													
5. Subordinate Organizational Tenure	132	7.26	6.08	.04	.15	.16	.03	—												
6. Subordinate Positive Affect	132	2.98	0.56	–.02	.22*	.03	.12	.02	(0.77)											
7. Subordinate Tenure with Supervisor	131	4.42	4.00	.04	–.07	.23**	.18*	.33**	–.24**	—										
8. Supervisor Gender	131	—	—	.18*	.01	–.20*	–.12	–.02	–.17	–.05	—									

(Continued on next page)

TABLE 2. Descriptive Statistics and Correlation Matrix *(Continued)*

	Descriptive Statistics			Correlation Matrix																
Variables	N	Mean	SD	1	2	3	4	5	6	7	8	9	10	11	12	13	14	15	16	17
9. Supervisor mid-level manager[c]	131	—	—	.04	.13	–.05	–.14	.05	–.16	–.07	.03	—								
10. Supervisor high-level manager[c]	131	—	—	–.15	–.10	.36**	.28**	.02	.11	.23**	–.15	–.55**	—							
11. Supervisor Organizational Tenure	131	10.42	8.04	.02	.07	.12	–.09	.54**	–.09	.31*	.21**	.02	.07	—						
12. Supervisor Positive Affect	128	3.00	0.56	.06	.12	.08	.25**	.01	.13	–.08	–.13	–.02	.27**	–.04	(0.77)					
Antecedent Variable																				
13. Supervisor PSNS[d]	132	4.23	1.20	–.17	.02	–.07	.21*	.05	.09	–.02	.11	.02	.05	.04	.23**	(0.94)				
Mediating Variable[d]																				
14. Subordinate PSNS	132	4.10	1.30	–.10	.09	.02	.16	–.02	.19*	.08	–.06	.09	.13	.09	.17	.35**	(0.93)			
Moderating Variables																				

15. In-group/Out-group[e]	123	—	—	–.10	–.08	.08	–.09	.02	–.04	–.14	–.21*	–.04	–.05	–.04	–.22*	–.06	–.18*	—		
Outcome Variables																				
16. Subordinate OCB-I[f]	131	5.79	0.84	.07	.12	.10	.16	.19*	.06	.21*	–.01	–.04	.14	.09	.37**	.17	.35**	–.27**	(0.94)	
17. Subordinate OCB-O[f]	131	5.76	0.80	–.03	.08	.13	.27**	.20*	.09	.30**	–.14	–.11*	.21*	.10	.43**	.19*	.34**	–.22*	.84**	(0.94)

Note. Pairwise deletion, $N = 123–132$. Values on the diagonal are Cronbach's α.
[a]Gender is coded as 1 = men and 2 = women.
[b]Regarding subordinate position, three dummy variables are created (i.e., subordinate low-level manager, subordinate mid-level manager, and subordinate high-level manager) and staff is the referent category.
[c]Regarding supervisor position, two dummy variable are created (i.e., supervisor mid-level manager and supervisor high-level manager) and low-level manager is the referent category.
[d]PSNS = perceived supervisory non-work support.
[e]In-group/Out-group refers to supervisors' perceived in-group/out-group of the subordinate, and it is coded as 1 = in-group and 2 = out-group.
[f]OCB-I = organizational citizenship behaviors toward specific individuals. OCB-O = organizational citizenship behaviors toward the organization.
$^{*}p < .05$. $^{**}p < .01$.

TABLE 3. The Main Effect of Supervisor Perceived Non-Work Supervisory Support and Moderating Effect of Supervisors' Perceived In-Group/Out-Group Membership of Subordinates (The Beta Coefficients in this Table are Standardized Beta Coefficients)

	Subordinate PSNS[a]			
	Model 1	Model 2	Model 3	Model 4
Control Variables				
Supervisor Gender[b]	–.11	–.17	–.23*	–.23*
Supervisor Mid-level Manager[c]	–.02	–.01	–.02	–.03
Supervisor High-level Manager[c]	–.03	–.01	–.00	.01
Supervisor Organizational Tenure	.11	.11	.12	.14
Subordinate Tenure with Supervisor	.07	.07	.04	.03
Supervisor Positive Affect	.17	.08	.03	.04
(ΔR^2)	(.06)			
Antecedent Variable				
Supervisor PSNS[a]		.35**	.36**	.41**
(ΔR^2)		(.11)**		
Moderating Variable				
In-group/Out-group (IO)[d]			–.20*	–.14
(ΔR^2)			(.04)*	
Interaction				
SS x IO				.19*
(ΔR^2)				(.03)*
Total R^2	.06	.17	.20	.23
Adjusted R^2	.00	.11	.14	.17
F value	1.08	3.06**	3.34**	3.53**
Degree of freedom	6, 108	7, 107	8, 106	9, 105

Note. $N = 115$. Standardized beta coefficients are shown. Values in parentheses are ΔR^2.
[a]PSNS is the abbreviation of perceived supervisory non-work support.
[b]Gender is coded as 1 = men and 2 = women.
[c]Regarding supervisor position, two dummy variable are created (i.e., supervisor mid-level manager and supervisor high-level manager) and low-level manager is the referent category.
[d]In-group/Out-group (IO) refers to Supervisors' perceived in-group/out-group membership of subordinates. It is coded as 1 = in-group and 2 = out-group.
$^*p < .05$. $^{**}p < .01$.

Tests of Hypotheses

Regarding Hypothesis 1 (supervisors' PSNS → subordinates' PSNS), the result of hierarchical regression analyses (Model 2 in Table 3) showed that after controlling for the effect of supervisor-related background variables and

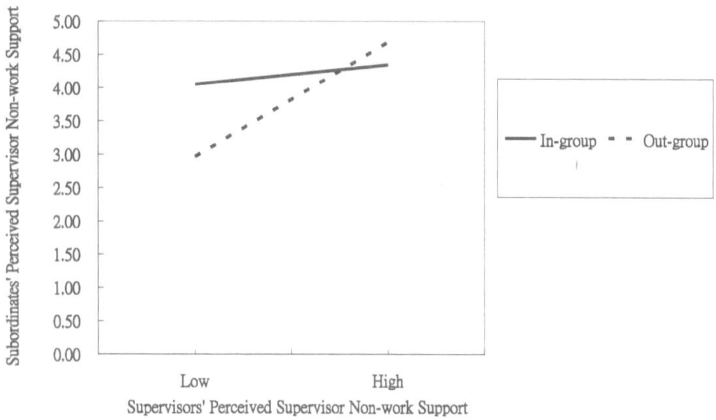

FIGURE 2. The interaction between supervisors' PSNS and supervisors' perceived in-group/out-group membership of subordinates on subordinates' PSNS. (Color figure available online).

supervisors' positive affect, the supervisors' PSNS still related positively to subordinates' PSNS ($\beta = .35$, $p < .01$). Hypothesis 1 was supported.

Regarding Hypothesis 2 (moderating effect of subordinate's in-group/out-group membership), we entered the control variables, antecedent variable (supervisors' PSNS), moderator (in-group/out-group membership), and interaction term (supervisors' PSNS x in-group/out-group membership) into the regression model respectively to predict subordinate's PSNS. The results (Model 4 in Table 3) showed that the interaction term significantly predicted subordinates' PSNS ($\beta = .19$, $p < .05$). We further drew the moderation model based on Aiken and West's (1991) procedure. As shown in Figure 2, the relationship between supervisors' PSNS and subordinates' PSNS was stronger for out-group subordinates but weaker for in-group subordinates. Hypothesis 2 was supported.

Regarding Hypothesis 3 (subordinates' PSNS→subordinates' OCB-I/OCB-O), the result (Model 3 and 6 in Table 4) showed that after controlling for the effect of subordinates' background variables, subordinate's positive affect, and supervisor's PSNS, the subordinates' PSNS still related positively to both subordinates' OCB-I ($\beta = .31$, $p < .01$) and OCB-O ($\beta = .25$, $p < .01$). Hypothesis 3 was supported.

Last, regarding Hypothesis 4 (supervisors' PSNS → subordinates' PSNS → subordinates' OCB-I/OCB-O), we adopted Baron and Kenny's (1986) procedure to test the mediation hypothesis. Table 4 showed that (1) the antecedent (supervisors'

TABLE 4. The Main Effect of Supervisor Perceived Supervisory Non-Work Support and Mediating Effect of Subordinate Perceived Non-Work Supervisor Support (The Beta Coefficients in this Table are Standardized Beta Coefficients)

Dependent Variable	Subordinate OCB-I[a]			Subordinate OCB-O[a]		
	Model 1	Model 2	Model 3	Model 4	Model 5	Model 6
Control Variables						
Subordinate Gender[b]	.13	.15	.16	.03	.06	.06
Subordinate low-level Manager[c]	.17	.17	.14	.15	.15	.12
Subordinate mid-level Manager[c]	.18	.19	.18	.17	.18	.16
Subordinate high-level Manager[c]	.22*	.19	.17	.28**	.25**	.23*
Subordinate Organizational Tenure	.09	.08	.11	.08	.07	.09
Subordinate Tenure with Supervisor	.11	.12	.07	.21*	.22*	.18
Supervisor Positive Affect	.02	.01	–.05	.06	.06	.01
(ΔR^2)	(.13*)			(.19***)		
Antecedent Variable						
Supervisor PSNS[d]		.16 [f]	.06		.15 [f]	.07
Mediating Variables						
Subordinate PSNS[d]			.31**			.25**
(ΔR^2)[d]		(.02)	(.09**)		(.02)	(.05**)
Total R^2	.13	.15	.23	.18	.26	.26
Adjusted R^2	.08	.09	.17	.15	.22	.22
F value	2.51*	2.65*	3.91***	5.50**	7.01**	6.14**
Degree of Freedom	7, 122	8, 121	9, 120	5, 124	6, 123	7, 122

Note. $N = 130$. Standardized beta coefficients are shown. Values in parentheses are ΔR^2.
[a]OCB-I refers to organizational citizenship behaviors toward specific individuals; OCB-O refers to organizational citizenship behaviors toward the organization.
[b]Gender is coded as 1 = men and 2 = women.
[c]Regarding subordinate position, three dummy variables are created (i.e., subordinate low-level manager, subordinate mid-level manager, and subordinate high-level manager) and staff is the referent category.
[d]PSNS is the abbreviation of perceived supervisory non-work support.
[e]The ΔR^2 of Model 2 and Model 3 is above and beyond the total R^2 of Model 1; the ΔR^2 of Model 5 and Model 6 is above and beyond the total R^2 of Model 4.
[f]Both total effects of supervisor PSNS on OCB-I ($\beta = .16$) and OCB-O ($\beta = .15$) reach marginal statistical significance ($p < .10$)
*$p < .05$. **$p < .01$.

PSNS) was related to outcomes (for OCB-I, $\beta = .16, p < .10$; for OCB-O, $\beta = .15, p < .10$) only to a degree of marginal significance (Model 2 and 5 in Table 4); (2) the antecedent (supervisors' PSNS) was significantly related to the mediator (subordinates' PSNS), $\beta = .35, p < .01$ (Model 2 in Table 3); and (3) after entering both antecedent and mediator into the regression model to predict outcomes, the mediator (subordinates' PSNS) still significantly related to OCB-I ($\beta = .31, p < .01$) and OCB-O ($\beta = .25$, $p < .01$), but the antecedent's (supervisors' PSNS) relationship with outcomes became non-significance (for OCB-I, $\beta = .06$, *n.s.*; for OCB-O, $\beta = .07$, *n.s.*; Models 3 and 6 in Table 4). As can be seen in Table 4, the total effect (i.e., the effect of supervisors' PSNS on subordinates' OCB-I/OCB-O) was only marginal significant, which did not well fit Baron and Kenny's (1986) first condition of mediator effect. However, some methodologists have questioned the necessity to include the first condition (i.e. the effect of antecedents on outcomes) when testing mediation effect (e.g., Collins, Graham, & Flaherty, 1998; LeBreton, Wu, & Bing, 2009; MacKinnon, 2000). Specifically, as the mediation process becomes more distal (as in the trickle-down process), the association between antecedents and outcomes turns weaker (Cole, Walter, & Bruch, 2008), which may lead to statistical insignificance. In fact, specifically, Kenny, Kashy, and Bolger (1998) provided an revised version of Baron and Kenny (1986) and argued that the first condition is no longer essential in exploring mediation effect (p. 260). In addition, to ensure that the mediation effect does exist, it is recommended to test the indirect effect (LeBreton et al., 2009). Therefore, in our study, we disregarded the first condition of mediator effect and tested the indirect effect via Sobel test as a supplement. Above all, based on Kenny et al.'s (1998) revised procedure, our results showed complete mediation, supporting H4. Also, the results of Sobel test demonstrated the significance of indirect effect. That is, subordinates' PSNS mediated the relationship of supervisors' PSNS with subordinates' OCB-I ($z = 2.55, p < .05$) and OCB-O ($z = 2.31, p < .05$).

Supplementary Analyses

Two issues require additional analysis. First, our study involved only PSNS, not PSWS (i.e., perceived supervisory work support). This raises an issue of whether PSNS and PSWS are really two distinct constructs. In order to examine whether PSNS is a different construct from PSWS, we obtained another sample of 101 full-time employees who had an immediate supervisor. The participants had an average tenure in the current organization of 8.63 years ($SD = 7.99$) and 58.3% were male. Participants were asked to complete the PSNS and PSWS scales. We measured PSNS using aforementioned Chou and Farh's (2000) five items. We measured the PSWS using nine-item supervisory work support scale developed by Greenhaus et al. (1990). Example items of PSWS are "My supervisor takes time to learn about my career goals and aspirations" and "My supervisor cares about whether or not I achieve my career goals." We performed confirmatory factor analysis (CFA) for these two variables (PSNS and PSWS). The results showed

TABLE 5. Simple Effects Across In-Group and Out-Group

Model	Level of Moderator	First stage	Second stage	Direct effects
Supervisors' PSNS[a] → Subordinates' PSNS → Subordinates' OCB-I[b]	Out-group	.60**	.25	.13
	In-group	.16	.47	–.07
	Difference[c]	.44*	–.22	.20
Supervisors' PSNS → Subordinates' PSNS → Subordinates' OCB-O[b]	Out-group	.60**	.12	.36
	In-group	.16	.52	–.10
	Difference	.44*	–.40	.46

Note. $N = 128$. The coefficients in this Table were based on bias-corrected confidence intervals derived from 1,000 bootstrap estimates.
[a]PSNS is the abbreviation of perceived supervisory non-work support.
[b]OCB-I refers to organizational citizenship behaviors toward specific individuals; OCB-O refers to organizational citizenship behaviors toward the organization.
[c]Difference = Out-group - In-group.
$^{*}p<.05$. $^{**}p<.01$.

that two-factor model (PSNS and PSWS) fits the data well ($\chi^2_{(76)} = 245.22$, $p < .01$, SRMR = .076, NNFI = .93, CFI = .94). We further compared the two-factor model to a single-factor model where PSNS and PSWS were integrated into a single "supervisory support" factor. The results showed that two-factor model provides a better fit compared to single-factor model ($\chi^2_{(77)} = 422.26$, $p < .01$, $p < .01$, SRMR = .12, NNFI = .86, CFI = .88). The chi-square difference between the one-factor model and the two factor model was significant ($\chi^2_{(1)} = 177.04$, $p < .01$), suggesting that the PSNS is a distinct construct that differs from PSWS.

Second, we explored both mediation (supervisors' PSNS → subordinates' PSNS → subordinates' OCB) and moderation (subordinates' in-group/out-group membership on supervisors' PSNS-subordinates' PSNS relationship) in our model, but we test their effects separately. This raises an issue of whether the mediating effect and (or) moderating effect still exist if we test moderation and mediation together. To explore this issue, we applied Edwards and Lambert's (2007) procedure for testing total effect model and examined whether the paths involved in mediation(first stage: antecedent → mediator; second stage: mediator → consequence; direct effect, antecedent → consequence) would be moderated by subordinates' in-group/out-group membership. If subordinates' in-group/out-group membership moderated the first-stage path but not other paths, Hypothesis 4 would be supported with sounder evidence.

Table 5 shows the simple effects for the in-group and out-group conditions as well as the differences in these effects. In in-group condition, both the first-stage and second-stage coefficients were not significant for OCB-I (first stage: $\beta = .16$, *ns*; second stage: $\beta = .47$, *ns*) and OCB-O (first stage: $\beta = .16$, *ns*; second stage: $\beta = .52$, *ns*). In out-group condition, the first-stage coefficient was significant for OCB-I ($\beta = .60, p < .01$) and OCB-O ($\beta = .60, p < .01$), whereas the second-stage coefficient was not significant for OCB-I ($\beta = .25$, *ns*) and OCB-O ($\beta = .12$, *ns*). Moreover, the differences in first-stage coefficients between in-group condition and out-group conditions reached statistical significance for OCB-I (difference = .44, $p < .01$) and OCB-O (difference = .44, $p < .01$); however, other differences (i.e., second stage, direct effect) did not reach statistical significance. These results implied that supervisors' perceived subordinate's in-group/out-group membership moderated only the first-stage path (i.e., supervisors' PSNS → subordinates' PSNS) and not other paths (subordinates' PSNS → OCB-I/OCB-O, supervisors' PSNS → OCB-I/OCB-O)

Taken together, the results of analysis following Edwards and Lambert's procedure (2007) showed that supervisors' perceived in-group/out-group membership of the subordinates moderated only the supervisors' PSNS-subordinates' PSNS relationship not other relationships, which provides additional evidence to support Hypothesis 4.

Discussion

Our findings supported the idea that when supervisors perceive more non-work support from their higher-level supervisors, they also provide more non-work support to their subordinates, which in turn increases subordinates' OCB. In fact, trickle-down model has been applied to discuss the top-down cascading process in various areas, including work supportive behavior (e.g., Shanock & Eisenberger, 2006; Tepper & Taylor, 2003), abusive supervision (e.g., Aryee et al., 2007), ethical leadership (e.g., Mayer et al., 2009), and psychological contract breach (e.g., Bordia et al., 2010). Therefore, our study not only was consistent with trickle-down model of leadership influence process, but also extended trickle-down model to a new area, non-work support, broadening the application range of trickle-down model.

In addition, our findings were in line with the prediction of justice perception perspective, social learning theory, and social exchange theory, and we went one step further by embedding these three theories within the framework of trickle-down model. Specifically, if we adopted only these three theories in our study, we could merely explain the supervisors' PSNS-subordinates' PSNS relationship and subordinates' PSNS-subordinate OCB relationship separately, rather than integrating these two relationships to describe the complete flow process from upper-level managers' non-work support to subordinates' OCB. By using trickle-down model as an overarching framework, we bridged the antecedent, mediator, and outcomes in the top-down flow process. Moreover, trickle-down model makes us aware that social learning, social exchange, and justice perception not only occurs in the dyadic relationship between supervisor and subordinate, but also extends to the complex hierarchical chain relationship among higher-level managers, lower-level supervisors, and subordinates. That is, the effect of social learning, social exchange, and justice perception, which come from upper-level managers, may flow down to subordinates via lower-level supervisors. Accordingly, trickle-down model contributes to the existing literature by offering us a new perspective to re-think the social learning theory, social exchange theory, and justice perception theory.

Our research also revealed that supervisors' categorization of subordinates moderates the flow from supervisors' PSNS to subordinates' PSNS. According to the results, supervisors provided non-work support to in-group subordinates because of their high-quality relationship with the subordinates, regardless of whether the supervisors observed and learned from the higher management or whether the supervisors felt the obligation to reciprocate higher-level managers' non-work support. Therefore, the cascading effect from supervisors' PSNS to subordinates' PSNS was less strong for in-group subordinates than for out-group subordinates. Although some previous studies also explored the boundary conditions of trickle-down process, they focused only on the supervisors' perception of their own job role (e.g., role definition) (Tepper & Taylor, 2003) and leadership style (e.g., authoritarian leadership style) (Aryee et al., 2007) and not on supervisors' perception of their subordinates and their exchange relationships. Our study filled this research gap by considering supervisors' perceived in-group/out-group membership of the subordinates as a moderator in supervisors' PSNS-subordinates' PSNS relationship, highlighting the importance of leader-member exchange relationship and social categorization process in the trickle-down process.

Theoretical Implications

The present research has a number of theoretical implications regarding non-work support. First, our findings extend the existing literature on supervisory support by considering the effect of supervisory non-work support on subordinates' attitude and behaviors. Although Farh and Cheng (2000) argued that managers tend to give holistic consideration to subordinates rather than focus merely on one single aspect of support, most studies on supervisory support have focused on supervisory work support (e.g., Greenhaus et al., 1990; Yoon & Thye, 2000). It is obvious that this focus has led to the research gap on the non-work aspect of supervisory support and therefore merits more research attention. In addition, many collectivistic cultures (e.g., Middle East, Latin America, and Pacific Asia) place much emphasis on family ties. Managers in these cultural contexts tend to extend the way they take care of their family members to the way they take care of subordinates by providing non-work support (Pellegrini & Scandura, 2008). Accordingly, the examination of supervisory non-work support is particularly relevant from the perspective of the cultural context.

Second, we applied trickle-down model to examine the effect of non-work support from high-level supervisor to subordinate via the mediating role of the lower-level supervisor. Although trickle-down model has been used to examine the flow process of perceived organization support or leadership behavior (Shanock & Eisenberger, 2006; Tepper & Taylor, 2003), it has been applied mainly within the work-related context. It has never been used to examine whether supervisory non-work support follows similar flow process. Furthermore, although studies by both Shanock and Eisenberger and Tepper and Taylor applied the trickle-down framework to evaluate supervisors' supportive behaviors, none of these studies used a specific individual, such as a higher-level manager as the starting point of flow process. Rather, both studies used a generic concept "my organization" as the starting point of the flow process. It appears that the target being evaluated at the supervisor level (my organization) is different from the target being evaluated at the subordinate level (my supervisor). Therefore, it would be difficult to understand the role of higher-level managers in the trickle-down process and to separate the influence of higher-level mangers from work climate or culture. In fact, Tangirala et al. (2007) suggested that in organizational hierarchy, the "boss's boss" is influential on file-and-rank employees' work behaviors and attitudes. By applying higher-level managers as the starting point of the flow in order to examine the trickle-down effect in PSNS, we extended the application of trickle-down model and at the same time filled the research gap of the studies by Shanock and Eisenberger and Tepper and Taylor.

Last, previous studies on LMX tended to focus on the outcome of LMX (e.g., employees' task performance, OCB, satisfaction, or organizational commitment) or potential antecedents of LMX (e.g., perceived similarity, transformational leadership) (Engle & Lord, 1997; Gerstner & Day, 1997; Wang et al., 2005). We were not aware of any study that would examine whether LMX strengthens or weakens the effect of supervisory support on subordinates, specifically in non-work area. Our study is the first to incorporate the concept of LMX into the boundary conditions of trickle-down effect. Our findings support the moderating role of LMX in that when supervisors perceive subordinates as in-group members, the supervisors show non-work support without requiring the social learning process from higher-level managers or a sense of generalized exchange.

Limitations and Future Research Directions

There are several limitations and research directions to note in our study. First, we used a cross-sectional design, which makes it difficult to draw causal inferences. However, in the trickle-down model, the influence of managers should be from higher organizational ranks to lower organizational ranks (Bass et al., 1987). Therefore, our study framework is in line with the trickle-down model. Despite of this, a longitudinal design would be preferred. By collecting supervisors' PSNS at time 1, followed by subordinates' PSNS (time 2), and then OCB (time 3), the problem of causal confusion could be avoided.

Second, we collected data within the Chinese context, which may limit the generalization. Because Chinese societies are more collectivistic, such cultural values stress group and family relationship more than individual well-beings. The role of the parents in the family often transmits to the role of the supervisor in the workplace, and this process is called pan-familism process (Yang, 1993). In this cultural context, supervisors may take on a parents-like role and care for the employees whole lives (Pellegrini & Scandura, 2008), focusing not only on work life but also non-work life (Gelfand, Erez, & Aycan, 2007; Pasa, Kabasakal, & Bodur, 2001). The subordinates may perceive the non-work support as appropriate or even expect the leaders to extend their considerations from work to non-work setting (Farh & Cheng, 2000; Pellegrini & Scandura, 2008). On the contrary, Western societies are more individualistic. People in individualistic cultures define their self-concepts in terms of their personal choices rather than their relationship with others (Ersoy, Born, Derous, & van der Molen, 2012), and thus they expect a clear distinction between self and others (Markus & Kitayama, 1991). In such cultural context, the boundary between work and non-work area is clear, and subordinates may consider supervisory non-work support as offensive to their privacy (Farh & Cheng, 2000). To prevent the invasion of self-independence and uniqueness, they may not expect supervisors to be involved in the non-work context of subordinates. Therefore, the trickle-down effect of PSNS may be more relevant in a more collectivistic cultural context, such as Chinese society, rather than a more individualistic cultural context. It is worth investigating whether the trickle-down effect of PSNS can be applied to individualistic cultural contexts. Future studies may include Western employees to examine whether the PSNS has similar effect on Western supervisors. Future studies may also examine whether cultural values, such as Chinese traditionality, power distance, and individualism/collectivism, moderate the trickle-down effect (Farh, Hackett, & Liang, 2007; Hofstede, 1980; Yang, Yu, & Yeh, 1989).

Third, we used a single dichotomous item to measure supervisors' perceived in-group/out-group membership of the subordinate. Such measure is less preferable as it restricts the potential variance of a variable. Future studies may employ a Likert-type scale, semantic different scale, or the LMX scale (Graen & Uhl-Bien, 1995) to operationalize this variable.

Fourth, we argued that by distinguishing PSNS from PSWS, we could gain a comprehensive understanding of the spectrum of supervisory support. However, we did not include PSWS in our study framework. Therefore, future studies can include both PSNS and PSWS in one study to examine their discriminant validity as well as their differential relationships with other organizational behavior variables. By doing so, we can accumulate the evidence of nomological network of supervisory support. Furthermore, future studies can also examine whether the flow process of PSNS and PSWS are the same. For example, we may examine whether PSNS has a greater influence on extra-role behavior or whether PSWS has greater influence on in-role behaviors. We may also investigate whether PSNS has a stronger relationship with life satisfaction or whether PSWS has a stronger relationship with job satisfaction.

Fifth, our study examined the trickle-down effect from high-level supervisors' non-work support to subordinates' OCB, but we did not investigate the role that coworkers play in the trickle-down process of PSNS. In fact, both coworker support and supervisory support are important for employee's well-beings, job attitudes, and work behaviors (Halbesleben, 2006; Ng & Sorensen, 2008). In addition, coworkers are more proximal compared to supervisors, and the coworker exchange relationship may make employees feel more informal, relaxed, and comfortable compared to leader-member exchange relationship. Therefore, the non-work support provided by coworker may also have profound effect as well as that of supervisors. Accordingly, future studies can investigate the ripple effect from coworkers (Barsade, 2002), specifically coworkers' non-work support.

Last, the difference between in-group and out-group membership may affect subordinates' attitudes and reactions toward PSNS. For in-group subordinates, the high-quality exchange relationship may make them more willing to accept supervisors' non-work support, and in-group subordinates may also believe that the motive behind supervisors' non-work support are sincere or authentic. On the contrary, for out-group subordinates, the low quality exchange relationship makes them feel incongruent when receiving supervisors' non-work support (e.g., "I do not have specifically good relationship with my supervisor. Why does she/he treat me so nice?") Such incongruence may lead out-group subordinates to attribute the motive behind supervisors' non-work support to be inauthentic or manipulative (e.g., what does my subordinate really want from me?") (Dasborough & Ashkanasy, 2002). Given that our study did not measure subordinates' attribution of supervisors' intentionality as well as investigate its effect on subordinates' preference for PSNS, future research may consider the interplay among PSNS, in-group/out-group membership, preference for PSNS, and attributions of intentionality.

Practical Implications

We offer three practical implications based on our findings. First, our findings highlight the influences of higher-level managers' behaviors on employees in organizations. Indeed, higher-level management is the figurehead and their behaviors are targets for imitation. Therefore, through the trickle-down process that happens at different levels, attitude and behaviors of top management are passed on to lower-level mangers and the influence can penetrate to every lower organizational rank (Mayer & Davis, 1999). Therefore, top managers should be careful about the way they interact with lower-level supervisors (their direct subordinates) because lower-level supervisors will imitate their behaviors, whether good and bad, and these behaviors can spill over to subordinates. For example, if top managers display positive behavior toward supervisors (e.g., ethical behavior, supportive behavior), it generates a "positive flow" from top managers to subordinates, which also elicits positive work behaviors and job attitudes at the subordinate level (Mayer et al., 2009; Tepper & Taylor, 2003). On the contrary, if top managers display negative behavior toward supervisors (e.g., abusive supervision, psychological contract breach) (Tepper & Taylor, 2003), it develops a "negative flow" from top managers to subordinates, which may destroy positive work behaviors and job attitudes or even induce deviance at the subordinate level (Aryee et al., 2007; Bordia et al., 2010).

Second, supervisors' PSNS can promote subordinates' extra-role behaviors. Therefore, organizations may encourage supervisors to provide non-work support beyond regular work support. For example, organizations may encourage supervisors to greet subordinates and care for their personal well-beings. Such personal care beyond the work support can easily gain subordinates' payoffs. Furthermore, organization may incorporate the ideas and skills from employee assistance programs (EAPs) and employee counseling into supervisor training. By doing so, supervisors may be able to develop new, more sophisticated skills that would allow them to take care of employees' non-work and work lives. Notably, employees with different cultural backgrounds may perceive the importance of personal privacy differently. Therefore, supervisors may need to consider this aspect while providing non-work support to avoid that their good intentions are mistakenly perceived as over-involvement by subordinates.

Last, based on our results, which showed that supervisors' perceived in-group/out-group membership of the subordinates moderated the relationship between supervisors' PSNS and subordinates' PSNS, organization should be aware that the supervisors' display of non-work support not only depends on the supervisor-subordinate relationship (i.e., the LMX between supervisors and subordinates), but also involves an interplay with supervisor-supervisor relationship (i.e., LLM, leader-leader exchange, between supervisor and higher-level manager). In fact, past literature has shown that higher-lever manager also plays a significant role in the interaction between lower-level supervisor and the subordinate (Tangirala et al., 2007). Above all, if the organization encouraged supervisors to provide supportive behaviors to the subordinates, it could develop different strategies for different categories of subordinate. For in-group subordinates, the facilitating factor may be the LMX relationship between supervisor and supervisor. For out-group subordinate, the facilitating factor may be the cascading effect of higher-level managers' behaviors and attitudes.

Conclusion

Most previous studies on supervisory support have focused on work support and ignored non-work support. Using the trickle-down model as the foundation, we examined how supervisors' PSNS influences PSNS of subordinates, which in turn affects subordinates' OCB. We also investigated how supervisors' categorization of subordinates as in-group or out-group members moderates the above flow process. Although past research has shown that trickle-down model can be applied to the cascading process of supervisory work support (Shanock & Eisenberger, 2006; Tepper & Taylor, 2003), our study went beyond work support and further suggested that trickle-down model can also be applied to non-work support. In addition, our study integrated LMX and trickle-down effect by showing that in-group membership weakens the hierarchical chain from supervisors' PSNS to subordinates' PSNS. To our knowledge, this is the first study to examine trickle-down effect under the context of in-group/out-group categorization. Taken together, our study not only extended the application of trickle-down model, but also incorporated the idea of LMX in order to clarify the boundary condition of trickle-down model. Therefore, our study contributes to the literature on both trickle-down model and LMX theory.

FUNDING

This research was supported by National Science Council of Taiwan (Grand NSC 98-2410-H-031-005-MY2).

REFERENCES

Aiken, L. S., & West, S. G. (1991). *Multiple regression: Testing and interpreting interactions*. Newbury Park, CA: Sage Publications.

Anderson, J. C., & Gerbing, D. W. (1988). Structural equation modeling in practice: A review and recommended two-step approach. *Psychological Bulletin, 103*, 411–423.

Aryee, S., Chen, Z.-X., Sun, L.-Y., & Debrah, Y. A. (2007). Antecedents and outcomes of abusive supervision: Test of a trickle-down model. *Journal of Applied Psychology, 92*, 191–201. doi: 10.1037/0021-9010.92.1.191

Bandura, A. (1977). *Social Learning Theory*. Englewood Cliffs, NJ: Prentice-Hall.
Bandura, A. (1986). *Social foundations of thought and action: A social-cognitive view*. Englewood Cliffs, NJ: Prentice Hall.
Baron, R. M., & Kenny, D. A. (1986). The moderator mediator variable distinction in social psychological research: conceptual, strategic, and statistical considerations. *Journal of Personality and Social Psychology*, *51*, 1173–1182. doi: 10.1037/0022-3514.51.6.1173
Barsade, S. G. (2002). The ripple effect: Emotional contagion and its influence on group behavior. *Administrative Science Quarterly*, *47*, 644–675. doi: 10.2307/3094912
Bass, B. M., Waldman, D. A., Avolio, B. J., & Bebb, M. (1987). Transformational leadership and the falling dominoes effect. *Group and Organization Studies*, *12*, 73–87. doi: 10.1177/105960118701200106
Bauer, T. N., & Green, S. G. (1996). Development of leader-member exchange: A longitudinal test. *Academy of Management Journal*, *39*, 1538–1567. doi: 10.2307/257068
Blau, P. (1964). *Exchange and power in social life*. New York, NY: Wiley.
Bolino, M. C., Varela, J. A., Bande, B., & Turnley, W. H. (2006). The impact of impression-management tactics on supervisor ratings of organizational citizenship behavior. *Journal of Organizational Behavior*, *27*, 281–297. doi: 10.1002/job.379
Bordia, P., Restubog, S. L. D., Bordia, S., & Tang, R. L. (2010). Breach beget breach: Trickle-down effects of psychological contract breach on customer service. *Journal of Management*, *36*, 1578–1607. doi: 10.1177/0149206310378366
Brief, A. P., & Motowidle, S. J. (1986). Prosocial organizational behavior. *Academy of Management Review*, *10*, 173–202. doi: 10.5465/AMR.1986.4283909
Brislin, R. (1980). Translation and content analysis of oral and written material. In H. C. Triandis & J. W. Berry (Eds.), *Handbook of cross-culture psychology* (Vol. 2, pp. 389–444). Boston: Allyn & Bacon.
Chen, C.-C., & Chiu, S.-F. (2008). An integrative model linking supervisor support and organizational citizenship behavior. *Journal of Business & Psychology*, *23*, 1–10. doi: 10.1007/s10869-008-9084-y
Cheng, B.-S. (1995). Hierarchical structure and Chinese organizational behavior. *Indigenous Psychological Research in Chinese Societies*, *3*, 142–219.
Cheng, B.-S., Chou, L.-F., & Farh, J.-L. (2000). A triad model of Paternalistic Leadership: The constructs and measurement. *Indigenous Psychological Research in Chinese Societies*, *14*, 3–64.
Cheng, B.-S., Chou, L.-F., Wu, T.-Y., Huang, M.-P., & Farh, J.-L. (2004). Paternalistic leadership and subordinate responses: Establishing a leadership model in Chinese organizations. *Asian Journal of Social Psychology*, *7*, 89–117. doi: 10.1111/j.1467-839X.2004.00137.x
Cheng, B.-S., Huang, M.-P., Chou, L.-F., Farh, J.-L., & Peng, S. (2003). A triad model of paternalistic leadership: Evidence from business organizational in Mainland China. *Journal of Psychology in Chinese Societies*, *20*, 209–250.
Cheng, B.-S., Shieh, P. Y., & Chou, L.-F. (2002). The principal's leadership, leader-member exchange quality, and the teacher's extra-role behavior: The effects of transformational and paternalistic leadership. *Indigenous Psychological Research in Chinese Societies*, *17*, 105–161.
Chu, C.-M. (2000). The effects of confidant relationship on performance appraisal: A differential matrices perspective. *Management Review*, *19*, 125–147.
Cole, M. S., Walter, F., & Bruch, H. (2008). Affective mechanisms linking dysfunctional behavior to performance in work teams: A moderated mediation study. *Journal of Applied Psychology*, *93*, 945–958. doi: 10.1037/0021-9010.93.5.945
Collins, L. M., Graham, J. W., & Flaherty, B. P. (1998). An alternative framework for defining mediation. *Multivariate Behavioral Research*, *33*, 295–312. doi: 10.1207/s15327906mbr3302_5

Cropanzano, R., & Mitchell, M. S. (2005). Social exchange theory: An interdisciplinary review. *Journal of Management, 31*, 874–900. doi: 10.1177/0149206305279602
Dansereau, F., Graen, G. B., & Haga, W. (1975). A vertical dyad linkage approach to leadership in formal organization. *Organization Behavior and Human Performance, 13*, 46–78. doi: 10.1016/0030-5073(75)90005-7
Das, T. K., & Teng, B.-S. (2002). Alliance constellations: A social exchange perspective. *Academy of Management Review, 27*, 445–456. doi: 10.5465/AMR.2002.7389937
Dasborough, M. T., & Ashkanasy, N. M. (2002). Emotion and attribution of intentionality in leader-member relationships. *The Leadership Quarterly, 13*, 615–634. doi: 10.1016/S1048-9843(02)00147-9
Derlega, V. J., Barbee, A. P., & Winstead, B. A. (1994). Friendship, gender, and social support: Laboratory studies of supportive interactions. In B. R. Burleson, T. L. Albrecht, & I. G. Sarason (Eds.), *Communication of social support: Messages, interactions, relationships, and community* (pp. 136–151). Thousand Oaks, CA: Sage.
Dienesch, R. M., & Liden, R. C. (1986). Leader-member exchange model of leadership: A critique and future development. *Academy of Management Review, 11*, 618–634. doi: 10.5465/AMR.1986.4306242
Edwards, J. R., & Lambert, L. S. (2007). Methods for integrating moderation and mediation: A general analytical framework using moderated path analysis. *Psychological Methods, 12*(1), 122. doi: 10.1037/1082-989X.12.1.1
Ekeh, P. P. (1974). *Social exchange theory: The two traditions*. Cambridge, MA: Harvard University Press.
Eisenberger, R., Stinglhamber, F., Vandenberghe, C., Sucharski, I. L., Rhoades, L. (2002). Perceived supervisor support: Contributions to perceived organizational support and employee retention. *Journal of Applied Psychology, 87*(3), 565–573. doi: 10.1037//0021-9010.87.3.565
Engle, E. M., & Lord, R. G. (1997). Implicit theories, self-schemas, and leader-member exchange. *Academy of Management Journal, 40*, 988–1010. doi: 10.2307/256956
Ersoy, N. C., Born, M. P., Derous, E., & van der Molen, H. (2012). The effect of cultural orientation and leadership style on self- versus other-oriented organizational citizenship behaviour in Turkey and the Netherlands. *Asian Journal of Social Psychology, 15*, 249–260. doi: 10.1111/j.1467–839X.2012.01380.x
Farh, J.-L., & Cheng, B.-S. (2000). A Cultural analysis of paternalistic leadership in Chinese organizations. In J. T. Li, A. S. Tsui, & E. Weldon (Eds.), *Management and organizations in the Chinese context* (pp. 94–127). London: Macmillan.
Farh, J.-L., Hackett, R. D., & Liang, J. (2007). Individual-level cultural values as moderators of perceived organizational support-employee outcome relationships in China: Computing the effects of power distance and traditionality. *Academy of Management Journal, 50*, 715–729. doi: 10.5465/AMJ.2007.25530866
Furst, S. A., & Cable, D. M. (2008). Employee resistance to organizational change: Managerial influence tactics and leader-member exchange. *Journal of Applied Psychology, 93*, 453–462. doi: 10.1037/0021-9010.93.2.453
Gelfand, M. J., Erez, M., & Aycan, Z. (2007). Cross-cultural organizational behavior. *Annual Review of Psychology, 58*, 479–514. doi: 10.1146/annurev.psych.58.110405.085559
George, J. M. (1991). State or trait: Effects of positive mood on prosocial behaviors at work. *Journal of Applied Psychology, 76*(2), 299–307. doi:10.1037/0021-9010.76.2.299
Gerstner, C. R., & Day, D. V. (1997). Meta-analytic review of leader-member exchange theory correlates and construct issues. *Journal of Applied Psychology, 82*, 827–844. doi: 10.1037/0021-9010.82.6.827
Gouldner, A. W. (1960). The norm of reciprocity: A preliminary statement. *American Sociological Review, 25*, 161–178. doi: 10.2307/2092623

Graen, G. B., & Scandura, T. A. (1987). Toward a psychology of dyadic organizing. *Research in Organizational Behavior*, *9*, 175–208.
Graen, G. B., & Uhl-Bien, M. (1995). Relationship-based approach to leadership: Development of leader-member exchange (LMX) theory of leadership over 25 years: Applying a multi-level multi-domain perspective. *The Leadership Quarterly*, *6*, 219–247. doi: 10.1016/1048-9843(95)90036-5
Grandey, A. A. (2003). When "the show must go on": Surface acting and deep acting as determinants of emotional exhaustion and peer-rated service delivery. *Academy of Management Journal*, *46*, 86–96. doi: 10.2307/30040678
Greenhaus, J. H., Parasuraman, S., & Wormley, W. M. (1990). Effects of race on organizational experiences, job performance evaluations, and career outcomes. *Academy of Management Journal*, *33*, 64–86. doi: 10.2307/256352
Halbesleben, J. R. B. (2006). Sources of social support and burnout: A meta-analytic test of the conservation of resources model. *Journal of Applied Psychology*, *91*, 1134–1145. doi: 10.1037/0021-9010.91.5.1134
Harrison, D. A., Price, K. H., Gavin, J. H., & Florey, A. T. (2002). Time, teams, and task performance: Changing effects of diversity on group functioning. *Academy of Management Journal*, *45*, 1029–1045. doi: 10.2307/3069328
Hofstede, G. H. (1980). *Culture's consequences: International differences in work-related values*. Beverly Hill, CA: Sage.
Hsu, C.-T., Hu, H.-H., Ling, H.-C., Cheng, B.-S., & Chou, L.-F. (2004). The relationships between paternalistic leadership and organizational citizenship behaviors: The mediating effects of leader-member relationship quality. *Chiao Da Management Review*, *24*, 119–149.
Hsu, W.-L. (2004). *The differential leadership in Mainland China and Taiwan: A process analysis*. Taipei: Doctor, National Taiwan University.
Hu, L.-T., & Bentler, P. M. (1999). Cutoff criteria for fit indexes in covariance structure analysis: Conventional criteria versus new alternatives. *Structural Equation Modeling*, *6*, 1–55.
Jackson, S. E., May, K. E., & Whitney, K. (1995). Understanding the dynamics of diversity in decision-making teams. In R. A. Guzzo & E. Salas (Eds.), *Team decision-making effectiveness in organizations* (Vol. 204–261). San Francisco: Jossey-Bass.
Kenny, D. A., Kashy, D. A., & Bolger, N. (1998). Data analysis in social psychology. In D. T. Gilbert & S. T. Fiske (Eds.), *The handbook of social psychology* (4 ed., Vol. 1, pp. 233–265). New York: McGraw-Hill.
Kidder, D. L. (2002). The influence of gender on the performance of organizational citizenship behaviors. *Journal of Management*, *28*, 629–648. doi: 10.1177/014920630202800504
LeBreton, J. M., Wu, J., & Bing, M. N. (2009). The truth(s) on testing for mediation in the social and organizational sciences. In C. E. Lance & R. J. Vandenberg (Eds.), *Statistical and methodological myths and urban legends* (pp. 107–141). New York: Routledge.
Lee, K., & Allen, N. J. (2002). Organizational citizenship behavior and workplace deviance: The role of affect and cognitions. *Journal of Applied Psychology*, *87*, 131–142. doi: 10.1037/0021-9010.87.1.131
Levi-Strauss, C. (1969). *The elementary structures of kinship*. Boston: Beacon Press.
Levinson, H. (1965). Reciprocation: The relationship between man and organization. *Administrative Science Quarterly*, *9*(4), 370–390. doi:10.2307/2391032
Lin, N., Ensel, W. M., & Vaughn, J. C. (1981). Social resources and strength of ties: Structural factors in occupational status attainment. *American Sociological Review*, *46*, 393–405.

Liu, W., Zhu, R., & Yang, Y. (2010). I warn you because I like you: Voice behavior, employee identifications, and transformational leadership. *The Leadership Quarterly*, *21*, 189–202. doi: 10.1016/j.leaqua.2009.10.014

MacKinnon, D. P. (2000). Multivariate applications in substance use research: New methods for new questions. In J. S. Rose, L. Chassin, C. C. Presson, & S. J. Sherman (Eds.), *Contrasts in multiple mediator models* (pp. 141–160). Mahwah, NJ: Erlbaum.

Markus, H. R., & Kitayama, S. (1991). Culture and the self: Implications for cognition, emotion, and motivation. *Psychological Review*, *98*, 224–253. doi: 10.1037/0033-295X.98.2.224

Masterson, S. S. (2001). A trickle-down model of organizational justice: Relating employees' and customers' perceptions of and reactions to fairness. *Journal of Applied Psychology*, *86*, 594–604. doi: 10.1037/0021-9010.86.4.594

Mayer, D. M., Kuenzi, M., Greenbaum, R., Bardes, M., & Salvador, R. (2009). How low does ethical leadership flow? Test of a trickle-down model. *Organizational Behavior and Human Decision Processes*, *108*, 1–13. doi: 10.1016/j.obhdp.2008.04.002

Mayer, R. C., & Davis, J. H. (1999). The effect of the performance appraisal system on trust for management: A field quasi-experiment. *Journal of Applied Psychology*, *84*, 123–136. doi: 10.1037/0021-9010.84.1.123

Milliken, F. J., & Martins, L. L. (1996). Searching for common threads: Understanding the multiple effects of diversity in organizational groups *Academy of Management Review*, *21*, 402–433. doi: 10.5465/AMR.1996.9605060217

Molm, L. D., Collett, J. L., & Schaefer, D. R. (2007). Building solidarity through generalized exchange: A theory of reciprocity. *American Journal of Sociology*, *13*, 205–242. doi: 10.1086/517900

Morrison, E. W. (1994). Role definitions and Organizational citizenship behaviors: The importance of the employee's perspective. *Academy of Management Journal*, *37*, 1543–1567. doi: 10.2307/256798

Ng, T. W. H., & Sorensen, K. (2008). Toward a further understanding of the relationships between perceptions of support and work attitudes: A meta-analysis. *Group & Organization Management*, *33*, 243–268. doi: 10.1177/1059601107313307

Organ, D. W. (1988). *Organizational citizenship behavior: The good soldier syndrome. Lexington*: MA: Lexington Books.

Pasa, S. F., Kabasakal, H., & Bodur, M. (2001). Society, organizations, and leadership in Turkey. *Applied Psychology: An International Review*, *50*, 559–589. doi: 10.1111/1464-0597.00073

Pellegrini, E. K., & Scandura, T. A. (2008). Paternalistic leadership: A review and agenda for future research. *Journal of Management*, *34*, 566–593. doi: 10.1177/0149206308316063

Podsakoff, P. M., MacKenzie, S. B., Lee, J.-Y., & Podsakoff, N. P. (2003). Common method biases in behavioral research: A critical review of the literature and recommended remedies. *Journal of Applied Psychology*, *88*, 879–903. doi: 10.1037/0021-9010.88.5.879

Podsakoff, P. M., MacKenzie, S. B., Paine, J. B., & Bachrach, D. G. (2000). Organizational citizenship behaviors: A critical review of the theoretical and empirical literature and suggestions for future research. *Journal of Management*, *26*, 513–563. doi: 10.1177/014920630002600307

Rafaeli, A., & Sutton, R. I. (1989). The expression of emotion in organizational life. *Research in organizational behavior*, *11*, 1–42.

Riordan, C. M. (2000). Relational demography within groups: Past developments, contradictions, and new directions. *Research in Personnel and Human Resources Management*, *19*, 131–173. doi: 10.1016/S0742-7301(00)19005-X

Schriesheim, C. A., Castro, S. L., & Cogliser, C. C. (1999). Leader-member exchange (LMX) research: A comprehensive review of theory, measurement, and data-analytic practices. *Leadership Quarterly*, *10*, 63–113. doi: 10.1016/S1048-9843(99)80009-5

Schriesheim, C. A., Neider, L. L., & Scandura, T. A. (1998). Delegation and leader-member exchange: Main effects, moderators, and measurement issues. *Academy of Management Journal*, *41*, 298–318. doi: 10.2307/256909

Shanock, L. R., & Eisenberger, R. (2006). When supervisors feel supported: Relationships with subordinates' perceived supervisor support, perceived organizational support, and performance. *Journal of Applied Psychology*, *91*, 689–695. doi: 10.1037/0021-9010.91.3.689

Shapcott, K. M., Carron, A. V., Burke, S. M., Bradshaw, M. H., & Estabrooks, P. A. (2006). Member diversity and cohesion and performance in walking groups. *Small Group Research*, *37*, 701–720. doi: 10.1177/1046496406294545

Smith, C. A., Organ, D. W., & Near, J. P. (1983). Organizational citizenship behavior: Its nature and antecedents. *Journal of Applied Psychology*, *68*, 653–663. doi: 10.1037/0021-9010.68.4.653

Sousa-Lima, M., Michel, J. W., & Caetano, A. (2013). Clarifying the importance of trust in organizations as a component of effective work relationships. *Journal of Applied Social Psychology*, *43*, 418–427. doi: 10.1111/j.1559-1816.2013.01012.x

Sullivan, I. G. (1989). Burnout: A study of a psychiatric center. *Loss, Grief & Care*, *3*, 83–93. doi: 10.1300/J132v03n01_11

Tangirala, S., Green, S. G., & Ramanujam, R. (2007). In the shadow of the boss's boss: Effects of supervisors' upward exchange relationships on employees. *Journal of Applied Psychology*, *92*, 309–320. doi: 10.1037/0021-9010.92.2.309

Tepper, B. J. (2000). Consequences of abusive supervision. *Academy of Management Journal*, *43*, 178–190. doi: 10.2307/1556375

Tepper, B. J., & Taylor, E. C. (2003). Relationship among supervisors' and subordinates' procedural justice perceptions and organizational citizenship behaviors. *Academy of Management Journal*, *46*, 97–105. doi: 10.2307/30040679

van Emmerik, I. J. H., & Brenninkmeijer, V. (2009). Deep-level similarity and group social capital: Associations with team functioning. *Small Group Research*, *40*, 650–669. doi: 10.1177/1046496409346550

Wagner, D., G., & Berger, J. (1985). Do sociological theories grow? *The Academy Journal of Sociology*, *90*, 697–728.

Wang, H., Law, K. S., Hackett, R. D., Wang, D., & Chen, Z. X. (2005). Leader-member exchange as a mediator of the relationship between transformational leadership and followers' performance and organizational citizenship behavior. *Academy of Management Journal*, *48*, 420–432. doi: 10.5465/AMJ.2005.17407908

Watson, D., Clark, L. A., & Tellegen, A. (1988). Development and validation of brief measures of positive and negative affect: The PANAS scales. *Journal of Personality and Social Psychology*, *54*, 1063–1070. doi: 10.1037/0022-3514.54.6.1063

Wayne, S. J., Shore, L. M., & Liden, R. C. (1997). Perceived organizational support and leadermember exchange: A social exchange perspective. *Academy of Management Journal*, *40*(1), 82–111. doi:10.2307/257021

Williams, L. J., & Anderson, S. E. (1991). job satisfaction and organizational commitment as predictors of organizational citizenship and in-role behaviors. *Journal of Management*, *17*, 601–617. doi: 10.1177/014920639101700305

Williams, S., & Shiaw, W. T. (1999). Mood and organizational citizenship behavior: The effects of positive affect on employee organizational citizenship behavior intentions. *The Journal of Psychology*, *133*(6), 656–668. doi: 10.1080/00223989909599771

Wu, T.-Y., & Hu, C. (2009). Abusive supervision and employee emotional exhaustion: Dispositional antecedents and boundaries. *Group and Organization Management, 34*, 143–169. doi: 10.1177/1059601108331217

Yang, K.-S. (1993). Chinese social orientation: An integrative analysis. In L. Y. Cheng, F. M. C. Cheung, & C. N. Chen (Eds.), *Psychotherapy for the Chinese (selected papers from the first international conference)* (pp. 19–56), Hong Kong: The Chinese University of Hong Kong.

Yang, K.-S., Yu, A. B., & Yeh, M. H. (1989). Chinese individual modernity and traditionality: Construct definition and measurement. In K. S. Yang & A. B. Yu (Eds.), *Chinese psychology and behavior* (pp. 241–306). Taipei: Laureat.

Yoon, J., & Thye, S. (2000). Supervisor support in the work place: Legitimacy and positive affectivity. *The Journal of Social Psychology, 140*, 295–316. doi: 10.1080/00224540009600472

Zellars, K. L., & Tepper, B. J. (2003). Beyond social exchange: New directions for organizational citizenship behavior theory and research. In J. J. Martocchio & G. R. Ferris (Eds.), *Research in personnel and human resources management, Vol 22. Research in personnel and human resources management* (pp. 395–424). Oxford, England: Elsevier Science Ltd.

Original manuscript received November 11, 2011
Final version accepted December 28, 2012

Index

Note: **Bold** page numbers refer to tables; *italic* page numbers refer to figures and page numbers followed by 'n' denote endnotes.